Programming Microsoft® ASP.NET 2.0 Applications: Advanced Topics

Dino Esposito
(Solid Quality Learning)

PUBLISHED BY
Microsoft Press
A Division of Microsoft Corporation
One Microsoft Way
Redmond, Washington 98052-6399

Library of Congress Control Number 2005939240

Printed and bound in the United States of America.

1 2 3 4 5 6 7 8 9   QWT   0 9 8 7 6

Distributed in Canada by H.B. Fenn and Company Ltd.

A CIP catalogue record for this book is available from the British Library.

Microsoft Press books are available through booksellers and distributors worldwide. For further information about international editions, contact your local Microsoft Corporation office or contact Microsoft Press International directly at fax (425) 936-7329. Visit our Web site at www.microsoft.com/mspress. Send comments to mspinput@microsoft.com.

Active Directory, ActiveX, InfoPath IntelliSense, JScript, Microsoft Press, MSDN, SharePoint, Tahoma, Verdana, Visio, Visual Basic, Visual Studio, Webdings, WebTV, Win32, Windows, Windows CE, Windows NT, and Windows Server are either registered trademarks or trademarks of Microsoft Corporation in the United States and/or other countries. Other product and company names mentioned herein may be the trademarks of their respective owners.

The example companies, organizations, products, domain names, e-mail addresses, logos, people, places, and events depicted herein are fictitious. No association with any real company, organization, product, domain name, e-mail address, logo, person, place, or event is intended or should be inferred.

This book expresses the author's views and opinions. The information contained in this book is provided without any express, statutory, or implied warranties. Neither the authors, Microsoft Corporation, nor its resellers, or distributors will be held liable for any damages caused or alleged to be caused either directly or indirectly by this book.

Acquisitions Editor: Ben Ryan
Project Editor: Lynn Finnel
Technical Editor: Kenn Scribner
Copy Editor: Roger LeBlanc
Indexer: Lynn Armstrong

Body Part No. X11-53582

To Francesco

(I often forget to say how much I love you)

"Imagination is more important than knowledge."

–Albert Einstein

Contents at a Glance

Table of Contents

Acknowledgments

A good ensemble of people made this book happen: Ben Ryan, Lynn Finnel, Kenn Scribner, Roger LeBlanc, and Robert Lyon. To all of them, I feel I owe a monumental "Thank You" for being so kind, patient, and accurate. They reviewed, edited, reworked, and tested all the text and code this book is made of.

Kenn—how can I thank you enough? I knew you from when we worked together in the past. I wanted you to be the technical editor of the book just because I knew you. Sure, you tend to write too many comments sometimes, which alters my internal state. But much more than this, you always write the comments that MUST be written. You catch everything; and I'll catch you for any other books I might be writing in the future. (And I do have quite a few ideas I'm quietly composing and that are taking form and substance in my mind already.)

Lynn—your commitment and dedication were absolutely total. And I cross my fingers that I'll have you on board again. Or is it the other way around, and I should hope you accept me again? No matter what, I'm looking forward to working with you again. And I'm very keen on this point.

Roger and Robert—I was going to write separate notes but then I realized I was going to say the same to both of you. Roger for the text and Robert for the code, you made this book much smoother and often read between the lines and understood my intentions better than me.

Ben—you're the entry point in the pipeline. You made it; and I was just a tool. Hopefully, an intelligent tool.

Other people contributed in various ways to improve the overall quality of the book you hold in your hands. An unordered list of names certainly includes Fernando Guerrero and all the folks at Solid Quality Learning, Marius Constantinescu, Marco Bellinaso, Steve Toub, Jay Greenfield, Andrea Saltarello, and Raffaele Rialdi.

Matthew Gibbs, Nikhil Kothari, David Ebbo, Simon Calvert, Dmitri Robsman, and Jonathan Hawkins on the ASP.NET team provided significant help and contributed a lot to transform my hunches and hypotheses into correct statements. And thanks to Scott Guthrie for being so surprisingly quick with his answers.

A special mention goes to Lutz Roeder and his wonderful tool, .NET Reflector, which I extensively used to dissect the internal plumbing of ASP.NET classes and controls. If you don't know it (really?) get it now at *http://www.aisto.com/roeder/dotnet*.

Another special mention is for the people at Openwave, in particular my friends Luca Passani and Ron Mandel. Thanks for supporting me and for the great Openwave Simulator tool.

It was a great pleasure!

—Dino

PS: After years of practice, this 800 page book was usual business for Silvia and kids (Francesco and Michela). It was nothing special, just everyday work. They know me, and how to handle me.

PPS: This book completes a project that started about nine months ago. An important change in my personal life occurred during this time—I rediscovered the importance of fitness and sport. So I started running and got back to my real and unique love (as far as sport is concerned)—tennis. Believe it or not, I found the solution to tricky issues related to the code and the organization of this book just waiting for me at the end of tough matches. This is my way of mentioning all my friends at the Monterotondo Tennis Club.

Introduction

I started making plans for an ASP.NET 2.0 "big" book in the summer of 2004. The first outline I came up with listed more than 1,600 pages: definitely too much for a book, no matter how interesting the contents could be and regardless of how brilliant and entertaining the author could be. It's clear that 1,600 pages make up a tome that is way too difficult to manage—in every sense.

A book that size would be difficult to manage for the author because of the tremendous amount of information to learn, digest, dissect, test, and then organize and present. It would be difficult to manage for the family of the author because such a big book would take no less than nine months of constant work, work that consumes the "day job" as well as kills spare time, kid time, wife time, and any other concept of time one may have.

It would be difficult to manage for the editors who are charged with the critical task of making the whole tome readable and making it flow as smoothly as possible. It would be tough for the technical reviewers, who must ensure that the sample code works and that the pseudo-code looks like it should work.

And finally, it would be difficult to manage for you—the reader—because a 1,600-page book is definitely heavy to move and cumbersome to thumb through.

So we decided to split the original "big" book into two books—*Programming Microsoft ASP.NET 2.0: Core Reference* and this one, *Programming Microsoft ASP.NET 2.0 Applications: Advanced Topics*. The sum of the two provides you with full coverage of the ASP.NET platform.

We cut the original table of contents into two parts, inspired by the following principle: distinguish between what the typical ASP.NET developer wants to know first so that they will be able to cook up quality ASP.NET 2.0 applications quickly, and other topics that, while important, were either more advanced or didn't fall into the "must know first" category. These first-principle topics formed the contents of the *Core Reference* book. Other topics were left for this book. The descriptive title—*Advanced Topics*—indicates that this book digs into topics you typically need to know about at a later time—after you've gained a good understanding of the core of the ASP.NET platform.

On the other hand, thousands of developers followed the evolution of ASP.NET 2.0 from the beginning by participating in various programs and practicing with builds and tech previews. These potential readers might want to skip the first steps and start directly with, say, the compilation model or custom controls.

All in all, ASP.NET is one big subject and my goal here is to provide you with the most accurate and insightful information possible. This requires a page count that exceeds any reasonable size for a book. So we split the subject into two mostly standalone books with minimal overlap while covering classic topics and more advanced topics, respectively. Individually, neither book covers the full set of ASP.NET topics, but together they provide state-of-the-art knowledge of the entire ASP.NET platform.

This book is *not* a revamped and more in-depth version of the first. It simply extends and complements the other by drilling down into some topics that were briefly mentioned in the other (for example, providers, controls, and compilation) and adds some new, more advanced topics (such as Web Parts, mobile controls, navigation, configuration and deployment).

When you break up a subject that represents a single block of knowledge into pieces, you generally must do so in an arbitrary, personal, and therefore arguable (to some) way. But it was necessary to make these choices to provide accurate and insightful ASP.NET coverage in a reasonably sized book.

Who Is This Book For?

There are two reasons that this is not a book for novice developers. It builds inevitably on some material discussed in *Programming Microsoft ASP.NET 2.0 Core Reference*, and it requires either that you have read that volume or that you have already obtained the same knowledge. In addition, in this book you won't find screen shots illustrating Microsoft Visual Studio 2005 wizards and there's no mention of Microsoft Visual Studio options to select or deselect that elicit specific behavior from your code. Of course, this doesn't mean that I hate Visual Studio 2005! And it most certainly doesn't mean that I'm not recommending Visual Studio 2005 to develop ASP.NET applications. Visual Studio 2005 is a great tool with which to write ASP.NET 2.0 applications, but judged purely from an ASP.NET technological perspective, it is merely a working tool. This book, instead, is all about ASP.NET as a technology as well as its internal plumbing.

I do recommend this book to developers who have read and digested *Programming Microsoft ASP.NET 2.0: Core Reference* or who have come to the same ASP.NET understanding in other ways. There are topics in this book, though, that have no prerequisites. They are Web parts, mobile controls, ASP.NET configuration, and, to some extent, the whole of Part III, which is devoted to controls.

Organization of This Book

The book is divided into three parts: "Inside the ASP.NET Machinery," "Special Features," and "ASP.NET Special Controls."

Part I details the compilation model, customization and configuration of the runtime environment, and the provider model. Chapter 5 provides some examples of advanced features and techniques to make your pages richer and more effective.

Part II highlights special capabilities of the platform that you can leverage to build special features in your pages and applications. This includes scripting and, in particular, script callbacks, Web Parts for creating portal-like applications, mobile applications for wireless devices, and the navigation API to improve the management of large and complex sites.

Part III focuses entirely on controls. I cover a couple of low-level iterative controls (*Repeater* and *DataList*) that, although overtaken by the new family of "view" controls (*GridView*, *DetailsView*, and *FormView*), still represent the only resources you have to create free-form user interfaces. In addition, this last section hosts a discussion of Web user controls and provides you with a crash-course covering custom controls, templates, data binding, and how you would add design-time features to your own controls.

System Requirements

You'll need the following hardware and software to build and run the code samples for this book:

- Microsoft Windows XP with Service Pack 2, Microsoft Windows Server 2003 with Service Pack 1, or Microsoft Windows 2000 with Service Pack 4.

- Microsoft Visual Studio 2005 Standard Edition or Microsoft Visual Studio 2005 Professional Edition.

- Internet Information Services (IIS) is not strictly required by Visual Studio for writing ASP.NET applications and debugging, but it is required by the sample code installation software.

- Microsoft SQL Server 2005 Express (included with Visual Studio 2005) or Microsoft SQL Server 2005.

- The Northwind Traders database of Microsoft SQL Server 2000 is used in most examples in this book to demonstrate data-access techniques throughout the book. If you are using SQL Server 2005, you can download installation scripts for the Northwind database from *http://www.microsoft.com/downloads/details.aspx?FamilyId=06616212-0356-46A0-8DA2-EEBC53A68034&displaylang=en*.

- 766-MHz Pentium or compatible processor (1.5 GHz Pentium recommended).

- 256 MB RAM (512 MB or more recommended).

- Video (800 × 600 or higher resolution) monitor with at least 256 colors (1024 × 768 high color 16-bit recommended).

- CD-ROM or DVD-ROM drive.

- Microsoft Mouse or compatible pointing device.

Configuring SQL Server 2005 Express Edition

Some of the sample code included with of this book requires that you have access to SQL Server 2005 Express Edition (or SQL Server 2005) to create and use the Northwind Traders database. If you are using SQL Server 2005 Express Edition, log in as Administrator on your computer and follow these steps to grant access to the user account that you will be using for performing the exercises in these chapters:

1. On the Windows Start menu, click All Programs, click Accessories, and then click Command Prompt to open a command prompt window.

2. In the command prompt window, type the following command:

   ```
   sqlcmd –S YourServer\SQLExpress –E
   ```

   Replace *YourServer* with the name of your computer.

   You can find the name of your computer by running the *hostname* command in the command prompt window, before running the *sqlcmd* command.

3. At the 1> prompt, type the following command, including the square brackets, and then press **Enter**:

   ```
   sp_grantlogin [YourServer\UserName]
   ```

   Replace *YourServer* with the name of your computer, and replace *UserName* with the name of the user account you will be using.

4. At the 2> prompt, type the following command and then press **Enter**:

   ```
   go
   ```

   If you see an error message, make sure you have typed the **sp_grantlogin** command correctly, including the square brackets.

5. At the 1> prompt, type the following command, including the square brackets, and then press **Enter**:

   ```
   sp_addsrvrolemember [YourServer\UserName], dbcreator
   ```

6. At the 2> prompt, type the following command and then press **Enter**:

   ```
   go
   ```

   If you see an error message, make sure you have typed the **sp_addsrvrolemember** command correctly, including the square brackets.

7. At the 1> prompt, type the following command and then press **Enter**:

   ```
   exit
   ```

8. Close the command prompt window.

Technology Updates

As technologies related to this book are updated, links to additional information will be added to the Microsoft Press Technology Updates Web page. Visit this page periodically at the following address for updates on Visual Studio 2005 and other technologies:

http://www.microsoft.com/mspress/updates/

Code Samples

All of the code samples discussed in this book can be downloaded from the book's companion content page at the following address:

http://www.microsoft.com/mspress/companion/0-7356-2177-2/

Support for This Book

Every effort has been made to ensure the accuracy of this book and the companion content. As corrections or changes are collected, they will be added to a Microsoft Knowledge Base article.

Microsoft Press provides support for books and companion content at the following Web site:

http://www.microsoft.com/learning/support/books/

Questions and Comments

If you have comments, questions, or ideas regarding the book or the companion content, or questions that are not answered by visiting the sites previously listed, please send them to Microsoft Press via e-mail to

mspinput@microsoft.com

Or via postal mail to

Microsoft Press
Attn: *Programming Microsoft ASP.NET: Advanced Topics Editor*
One Microsoft Way
Redmond, WA 98052-6399

Please note that Microsoft software product support is not offered through the preceding addresses.

Part I
Inside the ASP.NET Machinery

Chapter 1

The ASP.NET Compilation Model

With very few exceptions, all files that the Microsoft ASP.NET runtime environment can serve are automatically compiled on-demand when first required by a Web application. This basic fact is one of the pillars of the whole ASP.NET compilation and programming model. In ASP.NET 1.x, dynamic compilation is supported only for a small set of requested resources, including ASP.NET pages (*.*aspx*), ASP.NET Web services (*.*asmx*), HTTP handlers (*.*ashx*), the *global.asax* file, and class files. In particular, ASP.NET pages are compiled upon first request, whereas *global.asax* is dynamically compiled the first time any page is requested inside the application, even before the target page is compiled.

ASP.NET pages are made of markup and code files. To take advantage of the benefits that compiled code has over the interpreted code in classic ASP, the markup must be compiled. The compilation process consists of two main steps. First, the markup is converted into a C# or Microsoft Visual Basic .NET temporary class that fits in the ASP.NET class hierarchy. Second, the class is compiled to an assembly. The final assembly is then loaded into the application domain (AppDomain) that hosts the application.

The user making the request doesn't see much of this process. The first user to hit the page might experience a little delay on the first access. The originally requested resource (say, an *.aspx* file) is tracked and automatically invalidated and recompiled in case of changes. The first user to request the resource after the change will again experience a little delay as a result of the compilation step.

This mechanism presents two key benefits. On one end, it enables programmers to quickly develop applications as they just hit save and immediately cause code changes to take effect. On the other hand, pages served to end users originate from compiled code and run much faster. You get the testing ease of interpreted code and the performance and robustness of compiled code.

In ASP.NET 2.0, this compilation model is extended to account for other file types such as XSD, WSDL, resource files, themes, and master pages. In addition, ASP.NET 2.0 provides an extensibility model allowing for user-defined file types to be added to the list of supported types. Unlike ASP.NET 1.x, the compilation model of ASP.NET 2.0 doesn't need an explicit compilation step driven by Microsoft Visual Studio .NET. All compilation work is delegated to the Web server.

In this chapter, I'll explore the internals of the ASP.NET runtime environment to unveil how an ASP.NET page is transformed into a class, the benefits and costs of site precompilation, and what you can do to customize and extend the compilation engine.

The ASP.NET Runtime Environment

Any incoming request that Internet Information Server (IIS) captures is examined and mapped to an external module for actual processing. There are a couple of exceptions to this rule. IIS, in fact, directly serves requests for static resources such as image files and HTML pages, as well as requests that hit kernel-cached pages. A kernel-cached page is an ASP.NET page configured for page output caching that doesn't expose any settings or features that prevent kernel-level caching. This topic is covered in detail in Chapter 14 of my related book *Programming Microsoft ASP.NET 2.0: Core Reference* (Microsoft Press, 2005).

The external module in charge of processing incoming ASP.NET requests is a dynamic-link library (DLL) named *aspnet_isapi*. This module is not just a plain DLL—it's an IIS Internet Server Application Programming Interface (ISAPI) module. An ISAPI module is a DLL that implements a special protocol to enable communication with the IIS executable file.

> **Note**   An ISAPI module is a Microsoft Win32 DLL that exports a couple of functions with a given name and prototype. These functions are *GetExtensionVersion* and *HttpExtensionProc*— the real heart of the module. IIS calls *HttpExtensionProc* for processing the request, and the function generates the response.

The binding between resource extensions and the *aspnet_isapi* module is set in the IIS metabase, and it can be changed through the Properties dialog box of the IIS Web application. (See Figure 1-1.)

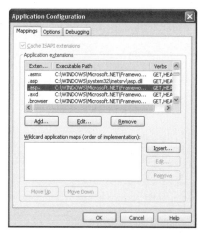

Figure 1-1   The list of mapped extensions for an ASP.NET application.

The tasks the *aspnet_isapi* extension is in charge of, and subsequently its workings, vary quite a bit with the process model in use. The ASP.NET process model is a series of steps that processes a request and generates a response for the browser. Let's review the details.

The ASP.NET Process Model

ASP.NET supports two process models named after the version of IIS where each is the default option. The IIS 5 process model is the only option available when ASP.NET runs under IIS 5.x. It can also be enabled under IIS 6.0 or later, but that is not the default option.

IIS 5.0 Process Model

According to this processing model, *aspnet_isapi* doesn't process the requested resource but instead acts as a dispatcher. It collects all the information available about the invoked URL, and then it routes the request toward another distinct process—the ASP.NET worker process named *aspnet_wp.exe*. The communication between the ISAPI extension and worker process takes place through named pipes. By default, the worker process runs under the ASPNET account. This account is created when ASP.NET is installed.

A single copy of the worker process runs all the time and hosts all the active Web applications, each in a distinct AppDomain. In a Web-garden scenario, multiple worker processes run simultaneously, one for each affinitized CPU.

If a client requests a page from an already running Web application, the ASP.NET runtime simply forwards the request to the existing AppDomain associated with that virtual directory. If the assembly needed to process the page is not available in the AppDomain, it will be created on the fly; otherwise, if it was already created upon the first call, it will simply be re-used. The creation of the assembly is the core topic I'm going to cover in this chapter.

The flow diagram of the IIS 5.0 process model is illustrated in Figure 1-2.

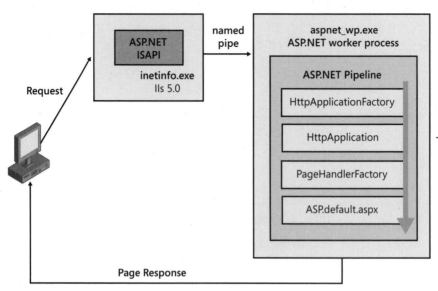

Figure 1-2   The IIS 5.0 process model.

IIS 6.0 Process Model

IIS 6.0 employs a different pipeline of internal modules to process an inbound request and can mimic the behavior of IIS 5.0 only if running in emulation mode. The IIS 6.0 process model, also known as the *worker process isolation mode*, is centered around the concept of an *application pool*. An application pool is a group of Web applications that share the same copy of the worker process, thus separating essential parts of the Web server from potentially malfunctioning applications. You can configure each application pool and its copy of the worker process with a different set of properties.

When running under the default IIS 6.0 process model, an ASP.NET application uses a generic, ASP.NET-agnostic worker process—the same worker process that serves all applications hosted by the Web server. This program is named *w3wp.exe*. A copy of this executable is shared by all Web applications assigned to the same application pool. Another key component of the IIS 6.0 architecture is the kernel-mode device driver named *http.sys*. This driver is the HTTP listener in charge of capturing and servicing any incoming requests.

When a request arrives, *http.sys* routes it to the queue managed by the application pool that the invoked application belongs to. There's one queue per application pool. In IIS 5.0 emulation mode, *http.sys* places requests in a unique, shared request queue.

Note   For more information on the internal architecture of IIS 6.0, you can take a look at *Internet Information Services (IIS) 6.0 Resource Kit* (Microsoft Press, 2004).

The *w3wp.exe* worker process loads *aspnet_isapi.dll*; the ISAPI extension, in turn, loads the common language runtime (CLR) and starts the ASP.NET runtime pipeline to process the request. When the IIS 6.0 process model is in use, the built-in ASP.NET worker process is disabled.

The flow diagram of the IIS 6.0 process model is illustrated in Figure 1-3.

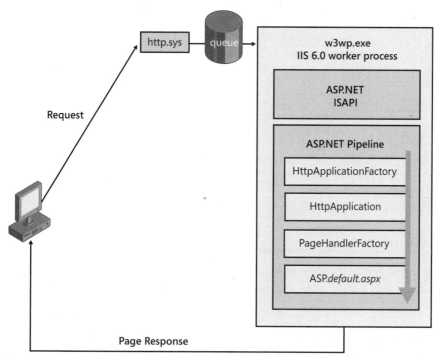

Figure 1-3   The IIS 6.0 process model.

The worker process uses *http.sys* to get requests and send responses to the client. The worker process runs under the NETWORK SERVICE account, which is the account with the least set of privileges compatible with the functionality it is expected to allow.

More Info   For more information about the steps to take to make the runtime generate a page response, you can refer to Chapter 3 of *Programming Microsoft ASP.NET 2.0: Core Reference* (Microsoft Press, 2005). In this chapter, I'll focus on one specific aspect of the page response generation that simply didn't find its way into the other book: the dynamic page compilation step.

The ASP.NET Pipeline

The ASP.NET process model determines how the original request flows from the IIS gate into the CLR instance for further processing. Inside the CLR, a pipeline of components services the request by actually processing the contents of the requested resource and returning any generated response. The managed modules that participate in the ASP.NET pipeline can read and edit the request, access and create cookies, and even order browser redirects. At the end of the pipeline, the request has morphed into an instance of a class that represents the requested ASP.NET page.

In ASP.NET 2.0, this process has been significantly refactored and now involves several new components, most of which are customizable to various extents by developers.

Each request for an *.aspx* resource is processed through the pipeline of modules you see in Figure 1-2 and Figure 1-3. The ultimate goal of the pipeline is to find a class that fully represents the requested page. If not found, such a class is created on the fly, compiled, and loaded in the AppDomain where the ASP.NET application runs. The entry point in the ASP.NET pipeline is the *HttpRuntime* class. The HTTP pipeline is a fully extensible chain of managed objects that works according to the classic concept of a pipeline. The various components are listed in Table 1-1.

Table 1-1   Components of the HTTP Pipeline

Component	Description
HttpApplicationFactory	An instance of this class is responsible for returning a valid *HttpApplication* object that can handle the request. The *HttpApplicationFactory* object maintains a pool of *HttpApplication* objects, and when invoked, it verifies that an AppDomain exists for the virtual folder targeted by the request. If the application is already running, the factory picks an *HttpApplication* out of the pool and passes it the request. A new *HttpApplication* object is created if an existing object will not be available.
HttpApplication	A running ASP.NET application is represented by a dynamically created class that inherits from *HttpApplication*. The source code of this dynamically generated class is created by parsing the contents of the *global.asax* file. The *HttpApplication* object determines the class that represents the resource being requested—typically, an ASP.NET page, a Web service, or perhaps a user control—and uses the proper handler factory to get an object that represents the requested resource.
HTTP modules	The *HttpApplication* maintains a list of HTTP module objects that can filter and even modify the content of the request. Registered modules are called during various moments of the elaboration as the request passes through the pipeline. Built-in HTTP modules are responsible for Forms authentication, output caching, session state management, and user profiling.
PageHandlerFactory	The page handler factory creates an instance of an object that represents the particular page requested. Analogous factory objects will do the same for other requested resources such as Web services or custom HTTP handlers.
IHttpHandler	The page object created by the page factory inherits from the *System .Web.UI.Page* class (or a class derived from this), which in turn implements the *IHttpHandler* interface. The final step accomplished by the ASP.NET runtime is calling the *IHttpHandler*'s *ProcessRequest* method on the page object. This call causes the page to execute the user-defined code and generate the markup for the client.

A graphical perspective of the HTTP pipeline is shown in Figure 1-4.

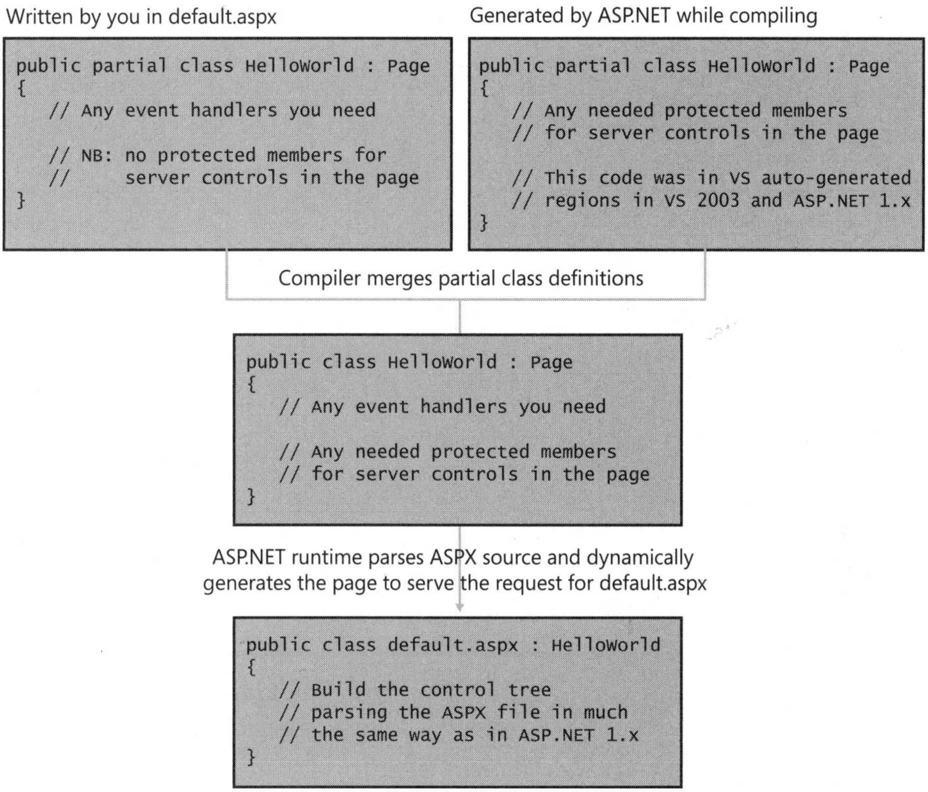

Written by you in default.aspx

```
public partial class HelloWorld : Page
{
    // Any event handlers you need

    // NB: no protected members for
    //     server controls in the page
}
```

Generated by ASP.NET while compiling

```
public partial class HelloWorld : Page
{
    // Any needed protected members
    // for server controls in the page

    // This code was in VS auto-generated
    // regions in VS 2003 and ASP.NET 1.x
}
```

Compiler merges partial class definitions

```
public class HelloWorld : Page
{
    // Any event handlers you need

    // Any needed protected members
    // for server controls in the page
}
```

ASP.NET runtime parses ASPX source and dynamically
generates the page to serve the request for default.aspx

```
public class default.aspx : HelloWorld
{
    // Build the control tree
    // parsing the ASPX file in much
    // the same way as in ASP.NET 1.x
}
```

Figure 1-4   The HTTP pipeline processing for a page.

Each Web application has its own copy of the HTTP runtime and runs in a separate AppDomain. The runtime object creates the HTTP context for the request, and it initializes the cache and the file system monitor used to detect changes in the application files. The worker process (either *aspnet_wp.exe* or *aspnet_isapi* inside *w3wp.exe*) activates the HTTP pipeline by creating a new instance of the *HttpRuntime* class and then calling its *ProcessRequest* method.

As mentioned, the ultimate goal of the HTTP pipeline is finding in the current AppDomain a managed class that fully represents the requested ASP.NET resource. For pages, this class derives either directly or indirectly from *Page* and follows a particular naming convention. For a page named *xxx.aspx*, the default class name is *ASP.xxx_aspx*. (If the page features the *Class-Name* attribute in the *@Page* directive, the actual class name will be *ASP.ClassName*.) If such a class is available in the current AppDomain, it is instantiated and invoked through the methods of the *IHttpHandler* interface. Otherwise, such a class is dynamically created by the page handler factory object. (As we'll see in a moment, ASP.NET knows exactly from the contents of temporary files if the page class exists and where it is located.)

> **Note**   The dynamic creation of a page class occurs at least the first time the page is requested right after deployment. The class is shared by all sessions, and only the very first user to hit it after the application is started experiences the compilation delay. After that, the page is recompiled only in case of changes to its source code or any of its dependencies, such as a master page. The first-hit delay can be avoided if the site is deployed in a precompiled form. If the page is precompiled, no dynamic creation occurs. I'll have more to say on this topic in a moment.

Let's focus on the mechanics of the page class dynamic creation and compilation.

The Page Handler Factory

The *HttpApplication* object retrieves from *machine.config* the name of the handler object to serve requests of a particular type. The following code snippet shows the standard setting that associates the *PageHandlerFactory* class with *.aspx* resources. Similar mappings are shown for *.asmx* (Web services) and *.ashx* (custom HTTP handler) resources.

```
<httpHandlers>
    <add path="*.aspx" verb="*" type="System.Web.UI.PageHandlerFactory"
        validate="True" />
    <add path="*.ashx" verb="*" type="System.Web.UI.SimpleHandlerFactory"
        validate="True" />
    <add path="*.asmx" verb="*"
        type="System.Web.Services.Protocols.WebServiceHandlerFactory,
            System.Web.Services, Version=2.0.0.0, Culture=neutral,
            PublicKeyToken=b03f5f7f11d50a3a"
        validate="False" />
    :
</httpHandlers>
```

The *PageHandlerFactory* class implements the *IHttpHandlerFactory* interface, detailed in Table 1-2.

Table 1-2   The *IHttpHandlerFactory* Interface

Method	Description
GetHandler	Returns an instance of a class that implements the *IHttpHandler* interface and can serve the request. For pages, this class derives from *Page*. Arguments to the method include the HTTP verb, the raw URL, and the context of the request.
ReleaseHandler	Does whatever is needed to enable the factory to reuse the specified handler instance. The default page HTTP handler's implementation of this method simply returns void.

The page handler factory is responsible for either finding the assembly that contains the page class or dynamically creating an ad hoc assembly. The source code for the class is created by parsing the source code of the requested *.aspx* resource, and it's temporarily saved in the following ASP.NET temporary folder:

```
%SystemRoot%\Microsoft.NET\Framework\[version]\Temporary ASP.NET Files
```

In ASP.NET 1.x, the page class inherits from the code-behind class you created with Visual Studio. In ASP.NET 2.0, the page class is an enhanced and completed version of the partial class in the Visual Studio .NET code file. In particular, the partial class in the project is completed with a second partial class dynamically arranged by the ASP.NET HTTP runtime.

> **Important**   The code-behind model of ASP.NET 1.x is still fully supported by the ASP.NET runtime engine. Unfortunately, it is not supported by Visual Studio 2005.

Figure 1-5 provides a graphical demonstration of how the source code of the dynamic page class is built.

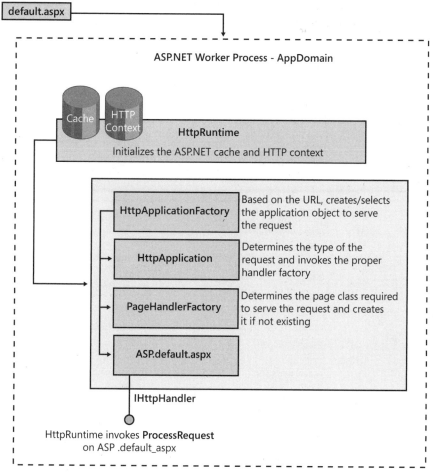

Figure 1-5 ASP.NET generates the source code for the dynamic class that will serve a request.

Next, the class is compiled and loaded in memory to serve the request. When a new request for the same page arrives, the class is ready and no compile step will ever take place. (The class will be re-created and recompiled only if the timestamp of the *.aspx* source changes.)

The Role of Partial Classes

Partial classes are a new feature of .NET Framework 2.0 compilers that allow you to break up the definition of a class into multiple, partial files. Each constituent class appears to be a perfectly valid and legal class definition, except that each is missing some of the logic and features expected of the overall class. The compiler will then take care of merging partial classes into a regular, nonpartial class that can be compiled to an assembly.

Partial classes are a source-level and assembly-limited way to extend the behavior of a class. In this regard, partial classes are *not* an object-oriented feature. Partial classes save time during the development cycle. They enable multiple teams to work on the same component at the same time, and they provide an elegant way to add functionality to a class incrementally by adding a new class instead of touching existing file classes.

Partial classes are used in ASP.NET 2.0 to overcome the brittleness of tool-generated code such as that found in ASP.NET 1.x projects. If you ever developed applications with Visual Studio .NET 2003, you should be familiar with those weird, auto-generated, semihidden regions of code that Visual Studio .NET 2003 inserts to support page designers. That code is required to extend code-behind classes with members that link to server controls dropped onto the underlying Web Form. Keeping the code-behind class in sync with the evolution of the Web Form might not be easy if you tend to edit the *aspx source* directly from the HTML editor. Partial classes remove the issue at the root: no more tool-generated code during the development phase. At compile time, the partial code-behind class is completed with member definitions, and this code is completely hidden from developers.

ASP.NET Temporary Files

Generating an assembly for a particular *.aspx* resource is a two-step process. First, a class file is created that fully represents the markup of the *.aspx* file. Second, the dynamically generated class is compiled into an assembly and cached in the *Temporary ASP.NET Files* folder. There will be a distinct folder for each installed version of ASP.NET.

Hidden Files and Assemblies

The Temporary ASP.NET Files folder has one child directory for each application ever executed. The name of the subfolder matches the name of the virtual directory of the application. Pages that run from the Web server's root folder are grouped under the Root subfolder. Page-specific assemblies are actually cached in a subdirectory placed a couple of levels down the virtual directory folder. The names of these child directories are the result of a hash algorithm based on some randomized factor along with the application name. A typical path is shown below. The last two directories (in boldface) here have fake but realistic names.

```
\Framework
  \[version]
    \Temporary ASP.NET Files
      \MyWebApp
        \3678b103
          \e60405c7
```

Regardless of the actual algorithm implemented to determine the folder names, from within an ASP.NET application, the full folder path is retrieved using the following, pretty simple, code:

```
string tempAspNetDir = HttpRuntime.CodegenDir;
```

So much for the location of the dynamic assembly. How does the ASP.NET runtime determine the assembly name for a particular *.aspx* page?

For each processed page, the application's temporary folder contains a file with the following name:

```
[page].aspx.XXXXX.compiled
```

Obviously, *[page]* represents the name of the *.aspx* resource. The *XXXXX* placeholder is a hash value based on the directory, so all *.aspx* files from the same folder have the same hash. All page files are compiled in the same folder, regardless of the fact that they might originate from different source folders. The hash value disambiguates files that have the same name but originally belonged to different originating source folders. An internally stored cache of hash values allows the ASP.NET runtime system to quickly identify hash values for any given resource name. The following listing shows the contents of a *.compiled* file.

```
<preserve virtualPath="/Compilation/Test.aspx"
          hash="7421446ce"
          filehash="4d443b62d9942247"
          flags="10000"
          assembly="App_Web_g5u1sfqg"
          type="ASP.Test_aspx">
    <filedeps>
        <filedep name="/Compilation/Test.aspx" />
        <filedep name="/Compilation/Test.aspx.cs" />
    </filedeps>
</preserve>
```

Note   The syntax of *.compiled* files is not documented and might change in the future. I'm showing it here for purely educational purposes and to help you form an idea of how things work under the hood. Be careful before you plan applications that rely on these features.

The *<preserve>* node contains a reference to the original source file (*test.aspx*), the name of the class created upon it (*ASP.Test_aspx*), and more importantly, the name of the assembly that contains a compiled version of the class.

The *<filedeps>* node lists the source files that concur with the definition of the dynamic assembly for the page.

Once the HTTP handler has identified the name of the class that represents the requested page, the *.compiled* file helps to figure out the assembly name, if any, that contains it. If no *.compiled* file exists, or if the linked assembly is missing or outdated, the *.aspx* source is parsed to create a temporary C# or Visual Basic .NET class file. This class file is then compiled to a new assembly whose name is randomly generated.

> **Note**   In ASP.NET 2.0, the name of dynamically created assemblies that represent pages always begins with *App_Web_*. Other dynamically created assemblies that represent themes, application code, resources, and *global.asax* have different prefixes.

Detecting Page Changes

The dynamically compiled page assembly is cached and used to serve any future request for the page. However, changes made to an *.aspx* file will automatically invalidate the assembly, which will be recompiled to serve the next request. The link between the assembly and the source *.aspx* files is kept in the aforementioned *.compiled* file. Any changes to any of the files listed in the *<filedeps>* section will also invalidate the assembly. To detect changes, the ASP.NET runtime installs a file monitor infrastructure based on the Win32 file notification system.

When a page is changed, it's recompiled as a single assembly and reloaded. ASP.NET ensures that the next request will be served the new page outfit by the new assembly. Current requests, on the other hand, will continue viewing the old page served by the old assembly. The two assemblies are given different (because they are randomly generated) names and therefore can happily live side by side in the same folder as well as be loaded in the same AppDomain.

How ASP.NET Replaces Page Assemblies

When a new assembly is created for a page as the result of an update, ASP.NET verifies whether the old assembly can be deleted. If the assembly contains only that page class, ASP.NET attempts to delete the assembly. Often, though, it finds the file loaded and locked, and the deletion fails. In this case, the old assembly is renamed by adding a *.delete* extension. (All executables loaded in Microsoft Windows can be renamed at any time, but they cannot be deleted until they are released.) Renaming an assembly in use is no big deal in this case because the image of the executable is already loaded in memory and there will be no need to reload it later. The file, in fact, is destined for deletion. Notice that *.delete* files are cleaned up when the directory is next accessed in *sweep* mode, so to speak. The directory, in fact, is not scavenged and cleaned each time it is accessed but only when the application is restarted or an application file (*global.asax* or *web.config*) changes.

Each ASP.NET application is allowed a maximum number of recompiles (with 15 as the default) before the whole application is restarted. The threshold value is set in the configuration file. If the latest compilation exceeds the threshold, the AppDomain is unloaded, and an application shutdown is scheduled to occur as soon as possible. Bear in mind that the atomic unit of code you can unload in the common language runtime (CLR) is the AppDomain, not the assembly. Put another way, you can't unload a single assembly without unloading the whole AppDomain.

> **Important**   When a page is recompiled, the assembly representing its old version stays in memory until the AppDomain is unloaded. There's no way this assembly can be freed up because this is one of the pillars of the whole CLR machinery. To avoid having too many recompiles flood the memory with too many assemblies (all of which are useless), the ASP.NET runtime periodically restarts the application and imposes an upper limit to the number of allowed recompiles.

Getting Runtime Information

The window shown in Figure 1-6 (*showruntimeinfo.aspx* in the book samples) displays some run-time information about the running application and AppDomains. Obtained from properties of the *HttpRuntime* class, the information includes the ID, path, and virtual path of the current AppDomain, plus useful paths such as the directory in which ASP.NET generates dynamic assemblies (*CodegenDir*) and the *Bin* directory of the application (*BinDirectory*).

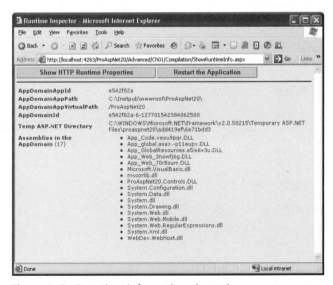

Figure 1-6   Run-time information about the current page.

The window also lists all the assemblies currently loaded in the AppDomain. The sample page needs 17 system assemblies, including those specific to the application—*global.asax* and the page class. This number increases each time you save the *.aspx* file because after a page update, a new assembly is loaded, but the old one is not unloaded until the whole AppDomain is unloaded. If you save the *.aspx* file several times (by just opening the file and pressing Ctrl+S), you see that after 15 recompiles, the AppDomain ID changes, and the number of loaded assemblies reverts back to 17 or whatever it was originally. This number, in fact, depends upon the number of referenced assemblies you included with your page.

The Hidden Code of an ASP.NET Page

To understand how the compilation process works, let's consider a practical example that involves the following page—*test.aspx*. The page is assumed to live in a folder named Compilation.

```
<%@ Page Language="C#" CodeFile="Test.aspx.cs" Inherits="Test" %>
<html>
<head runat="server">
    <title>Sample page</title>
</head>
<body>
    <form id="form1" runat="server">
    <div>
        <h1>Enter some text and click.</h1>
        <h2><asp:Label ID="Today" runat="server"
                Text='<%# DateTime.Now %>' /></h2>
        <asp:TextBox ID="TextBox1" runat="server" Text="Type here" />
        <asp:Button ID="Button1" runat="server" Text="Reverse"
            OnClick="ReverseText" />
        <hr />
        <asp:Label ID="Label1" runat="server" />
    </div>
    </form>
</body>
</html>
```

The code file for the page is as follows:

```
using System;
using System.Web.UI;
using System.Web.UI.WebControls;
using System.Text;

public partial class Test : System.Web.UI.Page
{
    protected void Page_Load(object sender, EventArgs e)
    {
        DataBind();
    }
    protected void ReverseText(object sender, EventArgs e)
    {
```

```
        string reverseText = Reverse(TextBox1.Text);
        Label1.Text = reverseText;
    }
    private string Reverse(string text)
    {
        if (text.Length == 1)
            return text;
        else
        {
            char[] rg = text.ToCharArray();
            Array.Reverse(rg);
            return new string(rg);
        }
    }
}
```

The page contains a text box to grab some user-typed text and a button to trigger a server-side operation that reverses the text. The results are shown in a label control, while another label control displays the current time through a data-bound expression. (For more information on data-bound expressions, refer to my related book *Programming Microsoft ASP.NET 2.0: Core Reference.*)

These features represent two of the most common operations you find on Web Forms pages—postbacks and declarative data binding. Let's examine in more detail how the *test.aspx* page is converted into a class and compiled into an assembly.

Involved Files

The source code of the page class to render *test.aspx* is created in the temporary folder and deleted immediately after compiling. You can make it persist, although only for educational purposes, by setting the *debug=true* attribute in the @*Page* directive. Execute the page, and once the page shows up in the browser, open the *compilation* browser under the ASP.NET temporary folder. Figure 1-7 shows the path to the folder where temporary files for the page are created.

Figure 1-7   The directory tree of the temporary folder for the */compilation* application.

Figure 1-8 lists the temporary files created to serve *test.aspx*. Note that some of these files are deleted after use on a production machine that serves nondebug pages.

Name ▲	Size	Type	Date Modified
App_Web_xgqc4cgb.dll	8 KB	Application E...	9/5/2005 3:50 PM
App_Web_xgqc4cgb.pdb	24 KB	PDB File	9/5/2005 3:50 PM
App_Web_z5fao-3h.dll	7 KB	Application E...	9/5/2005 3:50 PM
hash.web	1 KB	WEB File	9/5/2005 3:50 PM
test.aspx.2fb6c859.compiled	1 KB	COMPILED File	9/5/2005 3:50 PM
test.aspx.cdcab7d2.compiled	1 KB	COMPILED File	9/5/2005 3:50 PM
test.aspx.cdcab7d2_CBMResult.ccu	19 KB	CCU File	9/5/2005 3:50 PM
test.aspx.cdcab7d2_CBMResult.compiled	1 KB	COMPILED File	9/5/2005 3:50 PM
xgqc4cgb.0.cs	19 KB	Visual C# So...	9/5/2005 3:50 PM
xgqc4cgb.1.cs	2 KB	Visual C# So...	9/5/2005 3:50 PM
xgqc4cgb.2.cs	1 KB	Visual C# So...	9/5/2005 3:50 PM
xgqc4cgb.cmdline	2 KB	CMDLINE File	9/5/2005 3:50 PM
xgqc4cgb.err	0 KB	ERR File	9/5/2005 3:50 PM
xgqc4cgb.out	2 KB	OUT File	9/5/2005 3:50 PM

Figure 1-8   Temporary files created to serve *test.aspx*.

Table 1-3 provides more details about each of these files. Note that xgpc4gcp is a randomly generated prefix. You will get a different name each time you recompile the page.

Table 1-3   Key Temporary Files for *test.aspx*

File name	Description
hash.web	Contains the hash value for the folder, which will be used to calculate hash values for individual resources.
*App_Web_**xxx**.dll*	The dynamic assembly created for the pages in the folder named *test.aspx*. The *xxx* placeholder indicates the hash value that makes the *test.aspx* page unique even if multiple pages with the same name exist in different subdirectories.
*Test.aspx.**xxx**.compiled*	XML file that contains information about the dependencies that *test.aspx* has with external files. It also links *test.aspx* to the randomly generated assembly name.
*xgpc4cgb.**x**.cs*	Source code for the C# class code created after parsing *test.aspx* and all its dependencies. These files will be Visual Basic .NET class files if Visual Basic .NET is the language of the page. The *x* placeholder indicates a 0-based index used to distinguish relevant constituent files. *This file is deleted unless the* debug *attribute is turned on in the page.*
xgpc4cgb.cmdline	Text file that contains the command line used to compile the preceding class file. *This file is deleted unless the debug attribute is turned on in the page.*
xgpc4cgp.err	Text file that contains any output the compiler sends to the standard error stream. *This file is deleted unless the debug attribute is turned on in the page.*
xgpc4cgb.out	Text file that contains any output text generated by the compiler. *This file is deleted unless the debug attribute is turned on in the page.*

Let's take a look at the source code of the *xgpc4cgb.**x**.cs* files. For *test.aspx*, you count three distinct constituent source files. The *x* placeholder, therefore, varies from 0 through 2, in this case, as discussed in Table 1-4.

Table 1-4   Constituent Files for *test.aspx*

File	Class	Contents
xgpc4cgb.0.cs	*(partial)* Test, ASP.test_aspx	It contains two classes. The first is the partial class *Test* that completes the code file written by the author to back up *test.aspx*. The second is the page handler class used to serve the *test.aspx* resource.
xgpc4cgb.1.cs	*(partial)* Test	The code file class created by the page author as *test.aspx.cs*.
xgpc4cgb.2.cs	ASP.FastObjectFactory	Internal-use factory class created to avoid reflection and maximize speed when instantiating the page handler class.

The contents in the partial class defined as *xxx.1.cs* are the code of the code file class associated with the ASP.NET page. This partial class—named *Test* as in the *Inherits* attribute of the *@Page* directive—is completed with a dynamically generated partial class that adds members for each server control. Here's what the second partial class looks like:

```
public partial class Test : IRequiresSessionState
{
    protected Label Today;
    protected TextBox TextBox1;
    protected Button Button1;
    protected Label Label1;
    protected HtmlForm form1;

    protected DefaultProfile Profile {
        get {return (DefaultProfile) Context.Profile;}
    }
    protected HttpApplication ApplicationInstance {
        get {return (HttpApplication) Context.ApplicationInstance;}
    }
}
```

The boldfaced lines indicate the members corresponding to server controls—the code that in ASP.NET 1.x is generated by Visual Studio .NET 2003 in hidden regions.

The *FastObjectFactory* class is also worth a quick mention. Here's the typical source code:

```
namespace ASP {
    internal class FastObjectFactory
    {
        private FastObjectFactory() {}
        static object Create_ASP_Test_aspx()
    {
        return new ASP.Test_aspx();
    }
  }
}
```

It merely contains a static method that instantiates the page handler class in a strong-typed, early-bound manner. Because the compiled page type is known at run time, .NET reflection would be the only option left to instantiate a class. This trick allows you to gain a little bit of performance on a very frequently executed operation.

> **Warning**   This code is shown for educational purposes only and in a slightly edited format that makes it read well in the context of a book chapter. If you plan to use this information for building real-world applications, make sure that you verify and cross-check any line of code to ensure that it works in your context, too. Note also that this is ASP.NET internal code; as such, it might change in future builds without being noted.

Structure of the Page

The page class created to service requests for *test.aspx* inherits from the class specified through the *Inherits* attribute in the markup file—*Test* in this case. As mentioned, the *Test* class is a partial class defined in *test.aspx.cs* and derives, directly or indirectly, from *Page*. A second, ASP.NET-generated partial class will complete the definition of *Test*. The page handler for *test.aspx* has a fixed name—*ASP.Test_aspx*. Let's explore its internals:

```
namespace ASP {
  public class Test_aspx : Test {
    private static bool __initialized;
    private static object __fileDependencies;

    public Test_aspx() {
      string[] dependencies;
      AppRelativeVirtualPath = "~/Test.aspx";
      if (__initialized == false) {
          dependencies = new string[2];
          dependencies[0] = "~/Test.aspx";
          dependencies[1] = "~/Test.aspx.cs";
          __fileDependencies = GetWrappedFileDependencies(dependencies);
          __initialized = true;
        }
      Server.ScriptTimeout = 30000000;
    }

    protected override void FrameworkInitialize() {
      base.FrameworkInitialize();
      __BuildControlTree(this);
      AddWrappedFileDependencies(__fileDependencies);
      Request.ValidateInput();
    }

    public override int GetTypeHashCode() {
        // This static number is generated dynamically when the source
        // code of this page is generated dynamically
      return 850224717;
    }
      :
}
```

The class has two static members to indicate the initialization state of the class and the list of its file dependencies. These two members are initialized in the class constructor. Next, the *ASP.Test_aspx* overrides two methods on the base *Page* class, as detailed in Table 1-5.

Table 1-5   Overrides of *ASP.Test_aspx*

Method	Description
FrameworkInitialize	Governs the creation of the page's control tree.
GetTypeHashCode	Returns the hash code for the page that uniquely identifies the page's control hierarchy. The method should not be confused with *GetHash-Code* that all .NET Framework classes inherit from *System.Object*, although both methods pursue similar goals—returning values to identify the contents of objects. *GetTypeHashCode* is more specific than *GetHashCode* and bases its value on the page's control tree. The number is generated on the fly when the source code of the page is generated.

There are two key things going on in the override of *FrameworkInitialize*. First, the *__BuildControlTree* method is invoked to fill the *Controls* collection of the page class, thus determining the control tree of the page. The *__BuildControlTree* method is autogenerated by ASP.NET. We'll take a look at it in a moment. Second, *ValidateInput* is invoked on the *Request* object to ensure that no potentially dangerous input is being processed by the page. *ValidateInput* is controlled by the *ValidateRequest* attribute in the *@Page* directive and simply applies some standard regular expressions to all inbound data. You should never rely on *ValidateInput* alone to secure your application.

The Control Tree

The *__BuildControlTree* is the entry point in the code that physically builds a class from the ASPX markup. It uses an *IParserAccessor* reference to the current page object to find all subobjects in the specified graph and add them to the *Controls* collection of the page being processed.

```
private void __BuildControlTree(Test_aspx __ctrl)
{
    // Get the parser interface from the page
    IParserAccessor __parser = (IParserAccessor) __ctrl);

    // Build the <head> node and add it to the tree
    HtmlHead __ctrl1 = __BuildControl__control2();
    __parser.AddParsedSubObject(__ctrl1);

    // Build a subtree for a literal expression
    __parser.AddParsedSubObject(new LiteralControl("<body>"));

    // Build the <form> node and add it to tree
    HtmlForm __ctrl2 = __BuildControlform1();
    __parser.AddParsedSubObject(__ctrl2);
```

```
// Build a subtree for a literal expression
__parser.AddParsedSubObject(new LiteralControl("</body></html>"));
}
```

The contents of the *<head>* tag is processed to obtain a subtree of controls, and the same process occurs with the *<form>* tag and all of its contents. Any literal expression, such as *<body>*, is processed as a control as well. Any consecutive text found between two server controls is converted into a literal control and added to the tree.

> **Tip**   In light of this behavior, you should avoid using carriage return/linefeed pairs between server controls. In fact, the sequence */r/n* is added to the generated tree as a literal control. The sequence has no impact on the HTML rendering—it simply makes the source more easily readable—but it charges a slight performance penalty at run time.

Each server control originates a procedure like the following one, which builds the *TextBox1* text box control:

```
private TextBox __BuildControlTextBox1()
{
    TextBox __ctrl = new TextBox();
    this.TextBox1 = __ctrl;
    __ctrl.ApplyStyleSheetSkin(this);
    __ctrl.ID = "TextBox1";
    __ctrl.Text = "Type here";
    return __ctrl;
}
```

The preceding code is the result of the following markup:

```
<asp:TextBox ID="TextBox1" runat="server" Text="Type here" />
```

The build method for the *<form>* tag calls build methods for all contained controls. Build methods have fixed names: *__BuildControl*name, where *name* stands for the ID of the control. It will be *control*N for unnamed controls.

Event Handlers and Data-Binding Expressions

What if the control has an event handler or a data-binding expression? Let's first consider the case of a button with the *Click* event handler. The code is nearly identical to the preceding code snippet, except of course that a *Button* class is used instead of a *TextBox*. In addition, you'll find the following:

```
__ctrl.Click += new EventHandler(this.ReverseText);
```

For data-binding expressions <%# ... %>, the code generated is similar except that the *Data-Binding* event is used.

```
__ctrl.DataBinding += new EventHandler(__DataBindingToday);
```

The code associated with the handler depends on the nature of the bound control and the code being bound. In this relatively simple case, it looks like the following fragment:

```
public void __DataBindingToday(object sender, EventArgs e)
{
    Label target = (Label) sender;
    target.Text = Convert.ToString(DateTime.Now,
                                   CultureInfo.CurrentCulture);
}
```

The $-expressions introduced in ASP.NET 2.0 are processed in a different way, as they are not bound to the data-binding process. We'll delve deep into $-expressions in Chapter 5.

Reusing Dynamically Compiled Page Classes

Now that you know about internal classes being created to service *.aspx* resources, the obvious next step seems to be to think of ways to reuse this assembly to build similar-looking pages more quickly. Is the dynamically generated class reusable to build other similar pages in a sort of visual-inheritance à la Windows Forms? If the answer has to be yes or no, my answer would be no.

You can certainly make a copy of the dynamic assembly and import it into the *Bin* folder of an application. You can also modify the parent class in the code file of a page you want to build based on an existing one. It also compiles without significant warnings. It doesn't run, though, because ASP.NET pages are allowed to have at most one server-side *<head>* and *<form>* tag. The derived class will just add its own header and form to the existing one, thus producing prohibited duplicates. You can perhaps avoid that by writing the derived class in a particular way. But whatever efforts you put into it are not worth the cost, especially with master pages available in ASP.NET 2.0 that enjoy full support from the system. (See Chapter 6 in *Programming Microsoft ASP.NET 2.0: Core Reference* for full coverage of master pages and feasible forms of visual inheritance in ASP.NET.)

If you're going to reuse a bunch of pages or user controls in another Web application, you can consider delivering the dynamically created assembly instead of the source code. This approach makes sense in the context of large applications, in which you have quite a few pages and user controls (for example, *.ascx* files, which we'll cover in Chapter 12) that represent "closed" and not further updatable UI blocks. Instead of deploying them as source code, you sort of precompile them into a class library, thus obtaining a fully reusable piece of code. You create an ad hoc Web project in Visual Studio 2005, paying attention not to include *global.asax* and handling carefully any contents for which *web.config* is required. The fewer dependencies on application files, the better off you are. At this point, you publish the application using the Build|Publish menu option. From the target output directory, you pick up the generated assemblies, and you're done. You can do the same outside of Visual Studio 2005 by using the *MSBuild* tool. In all cases, make sure that you flag the Fixed Names check box, which will give assemblies more human-readable names.

The bottom line is that dynamically compiled page assemblies can be reused as is, but they cannot be used to build a hierarchy of pages in an object-oriented fashion.

Application Precompilation

By default, each public resource of an ASP.NET site is compiled on the fly only upon its first request. This introduces a first-hit delay as a result of the compilation process. Since the advent of ASP.NET 1.0, developers have raised the issue of site precompilation. Site precompilation brings a double benefit: no delay for requests because of compilation and no need of deploying source code to the Web server. Precompilation comes in two forms, each targeting a specific scenario: *in-place* and *deploy precompilation*. The former prepares all the resources in a site to be served without delay. It generates all needed dynamic assemblies for all pages and resources that need be compiled. In-place precompilation occurs on an already deployed application. It generates a site layout made only of assemblies that can be packaged and deployed to a production machine. This form of precompilation occurs on a development machine and is suited for out-of-the-box sites that, like classic Windows executable files, are not subject to dynamic changes. As do classic Windows executables, precompiled sites offer a high degree of protection against violations of the intellectual property behind the work.

In-Place Precompilation

In-place precompilation is merely a form of performance improvement. You deploy the application as usual using whatever technique you like or can afford—FTP, xcopy, or setup packages. Once the site is up and running on the production server, you precompile it before it goes public. Precompilation ensures that each page is accessed and each required dynamic assembly is created. In this way, even the first user hitting the page will be served quickly because the required assembly is already available. In-place precompilation essentially primes a site, meaning that no end user will ever wait for pages and their references to be compiled before being served a response.

Conditions for In-Place Precompilation

In-place precompilation assumes that the site is running under IIS, and it requires that .NET compilers are available on the target machine for the languages used by the pages. Precompilation will fail on the application if any file fails.

The in-place precompilation model preserves the full site structure and still allows sites to be extended with new pages or newer versions of existing pages. Needless to say, if new or modified pages are uploaded without stopping and recompiling the site, the first user hitting modified pages will experience the first-hit delay. When precompiling a site, though, only new or modified files are actually processed. Up-to-date files are skipped, thus minimizing the impact of the operation on the running sites.

The *aspnet_compiler* Utility

In-place precompilation consists essentially of running a batch compiler. It's analogous to manually requesting all the pages on the site to make sure all the code is compiled. The executable in charge of all forms of precompilation is *aspnet_compiler.exe*. You find it in the ASP.NET installation path:

```
%WINDOWS%\Microsoft.NET\Framework\[version]
```

To precompile a site in-place, you use the following command, where */proaspnet20* indicates the virtual folder of the application:

```
aspnet_compiler –v /proaspnet20
```

Table 1-6 lists the command-line switches supported by the utility that are relevant to in-place compilation.

Table 1-6   Command-Line Switches for *aspnet_compiler*

Switch	Description
-m	Indicates the full IIS metabase path of the application. This switch cannot be combined with the -v or -p switches.
-v	Indicates the virtual path of the application to be compiled. If -p is also specified, the physical path is used to locate the application. If no virtual path is specified, the application is assumed to be in the default site: *W3SVC/1/Root*.
-p	Indicates the physical path of the application to be compiled. If missing, the IIS metabase is used to locate the application. This switch must be combined with -v.
-d	If specified, the debug information is emitted during compilation.
-c	If specified, the precompiled application is fully rebuilt. Any previously compiled components will be recompiled.
-keyfile	Indicates the physical path to the key file for strong names.
-keycontainer	Indicates the name of the key container for strong names.
-aptca	If specified, compiled assemblies will allow partially trusted callers.
-delaysign	If specified, compiled assemblies are not fully signed when created.
-fixednames	If specified, the compiled assemblies will be given fixed names.

Let's look at an example of in-place precompilation.

Effects of In-Place Precompilation

After running the aforementioned command line, the utility runs and recursively scans all the pages and related dependencies in the virtual folder and child applications. Assemblies are generated in the code-gen directory and remain there to serve requests. Figure 1-9 shows the utility in action while the code-gen directory fills up.

To see it live, I suggest that you delete any temporary folder for your application and then run the utility from the command prompt. The folder fills up before your eyes, and when the tool completes, all required dynamic assemblies have been generated.

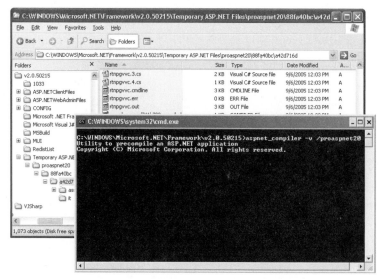

Figure 1-9 The *aspnet_compiler* in action precompiling a site in-place.

Note that *aspnet_compiler* requires *localhost* access and administrative rights on the machine to operate.

Precompilation for Deployment

Precompilation for deployment pursues different goals than in-place precompilation. Conceptually, it tends to transform the ASP.NET application into a closed executable that preserves intellectual property by hiding source code (both markup and classes). Precompilation generates a file representation of the site made of assemblies, static files, and configuration files that can be later packaged into a CAB, ZIP, or MSI file for actual deployment. As a pleasant side effect, it also saves your users from first-hit compilation delay. Precompilation for deployment has two variants that allow for nonupdatable or updatable sites.

You use the same utility—*aspnet_compiler*—to build manifests of a Web site. Table 1-7 lists additional command-line switches that are useful here.

Table 1-7   Additional Switches for *aspnet_compiler*

Switch	Description
-u	If specified, indicates that the precompiled application is updatable.
-f	Indicates that the target directory will be overwritten if it already exists and existing contents are lost.
targetDir	Indicates the physical path to which the application is compiled. If not specified, the application is precompiled in-place.

Nonupdatable Precompilation

The big difference between in-place and deploy precompilation is that the latter can work on the development machine and creates a deployable image of the site in the specified target directory. Try the following command:

```
aspnet_compiler -v /ProAspNet20 c:\Deliverable
```

You get the output shown in Figure 1-10.

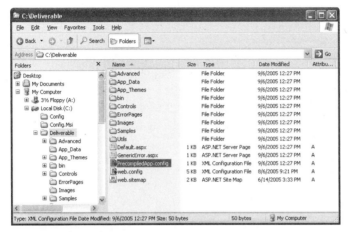

Figure 1-10   The site precompiled and ready for deployment.

The first thing that you notice is the presence of an additional small file named *precompiledapp.config* whose contents are shown here:

```
<precompiledApp version="2" updatable="false"/>
```

The file is a marker to inform the ASP.NET runtime that the application is precompiled. In the figure, you also see that *web.config* and *web.sitemap* have a different date. This is because static files such as images, *web.config*, *web.sitemap*, and HTML pages are not compiled. They are just copied to the target destination.

On the surface, the structure of the site is intact. However, if you delve a bit deeper, you see a lot of differences. First, all *.aspx* files are empty. To be more precise, they contain a string of text that warns you not to remove *.aspx* files even though they don't appear to contain any significant text.

In a precompiled solution, ASP.NET pages are marker files and should not be deleted. In other words, they represent a necessary endpoint and must be deployed. However, their contents won't be parsed or processed. You can also replace the text to display a custom message before you package the layout into a deliverable file.

The *Bin* folder of the application also contains a different set of assemblies, as in the original project. In addition to the referenced assemblies, the folder now contains one *App_Web_xxx* assembly for each page in the application.

Sites packaged for deployment only are not sensitive to file changes. When a change is required, you modify the original files, recompile the whole site, and redeploy the new layout. The only exception is the site configuration; you can update *web.config* or *web.sitemap* on the production server without having to recompile the site.

Updatable Precompilation

By adding a –*u* switch to the batch compiler utility, you can precompile a site to be updatable. In this case, *.aspx* files are slightly touched to remove the *CodeFile* attribute and change the *Inherits* attribute. Other files, on the other hand, are compiled as usual. In this way, you are allowed to make limited changes to the ASP.NET pages after compiling them. For example, you can change the position of controls or settings regarding colors, fonts, and other visual parameters. You can also add new controls to existing pages as long as they do not require event handlers or other code.

Code files are not deployed as source code, so you can't update the logic of the page without recompiling and redeploying the layout. Updatable sites won't save users from first-hit compilation delay when each page is accessed for the first time after a change is made.

> **Note** Updatable precompilation in ASP.NET 2.0 is nearly identical to the compilation and deployment model of ASP.NET 1.1, in which *.aspx* files are deployed in source and all classes (including code-behind classes) are compiled to assemblies.

Programmatic Precompilation

Site precompilation is also possible programmatically. The *ClientBuildManager* class exposes an API to invoke precompilation on an ASP.NET application. The *aspnet_compiler* utility simply creates an instance of the class and works through its public interface. The method to start the precompilation is *PrecompileApplication*.

The class constructors allow you to specify virtual and physical directories for the source and the target directory for the output. In addition, one of the constructors can accept additional parameters, such as precompilation flags and strong name attributes.

```
ClientBuildManagerParameter params = new ClientBuildManagerParameter();
params.PrecompilationFlags = PrecompilationFlags.Updatable |
                             PrecompilationFlags.OverwriteTarget;
ClientBuildManager cbm;
cbm = new ClientBuildManager(vdir, sourceDir, targetDir, params);
cbm.PrecompileApplication();
```

The *PrecompilationFlags* enum type is defined as follows:

```
public enum PrecompilationFlags {
     AllowPartiallyTrustedCallers = 0x20,
     Clean = 8,
     CodeAnalysis = 0x10,
     Default = 0,
     DelaySign = 0x40,
     FixedNames = 0x80,
     ForceDebug = 4,
     OverwriteTarget = 2,
     Updatable = 1
}
```

All classes are located in the *System.Web.Compilation* namespace.

Building Blocks of ASP.NET Compilation

The ASP.NET compilation machinery involves two main manager classes and a family of components named *build providers*. The two classes are the aforementioned *ClientBuildManager* and *BuildManager*.

ClientBuildManager acts a proxy between client applications such as Visual Studio and the ASP.NET back-end system that actually compiles pages and resources. *BuildManager* governs the physical compilation process from within the ASP.NET environment. It creates and uses build-provider components to process specific resources. Finally, *build providers* supply an object model to parse file types and generate code.

Behind each C# or Visual Basic .NET class dynamically compiled to an assembly from whatever application folder, there's a build provider. For example, a build provider governs the compilation of ASP.NET pages, themes, and profile information. You can define and register custom build providers to extend and enhance the set of file types that ASP.NET can handle. You'll see a sample custom build provider later in this book.

Let's start the tour of the ASP.NET compilation machinery with a look at the available configuration options.

Options for Compilation

The ASP.NET compilation environment is subject to a number of attributes defined in the *web.config* file. The section to check out is *<compilation>*. It is composed of four child sections, as listed in Table 1-8.

Table 1-8   Child Sections of *<compilation>*

Section	Description
<assemblies>	Lists the assemblies that are used during the compilation of an ASP.NET resource.
<codeSubDirectories>	Lists subdirectories containing code files to be compiled at run time. Typically, they are children of the *App_Code* folder. I'll return to this subject later.
<buildProviders>	Lists all registered build providers. I'll return to this subject later.
<expressionBuilders>	Lists all registered expression builders. (I'll cover expression builders in Chapter 5.)

Before going any further with child sections of the *<compilation>* block, let's explore the attributes available to *<compilation>*. The *Debug* attribute indicates whether to compile retail or debug binaries. The default is *false*. The *DefaultLanguage* attribute indicates the language to default to if the page lacks this information. The default is Visual Basic .NET. *Strict* and *Explicit* turn on and off the corresponding flags on the Visual Basic compiler. Finally, *TempDirectory* specifies the directory to use for temporary file storage during compilation.

Linked Assemblies

The *<assemblies>* section lists the assemblies automatically linked to each page class being compiled. The default contents of the section are shown here:

```
<assemblies>
    <add assembly="mscorlib" />
    <add assembly="System, ..." />
    <add assembly="System.Configuration, ..." />
    <add assembly="System.Web, ..." />
    <add assembly="System.Data, ..." />
    <add assembly="System.Web.Services, ..." />
    <add assembly="System.Xml, ..." />
    <add assembly="System.Drawing, ..." />
    <add assembly="System.EnterpriseServices, ..." />
    <add assembly="System.Web.Mobile, ..." />
    <add assembly="*" />
</assemblies>
```

The final *<add>* line dictates that all assemblies found in the */Bin* folder are to be loaded for the application. In application-specific *web.config* files, you can modify this list at will by using the *<clear />*, *<remove />*, and *<add />* nodes. They let you respectively empty the previous list, remove a particular assembly, and add a particular assembly.

Batch Compilation

ASP.NET attempts to batch into a single compiled assembly as many pages as possible without exceeding the configured maximum batch size. Batch compilation is a form of optimization that attempts to minimize the number of assemblies loaded into an application.

Batch compilation attempts to group in the same assembly pages resident in the same directory that are using the same language. Batch compilation is attempted only in Web directories containing page content such as *.aspx* and *.ascx* files. Reserved directories such as *App_Code* are always compiled atomically into a single assembly. Pages with parsing errors are excluded from compilation. When a page has a compile error, the result of the failed compilation is not included in the final assembly (see Table 1-9).

The batch system is governed by configuration directives in the *<compilation>* section of the configuration file.

Table 1-9   Batch Compilation Options

Attribute	Description
batch	Enables batch compilation. Set to *true* by default.
batchTimeout	Indicates, in seconds, the timeout period for batch compilation. If compilation cannot be completed within the timeout period, the compiler reverts to single compilation mode for the current page. *Note that in ASP.NET 2.0, this is no longer supported, and it is ignored.*
maxBatchSize	Indicates the maximum number of pages to be grouped together per batch compilation.
maxBatchGeneratedFileSize	Maximum combined size (in KB) of the generated source file per batch compilation.

Fine-tuning parameters in the *<compilation>* section of the configuration file is important and should save you from both having (and loading) 1000 different assemblies for as many pages and from having a single huge assembly with 1000 classes inside. Notice, though, that the problem here is not only with the size and the number of the assemblies but also with the time needed to recompile the assemblies in case of updates.

No-Compile Pages

In ASP.NET 2.0, *no-compile* pages are special pages that are just never compiled. You create a no-compile page by setting the *CompilationMode* attribute on the *@Page* directive to *Never*. What's the purpose of no-compile pages, and what's the difference between ASP.NET no-compile pages and static HTML pages?

First and foremost, no-compile pages are not for every application. No-compile pages are designed for improving scalability on very large Web sites with thousands of pages. A no-compile page is written like any other ASP.NET page and is, therefore, made of server controls. It is not allowed to contain code in its code-behind file, though. You can't have it bound to a code file, nor can it contain a server-side *<script>* block. The only executable piece of code allowed in a no-compile page are $-expressions. In Chapter 5, in the discussion of custom $-expressions, you'll learn that they can optionally be defined to work inside no-compile pages.

There are two main benefits of no-compile pages. In a secure environment such as Microsoft SharePoint Services, no-compile pages prevent developers from writing potentially buggy code that can cause problems to the hosting environment and even tear it down if the code crashes. In a large content-based Web site, no-compile pages avoid the need to compile thousands of pages. It should be noted that Windows operating systems have a limit on the number of DLLs that can be loaded into an application. As you hit this limit, the performance degrades significantly. For such large Web sites, no-compile pages offer a way to unload from memory and garbage-collect individual pages. Note that as regular assemblies, pages can't be unloaded without unloading the whole AppDomain. In theory, a no-compile site can serve an infinite number of pages without ever needing an AppDomain restart.

No-compile pages are a scalability feature rather than a performance feature. As far as raw performance is concerned, you should not expect any tangible benefit from the adoption of no-compile pages; in fact, it's probably even a little bit slower.

It's known that ASP.NET pages differ from HTML pages because of compilation. So what's the deal with no-compile ASP.NET pages? How do they work? The point of no-compile pages is that no assembly is created and persisted to disk. Rather, the control builder of the page is saved in memory and reused to create the page for each and every request. This cache is updated whenever, for whatever reason, the application is restarted.

ASP.NET Reserved Folders

There are a number of reserved folders (see Table 1-10) in an ASP.NET application.

Table 1-10   ASP.NET Reserved Folders

Folder name	File Types	Notes
Bin	.dll	Contains any prebuilt assemblies required by the application.
App_Browsers	.browser	Contains application-specific browser definition files that ASP.NET uses to identify individual browsers and determine their capabilities.
App_Code	.cs, .vb, .xsd, custom file types	Contains source class files to compile as part of the application. ASP.NET compiles the code in this folder when pages are requested. Code in the folder is referenced automatically in applications.
App_Data	.mdb, .mdf, .xml	Contains Microsoft Office Access and SQL Express files as well as XML files or other data stores.
App_GlobalResources	.resx	Contains resource files to be used programmatically in the localization of an application.
App_LocalResources	.resx	Contains page-scoped resource files.
App_Themes	.skin, .css, .xsl, auxiliary files	Contains a collection of files that define the appearance of ASP.NET pages and controls.
App_WebReferences	.wsdl	Contains WSDL files to generate proxy classes and other files associated with using Web services in your application.

The Bin Folder

The Bin folder contains all deployable assemblies required by the application for controls, components, or other code that you want to reference. Any *.dll* files found in the directory will be automatically linked to the application. If unused or outdated files are left around, the risk is that you'll get "ambiguous reference" exceptions. In other words, if two distinct assemblies define the same class (same namespace and class name), the ASP.NET runtime can't resolve which one to use and raises an exception. This is a common error when, at development time, you rename a project or an assembly name. To avoid that, make sure that no unnecessary assembly is found or at least remove the following line from the *<assemblies>* section in the configuration file:

```
<add assembly="*" />
```

Of all the folders listed in Table 1-10, only *Bin* is recognized also by ASP.NET 1.x applications. This folder is mandatory.

The *App_Browsers* Folder

This optional folder contains *.browser* files. A *.browser* file describes characteristics and capabilities of a browser—be it a mobile device or a desktop browser. ASP.NET installs a bunch of *.browser* files in the *Config\Browsers* folder under the installation path. These files are shared by all applications. You place under the *App_Browsers* folder only the browser files specific to the current application. The content of the *.browser* file is compiled on the fly to provide up-to-date browser information to the ASP.NET runtime.

Let's briefly address a scenario in which having a custom *.browser* file might be helpful. Imagine that your application uses a control that doesn't render effectively under a certain browser. You can write a *.browser* file to force ASP.NET to use a different adapter to render that control when the host page is served by the specified browser.

```
<browsers>
<browser id="browserID">
  <controlAdapters>
    <adapter controlType="Samples.CustomControl"
             adapterType="Samples.Adapters.CustomControlAdapter" />
  </controlAdapters>
</browser>
</browsers>
```

Assuming that *browserID* matches one of the standard browsers recognized by ASP.NET, the *.browser* file just shown dictates that *CustomControlAdapter* be used to render *CustomControl* under the specified browser.

The *App_Code* Folder

The *App_Code* subdirectory lives immediately underneath the Web application's root and stores all class files that should be dynamically compiled as part of the application. These class files get automatically linked to the application and don't require you to add any explicit directive or declaration in the page to create the dependency. Class files placed in the *App_Code* folder can contain any recognized ASP.NET component—custom controls, helper classes, build providers, business classes, custom providers, HTTP handlers, and so on.

> **Note**   At development time, changes to the *App_Code* folder cause the whole application to be recompiled. For large projects, this can be undesirable and time-consuming. For this reason, I encourage you to modularize your code into distinct class libraries in which you group logically related sets of classes. Mostly helper classes specific to the application should make their way into the *App_Code* folder.

All class files dropped into the *App_Code* folder should use the same language. If you have class files written in two or more languages, you must create language-specific subdirectories to contain classes for each language you support. Once files have been grouped by language, you add an entry to the *web.config* file for each subdirectory:

```
<compilation>
    <codeSubDirectories>
        <add directoryName="VBFolder" />
    </codeSubDirectories>
</compilation>
```

It is important that the language-specific subdirectory is registered in the *web.config* file; otherwise, all files underneath *App_Code* will be compiled to a single assembly regardless of the folder they belong to. The preceding configuration script delineates a situation in which all, say, C# files are in the root *App_Code,* and a few Visual Basic .NET class files are moved into the *VBFolder* directory. If a directory mentioned in the *<codeSubDirectories>* section doesn't exist, you'll receive a compilation error.

Files in the root *App_Code* folder are compiled to *App_Code_xxx.dll* assembly, where *xxx* is a randomly generated sequence of characters. Files in a given subdirectory will be compiled to a dynamically created assembly named *App_SubCode_xxx_yyy.dll*, where *xxx* indicates the name of the subdirectory and *yyy* is a random sequence of characters. The *<codeSubDirectories>* section is valid only if it is set in the *web.config* file in the application root.

A strongly named assembly can be created by dropping an *assemblyinfo.cs* file in the *App_Code* directory or any other subdirectory you might have. Obviously, you'll use an *assemblyinfo.vb* file if the folder contains Visual Basic .NET files. The assembly configuration file may refer to an *.snk* file to contain the key for the strong name.

Note   To sign an assembly with a strong name, you must first obtain a public/private key pair. You can get such a key pair by using the Strong Name tool (*sn.exe*), one of the SDK binaries you'll find in the installation path of the .NET Framework. Key pair files usually have an *.snk* extension. You save this file to an application folder and reference it in the *assemblyinfo.cs* file, as shown here:

```
[assembly: AssemblyKeyFileAttribute(@"yourKeyPair.snk")]
```

Note that Visual Basic .NET looks for the key file in the directory containing the Visual Studio Solution, whereas the C# compiler looks for the key file in the directory containing the binary. In light of this, adjust the path you use with the attribute, or place the key file in the proper folder.

On any subsequent rebuild, the name for assemblies change, and as soon as the old AppDomain requests cycle out, the old assemblies are removed.

The *App_Code* folder can contain more than just class files. In particular, it can contain and automatically process XSD files representing a schema of data. When an XSD file is added to the folder, the compiler will parse it to a typed *DataSet* class, which will be added to the application scope. In ASP.NET 1.x, this work is accomplished by a Visual Studio .NET wizard and uses a command-line utility under the hood—*xsd.exe*.

Note   When you register a component (for example, a custom server control or a custom HTTP handler) with the *web.config* file, you are typically requested to specify the name of the assembly that contains the code. If the component is defined in the *App_Code* folder, which name should you indicate for the assembly? In this case, you just omit the assembly information and specify only the full class name. When no assembly is specified, the ASP.NET runtime attempts to load the class from any loaded assemblies, including the dynamically created assembly for the *App_Code* folder.

The *App_Data* Folder

The *App_Data* folder is expected to contain data stores local to the application. It typically contains data stores in the form of files such as Microsoft Access or Microsoft SQL Server Express databases, XML files, text files, and whatever else your application can support. The contents of the folder are not processed by ASP.NET. The folder is the default location where ASP.NET providers store their data.

Note   The default ASP.NET account is granted full permissions on the folder. If you happen to change the ASP.NET account, make sure that the new account is granted read/write permissions on the folder.

The *App_GlobalResources* Folder

Just like other applications, an ASP.NET application can, and often should, use resources. Resources are an effective way to isolate localizable portions of the application's user interface. In general, a resource is nonexecutable text associated with the program. Typical resources are images, icons, text, and auxiliary files, but any serializable object can be considered a resource. Application resources are stored outside of the application so that they can be recompiled and replaced without affecting and recompiling the application itself.

An ASP.NET application needs to have a primary assembly to contain the default or neutral resources for the application. In addition, you deploy a number of satellite assemblies, each containing localized resources for a particular culture you want to support. In ASP.NET 1.x, compiling resources inside an assembly is a bit boring. You have to manually compile XML-based resource files (those with a *.resx* extension) into a *.resources* binary file. These files can be either embedded in a .NET executable or compiled into satellite assemblies. You use the Resource File Generator (*resgen.exe*) utility to convert text and XML-based resource files into *.resources* files. The resource file names follow the naming convention *baseName.culture-Name.resources*. Typically, the base name is the name of the application.

```
resgen.exe ProAspNet20.resx ProAspNet20.it.resources
```

Once created, the *.resources* file should be embedded into an assembly, or it can even be used as is as a resource container. To embed the resource file into a satellite assembly, you use the Assembly Linker tool (*al.exe*). On the command line, you indicate the culture (*it* in the next example, which represents Italian) and the name of the assembly.

```
al /out:ProAspNet20.resources.dll /c:it /embed:ProAspNet20.it.resources
```

After you compile your satellite assemblies, they will all have the same name. You deploy them in distinct subdirectories, each named after the culture.

Fortunately, with ASP.NET 2.0, gone are the days of satellite assemblies. More precisely, satellite assemblies are still there, but they are a thing of the past for developers thanks to the *App_GlobalResources* reserved folder.

Any *.resx* files located within the folder are automatically compiled to satellite assemblies. The name of the *.resx* file contains culture information to help the ASP.NET runtime environment with the assembly generation. The following files—*resources.resx*, *resources.it.resx*, *resources .fr.resx*—generate the neutral assembly and satellite assemblies for the Italian and French cultures. The neutral assembly is the default culture resource used by the application if no specific culture is called for.

Resource files located in the *App_GlobalResources* folder are global to the application and can be referenced from within any page. Resource reading results are greatly simplified from ASP.NET 1.x, too:

```
<asp:Label Runat="server" Text="<%$ Resources:ResxFile, MyResName %>" />
```

You can bind global resources declaratively using the newest $-expression named *Resources*. (I'll cover $-expressions in more detail in Chapter 5.) The expression takes two parameters—the name of the *.resx* source file (no extension), and the name of the resource to retrieve. To access resources programmatically, you resort to the following code:

```
HttpContext.GetGlobalResourceObject(resxFile, MyResName)
```

Both parameters are strings and have the same role as the parameters in the $-expression. Moreover, the implementation of the $- expression *Resources* uses *GetGlobalResourceObject* internally.

The *App_LocalResources* Folder

App_LocalResources is a subdirectory located below the folder that contains some ASP.NET pages. The folder can be filled with *.resx* files named after the pages located one level upper in the hierarchy. Assuming that the parent folder contains *test.aspx*, here are few feasible resource files you can find in the *App_LocalResources* folder: *test.aspx.resx, test.aspx.it.resx, test.aspx.fr.resx*. Obviously, resources stored in the aforementioned files have an effect only on *test.aspx* and are visible (and can be used) only from within the linked page.

How do you access a page-specific resource? For programmatic access, you use the following code:

```
HttpContext.GetLocalResourceObject("/ProAspNet20/ResPage.aspx",
                                   "PageResource1.Title")
```

The first parameter indicates the virtual path of the page; the second parameter is the resource name. For declarative access, you use the *meta:ResourceKey* attribute. Here's an example:

```
<asp:Button Runat="server" meta:resourcekey="ButtonResource1" />
```

The declaration associates a unique resource key with the specified button instance. The local *.resx* file will contain entries of the form *prefix.name*, where *prefix* is a resource key and *name* is a property name on the bound control. To give the button a localizable caption (the *Text* property), you simply create a *ButtonResource1.Text* entry in the resource file.

Resource files found in the both the local and global resource folders are compiled to create classes for satellite assemblies. The net effect is that developers create *.resx* files and test the page. The ASP.NET compilation machinery does the rest.

The *App_Themes* Folder

The *App_Themes* folder defines themes for ASP.NET controls. Each theme takes a folder under *App_Themes*. Defined, a theme is a collection of files with style information. Compiled, the contents of the files in a theme folder generate a class that, invoked by the page, programmatically sets styles on themed controls.

The *App_Themes* folder lists themes local to the application. An application can also inherit global themes defined in the following folder:

```
%WINDOWS%\Microsoft.NET\Framework\[version]\ASP.NETClientFiles\Themes
```

From the compilation perspective, there's no difference between global and local themes. If a theme with a given name exists both locally to the application and globally to the server machine, the local theme takes precedence.

The *App_WebReferences* Folder

In Visual Studio .NET 2003, an ASP.NET application that requires access to a Web service will obtain the corresponding *.wsdl* file through the Add Web Reference dialog box. The Web Service Description Language (WSDL) document for the Web service is not sufficient to make the Web service usable from the page. An ASP.NET page is ultimately a managed class and needs another managed class to talk to. So the Web service is wrapped by a proxy class. The proxy class is created by Visual Studio using the services of a command-line tool–*wsdl.exe*. The proxy class contains as many methods as there are Web methods on the Web service, and it incorporates any custom data type defined by the public interface of the Web service.

There are no significant costs for developers in this operation. However, developers are clearly dependent on Visual Studio to generate the proxy class. Wouldn't it be easier and simpler if you could just drop the *.wsdl* file somewhere in the application's tree and have ASP.NET deal with the rest? This is just what the *App_WebReferences* folder is for.

It recognizes *.wsdl* files describing bound Web services, and it generates runtime proxy classes so that ASP.NET pages can place calls to the Web service in a type-safe manner. The *App_WebReferences* folder can contain subfolders. The name of the subfolder drives the namespace of the resulting proxy class, whereas the WSDL file defines the classname. For example, the *samples.wsdl* file ProAspNet20 subfolder will originate a proxy class named *ProAspNet20.Samples*. The dynamically created assembly is named *App_WebReferences.xxx.dll*, where *xxx* is a random sequence of characters.

Build Providers

In ASP.NET 1.x, only a few file types are dynamically compiled into assemblies–ASP.NET pages, user controls, ASP.NET Web services, and custom HTTP handlers. In ASP.NET 2.0, a completely revisited compilation model extended this model to virtually any file type that you use in your application. In ASP.NET 2.0, commonly used file types are bound to a special breed of component–the build provider–which communicates with the ASP.NET infrastructure and provides the code representation of the contents of the specified file. Hence the build provider registered to process *.aspx* files will parse the *.aspx* markup and build a class according to the rules we examined in "The Hidden Code of an ASP.NET Page" section. This class will then be transformed into an assembly with a given scope.

ASP.NET developers are familiar with this model. The great news is that ASP.NET 2.0 applies this same model to a wide range of file types, such as class files (*.cs*, *.vb*), resource files (*.resx*), Web service references (*.wsdl*), typed DataSet (*.xsd*), themes, and so on. Certain file types undergo a runtime transformation process when dropped in some reserved folders. This transformation is driven by native build providers with the same internal architecture and mechanics of providers that build ASP.NET pages.

What's a Build Provider, Anyway?

A *build provider* is a component that can plug into the ASP.NET compilation system and provide custom compilation support for some file types. Build providers can automatically generate an appropriate proxy class by interpreting at compile time the contents of the source file. A build provider generates compilable code and keeps it in sync with the source file; as the source file changes, the build provider kicks in again and updates everything.

To solidify a discussion of build providers that so far has been a bit abstract, I suggest taking a look at the following excerpt from the default configuration file. It illustrates the built-in bindings between file types and native build providers.

```
<compilation>
  <buildProviders>
    <add extension=".aspx"
        type="System.Web.Compilation.PageBuildProvider" />
    <add extension=".ascx"
        type="System.Web.Compilation.UserControlBuildProvider" />
    <add extension=".master"
        type="System.Web.Compilation.MasterPageBuildProvider" />
    <add extension=".asmx"
          type="System.Web.Compilation.WebServiceBuildProvider" />
    <add extension=".ashx"
        type="System.Web.Compilation.WebHandlerBuildProvider" />
    <add extension=".resx"
        type="System.Web.Compilation.ResXBuildProvider" />
    <add extension=".resources"
        type="System.Web.Compilation.ResourcesBuildProvider" />
    <add extension=".wsdl"
        type="System.Web.Compilation.WsdlBuildProvider" />
    <add extension=".xsd"
        type="System.Web.Compilation.XsdBuildProvider" />
     <add extension=".js"
        type="System.Web.Compilation.ForceCopyBuildProvider" />
  </buildProviders>
</compilation>
```

All these build providers are nonpublic, internal classes defined in the *System.Web.Compilation* namespace inside the *system.web* assembly. All these classes derive from one common root—the *BuildProvider* class. (We'll get to the nitty-gritty details of *BuildProviders* in a moment.) Figure 1-11 shows the conceptual layout of the ASP.NET compilation model.

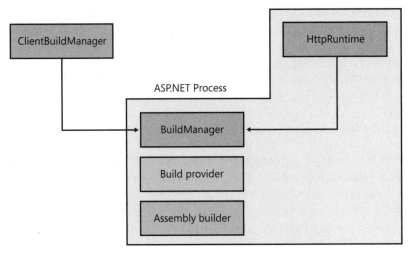

Figure 1-11   Conceptual layout for the ASP.NET compilation system.

The host environment receives input from external components—a client (for example, Visual Studio 2005 or precompilation utilities) using the *ClientBuildManager* API or the ASP.NET pipeline—and activates the build manager. The build manager, in turn, invokes the build provider in charge of the resource. When the proxy class has been generated, the assembly builder kicks in to compile the source.

> **Note**   Build providers are an important building block in the overall ASP.NET infrastructure, but they are certainly not the kind of component you'll have to tinker with every day. You should know that they exist and how they work. In the end, however, you'll rarely run into them unless you need to adjust the way certain files are processed by ASP.NET. In addition, build providers can be used to significantly enhance the runtime environment, as I'll show in the next section.

Most native build providers process some source file and generate a managed class for it that is then compiled to an application-scoped assembly. There are a couple of notable exceptions, though.

Build providers kick in during compilation, but compilation can occur for two different reasons—to service a user request at run time and to precompile an application. A file for which a build provider is registered is passed to the provider and processed. What happens next depends on the build provider logic. Application files mapped to a .NET language (for example, *.cs* or *.vb* files) are passed to the respective compilers and processed, but they are not deployed. Files that are bound neither to compilers nor build providers are ignored during the compilation step. The precompilation for the deployment mechanism, though, copies them verbatim to the final layout.

There are two points left open: What happens with *.js* files? And what if you want to exclude some files from deployment? *ForceCopyBuildProvider* addresses the former, while *IgnoreFileBuildProvider* is used for the latter.

The *ForceCopyBuildProvider* Provider

Specifically designed for *.js* files, this provider ensures that *.js* files are always copied during the precompilation for deployment. The issue is that *.js* is the extension of a standard .NET language—JScript. According to the rules I just outlined, Javascript files wouldn't be deployed. However, a *.js* file is often a client-side file, the lack of which can compromise an application. To avoid that, the *.js* extension is bound to *ForceCopyBuildProvider*, and *.js* files are then always copied when you deploy your Web site through the Copy Web Site operation in Visual Studio 2005.

The *IgnoreFileBuildProvider* Provider

Whereas *ForceCopyBuildProvider* always copies files, the *IgnoreFileBuild* provider always excludes files of a certain type from participating in any compiling or publishing operation. The ignore-file provider is particularly useful for development-only files you maintain for internal purposes but that have no reasons for being deployed—for example, a Microsoft Office Word document, Microsoft Office Visio diagrams, and so on. Enter the following script in your *web.config* file to let the compilation system ignore *.doc* files.

```
<compilation>
<buildProviders>
    <add extension=".doc"
        type="System.Web.Compilation.IgnoreFileBuildProvider" />
</buildProviders>
</compilation>
```

The *IgnoreFileBuildProvider* prevents mapped files from being deployed during a publish-Web or compilation operation.

Architecting a Custom Build Provider

Build providers are a constituent part of the compilation machinery and participate in build operations regardless of the starter—be it Visual Studio 2005 or the ASP.NET runtime. As a developer, you can implement your own provider to add custom semantics to ASP.NET compilation.

The canonical example consists of adding logic to process files with a given extension whose contents represent a mapping with one or more database tables. (I'll demonstrate this in a moment.) The provider could then dynamically generate strongly typed classes to render columns in the table. Classes will be generated any time one of these files is added to the project. Nicely enough, build providers also get you full IntelliSense support within Visual Studio 2005.

> **Note**   Have you ever wondered what the magic is that allows Visual Studio 2005 to recognize control properties through IntelliSense on the code-behind class of an *.aspx* page? In ASP.NET 1.x, Visual Studio .NET 2003 created ad hoc members to represent controls in protected regions so that the class was complete for a .NET reflection analysis. In ASP.NET 2.0, members that represent server controls are created at compile time thanks to the mechanism of partial classes. So how can IntelliSense work correctly on code files?
>
> The answer is that Visual Studio 2005 has the *.aspx* build provider generate the dynamic source code of the class with all missing declarations. The resulting assembly is loaded in the Visual Studio 2005 process; the resulting type of the page is scanned through reflection to populate the IntelliSense drop-down lists.

Goal of the *OrmBuildProvider* Provider

Let's look at an example. When building a data access layer (DAL) for your Web application, would you use ADO.NET *DataSet* objects or would you rather opt for custom collection classes? *DataSets* are ready-made objects and provide quite a few powerful functionalities such as sorting, filtering, and support for relationships. On the other hand, with collections of custom classes, you can create a data model that better fits the real entities of your problem domain. Custom collections have a more compact memory footprint, but they must be coded manually. Even though there are plenty of base classes in the .NET Framework, writing a realistic custom collection is still a time-consuming task. In the .NET Framework 2.0, the advent of generics greatly simplifies the creation of custom collection classes. A custom collection is no more complex than the following code:

```
public class CustomerCollection : Collection<Customer> {
}
```

You still have to code the *Customer* class, which will be dependent on the schema of some table in some database. Wouldn't it be nice if you could drop into the Web project some text file with a description of what you want and have ASP.NET do the rest? The pattern behind doesn't look much different from what happens with *.xsd* or *.resx* files. Both are XML files and describe some data; yet the ASP.NET compilation machinery can create classes out of them. To get this, you need a build provider to process the text file (or whatever format you want to use) and build a representation of the contents that can be compiled to an assembly.

The representation of the source file contents can be some plain text that forms one or more classes in the language being used by the application, or it can be an abstract, language-agnostic representation of the class created using the CodeDOM API. (I'll say more about this topic shortly.) The *BuildProvider* base class has a number of helper methods to make it easy to read-in the contents of the source file and build the resulting assembly.

The *OrmBuildProvider* I'm going to build will process *.map* files containing an XML description of a database table for which an entity class and a related collection class are required.

Structure of the *.map* Source File

It is agreed that any investments in the building of a collection-based DAL pays off only when the overall size of the application exceeds a certain threshold of complexity. In other words, for simple-minded applications, *DataSets* are just fine. However, I believe that if there were a quick and easy way to inject collections, even the laziest developer would be pleased to experiment with custom collections. The *.map* files and their underlying *OrmBuildProvide* are exactly what we need to fill this gap.

> **Note**   There's a lot to say about *DataSets* and custom collections and which of them fits better in various scenarios. Custom collections and *DataSets* are not functionally equivalent, although they are two ways of solving the same problem: containing and marshaling data across application tiers. Custom collections allow for a closer representation of real data, whereas *DataSets* implement an interesting number of features out-of-the-box. For more information, you can read the following article: *http://msdn.microsoft.com/msdnmag/issues/05/08/CuttingEdge*.

The format of the *.map* file is arbitrary, and it doesn't even have to be XML. However, I'm using the following XML schema:

```
<mappings namespace="ProAspNet20.Components">
    <mapping connectionString="SERVER=.;DATABASE=northwind;UID=...;"
        tableName="Customers"
        className="Customer"
        selectCommand="SELECT companyname AS CompanyName,
                              contactname AS Contact,
                              country As Country FROM customers"
        allowPartialClass="true"
        allowCollectionClass="true"
        collectionClassName="CustomerCollection">
    </mapping>
    ⋮
</mappings>
```

The <*mappings*> node is the outermost container of a list of <*mapping*> nodes, each representing a mapping between a group of classes and a database table. All the generated classes will belong to the same namespace, whose details are set in the <*mappings*> node. Table 1-11 lists the attributes of the <*mapping*> node.

Table 1-11   **Attributes of** *<mapping>*

Attribute	Description
allowCollectionClass	Indicates whether or not a collection class is required.
allowPartialClass	Indicates whether or not the entity class is partial.
className	Name of the entity class to be created.
collectionClassName	Name of the collection of entity classes.
connectionString	Connection string to access schema information.
selectCommand	Command used to retrieve schema information. Lists the columns and the name with which they will be mapped to class members.
tableName	Name of the table the entity class is based on.

Basically, you choose a table on a database and select a bunch of columns through the specified select command. The returned column information is used to build a .NET class with as many members as there are columns in the query. Each member takes the name and type of the column. The class ends up being a representation of the logical entity—such as employee, customer, or product—mapped to the table. The entity class can be flagged as partial and equipped with an optional collection class and possibly even a gateway class. The sample *.map* file I just outlined is expected to create the following classes:

- **Employee**   This class represents a logical entity in the problem domain. The class has as many members as there are columns in the specified select command. Each member is named after the public name of the column as modified by the *AS* clause.

- **EmployeeCollection**   A collection of *Employee* objects.

Once a *.map* file is dropped onto the *App_Code* folder, the registered build provider takes control of it, reads-in the contents, and generates dynamic classes. Let's see how.

> **Note**   You can extend the *.map* schema further. For example, if you intend to build your DAL according to the Data Mapper (DM) design pattern, you can enhance the schema and underlying build provider to generate a stub for a gateway class. In the DM pattern, the gateway class groups methods that represent the behavior of an entity class. According to DM rules, the gateway is a singleton class that can serve multiple instances of the entity class. In most cases, it is implemented as a set of static methods.

Implementing the Build Provider

A build provider is a class that inherits from *BuildProvider*. At a minimum, the derived class overrides the method *GenerateCode*. Here's the typical outline of the class:

```
public class OrmBuildProvider : BuildProvider
{
    public OrmBuildProvider() {
    }

    public override void GenerateCode(AssemblyBuilder ab)
```

```
    {
        // Get the virtual path to the source file
        string fileName = base.VirtualPath;

        // Get the tree representing the generated code
        CodeCompileUnit code = BuildCodeTree(fileName);

        // Build an assembly using the code tree
        ab.AddCodeCompileUnit(this, code);
    }
}
```

As the name suggests, the method *GenerateCode* processes the input *.map* file and generates one or more source classes with the collected information. The classes are described in a tree-based structure according to the CodeDOM model. When done, the code is passed to the assembly builder class and compiled. As you can see, overriding *GenerateCode* is as simple as writing a helper method to generate the source code of a compilable class based on the contents of the input file. Here's an example:

```
private CodeCompileUnit BuildCodeTree(string fileName)
{
    OrmDescriptor desc = ExtractInfo(fileName);
    return GenerateCodeDomTree(desc);
}
```

The method is articulated in two steps—reading in information from the *.map* file and generating the code tree. Information from the *.map* file is packed into an *OrmDescriptor* class defined, as shown here:

```
class OrmDescriptor
{
    public string Namespace;
    public OrmTableDescriptor[] Descriptors;
}
class OrmTableDescriptor
{
    public string ConnectionString;
    public string TableName;
    public string ClassName;
    public string SelectCommand;
    public bool IsPartial;
    public bool AllowCollectionClass;
    public string CollectionClassName;
}
```

The helper method *ExtractInfo* uses the XML Document Object Model (XMLDOM) API to parse the *.map* file and populate the descriptor.

```
OrmDescriptor ExtractInfo(string fileName)
{
    // Load the document
    XmlDocument doc = new XmlDocument();
    using (Stream file = VirtualPathProvider.OpenFile(fileName))
        {
            // Consider using a validating reader here for both
            // better performance and to check on the schema of the
            // document being loaded
            doc.Load(file);
        }

    // Get namespace information
    XmlNode root = doc.DocumentElement;
    string ns = root.Attributes["namespace"].Value;

    // Visit the <mapping> nodes
    XmlNodeList mappings = doc.SelectNodes("mappings/mapping");
    OrmTableDescriptor[] descriptors;
    descriptors = new OrmTableDescriptor[mappings.Count];
    for(int i=0; i<descriptors.Length; i++)
    {
        XmlNode mapping = mappings[i];
        OrmTableDescriptor t = new OrmTableDescriptor();
        descriptors[i] = t;

        t.ConnectionString = mapping.Attributes["connectionString"].Value;
        t.ClassName = mapping.Attributes["className"].Value;
        t.TableName = mapping.Attributes["tableName"].Value;
        t.SelectCommand = mapping.Attributes["selectCommand"].Value;

        bool isPartial = false;
        Boolean.TryParse(
            mapping.Attributes["allowPartialClass"].Value,
            out isPartial);
        t.IsPartial = isPartial;

        bool allowCollection = false;
        Boolean.TryParse(
            mapping.Attributes["allowCollectionClass"].Value,
            out allowCollection))
        t.AllowCollectionClass = allowCollection;
        if (allowCollection)
        {
            string coll = mapping.Attributes["collectionClassName"].Value;
            t.CollectionClassName = coll;
        }

        // Pack all info and return
        OrmDescriptor desc = new OrmDescriptor();
        desc.Namespace = ns;
        desc.Descriptors = descriptors;
        return desc;
    }
}
```

There are two ways in which a class can be generated as source code. The simplest option entails that you concatenate strings of text that represent instructions of a particular language. The second option is illustrated in the next section and uses the language-agnostic CodeDOM model. The CodeDOM model is a far more sophisticated solution but requires familiarity with a quirky and abstract API. Let's tackle this option first.

The CodeDOM Object Model

The Code Document Object Model (CodeDOM) is the .NET Framework API for code generation. Used extensively by ASP.NET native build providers, the CodeDOM API is located in the *System.CodeDom* namespace. It contains a bunch of classes that can be used to render a code graph in either Visual Basic .NET or C#. You outline the structure of the code you want to obtain by building a hierarchy of code elements and then ask the CodeDOM internal classes to render it in the language of choice. The *System.CodeDom* classes let you indicate the type of statement you want and its parameters. Next, when it comes to generating code, that generic description is turned into the real syntax. In the .NET Framework 2.0, the CodeDOM API has been further enhanced to support new language features such as partial classes and generics.

The *GenerateCodeDomTree* routine you met earlier uses CodeDOM to build entity and collection classes. The entity class will be (optionally) a partial class with a few property members. The collection class will be a generic-based list of entity classes. The following code shows how to build this tree:

```
CodeCompileUnit GenerateCodeDomTree(OrmDescriptor desc)
{
    CodeCompileUnit code = new CodeCompileUnit();

    // Import required namespaces
    CodeNamespaceImport import;
    import = new CodeNamespaceImport("System.Collections.Generic");

    // Create the namespace and add it to the code unit
    CodeNamespace ns = new CodeNamespace(desc.Namespace);
    ns.Imports.Add(import);
    code.Namespaces.Add(ns);

    // Loop through the mappings and add classes
    for (int i = 0; i < desc.Descriptors.Length; i++)
    {
        // Get the descriptor for the current mapping
        OrmTableDescriptor t = desc.Descriptors[i];

        // Create the class to represent the table
        CodeTypeDeclaration cls = new CodeTypeDeclaration(t.ClassName);
        cls.IsPartial = t.IsPartial;
        ns.Types.Add(cls);
```

```
// Loop through the selected table columns and add members
SqlDataAdapter adapter = new SqlDataAdapter(
    t.SelectCommand, t.ConnectionString);
DataTable dt = new DataTable();
adapter.FillSchema(dt, SchemaType.Mapped);

for(int j=0; j<dt.Columns.Count; j++)
{
    DataColumn column = dt.Columns[j];
    string colName = column.ColumnName;
    Type colType = column.DataType;
    string fieldName = "_" + colName.ToLower();

    //
    // Add a property for each column
    //

    // Add the private field to store the data
    CodeMemberField fld = new CodeMemberField(colType, fieldName);
    cls.Members.Add(fld);

    // Add property declaration and get/set accessors
    CodeMemberProperty prop = new CodeMemberProperty();
    prop.Name = column.ColumnName;
    prop.Type = new CodeTypeReference(column.DataType);
    prop.Attributes = MemberAttributes.Public;

    // Define the codeDOM reference for the property's private field
    CodeFieldReferenceExpression fldRef;
    fldRef = new CodeFieldReferenceExpression();
    fldRef.TargetObject = new CodeThisReferenceExpression();
    fldRef.FieldName = fieldName;

    // Get
    CodeMethodReturnStatement ret;
    ret = new CodeMethodReturnStatement(fldRef);
    prop.GetStatements.Add(ret);

    // Set
    CodeAssignStatement assign = new CodeAssignStatement();
    assign.Left = fldRef;
    assign.Right = new CodePropertySetValueReferenceExpression();
    prop.SetStatements.Add(assign);

    cls.Members.Add(prop);
}

// Create the collection class if required
if (t.AllowCollectionClass)
{
    string collName = t.CollectionClassName;
    CodeTypeDeclaration coll = new CodeTypeDeclaration(collName);
```

```
CodeTypeReference type = new CodeTypeReference("List",
    CodeTypeReferenceOptions.GenericTypeParameter);
type.TypeArguments.Add(t.ClassName);
coll.BaseTypes.Add(type);
ns.Types.Add(coll);
    }
  }
}
```

The most interesting part of this code is the generation of a collection class based on generics. Assuming that the entity class name is *Customer*, the final code will be the following:

```
public class CustomerCollection : List<Customer> {}
```

You first create a *CodeTypeDeclaration* object with the name of the collection class. Next, you create the CodeDOM reference to a type—the *CodeTypeReference* class. In the preceding code, the type is *List<T>*. Obviously, a generic type needs a type argument to replace the *T* in the declaration. The *Customer* type to qualify the collection is added through the *TypeArguments* collection. Finally, the resulting *List<Customer>* type is set as the base type for the collection being defined.

At this point, let's drop the *.map* file we saw earlier in the *App_Code* folder and see what happens.

> **Note**   When creating generic collection classes, should you use *List<T>* or *Collection<T>*? The difference is minimal and matches exactly the difference between the core interfaces—*IList* and *ICollection*. The general guideline is to use *List<T>* for internal members and go with *Collection<T>* for public members of a class.

Putting It All Together

To enable *.map* files, you need to tweak the *Web.config* file by adding an entry under *<buildProviders>*.

```
<buildProviders>
    <add extension=".map"
        type="Samples.OrmBuildProvider,OrmBuildProvider" />
</buildProviders>
```

The *extension* attribute indicates the extension for source files. The *type* attribute provides class name and assembly information. Note that custom files such as *.map* files can be deployed only to *App_Code*. Adding a new file to *App_Code* automatically restarts the application. The *.map* file is detected, and a proper source file is compiled and loaded in the AppDomain. The temporary source files are created in a subdirectory named *Sources_App_Code* below the code-gen directory.

Figure 1-12 shows the contents of this folder and the generated C# file that contains the entity class and related collection.

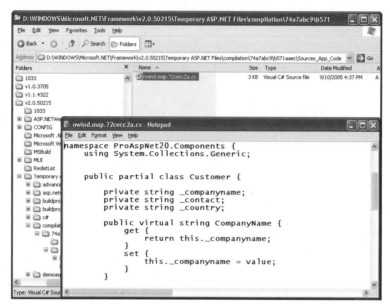

Figure 1-12   The source class file generated out of the *.map* file.

To use the dynamically created classes in your pages, all that you have to do is import the namespace specified in the *<mappings>* node. The following code works just fine. Developers don't have to write entity and collection classes but can use collections in their DAL and for binding operations.

```
public CustomerCollection GetCustomers()
{
    SqlDataAdapter adapter = new SqlDataAdapter(
        "SELECT companyname, contactname, country FROM customers",
        "SERVER=...;DATABASE=...;UID=...");
    DataTable dt = new DataTable();
    adapter.Fill(dt);

    CustomerCollection coll = new CustomerCollection();
    foreach (DataRow row in dt.Rows) {
        Customer c = new Customer();
        c.CompanyName = (string) row[0];
        c.Contact = (string) row[1];
        c.Country = (string) row[2];
        coll.Add(c);
    }

    return coll;
}
```

If you instruct the build provider to create a partial entity class, you can then extend it further in the project. Here's how to add an overridden *ToString* method to the *Customer* class:

```
public partial class Customer
{
    public override string ToString()
    {
        return String.Format("{0} ({1})", this.CompanyName, this.Country);
    }
}
```

Interestingly enough, the project contains no static definition for a partial class named *Customer*, yet the system can find one if you have a proper *.map* file in the *App_Code* folder.

Using a *TextWriter* Object

When it comes to generating a class based on the contents of a descriptor file, CodeDOM is not the only possible option. You can construct the final source code also by concatenating strings. In this case, the code of the overridden *GenerateCode* method looks slightly different:

```
public override void GenerateCode(AssemblyBuilder ab)
{
    TextWriter tw = ab.CreateCodeFile(this);
    if (tw == null)
        return;
    try {
        // Parse the file and generate the code we want from it
        string code = ParseFileAndCreateCode(base.VirtualPath);
        tw.Write(code);
    }
    catch {
        throw new ApplicationException("Can't build class");
    }
    finally {
        tw.Close();
    }
}
string ParseFileAndCreateCode(string fileName) {
    StringBuilder sb = new StringBuilder();
    sb.Append("public class Customer {");
    :
    return sb.ToString();
}
```

Using a text-writer binds you to a particular language, but it allows you to write code more quickly. The CodeDOM API is more abstract and certainly more complex and quirky to write. CodeDOM requires a larger memory footprint than a text-writer based solution. In terms of readability, no approach is perfect. CodeDOM is hard to read because of its level of abstraction; a text-writer solution has code interspersed with strings and placeholders, and it can be dangerously error-prone to modify and maintain. In the end, using a text-writer or CodeDOM is mostly a matter of preference.

> **Note**   Build providers are a feature specific to ASP.NET 2.0 and are not supported by Windows Forms projects. However, you could write an *MSBuild* action to perform a preconversion to accomplish something similar. The MSBuild custom action serves the purpose of emulating in Windows Forms the extra steps of ASP.NET compilation. From within MSBuild, you then invoke the same transformation code you host in the ASP.NET build provider. A discussion of this technique can be found here: *http://msdn.microsoft.com/msdnmag/issues/06/02/CuttingEdge.*

Virtual Path Providers

Before the advent of ASP.NET 2.0, a source ASP.NET page could be only an *.aspx* file deployed on the server and located in a particular folder. A one-to-one correspondence is required between *.aspx* resources and files on disk. In ASP.NET 2.0, the virtual path provider mechanism allows you to virtualize a bunch of files and even a structure of directories. You can abstract Web content away from the physical structure of the file system. Created to serve the needs of Share-Point—the next version of SharePoint will be built on top of ASP.NET 2.0—virtual path providers prove extremely useful to ASP.NET developers too. For example, you can register a path provider and serve ASP.NET the source code of your pages reading from a database. (Sound familiar? Yep, this is just what SharePoint does today and will do tomorrow, based on ASP.NET 2.0.)

Structure of a Virtual Path Provider

A *virtual path provider* (VPP) is a class that inherits from the *VirtualPathProvider* class and implements a virtual file system for a Web application. In such a virtual file system, you're essentially using for files and directories a custom data store other than the file system. Most files involved with the processing of an ASP.NET request can be stored in a virtual file system. The list includes ASP.NET pages, themes, master pages, user controls, custom resources mapped to a build provider, and static Web resources such as HTML pages and images.

A VPP can't serve global resources—such *global.asax* and *web.config*—and the contents of reserved folders—such as *Bin*, *App_Code*, *App_Data*, *App_GlobalResources*, and any *App_LocalResources*. Table 1-12 details the members to override in a sample VPP component.

Table 1-12   Members of the *VirtualPathProvider* Class

Member	Description
CombineVirtualPaths	Combines a base path with a relative path to return a complete path to a virtual resource
DirectoryExists	Indicates whether a directory exists in the virtual file system
FileExists	Indicates whether a file exists in the virtual file system
GetCacheDependency	Creates a cache dependency based on the specified virtual paths
GetCacheKey	Returns a cache key to use for the specified virtual path
GetDirectory	Gets a reference to a *VirtualDirectory*-derived class that represents the virtual directory the requested resource is mapped to

Table 1-12   Members of the *VirtualPathProvider* Class

Member	Description
GetFile	Gets a reference to a *VirtualFile* derived class that represents the virtual file the requested resource is mapped to
GetFileHash	Returns a hash of the specified virtual paths
Previous	Protected property, gets a reference to a previously registered VPP object to ensure that the resource can be resolved either by a registered VPP or the default one

When writing a custom VPP, it is important that you override *GetFile* and *GetDirectory* and use the *Previous* property carefully. Here's an example:

```
public override VirtualFile GetFile(string virtualPath)
{
    if (IsPathVirtual(virtualPath))
        return new YourVirtualFile(virtualPath, this);
    else
        return Previous.GetFile(virtualPath);
}
```

In the preceding code, *IsPathVirtual* is a private function that simply establishes whether your VPP is able to process the virtual path. If not, you pass the request down to the next VPP in the ASP.NET chain. If you omit the call to *Previous*, the request won't be processed.

```
private bool IsPathVirtual(string virtualPath)
{
    // For example
    // Check the virtual path against your data store
}
```

For more information and sample code, refer to the MSDN online documentation.

Structure of a Virtual File

A virtual path provider works by taking URLs and checking whether a VPP is registered to handle that URL. If so, the VPP is given a chance to return the ASP.NET source for that path. A VPP returns the source of a virtual path through an object that inherits from the class *VirtualFile*. Table 1-13 details the members to override in a virtual file class.

Table 1-13   Members of the *VirtualFile* Class

Member	Description
IsDirectory	Indicates whether this is a virtual resource that should be treated as a file
Name	Gets the display name of the virtual file
VirtualPath	Gets the path of the virtual file
Open	Returns a read-only stream that refers to the contents of the requested resource

The key thing to do when writing a custom virtual file class is to override the *Open* method and make it return a read-only stream to the contents of the virtual resource. In the *Open* method, you use the virtual path as the key to access the data store and retrieve the source code. For more information and sample code, refer to the MSDN online documentation.

Registering a Virtual Path Provider

Unlike most providers, a virtual path provider is not registered through the *web.config* file. You can register your VPP either in the *Application_Start* global event or by adding a static *AppInitialize* method to some class deployed in *App_Code*. Here's a sample class you can drop in *App_Code* to register a VPP:

```
public static class AppStart
{
    public static void AppInitialize()
    {
      // Add a new VPP to the chain
      MyPathProvider vpp = new MyPathProvider();
      HostingEnvironment.RegisterVirtualPathProvider(vpp);
    }
}
```

The name of the surrounding class is arbitrary; the name and signature of *AppInitialize* are not. If multiple static methods with this name exist in the different classes stored in *App_Code*, you get a compile error.

> **Important**   It is essential that a virtual path provider be registered prior to any page pars-ing or compilation. If a path provider is registered in other points in the application (for exam-ple, *web.config*) or page life cycle, some unexpected results may show up. There's no syntax requirement that prevents you from registering a VPP, say, in *Page_Load*. However, if the VPP is registered after the page assembly has been generated, there's no way to invalidate the link between that page and that assembly. As a result, when requesting that page, the VPP will be bypassed. It still makes sense to register a VPP from within a page event, but only if you do that from a page that is not designed to be served by the VPP and that is invoked prior to any page served by the VPP. As you can see, it's not a common situation.

Conclusion

Since its first version, ASP.NET has compiled a few file types on the fly—*.aspx* Web pages in particular. Page files are automatically compiled on-demand when first required by an applica-tion. Any changes made to the source of a dynamically compiled file automatically invalidates the corresponding assembly, which will then be re-created. This mechanism greatly simplifies application development, as developers need only save the file and refresh the page to imme-diately apply changes to the application.

In ASP.NET 2.0, while the top-level pattern remains intact, the underlying machinery has changed significantly. The new build system automatically manages quite a few file types, including ASP.NET pages, master and theme files, resources, and XSD schemas. These files provide a description of the expected results and makes use of a hidden component for parsing the contents and generating a compilable class. The new ASP.NET build system removes the need for an explicit precompilation step within the Visual Studio integrated development environment (IDE) and provides an extensibility model allowing new file types to be added. Essential to this model are build providers. By writing custom build providers, you can have ASP.NET take care of and compile your own resources. Build providers are the brains behind the superb IntelliSense capabilities in Visual Studio 2005, and they are the chief technology behind ASP.NET sites precompilation.

Just the Facts

- A request for an *.aspx* resource, namely an ASP.NET page, is mapped to a managed class that implements the *IHttpHandler* interface. This class is dynamically created if it is not found.

- Dynamic page compilation is a two-step process: the contents of the *.aspx* file are parsed, and a class file is built and compiled to an assembly. This model, which in ASP.NET 1.x works only for a few predefined file types, is refactored and extended to encompass custom file types.

- Build providers are system components that parse files with a given extension and return a class file to compile. Internally, a build provider will typically use the CodeDOM API to generate a code tree. You can write custom build providers to have ASP.NET generate your own classes from a text description.

- ASP.NET 2.0 defines several reserved folders to contain only certain types of resources, such as class files, page resources, and WSDL documents.

- In ASP.NET 2.0, a site can be precompiled in-place to save the first-hit compilation tax, or it can be precompiled for deployment. In the latter case, you get an image of the site where ASPX files are compiled to assemblies, and no source code or markup is ever deployed.

Chapter 2
HTTP Handlers and Modules

In the previous chapter, "The ASP.NET Compilation Model," I mentioned HTTP modules and HTTP handlers and introduced them as fundamental pieces of the Microsoft ASP.NET archi-tecture. HTTP handlers and modules are truly the building blocks of the Microsoft .NET Web platform. Any requests for an ASP.NET managed resource is always resolved by an HTTP han-dler and passes through a pipeline of HTTP modules. After the handler has processed the request, the request flows back through the pipeline of HTTP modules and is finally trans-formed into HTML code for the browser.

An HTTP handler is the component that actually takes care of serving the request. It is an instance of a class that implements the *IHttpHandler* interface. The *ProcessRequest* method of the interface is the central console that governs the processing of the request. For example, the *Page* class—the base class for all ASP.NET run-time pages—implements the *IHttpHandler* interface, and its *ProcessRequest* method is responsible for loading and saving the view state and for firing events such as *Init*, *Load*, *PreRender*, and the like.

ASP.NET maps each incoming HTTP request to a particular HTTP handler. A special breed of component—named the *HTTP handler factory*—provides the infrastructure for creating the physical instance of the handler to service the request. For example, the *PageHandlerFactory* class parses the source code of the requested *.aspx* resource and returns a compiled instance of the class that represents the page. An HTTP handler is designed to process one or more URL extensions. Handlers can be given an application or machine scope, which means that they can process the assigned extensions within the context of the current application or all applications installed on the machine. Of course, this is accomplished by making changes to either *machine.config* or a local *web.config* file, depending on the scope you desire.

HTTP modules are classes that implement the *IHttpModule* interface and handle runtime events. There are two types of public events that a module can deal with. They are the events raised by *HttpApplication* (including asynchronous events) and events raised by other HTTP modules. For example, *SessionStateModule* is one of the built-in modules provided by ASP.NET to supply session-state services to an application. It fires the *End* and *Start* events that other modules can handle through the familiar *Session_End* and *Session_Start* signatures.

HTTP handlers and HTTP modules have the same functionality as ISAPI extensions and ISAPI filters, respectively, but with a much simpler programming model. ASP.NET allows you to create custom handlers and custom modules. Before we get into this rather advanced aspect of Web programming, a review of the Internet Information Services (IIS) extensibility model is in order because this model determines what modules and handlers can and cannot do.

Note   ISAPI stands for Internet Server Application Programming Interface and represents the protocol by means of which IIS talks to external components. The ISAPI model is based on a Microsoft Win32 unmanaged dynamic-link library (DLL) that exports a couple of functions. This model will be significantly expanded in IIS 7.0 and will coincide with the ASP.NET extensibility model, which is based on HTTP handlers and modules. I'll return to this topic shortly.

Quick Overview of the IIS Extensibility API

A Web server is primarily a server application that can be contacted using a bunch of Internet protocols such as HTTP, File Transfer Protocol (FTP), Network News Transfer Protocol (NNTP), and the Simple Mail Transfer Protocol (SMTP). IIS—the Web server included with the Microsoft Windows operating system—is no exception.

A Web server generally also provides a documented application programming interface (API) for enhancing and customizing the server's capabilities. Historically speaking, the first of these extension APIs was the Common Gateway Interface (CGI). A CGI module is a new application that is spawned from the Web server to service a request. Nowadays, CGI applications are almost never used in modern Web applications because they require a new process for each HTTP request. As you can easily understand, this approach is rather inadequate for high-volume Web sites and poses severe scalability issues. IIS supports CGI applications, but you seldom use this feature unless you have serious backward-compatibility issues. More recent versions of Web servers supply an alternative and more efficient model to extend the capabilities of the module. In IIS, this alternative model takes the form of the ISAPI interface.

The ISAPI Model

When the ISAPI model is used, instead of starting a new process for each request, IIS loads an ISAPI component—namely, a Win32 DLL—into its own process. Next, it calls a well-known entry point on the DLL to serve the request. The ISAPI component stays loaded until IIS is shut down and can service requests without any further impact on Web server activity. The downside to such a model is that because components are loaded within the Web server process, a single faulty component can tear down the whole server and all installed applications. Starting with IIS 4.0, though, some countermeasures have been taken to address this problem. Before the advent of IIS 6.0, you were allowed to set the protection level of a newly installed application, choosing from three options: low, medium, and high.

If you choose low protection, the application (and its extensions) will be run within the Web server process (*inetinfo.exe*). If you choose medium protection, applications will be pooled together and hosted by an instance of a different worker process (*dllhost.exe*). If you choose high protection, each application set to High will be hosted in its own individual worker process (*dllhost.exe*).

Under IIS 6.0, Web applications are grouped in pools, and the choice you can make is whether you want to join an existing pool or create a new one. All applications in a pool share the same run-time and security settings and the same worker process—*w3wp.exe*. Figure 2-1 shows the dialog box you use in IIS 6.0 and Microsoft Windows Server 2003 to select an application pool for your Web application.

Figure 2-1   Selecting an application pool for a Web application in IIS 6.0 under Windows Server 2003.

Illustrious Children of the ISAPI Model

The ISAPI model has another key drawback—the programming model. An ISAPI component represents a compiled piece of code—a Win32 DLL—that retrieves data and writes HTML code to an output console. It has to be developed using C or C++, it should generate multithreaded code, and it must be written with extreme care because of the impact that bugs or run-time failures can have on the application.

Microsoft attempted to encapsulate the ISAPI logic in the Microsoft Foundation Classes (MFC), but even though the effort was creditable, it didn't pay off very well. MFC tended to bring more code to the table than high-performance Web sites would perhaps like, and worse, the resulting ISAPI extension DLL suffered from a well-documented memory leak.

Active Server Pages (ASP), the predecessor of ASP.NET, is, on the other hand, an example of a well-done ISAPI application. ASP is implemented as an ISAPI DLL (named *asp.dll*) registered to handle HTTP requests with an *.asp* extension. The internal code of the ASP ISAPI extension DLL parses the code of the requested resource, executes any embedded script code, and builds the page for the browser.

In IIS 6.0 and later versions, any functionality built on top of IIS must be coded according to the guidelines set by the ISAPI model. ASP and ASP.NET are no exceptions. Today, the whole ASP.NET platform works closely with IIS, but it is not part of it. The *aspnet_isapi.dll* core component is the link between IIS and the ASP.NET runtime environment. When a request for *.aspx* resources comes in, IIS passes the control to *aspnet_isapi.dll*, which in turn hands the request to the ASP.NET pipeline inside an instance of the common language runtime (CLR).

As of this writing, to extend IIS, you can write a Win32 DLL only with a well-known set of entry points. This requirement is going to change with IIS 7.0.

Structure of ISAPI Components

An ISAPI extension is invoked through a URL that ends with the name of the DLL that implements the function, as shown in the following URL:

```
http://www.contoso.com/apps/hello.dll
```

The DLL must export a couple of functions—*GetExtensionVersion* and *HttpExtensionProc*. The *GetExtensionVersion* function sets the version and the name of the ISAPI server extension. When the extension is loaded, the *GetExtensionVersion* function is the first function to be called. *GetExtensionVersion* is invoked only once and can be used to initialize any needed variables. The function is expected to return true if everything goes fine. In case of errors, the function should return false and the Web server will abort loading the DLL and put a message in the system log.

The core of the ISAPI component is represented by the *HttpExtensionProc* function. The function receives basic HTTP information regarding the request (for example, the query string and the headers), performs the expected action, and prepares the response to send back to the browser.

Note   Certain handy programming facilities, such as the session state, are abstractions that the ISAPI programming model lacks entirely. The ISAPI model is a lower-level programming model than, say, ASP or ASP.NET.

The ISAPI programming model is made of two types of components–ISAPI extensions and ISAPI filters.

ISAPI Extensions

ISAPI extensions are the IIS in-process counterpart of CGI applications. As mentioned, an ISAPI extension is a DLL that is loaded in the memory space occupied by IIS or another host application. Because it is a DLL, only one instance of the ISAPI extension needs to be loaded at a time. On the downside, the ISAPI extension must be thread-safe so that multiple client requests can be served simultaneously. ISAPI extensions work in much the same way as an ASP or ASP.NET page. It takes any information about the HTTP request and prepares a valid HTTP response.

Because the ISAPI extension is made of compiled code, it must be recompiled and reloaded at any change. If the DLL is loaded in the Web server's memory, the Web server must be stopped. If the DLL is loaded in the context of a separate process, only that process must be stopped. Of course, when an external process is used, the extension doesn't work as fast as it could when hosted in-process, but at least it doesn't jeopardize the stability of IIS.

ISAPI Filters

ISAPI filters are components that intercept specific server events before the server itself handles them. Upon loading, the filter indicates the event notifications that it will handle. If any of these events occur, the filter can process them or pass them on to other filters.

You can use ISAPI filters to provide custom authentication techniques or to automatically redirect requests based on HTTP headers sent by the client. Filters are a delicate gear in the IIS machinery. They can facilitate applications but also degrade performance if not written carefully. Filters, in fact, can run only in-process. Starting with IIS 5.0, filters can be loaded for the Web server as a whole or for specific Web sites.

ISAPI filters can accomplish tasks such as implementing custom authentication schemes, compression, encryption, logging, and request analysis. The ability to examine, and if necessary modify, both incoming and outgoing streams of data makes ISAPI filters very powerful and flexible. This last sentence shows the strength of ISAPI filters but also indicates their potential weakness, which would be performance hindrances if they're not written well.

Changes Coming Soon in IIS 7.0

ASP.NET 1.0 was a self-contained, brand new runtime environment bolted onto IIS. With the simultaneous release of ASP.NET 1.1 and IIS 6.0, the Web development and server platforms have gotten closer and started sharing some services such as process recycling and output caching. The advent of ASP.NET 2.0 doesn't change anything, but the release of IIS 7.0 will.

A Unified Runtime Environment

In a certain way, IIS 7.0 represents the unification of the ASP.NET and IIS platforms. HTTP handlers and modules, the runtime pipeline, and configuration files will become constituent elements of a common environment. The whole IIS internal pipeline will be componentized to originate a distinct and individually configurable component. A new section will be added to the *web.config* schema to configure the IIS environment.

Put another way, it will be as if the ASP.NET runtime expanded to incorporate and replace the surrounding Web server environment. It's hard to say whether things really went this way or whether it was the other way around. As a matter of fact, the same concepts and instruments you know from ASP.NET will be available in IIS 7.0 at the Web server level. To exemplify, you can use Forms authentication to protect access to any resources available on the server and not just ASP.NET-specific resources.

Managed ISAPI Extensions and Filters

Today if you want to take control of an incoming request in IIS, you have no choice other than writing a C or C++ DLL, using either MFC or perhaps the ActiveX Template Library (ATL). More user-friendly HTTP handlers and modules are an ASP.NET-only feature, and they can be applied only to ASP.NET-specific resources and only after the request has been authenticated by IIS and handed over to ASP.NET.

In IIS 7.0, you can write HTTP handlers and modules to filter *any* requests and implement any additional features using .NET code for whatever resources the Web server can serve. More precisely, you'll continue writing HTTP handlers and modules as you do today for ASP.NET, except that you will be given the opportunity to register them for any file type. Needless to say, old-style ISAPI extensions will still be supported, but unmanaged extensions and filters will likely become a thing of the past.

Writing HTTP Handlers

ASP.NET comes with a small set of built-in HTTP handlers. There is a handler to serve ASP.NET pages, one for .NET Web services, and yet another to accommodate .NET Remoting requests for remote objects hosted by IIS. Other helper handlers are defined to view the tracing of individual pages in a Web application (*trace.axd*) and to block requests for prohibited resources such as *.config* or *.asax* files. In ASP.NET 2.0, you'll also find a handler (*webresource.axd*) to inject assembly resources and script code into pages. We'll return to the built-in handler for Web resources in Chapter 9.

You can write custom HTTP handlers whenever you need ASP.NET to process certain requests in a nonstandard way. The list of useful things that you can do with HTTP handlers is limited only by your imagination. Through a well-written handler, you can have your users invoke any sort of functionality via the Web. For example, you could implement click counters and any sort of image manipulation, including dynamic generation of images, server-side caching, or obstructing undesired linking to your images.

> **Note**   An HTTP handler can either work synchronously or operate in an asynchronous way. When working synchronously, a handler doesn't return until it's done with the HTTP request. An asynchronous handler, on the other hand, launches a potentially lengthy process and returns immediately after. A typical implementation of asynchronous handlers are asynchronous pages, which we'll cover in Chapter 5. Later in this chapter, though, we'll take a look at the mechanics of asynchronous handlers, of which asynchronous pages are a special case.

Conventional ISAPI extensions and filters should be registered within the IIS metabase. In contrast, HTTP handlers are registered in the *web.config* file if you want the handler to participate in the HTTP pipeline processing of the Web request. In a manner similar to ISAPI extensions, you can also invoke the handler directly via the URL. As mentioned, with the advent of IIS 7.0, only the *web.config* registration model will remain in place, although you might still call the handler directly via the URL. I'll first discuss registered handlers and then show you how to deploy them directly.

The *IHttpHandler* Interface

Want to take the splash and dive into HTTP handler programming? Well, your first step is getting the hang of the *IHttpHandler* interface. An HTTP handler is just a managed class that implements that interface. More exactly, a synchronous HTTP handler implements the *IHttpHandler* interface; an asynchronous HTTP handler, on the other hand, implements the *IHttpAsyncHandler* interface. Let's tackle synchronous handlers first.

The contract of the *IHttpHandler* interface defines the actions that a handler needs to take to process an HTTP request synchronously.

Members of the *IHttpHandler* Interface

The *IHttpHandler* interface defines only two members—*ProcessRequest* and *IsReusable*, as shown in Table 2-1. *ProcessRequest* is a method, whereas *IsReusable* is a Boolean property.

Table 2-1   Members of the *IHttpHandler* Interface

Member	Description
IsReusable	This property gets a Boolean value indicating whether another request can use the current instance of the HTTP handler.
ProcessRequest	This method processes the HTTP request.

The *IsReusable* property on the *Page* class returns false, meaning that a new instance of the HTTP request is needed to serve a page request. You typically make it return false in all situations in which some significant processing is required that depends on the request payload.

Handlers used as simple barriers to filter special requests can set *IsReusable* to true to save some CPU cycles. I'll return to this subject with a concrete example in a moment.

The *ProcessRequest* method has the following signature:

```
void ProcessRequest(HttpContext context);
```

It takes the context of the request as the input and ensures that the request is serviced. In the case of synchronous handlers, when *ProcessRequest* returns, the output is ready for being forwarded to the client.

A Very Simple HTTP Handler

Again, an HTTP handler is simply a class that implements the *IHttpHandler* interface. The output for the request is built within the *ProcessRequest* method, as shown in the following code:

```
using System.Web;

namespace ProAspNet20.Advanced.CS.Components
{
    public class SimpleHandler : IHttpHandler
    {
        // Override the ProcessRequest method
        public void ProcessRequest(HttpContext context)
        {
            context.Response.Write("<H1>Hello, I'm an HTTP handler</H1>");
        }

        // Override the IsReusable property
        public bool IsReusable
        {
            get { return true; }
        }
    }
}
```

You need an entry point to be able to call the handler. In this context, an entry point into the handler's code is nothing more than an HTTP endpoint—that is, a public URL. The URL must be a unique name that IIS and the ASP.NET runtime can map to this code. When registered, the mapping between an HTTP handler and a Web server resource is established through the *web.config* file.

```
<configuration>
    <system.web>
        <httpHandlers>
            <add verb="*" path="myHandler.aspx"
                type="ProAspNet20.Advanced.CS.Components.SimpleHandler" />
        </httpHandlers>
    </system.web>
</configuration>
```

The *<httpHandlers>* section lists the handlers available for the current application. These settings indicate that *SimpleHandler* is in charge of handling any incoming requests for an endpoint named *myHandler.aspx*. Note that the URL *myHandler.aspx* doesn't have to be a physical resource on the server; it's simply a public resource identifier. The *type* attribute references the class and assembly that contains the handler. It's canonical format is *type[,assembly]*. You omit the assembly information if the component is defined in the *App_Code* or other reserved folders.

> **Note**   If you enter the settings shown previously in the *machine.config* file, you will register the *SimpleHandler* component as callable from within all Web applications hosted by the server machine.

If you invoke the *myHandler.aspx* URL, you obtain the results shown in Figure 2-2.

Figure 2-2   A sample HTTP handler that answers requests for *myHandler.aspx*.

The technique discussed here is the quickest and simplest way of putting an HTTP handler to work, but there is more to know about registration of HTTP handlers, and there are many more options to take advantage of. Now let's consider a more complex example of an HTTP handler.

An HTTP Handler for Quick Data Reports

With its relatively simple programming model, HTTP handlers give you a means of interacting with the low-level request and response services of IIS. In the previous example, we returned only constant text and made no use of the request information. In the next example, we'll configure the handler to intercept and process only requests of a particular type and generate the output based on the contents of the requested resource.

The idea is to build an HTTP handler for custom *.sqlx* resources. A SQLX file is an XML document that represents an SQL query. The handler grabs the information about the query, executes it, and finally returns the result set formatted as a grid. Figure 2-3 shows the expected outcome.

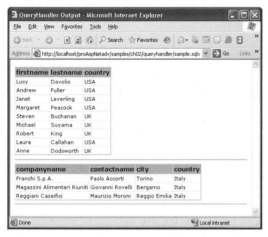

Figure 2-3   A custom HTTP handler in action.

To start, let's examine the source code for the *IHttpHandler* class.

> **Warning**   Take this example for what it really is—merely a way to process a custom XML file with a custom extension doing something more significant than outputting a "hello world" message. *Do not* take this handler as a realistic prototype for exposing your Microsoft SQL Server databases over the Web.

Building a Query Manager Tool

The HTTP handler should get into the game whenever the user requests an *.sqlx* resource. Assume for now that this aspect has been fully configured, and focus on what's needed to execute the query and pack the results into a grid. To execute the query, at a minimum, we need the connection string and the command text. The following text illustrates the typical contents of an *.sqlx* file:

```
<queries>
  <query connString="DATABASE=northwind;SERVER=localhost;UID=…;">
    SELECT firstname, lastname, country FROM employees
  </query>
  <query connString="DATABASE=northwind;SERVER=localhost;UID=…;">
    SELECT companyname FROM customers WHERE country='Italy'
  </query>
</queries>
```

The XML document is formed by a collection of *<query>* nodes, each containing an attribute for the connection string and the text of the query.

The *ProcessRequest* method extracts this information before it can proceed with executing the query and generating the output.

```
class SqlxData
{
    public string ConnectionString;
    public string QueryText;
}

public class QueryHandler : IHttpHandler
{
    public void ProcessRequest(HttpContext context)
    {
        // Parses the SQLX file
        SqlxData[] data = ParseFile(context);

        // Create the output as HTML
        StringCollection htmlColl = CreateOutput(data);

        // Output the data
        context.Response.Write("<html><head><title>");
        context.Response.Write("QueryHandler Output");
        context.Response.Write("</title></head><body>");
        foreach (string html in htmlColl)
        {
            context.Response.Write(html);
            context.Response.Write("<hr />");
        }
        context.Response.Write("</body></html>");
    }

    // Override the IsReusable property
    public bool IsReusable
    {
        get { return false; }
    }

    ⋮
}
```

The *ParseFile* helper function parses the source code of the *.sqlx* file and creates an instance of the *SqlxData* class for each query found.

```
private SqlxData[] ParseFile(HttpContext context)
{
    XmlDocument doc = new XmlDocument();
    string file = context.Request.Path;
    using (Stream file = VirtualPathProvider.OpenFile(file))  {
        doc.Load(file);
    }

    // Visit the <mapping> nodes
    XmlNodeList mappings = doc.SelectNodes("queries/query");
    SqlxData[] descriptors = new SqlxData[mappings.Count];
    for (int i=0; i < descriptors.Length; i++)
    {
        XmlNode mapping = mappings[i];
        SqlxData query = new SqlxData();
        descriptors[i] = query;
```

```
        try {
            query.ConnectionString =
                mapping.Attributes["connString"].Value;
            query.QueryText = mapping.InnerText;
        }
        catch {
            context.Response.Write("Error parsing the input file.");
        }
    }
    return descriptors;
}
```

The *SqlxData* internal class groups the connection string and the command text. The information is passed to the *CreateOutput* function, which will actually execute the query and generate the grid.

```
private StringCollection CreateOutput(SqlxData[] descriptors)
{
    StringCollection coll = new StringCollection();

    foreach (SqlxData data in descriptors)
    {
        // Run the query
        DataTable dt = new DataTable();
        SqlDataAdapter adapter = new SqlDataAdapter(data.QueryText,
            data.ConnectionString);
        adapter.Fill(dt);

        // Prepare the grid
        DataGrid grid = new DataGrid();
        grid.DataSource = dt;
        grid.DataBind();

        // Get the HTML
        string html = Utils.RenderControlAsString(grid);
        coll.Add(html);
    }
    return coll;
}
```

After executing the query, the method populates a dynamically created *DataGrid* control. In ASP.NET pages, the *DataGrid* control, like any other control, is rendered to HTML. However, this happens through the care of the special HTTP handler that manages *.aspx* resources. For *.sqlx* resources, we need to provide that functionality ourselves. Obtaining the HTML for a Web control is as easy as calling the *RenderControl* method on an HTML text writer object. This is just what the helper method *RenderControlAsString* does.

```
static class Utils
{
    public static string RenderControlAsString(Control ctl)
    {
        StringWriter sw = new StringWriter();
        HtmlTextWriter writer = new HtmlTextWriter(sw);
```

```
        ctl.RenderControl(writer);
        return sw.ToString();
    }
}
```

> **Note**   An HTTP handler that needs to access session state values must implement the
> *IRequiresSessionState* interface. Like *INamingContainer*, it's a marker interface and requires no
> method implementation. Note that the *IRequiresSessionState* interface indicates that the HTTP
> handler requires read and write access to the session state. If read-only access is needed,
> use the *IReadOnlySessionState* interface instead.

Registering the Handler

An HTTP handler is a class and must be compiled to an assembly before you can use it. The
assembly must be deployed to the *Bin* directory of the application. If you plan to make this
handler available to all applications, you can copy it to the global assembly cache (GAC). The
next step is registering the handler with an individual application or with all the applications
running on the Web server. You register the handler in the configuration file.

```
<system.web>
  <httpHandlers>
    <add verb="*"
      path="*.sqlx"
      type= "ProAspNet20.CS.Components.QueryHandler,ProAspCompLib" />
  </httpHandlers>
</system.web>
```

You add the new handler to the *<httpHandlers>* section of the local or global *web.config* file.
The section supports three actions: *<add>*, *<remove>*, and *<clear>*. You use *<add>* to add a new
HTTP handler to the scope of the *.config* file. You use *<remove>* to remove a particular handler.
Finally, you use *<clear>* to get rid of all the registered handlers. To add a new handler, you need
to set three attributes: *verb*, *path*, and *type*, as shown in Table 2-2.

Table 2-2   Attributes Needed to Register an HTTP Handler

Attribute	Description
verb	Indicates the list of the supported HTTP verbs—for example, *GET*, *PUT*, and *POST*. The wildcard character (*) is an acceptable value and denotes all verbs.
path	A wildcard string or a single URL that indicates the resources the handler will work on—for example, **.aspx*.
type	Specifies a comma-separated class/assembly combination. ASP.NET searches for the assembly DLL first in the application's private *Bin* directory and then in the system global assembly cache.

These attributes are mandatory. An optional attribute is also supported—*validate*. When
validate is set to *false*, ASP.NET will delay as much as possible loading the assembly with the
HTTP handler. In other words, the assembly will be loaded only when a request for it arrives.

ASP.NET will not try to preload the assembly until it is required, thus catching any errors or problems with the assembly at the latest possible moment. If the assembly were preloaded, your execution logic may not be prepared for potential errors and the system may become unstable.

So far you have correctly deployed and registered the HTTP handler, but if you try invoking an *.sqlx* resource, the results you produce are not what you'd expect. The problem lies in the fact that so far you configured ASP.NET to handle only *.sqlx* resources, but IIS still doesn't know anything about them!

A request for an *.sqlx* resource is managed by IIS in the first place. If you don't register an ISAPI extension to handle that, IIS will treat it as a static resource and serve the request by sending back the source code of the file. The extra step required is registering the *.sqlx* extension with the IIS metabase, as shown in Figure 2-4.

Figure 2-4   Registering the *.sqlx* extension with the IIS metabase.

The dialog box in the figure is obtained by clicking on the properties of the application in IIS Manager and then the and then the Web Site tab on the resulting dialog box. To involve the HTTP handler, you must choose *aspnet_isapi.dll* as the ISAPI extension. In this way, all *.sqlx* requests are handed out to ASP.NET and processed through the specified handler. Make sure that you select *aspnet_isapi.dll* from the folder of the ASP.NET version that you plan to use.

> **Caution**   In Microsoft Visual Studio 2005, if you test a sample *.sqlx* resource by using the local embedded Web server, nothing happens that forces you to register the *.sqlx* resource with IIS. This is just the point, though—you're not using IIS! In other words, if you use the local Web server, you have no need to touch IIS; you do need to register any custom resource you plan to use with IIS before you get to production.

If your Web application manages resources of a type that you don't want to make publicly available over the Web, you must instruct IIS not to display those files. A possible way to accomplish this consists of forwarding the request to *aspnet_isapi* and then binding the extension to one of the built-in handlers—the *HttpForbiddenHandler* class.

```
<add verb="*" path="*.xyz" type="System.Web.HttpForbiddenHandler" />
```

Any attempt to access an *.xyz* resource results in an error message being displayed.

Deploying Your Handler as an ASHX Resource

An alternative way to define an HTTP handler is through an *.ashx* file. When a request for a specified *.ashx* resource is received, the handler will get executed. The association between the HTTP handler and the *.ashx* resource is established within the *.ashx* source file by using a special directive: *@WebHandler*. All *.ashx* files must begin with a directive like the following one:

```
<%@ WebHandler Language="C#" Class="Namespace.MyHandler" %>
```

When the URL that corresponds to the *.ashx* resource is invoked, the *MyHandler* class is automatically invoked. Here's a sample *.ashx* file. As you can see, it is the plain class file plus the special *@WebHandler* directive.

```
<%@ WebHandler Language="C#" Class="MyHandler" %>

using System.Web;

public class MyHandler : IHttpHandler {

    public void ProcessRequest (HttpContext context) {
        context.Response.ContentType = "text/plain";
        context.Response.Write("Hello World");
    }

    public bool IsReusable {
        get {
            return false;
        }
    }
}
```

When *.ashx* resources are used to implement an HTTP handler, no deployment setup is needed. In particular, you don't need to arrange for a *web.config* file and for a new *<httpHandlers>* section. You just deploy the source file, and you're done. Just as for Web services, the source file will be loaded and compiled only on demand. Because ASP.NET adds a special entry to the IIS metabase for *.ashx* resources, you don't even need to enter changes to the Web server configuration.

Resources with an *.ashx* extension are handled by an HTTP handler class named *SimpleHandleFactory*. Note that *SimpleHandleFactory* is actually an HTTP handler factory class, not a simple HTTP handler class. We'll discuss handler factories in a moment.

The *SimpleHandleFactory* class looks for the *@WebHandler* directive at the beginning of the file. The *@WebHandler* directive tells the handler factory the name of the HTTP handler class to instantiate once the source code has been compiled.

> **Important**   You can build HTTP handlers both as regular class files compiled to an assembly
> and via *.ashx* resources. There's no significant difference between the two approaches except
> that *.ashx* resources, like ordinary ASP.NET pages, will be compiled on the fly upon the first
> request.

HTTP Handlers vs. ASP.NET Pages

You should resort to HTTP handler resources to implement application-specific functionality that needs to be processed faster than regular Web pages. In any case, an HTTP handler returns a valid HTTP response with a content type and a body. Serving an *.ashx* request, or any other request managed by a custom handler, may result in faster code than serving an *.aspx* resource. Processing a custom handler is generally faster because no intermediate events (for example, *Init*, *Load*) are raised to the user code, no view state is managed, and no postback mechanism is supported. Roughly speaking, a request for a custom HTTP handler is like a request for an *.aspx* resource in which only the rendering step ever takes place. In addition, finding the right HTTP handler to serve a page request might take a while longer because a page handler factory intermediate object should be involved.

This said, bear in mind that an ASP.NET page is just an HTTP handler—although a quite complex and sophisticated one. The underlying processing mechanism is exactly the same. If custom HTTP handlers serving a particular need are generally faster than pages, it is because they are generally implemented to go straight to the point of producing a given result. For example, imagine that you want to display an image taken out of a database—a topic that we'll cover in detail in Chapter 9. You still need to bind an *Image* control to a URL serving the appropriate MIME type. Should this URL be a page? It can certainly be a page; however, if you use a custom HTTP handler, you generally get faster code.

An ASP.NET page is a complex object and is served by a tailor-made, and necessarily complex, HTTP handler—the *Page* class. When it comes to serving custom resources, you should make sure that an appropriate handler is used that contains only the necessary intelligence and complexity. To illustrate this point, consider that to run a query and serve the bytes of an image stored in a database, you don't need view-state and postback management, nor do you need to fire events to the application.

Should you use generic *.ashx* resources or go for a custom extension? That mostly depends on the function you want to implement. The ASHX approach is designed for relatively simple scenarios in which you have few parameters to pass (or no parameters at all) and for which you use the query string to bring them in. A custom extension is preferable if you have a custom document to process with a variety of information organized in a nonflat or complex layout.

The Picture Viewer Handler

Let's examine another scenario that involves custom HTTP handlers. Thus far, we have explored custom resources and the built-in *.ashx* extension and realized how important it is to register custom extensions with IIS.

To speed up processing, IIS claims the right of personally serving some resources that typically form a Web application without going down to a particular ISAPI extension. The list includes static files such as images and HTML files. What if you request a GIF or a JPG file directly from the address bar of the browser? IIS retrieves the specified resource, sets the proper content type on the response buffer, and writes out the bytes of the file. As a result, you'll see the image in the browser's page. So far so good.

What if you point your browser to a virtual folder that contains images? In this case, IIS doesn't distinguish the contents of the folder and returns a list of files, as shown in Figure 2-5.

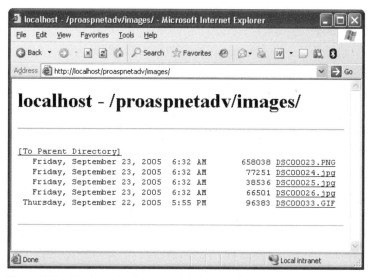

Figure 2-5   The standard IIS-provided view of a folder.

Wouldn't it be nice if you could get a preview of the contained pictures?

Designing the HTTP Handler

You need a particular extension that filters the contents of the folder, selects images, and arranges a tabular view. For doing this at the IIS level, you need to write an unmanaged ISAPI extension or just wait for IIS 7.0 to ship. An alternate approach consists of writing a managed HTTP handler with ASP.NET and convincing IIS to yield to ASP.NET when a folder with images is requested.

The idea is binding our picture viewer handler to a particular endpoint—say, *view.axd*. As mentioned earlier in the chapter, a fixed endpoint for handlers doesn't have to be necessarily an existing, deployed resource. You make the *view.axd* endpoint follow the folder name, as shown here:

```
http://www.contoso.com/images/misc/view.axd
```

The handler will process the URL, extract the folder name, and select all the contained pictures.

> **Note** In ASP.NET, the *.axd* extension is commonly used for endpoints referencing a special service. *Trace.axd* for tracing and *WebResource.axd* for script and resources injection are two popular examples. In particular, the *Trace.axd* handler implements the same logic described here. You append its name to the URL, and it will trace all requests for pages in that application.

Implementing the HTTP Handler

The picture viewer handler will return a page composed of a multirow table showing as many images as there are in the folder. Here's the skeleton of the class:

```
class PictureViewerInfo
{
    public PictureViewerInfo() {
        DisplayWidth = 200;
        ColumnCount = 3;
    }
    public int DisplayWidth;
    public int ColumnCount;
    public string FolderName;
}

public class PictureViewerHandler : IHttpHandler
{
    // Override the ProcessRequest method
    public void ProcessRequest(HttpContext context)
    {
        PictureViewerInfo info = GetFolderInfo(context);
        string html = CreateOutput(info);

        // Output the data
        context.Response.Write("<html><head><title>");
        context.Response.Write("Picture Web Viewer");
        context.Response.Write("</title></head><body>");
        context.Response.Write(html);
        context.Response.Write("</body></html>");
    }

    // Override the IsReusable property
    public bool IsReusable
    {
        get { return false; }
    }
    ⋮
}
```

Retrieving the actual path of the folder is as easy as stripping off the *view.axd* string from the URL and trimming any trailing slashes or backslashes. Next, the URL of the folder is mapped to a server path and processed using the .NET Framework API for files and folders.

```
private ArrayList GetAllImages(string path)
{
    string[] fileTypes = { "*.bmp", "*.gif", "*.jpg", "*.png" };
    ArrayList images = new ArrayList();
    DirectoryInfo di = new DirectoryInfo(path);
    foreach (string ext in fileTypes)
    {
        FileInfo[] files = di.GetFiles(ext);
        if (files.Length > 0)
            images.AddRange(files);
    }
    return images;
}
```

The *DirectoryInfo* class provides some helper functions on the specified directory; for example, the *GetFiles* method selects all the files that match the given pattern. Each file is wrapped by a *FileInfo* object. The method *GetFiles* doesn't support multiple search patterns; to search for various file types, you need to iterate for each type and accumulate results in an array list or equivalent data structure.

Once you get all the images in the folder, you move on to building the output for the request. The output is a table with a fixed number of cells and a variable number of rows to accommodate all selected images. The image is not downloaded as a thumbnail, but it is more simply rendered in a smaller area. For each image file, a new *<img>* tag is created through the *Image* control. The *width* attribute of this file is set to a fixed value (say, 200 pixels), causing most modern browsers to automatically resize the image. Furthermore, the image is wrapped by an anchor that links to the same image URL. As a result, when the user clicks on an image, the page refreshes and shows the same image at its natural size.

```
string CreateOutputForFolder(PictureViewerInfo info)
{
    ArrayList images = GetAllImages(info.FolderName);
    Table t = new Table();

    int index = 0;
    bool moreImages = true;
    while (moreImages)
    {
        TableRow row = new TableRow();
        t.Rows.Add(row);
        for (int i = 0; i < info.ColumnCount; i++)
        {
            TableCell cell = new TableCell();
            row.Cells.Add(cell);

            // Create the image
            Image img = new Image();
            FileInfo fi = (FileInfo)images[index];
```

```
img.ImageUrl = fi.Name;
img.Width = Unit.Pixel(info.DisplayWidth);

// Wrap the image in an anchor so that a larger image is
// shown when the user clicks
HtmlAnchor a = new HtmlAnchor();
a.HRef = fi.Name;
a.Controls.Add(img);
cell.Controls.Add(a);

// Check if there are more images to show
index++;
moreImages = (index < images.Count);
if (!moreImages)
    break;
    }
  }
}
```

You might want to make the handler accept some optional query string parameters, such as width and column count. These values are packed in an instance of the helper class *Picture-ViewerInfo* along with the name of the folder to view. Here's the code to process the query string of the URL to extract parameters if any are present:

```
PictureViewerInfo info = new PictureViewerInfo();
object p1 = context.Request.Params["Width"];
object p2 = context.Request.Params["Cols"];
if (p1 != null)
    Int32.TryParse((string)p1, out info.DisplayWidth);
if (p2 != null)
    Int32.TryParse((string)p2, out info.ColumnCount);
```

Figure 2-6 shows the handler in action.

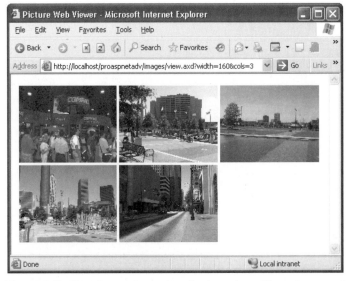

Figure 2-6   The picture viewer handler in action with a given number of columns and width.

Registering the handler is easy, too. You just add the following script to the *web.config* file:

```
<add verb="*" path="view.axd"
    type="ProAspNet20.CS.Components.PictureViewerHandler,ProAspCompLib" />
```

You would place the assembly in the GAC and move the configuration script to *machine.config* to extend the settings to all applications on the machine.

Advanced HTTP Handler Programming

In a conventional HTTP handler, the *ProcessRequest* method takes the lion's share of the overall set of functionality. The second member of the *IHttpHandler* interface—the *IsReusable* property—is used only in particular circumstances. By calling *IsReusable*, an HTTP handler factory can query a handler to determine whether the same instance can be used to service multiple requests.

The Boolean value returned by *IsReusable* also indicates whether the handler object can be pooled. This is certainly true for *HttpApplication* objects—this class, too, implements the interface—called to serve a request, but it's patently false for handlers representing a Web Forms page. If you set the *IsReusable* property to return true, the handler is not unloaded from memory after use.

In all the cases considered so far, we never had the need to distinguish between two or more distinct handlers for a request. In situations in which the HTTP handler for a request is not uniquely identified, you might want to use an HTTP handler factory object.

HTTP Handler Factories

An HTTP request can be directly associated with an HTTP handler or with an HTTP handler factory object. An HTTP handler factory is a class that implements the *IHttpHandlerFactory* interface and is in charge of returning the actual HTTP handler to use to serve the request. The *SimpleHandlerFactory* class provides a good example of how a factory works. The factory is mapped to requests directed at *.ashx* resources. When such a request comes in, the factory determines the actual handler to use by looking at the *@WebHandler* directive in the source file.

In the .NET Framework, HTTP handler factories are used to perform some preliminary tasks on the requested resource prior to passing it on to the handler. Another good example of a handler factory object is represented by an internal class named *PageHandlerFactory*, which is in charge of serving *.aspx* pages. In this case, the factory handler figures out the name of the handler to use and, if possible, loads it up from an existing assembly.

HTTP handler factories are classes that implement a couple of methods on the *IHttpHandlerFactory* interface—*GetHandler* and *ReleaseHandler*, as shown in Table 2-3.

Table 2-3   Members of the *IHttpHandlerFactory* Interface

Method	Description
GetHandler	Returns an instance of an HTTP handler to serve the request
ReleaseHandler	Takes an existing HTTP handler instance and frees it up or pools it

The *GetHandler* method has the following signature:

```
public virtual IHttpHandler GetHandler(HttpContext context,
    string requestType, string url, string pathTranslated);
```

The *requestType* argument is a string that evaluates to *GET* or *POST*—the HTTP verb of the request. The last two arguments represent the raw URL of the request and the physical path behind it. The *ReleaseHandler* method is a mandatory override for any class that implements *IHttpHandlerFactory*; in most cases, it will just have an empty body.

The following listing shows a sample HTTP handler factory that returns different handlers based on the HTTP verb (*GET* or *POST*) used for the request:

```
class MyHandlerFactory : IHttpHandlerFactory
{
    public IHttpHandler GetHandler(HttpContext context,
        string requestType, String url, String pathTranslated)
    {
        if(context.Request.RequestType.ToLower() == "get")
            return (IHttpHandler) new MyGetHandler();
        else if(context.Request.RequestType.ToLower() == "post")
            return (IHttpHandler) new MyPostHandler();
        return null;
    }

    public void ReleaseHandler(IHttpHandler handler)
    {
        // nothing to do
    }
}
```

When you use an HTTP handler factory, it's the factory, not the handler, that needs to be registered with the ASP.NET configuration file. If you register the handler, it will always be used to serve requests. If you opt for a factory, you have a chance to decide dynamically and based on runtime conditions which handler is more appropriate for a certain request.

Asynchronous Handlers

An asynchronous HTTP handler is a class that implements the *IHttpAsyncHandler* interface. The system initiates the call by invoking the *BeginProcessRequest* method. Next, when the method ends, a callback function is automatically invoked to terminate the call. In the .NET Framework, the sole *HttpApplication* class implements the asynchronous interface. The members of *IHttpAsyncHandler* interface are shown in Table 2-4.

Table 2-4   Members of the *IHttpAsyncHandler* Interface

Method	Description
BeginProcessRequest	Initiates an asynchronous call to the specified HTTP handler
EndProcessRequest	Terminates the asynchronous call

The signature of the *BeginProcessRequest* method is as follows:

```
IAsyncResult BeginProcessRequest(HttpContext context,
    AsyncCallback cb, object extraData);
```

The *context* argument provides references to intrinsic server objects used to service HTTP requests. The second parameter is the *AsyncCallback* object to invoke when the asynchronous method call is complete. The third parameter is a generic cargo variable that contains any data you might want to pass to the handler.

> **Note**   An *AsyncCallback* object is a delegate that defines the logic needed to finish process-ing the asynchronous operation. A delegate is a class that holds a reference to a method. A del-egate class has a fixed signature, and it can hold references only to methods that match that signature. A delegate is equivalent to a type-safe function pointer or a callback. As a result, an *AsyncCallback* object is just the code that executes when the asynchronous handler has completed its job.

The *AsyncCallback* delegate has the following signature:

```
public delegate void AsyncCallback(IAsyncResult ar);
```

It uses the *IAsyncResult* interface to obtain the status of the asynchronous operation. To illus-trate the plumbing of asynchronous handlers, I'll show you the pseudocode that the HTTP runtime employs when it deals with asynchronous handlers. The HTTP runtime invokes the *BeginProcessRequest* method as illustrated by the following pseudocode:

```
// Sets an internal member of the HttpContext class with
// the current instance of the asynchronous handler
context.AsyncAppHandler = asyncHandler;

// Invokes the BeginProcessRequest method on the asynchronous HTTP handler
asyncHandler.BeginProcessRequest(context, OnCompletionCallback, context);
```

The *context* argument is the current instance of the *HttpContext* class and represents the con-text of the request. A reference to the HTTP context is also passed as the custom data sent to the handler to process the request. The *extraData* parameter in the *BeginProcessRequest* signa-ture is used to represent the status of the asynchronous operation. The *BeginProcessRequest* method returns an object of type *HttpAsyncResult*–a class that implements the *IAsyncResult* interface. The *IAsyncResult* interface contains a property named *AsyncState* that is set with the *extraData* value–in this case, the HTTP context.

The *OnCompletionCallback* method is an internal method. It gets automatically triggered when the asynchronous processing of the request terminates. The following listing illustrates the pseudocode of the *HttpRuntime* private method:

```
// The method must have the signature of an AsyncCallback delegate
private void OnHandlerCompletion(IAsyncResult ar)
{
```

```
    // The ar parameter is an instance of HttpAsyncResult
    HttpContext context = (HttpContext) ar.AsyncState;

    // Retrieves the instance of the asynchronous HTTP handler
    // and completes the request
    IHttpAsyncHandler asyncHandler = context.AsyncAppHandler;
    asyncHandler.EndProcessRequest(ar);

    // Finalizes the request as usual
    ⋮
}
```

The completion handler retrieves the HTTP context of the request through the *AsyncState* property of the *IAsyncResult* object it gets from the system. As mentioned, the actual object passed is an instance of the *HttpAsyncResult* class—in any case, it is the return value of the *BeginProcessRequest* method. The completion routine extracts the reference to the asynchronous handler from the context and issues a call to the *EndProcessRequest* method.

```
void EndProcessRequest(IAsyncResult result);
```

The *EndProcessRequest* method takes the *IAsyncResult* object returned by the call to *Begin-ProcessRequest*. As implemented in the *HttpApplication* class, the *EndProcessRequest* method does nothing special and is limited to throwing an exception if an error occurred.

Implementing Asynchronous Handlers

Asynchronous handlers essentially serve one particular scenario—when the generation of the markup is subject to lengthy operations, such as time-consuming database stored procedures or calls to Web services. In these situations, the ASP.NET thread in charge of the request is stuck waiting for the operation to complete. Because the thread is a valuable member of the ASP.NET thread pool, lengthy tasks are potentially the perfect scalability killer. However, asynchronous handlers are here to help.

The idea is that the request begins on a thread-pool thread, but that thread is released as soon as the operation begins. In *BeginProcessRequest*, you typically create your own thread and start the lengthy operation. *BeginProcessRequest* doesn't wait for the operation to complete; therefore, the thread is returned to the pool immediately.

There are a lot of tricky details that this bird's-eye description just omitted. In the first place, you should strive to avoid a proliferation of threads. Ideally, you should use a custom thread pool. Furthermore, you must figure out a way to signal when the lengthy operation has terminated. This typically entails creating a custom class that implements *IAsyncResult* and returning it from *BeginProcessRequest*. This class will embed a synchronization object—typically a *ManualResetEvent* object—that the custom thread carrying the work will signal upon completion.

In the end, building asynchronous handlers is definitely tricky and not for novice developers. Very likely, you are more interested in asynchronous pages than in asynchronous HTTP handlers—that is, the same mechanism but applied to *.aspx* resources. In this case, the "lengthy task" is merely the *ProcessRequest* method of the *Page* class. (Obviously, you configure the page to execute asynchronously only if the page contains code that might start I/O-bound and potentially lengthy operations.)

In ASP.NET 2.0, you find ad hoc support for building asynchronous pages more easily and comfortably. We'll take a look at the API that provides this functionality in Chapter 5.

Writing HTTP Modules

So we've learned that ASP.NET runs as an ISAPI extension within the IIS process. Any incoming requests for ASP.NET resources are handed over to the worker process for the actual processing within the context of the CLR. Both in IIS 5.0 and 6.0, the worker process is a distinct process from IIS, so if one ASP.NET application crashes, it doesn't bring down the whole server. (In IIS 6.0, the handing over between the Web server and the worker process is more direct and faster.)

ASP.NET manages a pool of *HttpApplication* objects for each running application and picks up one of the pooled instances to serve a particular request. As discussed in Chapter 1, these objects are based on the class defined in your *global.asax* file or on the base *HttpApplication* class if *global.asax* is missing. The ultimate goal of the *HttpApplication* object in charge of the request is getting an HTTP handler.

On the way to the final HTTP handler, the *HttpApplication* object makes the request pass through a pipeline of HTTP modules. An HTTP module is a .NET Framework class that implements the *IHttpModule* interface. The HTTP modules that filter the raw data within the request are configured on a per-application basis within the *web.config* file. All ASP.NET applications, though, inherit a bunch of system HTTP modules configured in the *machine.config* file.

Generally speaking, an HTTP module can pre-process and post-process a request, and it intercepts and handles system events as well as events raised by other modules. The good news is that you can write and register your own HTTP modules and make them plug into the ASP.NET runtime pipeline, handle system events, and fire their own events.

The *IHttpModule* Interface

The *IHttpModule* interface defines only two methods—*Init* and *Dispose*. The *Init* method initializes a module and prepares it to handle requests. At this time, you subscribe to receive notifications for the events of interest. The *Dispose* method disposes of the resources (all but memory!) used by the module. Typical tasks you perform within the *Dispose* method are closing database connections or file handles.

The *IHttpModule* methods have the following signatures:

```
void Init(HttpApplication app);
void Dispose();
```

The *Init* method receives a reference to the *HttpApplication* object that is serving the request. You can use this reference to wire up to system events. The *HttpApplication* object also features a property named *Context* that provides access to the intrinsic properties of the ASP.NET application. In this way, you gain access to *Response*, *Request*, *Session*, and the like.

Table 2-5 lists the events that HTTP modules can listen to and handle.

Table 2-5   *HttpApplication* Events

Event	Description
AcquireRequestState, *PostAcquireRequestState*	Occurs when the handler that will actually serve the request acquires the state information associated with the request. *The post event is not available in ASP.NET 1.x.*
AuthenticateRequest, *PostAuthenticateRequest*	Occurs when a security module has established the identity of the user. *The post event is not available in ASP.NET 1.x.*
AuthorizeRequest, *PostAuthorizeRequest*	Occurs when a security module has verified user authorization. *The post event is not available in ASP.NET 1.x.*
BeginRequest	Occurs as soon as the HTTP pipeline begins to process the request.
Disposed	Occurs when the *HttpApplication* object is disposed of as a result of a call to *Dispose.*
EndRequest	Occurs as the last event in the HTTP pipeline chain of execution.
Error	Occurs when an unhandled exception is thrown.
PostMapRequestHandler	Occurs when the HTTP handler to serve the request has been found. *The event is not available in ASP.NET 1.x.*
PostRequestHandlerExecute	Occurs when the HTTP handler of choice finishes execution. The response text has been generated at this point.
PreRequestHandlerExecute	Occurs just before the HTTP handler of choice begins to work.
PreSendRequestContent	Occurs just before the ASP.NET runtime sends the response text to the client.
PreSendRequestHeaders	Occurs just before the ASP.NET runtime sends HTTP headers to the client.
ReleaseRequestState, *PostReleaseRequestState*	Occurs when the handler releases the state information associated with the current request. *The post event is not available in ASP.NET 1.x.*
ResolveRequestCache, *PostResolveRequestCache*	Occurs when the ASP.NET runtime resolves the request through the output cache. *The post event is not available in ASP.NET 1.x.*
UpdateRequestCache, *PostUpdateRequestCache*	Occurs when the ASP.NET runtime stores the response of the current request in the output cache to be used to serve subsequent requests. *The post event is not available in ASP.NET 1.x.*

All these events are exposed by the *HttpApplication* object that an HTTP module receives as an argument to the *Init* method.

A Custom HTTP Module

Let's come to grips with HTTP modules by writing a relatively simple custom module named *Marker* that adds a signature at the beginning and end of each page served by the application. The following code outlines the class we need to write:

```
using System;
using System.Web;

namespace ProAspNet20.CS.Components
{
    public class MarkerModule : IHttpModule
    {
        public void Init(HttpApplication app)
        {
            // Register for pipeline events
        }

        public void Dispose()
        {
            // Nothing to do here
        }
    }
}
```

The *Init* method is invoked by the *HttpApplication* class to load the module. In the *Init* method, you normally don't need to do more than simply register your own event handlers. The *Dispose* method is, more often than not, empty. The heart of the HTTP module is really in the event handlers you define.

Wiring Up Events

The sample *Marker* module registers a couple of pipeline events. They are *BeginRequest* and *EndRequest*. *BeginRequest* is the first event that hits the HTTP application object when the request begins processing. *EndRequest* is the event that signals that the request is going to be terminated and that it's your last chance to intervene. By handling these two events, you can write custom text to the output stream before and after the regular HTTP handler—the *Page*-derived class.

The following listing shows the implementation of the *Init* and *Dispose* methods for the sample module:

```
public void Init(HttpApplication app)
{
    // Register for pipeline events
    app.BeginRequest += new EventHandler(OnBeginRequest);
    app.EndRequest += new EventHandler(OnEndRequest);
}

public void Dispose()
{
}
```

The *BeginRequest* and *EndRequest* event handlers have a similar structure. They obtain a reference to the current *HttpApplication* object from the sender and get the HTTP context from there. Next, they work with the *Response* object to append text or a custom header.

```
public void OnBeginRequest(object sender, EventArgs e)
{
    HttpApplication app = (HttpApplication) sender;
    HttpContext ctx = app.Context;

        // More code here
        ⋮

    // Add custom header to the HTTP response
    // PageHeaderText is a constant string defined elsewhere
    ctx.Response.AppendHeader("Author", "DinoE");
    ctx.Response.Write(PageHeaderText);
}

public void OnEndRequest(object sender, EventArgs e)
{
    // Get access to the HTTP context
    HttpApplication app = (HttpApplication) sender;
    HttpContext ctx = app.Context;

        // More code here
        ⋮

    // Append some custom text
    // PageFooterText is a constant string defined elsewhere
    ctx.Response.Write(PageFooterText);
}
```

OnBeginRequest writes standard page header text and also adds a custom HTTP header. *OnEndRequest* simply appends the page footer. The effect of this HTTP module is visible in Figure 2-7.

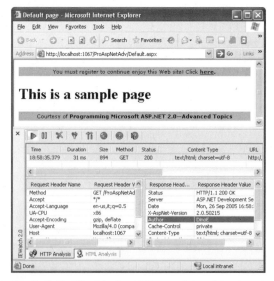

Figure 2-7   The *Marker* HTTP module adds a header and footer to each page within the application.

Note   The tool in the figure—IEWatch 2.0—is a plug-in for Microsoft Internet Explorer that allows you to analyze HTTP/HTTPS requests and the HTML source code. You can get it at *http://www.iewatch.com*.

The dockable window at the bottom of Internet Explorer shows all the HTTP headers being sent and received by the browser. The custom header in the response text is clearly visible.

Registering with the Configuration File

You register a new HTTP module by adding an entry to the *<httpModules>* section of the configuration file. The overall syntax of the *<httpModules>* section closely resembles that of HTTP handlers. To add a new module, you use the *<add>* node and specify the *name* and *type* attributes. The *name* attribute contains the public name of the module. This name will be used to select the module within the *HttpApplication*'s *Modules* collection. If the module fires custom events, this name is also used as the prefix for building automatic event handlers in the *global.asax* file.

```
<system.web>
  <httpModules>
    <add name="Marker"
      type="ProAspNet20.CS.Components.MarkerModule,ProAspCompLib" />
  </httpModules>
</system.web>
```

The *type* attribute is the usual comma-separated string that contains the name of the class and the related assembly. The configuration settings can be entered into the application's configuration file as well as into the machine configuration file. In the former case, only pages within the application will be affected; in the latter case, all pages within all applications will be processed by the specified module.

The order in which modules are applied depends on the physical order of the modules in the configuration list. You can remove a system module and replace it with your own that provides a similar functionality. In this case, in the application's *web.config* file, you use the *<remove>* node to drop the default module and then use *<add>* to insert your own. If you want to completely redefine the order of HTTP modules for your application, you could clear all the default modules by using the *<clear>* node and then re-register them all in the order you prefer.

Accessing Other HTTP Modules

The sample just discussed demonstrates how to wire up pipeline events—that is, events fired by the *HttpApplication* object. But what about events fired by other modules? The *HttpApplication* object provides a property named *Modules* that gets the collection of modules for the current application.

The *Modules* property is of type *HttpModuleCollection* and contains the names of the modules for the application. The collection class inherits from the abstract class *NameObjectCollection-Base*, which is a collection of pairs made of a string and an object. The string indicates the public name of the module; the object is the actual instance of the module. To access the module that handles the session state, you need code like this:

```
SessionStateModule sess = app.Modules["Session"];
sess.Start += new EventHandler(OnSessionStart);
```

As mentioned, you can also handle events raised by HTTP modules within the *global.asax* file and use the *ModuleName_EventName* convention to name the event handlers. The name of the module is just one of the settings that you need to define when registering an HTTP module.

The Page Refresh Feature

Let's examine a practical situation in which the ability to filter the request before it gets processed by an HTTP handler helps to implement a feature that would otherwise be impossible. The postback mechanism has a nasty drawback—if the user refreshes the currently displayed page, the last action taken on the server is blindly repeated. If a new record were added as a result of a previous posting, for example, the application would attempt to insert an identical record upon another postback. Of course, this results in the insertion of identical records and should result in an exception. This snag has existed since the dawn of Web programming and was certainly not introduced by ASP.NET. To implement nonrepeatable actions, some countermeasures are required to essentially transform any critical server-side operation into an idempotency. In algebra, an operation is said to be *idempotent* if the result doesn't change no matter how many times you execute it. For example, take a look at the following SQL command:

```
DELETE FROM employees WHERE employeeid=9
```

You can execute the command 1000 consecutive times, but only one record at most will ever be deleted—the one that satisfies the criteria set in the WHERE clause. Consider this one, instead:

```
INSERT INTO employees VALUES (...)
```

Each time you execute the command, a new record might be added to the table. This is especially true if you have auto-number key columns or nonunique columns. If the table design requires that the key be unique and specified explicitly, a SQL exception would be thrown the second time you run the command.

Although the particular scenario we considered is typically resolved in the data access layer (DAL), the underlying pattern represents a common issue for most Web applications. So the open question is how can we detect whether the page is being posted as the result of an explicit user action or because the user simply hit F5 or the page refresh toolbar button?

The Rationale Behind Page Refresh Operations

The page refresh action is a sort of internal browser operation for which the browser doesn't provide any external notification in terms of events or callbacks. Technically speaking, the page refresh consists of the "simple" reiteration of the latest request. The browser caches the latest request it served and reissues it when the user hits the page refresh key or button. No browsers that I'm aware of provide any kind of notification for the page refresh event—and if there are any that do, it's certainly not a recognized standard.

In light of this, there's no way that the server-side code (for example, ASP.NET, classic ASP, or ISAPI DLLs) can distinguish a refresh request from an ordinary submit or postback request. To help ASP.NET detect and handle page refreshes, you need to build surrounding machinery that makes two otherwise identical requests look different. All known browsers implement the refresh by resending the last HTTP payload sent; to make the copy look different from the original, an extra service must add additional parameters, and the ASP.NET page must be capable of catching them.

I considered some additional requirements. The solution should not rely on session state and should not tax the server memory too much. It should be relatively easy to deploy and as unobtrusive as possible.

Outline of the Solution

The solution is based on the idea that each request be assigned a ticket number and the HTTP module will track the last-served ticket for each distinct page it processes. If the number carried by the page is lower than the last-served ticket for the page, it can mean only that the *same* request has been served already—namely, a page refresh. The solution consists of a couple of building blocks: an HTTP module to make preliminary checks on the ticket numbers and a custom page class that automatically adds a progressive ticket number to each served page. Making the feature work is a two-step procedure: first, register the HTTP module; second, change the base code-behind class of each page in the relevant application to detect browser refreshes.

The HTTP module sits in the middle of the HTTP runtime environment and checks in every request for a resource in the application. The first time the page is requested (when not posting back), there will be no ticket assigned. The HTTP module will generate a new ticket number and store it in the *Items* collection of the *HttpContext* object. In addition, the module initializes the internal counter of the last-served ticket to 0. Each successive time the page is requested, the module compares the last-served ticket with the page ticket. If the page ticket is newer, the request is considered a regular postback; otherwise, it will be flagged as a page refresh. Table 2-6 summarizes the scenarios and related actions.

Table 2-6   Scenarios and Actions

Scenario	Action
Page has no ticket associated.	Counter of the last ticket served is set to 0.
■ No refresh.	The ticket to use for the next request of the current page is generated and stored in *Items*.
Page has a ticket associated.	Counter of the last ticket served is set with the ticket associated with the page.
■ Page refresh occurs if the ticket associated with the page is lower than the last served ticket.	The ticket to use for the next request of the current page is generated and stored in *Items*.

Some help from the page class is required to ensure that each request—except the first—comes with a proper ticket number. That's why you need to set the code-behind class of each page that intends to support this feature to a particular class—a process that we'll discuss in a moment. The page class will receive two distinct pieces of information from the HTTP module—the next ticket to store in a hidden field that travels with the page, and whether or not the request is a page refresh. As an added service to developers, the code-behind class will expose an extra Boolean property—*IsRefreshed*—to let developers know whether or not the request is a page refresh or a regular postback.

> **Important**   The *Items* collection on the *HttpContext* class is a cargo collection purposely created to let HTTP modules pass information down to pages and HTTP handlers in charge of physically serving the request. The HTTP module we employ here sets two entries in the *Items* collection. One is to let the page know whether the request is a page refresh; another is to let the page know what the next ticket number is. Having the module pass the page the next ticket number serves the purpose of keeping the page class behavior as simple and linear as possible, moving most of the implementation and execution burden on to the HTTP module.

Implementation of the Solution

There are a few open points with the solution I just outlined. First, some state is required. Where do you keep it? Second, an HTTP module will be called for each incoming request. How do you distinguish requests for the same page? How do you pass information to the page? How intelligent do you expect the page to be?

It's clear that each of these points might be designed and implemented in a different way than shown here. All design choices made to reach a working solution here should be considered arbitrary, and they can possibly be replaced with equivalent strategies if you want to rework the code to better suit your own purposes. Let me also add this disclaimer: I'm not aware of commercial products and libraries that fix this re-posting problem. In the past couple of years, I've been writing articles on the subject of re-posting and speaking to various user groups. The version of the code presented in this next example incorporates the most valuable suggestions I've collected along the way. One of these suggestions is to move as much code as possible into the HTTP module, as mentioned in the previous note.

The following code shows the implementation of the HTTP module:

```
public class RefreshModule : IHttpModule
{
    public void Init(HttpApplication app) {
        app.BeginRequest += new EventHandler(OnAcquireRequestState);
    }
    public void Dispose() {
    }
    void OnAcquireRequestState(object sender, EventArgs e) {
        HttpApplication app = (HttpApplication) sender;
```

```
        HttpContext ctx = app.Context;
        RefreshAction.Check(ctx);
        return;
    }
}
```

The module listens to the *BeginRequest* event and ends up calling the *Check* method on the helper *RefreshAction* class.

```
public class RefreshAction
{
    static Hashtable requestHistory = null;

    // Other string constants defined here
    ⋮

    public static void Check(HttpContext ctx) {
        // Initialize the ticket slot
        EnsureRefreshTicket(ctx);

        // Read the last ticket served in the session (from Session)
        int lastTicket = GetLastRefreshTicket(ctx);

        // Read the ticket of the current request (from a hidden field)
        int thisTicket = GetCurrentRefreshTicket(ctx, lastTicket);

        // Compare tickets
        if (thisTicket > lastTicket ||
        (thisTicket==lastTicket && thisTicket==0)) {
            UpdateLastRefreshTicket(ctx, thisTicket);
        ctx.Items[PageRefreshEntry] = false;
        }
        else
            ctx.Items[PageRefreshEntry] = true;
    }

    // Initialize the internal data store
    static void EnsureRefreshTicket(HttpContext ctx)
    {
        if (requestHistory == null)
            requestHistory = new Hashtable();
    }

    // Return the last-served ticket for the URL
    static int GetLastRefreshTicket(HttpContext ctx)
    {
        // Extract and return the last ticket
        if (!requestHistory.ContainsKey(ctx.Request.Path))
            return 0;
        else
            return (int) requestHistory[ctx.Request.Path];
    }
```

```
// Return the ticket associated with the page
static int GetCurrentRefreshTicket(HttpContext ctx, int lastTicket)
{
    int ticket;
    object o = ctx.Request[CurrentRefreshTicketEntry];
    if (o == null)
        ticket = lastTicket;
    else
        ticket = Convert.ToInt32(o);
    ctx.Items[RefreshAction.NextPageTicketEntry] = ticket + 1;
    return ticket;
}

// Store the last-served ticket for the URL
static void UpdateLastRefreshTicket(HttpContext ctx, int ticket)
{
    requestHistory[ctx.Request.Path] = ticket;
}
}
```

The *Check* method performs the following actions. It compares the last-served ticket with the ticket (if any) provided by the page. The page stores the ticket number in a hidden field that is read through the *Request* object interface. The HTTP module maintains a hashtable with an entry for each distinct URL served. The value in the hashtable stores the last-served ticket for that URL.

> **Note**   The *Item* indexer property is used to set the last-served ticket instead of the *Add* method because *Item* overwrites existing items. If the item already exists, the *Add* method just returns.

In addition to creating the HTTP module, you also need to arrange a page class to use as the base for pages wanting to detect browser refreshes. Here's the code:

```
// Assume to be in a custom namespace
public class Page : System.Web.UI.Page
{
  public bool IsRefreshed {
    get {
      HttpContext ctx = HttpContext.Current;
      object o = ctx.Items[RefreshAction.PageRefreshEntry];
      if (o == null)
        return false;
      return (bool) o;
    }
  }

  // Handle the PreRenderComplete event
  protected override void OnPreRenderComplete(EventArgs e) {
    base.OnPreRenderComplete(e);
    SaveRefreshState();
  }
```

```
// Create the hidden field to store the current request ticket
private void SaveRefreshState() {
    HttpContext ctx = HttpContext.Current;
    int ticket = (int) ctx.Items[RefreshAction.NextPageTicketEntry];
    ClientScript.RegisterHiddenField(
        RefreshAction.CurrentRefreshTicketEntry,
        ticket.ToString());
}
}
```

The sample page defines a new public Boolean property, *IsRefreshed*, that you can use in code in the same way you would use *IsPostBack* or *IsCallback*. It overrides *OnPreRenderComplete* to add the hidden field with the page ticket. As mentioned, the page ticket is received from the HTTP module through an ad hoc (and arbitrarily named) entry in the *Items* collection.

Figure 2-8 shows a sample page in action. Let's take a look at the source code of the page.

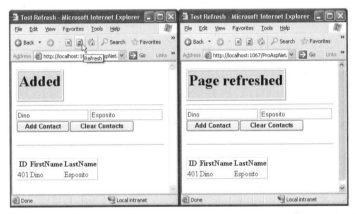

Figure 2-8   The page doesn't repeat a sensitive action if the user refreshes the browser's view.

```
public partial class TestRefresh : ProAspNet20.CS.Components.Page
{
    protected void AddContactButton_Click(object sender, EventArgs e)
    {
        Msg.InnerText = "Added";
        if (!this.IsRefreshed)
            AddRecord(FName.Text, LName.Text);
        else
            Msg.InnerText = "Page refreshed";

        BindData();
    }
    ⋮
}
```

The *IsRefreshed* property lets you decide what to do when a postback action is requested. In the preceding code, the *AddRecord* method is not invoked if the page is refreshing. Needless to say, *IsRefreshed* is available only with the custom page class presented here. The custom page class doesn't just add the property, it also adds the hidden field, which is essential for the machinery to work.

Conclusion

HTTP handlers and HTTP modules are the building blocks of the ASP.NET platform. ASP.NET includes several predefined handlers and HTTP modules, but developers can write handlers and modules of their own to perform a variety of tasks. HTTP handlers, in particular, are faster than ordinary Web pages and can be used in all circumstances in which you don't need state maintenance and postback events. To generate images dynamically on the server, for example, an HTTP handler is more efficient than a page.

Everything that occurs under the hood of the ASP.NET runtime environment occurs because of HTTP handlers. When you invoke a Web page or a Web service method, an appropriate HTTP handler gets into the game and serves your request. At the highest level of abstraction, the behavior of an HTTP handler closely resembles that of an ISAPI extension. While the similarity makes sense, a key difference exists: HTTP handlers are .NET components and are therefore managed and execute within the CLR's runtime environment. The CLR, in turn, is hosted by the worker process. An ISAPI extension, on the other hand, is a Win32 library that can live within the IIS process. In the ASP.NET process model, the *aspnet_isapi* component is a true ISAPI extension that collects requests and dispatches them to the worker process. ASP.NET internally implements an ISAPI-like extensibility model in which HTTP handlers play the role of ISAPI extensions in the IIS world. This model will change in IIS 7.0, at which point managed HTTP modules and extensions will also be recognized within the IIS environment.

HTTP modules are to ISAPI filters what HTTP handlers are to ISAPI extensions. HTTP modules are good at performing a number of low-level tasks for which a tight interaction and integration with the request/response mechanism is a critical factor. Modules are sort of interceptors that you can place along an HTTP packet's path, from the Web server to the ASP.NET runtime and back. Modules have read and write capabilities, and they can filter and modify the contents of both inbound and outbound requests.

We have touched on configuration files several times in the first two chapters of the book. It's about time we take the plunge into the *web.config* file and its rather rich schema. This is good fodder for the next chapter.

Just the Facts

- HTTP handlers and modules are like classic ISAPI extensions and filters except that they are managed components and provide a much simpler, less error-prone programming model.

- An HTTP handler is the ASP.NET component in charge of handling a request. In the end, an ASP.NET page is just an instance of an HTTP handler.

- HTTP handlers are classes that implement the *IHttpHandler* interface and take care of processing the payload of the request.

- HTTP modules are classes that implement the *IHttpModule* interface and listen to application-level events.

- Custom HTTP handlers and modules must be registered with the application or all applications in the server machine, through special sections in the *web.config* file.

Chapter 3
ASP.NET Configuration

The Microsoft .NET Framework defines a tailor-made, XML-based application programming interface (API) to access configuration files and, in doing so, forces developers to adopt a common, rich, and predefined schema for storing application settings. In the more general context of the .NET configuration scheme, ASP.NET applications enjoy specific features such as a hierarchical configuration scheme that allows settings inheritance and overriding at various levels—machine, application, or specific directories.

Configuration files are typically created offline or during the development of the application. They are deployed with the application and can be changed at any time by administrators. Changes to such critical files are promptly detected by the ASP.NET runtime and cause all the pages to recompile. ASP.NET pages can use the classes in the *System.Configuration* namespace to read from—and in ASP.NET 2.0, also to write to—configuration files.

In this chapter, we'll specifically delve into the ASP.NET configuration machinery. We'll see how to fine-tune the ASP.NET runtime and review the whole collection of parameters you can set for an individual application.

The ASP.NET Configuration Hierarchy

Configuration files are standard XML files that rigorously follow a given schema. The schema defines all possible settings for machine, security, and application files. All configuration files begin with a *<configuration>* node and then differentiate their contents and child nodes according to their final goal and the information they contain. Configuration in ASP.NET is hierarchical and is based on a unique, machine-specific file named *machine.config* plus any number of *web.config* files.

Wise use of the settings in *machine.config* and *web.config* files allows you to declaratively restrict access to given folders and even enable a different set of features. For example, the following *web.config* file restricts access to the folder that contains it to all users except the administrator:

```
<configuration>
    <system.web>
        <authorization>
            <allow users="YourDomain\Administrator" />
            <deny users="*" />
        </authorization>
    </system.web>
</configuration>
```

You simply have to add the code in bold type to the *web.config* file in another directory to activate the same restriction.

> **Warning**   ASP.NET protects its configuration files from direct Web access by instructing Internet Information Server (IIS) to block browser access to configuration files. An HTTP access 403 Forbidden error is returned to all browsers that attempt to request a .config as a URL. The mechanism for accomplishing this is, interestingly enough, performed through a "forbidden file" handler, as we examined in the previous chapter.

Configuration Files

The syntax of *machine.config* and *web.config* files is identical—both are XML files based on the same schema. The ASP.NET runtime processes configuration information hierarchically, proceeding from a root common to all applications on the machine—*machine.config*—down to all the *web.config* files found in the various folders of the particular application.

> **Note**   The *machine.config* file is located in the Config directory under the ASP.NET installation folder. The installation folder is located under the Windows directory at the following path: \Microsoft.NET\Framework\[version]\. If you take a look at the contents of the Config directory, you'll find three similar files: *machine.config*, *machine.config.default*, and *machine.config.comments*. Provided for educational purposes, the latter two files provide description and default values of each configuration section. To improve performance, the *machine.config* file contains only the settings that differ from their defaults.

The Tree of Configuration Files

When an ASP.NET application starts, all configurable parameters are set to the default values defined in *machine.config*. These values can be overridden in the first place by a *web.config* file placed in the root folder of the application. The *web.config* file can also add new application-specific settings. In theory, a root *web.config* file can also clear all the settings in the original machine configuration and replace them altogether. However, in practice it is very rare that you would reconfigure ASP.NET for your application to this extreme.

You can also define additional *web.config* files in child folders to apply other settings to all the resources contained in the subtree rooted in the folder. Also in this case, the innermost *web.config* can overwrite, restrict, or extend the settings defined at upper levels. Figure 3-1 illustrates how ASP.NET processes system and application settings for each page in the Web site.

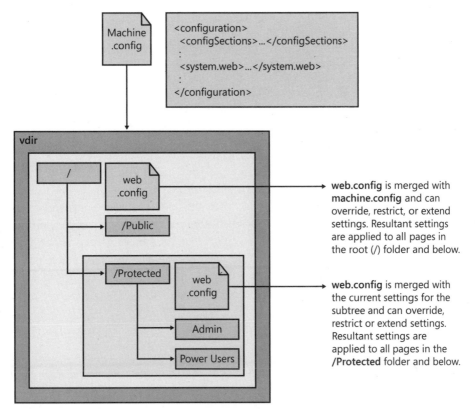

Figure 3-1   Hierarchical nature of ASP.NET configuration.

Configuring the machine file is an administrative task and should be performed with the server offline when the application is deployed or during periodical maintenance. Applications, on the other hand, might have the need to read from *web.config* files—that is, the application-specific repository for configuration information. Data that applications might want to read from *web.config* is applicationwide data, such as connection strings to databases, URLs to connect to user interface elements, and pieces of software that need to be enabled or disabled.

Important   In ASP.NET 2.0, a new level of configuration—the Web site *web.config* file—is added to the hierarchy shown in Figure 3-1. This file is a *web.config* file located in the same folder as *machine.config,* whose contents are merged with those of *machine.config.* This additional level is simply a way to spread the contents of *machine.config* over more files. In light of this, you should try to use the site root *web.config* file instead of *machine.config* for global settings.

Reading and Writing Configuration Files

Only in very special cases should the application write to either *machine.config* or *web.config*. If you need to persist some data on the server (for example, user profile data), you should take advantage of the user profile API and the profile provider. The need for writing to a configuration file should be taken as an alarm bell that warns you against possible bad design choices.

> **Note**   For more information on the core profile API, take a look at Chapter 5 of *Programming Microsoft ASP.NET 2.0: Core Reference* (Microsoft Press, 2005). We'll cover custom providers, and touch on user profiling again, in the next chapter.

In version 2.0, ASP.NET comes with a full I/O API for reading and writing configuration files. A set of tailor-made classes maps all the feasible sections and nodes in the configuration schema and exposes methods to read and write. Any modification to *web.config* automatically invalidates all the dynamic assemblies created for the application. Hence, all the pages are recompiled with the next request to reflect the changes in the configuration. You can understand, then, that especially for large-scale Web sites with hundreds of pages, repeated and generalized compilations are a serious issue that lead to dramatic performance hits. For this reason, user profile data—the most common and perhaps the only reasonable type of configuration data to persist—boasts its own persistence service, the aforementioned profile provider.

The Configuration Schema

All configuration files have their root in the *<configuration>* element. Table 3-1 lists the main first-level children of the *<configuration>* element. Each node has a specified number of child elements that provide a full description of the setting. For example, the *<system.web>* element optionally contains the *<authorization>* tag, in which you can store information about the users who can safely access the ASP.NET application.

Table 3-1   Main Children of the *<configuration>* Element

Element	Description
<appSettings>	Contains custom application settings.
<configSections>	Describes the configuration sections for custom settings. If this element is present, it must be the first child of the *<configuration>* node.
<connectionStrings>	Lists predefined connection strings that are useful to the application. *Not supported in ASP.NET 1.x.*
<configProtectedData>	Contains ciphered data for sections that have been encrypted. *Not supported in ASP.NET 1.x.*
<runtime>	Run-time settings schema; describes the elements that configure assembly binding and run-time behavior such as probing and assembly redirect.

Table 3-1   Main Children of the *<configuration>* Element

Element	Description
<startup>	Startup settings schema; contains the elements that specify which version of the common language runtime (CLR) must be used.
<system.diagnostics>	Describes the elements that specify trace switches and listeners that collect, store, and route messages.
<system.net>	Network schema; specifies elements to indicate how the .NET Framework connects to the Internet, including the default proxy, authentication modules, and connection parameters.
<system.runtime.remoting>	Settings schema; configures the client and server applications that exploit .NET remoting.
<system.web>	The ASP.NET-specific configuration section; contains the elements that control all aspects of the behavior of an ASP.NET application.

Because we're focusing on ASP.NET applications, only the *<system.web>* section has particular importance for us and will be covered in detail. Other sections for which you'll find significant coverage here are *<connectionStrings>* and *<configProtectedData>*. However, this doesn't mean that, as an ASP.NET developer, you'll never use other sections—most certainly not!

For example, the *<configSections>* element defines the sections that will be used to group information in the rest of the document. The *<appSettings>* element contains user-defined nodes whose structure has been previously defined in the *<configSections>* node. You might need to interact with the *<system.diagnostics>* section if you want to use a custom trace listener that logs its results to an application-defined file. You'll probably need *<runtime>* if some special rules for probing assemblies are required. Furthermore, if the ASP.NET application performs calls to some remote component, you must adjust settings in the *<system.runtime.remoting>* section.

Sections and Section Groups

All sections used in a configuration file must be declared in the initial *<configSections>* section. The following code example demonstrates how the *<system.web>* section is declared in *machine.config*:

```
<configSections>
    <sectionGroup name="system.web"
          type="System.Web.Configuration.SystemWebSectionGroup, ...">
        <section name="authentication"
            type="System.Web.Configuration.AuthenticationSection, ..."
            allowDefinition="MachineToApplication" />
        ⋮
    </sectionGroup>
</configSections>
```

The *<sectionGroup>* element has no other role than marking and grouping a few child sections, thus creating a sort of namespace for them. In this way, you can have sections with the same name living under different groups. The *<section>* element takes two attributes—*name* and *type*. The *name* attribute denotes the name of the section being declared. The *type* attribute indicates the name of the managed class that reads and parses the contents of the section from the configuration file. The value of the *type* attribute is a comma-separated string that includes the class and full name of the assembly that contains it.

The *<section>* element also has two optional attributes—*allowDefinition* and *allowLocation*. The *allowDefinition* attribute specifies the configuration files in which the section can be used. Feasible values for the *allowDefinition* attribute are listed in Table 3-2.

Table 3-2   Values for the *allowDefinition* Attribute

Value	Description
Everywhere	The section can be used in any configuration file. (Default.)
MachineOnly	The section can be used only in the *machine.config* file.
MachineToApplication	The section can be used in the *machine.config* file and in the application's *web.config* file. You cannot use the section in *web.config* files located in subdirectories of the virtual folder.

The *allowLocation* attribute determines whether the section can be used within the *<location>* section. The *<location>* section in a *machine.config* file allows you to apply the specified machinewide settings only to the resources below a given path. (I'll say more about the *<location>* section shortly.)

Many sections in the configuration files support three special elements, named *<add>*, *<remove>*, and *<clear>*. The *<add>* element adds a new setting to the specified section, whereas *<remove>* removes the specified one. The *<clear>* element clears all the settings that have previously been defined in the section. The *<remove>* and *<clear>* elements are particularly useful in ASP.NET configuration files in which a hierarchy of files can be created. For example, you can use the *<remove>* element in a child *web.config* file to remove settings that are defined at a higher level in the configuration file hierarchy.

The *<remove>* and *<clear>* elements don't affect the actual data stored in the configuration file. Removing a section doesn't erase the related data from the file; it simply removes the data from the in-memory tree of settings that ASP.NET builds and maintains for an application.

> **Note**   Sections are a necessary syntax element in configuration files. However, you don't need to declare sections in all application-specific *web.config* files. When processing a *web.config* file, in fact, ASP.NET builds a configuration tree starting from the root *machine.config* file. Because all standard sections are already declared in the *machine.config* file that ships with the .NET Framework, your application needs to declare only custom sections you plan to use.
>
> Finally, bear in mind that an exception is thrown when a configuration section lacks a corresponding entry in the *<configSections>* section and when the layout of the data does not match the declaration.

Let's start our tour of the configuration schema with a closer look at the *<location>* section.

The *<location>* Section

The *<location>* section serves one main purpose in two distinct scenarios. The section provides an alternative technique to apply different settings to various parts of an application. You typically employ the *<location>* section to apply different settings to subdirectories of the same application and to configure distinct applications installed on the same machine.

When defined inside an application's root *web.config* file, it allows you to apply different settings to different subdirectories. Instead of defining child *web.config* files, you can create a single *web.config* file in the root folder and specify settings on a per-directory basis. Basically, the *<location>* element lets you create embedded configuration sections associated with a particular directory. From a functional point of view, this is equivalent to having a *web.config* file in each directory.

When defined inside the *machine.config* file, or in a site's root *web.config* file, the *<location>* section enables you to specify different machinewide settings for various Web applications. Used in this way, the section turns out to be an extremely powerful tool to let multiple applications apply individual machinewide settings in an ISP scenario.

> **Caution**   Note the difference between the application's root *web.config* file and the site's root *web.config* file. The application's root configuration file is the *web.config* file you find in the application's root folder. You use this file to adapt ASP.NET settings to the needs of the particular application and its subdirectories. In contrast, the site's root *web.config* file is located in the same folder as *machine.config*, and therefore well outside the Web space of any deployed applications. This file is a sort of appendix of *machine.config* and should be used as an additional level of settings personalization. A *<location>* element defined in this file can be scoped to any applications on the machine. A *<location>* element without the *Path* attribute will affect all applications in the machine.

Centralized Configuration

The *<location>* section has two attributes: *Path* and *allowOverride*. The *Path* attribute represents the virtual path to which the embedded settings apply. The following example shows how it works. The code shown is taken from a *web.config* file. Note that the name of the folder must be relative and should not begin with slashes, backslashes, or dots.

```
<configuration>
    <system.web>
        <!-- Settings for the application go here -->
    </system.web>

    <location path="Reserved">
        <system.web>
            <!-- Settings for the /Reserved folder go here -->
        </system.web>
    </location>
</configuration>
```

The defining characteristic of this approach is that you have a single, centralized *web.config* file to maintain and can still configure subdirectories individually and independently. This feature saves you from the burden of maintaining several *web.config* files, but it also introduces some unpleasant side effects that in the long run can turn out to be quite harsh. For example, any change to the file results in a new compilation for all the pages in the application. If you maintain distinct *web.config* files, the compilation occurs only for the pages really affected by the change.

> **Note**   If the *path* attribute is omitted in the *<location>* element, the embedded settings apply to all subfolders of the application in the case of an application's root *web.config*. Settings affect all installed applications on the server machine if the *<location>* element that is missing the *path* attribute is found in the site's root *web.config* or *machine.config*.

Machinewide Settings

Used within the *machine.config* file or the site's root *web.config* file, the *<location>* element lets you specify different machinewide settings for all the Web applications hosted on the server machine. Note that in this case, though, you must indicate the name of the application you're configuring, prefixed by the IIS name of the Web site. The Web site name is read in the IIS Manager. The following script applies to the *ProAspNet20* application in the Web site shown in Figure 3-2:

```
<location path="Default Web Site/ProAspNet20">
    <system.web>
        <!-- Settings for the Web site go here -->
    </system.web>
</location>
```

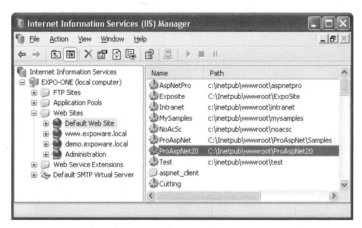

Figure 3-2   Default Web site of a sample IIS-equipped server machine.

When you develop the ASP.NET code, you typically test it on a development machine with its own copies of *machine.config* and site *web.config* files. When you deploy the application on a production box, especially in an ISP scenario, you might not be able to restore the same settings. One possible reason is that the administrator does not want you to modify the current settings because they are too high for other applications or because of security concerns.

You can work around the issue by simply replicating any needed global settings into the application's root *web.config*. If you are deploying your code to a service provider, you might find that many configuration elements have been locked down and cannot be overridden. (I'll say more about this aspect shortly.) In this case, a new application-specific *<location>* section created in *machine.config* or the site's *web.config* can contain all the machine settings needed for your application without breaking others.

Whenever possible, though, you should try to replicate needed changes into the application's *web.config*. This should always be the first option considered because it makes the entire application self-contained.

> **Important**   When you register components (say, an HTTP handler) in the *<location>* section of a *machine.config* file, make sure the assembly you use is strongly named and installed in the global assembly cache (GAC). Refer to Chapter 1 for a quick overview of strongly named assemblies. In the configuration script, you also have to specify the full name of the assembly. Here's how to register the *view.axd* HTTP handler in the *machine.config* file for the *ProAspNet20* application.
>
> ```
> <location path="Default Web site/proaspnet20">
>   <system.web>
>     <httpHandlers>
>       <add verb="*" path="view.axd"
>           type="ProAspNet20.CS.Components.PictureViewerHandler,
>               ProAspCompLib, Version=1.0.0.0, Culture=neutral,
>               PublicKeyToken=54943ebb40058fcb" />
>     </httpHandlers>
>   </system.web>
> </location>
> ```
>
> Note that additional information in the strong name might vary upon creation. See Chapter 2 for more details on *view.axd*.

Unmodifiable Settings

The second *<location>* attribute you can specify—*allowOverride*—allows you to lock some settings at either the machine or application level. By grouping settings in a *<location>* element with the *allowOverride* attribute set to *false*, you tell the ASP.NET configuration system to raise an exception whenever a protected setting is overridden in a lower-level configuration file.

```
<location path="Default Web Site/ProAspNet20" allowOverride="false">
    <system.web>
        <!-- These settings cannot be overridden -->
    </system.web>
</location>
```

The ultimate goal of this feature is to enable administrators to control the settings of a server that provides ASP.NET hosting. When a new application is installed in production, changes might be required on the target machine to reflect the native environment of the application. Updating the *machine.config* file on the production machine is not an issue as long as yours is the only application running or you can directly control and configure all the applications hosted on that machine. However, in an application-hosting scenario, the administrator might decide to lock some machine settings to prevent installed applications from modifying them. In this way, the administrator can preserve, to the extent possible, the integrity of the hosting environment and guarantee that all applications run under the same conditions.

> **Note**   By default, nearly all predefined sections can appear within a *<location>* section. The exceptions are *<runtime>*, *<mscorlib>*, *<system.runtime.remoting>*, and *<startup>*. In general, sections can be disallowed from appearing in *<location>* by using the *allowLocation* attribute. The *allowLocation* attribute of the *<section>* element determines the section's capability of being customized for a particular path. Set it to *false*, and the section is not allowed to be used within a *<location>* section.

The *<system.web>* Section

The *<system.web>* section contains all the configuration elements that set up the ASP.NET runtime environment and controls how ASP.NET applications behave. Table 3-3 lists all feasible first-level elements and their override level.

Table 3-3   Sections Allowed Within *<system.web>*

Section	Overridable	Description
<anonymousIdentification>	Machine, application	Configures identification for users who are not authenticated. *Not supported in ASP.NET 1.x.*
<authentication>	Machine, application	Sets the authentication mechanism.
<authorization>	Everywhere	Indicates authorized users.
<browserCaps>	Everywhere	Lists known browser capabilities.
<clientTarget>	Everywhere	Lists predefined client targets.
<compilation>	Everywhere	Settings for batch compilation. (See Chapter 1.)
<customErrors>	Machine, application	Settings for custom error pages.
<deployment>	Everywhere	Indicates how the application is deployed. *Not supported in ASP.NET 1.x.*
<deviceFilters>	Everywhere	Lists known mobile browser capabilities. (See Chapter 9.) *Not supported in ASP.NET 1.0.*
<globalization>	Everywhere	Settings for application localization.
<healthMonitoring>	Machine, application	Configures an application for health monitoring. *Not supported in ASP.NET 1.x.*

Table 3-3   Sections Allowed Within *<system.web>*

Section	Overridable	Description
<hostingEnvironment>	Machine, application	Defines configuration settings that control the behavior of the application hosting environment. *Not supported in ASP.NET 1.x.*
<httpCookies>	Everywhere	Configures properties for cookies used by an ASP.NET application. *Not supported in ASP.NET 1.x.*
<httpHandlers>	Everywhere	Lists registered HTTP handlers. (See Chapter 2.)
<httpModules>	Everywhere	Lists registered HTTP modules. (See Chapter 2.)
<httpRuntime>	Everywhere	Lists HTTP runtime settings.
<identity>	Everywhere	Sets impersonation.
<machineKey>	Everywhere	Encryption key for sensitive data.
<membership>	Machine, application	Defines settings for user authentication through ASP.NET membership. *Not supported in ASP.NET 1.x.*
<mobileControls>	Everywhere	Lists device-specific class adapters for Web controls. (See Chapter 8.) *Not supported in ASP.NET 1.0.*
<pages>	Everywhere	Controls features of ASP.NET pages.
<processModel>	Machine	Configures the process model.
<profile>	Machine, application	Defines settings for user profile's data model. *Not supported in ASP.NET 1.x.*
<protocols>	Machine, application	Specifies the protocols that an ASP.NET Web service can use. *Not supported in ASP.NET 1.x.*
<roleManager>	Machine, application	Defines settings for role management. *Not supported in ASP.NET 1.x.*
<securityPolicy>	Machine, application	Defines allowed trust levels.
<sessionState>	Machine, application	Configures the *Session* object.
<siteMap>	Machine, application	Defines settings used to support the navigation infrastructure. (See Chapter 10.) *Not supported in ASP.NET 1.x.*
<trace>	Everywhere	Configures the tracing system.
<trust>	Machine, application	Defines the default trust level.
<webControls>	Everywhere	Locates client scripts.
<webParts>	Everywhere	Defines settings for Web Parts. (See Chapter 7.) *Not supported in ASP.NET 1.x.*
<webServices>	Everywhere	Configures Web services.
<xhtmlConformance>	Everywhere	Defines settings for XHTML conformance. *Not supported in ASP.NET 1.x.*

Each of the elements listed in Table 3-3 features its own schema and provides attributes and enumerations to pick values from.

In addition to the sections listed in Table 3-3, the *<system.web>* group contains a subgroup named *<Caching>*. Table 3-4 lists the child elements.

Table 3-4   Sections Allowed Within *<Caching>*

Section	Overridable	Description
<cache>	Machine, application	Configures the global cache settings for an ASP.NET application. *Not supported in ASP.NET 1.x.*
<outputCache>	Machine, application	Configures the output cache for a Web application. *Not supported in ASP.NET 1.x.*
<outputCacheSettings>	Machine, application	Defines caching profiles. *Not supported in ASP.NET 1.x.*
<sqlCacheDependency>	Machine, application	Configures the SQL cache dependencies for an ASP.NET application. *Not supported in ASP.NET 1.x.*

Let's examine some of the aforementioned sections in a bit more detail. For a complete reference, though, you might want to check out the excellent MSDN online documentation.

> **Note**   Some of the sections listed in Table 3-3 and Table 3-4 are covered in depth in other chapters throughout the book. To avoid over-coverage, these section are not covered here. Note also that other sections such as *<sessionState>*, *<authentication>*, and *<membership>* that are briefly explained here are fully covered in *Programming Microsoft ASP.NET 2.0: Core Reference* (Microsoft Press, 2005), in the chapters dedicated to their respective topics.

The *<anonymousIdentification>* Section

Anonymous identification is a new ASP.NET 2.0 feature that assigns a predefined identity to users who connect anonymously to an application. Anonymous identification has nothing to do with the anonymous user you can set at the IIS level, nor does it affect the authentication mechanism of ASP.NET. The feature is designed to work with the user profile API to simplify the way you write code in scenarios where both authenticated and unauthenticated users can use the site.

The *<anonymousIdentification>* section allows you to configure how it works. Here's the overall schema of the section.

```
<anonymousIdentification
    enabled="[true | false]"
    cookieless="[UseUri | UseCookies | AutoDetect | UseDeviceProfile]"
    cookieName=""
    cookiePath=""
```

```
      cookieProtection="[None | Validation | Encryption | All]"
      cookieRequireSSL="[true | false]"
      cookieSlidingExpiration="[true | false]"
      cookieTimeout="[DD.HH:MM:SS]"
      domain="cookie domain"
/>
```

Basically, anonymous identification creates a cookied or cookieless ticket and associates it with the ongoing request. The *enabled* attribute turns the feature on and off; the *cookieless* attribute instructs the ASP.NET runtime about cookie usage. Table 3-5 illustrates the options for the *cookieless* attribute.

Table 3-5   Options for the *cookieless* Attribute

Value	Description
AutoDetect	Uses cookies if the browser has cookie support currently enabled. It uses the cookieless mechanism otherwise.
UseCookie	Always uses cookies, regardless of the browser capabilities.
UseDeviceProfile	Uses cookies if the browser supports them, and uses the cookieless mechanism otherwise. When this option is used, no attempt is made to check whether cookie support is really enabled for the requesting device. This is the default option.
UseUri	Never uses cookies, regardless of the browser capabilities.

All other attributes relate to the cookie, if one is created. You can set its name—the default name is *.ASPXANONYMOUS*—path, domain, protection, expiration, and timeout. You can also indicate whether Secure Sockets Layer (SSL) should be used to transmit the cookie.

The *<authentication>* Section

The *<authentication>* section allows you to configure a Web site for various types of user authentication, including forms-based authentication as well as Microsoft Passport and IIS-driven authentication. This section uses two mutually exclusive subsections—*<forms>* and *<passport>*—and the *mode* attribute to control the authentication mode requested by an application. Allowable values for the *mode* attribute are shown in Table 3-6.

Table 3-6   Supported Authentication Modes

Value	Description
Forms	Makes use of a custom form to collect logon information.
Passport	Exploits the authentication services of Microsoft Passport.
None	Indicates ASP.NET should not enforce any type of authentication, which means only anonymous users can connect or the application itself provides a built-in mechanism.
Windows	Exploits any authentication services of IIS—basic, digest, NTLM\Kerberos, or certificates. This is the default mode.

When using the forms authentication, you are allowed to specify a few additional parameters, such as *name*, *loginURL*, *protection*, and *cookieless*. Table 3-7 lists the attributes of the *<forms>* element.

Table 3-7   Attributes of the *<forms>* Element

Attribute	Description
cookieless	Defines whether and how cookies are used for authentication tickets. Feasible values are the same as those listed in Table 3-5. *Not supported in ASP.NET 1.x.*
defaultUrl	Defines the URL to redirect after authentication. The default is *default.aspx*. *Not supported in ASP.NET 1.x.*
domain	Specifies a domain name to be set on outgoing authentication cookies. *Not supported in ASP.NET 1.x.*
enableCrossApp-Redirects	Indicates whether users can be authenticated by external applications when authentication is cookieless. The setting is ignored if cookies are enabled. When cookies are enabled, cross-application authentication is always possible. *Not supported in ASP.NET 1.x.*
loginUrl	Specifies the URL to which the request is redirected for login if no valid authentication cookie is found.
name	Specifies the name of the HTTP cookie to use for authentication. The default name is *.ASPXAUTH*.
path	Specifies the path for the authentication cookies issued by the application. The default value is a slash (/). Note that some browsers are case sensitive and will not send cookies back if there is a path case mismatch.
protection	Indicates how the application intends to protect the authentication cookie. Feasible values are *All*, *Encryption*, *Validation*, and *None*. The default is *All*.
requireSSL	Indicates whether an SSL connection is required to transmit the authentication cookie. The default is *false*. If *true*, ASP.NET sets the *Secure* property on the authentication cookie object so that a compliant browser does not return the cookie unless the connection is using SSL. *Not supported in ASP.NET 1.0.*
slidingExpiration	Indicates whether sliding expiration is enabled. The default is *false*, meaning that the cookie expires at a set interval from the time it was originally issued. The interval is determined by the *timeout* attribute. *Not supported in ASP.NET 1.0.*
timeout	Specifies the amount of time, in minutes, after which the authentication cookie expires. The default value is *30*.

Note that the description of cookie-related attributes in Table 3-7 works also for similar attributes in the *<anonymousIdentification>* section.

More Info   This section is covered in greater detail in Chapter 15 of *Programming Microsoft ASP.NET 2.0: Core Reference* (Microsoft Press, 2005).

The *<authorization>* Section

The *<authorization>* section is used to define a declarative filter to control access to the resources of the application. The *<authorization>* section contains two subsections named *<allow>* and *<deny>*, which can be used to allow and deny access to users. Both elements feature three attributes—*users*, *roles*, and *verbs*—filled with a comma-separated list of names, as the following code demonstrates:

```
<authorization>
    <allow users="comma-separated list of users"
           roles="comma-separated list of roles"
           verbs="comma-separated list of verbs" />

    <deny users="comma-separated list of users"
          roles="comma-separated list of roles"
          verbs="comma-separated list of verbs" />
</authorization>
```

The *<allow>* element authorizes access to any user whose name appears in the list—that is, to all users with any of the specified roles. Authorized users can execute only the HTTP verbs (for example, *POST* and *GET*) indicated by the *verbs* attribute.

Conversely, the *<deny>* element prohibits listed users from executing the specified actions. The default setting allows all users free access to the resources of the application. When specifying the user name, a couple of shortcuts are allowed. The asterisk (*) means all users, whereas the question mark (?) stands for the anonymous user.

> **More Info**   This section is covered in greater detail in Chapter 15 of *Programming Microsoft ASP.NET 2.0: Core Reference* (Microsoft Press, 2005).

The *<browserCaps>* Section

The *<browserCaps>* section enumerates the characteristics and capabilities of the supported browsers, including—in version 1.1 of the .NET Framework—mobile devices. The *<browserCaps>* section is tightly coupled with the *HttpBrowserCapabilities* class (and *MobileCapabilities* in version 1.1), which allows the ASP.NET runtime to gather technical information about the browser that is running on the client. An ASP.NET application identifies the browser through the *Browser* property of the intrinsic *Request* object. Internally, the *Request* object first looks at the user-agent information that comes with the HTTP request and then matches this information with the content of the *<browserCaps>* section. If a match is found, an instance of the *HttpBrowserCapabilities* class is created and filled with the available information. The newly created object is then made available to the application through the *Browser* property.

Under the *<browserCaps>* section, you find a fair number of commercial browsers described in terms of their run-time capabilities, such as cookies, tables and frames support, script languages accepted, XML DOM, and operating system. The element can be declared at any level in the application, thus making it possible for you to enable certain levels of browser support for certain applications. The list of available browsers can be updated as required to detect future browsers and browser capabilities.

> **Important**   Using the *<browserCaps>* element to define browsers is deprecated in ASP.NET 2.0, although it is fully supported. Any data found in this element is merged with the information read from the corresponding .browser file located in the *systemroot*\Microsoft.NET\ Framework\[version]\CONFIG\Browsers folder and any existing application-level App_Browsers folders. In a pure ASP.NET 2.0 application, you should rely on .browser files only.

The *<caching>* Section

The *<caching>* section configures the cache settings for an ASP.NET application. It consists of four child sections: *cache*, *outputCache*, *outputCacheSettings*, and *sqlCacheDependency*.

The *<cache>* section defines a few applicationwide settings that relate to caching. For example, the *percentagePhysicalMemoryUsedLimit* and *privateBytesLimit* attributes indicate the maximum size of memory (percentage and bytes) that can be occupied before the cache starts flushing expired items and attempting to reclaim memory. Here's the schema of the section with default values:

```
<cache disableMemoryCollection = "false"
    disableExpiration = "false"
    privateBytesLimit = "0"
    percentagePhysicalMemoryUsedLimit = "89"
    privateBytesPollTime = "00:02:00" />
```

The default time interval between polling for the memory usage is 2 minutes. Note that by setting the *disableExpiration* attribute, you can disable the automatic scavenging of expired cache items—the most defining trait of ASP.NET cache.

The *<outputCache>* section takes care of output caching. Here is the schema of the section with default values:

```
<outputCache enableOutputCache = "true"
    enableFragmentCache = "true"
    sendCacheControlHeader = "true"
    omitVaryStar = "false">
</outputCache>
```

If output or fragment caching is disabled in the configuration file, no pages or user controls are cached, regardless of the programmatic settings. The *sendCacheControlHeader* attribute indicates whether the *cache-control:private* header is sent by the output cache module by default. Similarly, the *omitVaryStar* attribute enables or disables sending an HTTP *Vary: ** header in the response.

The *<outputCacheSettings>* section contains groups of cache settings that can be applied to pages through the *@OutputCache* directive. The section contains only one child section, named *<outputCacheProfiles>*. An output cache profile is simply a way of referencing multiple settings with a single name. Here's an example:

```
<outputCacheSettings>
  <outputCacheProfiles>
    <add name="ServerOnly"
      duration="60"
      varyByCustom="browser" />
  </outputCacheProfiles>
</outputCacheSettings>
```

The *ServerOnly* profile defines a cache duration of 60 seconds and stores different versions of the page based on browser type. Here is the schema of *<outputCacheProfiles>*:

```
<outputCacheProfiles>
  <add name = ""
    enabled = "true"
    duration = "-1"
    location = ""
    sqlDependency = ""
    varyByCustom = ""
    varyByControl = ""
    varyByHeader = ""
    varyByParam = ""
    noStore = "false"/>
</outputCacheProfiles>
```

A database dependency is a special case of custom dependency that consists of the automatic invalidation of some cached data when the contents of the source database table changes. In ASP.NET 2.0, this feature is implemented through the *SqlCacheDependency* class. The *<sqlCacheDependency>* section defines the settings used by the *SqlCacheDependency* class when you use database caching and table-based polling against SQL Server 7.0 or SQL Server 2000.

```
<sqlCacheDependency enabled="true" pollTime="1000">
  <databases>
    <add name="Northwind" connectionStringName="LocalNWind" />
  </databases>
</sqlCacheDependency>
```

The *pollTime* attribute indicates (in milliseconds) the interval of the polling. In the preceding sample, any monitored table will be checked every second. Under the *<databases>* node, you find a reference to monitored databases. The *name* attribute is used only to name the dependency. The *connectionStringName* attribute points to an entry in the *<connectionStrings>* section of the *web.config* file and denotes the connection string to access the database. Which tables in the listed databases will really be monitored depends on the effects produced by another tool—*aspnet_regsql.exe*—that we'll cover later in the chapter.

Any values stored in the *<sqlCacheDependency>* section have no effect when you use *SqlCacheDependency* in conjunction with query notifications on SQL Server 2005.

The *<clientTarget>* Section

The *<clientTarget>* section adds aliases for specific user agents that ASP.NET pages can target through the *ClientTarget* property. In other words, the *<clientTarget>* section defines the allowable values for the *ClientTarget* property of the *Page* class. By default, the following aliases are defined: *ie5*, *ie4*, *uplevel*, and *downlevel*. As the names suggest, the first two aliases indicate Internet Explorer 5.5 and Internet Explorer 4.0, respectively. Notice that in ASP.NET, an up-level browser is meant to be Internet Explorer 4.0 (the first browser to support dynamic HTML), whereas a down-level browser is currently undefined.

```
<clientTarget>
  <add alias="ie5" userAgent="Mozilla/4.0 (compatible; MSIE 5.5; ...)"/>
  <add alias="ie4" userAgent="Mozilla/4.0 (compatible; MSIE 4.0; ...)"/>
  <add alias="uplevel" userAgent="Mozilla/4.0 (compatible; MSIE 4.0; ...)/>
  <add alias="downlevel" userAgent="Unknown"/>
</clientTarget>
```

Bear in mind that setting the *ClientTarget* property to one of the values listed in the section forces the *HttpBrowserCapabilities* object for the page to return the capabilities of the specified browser rather than the capabilities of the actual requesting client.

The *<customErrors>* Section

The *<customErrors>* section specifies the error-handling policy for an ASP.NET application. By default, when an error occurs on a page, the local host sees the detailed ASP.NET error page, whereas remote clients are shown a custom error page or a generic page if no custom page is specified. This policy is controlled through the *Mode* attribute. The *Mode* attribute can be set to *On*, *Off*, or *RemoteOnly*, which is the default. If the attribute is set to *On*, custom error pages are displayed both locally and remotely; if set to *Off*, no special error-handling mechanism is active and all users receive the typical ASP.NET error page with the original runtime's or compiler's error message and the stack trace.

Error pages can be specified in two ways: You can provide a generic error page as well as error-specific pages. The custom but generic error page is set through the *defaultRedirect* attribute of the *<customErrors>* element. This setting is ignored if the mode is *Off*.

```
<customErrors defaultRedirect="Errors/appGenericErr.aspx" mode="On">
    <error statusCode="404" redirect="Errors/notfound.aspx" />
    <error statusCode="500" redirect="Errors/internal.aspx" />
</customErrors>
```

The *<customErrors>* section supports a repeatable child *<error>* tag that is used to associate a custom page with a particular error code. You should note that only certain status codes are supported. Some error codes, such as 403, might come directly from IIS and never get to ASP.NET. The *<error>* tag has two optional attributes: *redirect* and *statusCode*. The *redirect* attribute points to the URL of the page, whereas the *statusCode* attribute specifies the HTTP status code that will result in an error. If custom mode is enabled but no error-specific page is known, the default redirect is used. If custom mode is enabled but no custom page is specified, the ASP.NET generic error page is used.

The *<deployment>* Section

The *<deployment>* section indicates the deployment mode of the application and has only one Boolean attribute, named *retail*. The attribute indicates whether the application is intended to be deployed for production (*retail* equals *true*) or test (*retail* equals *false*). When *retail* is set to *true*, ASP.NET will automatically disable certain configuration settings such as trace output, custom errors, and debug capabilities. When the default value of retail is *false*, each application is automatically deployed for testing.

In ASP.NET 1.x, you have to manually turn off all development and testing run-time features that might slow down an application in production.

```
<deployment retail="true" />
```

In ASP.NET 2.0, it suffices that you add the preceding script to the deployed *web.config* file.

The *<globalization>* Section

The *<globalization>* section configures the globalization settings of ASP.NET applications so that requests and responses take into account encoding and culture information. The attributes of the *<globalization>* section are shown in Table 3-8.

Table 3-8   Globalization Attributes

Attribute	Description
requestEncoding	Specifies the assumed encoding of each request, including posted data and the query string. The default is UTF-8.
responseEncoding	Specifies the content encoding of responses. The default is UTF-8.
fileEncoding	Specifies the encoding for ASP.NET resource files (.aspx, .asmx, and .asax). Unicode and UTF-8 files saved with the byte order mark prefix are recognized regardless of the value of the attribute.
culture	Specifies the culture to be used to process requests.
uiCulture	Specifies the culture name to be used to look up locale-dependent resources at run time.

Note that, if specified, the *Accept-Charset* attribute in the request overrides the default *request-Encoding* setting. If you remove any encoding setting from the configuration files, ASP.NET defaults to the server's locale. In the majority of cases, *requestEncoding* and *responseEncoding* have the same value.

Valid names for the *culture* and *uiCulture* attributes are non-neutral culture names such as *en-US*, *en-AU*, and *it-IT*. A culture name is made of two elements—the language and country—and both are to be specified in this context.

The *<healthMonitoring>* Section

In ASP.NET 2.0, health monitoring is a system feature that allows the production staff to monitor the status of a deployed application and track significant events related to performance, failures, and anomalies. The ASP.NET health monitoring system works by firing events to providers. The event contains actual information about what happened. The provider processes the information. Here is the overall schema:

```
<healthMonitoring
    enabled="true|false"
    heartbeatInterval="HH:MM:SS">
    <bufferModes>...</bufferModes>
    <providers>...</providers>
    <eventMappings>...</eventMappings>
    <profiles>...</profiles>
    <rules>...</rules>
</healthMonitoring>
```

The *enabled* attribute specifies whether health monitoring is enabled. It is *true* by default. The *heartbeatInterval* attribute indicates how often the *heartbeat* event is raised. The heartbeat event serves as a timer for the whole subsystem and is raised at regular intervals to capture useful runtime state information. The heartbeat is just one of the events that the health monitoring system can detect. Other events track unhandled exceptions, request processing, application lifetime, and success and failure audits. Child sections, listed in Table 3-9, let you configure the whole subsystem.

Table 3-9   Elements for Health Monitoring

Element	Description
bufferModes	It is used with Microsoft SQL Server and Web event providers (with built-in e-mail capability) to determine how often to flush the various events to the provider and the size of the intermediate buffer.
eventMappings	Maps friendly event names to the event classes. You use this element to register custom event types.
profiles	Defines parameter sets to use when configuring events.
providers	Defines the health monitoring providers that process events. Predefined providers write to a SQL Server table and the Event Log, and they send e-mail messages. You use this element to register custom Web event providers.
rules	Maps events to providers.

The interval for the *heartbeat* event is set to *0* by default, meaning that no heartbeat event is raised by default.

The *<hostingEnvironment>* Section

The *<hostingEnvironment>* section defines configuration settings that control the behavior of the application hosting environment. As you can see in the following code segment, the section has three attributes: *idleTimeout*, *shadowCopyBinAssemblies*, and *shutdownTimeout*.

```
<hostingEnvironment idleTimeout="HH:MM:SS"
                    shadowCopyBinAssemblies="true|false"
                    shutdownTimeout="number"/>
```

The *idleTimeout* attribute sets the amount of time, in minutes, to wait before unloading an inactive application. It is set to *Infinite* by default, meaning that inactive applications are not automatically unloaded. Note also that "inactive" doesn't mean nonresponsive; an application is inactive if no user is working with it, and this is normally not by itself a good reason to kill it. The *shadowCopyBinAssemblies* attribute indicates whether the assemblies of an application in the *Bin* directory are shadow-copied to the application's ASP.NET temporary files directory. It is *true* by default. Finally, the *shutdownTimeout* attribute sets the number of seconds (30 by default) to wait before closing the application.

> **Note**   Shadow-copy is a .NET Framework feature that ASP.NET uses extensively. When shadow-copy is enabled on an AppDomain, assemblies loaded in that AppDomain will be copied to an internal cache directory and used from there. In this way, the original file is not locked and can be changed at will. Shadow-copy is enabled on every AppDomain created by ASP.NET 1.x. You can control the feature through the *shadowCopyBinAssemblies* in ASP.NET 2.0.

The *<httpCookies>* Section

The *<httpCookies>* section is used to configure properties for cookies used by ASP.NET applications. Here is the overall schema:

```
<httpCookies domain="string"
             httpOnlyCookies="true|false"
             requireSSL="true|false" />
```

The *domain* attribute indicates the default Internet domain of the cookie and is set to the empty string by default. The *requireSSL* attribute is *false* by default. If *true*, SSL is required for all cookies. The *httpOnlyCookies* attribute enables ASP.NET to output an extra *HttpOnly* cookie attribute that can help mitigate cross-site scripting threats that result in stolen cookies. When a cookie that has the *HttpOnly* attribute set to *true* is received by a compliant browser such as Internet Explorer 6.0 SP1, it is inaccessible to client-side script. Adding the *HttpOnly* attribute is as easy as appending the *;HttpOnly* string to the path of all response cookies. You can do that yourself in ASP.NET 1.x.

> **Warning**   For at least two reasons, the *HttpOnly* attribute is not a silver bullet that will stop cross-site scripting attacks. First and foremost, very few contemporary browsers recognize it. Second, any network monitor tool (for example, Fiddler, available at *http://www.fiddlertool.com*) could easily detect and remove it.

Any settings defined in the *<httpCookies>* section can be overridden by classes that actually create cookies in ASP.NET pages.

The *<httpRuntime>* Section

The *<httpRuntime>* section configures some run-time parameters for the ASP.NET pipeline. Interestingly enough, the section can be declared at any level, including subdirectory levels. This fact accounts for the great flexibility that allows you to set up the run-time environment with the finest granularity. Configurable attributes are listed in Table 3-10.

Table 3-10   ASP.NET Runtime Attributes

Attribute	Description
apartmentThreading	Enables apartment threading for classic ASP compatibility. The default is *false*. *Not supported in ASP.NET 1.x.*
appRequestQueueLimit	Specifies the maximum number of requests the application is allowed to queue before returning the 503 Server Too Busy error. The default is *100* for ASP.NET 1.x and *5000* for ASP.NET 2.0.
delayNotificationTimeout	Specifies the timeout for delaying notifications. The default is *5* seconds. *Not supported in ASP.NET 1.x.*
enable	Specifies whether the AppDomain is enabled to accept incoming requests. The default is *true*.
enableHeaderChecking	Specifies whether ASP.NET should check the request header for potential injection attacks. If an attack is detected, ASP.NET responds with an error. The default is *true*. *Not supported in ASP.NET 1.x.*
enableKernelOutputCache	Enables the *http.sys* cache on IIS 6.0 and later. The default is *true*. Ignored under IIS 5.0. *Not supported in ASP.NET 1.0.*
enableVersionHeader	Outputs a header with the ASP.NET version with each request. The default is *true*. Used only by Microsoft Visual Studio 2005; can be disabled for production sites. *Not supported in ASP.NET 1.0.*
executionTimeout	Specifies the maximum number of seconds a request is allowed to execute before ASP.NET automatically times it out. Default is *90* seconds in ASP.NET 1.x and *110* seconds in ASP.NET 2.0.
maxRequestLength	Indicates the maximum accepted size (in kilobytes) of a Web request. No request is accepted if its overall length exceeds the threshold of 4 MB.
minLocalRequestFreeThreads	Indicates the minimum number of free threads to allow execution of new local requests. The default threshold value is set to *4*.
minFreeThreads	Indicates the minimum number of free threads needed to allow execution of new Web requests. The default threshold value is set to *8*.

Table 3-10   **ASP.NET Runtime Attributes**

Attribute	Description
requestLengthDiskThreshold	Specifies the input stream buffering threshold limit in number of bytes. Its value should not exceed the *maxRequestLength*. The default is *256* bytes. *Not supported in ASP.NET 1.x.*
requireRootedSaveAsPath	Specifies whether the file name parameter in a *Request*'s *SaveAs* method must be an absolute path. *Not supported in ASP.NET 1.x.*
sendCacheControlHeader	Specifies whether to send a cache control header. *Not supported in ASP.NET 1.x.*
shutDownTimeout	Number of minutes that are allowed for the worker process to close. When the timeout expires, ASP.NET closes the worker process. *Not supported in ASP.NET 1.x.*
useFullyQualifiedRedirectUrl	Indicates whether client redirects must be automatically converted to fully qualified URLs (*true*) or used as specified in the page source code (*false*). The default is *false*.
waitChangeNotification, *maxWaitChangeNotification*	Indicate the minimum and maximum number of seconds to wait (*0* by default) before restarting the AppDomain after a file change notification. *Not supported in ASP.NET 1.x.*

Notice that ASP.NET won't process a request if not enough free threads are available in the thread pool. When this happens, the request is queued to the application until the threshold set by the *appRequestQueueLimit* is exceeded. But why, in the default case, does ASP.NET need at least eight free threads to execute a request? These free threads are at the disposal of ongoing requests (for example, download of linked images, style sheets, and user controls) should they issue child requests to complete processing.

Another small number of threads (four by default) are reserved for child requests coming through the local host. If the request has been generated locally—that is, the client IP is 127.0.0.1 or matches the server IP—it is scheduled on one of the threads in the pool reserved for local calls. Often local requests originate as child requests—for example, when an ASP.NET page invokes a Web service on the same server. There's no need in this case to consume two threads from the pool to serve two related requests, one of which is waiting for the other to terminate. By using an additional thread pool, you actually assign local requests a slightly higher priority and reduce the risk of deadlocks.

The *<identity>* Section

The *<identity>* section controls the identity of the ASP.NET application. It supports three attributes: *impersonate*, *userName*, and *password*. The key attribute is *impersonate*. It is set to *false* by default, which means that the application does not impersonate any client user.

```
<identity impersonate="true" />
```

When *impersonate* is set to *true*, each request is served by ASP.NET impersonating either the Windows user currently logged on or the user specified through the *userName* and *password* attributes.

> **Warning**   The user name and password are stored in clear text in the configuration file. Although IIS never serves requests for configuration files, a *web.config* file can be read by other means. You should consider forms of protection for the contents of the section. In ASP.NET 1.x, you can use the following convention:
>
> ```
> userName="registry:HKLM\Software\AspNetProcess,Name"
> password="registry:HKLM\Software\AspNetProcess,Pswd"
> ```
>
> *Name* and *Pswd* are two arbitrarily named registry entries in the specified node. Both entries are in REG_BINARY format and store contents encrypted by the Data Protection API (DPAPI) encryption functions. You use the command-line *aspnet_setreg.exe* tool to write to the registry. In ASP.NET 2.0, you simply encrypt the *<identity>* section by using XML Encryption. I'll say more about this topic later.

The *<machineKey>* Section

Valid at the machine and application levels, the *<machineKey>* section configures the keys to encrypt and decrypt forms authentication tickets and view-state data. Here's the schema:

```
<machineKey
    validationKey="AutoGenerate|value[,IsolateApps]"
    decryptionKey="AutoGenerate|value[,IsolateApps]"
    validation="[SHA1|MD5|3DES|AES]"
    decryption="[Auto|AES|3DES]" />
```

The *validationKey* and *decryptionKey* attributes specify the encryption and decryption keys. An encryption key is a sequence of characters whose length ranges from a minimum of 40 to a maximum of 128 characters. The *validation* attribute, on the other hand, indicates the type of encryption used to validate data. Allowable values are SHA1 (the default), MD5, AES, and 3DES. Finally, the *decryption* attribute indicates the type of hashing algorithm that is used for decrypting data. Feasible values are AES and 3DES. The default is *Auto*, meaning that ASP.NET determines which decryption algorithm to use based on configuration default settings.

The default value of both *validationKey* and *decryptionKey* attributes is *AutoGenerate,Isolate-Apps*. This means that keys are autogenerated at setup time and stored in the Local Security Authority (LSA). LSA is a protected subsystem of Windows NT–based operating systems that maintains information about all aspects of local security on a system. The *IsolateApps* modifier instructs ASP.NET to generate a key that is unique for each application.

Settings in the *<machineKey>* section are a critical element of applications hosted on multiple machines, such as in a Web farm or a failover cluster. All machines across a network must share the same *<machineKey>* settings. You might want to set *validationKey* and *decryptionKey* attributes manually to ensure consistent configuration.

The *<membership>* Section

The *<membership>* section defines parameters for managing and authenticating user accounts through the ASP.NET membership API. Here's the schema of the section:

```
<membership
    defaultProvider="provider name"
    userIsOnlineTimeWindow="number of minutes"
    hashAlgorithmType="SHA1">
    <providers>
      ⋮
    </providers>
</membership>
```

The *defaultProvider* attribute indicates the name of the default membership provider—it is *AspNetSqlMembershipProvider* by default. The attribute named *userIsOnlineTimeWindow* specifies how long a user can be idle and still be considered online. The interval is set to 15 minutes by default. The *hashAlgorithmType* refers to the name of the encryption algorithm that is used to hash password values.

```
<membership>
    <providers>
      <add name="MyProvider"
           type="Samples.MyMembershipProvider"
           connectionStringName="MyConnString"
           enablePasswordRetrieval="false"
           enablePasswordReset="true"
           requiresQuestionAndAnswer="true"
           passwordFormat="Hashed" />
      ⋮
    </providers>
</membership>
```

The *<providers>* child section lists all registered membership providers. You use this section to add custom membership providers. Each provider has its own set of attributes.

The *<pages>* Section

The *<pages>* section sets default values for many of the *@Page* directive attributes and declaratively configures the run-time environment for a Web page. Table 3-11 enumerates the supported attributes.

Table 3-11   Attributes to Configure ASP.NET Pages

Attribute	Description
asyncTimeout	Number of seconds to wait for an asynchronous handler to complete during asynchronous processing. The default is *45* seconds. *Not supported in ASP.NET 1.x.*
autoEventWireup	Indicates whether page events are automatically assigned to event handlers with a particular name (for example, *Page_Load*). Set to *true* by default.

Table 3-11 **Attributes to Configure ASP.NET Pages**

Attribute	Description
Buffer	Indicates whether response buffering is enabled. Set to *true* by default.
compilationMode	Indicates whether an ASP.NET page or control should be compiled at run time. Allowable values are *Never*, *Auto*, and *Always*—the default. *Auto* means that ASP.NET will not compile the page, if possible. *Not supported in ASP.NET 1.x.*
enableSessionState	Indicates whether session state is enabled. Set to *true* by default; also accepts as values *false* and *ReadOnly*. The session state is disabled altogether if the attribute is set to *false*; it is accessible only for reading if set to *ReadOnly*.
enableViewState	Specifies whether view state is enabled. Set to *true* by default.
enableViewStateMac	Specifies whether the view state of a page should be checked for tampering on each page postback. Set to *true* by default.
maintainScrollPosition-OnPostBack	If *true*, the page maintains the same scroll position after a postback. *Not supported in ASP.NET 1.x.*
masterPageFile	Specifies the master page for the pages in the scope of the configuration file. *Not supported in ASP.NET 1.x.*
maxPageStateFieldLength	Indicates the maximum length of the view-state field. A negative value indicates that no upper limit exists. If the size of the view state exceeds the maximum, the contents will be sent in chunks. *Not supported in ASP.NET 1.x.*
pageBaseType	Indicates the base code-behind class that *.aspx* pages inherit by default—that is, unless a code-behind class is explicitly provided. The default class is *System.Web.UI.Page*. The new class name must include assembly information.
pageParserFilterType	Specifies the type of filter class that is used by the ASP.NET parser to determine whether an item is allowed in the page at parse time. *Not supported in ASP.NET 1.x.*
smartNavigation	Specifies whether smart navigation is enabled. Set to *false* by default. Deprecated in favor of the *maintainScrollPositionOnPostBack* attribute.
styleSheetTheme	Name of the style-sheet theme used for the pages in the scope of the configuration file. *Not supported in ASP.NET 1.x.*
theme	Name of the theme used for the pages in the scope of the configuration file. *Not supported in ASP.NET 1.x.*
userControlBaseType	Indicates the code-behind class that *.ascx* user controls inherit by default. The default class is *System.Web.UI.UserControl*. The new class name must include assembly information.
validateRequest	Indicates that ASP.NET examines all input from the browser for potentially dangerous data. Set to *true* by default. *Not supported in ASP.NET 1.0.*
viewStateEncryptionMode	Indicates the encryption mode of the view state. Feasible values are *Always*, *Never*, and *Auto*. *Auto* means that the view state is encrypted only if a control requests it. *Not supported in ASP.NET 1.x.*

In particular, the *pageBaseType* attribute is an extremely powerful setting you might want to use when all your application pages inherit from a common code-behind class. In this case, instead of modifying all the pages, you centralize the setting in the *web.config* file at the level (machine, application, or subdirectory) you want.

A very interesting attribute is *maxPageStateFieldLength*. One of the problems developers experience with a too-large view state is that the underlying browser might not be capable of carrying all those bytes back and forth for a single input field. As a result, the content of the view state is truncated and the application fails. This is particularly likely to happen on pretty simple Web browsers such as Microsoft WebTV and personal digital assistants (PDAs). To solve the issue in ASP.NET 1.x, you have only a "take the bull by the horns" approach at your disposal. You derive a custom page class, override the methods that read and write view-state information, and make the class leave view-state information on the server. In ASP.NET 2.0, there's an easier way out: using *maxPageStateFieldLength*. If the real size of the view state exceeds the upper limit set through the attribute, ASP.NET automatically cuts the view state into chunks and sends it down using multiple hidden fields. For example, if you set *maxPageStateFieldLength* to 5, here's what the page contains:

```
<input type="hidden" id="__VIEWSTATEFIELDCOUNT" value="..." />
<input type="hidden" id="__VIEWSTATE" value="/wEPD" />
<input type="hidden" id="__VIEWSTATE1" value="wUKLT" />
<input type="hidden" id="__VIEWSTATE2" value="I2MjI" />
⋮
```

The final byte count of the client page is even a bit higher than in the default case, but at least your page won't fail because of a truncated view state on simple and not-too-powerful Web browsers.

The *<processModel>* Section

The *<processModel>* section configures the ASP.NET process model—that is, the procedure that brings a request to be processed in the HTTP pipeline. The attributes of the *<processModel>* section are actually read by unmanaged code—the *aspnet_isapi.dll* ISAPI extension. For this reason, you need to restart IIS to have changes applied. For the same reason, you can never override any attributes in the *<processModel>* section in a *web.config* file. The *<processModel>* section can exist only within a *machine.config* file, and it affects all ASP.NET applications that are running on the server. The following code example illustrates the schema of the section:

```
<processModel
    enable="true|false"
    timeout="hrs:mins:secs|Infinite"
    idleTimeout="hrs:mins:secs|Infinite"
    shutdownTimeout="hrs:mins:secs|Infinite"
    requestLimit="num|Infinite"
    requestQueueLimit="num|Infinite"
    restartQueueLimit="num|Infinite"
    memoryLimit="percent"
    webGarden="true|false"
```

```
cpuMask="num"
userName="username"
password="password"
logLevel="All|None|Errors"
clientConnectedCheck="hrs:mins:secs|Infinite"
comAuthenticationLevel="Default|None|Connect|Call|
            Pkt|PktIntegrity|PktPrivacy"
comImpersonationLevel="Default|Anonymous|Identify|
            Impersonate|Delegate"
responseDeadlockInterval="hrs:mins:secs|Infinite"
responseRestartDeadlockInterval="hrs:mins:secs|Infinite"
autoConfig="true|false"
maxWorkerThreads="num"
maxIoThreads="num"
minWorkerThreads="num"
minIoThreads="num"
serverErrorMessageFile=""
pingFrequency="Infinite"
pingTimeout="Infinite"
maxAppDomains="2000" />
```

When ASP.NET is running under IIS version 6.0 in native mode, the IIS 6.0 process model is used, and most of the attributes in the *<processModel>* section are ignored. To configure the process identity, recycling, or other process model values in IIS 6.0, you use the IIS Manager to configure the IIS worker process for your application, as shown in the Figure 3-3. You display the dialog box by right-clicking on the properties of the application pool to which your application belongs.

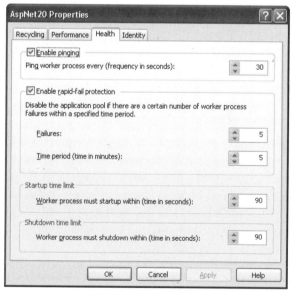

Figure 3-3   Configure the process model when the IIS 6.0 native process model is used.

Table 3-12 lists the *<processModel>* attributes that still apply when the IIS 6.0 native process model is employed.

Table 3-12   Configuring the ASP.NET Process Model

Attribute	Description
autoConfig	Indicates that ASP.NET automatically configures some critical attributes to achieve optimal performance. Default is *true*. For more details about the attributes fine-tuned and their suggested values, see Knowledge Base article 821268.
maxIoThreads	Indicates the maximum number of I/O threads per CPU in the thread pool. The default is *20* (indicating a total of 20–*N* threads on a machine with *N* CPUs).
maxWorkerThreads	Indicates the maximum number of worker threads per CPU in the thread pool. The default is *20* (meaning a total of 20–*N* threads on a machine with *N* CPUs).
minIoThreads	Configures the minimum number of I/O threads to use for the process on a per-CPU basis. The default is *1*.
minWorkerThreads	Configures the maximum amount of worker threads to use for the process on a per-CPU basis. The default is *1*.
requestQueueLimit	Indicates the number of requests the ASP.NET process can queue before returning the 503 Server Too Busy error. The default is *5000*.
responseDeadlockInterval	Indicates the time after which a process with queued requests that has not returned a response is considered deadlocked and is shut down. The default is 3 minutes.

Notice that time quantities are typically expressed in the HH:MM:SS format. For example, the 00:00:05 string is interpreted as 5 seconds. The word *Infinite* indicates an infinite time or an infinite number, as appropriate.

Important   If you're going with the IIS 5.0 process model, either in emulation mode or because your application runs under Windows 2000 Server, refer to the MSDN online documentation for more details on the attributes not included in Table 3-12. Note, though, that running ASP.NET in emulation mode on IIS 6.0 is not a great idea from a performance standpoint. If you're looking for ways of improving the performance of ASP.NET applications, take a look at Chapter 6, *Improving ASP.NET Performance*, of the Patterns & Practices series. The URL is *http://msdn.microsoft.com/library/en-us/dnpag/html/scalenetchapt06.asp*.

The *<profile>* Section

The *<profile>* section is used to configure the user-profiling feature introduced with ASP.NET 2.0. Basically, each user can be assigned a set of properties whose values are loaded and persisted automatically by the system when the request begins and ends. A profile provider takes care of any I/O activity by using a particular data store. The default profile provider, for example, uses the *AspNetDb.mdf* file and SQL Server 2005 Express. The *<profile>* section has the following schema:

```
<profile
    enabled="true|false"
    inherits="fully qualified type reference"
    automaticSaveEnabled="true|false"
    defaultProvider="provider name">
    <properties>...</properties>
    <providers>...</providers>
</profile>
```

The *enabled* attribute indicates whether user profiles are enabled. The default value is *true*. The set of properties that is associated with each authenticated user is defined in the *<properties>* child element.

```
<profile>
    <properties>
        <add name="BackColor" type="string" />
        <add name="ForeColor" type="string" />
    </properties>
</profile>
```

Table 3-13 lists the attributes allowed on a profile property.

Table 3-13   Attributes of a Profile Property

Attribute	Description
allowAnonymous	Allows storing values for anonymous users. Set to *false* by default.
customProviderData	Contains data for a custom profile provider.
defaultValue	Indicates the default value of the property.
name	Name of the property.
provider	Name of the provider to use to read and write the property.
readOnly	Specifies whether the property value is read-only. *False* by default.
serializeAs	Indicates how to serialize the value of the property. Possible values are *Xml, Binary, String,* and *ProviderSpecific.*
type	The .NET Framework type of property. It is a string object by default.

All properties are packaged in a dynamically created class that is exposed to user code through the *Profile* property on the *HttpContext* object. The *Inherits* attribute allows you to define the base class of this dynamically created profile class. The *automaticSaveEnabled* attribute specifies whether the user profile should be automatically saved at the end of the execution of an ASP.NET page. (The default is *true*.) Note that the profile is saved only if the HTTP module in charge of it detects that the profile has been modified.

The *<providers>* element lists all available profile providers. You use this section to register custom providers. The *defaultProvider* attribute indicates the currently selected provider that pages will use.

The *<roleManager>* Section

The *<roleManager>* section configures role management for an ASP.NET 2.0 application. Role management is carried out by two components: an HTTP module that intercepts incoming requests, and a role provider that retrieves and sets role information for the authenticated user. The provider acts as a proxy for the data store where the role information is stored. All available providers are listed in the *<providers>* child section. A new provider should be added here. The default provider is specified in the *defaultProvider* attribute. The overall schema of the section is shown here:

```
<roleManager
    cacheRolesInCookie="true|false"
    cookieName="name"
    cookiePath="/"
    cookieProtection="All|Encryption|Validation|None"
    cookieRequireSSL="true|false "
    cookieSlidingExpiration="true|false "
    cookieTimeout="number of minutes"
    createPersistentCookie="true|false"
    defaultProvider="provider name"
    domain="cookie domain">
    enabled="true|false"
    maxCachedResults="maximum number of role names cached"
    <providers>...</providers>
</roleManager>
```

Once the HTTP module receives the role information from the currently selected provider, it usually creates a cookie to cache the information for future requests. All cookie-related attributes you see in the schema configure a different aspect of the cookie. The default name is *.ASPXROLES.*

The *<securityPolicy>* Section

In the *<securityPolicy>* section, you define mappings between security levels and policy files. The section can be configured at the application level but not in subdirectories. The section contains one or more *<trustLevel>* elements with *name* and *policyFile* attributes. You also can use the section to extend the security system by providing your own named trust levels mapped to a custom security policy file. Here's an excerpt from the site's root *web.config* file that ASP.NET 2.0 installs:

```
<securityPolicy>
    <trustLevel name="Full"    policyFile="internal" />
    <trustLevel name="High"    policyFile="web_hightrust.config" />
    <trustLevel name="Medium"  policyFile="web_mediumtrust.config" />
    <trustLevel name="Low"     policyFile="web_lowtrust.config" />
    <trustLevel name="Minimal" policyFile="web_minimaltrust.config" />
</securityPolicy>
```

The *name* attribute can be set to *Full*, *High*, or *Low* in all versions of the .NET Framework. In version 1.1 and newer versions, *Minimal* and *Medium* levels are also allowed. Each trust level identifies a particular security level that you map to a policy file. Security policy files are XML files located in the same folder as *machine.config*.

Notice that in ASP.NET, the *Full* level of trust doesn't need to have an associated policy file full of permission sets and code-group definitions. The reason is that ASP.NET doesn't add extra security settings in case of *Full* trust, so in such cases the content of the *policyFile* attribute is ignored.

The *<sessionPageState>* Section

The *<sessionPageState>* section is responsible for configuring how to use session state to store view-state information on small devices that have limited page size or bandwidth requirements. For example, ASP.NET mobile controls typically use session state to store their view state. When it comes to this, how do you deal with Back and Forward browser requests? This is a non-issue when each page embeds its own view state. However, when the view state is stored on the server, you should guarantee that the view state for several previously requested pages is maintained to save the page history. How many pages? This is exactly where the *<sessionPageState>* section fits in.

<sessionPageState historySize="9" />

The section has a unique attribute—*historySize*—whose default value is 9. This attribute has effect only for ASP.NET mobile controls.

The *<sessionState>* Section

The *<sessionState>* section stores session-state settings for the current application. The section determines behavior and implementation details of the ASP.NET *Session* object. The *Session* object can work in different modes to accommodate the application's requirements for performance, robustness, and data reliability. In Table 3-14, you can see the list of acceptable attributes for the element. The *mode* attribute is the only mandatory attribute. Some attributes are mutually exclusive.

Table 3-14   Session-State Attributes

Attribute	Description
allowCustomSqlDatabase	If *true*, enables specifying a custom SQL Server database to store session data instead of using the default *ASPState* database. *Not supported in ASP.NET 1.x.*
cookieless	Specifies how to communicate the session ID to clients. Feasible values are those listed in Table 3-5.
cookieName	Name of the cookie, if cookies are used for session IDs. *Not supported in ASP.NET 1.x.*

Table 3-14   Session-State Attributes

Attribute	Description
customProvider	Name of the custom session-state store provider to use for storing and retrieving session-state data. *Not supported in ASP.NET 1.x.*
mode	Specifies the implementation mode of the session state. Acceptable values are *Off, InProc, Custom, StateServer*, and *SQLServer*. When set to *Off*, session-state management is disabled and the *Session* object is not available to the application. *InProc* is the default working mode and stores session data locally in the Web server's memory. Alternatively, the session state can be stored on a remote server (*StateServer*) or in a SQL Server database (*SQLServer*). In ASP.NET 2.0, the *Custom* option indicates that the application is using a custom data store.
partitionResolverType	Indicates type and assembly of the partition resolver component to be loaded to provide connection information when session state is working in *SQLServer* or *StateServer* mode. If a partition resolver can be correctly loaded, *sqlConnectionString* and *stateConnectionString* attributes are ignored. *Not supported in ASP.NET 1.x.*
regenerateExpiredSessionId	When a request is made with a session ID that has expired, if this attribute is *true*, a new session ID is generated; otherwise, the expired one is revived. The default is *false. Not supported in ASP.NET 1.x.*
sessionIDManagerType	Null by default. If set, it indicates the component to use as the generator of session IDs. *Not supported in ASP.NET 1.x.*
sqlCommandTimeout	Specifies the number of seconds an SQL command can be idle before it is canceled. The default is *30*.
sqlConnectionString	Used when *mode* is set to *SQLServer*; specifies the connection string for the SQL Server database to use for storing session data.
stateConnectionString	Used when *mode* is set to *StateServer*; specifies the server name and port where session state should be stored.
stateNetworkTimeout	Specifies the number of seconds the TCP/IP network connection between the Web server and the state server can be idle before the request is canceled. The default is *10*.
timeout	Specifies the number of minutes a session can be idle before it is abandoned. The default is *20*.
useHostingIdentity	Indicates that the ASP.NET process identity is impersonated to access a custom state provider or the *SQLServer* provider configured for integrated security. The default is *true. Not supported in ASP.NET 1.x.*

In addition, the child *<providers>* section lists custom session-state store providers. ASP.NET session state is designed to enable you to easily store user session data in different sources, such as a Web server's memory or SQL Server. A store provider is a component that manages the storage of session-state information and stores it in alternative media (for example, an Oracle database) and with an alternative layout.

The default connection string for the *SQLServer* mode is set to the following:

```
data source=127.0.0.1;Integrated Security=SSPI
```

As you can see, it doesn't contain the database name, which defaults to *AspState*. You create this database before the application is released using either T-SQL scripts or the *aspnet_regsql* command-line utility.

The default connection string for the *StateServer* mode is set to the following:

```
tcpip=127.0.0.1:42424
```

You can change at will the TCP/IP address and the port used. Note, though, that to change the port, you must edit the *Port* entry under the registry key:

```
HKEY_LOCAL_MACHINE\
    SYSTEM\CurrentControlSet\Services\aspnet_state\Parameters
```

Writing the new port number in the configuration file is not enough.

The *<siteMap>* Section

The *<siteMap>* section configures settings and providers for the ASP.NET site navigation system. The schema of the section is quite simple:

```
<siteMap
  enabled="true|false"
  defaultProvider="provider name">
  <providers>...</providers>
</siteMap>
```

The feature relies on site map providers—that is, made-to-measure components that return information representing the structure of the site. ASP.NET comes with one predefined provider—the *AspNetXmlSiteMapProvider* class. The default site map provider is specified through the *defaultProvider* attribute. All available providers, including custom providers, are listed in the *<providers>* section.

The *<trace>* Section

Tracing refers to the program's ability to send informative messages about the status of the execution. In general, tracing is a way to monitor the behavior of an application in a production environment, and debugging is used for development time testing. The *<trace>* section defines attributes that can modify the behavior of application-level tracing. The attributes are listed in Table 3-15.

Table 3-15   Application-Level ASP.NET Tracing Attributes

Attribute	Description
enabled	Specifies whether tracing is enabled for an application. The default is *false*. Tracing must be enabled in order to use the trace viewer (*trace.axd*) and other tracing facilities.
localOnly	If *true*, makes the trace viewer available only on the local host; if *false*, makes it available also remotely. The default is *true*. Note that *trace.axd* is one of the default HTTP handlers registered at installation time.
pageOutput	Specifies whether trace output is rendered at the end of each page. If *false*, trace output is accessible through the trace viewer only. The default is *false*. Regardless of this global setting, individual pages can enable tracing using the *Trace* attribute of the *@Page* directive.
requestLimit	Indicates the maximum number of trace results to store on the server and that are subsequently available through *trace.axd*. The default value is *10*. The maximum is *10000*.
traceMode	Indicates the criteria by which trace records are to be sorted and displayed. Acceptable values are *SortByTime* (the default) or *SortByCategory*. Sorting by time means that records are displayed in the order in which they are generated. A category, on the other hand, is a user-defined name that can be optionally specified in the trace text.
writeToDiagnosticsTrace	Set to *false* by default, specifies whether trace messages should be forwarded to the diagnostics tracing infrastructure, for any registered listeners. *Not supported in ASP.NET 1.x.*

In the .NET Framework, tracing is provided through a unified, abstract API that uses ad hoc drivers to physically output the messages. These drivers are called *listeners* and redirect the tracing output to the specified target—typically a log file or an output stream. Listeners are defined in the *<system.diagnostics>* section. When *writeToDiagnosticsTrace* is *true*, any ASP.NET-generated trace message is also forwarded to all registered listeners.

The *<trust>* Section

The *<trust>* section configures the trust level under which the application will be run and determines the code-access security restrictions applied to the application. By default, all ASP.NET applications run on the Web server as fully trusted applications and are allowed to do whatever their account is allowed to do. The CLR doesn't sandbox the code. Hence, any security restrictions applied to an application (for example, the inability to write files or write to the registry) are not the sign of partial trust but simply the effect of the underprivileged account under which ASP.NET applications normally run.

You act on the *<trust>* section if you want to run a Web application with less than full trust. The following code example shows the default *<trust>* setting in *machine.config*:

```
<trust level="Full" originUrl="" />
```

Allowable values for the *level* attribute are all the *<trustLevel>* entries defined in the *<security-Policy>* section.

The *originUrl* attribute is a sort of misnomer. If you set it, what really happens is quite simple: the application is granted the permission of accessing the specified URL over HTTP using either a *Socket* or *WebRequest* class. Of course, the Web permission is granted only if the specified *<trust>* level supports that. *Medium* and higher trust levels do.

In ASP.NET 2.0, the *<trust>* section supports an additional Boolean attribute—*processRequestInApplicationTrust*. If *true* (the default), the attribute dictates that page requests are automatically restricted to the permissions in the trust policy file applied to the application. If *false*, there's the possibility that a page request runs with higher privileges than set in the trust policy.

> **Note**   The *<trust>* section is allowed only at the machine level and application level because of technical reasons, not because of security concerns. An ASP.NET application runs in its own AppDomain, and the trust level for that application is set by applying the appropriate security policy to the AppDomain. Although policy statements can target specific pieces of code, the AppDomain is the lowest level at which a security policy can be applied. If the CLR has a policy level more granular than the AppDomain, you can define different trust levels for various portions of the ASP.NET application.

The following script shows how to specify *Medium* trust level settings for all applications on a server. The script is excerpted from a site's root *web.config* file. With *allowOverride* set to *false*, the trust level is locked and cannot be modified by the application's root *web.config* file.

```
<location allowOverride="false">
  <system.web>
    <trust level="Medium" originUrl="" />
  </system.web>
</location>
```

By adding the following script, you release the lock for a particular application on the machine:

```
<location allowOverride="true" path="Default Web Site/ProAspNet20">
  <system.web>
    <trust level="Medium" originUrl="" />
  </system.web>
</location>
```

The *<urlMappings>* Section

The *<urlMappings>* section contains a list of mappings between fake URLs and real endpoints in the application. Here's a quick example that is worth a thousand words:

```
<urlMappings enabled="true">
  <add url="~/main.aspx" mappedUrl="~/default.aspx?tab=main" />
</urlMappings>
```

The *url* attribute indicates the URL that users request from their browser. The *mappedUrl* attribute indicates the corresponding URL that is passed on to the application. Both URLs are application relative. In addition to the *<add>* node, the *<urlMappings>* section also supports the *<remove>* and *<clear>* nodes.

> **Note**   In ASP.NET 2.0, the *<urlMappings>* section is the declarative counterpart of the *RewritePath* method defined in the *HttpContext* class.

The *<webControls>* Section

The *<webControls>* section contains only the *clientScriptsLocation* attribute that specifies the default path to ASP.NET client script files. These files are included in the HTML code generated for *.aspx* pages when these pages require client-side functionalities such as smart navigation and client-side control validation.

```
<webControls clientScriptsLocation="/aspnet_client/{0}/{1}/" />
```

The preceding code example represents the default contents of the *<webControls>* section. The content of *clientScriptsLocation*, properly expanded, is the URL used for script includes. The *aspnet_client* directory is automatically created under the Web server's root when you install ASP.NET. The two placeholders in the string represent subdirectories whose names might change in future versions of ASP.NET. The first placeholder is always set to *system_web*. The second placeholder expands to a subdirectory name based on the version of the .NET Framework.

Unlike previous versions, ASP.NET 2.0 doesn't use this folder to store client script files. Client script files are, in fact, embedded as resources in the *system.web* assembly and are injected in pages through the *webresource.axd* HTTP handler.

You can use the client script folder to store script files employed by any custom ASP.NET control you might write.

The *<webServices>* Section

The *<webServices>* section controls the settings of Web services created using ASP.NET. The section contains several subsections to configure the supported protocols, SOAP extensions that need to run, the Web services Help page, and more. The schema of the section consists of no attributes and a variety of child sections. Table 3-16 lists the supported subsections.

Table 3-16   Sections Available to Configure Web Services

Section	Description
conformanceWarnings	Defines a collection of WS-I profiles that will be used to validate the Web services. *Not supported in ASP.NET 1.x.*
Protocols	Defines the transmission protocols that ASP.NET supports and can use to decrypt Web service client requests.
serviceDescriptionFormat- ExtensionTypes	Defines additional classes that extend how a service description is generated for all Web services.

Table 3-16 Sections Available to Configure Web Services

Section	Description
soapExtensionImporterTypes	Registers the SOAP extensions to run when a service description for a Web service is accessed to create a proxy class.
soapExtensionReflectorTypes	Registers the SOAP extensions to run when a service description is generated for all Web services.
soapExtensionTypes	Registers the SOAP extensions to run with all the Web services.
soapServerProtocolFactoryType	Sets an object that corresponds to the protocol used to call the Web service. *Not supported in ASP.NET 1.x.*
wsdlHelpGenerator	Specifies the *.aspx* page that generates the Web service help page displayed when an *.asmx* Web service is requested through the local browser.

By default, an ASP.NET Web service supports the following protocols:

```
<protocols>
    <add name="HttpSoap12" />
    <add name="HttpSoap" />
    <add name="HttpPostLocalhost" />
    <add name="Documentation" />
</protocols>
```

As you can see, HTTP-POST and HTTP-GET protocols have not been supported natively for security concerns since ASP.NET 1.1. If you would like to have them back to ease development and testing, you add the following:

```
<protocols>
    <add name="HttpPost" />
    <add name="HttpGet" />
</protocols>
```

The *Documentation* protocol is the key that enables the ASP.NET runtime to deliver a help page when you point your browser directly to an *.asmx* resource. If you disable the protocol, no help page is generated when a user navigates to a Web service URL; instead, a Requested Format Is Unrecognized error is displayed. If you want to maintain the help page functionality but change the structure and contents of the page, modify the *href* attribute of the *<wsdlHelp-Generator>* element:

```
<webServices>
    <wsdlHelpGenerator href="YourNewGeneratorPage.aspx" />
</webServices>
```

Of course, the help page can be customized for all hosted Web services or for only a particular Web service.

The *<xhtmlConformance>* Section

In ASP.NET 2.0, the *<xhtmlConformance>* section designates the XHTML rendering mode for an application. The default rendering for pages and controls is XHTML 1.0 Transitional. This is also the default for new pages created in Visual Studio 2005. You can configure the preferred rendering by setting options in the *<xhtmlConformance>* section, which enables you to select XHTML 1.0 Transitional, XHTML1.0 Strict, and legacy rendering.

```
<xhtmlConformance mode="Transitional|Legacy|Strict"/>
```

If you opt for *Legacy*, pages and controls will render as in ASP.NET 1.x.

Other Top-Level Sections

The sections under the *<system.web>* element don't exhaust the list of configuration elements that are useful to ASP.NET developers. At least three other sections should be known and mastered.

The *<appSettings>* Section

The *<appSettings>* section stores custom application configuration data such as file paths, URLs of interest, and any other applicationwide information.

```
<configuration>
    <appSettings>
        <add key="StockPickerWebServiceUrl" value="..." />
    </appSettings>
</configuration>
```

The syntax of the *<appSettings>* section is defined as follows:

```
<appSettings>
    <add key="..." value="..." />
    <remove key="..." />
    <clear />
</appSettings>
```

The *<add>* element adds a new setting to the internal collection. This new setting has a value and is identified by a unique key. The *<remove>* element removes the specified setting from the collection. The setting is identified using the key. Finally, the *<clear>* element clears all settings that have previously been defined in the section.

In ASP.NET 1.x, you typically use this section for storing database connection strings. In ASP.NET 2.0, a new tailor-made section has been added for connection strings. You should avoid storing user-specific information in *<appSettings>*. You use a handcrafted database solution in ASP.NET 1.x, and the user profile API in ASP.NET 2.0.

Any contents you design for storage in the *<appSettings>* section can be saved to an external XML file that is linked to the section through the *file* attribute.

```
<appSettings file="myfile.config" />
```

The contents of the file pointed to by the *file* attribute are read as if they are an *<appSettings>* section in the *web.config* file. Note that the root element of the file must match *<appSettings>*.

> **Note**   Changes to the external file are not detected until the application is restarted. If you incorporate *<appSettings>* in the *web.config* file, changes are detected in real time.

The *<connectionStrings>* Section

In the .NET Framework 2.0, configuration files define a new section specifically designed to contain connection strings. The section is named *<connectionStrings>* and is laid out as follows:

```
<connectionStrings>
    <add name="NWind"
        connectionString="SERVER=...;DATABASE=...;UID=...;PWD=...;"
        providerName="System.Data.SqlClient"  />
</connectionStrings>
```

You can manipulate the contents of the section by using *<add>*, *<remove>*, and *<clear>* nodes. Each stored connection is identified with a name you set through the *name* attribute. The connection parameters are set in the *connectionString* attribute. Finally, the *providerName* attribute indicates the ADO.NET data provider to use.

In ASP.NET 2.0, connection names are also used within the configuration file to link a connection string to other sections—typically the *<providers>* section of *<membership>* and *<profile>* nodes.

The *<configProtectedData>* Section

ASP.NET 2.0 introduces a system for protecting sensitive data stored in the configuration system. It uses industry-standard XML encryption to encrypt specific sections of configuration files that might contain sensitive data. XML encryption (which you can learn more about at *http://www.w3.org/TR/xmlenc-core*) is a way to encrypt data and represent the result in XML. Prior to version 2.0, only a few specific ASP.NET sections that contain sensitive data support protection of this data using a machine-specific encryption in a registry key. This approach requires developers to come up with a utility to protect their own secrets—typically connection strings, credentials, and encryption keys.

In the .NET Framework 2.0, encryption of configuration sections is optional, and you can enable it for any configuration sections you want by running a command-line tool, as we'll see later.

You can specify the type of encryption you want by selecting the appropriate provider from the list of available encryption providers. The .NET Framework 2.0 comes with two predefined providers: *DPAPIProtectedConfigurationProvider* and *RSAProtectedConfigurationProvider*. The former uses the Windows Data Protection API (DPAPI) to encrypt and decrypt data; the latter (the default provider) uses the RSA encryption algorithm to encrypt and decrypt data. Most configuration sections that are processed by the managed configuration system are eligible for protection. The *<configProtectedData>* section itself, though, can't be protected. In this case, clear text is necessary to describe the behavior of the system. Similarly, sections consumed by the CLR from Win32 code or from ad hoc managed XML parsers can't be protected by this system because they don't employ section handlers to consume their configuration. This includes at least the following sections: *<processModel>*, *<runtime>*, *<mscorlib>*, *<startup>*, and *<system.runtime.remoting>*.

Managing Configuration Data

Configuration data can be managed by developers and administrators in two main ways—programmatically through an ad hoc API, and manually through command-line utilities, XML editors, or perhaps the ASP.NET MMC snap-in. Let's take a closer look at these options.

Using the Configuration API

ASP.NET 2.0 includes a full configuration management API that enables you to navigate, read, and write an application's configuration files. Configuration settings are exposed as a set of strongly typed objects against which you can easily program. These classes—one for each section in the overall schema—are all defined in the *System.Configuration* namespace.

The configuration API is smart enough to provide a merged view of all the settings that apply to that level. When settings are modified, the API automatically writes changes to the correct node in the correct configuration file. The management API can be used to read and write configuration settings of local and remote applications. Custom configuration sections are automatically manageable through the API.

Retrieving Web Configuration Settings

You use the *WebConfigurationManager* class to get access to the ASP.NET configuration files. The class is the preferred way to work with configuration files related to Web applications. The following code example illustrates how to retrieve the HTTP handlers in use in the current application:

```
void Button1_Click(object sender, EventArgs e)
{
    string name = @"system.web/httpHandlers";
    Configuration cfg =
        WebConfigurationManager.OpenWebConfiguration("/");
    HttpHandlersSection hdlrs =
        (HttpHandlersSection)cfg.GetSection(name);
    EnumerateHandlers(hdlrs, ListBox1);
}

void EnumerateHandlers(HttpHandlersSection section, ListBox ctl)
{
    foreach (HttpHandlerAction h in section.Handlers)
        ctl.Items.Add(h.Path);
}
```

You open the configuration file using the *OpenWebConfiguration* method. The parameter you pass to the method indicates the level at which you want to retrieve information. If you specify null or /, you intend to capture configuration data at the site's root level. If you want information at the machine level, you resort to the *OpenMachineConfiguration* method.

The *OpenWebConfiguration* method returns a *Configuration* object on which you can call *GetSection* to retrieve the contents of a particular section. For HTTP handlers, you do as follows:

```
HttpHandlersSection section;
section = (HttpHandlersSection) cfg.GetSection(@"system.web/httpHandlers");
```

Each section class has a programming interface that closely reflects the attributes and child sections on the element. Figure 3-4 shows the preceding code in action.

Figure 3-4   Retrieving the list of HTTP handlers for an application.

The figure shows two list boxes. The first contains all the handlers visible at the site level; the second also includes those registered at the application level. The additional three HTTP handlers you see at the top of the second list box are due to the following script in the application's root *web.config*:

```
<httpHandlers>
    <add verb="*" path="myHandler.aspx" type="..." />
    <add verb="*" path="*.sqlx" type="..." />
    <add verb="*" path="view.axd" type="..." />
</httpHandlers>
```

To access configuration data at the application level, you pass the application's URL to the *OpenWebConfiguration* method.

```
string path = Request.CurrentExecutionFilePath;
Configuration cfg = WebConfigurationManager.OpenWebConfiguration(path);
```

To retrieve information about other sections, you use the same pattern illustrated earlier by changing section names and section classes.

Retrieving Application Settings

The *WebConfigurationManager* class is designed to work with settings specific to ASP.NET applications. As mentioned, most ASP.NET applications need to access data in sections outside the *<system.web>* element. Canonical examples are *<appSettings>* and *<connectionString>*. For sections not included in the *<system.web>* element, you normally use the *Configuration-Manager* class. However, *WebConfigurationManager* contains a couple of helper public properties to access *AppSettings* and *ConnectionStrings* collections. The following code example shows the implementation of these properties in *WebConfigurationManager*:

```
public static NameValueCollection AppSettings {
    get {return ConfigurationManager.AppSettings;}
}
public static NameValueCollection ConnectionStrings {
    get {return ConfigurationManager.ConnectionStrings;}
}
```

As you can see, to access application settings and connection strings, you can interchangeably use the *AppSettings* and *ConnectionStrings* collections on both *WebConfigurationManager* and *ConfigurationManager*. Here's how to obtain a registered connection string named *Northwind*:

```
WebConfigurationManager.ConnectionStrings["Northwind"].ConnectionString
```

For a value stored in the *<appSettings>* section, you need the following:

```
WebConfigurationManager.AppSettings["StockPickerWebServiceUrl"]
```

In case you need to access other sections outside *<system.web>*, the *ConfigurationManager* class supplies the *OpenMachineConfiguration* method to access the tree of configuration data. Here's the code to retrieve the supported protocol prefixes for Web requests (https, http, ftp, and the like):

```
string name = @"system.net/webRequestModules";
Configuration cfg = ConfigurationManager.OpenMachineConfiguration();
WebRequestModulesSection section;
section = (WebRequestModulesSection) cfg.GetSection(name);
foreach (WebRequestModuleElement m in section.WebRequestModules)
    ListBox3.Items.Add(m.Prefix);
```

Updating Application Settings

All the content of the configuration tree is exposed to applications through a sort of Document Object Model (DOM). This DOM is modifiable in memory. Once you're done, you can persist changes by calling the *Save* method on the corresponding *Configuration* class. The following code example shows how to programmatically add a new HTTP handler to the current application:

```
string name = @"system.web/httpHandlers";
string path = "/proaspnetadv";
```

```
Configuration cfg = WebConfigurationManager.OpenWebConfiguration(path);
HttpHandlersSection section;
section = (HttpHandlersSection)appConfig.GetSection(name);

HttpHandlerAction newHandler = new HttpHandlerAction("*.xyz",
        "System.Web.HttpForbiddenHandler", "*");
section.Handlers.Add(newHandler);
cfg.Save();
```

The newly added handler configures the system so that requests for *.xyz* files are blocked. The application's *web.config* file is modified as follows:

```
<httpHandlers>
    ⋮
  <add path="*.xyz"
       verb="*"
       type="System.Web.HttpForbiddenHandler" />
</httpHandlers>
```

Figure 3-5 shows what happens to an *.xyz* request with the forbidden handler active.

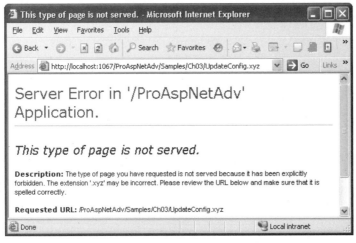

Figure 3-5   Resources with an *.xyz* extension are now no longer served.

To re-enable *.xyz* resources, you need to remove the handler that was just added. The following code shows how to proceed programmatically:

```
string name = @"system.web/httpHandlers";
string path = "/proaspnetadv";

Configuration cfg = WebConfigurationManager.OpenWebConfiguration(path);
HttpHandlersSection section;
section = (HttpHandlersSection)cfg.GetSection(name);
section.Handlers.Remove("*", "*.xyz");
appConfig.Save();
```

After this, any request for an *.xyz* resource is likely to produce the perhaps more familiar "Resource Not Found" message.

Encrypting a Section

With the exceptions listed earlier while discussing the *<protectedData>* section, all sections in a configuration file can be encrypted both programmatically, using the configuration API, and in offline mode, using a command-line tool. Let's tackle this latter option first.

You use the newest version of a popular system tool—*aspnet_regiis.exe*. Here's a sample use of the utility to encrypt connection strings for the */ProAspNetAdv* application. Note that the section names are case sensitive.

```
aspnet_regiis.exe -pe connectionStrings -app /ProAspNetAdv
```

After running this command, the *web.config* looks different. The *<connectionStrings>* section now incorporates a child *<EncryptedData>* section, which is where the ciphered content has been stored. If you open the *web.config* file after encryption, you see something like the following:

```
<configuration>
  <connectionStrings
     configProtectionProvider="RsaProtectedConfigurationProvider">
    <EncryptedData …>
       ⋮
      <CipherData>
        <CipherValue>cQyofWFQ… =</CipherValue>
      </CipherData>
    </EncryptedData>
  </connectionStrings>
</configuration>
```

To restore the *web.config* file to its original clear state, you use the **-pd** switch in lieu of **-pe** in the aforementioned command line.

The nice part of the story is that this form of encryption is completely transparent to applications, which continue working as before.

To encrypt and decrypt sections programmatically, you use the *ProtectSection* and *Unprotect-Section* methods defined on the *SectionInformation* object. Here's how to proceed:

```
string name = "connectionStrings";
string path = "/proaspnetadv";
string provider = "RsaProtectedConfigurationProvider";
Configuration cfg = WebConfigurationManager.OpenWebConfiguration(path);
ConnectionStringsSection section;
section = (ConnectionStringsSection) cfg.GetSection(name);
section.SectionInformation.ProtectSection(provider);
cfg.Save();
```

To unprotect, you change the call to *ProtectSection* with the following:

```
section.SectionInformation.UnprotectSection();
```

Note that to persist changes, it is still essential to place a call to the *Save* method on the *Configuration* object.

Choosing the Encryption Provider

Any page that uses protected sections works like a champ as long as you run it inside the local Web server embedded in Visual Studio 2005. You might get an RSA provider configuration error if you access the same page from within a canonical (and much more realistic) IIS virtual folder. What's up with that?

The RSA-based provider—the default protection provider, if you use the command-line tool—needs a key container to work. A default key container is created upon installation and is named *NetFrameWorkConfigurationKey*. The *aspnet_regiis.exe* utility provides a lot of command-line switches for you to add, remove, and edit key containers. The essential point is that you have a key container created before you dump the RSA-protected configuration provider. The container must not only exist, but it also must be associated with the user account attempting to call it. The system account (running the local Web server) is listed with the container; the ASP.NET account on your Web server might not be. Assuming you run ASP.NET under the NETWORK SERVICE account (the default on Windows Server 2003 machines), you need the following code to add access to the container for the user:

```
aspnet_regiis.exe -pa "NetFrameworkConfigurationKey"
        "NT AUTHORITY\NETWORK SERVICE"
```

It is important that you specify a complete account name, as in the preceding code. Note that granting access to the key container is necessary only if you use the RSA provider.

Both the RSA and DPAPI providers are great options for encrypting sensitive data. The DPAPI provider dramatically simplifies the process of key management—keys are generated based on machine credentials and can be accessed by all processes running on the machine. For the same reason, the DPAPI provider is not ideal to protect sections in a Web-farm scenario, where the same encrypted *web.config* file is deployed to several servers. In this case, either you manually encrypt all *web.config* files on each machine or you copy the same container key to all servers. To accomplish this, you create a key container for the application, export it to an XML file, and import it on each server that will need to decrypt the encrypted *web.config* file. To create a key container, you do as follows. (Using the command-line utility is mandatory here.)

```
aspnet_regiis.exe -pc YourContainerName -exp
```

Next, you export the key container to an XML file:

```
aspnet_regiis.exe -px YourContainerName YourXmlFile.xml
```

Next, you move the XML file to each server and import it as follows:

```
aspnet_regiis.exe -pi YourContainerName YourXmlFile.xml
```

As a final step, grant the ASP.NET account permission to access the container.

Creating Custom Configuration Sections

The predefined XML schema for configuration files fits the bill in most cases, but when you have complex and structured information to persist, none of the existing schemas appears to be powerful enough. At this point, you have two possible alternatives. You can simply avoid using a standard configuration file and instead use a plain XML file written according to the schema you feel is appropriate for the data. Alternatively, you can embed your XML configuration data in the standard application configuration file but provide a tailor-made configuration section handler to read it.

Creating a new section (plus an optional new section group) requires editing the *web.config* file to register the section (or section group). While registering the new section, you need to specify the section handler component—that is, the piece of software in charge of parsing the contents of the section to processable data. Depending on what kind of data you're going to store in the section, you can use one of the existing handlers or, more likely, create your own section handler.

In ASP.NET 1.x, a configuration section handler is a class that implements the *IConfiguration-SectionHandler* interface. The interface contains just one method—*Create*—which is expected to take the XML subtree as input, and output an object that contains the parsed information. In ASP.NET 2.0, the configuration section handler is a class that ultimately inherits from the *ConfigurationSection* class. The section handler class defines public properties and maps them to attributes in the XML element. In addition, these class properties are decorated with a special attribute named *ConfigurationProperty*. The following example shows how to create the handler for a new <*MyPages*> section with just one attribute—*pageBackColor*.

```
public class MyPagesSection : ConfigurationSection
{
   private static readonly ConfigurationProperty propPageBackColor = null;

   static MyPagesSection()
   {
      MyPagesSection.propPageBackColor = new ConfigurationProperty(
         "PageBackColor", typeof(string), "yellow",
          ConfigurationPropertyOptions.IsRequired);
   }

   [ConfigurationProperty("pageBackColor")]
   public string PageBackColor
   {
      get
      {
      return (string) base[MyPagesSection.propPageBackColor];
      }
      set
      {
      base[MyPagesSection.propPageBackColor] = value;
      }
   }
}
```

The mapping between a property and a section attribute is established through the *ConfigurationProperty* attribute. The parameter of the attribute constructor indicates the name of the section attribute used to feed the decorated property.

A custom section must be registered to work properly. Here's how to do it:

```
<configuration>
  <configSections>
    <section name="myPages"
             type="ProAspNet20.Components.MyPagesSection, ProAspCompLib" />
  </configSections>
  ⋮
<configuration>
```

The *type* property in the *<section>* tag indicates the class being used to read and write the contents of the section. For the sample *<myPages>* section, the system uses the *MyPagesSection* class in the specified assembly. If the assembly is strongly typed and located in the global assembly cache (GAC), you should indicate its full name.

Using Management Tools

ASP.NET 2.0 includes a full range of management tools that you can use to configure your applications. In addition to the Web Site Administration Tool integrated with all versions of Visual Studio 2005, you'll find a Microsoft Management Console (MMC) snap-in and a bunch of command-line utilities. All these tools, each within its expected behavior, access the configuration files and enter changes.

ASP.NET MMC Snap-In

The ASP.NET MMC snap-in is an additional property page added to the dialog box that IIS Manager displays when you right-click to see the properties of an ASP.NET application. (See Figure 3-6.)

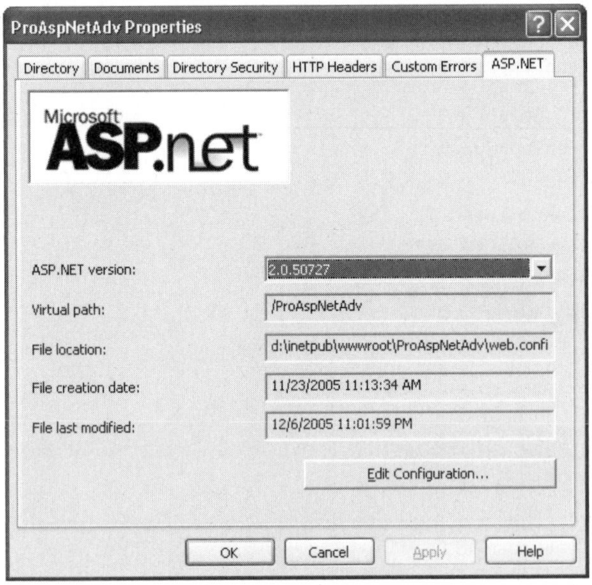

Figure 3-6   The ASP.NET MMC snap-in in action.

The snap-in allows you to change the ASP.NET version of any IIS application and to inspect and change many common settings. To display the dialog box shown in the figure, you take the following steps:

1. Select Administrative Tools/Internet Information Services, and open the IIS MMC console—that is, IIS Manager.

2. Select the application you want to configure, and select Properties from the Action menu or the context menu.

3. From the property sheet, click the ASP.NET tab.

The Edit Configuration button in the preceding figure opens a second tabbed dialog box, where you can choose settings to change by functional areas (for example, state management, authentication, and application) and you are provided a visual editor with all required bells and whistles. (See Figure 3-7.)

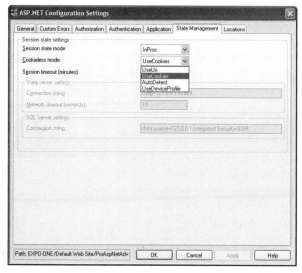

Figure 3-7   Configuring the ASP.NET application session state through the MMC snap-in.

As soon as you apply changes, the *web.config* file is updated.

Web Site Administration Tool

Figure 3-8 presents the Web Site Administration Tool (WSAT) in its full splendor. The tool is articulated in three main blocks (plus the home block), each covering a particular area of administration—security, application settings, and providers.

Figure 3-8   The Visual Studio 2005 ASP.NET Web Site Administration Tool.

WSAT is a distinct application installed with Visual Studio 2005 and ASP.NET 2.0. For security reasons, though, it is not publicly exposed through IIS. To access the interface in the figure, you must be working on the Visual Studio 2005 project for the application. To open the administration tool from an ASP.NET project, you select ASP.NET Configuration from the Web-site menu.

The Security tab of WSAT lets you manage all the security settings for your application. You can choose the authentication method, set up users and passwords, create roles and groups of users, and create rules for controlling access to specific parts of your application. A wizard can guide you through the steps needed to set up individual users and roles.

The Application tab provides a convenient way to edit the *<appSettings>* section of the *web.config* file. In addition to adjusting application settings, you can also configure error pages, debugging options, and e-mail settings.

Finally, if you want to change the default provider for a particular ASP.NET feature, you use the Provider tab. You also use the same page to register a new provider.

Extending WSAT with Custom Tabs

The WSAT administration tool is deployed with full source code and can be easily extended too! The full source code of WSAT is available at

```
%WINDOWS%\Microsoft.NET\Framework\[version]\ASP.NETWebAdminFiles
```

Extending WSAT requires a new page—the new tab displayed to users—and minor changes to a couple of existing pages to link the new tab. Let's see how to integrate a tab to add, remove, and edit HTTP handlers. (See Figure 3-9.)

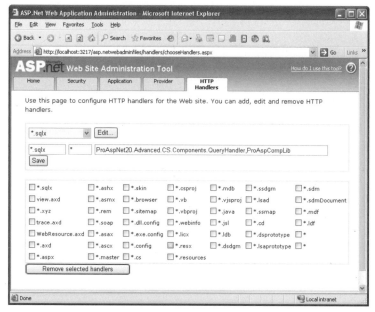

Figure 3-9   WSAT extended with a custom HTTP handlers tab.

The first thing to do is create the new page. Let's create a new subdirectory under the WSAT root and call it *Handlers*. Here you create an ASP.NET page with the following schema:

```
<%@ Page masterPageFile="~/WebAdmin.master"
        inherits="System.Web.Administration.HandlersPage" %>
<%@ MasterType virtualPath="~/WebAdmin.master" %>
<%@ Import Namespace="System.Web.Configuration" %>

<script runat="server" language="CS">
public void Page_Load()
{
}
</script>
<asp:content runat="server" contentplaceholderid="titleBar">
    <asp:literal runat="server" text="<%$ Resources:ConfigureHandlers %>"/>
</asp:content>
<asp:content runat="server" contentplaceholderid="content">
  ⋮
</asp:content>
```

The page (*manageHandlers.aspx*) is based on the same master page as all other WSAT pages. Public text used within the page is read from a local resources file (*manageHandlers.aspx.resx*) that you create in a child App_LocalResources folder. (See Chapter 1 for details on ASP.NET special folders.) Next, you fill the empty body of the page with controls and code up to the final result in Figure 3-9 or any other goal you have in mind. The base page class is shown here:

```
public class HandlersPage : WebAdminPage
{
    protected override void OnInit(EventArgs e)
    {
        NavigationBar.SetSelectedIndex(4);
        base.OnInit(e);
    }
}
```

The magic number in the preceding code (4) indicates the index of the tab in the overall WSAT application. The number indicates that this tab will be the fifth tab displayed. This is also the only required change to the base *WebAdminPage*. This page class also exposes an *ApplicationPath* property, which is set with the path of your application. This string is essential to access the configuration tree programmatically.

To link the new page to the remainder of the WSAT infrastructure, you need to tweak both *default.aspx* and *navigationBar.ascx*, which are located in the root of the WSAT application. *Default.aspx* is the WSAT home page and provides a table of links to the tabs, as shown in Figure 3-10. A new row for the HTTP Handlers tab must be explicitly added.

```
<tr class="gridRowStyle8">
    <td>
        <a id="ProviderLink" href="handlers/chooseHandlers.aspx">
        <asp:literal runat="server"
            text="<%$ Resources: HandlersConfig %>"/></a>
    </td>
    <td>
        <asp:literal runat="server"
            text="<%$ Resources: EnablesHandlers %>"/
>
    </td>
</tr>
```

The rows use text from the page resources; this requires changes to the *default.aspx.resx* file in the App_LocalResources folder of the WSAT root.

The *navigationBar* user control creates the tabs by reading information from an array list. You modify the source code to add a new entry.

Note   If you want to modify WSAT, make sure you first make a backup copy of the whole directory.

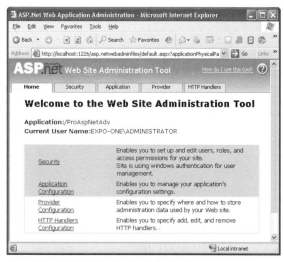

Figure 3-10   The new home page of WSAT.

Command-Line Tools

Two command-line utilities are frequently used in ASP.NET 2.0: *aspnet_regsql* and *aspnet_regiis*. You find both under the ASP.NET installation path:

```
%WINDOWS%\Microsoft.NET\Framework\[version]
```

The tool *aspnet_regsql.exe* configures a variety of services—session state, membership, user profiles, and SQL cache invalidation—that can use a SQL Server database. Each of these features requires the database to be configured with permissions and prepopulated as needed. The tool can be used either as a command-line tool or a wizard. To run the tool as a UI wizard, you run it without command-line arguments. If you prefer command-line switches, get the list of available options with *aspnet_regsql -?*.

The tool *aspnet_regiis.exe* is used to install and uninstall particular versions of ASP.NET. In ASP.NET 2.0, you can also use the tool to encrypt configuration sections. Note that each version of ASP.NET includes a different version of *aspnet_regiis*. To configure a particular version of ASP.NET, you need to locate and use the corresponding version of *aspnet_regiis*. Here's a brief list of typical usages:

```
aspnet_regiis -s W3SVC/1/ROOT/appName
```

The preceding command configures an IIS application to run the specific version of ASP.NET supported by the tool. The application is identified with its full IIS metabase path.

```
aspnet_regiis -lv
```

The preceding command lists all installed versions of ASP.NET on a computer.

```
aspnet_regiis -i
```

The preceding command installs the version of ASP.NET supported by the tool.

Conclusion

ASP.NET applications have many configurable settings. The various settings can all be controlled at different levels and overridden, extended, or restricted as appropriate. ASP.NET configuration is hierarchical and lets you apply different configuration schemes at various levels of granularity—the machine, the Web site, the application, and even the folder.

Configuration files are probably the most critical aspect to consider when you prepare to deploy ASP.NET applications. Arranging a setup program has never been as easy as it is with Visual Studio .NET (not considering third-party products), but deciding how to replicate the settings of the native environment might not be trivial. ASP.NET applications, in fact, can be deployed on a Web farm or in an ISP scenario, which requires particular care of the *machine.config* and *web.config* files. All in all, though, the deployment with ASP.NET is ultimately more effective and time saving than options previously available.

Just the Facts

- The ASP.NET configuration system builds an in-memory tree of the configuration data and uses it to control the way in which a given application executes.

- The schema of configuration files is extensible, and it is the same for all types of .NET Framework applications. Each configuration file can add custom sections. Each section is bound to a particular component—the section handler—which is responsible for parsing the XML data and returning processable data.

- The *machine.config* file contains machinewide settings shared by all applications installed on the server machine.

- The *<system.web>* section groups all the settings that are relevant to ASP.NET applications—from session state to compilation and from security to HTTP handlers.

- All sections defined in a configuration file can be encrypted using XML encryption. The encryption is optional and completely transparent for the code.

- Connection strings are stored in a tailor-made section, thus solving an old issue of Web applications.

- You can edit the configuration of an ASP.NET application in various ways: programmatically using the ASP.NET management API or through a variety of tools, including WSAT, IIS MMC snap-in, or command-line tools.

Chapter 4
Building Custom ASP.NET Providers

One of the most intriguing and powerful features that ASP.NET 2.0 introduces is the *provider model*. Based on common object-oriented principles such as inheritance and polymorphism, the provider model is an extensibility pattern for developers to replace or enhance native ASP.NET components. The provider model defines a common API for a variety of operations—membership, state management, and user profiling, just to name a few. Such an API is exposed as a pluggable component registered with the ASP.NET system. Developers learn a well-known API and always work with it, while internally the API can behave differently in different applications. Wherever in ASP.NET 2.0 the provider model is supported, the top-level API remains intact while the internal implementation (storage, validation, I/O, logic) can be changed to serve the particular needs of the application.

Generally, the provider model offers a simple, elegant, and effective pattern to make certain parts of an application customizable by clients and administrators. The ASP.NET implementation of the provider model makes you capable of customizing certain parts of the ASP.NET runtime environment through special classes (therefore, providers) from which you can derive your own.

Several ASP.NET native services employ the provider model and expose their internals through replaceable providers—for example, the user profiling subsystem. By writing a custom provider, you can change the schema of the data used to persist user preferences, store this data in an Oracle or DB2 database, and perhaps store data encrypted rather than as clear text.

The use of providers is not limited to ASP.NET native services. An application that implements a custom service can make it support providers. In this way, under the covers of a common and public interface, the new service will be as customizable as native built-in ASP.NET providers for data storage and management. In this chapter, we'll first take a detailed look at the structure of ASP.NET providers and then show the implementation of a custom provider for user profiling.

> **Note**   This chapter will provide just one example of how to write a custom provider for an ASP.NET native service—user profiles. For an insider's view and many more examples, check out the white paper "ASP.NET 2.0 Providers" available at *http://msdn.microsoft.com/asp.net/downloads/providers/*.

The Pattern of Providers

The provider infrastructure of ASP.NET is designed to allow developers to extend or replace some out-of-the-box functionalities such as user profiling, membership, and more. Figure 4-1 illustrates the big picture of providers.

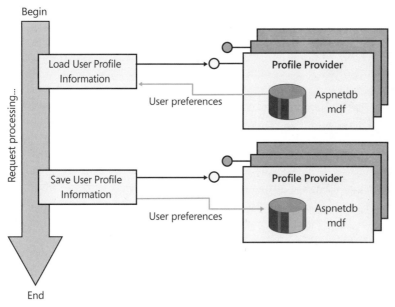

Figure 4-1   The big picture of the ASP.NET provider model.

The mainstream code of ASP.NET connects to a service (for example, a user profile) to accomplish a certain function (say, load user preferences). It actually connects to a component that exposes a well-known interface. The data exchange takes place polymorphically with mainstream code that barely knows the name and location of the component. The component providing the service (that is, the provider) can be replaced by other functionally similar components, either components natively shipped by ASP.NET or implemented by developers or third-party vendors.

Does this sound like a schema you're already familiar with? Or something you've already heard of somewhere? Well, actually, a few design patterns apply to the ASP.NET provider model, and design patterns are just recurring solutions to software issues you find again and again in real-world development. Let's briefly review some of the design patterns you (maybe unconsciously) use when working with ASP.NET providers.

Note   Both ASP.NET and Microsoft Windows Forms rely upon the provider model, though in different and curiously nonoverlapping areas. ASP.NET employs the provider model in key services such as membership and personalization, but not to manage application settings. Windows Forms, instead, takes advantage of the model only for storing user and application settings.

The Theory—Design Patterns

The provider model allows ASP.NET developers to become familiar with a single API to program a service regardless of how that particular service interoperates with the rest of the system and data storage layers. The theory behind this behavior is codified in the popular behavioral design pattern—the pattern *strategy*.

Note   There are countless books on the market and as many papers and Web sites available that provide excellent coverage of design patterns, with and without .NET and ASP.NET involved. When you face such a plethora of information, the main problem is finding exactly the information you need and finding it written at a level you can quickly understand. As far as design patterns are concerned, *http://www.dofactory.com* is my preferred Web site.

The Pattern "Strategy"

Defined, the strategy pattern indicates an expected behavior that can be implemented through a variety of interchangeable algorithms. Each application then selects the algorithm that best fits while keeping the public, observable behavior and programming API intact. Applied to an ASP.NET service such as user profiling, the pattern isolates in the replaceable algorithm the code to store and retrieve user preferences and serve them to the page through a common and unchangeable API.

The most notable feature of the strategy pattern is that it provides an abstract way for an object, or an entire subsystem, to expose its internals so that a client can unplug the default implementation and plug his own in. This is exactly what happens in ASP.NET for a number of services, including membership, roles and state management, user profiling, and site navigation. All in all, the ASP.NET provider model is the ASP.NET implementation of the strategy pattern.

The Pattern "Adapter"

Implemented in the framework, the pattern *strategy* enables ASP.NET developers to switch the underlying algorithm while preserving the overall behavior. There are more factors, though, that deserve a place in the list of key benefits supplied by the provider model. Imagine you're planning your own replacement strategy for a given service—let's consider user profiling again.

What kind of code are you going to put in the custom provider? You might simply want to change the default storage layer and, say, use your own database table. Or perhaps you might need to be untied from databases and use, say, an XML file or even the system registry. In this case, you simply write fresh code to meet your requirements. What if, instead, you are porting an existing application to ASP.NET 2.0? You might have some similar-looking code—for example, a handcrafted personalization subsystem—already in place. You can throw all that code away (and with it all the time and money invested) or *adapt* it to fit in the new model provided by ASP.NET 2.0 for that service. Another popular pattern helps out here—the pattern *adapter*.

The declared intent of the adapter pattern is to convert a class A to an interface B that a client C understands. So you wrap your existing code for user profiling into a new provider class that can be seamlessly plugged into the existing ASP.NET 2.0 framework. You change the underlying implementation of the ASP.NET personalization API and use your own schema and storage medium while keeping the top-level interface intact. And, more importantly, you get to fully reuse your code.

The Pattern "Factory"

As we saw in Chapter 3, there are several places in the configuration tree where you can register custom providers for existing ASP.NET services and select the default one. Next, at run time, ASP.NET creates an instance of the provider class designated as the default. By registering a provider in the *web.config* file, you actually define an interface for creating an object that is independent from the execution context. In other words, your ASP.NET page will end up creating an instance of an object that it might not know in advance. This model is referred to as the *factory* pattern.

The Practice—Implementation Details

In ASP.NET 2.0, providers are classes derived from a base class that override existing behaviors. To create your own provider for a given service, you start by defining a new class that inherits from the base class defined for that type of provider. All providers, for any supported services, derive from a common base class named *ProviderBase*. (See Figure 4-2.)

Three distinct elements make up the implementation of an ASP.NET provider—the base class, configuration layer, and storage layer. The base class provides core functionality mostly through abstract methods for you to override and customize. The configuration layer supplies information used to identify the actual provider so that the ASP.NET runtime can locate and instantiate it. Finally, the storage layer is the physical medium where data is stored. It can be a database table, an XML file, or whatever else makes sense for the feature.

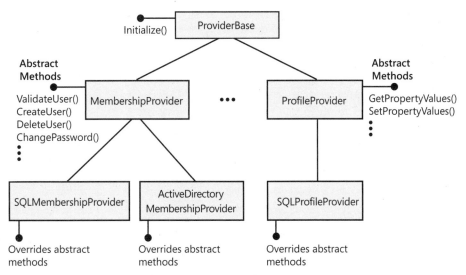

Figure 4-2   The hierarchy of ASP.NET provider classes.

The Base Class

A provider base class supplies the core functionality promised by a service's interface. For example, the base class for the user profile service defines two methods—*GetPropertyValues* and *SetPropertyValues*. (See Figure 4-2.) The former method contracts to return values that form the current user's profile; the latter method saves back to the storage layer the user's profile as determined by the current request. The client—that is, the ASP.NET page—is not required to know anything about the implementation details of the provider.

As mentioned, all provider base classes derive from a common class named *ProviderBase*. This base class provides one overridable method—*Initialize*—through which the run-time environment passes any pertinent settings from the configuration file. Each provider-based service has its own, more specific, base class that in most cases inherits directly from *ProviderBase*. Speaking of this, you should note that the diagram in Figure 4-2 is a bit oversimplified. The *ProfileProvider* class doesn't derive directly from *ProviderBase*. Instead, it derives from *Settings-Provider* which, in turn, descends from *ProviderBase*. We'll return to this matter later in the chapter.

The Configuration Layer

Each supported provider type is assigned a section in the configuration file, which is where the default provider for the feature is set and all available providers are listed. (See Chapter 3 for details on configuration files.) If the provider supports public properties, default values for these properties can be specified through attributes. The contents of the section are passed as an argument to the *Initialize* method of the *ProviderBase* class—the only method that all providers have in common. Within this method, each provider uses the passed information to initialize its own state.

The Storage Layer

All providers need to read and write information to a persistent storage medium. In many cases, two providers of the same type differ only for the storage they employ. Details of the storage medium are packed in the attributes of the provider in the *<providers>* section. For example, the *SqlProfileProvider* provider in Figure 4-2 is the predefined profile provider that reads and writes to a Microsoft SQL Server 2005 Express table named *aspnetdb.mdf*. Later in the chapter, we'll create a custom provider that just uses an alternative table name and layout. (This is a common situation if you are migrating some existing code from ASP.NET 1.x.)

Note that for a provider to work, any needed infrastructure (that is, the database, tables, relationships, and files) must exist. Setting up the working environment is a task typically accomplished at deployment time.

> **Note**   Providers are a hot new feature of ASP.NET 2.0. However, the patterns behind the provider model are common and recurring solutions that can be used also to empower services supplied by ASP.NET 1.x applications. No system services are available in ASP.NET 1.x based on the provider model; however, custom services implemented by ASP.NET 1.x applications can be designed to support customization through providers. Check out *http://msdn.microsoft.com/asp.net/beta2/providers* for more information and sample code.

Built-In ASP.NET Providers

In ASP.NET, the provider model is used to achieve several tasks, the most important of which are as follows:

- The implementation of a read/write mechanism to persist the user profile

- The creation of a user-defined repository of user credentials that supports most common operations, such as checking a user for existence, adding and deleting users, and changing passwords

- The creation of a user-defined repository for user roles

- The definition of the site map

- The introduction of newer types of data storage for the session state

Table 4-1 shows the list of the provider-based services and related classes available in ASP.NET 2.0.

Table 4-1   Available ASP.NET Provider Base Classes

Service	Base Class	Description
Membership and user's credentials	*MembershipProvider*	Base class for membership providers used to manage user account information
Web Parts personalization	*PersonalizationProvider*	Base class for managing personalization for Web Parts components
User profiling	*ProfileProvider*	Base class for personalization providers used to persist and retrieve user's profile information
Protected configuration section	*ProtectedConfiguration-Provider*	Base class for encryption providers used to encrypt information in configuration files
Role management	*RoleProvider*	Base class for role providers used to manage user role information
Session state management	*SessionStateStore-ProviderBase*	Base class for session state store providers. These providers are used to save and retrieve session state information from persistent storage media
Site mapping and navigation	*SiteMapProvider*	Base class for managing site map information
Web events and health monitoring	*WebEventProvider*	Base class for health monitoring providers that process system events.

The classes listed in Table 4-1 define an abstract method for each aspect that's customizable in the feature they represent. For example, regarding user profiling management, the class *ProfileProvider* exposes methods such as *GetPropertyValues* and *SetPropertyValues*. Note that you'll never use *ProfileProvider* in your code just because it's an abstract class. Instead, you'll use a derived class such as *SqlProfileProvider*. The same holds true for other types of providers.

Finally, if you're going to write a custom provider that replaces any predefined providers shipped by ASP.NET 2.0, you'd create a class that inherits from any of the classes listed in the table. Let's grab hold of these base classes.

The Membership Service

The membership provider defines the contract that ASP.NET implements to provide membership services to applications. The contract includes methods to validate users' credentials; change and reset passwords; and create, find, and delete user accounts.

In addition to users' credentials validation and management, a membership provider is also designed to supply advanced services regarding passwords. You can define the minimum acceptable length for a password, the number of mandatory punctuation characters, the hash format, and even a regular expression for valid passwords to comply with. In addition, you can enable or disable password reset and retrieval and bind both to the built-in implementation of the question/answer protocol. The provider also supplies a safeguard against password guessing. Users, in fact, are not allowed to try passwords for more than a fixed number of times in a given time interval.

> **Important**   All the methods and properties that form a provider's contract are marked as abstract. This means that all custom providers must implement all members; however, some providers might provide an empty implementation or just throw a "not supported" exception. This holds true for all types of providers.

The base class for providers of membership services is *MembershipProvider*. ASP.NET ships with two predefined providers: *SqlMembershipProvider* and *ActiveDirectoryMembershipProvider*. Both are defined in the *System.Web.Security* namespace.

The *SqlMembershipProvider* Provider

The *SqlMembershipProvider* provider reads and writes membership information in made-to-measure tables in the *aspnetdb.mdf* database in SQL Server 2005 Express. You create the SQL Server database by running the *aspnet_regsql.exe* utility from the command line. (See Chapter 3.) Alternatively, you can do the same from within the Web Site Administration Tool (WSAT) available from the Website menu in Microsoft Visual Studio 2005.

Once created, the *aspnetdb* database will contain at least the following tables: *aspnet_Applications*, *aspnet_Membership*, *aspnet_SchemaVersions*, and *aspnet_Users*. You also need to ensure that the current ASP.NET worker process account (typically, NT AUTHORITY/NETWORK SERVICE) is granted full access to the *aspnetdb* database.

> **Tip**   By changing the connection string in the *web.config* file of your application, you can make *SqlMembershipProvider* able to read and write data to a SQL Server 2000 or SQL Server 2005 database, as long as the layout of internal tables remains unchanged. Using SQL Express is recommended for small applications in Internet scenarios or if you simply want to experiment with the functionality. This holds true for all types of providers based on *aspnetdb.mdf* and SQL Server 2005 Express.

The AspNetDb Database

The *aspnetdb.mdf* database serves all the predefined providers in ASP.NET 2.0 that use SQL Server as the storage medium. As an application developer, you don't need to know much about this database's internals to use it; built-in providers make it completely transparent. However, a quick look at its tables is useful and becomes a source of inspiration should you have the need some day of writing an alternative and custom storage system. Figure 4-3 offers a view of *aspnetdb.mdf* in Server Explorer. To access the items shown in the figure, you only need to double-click the file in Solution Explorer.

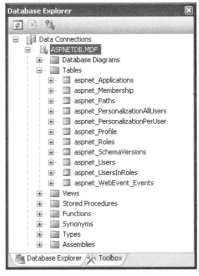

Figure 4-3   Aspnetdb: a view of the interior.

Table 4-2 lists and details the tables. Most of the tables are relevant to a particular provider.

Table 4-2   Tables in *aspnetdb.mdf*

Table	Contents
aspnet_Applications	Lists all the applications using this database.
aspnet_Membership	Lists all membership information for application users stored in the *aspnet_Users* and *aspnet_Applications* tables.
aspnet_Paths	Stores paths of pages using Web Parts.
aspnet_PersonalizationAllUsers	Stores layout information about application pages using Web Parts that apply to all users. Page path is taken from the *aspnet_Paths* table
aspnet_PersonalizationPerUser	Stores layout information about application pages using Web Parts that apply to a particular user. Page path is taken from the *aspnet_Paths* table. Users are taken from the *aspnet_Users* table.
aspnet_Profile	Stores profile data on a per-user basis. Users are defined in *aspnet_Users* and scoped by applications listed in the *aspnet_Applications* table.
aspnet_Roles	Lists all available roles.
aspnet_SchemaVersions	Contains versioning information about the table schema each feature currently supports.
aspnet_Users	Lists all registered users. This table is shared by all providers interested in user-specific information.
aspnet_UsersInRoles	Stores user/role mapping information.
aspnet_WebEvent_Events	Stores details about logged Web events.

As you can see, several providers share the same tables. For example, user names are stored in the *aspnet_Users* table and are read from here by all user-related providers—Web Parts, membership, profile, role. As an example, consider what happens when you add a new user through the membership provider. It first creates a new entry (with GUID and user name) in the *aspnet_Users* table and then adds a new record to the *aspnet_Membership* where other membership information (such as e-mail, password, and settings) is stored.

Each built-in SQL Server–based provider supports schema versioning. The *aspnet_SchemaVersions* helper table contains one record for each provider-enabled service (membership, profile, and so on) with a string column to indicate the supported schema version (1.0, 1.1, 2.0, and so on) and a Boolean column to signal whether the schema in the record is the current one. Each service can have multiple records in the table if there are versions of the provider around requiring different table schemas. The code of the built-in providers checks the schema once before issuing the first SQL command, and it throws an exception if the schema of the involved tables doesn't match the provider's expectation.

> **Note** Table schema versioning is a feature supported by all ASP.NET built-in providers that use the *aspnetdb.mdf* database. If you write custom providers, you might want to consider building a similar feature in your storage medium. You should take this information into account if, for some reason, you happen to write a custom provider for a feature that uses aspnetdb.mdf as the data store. An example could be a SQL provider for site mapping—the only provider-enabled feature to lack a SQL Server–based provider. But, again, this is just an example.

The *ActiveDirectoryMembershipProvider* Provider

The *ActiveDirectoryMembershipProvider* provider manages storage of membership information in Active Directory directory service and Active Directory Application Mode (ADAM) user stores. When using the Active Directory provider, you need to specify the connection string in the *web.config* file along with valid credentials to access the Active Directory server. If you do not specify account credentials, Active Directory will use the credentials of the ASP.NET worker process. What matters is that the account has sufficient permissions in Active Directory.

Note that the any security settings set at the Active Directory provider level must be verified against the settings in the Active Directory environment. For example, Active Directory doesn't accept a password shorter than seven characters devoid of noncharacter symbols. You could, in theory, configure your Active Directory provider to accept, say, passwords with only six characters. However, when setting the password for a given account, the Active Directory provider first checks the password against its parameters and then passes it on to Active Directory. If the password doesn't meet Active Directory requirements, the operation fails. As a result, the strongest security policy is always applied.

Note that the Active Directory provider supports account lockout as part of the membership provider contract. Basically, it tracks the number of failed password attempts (and failed password answer attempts) in the specified period and locks out a user when too many attempts are made. By default, users are not allowed to try it more than five times in ten minutes. How-ever, it is important to know that any account locked out by the Active Directory provider doesn't appear as locked out in the Active Directory environment. The account lockout simply prevents the user from accessing any application protected by the Active Directory–powered membership system. The user will still be able to log on to Windows using her perfectly valid Active Directory account.

Active Directory in Multiple Domains

You can use the *ActiveDirectoryMembershipProvider* provider also in an Active Directory sce-nario where multiple domains are defined. The provider doesn't need to work in a really dif-ferent way. The trick is using multiple provider entries in the *<membership>* section of the *web.config* file and authenticating each user against the relevant domain controller. Let's sup-pose you have two domains, each with a connection string entry in *<connectionStrings>* point-ing to the specific user database.

```
<connectionStrings>
   <add name="TestDomain1ConnString"
       connectionString="LDAP://TestDomain1.com/CN=Users,DC=..." />
   <add name="TestDomain2ConnString"
       connectionString="LDAP://TestDomain2.com/CN=Users,DC=..." />
</connectionStrings>
```

You define an instance of the Active Directory provider for each domain to support. Each entry will have different settings for its connection string and perhaps administrative account. Needless to say, you might want to encrypt this section if it is going to contain passwords.

```
<providers>
   <add name="TestDomain1"
       type="System.Web.Security.ActiveDirectoryMembershipProvider, ..."
       connectionStringName="TestDomain1ConnString"
       connectionUsername="TestDomain1\Admin"
       connectionPassword="..." />
   <add name="TestDomain2"
       type="System.Web.Security.ActiveDirectoryMembershipProvider, ..."
       connectionStringName="TestDomain2ConnString"
       connectionUsername="TestDomain2\Admin"
       connectionPassword="..." />
</providers>
```

What happens when a user attempts to log on to a page protected by the Active Directory membership provider? The user must indicate the domain as well in the logon page. You can either add an additional text box in the page to collect the relevant domain or require the user to express the account name in the form *domain/username* and then parse it out. Once you know the user's domain, you change the validation code of the login page as follows:

```
// These variables are initialized with the contents of
// the login page controls
string userName = "...";
string pswd = "...";
```

```
string domainName = "...";
  ⋮
MembershipProvider domainProvider;
if (domainName == "TestDomain1")
    domainProvider = Membership.Providers["TestDomain1"];
else if (domainName == "TestDomain2.test.com")
    domainProvider = Membership.Providers["TestDomain2"];

// Validate the user with the membership system
if (domainProvider.ValidateUser(userName, pswd) {
    ⋮
}
```

When to Replace

You typically plan to write a custom membership provider if you want to store membership information in a SQL Server table with a different schema or in a completely different database management system (DBMS), such as Oracle or DB2. A common scenario for a custom membership provider is when you have an existing membership system developed for an ASP.NET 1.x application to integrate in a new ASP.NET 2.0 solution.

A custom membership system is also reasonable if you want to use a non–Active Directory Lightweight Directory Access Protocol (LDAP) provider for authentication, a local or remote Web service, or, in general, a completely custom validation algorithm.

The Role Management Service

Roles in ASP.NET simplify the implementation of applications that require authorization. A role is just a logical attribute assigned to a user that indicates the logical role the user plays in the context of the application. Role information is usually attached to the identity object so that the application code can check it before the execution of critical operations. In ASP.NET, the role management feature simply takes care of maintaining the relationship between a user account and associated roles.

For its I/O activity, the role management service uses the provider model and a provider component. The contract established through the provider's interface includes methods to create and delete roles, add roles to users and users to roles, find users in roles, and check roles for existence.

The role provider base class is *RoleProvider*. ASP.NET 2.0 provides three concrete implementations of it—*SqlRoleProvider*, *WindowsTokenRoleProvider*, and *AuthorizationStoreRoleProvider*. All provider classes are defined in the *System.Web.Security* namespace. The *SqlRoleProvider* class—the default role provider—stores users-to-roles relationships to the aforementioned *aspnetdb.mdf* database file in SQL Server 2005 Express.

Note   You can view and edit the contents of the *aspnetdb.mdf* file either through WSAT or Server Explorer in Visual Studio 2005.

The *WindowsTokenRoleProvider* Provider

The *WindowsTokenRoleProvider* provider is a read-only role provider that retrieves role information for a Windows user based on Windows security groups. It is mostly useful to ASP.NET intranet applications that use Windows authentication and disable anonymous access. The role information returned by the provider is based on the user's membership in a particular Windows group. You can't use this provider to create or delete roles. Likewise, the provider doesn't support modifications of any user-role associations because this functionality is managed by the Windows operating system. The *WindowsTokenRoleProvider* class supports only a small subset of methods on the service contract. Only the *IsUserInRole* and *GetUsersInRole* methods of the *RoleProvider* abstract class enjoy a non-empty implementation. All other methods are limited to throwing an exception.

The *AuthorizationStoreRoleProvider* Provider

The *AuthorizationStoreRoleProvider* provider manages storage of role information for an authorization manager (AzMan) policy store. Supported on Microsoft Windows Server 2003, Windows XP Professional, and Windows 2000 Server, AzMan is a separate Windows download that enables you to group individual operations together to form tasks. You can then authorize roles to perform specific tasks, individual operations, or both. AzMan provides an MMC snap-in to manage roles, tasks, operations, and users. Role information is stored in a proper policy store, which can be an XML file, an Active Directory, or an ADAM server. Figure 4-4 shows a sample AzMan store with a configured task. You can display the snap-in in the figure by running *azman.msc* from the Windows command prompt.

Figure 4-4   A sample AzMan policy store with a configured task.

Through AzMan, you simply create abstract tasks and operations and associate them with users and roles. Next, you use the AzMan API to check role membership for a given user and even to query whether a given user is authorized to execute a given task or operation. In ASP.NET applications, by using the *AuthorizationStoreRoleProvider* role provider, you can use the role management API against an AzMan policy store.

Note, though, that the *AuthorizationStoreRoleProvider* provider enables you to use only a subset of the AzMan API. In particular, the role provider allows you to manage roles, add and remove users from roles, and check role membership. Through the role provider, you can't check whether a user is authorized to perform a named task or operation. To access the whole AzMan API, you need to reference the AzMan library in your ASP.NET application through COM Interop.

> **Note**   To learn more about AzMan, check the article you find at *http://msdn.microsoft.com/library/en-us/dnpag2/html/paght000019.asp*. You can download AzMan from *http://windows-update.microsoft.com* because it is part of most service packs.

To use the *AuthorizationStoreRoleProvider* provider with an ASP.NET application, you need to specify a connection string to point to the policy store. Here's an example:

```
<connectionString>
   <add name="LocalPolicyStore"
        connectionString="msxml://c:/mystore.xml" />
</connectionString>
<system.web>
   <roleManager>
      <providers>
         <add name="RoleManagerAzManProvider"
            type="System.Web.Security.AuthorizationStoreRoleProvider, ... "
            connectionStringName="LocalPolicyStore"
            applicationName="AzManDemo" />
      </providers>
   </roleManager>
</system.web>
```

Note that you need to prefix the path to the XML file with *msxml*. You will need to use a compatible connection string if you're going to use Active Directory or ADAM.

Comparing the ASP.NET Roles API to AzMan

What are the benefits, if any, that raw AzMan provides over the ASP.NET role provider API? First and foremost, AzMan represents a broader API for systemwide role and user management. AzMan is not limited to .NET applications, let alone to ASP.NET applications. It is a COM library designed to address the needs of a variety of applications and Windows platforms.

This said, AzMan provides one key advantage over ASP.NET roles. It provides a more fine-grained mechanism for role-based authorization with its ability of abstracting, also, operations and tasks. To take advantage of this extended capability, though, you need to use the native AzMan or wrap it in a custom role provider that extends the built-in *AuthorizationStoreRoleProvider* provider.

When to Replace

A custom role provider makes sense if you want a different data store or, more simply, a SQL Server table with a different schema. The desired schema typically matches what you have in the existing application you're migrating.

A custom role provider is also a viable choice when you want role management implemented through a separate module or Web service and when you need stronger role-based security in your middle tier. In this latter case, you might find that the full AzMan API or analogous API and products are a better option. AzMan is integrated with ASP.NET but not entirely. You need to extend the built-in *AuthorizationStoreRoleProvider* provider to get full support for the AzMan API.

The User's Profile Service

The user profiling service allows authenticated and anonymous users of a site to express preferences on customizable application settings. For the service to work, a few conditions must be met. First, the application must provide a data model—that is, a list of attributes that users can set at will and that the service will persist. Second, there must be one or more pages in the application to provide a visual editor so that users can express their preferences and edit later. Third, there must be at least some pages in the application that reflect the user's defined preferences in their own graphics. When visiting profile-enabled pages, users will experience the settings they entered in much the same way in which it works with controls and themes.

The data model is an XML fragment defined in the *web.config* file where you list application-wide properties that pages can consume and/or let users edit. It is important to note that the data model is scoped to the application, not to individual pages. When each page is loaded to serve a request, the HTTP context object contains a profile object that represents the data model for the application. The data stored in the profile object are specific to the connected user and are retrieved by the user's profile service through the selected provider. When the request ends, the same user's profile service takes care of saving the profile properties back to the data store.

The *SqlProfileProvider* Provider

The base class for providers of profile services is *ProfileProvider*. ASP.NET ships with one predefined provider—*SqlProfileProvider*—defined in the *System.Web.Profile* namespace. The provider reads and writes profile data in a table of the *aspnetdb.mdf* database in SQL Server 2005

Express. A profile provider is expected to read profile values from a data store when the request begins and save changed values back when the request ends.

The profile table contains one record for each user. User settings are packed in a sequence of values distinguishing between text and binary data, as shown in Figure 4-5.

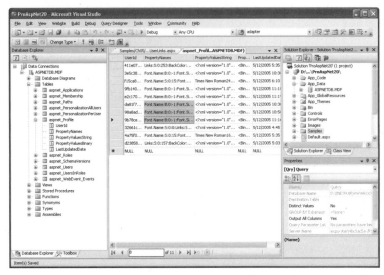

Figure 4-5   Sample contents of the *aspnet_Profile* table in the *aspnetdb* database.

When to Replace

You typically want to write a custom profile provider if you want to store profile information in a SQL Server table with a different schema or in a completely different DBMS system, such as Oracle or DB2. Likewise, you plan a custom provider to integrate an existing profile system in a new ASP.NET 2.0 solution. A custom provider is also recommended if you want to use any other storage medium (XML or Access file) or require any nonsupported features such as compression or encryption.

Later in the chapter, we'll discuss a custom profile provider that uses a custom SQL Server table as the storage medium.

The Session State Service

Session state management is one of the pillars of ASP.NET. It maintains a name/value collection for each valid user session and offers a read/write programming interface through the popular *Session* object. Internally, the ASP.NET 2.0 session state service relies on a number of components, including an HTTP module, a bunch of providers, and physical data stores.

The HTTP module serves ASP.NET the name/value collection of data forming the session state for the current user. When the request ends, the HTTP module receives from ASP.NET the modified session state and stores it. Session store providers represent the interface between the HTTP module and the data stores where data is physically kept for the duration of the session.

A session store provider is the component in charge of serving any data related to the current session. Invoked when the request needs to acquire state information, it retrieves data from a given storage medium and returns that to the module. Invoked by the module when the request ends, it writes the supplied data to the storage layer.

SessionStateStoreProviderBase is the base class for session store providers. It is defined in the *System.Web.SessionState* namespace. ASP.NET comes with three predefined providers, which store data in the worker process's memory, state server, and SQL Server.

> **Note**   In ASP.NET 1.x, you find a similar architecture that employs different but similar-looking components named *state client managers*. All of them implement a common interface—
> *IStateClientManager*. This interface has been lost in the transition to version 2.0, a victim of the refactoring process and the advent of the provider model.

The *InProcSessionStateStore* Provider

The default provider, *InProcSessionStateStore*, stores data as live objects in the ASP.NET *Cache*. Because stored data is ready to use, *InProcSessionStateStore* is the fastest option. However, bear in mind that the more data you store in a session, the more memory is consumed on the server, which increases the risk of performance hits. The memory actually used belongs to the ASP.NET worker process—*aspnet_wp.exe* if the IIS 5.0 process model is used or to an instance of *w3wp.exe* if the IIS 6.0 process model is employed.

Only when this provider is selected can the HTTP module fire the *Session_End* event to signal the end of the session so that applications can perform any clean-up code needed to terminate the session.

The *OutOfProcSessionStateStore* Provider

The *OutOfProcSessionStateStore* session state provider maintains data outside the ASP.NET worker process. More precisely, data is stored in the memory of a Microsoft Windows NT service named *aspnet_state.exe*. Stopped by default, the service requires a manual start. The executable file is located in the installation folder of ASP.NET:

```
%WINDOWS%\Microsoft.NET\Framework\[version]
```

The state service is a constituent part of ASP.NET and gets installed along with it, so you have no additional setup application to run. The communication between the HTTP module and the state server occurs over a TCP/IP port defined in the *web.config* file. (See Chapter 3.)

Using out-of-process storage scenarios gives the session state a longer life and your application a greater robustness. By separating the session state from the page itself, you can also scale an existing application to Web-farm and Web-garden architectures much more easily. In addition, the session state living in an external process eliminates at the root the risk of periodically losing data because of ASP.NET process recycling.

On the down side, note that in an out-of-process architecture, session values are to be copied from the native storage medium into the memory of the AppDomain that processes the request. A serialization/deserialization layer is needed to accomplish the task and is one of the major costs for out-of-process state providers.

The *SqlSessionStateStore* Provider

Maintaining the session state in an external process certainly makes the whole ASP.NET application more stable. Whatever happens to the worker process, the session state is still there, ready for further use. If the service is paused, the data is preserved and automatically retrieved when the service resumes. Unfortunately, if the state provider service is stopped or if a failure occurs, the data is lost. If robustness is key for your application, use the *SqlSessionStateStore* provider.

When you use the *SqlSessionStateStore* provider, the session data is stored in a made-to-measure SQL Server database. As a result, the session data survives even if SQL Server crashes, but you have to add higher overhead to the bill. You can store data on any connected machine, as long as the machine runs SQL Server 7.0 or newer. Besides the different medium, the storage mechanism is nearly identical to that of the *OutOfProcSessionStateStore* provider. In particular, the serialization and deserialization algorithm is the same, only it's a bit slower because of the characteristics of storage.

The database used by default is named *ASPState* and contains several stored procedures. You can choose between a temporary and a persistent table. If you opt for a temporary table, the session data is lost if the computer running SQL Server is restarted. You can declaratively choose to use another database (not the default *ASPState*), but the internal structure must be the same. Sessions are represented as rows in a helper table, and expired sessions are removed using a background job. You configure the *SqlSessionStateStore* provider using the *web.config* file.

When to Replace

There's just one fundamental reason to replace any of the predefined session state store providers with a custom one—using a DBMS other than SQL Server. There are a number of other things you can customize in a session state provider—for example, the structures used to physically store and return data—but the DBMS is by far the most compelling one.

Consider the following scenario: you have an enterprise application that uses Oracle databases. For your session state, you need the robustness that a database-powered solution can deliver. Why should you be willing to introduce another DBMS (for example, SQL Server) in your environment only to implement robust and reliable session state? In this case, you write (or buy) a custom session state provider that mimics the behavior of the *SqlSessionStateStore* provider, except that it is optimized for Oracle (or whatever other DBMS you're using).

> **Tip**   To write a state provider, you might find the methods of the *SessionStateUtility* class helpful. The class contains methods to serialize and deserialize session items to and from the storage medium. Likewise, the class has methods to extract the dictionary of data for a session and add it to the HTTP context and the *Session* property.

The Site Mapping Service

A site map is a hierarchical data structure that represents the internal structure of a Web site. There are many interesting scenarios in which a site map is useful. You can use the site map to display the location of the page in the site and links to parent pages. In ASP.NET 2.0, a site map can also be used in conjunction with rich controls such as *TreeView* and *Menu* to drive the structure of the site's home page. (We'll return to this topic in Chapter 10.) Where does a site map come from?

By default, ASP.NET applications read site maps from an XML file with a fixed name—*web.sitemap*—deployed in the application's root folder. This XML file and its schema are just one option, though. The service of retrieving site map information is, therefore, contracted out to a provider. By changing the underlying provider, you can change the data store and the way data is retrieved, but not the final format of site map that ASP.NET controls and pages expect.

The base class for site map providers is *SiteMapProvider*. The contract defined by this class requires that derived classes build a tree of site map node objects and supply methods for finding nodes from the site map. Each node contains a display name, a URL, a parent, a list of child nodes, and roles. Site map providers can be combined to form a hierarchy. This feature addresses a particular scenario: when different areas of the site are owned by different teams managing their own site maps and site map providers.

The *SiteMapProvider* contract also provides for security trimming. Providers that support this feature are able to include in the list of each node's children only nodes that are visible to the current user based on his or her roles. Finally, site map providers should support text localization by either indicating the RESX file from where each node will need to load the display text or by using an entirely custom mechanism and providing already localized text to ASP.NET. For example, the provider might build the tree from different data sources according to the current thread culture.

> **Note**   Once loaded in memory, the site map is not necessarily set in stone and can undergo a number of dynamic changes. For example, you can add, remove, and modify nodes on the fly by providing a handler for the provider's *SiteMapResolve* event.

The *XmlSiteMapProvider* Provider

The *XmlSiteMapProvider* provider inherits from an intermediate provider class named *Static-SiteMapProvider* which, in turn, inherits from *SiteMapProvider*. It builds the site map from the information read out of an XML file whose name is set by the *siteMapFile* attribute in the configuration file, as shown in the site's *web.config* excerpt that follows.

```
<siteMap>
   <providers>
      <add name="AspNetXmlSiteMapProvider"
           siteMapFile="web.sitemap"
           type="System.Web.XmlSiteMapProvider, System.Web, ... " />
   </providers>
</siteMap>
```

By default, the *web.sitemap* file is located at the application root; however, you can change the name and location of the file from which the *XmlSiteMapProvider* provider loads data. Note that you cannot change the extension of the file from which *XmlSiteMapProvider* reads data. The *XmlSiteMapProvider* provider recognizes only files with the *.sitemap* extension.

The schema of the source XML file is fixed, too. It consists of a unique *<siteMap>* node followed by any number of nested *<siteMapNode>* tags. The *<siteMapNode>* node corresponds to an instance of the *SiteMapNode* class. Any site map provider is ultimately required to return a *SiteMapNode* object that is the root of the site map hierarchy. Here's an example of an XML site map:

```
<siteMap>
   <siteMapNode title="Intro" url="intro.aspx" >
      <siteMapNode title="Acknowledgements" url="ack.aspx" />
      <siteMapNode title="References" url="ref.aspx" />
   </siteMapNode>
   <siteMapNode title="Samples" url="samples.aspx">
      ⋮
   </siteMapNode>
   ⋮
</siteMap>
```

The *SiteMapNode* class has various properties, among which the *Url* property stands out. The *XmlSiteMapProvider* uses the *Url* property as a key, meaning that in any *.sitemap* XML file, the URL of each node must be unique in the scope of the site map. A custom site map provider might want to use another *SiteMapNode* property—the *Key* property—to uniquely identify nodes. In this case, values assigned to the *Key* property must be unique in the scope of the site map.

Finally, note that the *XmlSiteMapProvider* monitors the XML file for changes and dynamically rebuilds the site map when the source file is modified by an administrator.

When to Replace

You might want to create a custom site map provider if you find that the XML schema of *.sitemap* files doesn't meet your requirements or if you don't want to use XML files at all. In this case, any other storage media are fine, in particular databases. Again, this approach is highly recommended if you have an existing site map infrastructure to migrate to ASP.NET 2.0.

When it comes to building a custom site map provider, consider deriving yours from *StaticSiteMapProvider* instead of *SiteMapProvider*. The *StaticSiteMapProvider* is still an abstract class, but it implements most of the virtual abstracts methods defined on the parent class. As a result, deriving from *StaticSiteMapProvider* usually simplifies things quite a bit.

The Web Event Handling Service

The ASP.NET health monitoring system instruments your application for a number of pre-defined and custom events related to performance, security, failures, and anomalies. Quite simply, the subsystem works by sending events to a number of registered listeners. In this case, listeners are just Web event providers. A Web event provider typically processes the information associated with a health event by recording the event on a persistent medium. Each event contains information such as type, code, and a descriptive message. Not all events are of interest to all providers. The mapping between providers and fired events is set in the *web.config* file, as discussed in Chapter 3.

The base class for Web event providers is *WebEventProvider*. Some built-in providers inherit from an intermediate class named *BufferedWebEventProvider*. All classes are defined in the *System.Web.Management* namespace.

The *EventLogWebEventProvider* Provider

The *EventLogWebEventProvider* provider works by logging health-monitoring events into the Windows Application Event Log. This is the only provider that is bound to some events by default.

```
<rules>
    <add name="All Errors Default" eventName="All Errors"
        provider="EventLogProvider" ... />
    <add name="Failure Audits Default" eventName="Failure Audits"
        provider="EventLogProvider" ... />
</rules>
```

As you can see from the excerpt from the site's *web.config* file, the *EventLogWebEventProvider* provider tracks failure audits and all other errors and records them in the Windows Application Event Log.

The *MailWebEventProvider* Provider

MailWebEventProvider is an intermediate, abstract class that inherits from another intermediate class—*BufferedWebEventProvider*. Classes derived from *BufferedWebEventProvider* maintain an internal queue where listed events are buffered to be flushed at a later time. The class *MailWebEventProvider* provides the base functionality for an event provider that sends e-mail for each tracked event. From it, two more specific classes derive—*SimpleMailWebEventProvider* and *TemplatedMailWebEventProvider*.

Registered as a Web event provider, *SimpleMailWebEventProvider* enables the health monitoring system to send e-mail notifications of an event. The following script code registers the *SimpleMailWebEventProvider* provider with details of the message to create:

```
<providers>
    <add name="CriticalMailEventProvider"
         type="System.Web.Management.SimpleMailWebEventProvider, ..."
         from="admin@contoso.com"
         to="someone@contoso.com"
         bodyHeader="Warning!"
         bodyFooter="Please investigate ASAP."
         subjectPrefix="Action required." />
</providers>
```

This script is not enough, though. It also requires an explicit link to be set between the Web event provider and one or more categories of events. The following script enables the mail provider to work on all errors that occur within an application:

```
<rules>
    <add name="All Errors by Email"
         eventName="All Errors"
         provider="CriticalMailEventProvider" />
</rules>
```

The *name* attribute is a nickname string and must be unique in the application scope. By default, the *All Errors* event name is also bound to the Event Log provider. Note, though, that in an ISP scenario, you're likely forbidden to write to the event log.

As a result, once the preceding script is added to the *web.config* file, you'll receive an e-mail and an event log notification for each error. As we learned in Chapter 3, *<rules>* and *<providers>* go under the *<healthMonitoring>* section.

To be precise, we still lack the final touch before e-mail messages can start going out—the *<add>* entry of Web event providers doesn't allow you to indicate the SMTP host. This setting is inherited from the *<mailSettings>* section of configuration files. Here's an example:

```
<system.net>
    <mailSettings>
        <smtp deliveryMethod="network">
            <network host="mail.contoso.com" />
        </smtp>
    </mailSettings>
</system.net>
```

Figure 4-6 illustrates the two notifications you get for an unhandled page exception.

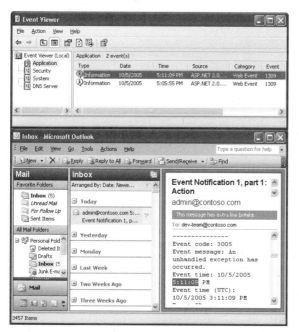

Figure 4-6   Notifications of Web events.

The format of the message sent through *SimpleMailWebEventProvider* can't be modified. If you want to build more sophisticated e-mail messages, you can use the *TemplatedMailWebEvent-Provider* provider instead. This provider has one more attribute—*template*—which references an ASP.NET page. Here's a sample page:

```
<%@ Page Language="C#" AutoEventWireup="true" Inherits="MyEmailTemplate"
        CodeFile="MyEmailTemplate.aspx.cs" %>
<html>
<body>
    <form id="form1" runat="server">
       <asp:Label runat="server" ID="TheMailBody" />
    </form>
</body>
</html>
```

In the code file, you access any event information available and build output.

```
using System.Web.Management;
public partial class MyEmailTemplate : System.Web.UI.Page
{
    protected void Page_Load(object sender, EventArgs e)
    {
       // Use a StringBuilder to buffer markup
       StringBuilder pageBody = new StringBuilder();
       ⋮
```

```
        // Loop through the events in the current notification
        WebBaseEventCollection events;
        events = TemplatedMailWebEventProvider.CurrentNotification.Events;
        foreach (WebBaseEvent e in events)
        {
            // Build your output here using the properties of
            // the WebBaseEvent object
            ⋮
        }

        // Push the markup to the page
        TheMailBody.Text = pageBody.ToString();
    }
}
```

The *TemplateMailWebEventProvider* class has one static member—*CurrentNotification*—that returns the collection of events in the current notification. *CurrentNotification* evaluates to an instance of the *MailEventNotificationInfo* class. The *Events* member on this latter class is a collection of *WebBaseEvent* objects.

The *SqlWebEventProvider* Provider

Just like mail providers, *SqlWebEventProvider* is also a buffered provider component. It writes event information to the configured SQL Server database. The target database is the same *aspnetdb.mdf* file that we met earlier for other types of providers. The table where data is flushed is *aspnet_WebEvent_Events*.

The *SqlWebEventProvider* is enabled by default but is not bound to any event. To start it writing to the *aspnetdb* database, you only need to add a proper *<rules>* section to your application's *web.config* that maps events to the provider.

The *TraceWebEventProvider* Provider

The *TraceWebEventProvider* provider sends intercepted health events out as ASP.NET trace messages viewable through the *trace.axd* utility. This provider is neither registered nor linked to any events. You need to tweak both the *<providers>* and *<rules>* sections of the configuration file to enable it.

```
<trace enabled="true" />
```

Furthermore, note that ASP.NET tracing must be enabled for the feature to work.

The *WmiWebEventProvider* Provider

The *WmiWebEventProvider* provider forwards the intercepted events to the Windows Management Instrumentation (WMI) system. In general, WMI is a component of the Windows operating system that allows administrators and developers to manage system information and control system modules. For example, an administrator can use WMI to query the status of applications and networks, whereas a developer might use WMI to create event-monitoring applications that report incidents and anomalies.

Knowledge Base article 893664 contains a sample WMI listener application that uses classes in the *System.Management* assembly to watch for WMI events. Figure 4-7 shows that sample console application in action on an ASP.NET application with the following *<rules>* section in the configuration:

```
<rules>
    <add name="All Errors to WMI" eventName="All Errors"
        provider="WmiWebEventProvider" />
</rules>
```

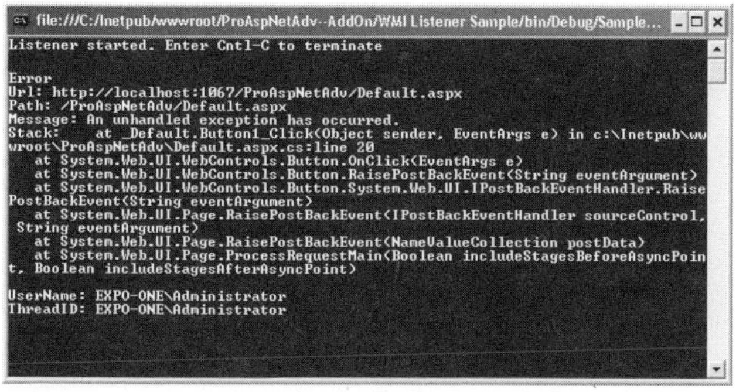

Figure 4-7   A sample WMI watcher application catching ASP.NET errors.

When to Replace

ASP.NET already provides a fair number of different Web event providers. In this case, the most common reason—if not the only one—for writing a custom provider is to record events in a different SQL Server database, in another DBMS system such as Oracle, or in some other mechanism such as Microsoft Message Queue (MSMQ).

You could even consider writing a custom provider to log events on a text/XML file with a particular format well suited to be processed by other services in your environment. If this is precisely your problem, consider that the Windows Event Log already provides various options to export the stored information and similar facilities can be built for a SQL Server table or perhaps WMI stores. In my opinion, it is preferable to stick to one of the predefined providers and devise some offline tool to adapt data to the format you need.

The Web Parts Personalization Service

ASP.NET Web Parts provide an infrastructure for creating Web applications that can handle rich content as well as large amounts of it. Using Web Parts, you can build sites that enable users to select and receive only the content they want. ASP.NET Web Parts are container components that aggregate different types of content.

You can think of a Web Part as a window of information available within the page. Users can close, minimize, or restore that window. A Web Part is essentially a container filled with the usual HTML stuff—static text, link, images, and other controls, including user controls and custom controls. By combining Web Parts and the personalization service, page developers can easily create pages and controls tailored to the individual user's needs. We'll cover Web Parts in Chapter 7.

The contents and layout of Web Parts are subject to user preferences. These user-specific settings are critical and are to be persisted somewhere. The personalization service of Web Parts accomplishes this task by employing the provider model.

The *SqlPersonalizationProvider* Provider

The base class for any Web Parts provider is *PersonalizationProvider*, an abstract class defined in the *System.Web.UI.WebControls.WebParts* namespace. ASP.NET comes with only one built-in provider—*SqlPersonalizationProvider*.

The provider saves its data in three tables inside the *aspnetdb.mdf* file. First, each page is saved with its own path in the *aspnet_Paths* table. Next, an entry is created to link paths and users with per-page and per-user settings. Per-user settings go in the *aspnet_PersonalizationPerUser* table. Shared settings go in the *aspnet_PersonalizationAllUsers* table.

When to Replace

Given the complexity of the data to store for a Web Part, you might want to consider writing a custom Web Parts personalization provider only if you need to use a different database server. If you don't want to use SQL Server 2005 Express, you can modify the connection string in the *web.config* file and make it point to a SQL Server database with the same schema.

If you do this, be aware that you are responsible for creating such a database. The *aspnet_regsql* utility does have command-line switches that can be of some help. See the MSDN online documentation for more information regarding the *aspnet_regsql* utility.

The Configuration Protection Service

As mentioned in Chapter 3, ASP.NET 2.0 allows you to use encryption to protect specific sections of the *web.config* file. A special breed of components—encryption providers—take care of encryption. The list of available protection providers can be found in the *<providers>* section of the *<protectedData>* section of the configuration.

The purpose of an encryption provider is quite simple—encrypt the contents of the specified section using a particular cryptographic engine and return the results as an XML node. Likewise, the provider must be able to decrypt the contents of a given XML node.

The base for encryption providers is *ProtectedConfigurationProvider,* which, in turn, inherits from *ProviderBase*. ASP.NET 2.0 defines a couple of built-in providers—one using the RSA algorithm, and one based on the Windows Data Protection API (DPAPI).

Internal Structure of Encryption Providers

An encryption provider is required to have two main methods whose prototypes are shown here:

```
public abstract class ProtectedConfigurationProvider : ProviderBase
{
     public abstract XmlNode Decrypt(XmlNode encryptedNode);
     public abstract XmlNode Encrypt(XmlNode node);
}
```

The provider receives an *XmlNode* object representing the configuration subtree to encrypt, does its own work, and returns an *XmlNode* object rooted in the tree, which will be inserted under the protected section. The following pseudo-code shows the behavior of *Encrypt*:

```
public override XmlNode Encrypt(XmlNode node)
{
    // Encrypt the contents of the node
    string clearText = node.OuterXml;
    string encText = EncryptText(clearText);

    // Build the XML string to return
    StringBuilder finalText = new StringBuilder();
    finalText.Append("EncryptedData><CipherData><CipherValue>");
    finalText.Append(encText);
    finalText.Append("</CipherValue></CipherData></EncryptedData>");

    // Build the XML subtree to insert in the web.config
    XmlDocument doc = new XmlDocument();
    doc.PreserveWhitespace = true;
    doc.LoadXml(finalText.ToString());
    return doc.DocumentElement;
}
```

The *Decrypt* method does the reverse.

```
public override XmlNode Decrypt(XmlNode encryptedNode)
{
    // Get the encrypted text and decrypt
    string cipherValue = TraverseToNodeValue(encryptedNode);
    string clearText = this.DecryptText(cipherValue);

    // Build the XML subtree to insert in the web.config
    XmlDocument doc = new XmlDocument();
    doc.PreserveWhitespace = true;
    doc.LoadXml(clearText);
    return doc.DocumentElement;
}
```

Note that code shown here is pseudo-code created to illustrate the internal behavior of a typical encryption provider. All the nitty-gritty details of the encryption/decryption are buried in the subroutines and strictly depend on the provider of choice. Providers differentiate from one another based on the cryptographic engine they employ.

The *RsaProtectedConfigurationProvider* Provider

The *RsaProtectedConfigurationProvider* provider employs the RSA algorithm—one of the most popular public-key encryption algorithms. In public key cryptography, a message is encrypted using a pair of keys—the private and public key. The private key is generally kept secret, while the public key can be openly distributed. The sender encrypts a message using the recipient's public key and sends it. The recipient will be able to decrypt the message using his own private key. Public and private keys are mathematically related so that it is virtually impossible to deduce the private key from the public key. Moreover, only the public key can be used to encrypt a message and only the corresponding private key can be used to decrypt it. Built into many popular software products, the RSA algorithm is the *de facto* standard for industrial-strength encryption.

In the .NET Framework, the *RSACryptoServiceProvider* class creates a public/private key pair when you use the default constructor. Keys can either be stored for use in multiple sessions or generated for one session only. To safely store keys (also often referred to as *asymmetric keys*), you should use a secure key container. This raises a potential issue with the *RsaProtectedConfigurationProvider* provider. Let's take a look at the *machine.config* file where built-in encryption providers are listed.

```
<protectedData defaultProvider="RsaProtectedConfigurationProvider">
    <providers>
        <add keyContainerName="NetFrameworkConfigurationKey"
             useMachineContainer="true"
             name="RsaProtectedConfigurationProvider"
             type="System.Configuration.RsaProtectedConfigurationProvider,
                   System.Configuration, ..." />
    </providers>
</protectedData>
```

As you can see, *RsaProtectedConfigurationProvider* is the default encryption provider and uses a key container named *NetFrameworkConfigurationKey*. This container is created and filled upon ASP.NET installation with the asymmetric keys to use for encrypting configuration sections. It is extremely important that the key container exist before the *RsaProtectedConfigurationProvider* provider is used.

There's an additional point to consider, though. Not only should the key container exist, but it must also be associated with the user account attempting to call it. By default, the system account is listed with the container, but the ASP.NET account on your Web server usually is not. What does this mean to you? If you attempt to use a protected section from within the local Web server embedded in Visual Studio 2005, it always works. If you move the same page in an IIS virtual folder and run it through IIS, the encryption provider fails. The reason is that, in this case, the access to the container is performed by the ASP.NET account, which might not be registered with the key container.

Assuming you run ASP.NET under the NETWORK SERVICE account (the default on computers running Windows Server 2003), you need to run the following command from the Windows command prompt:

```
aspnet_regiis.exe -pa "NetFrameworkConfigurationKey"
                "NT AUTHORITY\NETWORK SERVICE"
```

The command will add access to the container for the specified account. It is important that you specify a complete account name, including the domain "NT AUTHORITY", as in the preceding code. Note that granting access to the key container is necessary only if you use the RSA provider.

The *aspnet_regiis* utility provides various switches to let you create custom key containers and even to export them to other machines. If you create a custom container, though, remember to update the configuration (the site's or application's *web.config* file) to let the *RsaProtected-ConfigurationProvider* provider know about it.

Protecting Sections on a Web Farm

As we'll see more clearly in the next section, the RSA algorithm is the most viable option to protect configuration sections in a Web farm. When setting up a Web farm, you typically install the *same* set of application files on each machine, including the *web.config* file with protected sections. This *web.config* file has been created—and some section encrypted—on one particular development machine, or perhaps on a production machine. The installation of ASP.NET, though, creates a different pair of asymmetric keys on the various farm machines. As a result, a blind x-copy of the application files is not enough, as long as the *web.config* file contains protected sections.

The problem here is not that different machines might have different keys, but that each machine will likely have keys different from those used to originally encrypt the deployed *web.config* file. There are two ways to address this issue:

- Deploy a clear-text *web.config* file and encrypt it on each Web farm machine. Each machine ends up having a different and unique *web.config* file that can be read only with the keys stored on that machine.

- Use x-copy to deploy an already encrypted *web.config* file on all machines. At the same time, make sure that all machines share the same keys.

To accomplish the latter step, you first export the keys used to encrypt the *web.config* file. This operation must be run on the machine on which the encrypted *web.config* was created. You use the following command:

```
aspnet_regiis.exe -px "NetFrameworkConfigurationKey" MyKeys.xml
```

The command exports the default key container to *MyKeys.xml*. Needless to say, if you've used a different key container, use that in the call to *aspnet_regiis*.

The XML file needs be copied to all machines in the Web farm and then imported in the key container of choice. The key container name must be the same on all machines.

```
aspnet_regiis.exe -pi "NetFrameworkConfigurationKey" MyKeys.xml
```

As a final step, grant the ASP.NET account on each machine permission to access the container.

```
aspnet_regiis.exe -pa "NetFrameworkConfigurationKey"
                "NT AUTHORITY\NETWORK SERVICE"
```

The *DpapiProtectedConfigurationProvider* Provider

The *DpapiProtectedConfigurationProvider* provider uses the Windows Data Protection API (DPAPI) to encrypt sections of the *web.config* file. Introduced with Windows 2000, DPAPI is an operating system–level API and consists of two (unmanaged) functions: *CryptProtectData* and *CryptUnprotectData*.

> **Note**   In the .NET Framework 2.0, you can use DPAPI to protect your application's data through the new *ProtectedData* class. The class is a simple wrapper for the unmanaged API and uses P/Invoke calls internally. In the .NET Framework 1.x, you have to call P/Invoke yourself or resort to helper libraries, most of which are freely available. You can find an example here: *http://msdn.microsoft.com/library/en-us/dnnetsec/html/SecNetHT07.asp*.

The key difference between RSA and DPAPI is just in the keys. First, DPAPI is a symmetric algorithm, meaning that the same key is required to encrypt and decrypt text. Second, DPAPI automatically generates an encryption key.

In brief, DPAPI generates a master key and encrypts it using a key based on the logged-on user's password. Next, DPAPI derives a session key from the master key, some random data, and some optional entropy (random text) passed in by the user. The session key is actually used to do the encryption work.

DPAPI also provides a flag to work in machine mode rather than in user mode. In this case, machinewide information is used to generate the key that protects the master key. In case of machinewide protection, any process on a machine can decrypt text encrypted by any other process running on the same machine. This is the default working mode for the *DpapiProtect-edConfigurationProvider* provider. Here's the way the DPAPI provider is declared in the *machine.config* file.

```
<providers>
    <add useMachineProtection="true"
        name="DataProtectionConfigurationProvider"
        keyEntropy=""
        type="System.Configuration.DpapiProtectedConfigurationProvider,
            System.Configuration, ..." />
</providers>
```

If you use the DPAPI provider, you won't experience any difference between IIS and the Visual Studio 2005 embedded Web server. Using DPAPI on a Web farm is problematic if machine-wide protection is used—each machine is different, and there will be no reliable way to ensure that the key is the same. You might try with the same entropy value and setting the same logon account and password on all machines. All in all, I believe that the RSA-based provider is the best option for Web farms.

> **Note**   When working in user-mode, DPAPI is based on the user's password. What if the user changes his or her password? DPAPI hooks up the password-changing event and re-encrypts the master key. The user's password has no impact on the session key actually being used to encrypt and decrypt.

When to Replace

Playing and kidding around with encryption and security in general is never a safe practice. This is true even, or perhaps especially, when you do that armed with the best intentions of building a more secure environment. The golden rule as far as encryption is concerned is, "Do not build your own encryption library, but use any reliable library that exists."

To encrypt data in configuration files, you have two options with different characteristics but that are equally strong. I can't see any serious reason for building a custom provider that replaces the RSA and DPAPI providers. Adding a custom one, though, is technically possible and even relatively easy to do.

Basically, you might want to do that to use another encryption library. There might be application-specific reasons for doing this. However, make sure that the encryption library you bring in is a good one and not just your own little creation.

Roll Your Own Provider

Let's see a practical example of how to build a custom provider. In many of the preceding "When to Replace" sections, you found a common scenario. You might want to roll your own provider to integrate into an ASP.NET 2.0 application some existing and tested code that already implement a service that is provider-based in ASP.NET 2.0.

Some features are a pure necessity for most real-world ASP.NET applications—for example, membership, roles, user profiling, and site mapping. For these features, ASP.NET 2.0 supplies built-in solutions set in an extensible model—the provider model. What should you do? Throw your existing code out the window and blissfully embrace the dazzling new model of ASP.NET 2.0? While this might be an option, in most cases you'll probably want to take the best of everything—that is, stay with the ASP.NET 2.0 model while reusing your tested and reliable code. On the other hand, isn't this precisely the essence of the "adapter" pattern that we mentioned earlier in the chapter?

Let's suppose that you have some old ASP.NET 1.x code that implements user profiles using cookies. In other words, each registered user is given a cookie with some data that represents her preferences with regard to the visited pages. The cookie is presented with each request, and each page consumes part of the contents. (By the way, this is a very common practice, so this example has real-world applicability.) Let's see how to incorporate this code in a custom profile provider.

> **Note**   More than for the practical solution it offers, I think this example will be useful for the underlying pattern it illustrates—adapting existing, tested, reliable code to work in the context of an ASP.NET 2.0 provider. The extent to which you could integrate your code in a provider depends on both the service's contract (membership, profile) and the characteristics of your existing code. As far as the user profiling service is concerned, the reuse of existing code is even harder because of the data model that can be defined differently on a per-application basis. In the book code, you find two sample pages persisting preferences through cookies—one that uses a custom API, and one that uses the profile provider we're going to build. As you'll see, full reuse of the existing API in this case is unlikely. The contract of other services, such as membership or site mapping, makes the reuse of existing code feasible and relatively easy.

Design Considerations

All providers inherit from *ProviderBase*, and, therefore, all providers share an *Initialize* method and a couple of properties—*Name* and *Description*. The initialization of a provider is a critical step and must be coded with a few guidelines in mind. Let's start from here.

The Initialization of a Provider

The *Initialize* method of a provider receives a couple of parameters, as shown here:

```
public virtual void Initialize(string name, NameValueCollection config)
```

The *name* argument indicates the name of the provider as read from the configuration file. The *config* argument contains the collection of attributes found in the configuration file. The config collection should never be null; if it is, you should throw an exception.

```
if (config == null)
    throw new ArgumentNullException("Null configuration parameters");
```

Before the *Initialize* method on the base class is called, you should ensure that the *name* parameter is not null or empty.

```
if (String.IsNullOrEmpty(name))
        name = "CookieProfileProvider";
```

You can set it to any constant string you like—typically the name of the class. If the *name* attribute is set in the *web.config* file, that value is found here. Next, you call the base *Initialize* method. When the method returns, you take care of any custom attribute your provider requires. For example, a cookie-based profile provider might read the default name and expiration of the cookie.

```
_cookieName = config["cookieName"];
if (String.IsNullOrEmpty(_cookieName))
    _cookieName = ".PROF";
config.Remove("cookieName");
```

It is recommended that any recognized attribute be removed from the *config* collection. At the end of the method, the *config* collection should be empty, meaning that all attributes have been processed. If it is not empty, you should throw an exception. You should also throw an exception if a required attribute is not found and there's no valid default value you can or want to provide for it.

> **Important**   It depends on how the specific provider is designed, but calling any service-specific API from within the *Initialize* method of the provider is generally not a safe operation. You should avoid it or, at the very minimum, make sure that you don't risk a stack overflow. Be aware that there might be calls on provider-related objects that make a call back to *Initialize*.
>
> The code at risk is any code that has to do with the *Providers* property exposed by most service classes such as *Membership*, *ProfileManager*, or *Roles*. Using the *Providers* property likely places a call to the provider's *Initialize* method. If this happens from within the *Initialize* method itself, a stack overflow might be just around the corner.

Threading Issues

A provider is typically instantiated when the first request arrives that involves the corresponding service. For example, the profile provider is not loaded until some user requests a page that makes use of the user profile service. Subsequently, a provider is instantiated once per application and its lifetime is nearly identical to that of the application.

All requests in an application share the same instance of the provider, but different requests might go on different threads. It is also a reasonable assumption that multiple threads will be accessing the provider at the same time. In other words, a provider must be explicitly designed to be thread-safe.

The thread-safety constraint doesn't apply to the *Initialize* method. By design, in fact, access to this provider's method is automatically serialized. The explanation is all in what happens in the *ProviderBase*'s *Initialize* method—a stateful private variable indicates whether or not the provider has been already initialized. Access to this variable is properly wrapped by a *lock* statement.

Throwing Exceptions

A provider is part of an application's API. According to rules of good programming, you should signal any unexpected situation by throwing an exception. If you can find an existing exception class in the .NET Framework that matches closely what you intend to notify, by all means use that. *ArgumentException*, *NotImplementedException*, and *NullReferenceException* are examples of exceptions that a provider might commonly throw.

The .NET Framework also provides a *ProviderException* class that should be used to deliver detailed information regarding the exception. You should consider *ProviderException* as the base class for provider-specific exceptions. Either you use it or define your own exceptions deriving from it.

Implementation of a Cookie-Based Profile Provider

The *CookieProfileProvider* provider stores user profiles in a cookie. Cookies are named after the current user and can be given the desired expiration. All properties defined in the *web.config* data model are copied in a hash table, serialized, and then encoded to Base64 before storage. The sample code uses the binary serializer to make sure it can handle any serializable type of data. You might want to optimize the code by using simpler serialization policies for common and primitive types.

Methods to Override

The *CookieProfileProvider* class derives from *ProfileProvider*, which, in turn, derives from *SettingsProvider*. The methods to override are listed in Table 4-3.

Table 4-3 Overridable Methods for a Profile Provider

Method	Description
DeleteInactiveProfiles	Defined on *SettingsProvider*, deletes all profiles inactive since a given date
DeleteProfiles	Defined on *SettingsProvider*, deletes the profiles of the specified users
FindInactiveProfilesByUserName	Defined on *SettingsProvider*, finds all profiles inactive since a given date and matching a given user name
FindProfilesByUserName	Defined on *SettingsProvider*, finds all profiles matching a given user name
GetAllInactiveProfiles	Defined on *SettingsProvider*, finds all inactive profiles since a given date
GetAllProfiles	Defined on *SettingsProvider*, finds all profiles
GetNumberOfInactiveProfiles	Defined on *SettingsProvider*, returns the number of inactive profiles since a given date
GetPropertyValues	Defined on *ProfileProvider*, returns the property values as read from the storage medium
Initialize	Defined on *ProviderBase*, initializes the provider
SetPropertyValues	Defined on *ProfileProvider*, saves the current profile down to the storage medium

I'm not going to implement all methods inherited from the *SettingsProvider* base class. All of them will simply throw the "not supported" exception. Here's an example:

```
public override int DeleteProfiles(string[] usernames)
{
    throw new NotSupportedException();
}
```

The class has three public properties—*ApplicationName* (overridden) plus *CookieName* and *CookieExpires*.

```
public class CookieProfileProvider : ProfileProvider
{
    private string _cookieName;
    private int _cookieExpires;
    private string _appName;

    public CookieProfileProvider()
    {}

    public override string ApplicationName
    {
        get { return _appName; }
        set { _appName = value; }
    }

    public virtual string CookieName
    {
        get { return _cookieName; }
        set { _cookieName = value; }
    }

    public virtual int CookieExpires
    {
        get { return _cookieExpires; }
        set { _cookieExpires = value; }
    }
    ⋮
}
```

The *Initialize* Method

The *Initialize* method reads *cookieName* and *cookieExpires* attributes from the configuration section and initializes the public properties to their defaults.

```
public override void Initialize(string name, NameValueCollection config)
{
    if (config == null)
        throw new ArgumentNullException("Null configuration parameters");

    // Make sure the provider has a name
    if (String.IsNullOrEmpty(name))
        name = "CookieProfileProvider";
```

```
    // Call the base class method
    base.Initialize(name, config);

    // Read the application name
    _appName = config["applicationName"];
    if (String.IsNullOrEmpty(_appName))
        _appName = HostingEnvironment.ApplicationVirtualPath;
    config.Remove("applicationName");

    // Read the cookie name
    _cookieName = config["cookieName"];
    if (String.IsNullOrEmpty(_cookieName))
        _cookieName = ".PROF";
    config.Remove("cookieName");

    // Read the cookie expiration
    bool success = Int32.TryParse(config["cookieExpires"],
            out _cookieExpires);
    if (!success)
        _cookieExpires = 10;
    config.Remove("cookieExpires");

    // Throw an exception if there are still unknown attributes
    if (config.Count > 0)
    {
        string attrib = config.GetKey(0);
        if (!String.IsNullOrEmpty(attrib))
            throw new ProviderException("Unrecognized attribute: " + attrib);
    }
}
```

The *GetPropertyValues* Method

The *GetPropertyValues* method is intended to return the contents of the user profile. In this method, you should read data out of the data store and pack it into a tailormade collection. The collection you return will be consumed by ASP.NET to initialize the members of the profile object that pages will see. The arguments you get from the system include the list of profile properties for which you are expected to specify a value.

To avoid having any of the declared profile properties (in the *<profile>* section of the *web.config*) go uninitialized, it is essential that you do a first run on all requested properties and make sure all of them are added to the returned collection. Only at this point should you check for the availability of data in the store. Take a look at the following code:

```
public override SettingsPropertyValueCollection GetPropertyValues(
        SettingsContext context,
        SettingsPropertyCollection properties)
{
    SettingsPropertyValueCollection settings;
    settings = new SettingsPropertyValueCollection();

    // Check how many properties we are going to retrieve
    if (properties.Count == 0)
        return settings;
```

```
// Add all properties to the output collection.
// This guarantees that as many entries will be created (and not be
// null) on the Profile object
foreach (SettingsProperty property in properties) {
    SettingsPropertyValue pv = new SettingsPropertyValue(property);
    settings.Add(pv);
}

// Read the cookie (if any)
string username = (string)context["UserName"];
string cookie = CookieName + "_" + username;
HttpCookie cookieProfile = HttpContext.Current.Request.Cookies[cookie];
if (cookieProfile == null)
    return settings;

// Base64 decoding and binary deserialization
string data = cookieProfile["SerializedData"];
byte[] bits = Convert.FromBase64String(data);
Hashtable table = null;
using(MemoryStream mem = new MemoryStream(bits)
{
    BinaryFormatter bin = new BinaryFormatter();
    table = (Hashtable) bin.Deserialize(mem);
    mem.Close();
}

// Add data to the properties
foreach (SettingsPropertyValue spv in settings) {
    // The value we provide is immediately usable
    spv.Deserialized = true;
    spv.PropertyValue = table[spv.Name];
}

return settings;
}
```

The first for-each loop ensures that all requested properties have an entry in the returned collection. This guarantees that each object is initialized through its default constructor and that any value type defaults to its neutral value—*false* for Booleans and *0* for integers, empty strings, and so on. Only the properties added in the *settings* collection will be non-null in the page *Profile* object.

The cookie contains an encoded hashtable. The values in the hashtable match the properties in the data model. Let's dig out more on the structure of the cookie.

The *SetPropertyValues* Method

The *SetPropertyValues* method is intended to save the contents of the user profile at the end of each request. The method receives the collection of properties to save along with some context information. The context information is a hashtable class named *SettingsContext*. The *SettingsContext* class is instantiated and filled by the ASP.NET infrastructure. Specifically, the settings context is managed by the profile class—*ProfileBase*—established as the parent of the dynamically generated profile class. There are two entries created—*UserName* and *IsAuthenticated*;

the former is packed with the current user name and the latter with a Boolean value denoting whether the user is authenticated or anonymous.

The following code copies all properties to persist to an intermediate hashtable. For each entry, the key is given by the name of the property. The value is just the value of the property. The hashtable is then binary serialized and encoded to Base64. The resulting string is stored as a single entry–named *SerializedData*–in the cookie.

```
public override void SetPropertyValues(SettingsContext context,
        SettingsPropertyValueCollection properties)
{
    // Get information about the user
    string username = (string)context["UserName"];
    bool authenticated = (bool)context["IsAuthenticated"];

    // If no properties, return
    if (String.IsNullOrEmpty(username) || properties.Count == 0)
        return;

    // Prepare the cookie
    string cookie = CookieName + "_" + username;
    HttpCookie cookieProfile = HttpContext.Current.Request.Cookies[cookie];
    if (cookieProfile == null)
        cookieProfile = new HttpCookie(cookie);
    cookieProfile.Expires = DateTime.Now.AddMinutes(CookieExpires);

    // Prepare the data to store
    Hashtable table = new Hashtable();
    foreach (SettingsPropertyValue pp in properties)
    {
        if (!authenticated &&
            !(bool)pp.Property.Attributes["AllowAnonymous"])
            continue;
        table.Add(pp.Name, pp.PropertyValue);
    }

    // Encode and write the hashtable to the cookie
    BinaryFormatter bin = new BinaryFormatter();
    MemoryStream mem = new MemoryStream();
    bin.Serialize(mem, table);
    string data = Convert.ToBase64String(mem.GetBuffer(), 0,
        (int) mem.Length);
    cookieProfile["SerializedData"] = data;

    // Save
    HttpContext.Current.Response.AppendCookie(cookieProfile);
}
```

Underpinnings of the Profile Service

The page's code uses the *HttpContext.Profile* property to access the user profile. The property is bound to an instance of the *ProfileCommon* class. This class doesn't exist in the .NET Framework; rather, it is created on the fly after processing the contents of the *<profile>* section in the *web.config* and, more precisely, in the *<properties>* subsection. The *ProfileCommon* class is given as many properties as there are entries in the *<properties>* section. Each property has a number of attributes only a few of which are relevant to the creation of the *ProfileCommon* class. Table 4-4 lists the attributes of the profile property as you can specify them in the *<add>* element. (See Chapter 3 for details on the configuration.)

Table 4-4   Attributes of the *<add>* Element

Attribute	Description
allowAnonymous	Allows storing values for anonymous users. *False* by default.
defaultValue	Indicates the default value of the property.
customProviderData	Contains data for a custom profile provider.
name	Name of the property.
provider	Name of the provider to use to read and write the property.
readOnly	Specifies whether the property value is read-only. *False* by default.
serializeAs	Indicates how to serialize the value of the property. Possible values are *Xml*, *Binary*, *String*, and *ProviderSpecific*.
type	The .NET Framework type of the property. It is a string object by default.

Only *readOnly* and *type* influence the structure of the property in the *ProfileCommon* class. Other attributes are used for persistence in the provider's data store. The *ProfileCommon* class derives from a .NET Framework class—*ProfileBase*. *ProfileBase* is not an abstract class, but it contains quite a bit of code. It derives from *SettingsBase*. These two base classes lay the groundwork and invoke the provider's methods—*GetPropertyValues* and *SetPropertyValues*.

The list of properties to persist is read out of the *web.config* file. For each property, a descriptor class is created—*SettingsProperty*. Members of this class map to the attributes in Table 4-4. *GetPropertyValues* and *SetPropertyValues* receive a collection of *SettingsProperty* classes and are called to load or save corresponding values from the data store. Figure 4-8 recaps the interaction between a profile provider and a sample page.

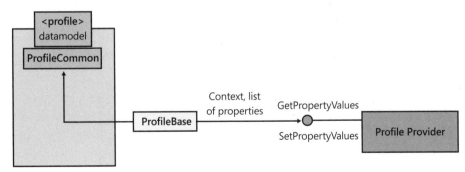

Figure 4-8   The interaction between profile classes and profile providers.

The *ProfileBase* class sports two methods—*Create* and *Save*—which are called by the page mainstream code before the page is initialized and after the page markup has been created. The call to *Create* originates a call to *GetPropertyValues*. The call to *Save* ends with a call to *SetPropertyValues*.

When *SetPropertyValues* is called, the property descriptor contains some information that might be used to implement some optimizations. In this case, the property descriptor is an instance of the *SettingsPropertyValue* class. Table 4-5 lists the properties.

Table 4-5   Properties of *SettingsPropertyValue*

Attribute	Description
Deserialized	Indicates whether the property value is deserialized. If false, ASP.NET will attempt to deserialize the value using the algorithm suggested by the *SerializeAs* attribute in the *SettingsProperty* descriptor. If the provider takes care of serialization, this attribute must always be true. This is the case with the sample provider discussed here.
IsDirty	Indicates whether the page's code modified the property value.
Name	Returns the name of the property.
Property	Returns the *SettingsProperty* descriptor of the property.
PropertyValue	The value of the property in the native, deserialized form.
SerializedValue	The value of the property in the serialized form. The format actually depends on the value of the *SerializeAs* attribute in the *SettingsProperty* descriptor.
UseDefaultValue	Indicates whether the property is set to its default value.

Typically, a profile provider won't save back properties that haven't been modified during the last request. The *IsDirty* property tells whether saving is required. Likewise, a profile provider can avoid saving default values to the store. The default value of a property is hard-coded in the *web.config* and will be automatically assigned to the property. The *UseDefaultValue* property tells you whether the default value is being currently assigned to the property.

Finally, a profile provider doesn't necessarily take care of property serialization. For better performance, the provider normally saves the serialized value (if any) as provided through the property descriptor. If no serialized value is provided, it then stores the original property value. Obviously, this approach will work only for primitive types. For the sake of simplicity, the sample provider, on the other hand, always takes native property values and serializes them to a byte array.

By looking at the value of the *Deserialized* property, the provider can figure out where to turn to get the value to store—*PropertyValue* if *true*, *SerializedValue* if *false*. Setting *Deserialized* to *true* and *PropertyValue* to *null* is the combination of values that tells the provider the property has a *null* value.

Note The profile service can be enabled or disabled in its entirety. You can't choose to have it on for certain pages and off for others. What if you want to use it only on a subset of application pages? This already happens just the way you would expect. The profile provider is invoked for reading only if the page places input calls to the *Profile* object, and it is invoked for writing if the caller page writes to the *Profile* object. No overhead results for pages not using the *Profile* object.

Scoping Data to Applications

The *ApplicationName* property that most providers share is meant to scope data being manipulated by providers to a particular application. For example, the default SQL Server–based providers use this property extensively to create records for users of a specific application. What's the advantage of this?

You could have multiple applications to share the same data store. This is unlikely to happen as long as the data store is an MDF file; but it gets real when you have your data stored in a DBMS or exposed through a Web service.

The cookie profile provider doesn't use the application name.

Putting It All Together

To be usable, a custom provider must not only be registered with the application, but it must also be selected as the default one. Furthermore, for a profile provider to work, you must define an applicationwide data model for the user's profile. The following code shows what's needed:

```
<anonymousIdentification enabled="true" />
<profile enabled="true" defaultProvider="CookieProfileProvider">
   <properties>
      <add name="BackColor" allowAnonymous="true"
         type="string" />
      <add name="ForeColor"
         type="string" allowAnonymous="true"/>
      <add name="Links" allowAnonymous="true"
         type="System.Collections.Specialized.StringCollection"
         serializeAs="Xml" />
   </properties>
   <providers>
      <clear />
      <add name="CookieProfileProvider"
         type="ProAspNet20.CS.Components.CookieProfileProvider,
             ProAspCompLib" />
   </providers>
</profile>
```

Note that properties can allow anonymous access or not allow it. If at least one property does, you must explicitly enable anonymous identification. Anonymous identification is a profile-specific feature that assigns a system-provided user name to users who access a site not authenticated. This feature has nothing to do with Forms authentication and security. It simply makes ASP.NET use a common user name to store preferences for all anonymous users. For more information on programming against the profile service, check out Chapter 5 in my other recent book, *Programming Microsoft ASP.NET 2.0: Core Reference* (Microsoft Press, 2005).

No changes are required to pages to make them support a custom provider. You just code against the *Profile* to get and set properties on the profile.

The Provider Model for Custom Services

The provider model is not limited to built-in services such as membership or session state. If your application exposes a custom service, you might well build a provider model around it. Suppose you want to provide a service to read global application settings from a number of possible locations and not just from the *<appSettings>* section of the *web.config* file.

The first step is creating a class with a bunch of static methods to expose the service to applications. Let's call this class *AppSettingsManager*. At the very minimum, this class will expose an *AppSettings* name/value collection property. The page will always call *AppSettingsManager.AppSettings* to get the application settings, regardless of how those values are retrieved. Internally, the *get* accessor of the *AppSettings* property will retrieve the registered provider, call a public method on it (say, *GetValues*), and return the values to the page.

Next, you define a provider base class and make it expose a few public methods that form the service contract—say, *GetValues*. This method will be abstract on the base class so that each derived provider must implement it.

Finally, a tailormade section in the *web.config* section is required for the new provider. The section has an ad hoc schema and requires a proper section handler component to deal with its contents. In addition to initialization attributes for the provider, the section should be able to list all registered providers and designate the current default provider.

Conclusion

The provider model is not an application feature that end users can see with their own eyes. In itself, it doesn't make an application show a richer content, run faster, or perhaps be more responsive. The provider model is an infrastructural feature that improves an application's architecture by enabling developers and architects to operate under the hood of some system components. At the same time, it enables developers to build new components that expose hooks for clients to plug in and customize behavior and settings.

ASP.NET 2.0 implements the model for a number of services, including membership, role management, user profiling, and session state. For each of these services, a base class defines the contract between the ASP.NET service and providers used for loading and saving data from different storage media. You can write a custom provider by inheriting from an existing provider class for the service you want. Whichever provider is in use, nothing changes for the top-level pages.

In this chapter, I reviewed all the built-in providers for the various services and discussed how to build a custom one.

Just the Facts

- Several built-in ASP.NET services (for example, membership, profiling, and session state) delegate certain common tasks to external and replaceable components known as providers.

- The provider model makes you capable of customizing certain parts of the ASP.NET runtime environment through special classes from which you can derive your own.

- Providers in ASP.NET 2.0 are classes that are derived from a base class and that implement a few abstract methods.

- To create your own provider for a given service, you start by defining a new class that inherits from the base class defined for that type of provider. All providers, for any supported services, derive from a common base class named *ProviderBase*.

- Providers are differentiated from one another mostly by how they do I/O. Typically, two providers for the same service will use different data stores—files, databases, Web services, or cookies, to name a few.

- Most of the ASP.NET built-in providers store their data to the *aspnetdb.mdf* database in use with SQL Server 2005 Express.

- Providers are instantiated once per application and must be written to be thread-safe because they serve all requests for pages in the application lifetime.

Chapter 5
Building Feature-Rich Pages

Not all ASP.NET pages are the same, and it's not just because each might behave differently and use a different set of controls. Certain behaviors that ASP.NET pages implement, in fact, might rely on potentially lengthy functions—for example, complex database operations and Web service calls. In all these cases, the classic and inherently synchronous processing model of ASP.NET pages is simply unfit. Asynchronous HTTP handlers have existed since ASP.NET 1.0, but only ASP.NET 2.0 provides specific support for asynchronous pages. In ASP.NET 2.0, the distinction between synchronous and asynchronous pages is easy to make and detect.

The bold arrival of declarative programming in ASP.NET 2.0 poses an additional problem—how can you set control properties with programmatic expressions? In ASP.NET 1.x, you have ASP-style code blocks and data-binding expressions. For various reasons, neither approach is appropriate for the scenarios that emerge in ASP.NET 2.0—in particular, scenarios in which data source controls are involved. So the ASP.NET team introduced dynamic expressions and an extensibility model based on expression builders. As a result, you can create custom expressions and use them to take the declarative programming model to the next level.

Finally, ASP.NET 2.0 lets you exercise some control on how the dynamically created source code of an *.aspx* resource is generated. You can filter the markup of any *.aspx* resource to ensure, for example, that only safe controls are employed. This behavior is obtained through a new breed of components—page parser filters—that contribute to making the page processing environment richer than ever.

In this chapter, I'll discuss three enhancements to the page programming model that help make complex features more accessible and, at the same time, unveil even more constituent parts of the underlying ASP.NET page machinery.

Building Asynchronous Pages

In Chapter 2, I hinted at the difference between synchronous and asynchronous HTTP handlers in serving ASP.NET requests. Let's briefly recap the rationale behind such an important point.

Each incoming ASP.NET request is assigned to a thread picked up from the ASP.NET thread pool. The request is served by an HTTP handler selected according to the type of the request and the *web.config*'s current settings. The HTTP handler is a registered object that implements the *IHttpHandler* interface—an interface that sports the *ProcessRequest* method to actually serve the request. The thread calls *ProcessRequest* on the handler and waits for it to terminate. For how long?

If the operation completes slowly or the requested resource is unresponsive, a synchronous page is blocked and is therefore the underlying thread. Using synchronous handlers for potentially long, non-CPU-bound operations puts application scalability at serious risk. In high-traffic sites, the application itself might eventually become unresponsive as the number of free pooled threads available to serve new requests approaches zero.

Asynchronous handlers are the only way out of this quagmire. In ASP.NET 1.x, asynchronous handlers require you to have a reasonably high level of familiarity with the asynchronous pattern found throughout the .NET Framework and HTTP runtime asynchronous events. It also requires a fair amount of nontrivial code for a correct implementation. In ASP.NET 2.0, you find a clear distinction between asynchronous HTTP handlers and asynchronous pages. For asynchronous pages only, a number of facilities greatly simplify the development.

Tools for Asynchronous ASP.NET Programming

The longer the thread hangs on to the request, the longer one thread is subtracted from the ASP.NET pool to serve new incoming requests. When no threads are available to serve new requests, requests are queued up. The request queue, though, is a finite resource. The size of the queue is statically determined in the configuration file through the *appRequestQueue-Limit* attribute of the *<httpRuntime>* section. The value indicates the maximum number of requests the application is allowed to queue before returning error 503—Server too busy. Note that the default queue limit is set to 100 for ASP.NET 1.x, but it can be up to 5000 in ASP.NET 2.0.

Synchronous pages engaged in lengthy tasks, and in general any form of synchronous HTTP handlers, are the ultimate scalability killer. In the best case, users experience delayed responses because the likelihood that a request gets queued is obviously higher when each thread takes a long time to complete. In the worst case, too many requests get queued up until the "Server too busy" error arrives on the scene.

> **Note**   It is interesting to point out that although the number of available pooled threads might approach zero, most of them, although engaged in an operation, are actually idle. In such situations, the CPU usage is likely to be minimal. For example, with a Web service call in process, the local thread is idle because most of the work occurs on a remote machine. So you have threads engaged while being idle, requests being queued, and low throughput for the end users—an unacceptable waste of resources.

The *IHttpAsyncHandler* Interface

In ASP.NET, HTTP handlers are synchronous by default. Asynchronous HTTP handlers must be explicitly architected and implemented by applying slightly different interfaces and programming rules. An asynchronous handler differs from a synchronous handler in one key way. It provides methods to handle the request asynchronously. Instead of using the synchronous *ProcessRequest* method, an asynchronous handler features the methods listed in Table 5-1. These methods are part of the *IHttpAsyncHandler* interface.

Table 5-1   The *IHttpAsyncHandler* Interface

Method	Description
BeginProcessRequest	Contains the code to process the request. This code should be designed to start the operation on a secondary thread and return immediately.
EndProcessRequest	Contains the code to terminate the request that was previously started.

In an asynchronous HTTP handler, the *IHttpAsyncHandler* interface replaces *IHttpHandler*. An asynchronous ASP.NET page consists of a page class that implements *IHttpAsyncHandler* instead of *IHttpHandler*. The *HttpRuntime* object, which governs the execution of ASP.NET requests, is already designed to distinguish and properly deal with asynchronous and synchronous handlers. (See Chapter 1.)

The *BeginProcessRequest* Method

The signature of the *BeginProcessRequest* method is shown here:

```
IAsyncResult BeginProcessRequest(
    HttpContext context,
    AsyncCallback cb,
    object extraData);
```

The *context* argument is a reference to the current HTTP context. Among other things, it provides access to intrinsic server objects such as *Request* and *Response*. The second parameter is the *AsyncCallback* object to invoke when the call is complete. The third parameter—*extraData*—is a generic cargo variable. It contains any additional data you want to be passed to the handler.

The *BeginProcessRequest* method is expected to create a new thread and make it execute a potentially lengthy, non-CPU-bound operation such as accessing a Web service, polling some hardware device, and running a complex database query or update. The *BeginProcessRequest* method is also expected to start the operation and return immediately.

The return value—an object implementing *IAsyncResult*—will be used to finalize the request and serve the page later once the non-CPU-bound activity is complete. What's *IAsyncResult*, anyway?

The *IAsyncResult* Interface

In brief, *IAsyncResult* is the interface that represents the status of an asynchronous operation. The interface is typically implemented by classes that work with asynchronous method calls. These classes are the preferred return type of methods that initiate an asynchronous operation. A good example is the *BeginRead* method of the *FileStream* class. *IAsyncResult*-based objects are also the input of methods that terminate asynchronous operations—such as *EndRead* on the *FileStream* class.

An object that implements the *IAsyncResult* interface stores state information for an asynchronous operation, and it usually provides a synchronization object to signal when the operation completes.

The *EndProcessRequest* Method

The *EndProcessRequest* method is called on the nonpooled thread that carries the potentially lengthy operation once the ongoing operation has completed. The method has the following prototype:

```
void EndProcessRequest(IAsyncResult result);
```

The incoming *IAsyncResult* parameter is the return value of the call to *BeginProcessRequest*.

> **Caution**   You can't access intrinsics from within *EndProcessRequest* because it will be called on manually created threads that are not initialized with a reference to the HTTP context. In other words, *HttpContext.Current* returns null.

In the end, asynchronous handlers play a key role and are a required feature in all situations in which long-running operations might be frequently invoked. In ASP.NET 1.x, there are no facilities to create asynchronous handlers more easily. In Chapter 2, I outlined the main steps for creating asynchronous handlers in ASP.NET 2.0.

ASP.NET 2.0 offers some facilities for building asynchronous pages very easily. Such facilities, though, exist only for *.aspx* pages. This means that if, for some reason, you need a custom HTTP handler to work asynchronously, you have to build it from the ground up just as in ASP.NET 1.x.

> **Note** For more information and some neat examples on asynchronous handlers in ASP.NET 1.x, take a look at *MSDN Magazine,* June 2003. The particular article I'm referring to is online at: *http://msdn.microsoft.com/msdnmag/issues/03/06/Threading.*

ASP.NET 2.0 Facilities

Two aspects characterize an asynchronous ASP.NET page: a new attribute on the *@Page* directive, and one or more tasks registered for asynchronous execution. The asynchronous task can be registered in either of two ways. You can define a *Begin/End* pair of asynchronous handlers for the *PreRenderComplete* event or create a *PageAsyncTask* object to represent an asynchronous task.

The page can wire up asynchronously to the *PreRenderComplete* event at any time in the life cycle, provided that it happens before the *PreRender* event fires. This is generally done in the *Page_Load* event, and the process consists of a call to the new method *AddOnPreRender-CompleteAsync* defined on the *Page* class.

The registration of an asynchronous task can also be done with a call to the *RegisterAsyncTask* method, passing a *PageAsyncTask* object, and it can happen at any time before the page enters its prerendering stage.

In both cases, the asynchronous task is started automatically when the page has progressed to a well-known point. Let's dig out more details.

> **Note** An ASP.NET asynchronous page is still a class that derives from *Page*. There are no special base classes to inherit for building asynchronous pages.

The *Async* Attribute

The new *Async* attribute on the *@Page* directive accepts a Boolean value to enable or disable asynchronous processing. The default value is *false.*

```
<%@ Page Async="true" ... %>
```

The *Async* attribute is merely a message for the page parser. When used, the page parser implements the *IHttpAsyncHandler* interface in the dynamically generated class for the *.aspx* resource. The *Async* attribute enables the page to register asynchronous handlers for the *PreRenderComplete* event. No additional code is executed at run time as a result of the attribute.

Let's consider a request for a *TestAsync.aspx* page marked with the *Async* directive attribute. The dynamically created class, named *ASP.TestAsync_aspx*, is declared as follows:

```
public class TestAsync_aspx : TestAsync, IHttpAsyncHandler
{
    ⋮
}
```

TestAsync is the code file class and inherits from *Page*, or a class that in turn inherits from *Page*. *IHttpAsyncHandler* is the canonical interface used for serving resources asynchronously since ASP.NET 1.0. We'll return to the built-in implementation of the *IHttpAsyncHandler* interface later.

The *AddOnPreRenderCompleteAsync* Method

The *AddOnPreRenderCompleteAsync* method adds an asynchronous event handler for the page's *PreRenderComplete* event. An asynchronous event handler consists of a *Begin/End* pair of event handler methods, as shown here:

```
AddOnPreRenderCompleteAsync (
    new BeginEventHandler(BeginTask),
    new EndEventHandler(EndTask)
);
```

The *BeginEventHandler* and *EndEventHandler* are delegates defined as follows:

```
IAsyncResult BeginEventHandler(
    object sender,
    EventArgs e,
    AsyncCallback cb,
    object state)
void EndEventHandler(
    IAsyncResult ar)
```

In the code file, you place a call to *AddOnPreRenderCompleteAsync* as soon as you can and always earlier than the *PreRender* event can occur. A good place is usually the *Page_Load* event. Next, you define the two asynchronous event handlers.

> **Note**   Placing the call to *AddOnPreRenderCompleteAsync* in *Page_Load* should be a choice made with ample forethought. It is a good choice as long as you have a page that is invoked by another page to execute the operation and display results. If the page needs to start the asynchronous operation on demand, you might want to place the call in the postback event handler. In this case, though, if the page is posted back through other controls, you risk losing the results of the asynchronous operation on refresh. We'll return to this point later. For now, let's just state that *Page_Load* is good most of the time, but you should think carefully about using it.

The *Begin* handler is responsible for starting any operation you fear can block the underlying thread for too long. The handler is expected to return an *IAsyncResult* object to describe the state of the asynchronous task. The *End* handler completes the operation and updates the page's user interface and controls. Note that you don't necessarily have to create your own object that implements the *IAsyncResult* interface. In most cases, in fact, to start lengthy operations, you just use built-in classes that already implement the asynchronous pattern and provide *IAsyncResult* ready-made objects.

> **Important**   The *Begin* and *End* event handlers are called at different times and generally on
> different pooled threads. In between the two methods calls, the lengthy operation takes place.
> From the ASP.NET runtime perspective, the *Begin* and *End* events are similar to serving distinct
> requests for the same page. It's as if an asynchronous request is split in two distinct steps—a
> *Begin* and *End* step. Each request is always served by a pooled thread. Typically, the *Begin* step
> is served by a thread picked up from the ASP.NET worker thread pool. The *End* step is served by
> a thread selected from the completion thread pool.

The page progresses up to entering the *PreRenderComplete* stage. You have a pair of asynchronous event handlers defined here. The page executes the *Begin* event, starts the lengthy operation, and is then suspended until the operation terminates. When the work has been completed, the HTTP runtime processes the request again. This time, though, the request processing begins at a later stage than usual. In particular, it begins exactly where it left off—that is, from the *PreRenderComplete* stage. The *End* event executes, and the page finally completes the rest of its life cycle, including view-state storage, markup generation, and unloading.

The Significance of *PreRenderComplete*

So an asynchronous page executes up until the *PreRenderComplete* stage is reached and then blocks while waiting for the asynchronous operation to complete. When the operation is finally accomplished, the page execution resumes from the *PreRenderComplete* stage. A good question to ask would be the following: "Why *PreRenderComplete*?" What makes *PreRender-Complete* such a special event?

By design, in ASP.NET 2.0 there's a single unwind point for asynchronous operations (also familiarly known as the *async point*). This point is located between the *PreRender* and *PreRenderComplete* events. When the page receives the *PreRender* event, the async point hasn't been reached yet. When the page receives *PreRenderComplete*, the async point has passed. As we'll see in more detail in the next section, requests for asynchronous pages are split in two parts—before and after the async point. The async point is designed to be around the *PreRenderComplete* event. That's why this event is so special and therefore why you need to understand it.

The *RegisterAsyncTask* Method

The *AddOnPreRenderCompleteAsync* method is not the only tool you have to register an asynchronous task. The *RegisterAsyncTask* method is, in most cases, an even better solution. *RegisterAsyncTask* is a void method and accepts a *PageAsyncTask* object. As the name suggests, the *PageAsyncTask* class represents a task to execute asynchronously. (We'll return to syntax and usage of *RegisterAsyncTask* later.)

Building a Sample Asynchronous Page

At this point of discussion, you're still missing a lot of details about the internal implementation of asynchronous pages. However, you know enough to arrange a quite simple but functionally significant page. Let's roll a first asynchronous test page to download and process some RSS feeds. The page markup is quite simple indeed:

```
<%@ Page Async="true" Language="C#" AutoEventWireup="true"
        CodeFile="TestAsync.aspx.cs" Inherits="TestAsync" %>
<html>
<body>
    <form id="form1" runat="server">
        <% = rssData %>
    </form>
</body>
</html>
```

The code file is shown next, and it attempts to download the RSS feed from my personal blog:

```
public partial class TestAsync : System.Web.UI.Page
{
    const string RSSFEED = "http://weblogs.asp.net/despos/rss.aspx";
    private WebRequest req;
    public string rssData;

    void Page_Load (object sender, EventArgs e)
    {
        AddOnPreRenderCompleteAsync (
            new BeginEventHandler(BeginTask),
            new EndEventHandler(EndTask));
    }

    IAsyncResult BeginTask(object sender,
                           EventArgs e, AsyncCallback cb, object state)
    {
        // Trace
        Trace.Warn("Begin async: Thread=" +
                   Thread.CurrentThread.ManagedThreadId.ToString());

        // Prepare to make a Web request for the RSS feed
        req = WebRequest.Create(RSSFEED);

        // Begin the operation and return an IAsyncResult object
        return req.BeginGetResponse(cb, state);
    }

    void EndTask(IAsyncResult ar)
    {
        // This code will be called on a pooled thread

        string text;
        using (WebResponse response = req.EndGetResponse(ar))
        {
            StreamReader reader;
            using (reader = new StreamReader(response.GetResponseStream()))
```

```
        {
            text = reader.ReadToEnd();
        }

        // Process the RSS data
        rssData = ProcessFeed(text);
    }

    // Trace
    Trace.Warn("End async: Thread=" +
            Thread.CurrentThread.ManagedThreadId.ToString());

    // The page is updated using an ASP-style code block in the ASPX
    // source that displays the contents of the rssData variable
}

string ProcessFeed(string feed)
{
    // Build the page output from the XML input
    ⋮
}
}
```

> **Important**   As you are probably aware, RSS stands for Really Simple Syndication. It's just a mechanism for publishing news feeds online. RSS is actually part of the XML vocabulary, but unlike most things XML, you won't find an RSS specification at the World Wide Web Consortium's Web site. Instead, the "official" RSS specification is published at *http://blogs.law.harvard.edu/tech/rss*.

As you can see, such an asynchronous page differs from a standard one only for the the aforementioned elements—the *Async* directive attribute and the pair of asynchronous event handlers. Figure 5-1 shows the sample page in action.

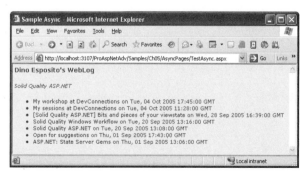

Figure 5-1   A sample asynchronous page downloading links from a blog.

It would also be interesting to take a look at the messages traced by the page. Figure 5-2 provides visual clues of it. The Begin and End stages are served by different threads and take place at different times.

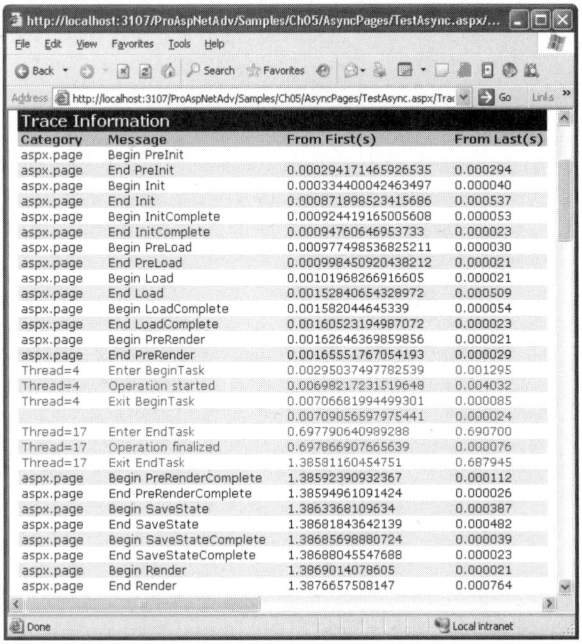

Trace Information

Category	Message	From First(s)	From Last(s)
aspx.page	Begin PreInit		
aspx.page	End PreInit	0.000294171465926535	0.000294
aspx.page	Begin Init	0.000334400042463497	0.000040
aspx.page	End Init	0.000871898523415686	0.000537
aspx.page	Begin InitComplete	0.000924419165005608	0.000053
aspx.page	End InitComplete	0.00094760646953733	0.000023
aspx.page	Begin PreLoad	0.000977498536825211	0.000030
aspx.page	End PreLoad	0.000998450920438212	0.000021
aspx.page	Begin Load	0.00101968266916605	0.000021
aspx.page	End Load	0.00152840654328972	0.000509
aspx.page	Begin LoadComplete	0.001582044645339	0.000054
aspx.page	End LoadComplete	0.00160523194987072	0.000023
aspx.page	Begin PreRender	0.00162646369859856	0.000021
aspx.page	End PreRender	0.00165551767054193	0.000029
Thread=4	Enter BeginTask	0.00295037497782539	0.001295
Thread=4	Operation started	0.00698217231519648	0.004032
Thread=4	Exit BeginTask	0.00706681994499301	0.000085
		0.00709056597975441	0.000024
Thread=17	Enter EndTask	0.697790640989288	0.690700
Thread=17	Operation finalized	0.697866907665639	0.000076
Thread=17	Exit EndTask	1.38581160454751	0.687945
aspx.page	Begin PreRenderComplete	1.38592390932367	0.000112
aspx.page	End PreRenderComplete	1.38594961091424	0.000026
aspx.page	Begin SaveState	1.3863368109634	0.000387
aspx.page	End SaveState	1.38681843642139	0.000482
aspx.page	Begin SaveStateComplete	1.38685698880724	0.000039
aspx.page	End SaveStateComplete	1.38688045547688	0.000023
aspx.page	Begin Render	1.3869014078605	0.000021
aspx.page	End Render	1.3876657508147	0.000764

Figure 5-2 The trace-request details clearly show the two steps needed to process a request asynchronously.

Note the time elapsed between the Exit BeginTask and Enter EndTask stages. It is much longer than intervals between any other two consecutive operations. It's in that interval that the lengthy operation–in this case, downloading and processing the RSS feed–took place. The interval also includes the time spent to pick up another thread from the pool to serve the second part of the original request.

Async-Compliant Operations

Which operations are good candidates to be implemented in asynchronous pages? Put another way, which required operations force, or at least strongly suggest, the adoption of an asynchronous page? Let's try to formalize the concept a bit.

Any operation can be roughly labeled in either of two ways: CPU bound or I/O bound. CPU bound indicates an operation whose completion time is mostly determined by the speed of the processor and amount of available memory. I/O bound indicates the opposite situation, in which the CPU mostly waits for other devices to terminate.

The need for asynchronous processing arises when an excessive amount of time is spent getting data in and out of the computer in relation to the time spent processing it. In such situations, the CPU is idle or underused and spends most of its time waiting for something to happen. In particular, I/O-bound operations in the context of ASP.NET applications are even more harmful because serving threads are blocked, too, and the pool of serving threads is a finite and critical resource.

You get real performance advantages if you use the asynchronous model on I/O-bound operations. In the .NET Framework implementation, therefore, when an asynchronous call is made, no threads are blocked while the operation is pending.

Typical examples of I/O-bound operations are all operations that require access to some sort of remote resource or interaction with external hardware devices. Operations on non-local databases and non-local Web service calls are the most common I/O-bound operations for which you should seriously consider building asynchronous pages.

In ASP.NET, lengthy CPU-bound operations (for example, a heavy algorithm acting on memory data) are still important to implement asynchronously to maintain the number of available pooled threads at a high enough level. In this case, though, the CPU is still loaded with some work, and the performance gain is lower than with I/O-bound operations.

Implementation of Asynchronous Pages

If your goal with this part of the chapter is simply getting hold of the main techniques to build asynchronous pages, you can skip this section and jump directly to the "Real-World Scenarios for Asynchronous Pages" section. If you have more ambitious goals, read on as we delve deep into the actual implementation of asynchronous pages in ASP.NET 2.0.

As mentioned, the *Async* attribute is simply a directive to the page parser. If specified, the final ASP.NET page will implement the *IHttpAsyncHandler* interface and will be recognized and processed by the ASP.NET runtime accordingly. If the HTTP handler for a given resource implements the *IHttpAsyncHandler* interface, the HTTP runtime uses an asynchronous processing model, as in the following pseudo-code:

```
// This pseudo-code is executed by the ProcessRequest method of
// HttpRuntime object (See Chapter 1)
if (requestHandler is IHttpAsyncHandler)
{
    // completionCallback points to the code that resumes execution
    // after the unwind point (PreRenderComplete)
    ctx.AsyncAppHandler = requestHandler;
    requestHandler.BeginProcessRequest(ctx, completionCallback, ctx);
}
else
{
    requestHandler.ProcessRequest(context1);
    FinishRequest(ctx.WorkerRequest, ctx, null);
}
```

The *Async* attribute modifies the code emitted for a page. If set to *true*, a page request will always execute asynchronously. However, if there are no asynchronous event handlers for *PreRenderComplete*, the call to *BeginProcessRequest* falls into the completion callback immediately after its end. The serving thread is the same. The bottom line is the following:

■ *Async* is not sufficient to start asynchronous processing on a page; the real trigger is that tasks are registered for asynchronous execution.

■ You should mark with *Async=true* only pages for which you really want an asynchronous behavior.

■ You can also have dual pages with nearly identical runtime costs. A *dual page* is a page that works asynchronously only in certain situations. For these pages, tasks are registered conditionally—for example, after a button is clicked. We'll return to this topic later with an example.

Let's take a look at the built-in implementation of the *IHttpAsyncHandler* interface provided by the ASP.NET runtime.

The *IHttpAsyncHandler* Interface Implementation

In Chapter 1, I explained some techniques to capture the source code of the dynamically generated class for a page you're developing. Let's apply them here. The following code comes from the source code of the class that serves the sample *TestAsync.aspx* page:

```
public virtual IAsyncResult BeginProcessRequest(
    HttpContext context, AsyncCallback cb, object data)
{
    return base.AsyncPageBeginProcessRequest(context, cb, data);
}
public virtual void EndProcessRequest(IAsyncResult ar)
{
    base.AsyncPageEndProcessRequest(ar);
}
```

The *AsyncPageBeginProcessRequest* is a protected method of the *Page* class in ASP.NET 2.0. The key thing that this method does is queue a task to execute on a pooled thread. The task is a "partial process request" that ends just before the async point—that is, before entering the *PreRender-Complete* stage. In other words, the *AsyncPageBeginProcessRequest* method orders the execution of the page request on a pooled thread and up to a certain point—the aforementioned async point.

Note   "Async point" and "unwind point" are synonymous and used interchangeably in this chapter. The async point is simply defined as the point of decision where the system establishes whether to process the page synchronously or asynchronously.

To queue the task, the *AsyncPageBeginProcessRequest* method creates a new *WaitCallback* delegate and makes it work on an internal function like the following one:

```
private void AsyncPageProcessRequestBeforeAsyncPoint(object state)
{
    this.ProcessRequest(true, false);
}
```

ProcessRequest is an overloaded version of the *Page*'s *ProcessRequest* method that is used to serve a page synchronously. It's essential now to make sense of the Boolean parameters. Let's review the method prototype. (You can easily track this by taking a look at the stack trace you get, for example, when the page execution reaches the *PreRender* stage.)

```
void ProcessRequest(
    bool includeStagesBeforeAsyncPoint,
    bool includeStagesAfterAsyncPoint)
```

Got the point? An asynchronous request is split in two parts—before and after the async point. The preceding overload of *ProcessRequest* dictates which one(s) to execute.

The *AsyncPageBeginProcessRequest* method also accomplishes another important task. After the page request has progressed to the async point, it invokes any registered asynchronous tasks. If the task was registered using asynchronous event handlers, it invokes the *Begin* handler. Otherwise, if the task was registered with *RegisterAsyncTask*, it calls into a new method of the *Page* class that is named *ExecuteRegisteredAsyncTasks*. This method starts all registered tasks, one after the next.

The *AsyncPageEndProcessRequest* method controls the process that starts the second step on the original request—that is, from the async point to the page markup. Figure 5-3 provides a graphical representation of the two steps of an asynchronous request and compares it to the execution of a synchronous request.

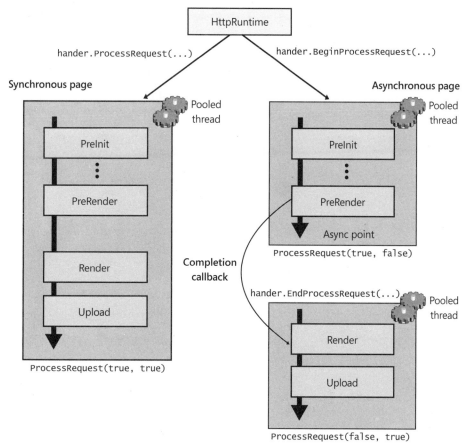

Figure 5-3 Each asynchronous request is split in two parts—before and after the async point.

It is essential to know that the two parts of an asynchronous request occur on distinct pooled threads.

The Modified Page Life Cycle

From the previous examination of the ASP.NET implementation of the *IHttpAsyncHandler* interface, we can see that a slightly different page life cycle emerges for asynchronous pages. Let's review the progression of events:

- The *HttpRuntime* object accepts the request and calls *BeginProcessRequest* on the asynchronous page handler. Execution begins on a worker thread from the ASP.NET pool. A completion callback waits for the request processing to terminate.

- The worker thread processes the page synchronously until the async point is reached. All events fire regularly up to, and including, *PreRender*.

- When the async point is reached, the asynchronous task begins and triggers an I/O-bound operation. The *Begin* handler returns an object that implements *IAsyncResult*. This object includes a completion callback function that will be called when the operation completes.

- The worker thread serving the request returns while the lengthy operation is going on. No threads are blocked at this time.

- When the operation is complete, the completion callback calls the *End* handler, executes, and finalizes the page with the results of the background operation. This operation is typically executed on a thread picked from the completion thread pool.

- The completion callback also queues a second "partial process request." But this time, the Boolean arguments are reversed and only stages after async points are executed. At this point, the execution of the original request is complete and the control returns to *HttpRuntime*.

- The HTTP runtime calls *EndProcessRequest* on the asynchronous page handler. The event handler does little work and raises an exception only if an error occurred.

- The handler phase is terminated, and the HTTP runtime finalizes the request by flushing the response and going through the usual sequence of applicationwide events up until *EndRequest*.

Figure 5-4 provides a detailed view of the steps involved in completing an asynchronous request.

Note that each framed region of code in the figure runs in its own pooled thread. Note also that two nested callbacks are involved. The outermost callback controls the termination of the whole request and is set up by the *HttpRuntime* object. The innermost callback concatenates logically the execution of the *Begin* and *End* handlers and contains user code. This callback refers to the two parts of the page life cycle—that is, before and after the async point.

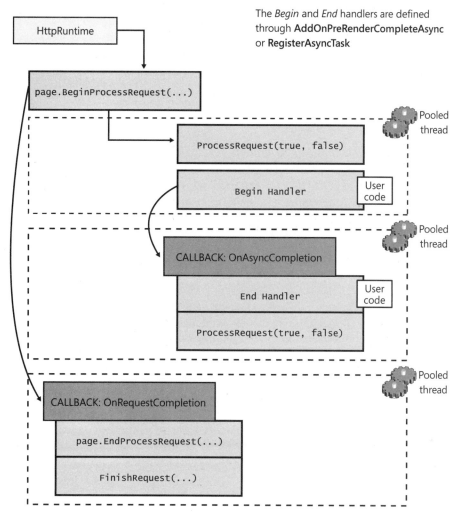

The *Begin* and *End* handlers are defined through **AddOnPreRenderCompleteAsync** or **RegisterAsyncTask**

Figure 5-4   Steps to complete an asynchronous request.

The outermost callback refers to infrastructure code and runs out of reach for page developers. The following listing examines an outermost callback in charge of intercepting the right time to finalize an asynchronous request:

```
private void OnHandlerCompletion(IAsyncResult ar)
{
    // This code runs under the control of HttpRuntime
    // when an asynchronous request completes its
    // page lifecycle. This code is an external wrapper
    // to the code you write for asynchronous pages

    HttpContext ctx = (HttpContext) ar.AsyncState;
    try {
        ctx.AsyncAppHandler.EndProcessRequest(ar);
    }
```

```
    catch (Exception ex) {
        // Recover from the exception
    }
    finally {
        // Reset the pointer to the async handler
        ctx.AsyncAppHandler = null;
    }

    // Finalize the request
    FinishRequest(ctx.WorkerRequest, ctx, ctx.Error);
}
```

The call to *EndProcessRequest* ultimately results in a call to the page internal *AsyncPageEnd-ProcessRequest* method. The *FinishRequest* method is internal to the *HttpRuntime* class. It simply flushes the page response, updates some performance counters, and terminates the request.

Asynchronous pages do not require full trust. They will also be usable from the medium level and above.

Note   Some code needs be run between the point in which the asynchronous operation is started and the async point, where the current thread is unwound. It is theoretically possible that the asynchronous operation can complete before the async point is reached. In any case, the callback is not fired until the async point is reached.

Real-World Scenarios for Asynchronous Pages

Let's examine a few common scenarios in which using asynchronous pages is appropriate and highly recommended.

Calling a Web Service

You bind a Web service to your ASP.NET application by adding a Web Service Description Language (WSDL) file to the project (a "Web Reference"). The build provider for WSDL files creates a client-based proxy class to be used to place calls to the Web service. The proxy class mirrors the Web methods of the Web service and adds a pair of *Begin/End* methods to each method to allow for asynchronous calls. Here's the core code of a typical asynchronous page calling a Web service:

```
private MyWeatherService weather;
private int temperature;
IAsyncResult BeginTask(object sender, EventArgs e,
        AsyncCallback cb, object state)
{
    weather = new MyWeatherService();
    return weather.BeginGetTemperature(cb, state);
}
```

```
void EndTask(IAsyncResult ar)
{
    temperature = weather.EndGetTemperature(ar);
}
```

The preceding *BeginTask* and *EndTask* methods form the pair of asynchronous handlers for the *PreRenderComplete* event.

> **Note** Nothing prevents you from also adding a synchronous *PreRenderComplete* event handler that fires immediately after the async point. For asynchronous pages, the synchronous *PreRenderComplete* event fires after the *End* asynchronous handler for the event.

The Web service proxy classes generated in ASP.NET 2.0 also supply an alternate way of calling into Web service methods. This second approach should be the preferred way to invoke Web service methods in ASP.NET 2.0.

For each published method, the proxy class contains an *xxxAsync* method and an *xxxCompleted* event. Your code will look like the following:

```
private MyWeatherService weather;
private int temperature;

// This code may be bound to a button in a page
protected void OnQueryWeather(object sender, EventArgs e)
{
    // Get an instance of the Web service proxy
    weather = new MyWeatherService();

    // Prepare the handler for the xxxCompleted event
    GetTempCompletedEventHandler hdlr;
    hdlr = new GetTemperatureCompletedEventHandler(GetTemperatureCompleted);
    weather.GetTemperatureCompleted += hdlr;

    // Call the Web method asynchronously
    weather.GetTemperatureAsync(...);
}

void GetTemperatureCompleted(object s, GetTemperatureCompletedEventArgs e)
{
    // Process the results you get from e.Result
}
```

Is there any difference between the two approaches? Differences are minimal as long as you're executing one single asynchronous call. If multiple and related asynchronous calls are being executed, the *MethodAsync* approach makes things go much more easily. The code in the proxy class, therefore, automatically synchronizes all queued calls and blocks page rendering until all classes have returned. To obtain that same effect with a *PreRenderComplete Begin/End* approach, be ready to handle the synchronization manually. In brief, this means piling up the synchronization handles of all *IAsyncResult* objects (the *AsyncWaitHandle* property) in an array and calling *WaitHandle.WaitAll* on the array. No worries, though, because you can use the *xxxAsync* method and have ASP.NET take care of everything else.

Another slight difference in favor of the *MethodAsync* approach is that the context for the thread running the *MethodCompleted* event is richer than the context for the thread serving the *End* event handler on *PreRenderComplete*. For example, the *MethodAsync* thread's context includes impersonation information, the HTTP context, and intrinsics such as *Server* and *Response*. In particular, the impersonation information means that you can successfully use the handler for things such as database access, which needs to rely on the thread impersonation context.

> **Note**   A call to a local Web service is served differently than calls to remote resources. As we saw in Chapter 3, ASP.NET reserves a small pool of threads for any child requests coming through the local host, including Web service calls. You control the size of the pool with *minLocalRequestFreeThreads*, an attribute in the *<httpRuntime>* configuration section. Whenever a page places a call to a local Web service, the call is not served through an ordinary pooled thread, but a thread from a secondary pool is picked up. This trick provides a better handling of cases where synchronous pages call into local Web services. Asynchronous pages, however, would enable a better performance in this case also.

Fire-and-Forget Web Service Calls

A fire-and-forget Web service call occurs when you want your page to place the call to the Web service and return without waiting for any kind of response. Logically speaking, a fire-and-forget call is when you omit the *End* handler in your asynchronous task.

Unfortunately, this is not supported in ASP.NET 2.0. If you replace the *End* event handler with null, a runtime exception is thrown complaining about exactly that. The best thing you can do is use an empty *End* handler and mark the Web service method with the *OneWay=true* attribute, and then call it using the synchronous method on the proxy class. This can be done either on a synchronous or asynchronous page, depending on the estimated latency of the network. When the Web service method is flagged with *OneWay*, the Web service immediately returns an HTTP 202 status code to the caller, which ends the communication between client and Web service.

A Web service method that intends to support the *OneWay* attribute should be void and should not support output parameters. In general, the one-way services are intended to simplify both ASP.NET and IIS processing on the server.

Running a Long Database Operation

In the .NET Framework 2.0, the .NET data provider for Microsoft SQL Server supports asynchronous commands. The support for asynchronous operations is built into the *SqlCommand* class and is limited to executing nonquery commands and getting a reader or an XML reader.

It is important to note that asynchronous commands are not implemented by creating a new thread and blocking execution on it. Among other things, ADO.NET is not thread-safe and blocking threads would be a serious performance hit. When asynchronous commands are enabled, ADO.NET opens the TCP socket to the database in overlapped mode and binds it to the I/O completion port.

Technically speaking, to improve the performance of ASP.NET pages engaged in long-running database transactions, it suffices that you employ asynchronous pages. In ASP.NET 1.x, you have to build your own asynchronous handlers; in ASP.NET 2.0, you can use the asynchronous facilities that I've been discussing in this chapter. However, if you limit yourself to employing asynchronous pages only, you execute database operations synchronously on a secondary thread. In this way, you block the thread until the operation is complete. This might not be a real issue in a Microsoft Windows desktop application; it soon becomes a source of serious trouble in case of server-side multithreaded applications such as ASP.NET applications. Sadly enough, this is also the only option you have in ASP.NET 1.x.

In ASP.NET 2.0, you can combine asynchronous pages and asynchronous commands. Let's see how.

The first step is registering the usual pair of asynchronous handlers for the *PreRenderComplete* event.

```
void Page_Load (object sender, EventArgs e)
{
    AddOnPreRenderCompleteAsync(
        new BeginEventHandler(BeginTask),
        new EndEventHandler(EndTask));
}
```

Next, when the page progression reaches the async point, the *BeginTask* handler is automatically invoked.

```
SqlConnection conn;
IAsyncResult BeginTask(object sender, EventArgs e,
        AsyncCallback cb, object state)
{
    // Trace (Utils.TraceThread is a custom utility discussed later)
    Utils.TraceThread("Enter BeginTask");

    // Prepare to execute an async command
    conn = new SqlConnection(GetConnectionString("LocalNWind"));

    // Fire the first command: get customer info
    cmd = new SqlCommand("SalesByCategory", conn);
    cmd.CommandType = CommandType.StoredProcedure;
    cmd.Parameters.Add("@CategoryName",
                        SqlDbType.NVarChar, 15).Value = "Seafood";
    cmd.Parameters.Add("@OrdYear",
                        SqlDbType.Int).Value = 1997;
```

```
    // Fire the command
    conn.Open();
    IAsyncResult ar = cmd.BeginExecuteReader(cb, state);
    Utils.TraceThread("Command started");

    // Trace
    Utils.TraceThread("Exit BeginTask");
    return ar;
}
string GetConnectionString(string cnEntry)
{
    string cs;
    cs = ConfigurationManager.ConnectionStrings[cnEntry].ConnectionString;
    return cs + ";Asynchronous Processing=true;";
}
```

Once the connection is open, you call *BeginExecuteReader* and pass it both the callback and the state object you get from the ASP.NET infrastructure. You return the *IAsyncResult* object that the ADO.NET method creates to track the asynchronous operation. When the database command ends, the following code executes:

```
void EndTask(IAsyncResult ar)
{
    using(SqlDataReader reader = cmd.EndExecuteReader(ar))
    {
        if (!reader.Read())
            return;

        // Bind to a grid
        GridView1.DataSource = reader;
        GridView1.DataBind();

        // Clean-up
        reader.Close();
        conn.Close();
    }
}
```

> **Caution**   *BeginExecuteReader* has an overload that accepts no parameters. If you use that, though, the page will never complete. This is because you don't pass a callback to the *Begin* method. Using the parameterless version of *BeginExecuteReader* is fine as long as you are not relying on callbacks to detect the completion of an asynchronous operation.

For brevity, I've omitted a few trace commands from the *EndTask* method. You see the traced messages in Figure 5-5.

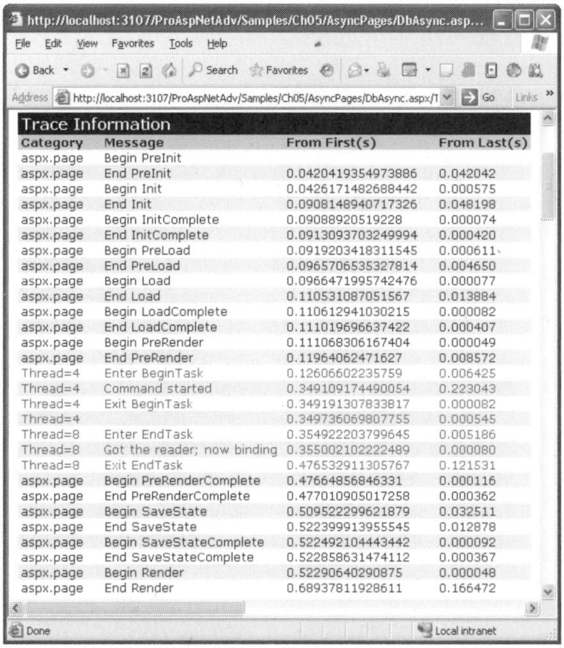

Figure 5-5   Tracing the execution of an asynchronous database operation.

I need to add a few side notes on asynchronous database operations. First and foremost, you need to explicitly enable asynchronous connections on the connection string. You can do that by adding the *Asynchronous Processing* attribute. Second, you normally don't want to use asynchronous pages for a query and data binding unless you need to run a very complex and long-stored procedure. It's more likely that you'll resort to asynchronous processing when you have a long transaction. Finally, in the *BeginTask* code snippet, I use the following utility to trace the ID of the current thread:

```
public static void TraceThread(string msg)
{
    string displayThread = "Thread=" +
        Thread.CurrentThread.ManagedThreadId.ToString();
    HttpContext.Current.Trace.Warn(displayThread, msg);
}
```

Being coded as a static method on a non-code-behind class, this utility has just one way to access the *Trace* object—using the *HttpContext.Current* object. As mentioned earlier, when you register an asynchronous operation through a *PreRenderComplete* pair of events, the context of the thread that runs the *End* handler doesn't include a reference to the *HttpContext.Current* object. This happens even though the thread used to serve the *End* handler is the same as that used to serve the *Begin* part..

> **Tip**   Tracepoints are a cool new feature of Microsoft Visual Studio 2005 that let you trace
> messages wherever you have a breakpoint. Tracepoints just save you from sprinkling lots of
> Trace messages around your code. To set a tracepoint, you first set a breakpoint and then right-
> click and select *When Hit*. You choose to print a message and also have the option of taking
> advantage of a number of predefined macros to output, say, the ID of the current thread.
> Unlike breakpoints, tracepoints don't necessarily stop the execution. You see the results in the
> Output window of Visual Studio 2005.

Starting Multiple Asynchronous Tasks

When you make a call to *AddOnPreRenderCompleteAsync*, you actually register *Begin* and *End*
delegate event handlers for an asynchronous page. The delegates involved, though, are multi-
cast delegates and can support multiple subscribers. This means that to start multiple asynchronous tasks, you can simply put multiple calls to *AddOnPreRenderCompleteAsync* in your
page and go. Here's an example:

```
void Page_Load (object sender, EventArgs e)
{
    AddOnPreRenderCompleteAsync(
        new BeginEventHandler(BeginTask1),
        new EndEventHandler(EndTask1));
    AddOnPreRenderCompleteAsync(
        new BeginEventHandler(BeginTask2),
        new EndEventHandler(EndTask2));
    AddOnPreRenderCompleteAsync(
        new BeginEventHandler(BeginTask3),
        new EndEventHandler(EndTask3));
}
```

The rendering of the page is automatically delayed until all tasks are terminated. Is there any
chink in this apparently solid armor? Let's put tracepoints through their paces and see what
happens. If you add a tracepoint at the beginning of *Page_Load* and all pairs of *Begin/End* handlers, run the page, and look at the Output window of Visual Studio 2005, you'll see a result
similar to the following script (edited to fit):

```
Page_Load(object, EventArgs), Thread: 0x230
BeginTask1(object, EventArgs, AsyncCallback, object), Thread: 0x230
EndTask1(IAsyncResult), Thread: 0x1228
BeginTask2(object, EventArgs, AsyncCallback, object), Thread: 0x1228
EndTask2(IAsyncResult), Thread: 0x230
BeginTask3object, EventArgs, AsyncCallback, object), Thread: 0x230
EndTask3(IAsyncResult), Thread: 0xD78
```

What does it mean to you? Tasks are always processed sequentially, one at a time, to guarantee
the consistency of the final page. The thread that ends the previous task triggers the next.

Serialized execution of tasks in the context of an asynchronous page is not a bad thing per se,
and it still produces a highly scalable page. Scalability is not at risk here, but throughput is. So
what if you want to gain in parallelism and make all pages run simultaneously?

Applications that don't require the sequential execution of tasks should use a single handler and launch multiple asynchronous operations from that handler. Here's the code outline:

```
void Page_Load (object sender, EventArgs e)
{
    AddOnPreRenderCompleteAsync(
        new BeginEventHandler(BeginTask),
        new EndEventHandler(EndTask));
}
IAsyncResult BeginTask(object sender, EventArgs e,
    AsyncCallback cb, object state)
{
    // Fire first task
    ⋮

    // Fire second task
    ⋮

}
void EndTask(IAsyncResult ar)
{
    // Finalize first task
    ⋮

    // Finalize second task
    ⋮

}
```

This poses another problem, though. You need an *IAsyncResult* object that signals the page when all operations are terminated. For individual operations, you can use the object you get from the *Begin* method; for multiple calls, you need a custom object. The goal of this composite *IAsyncResult* object is tracking all pending operations and signalling ASP.NET when all work is complete.

Writing a Custom *IAsyncResult* Object

In its simplest form, a custom class that implements the *IAsyncResult* interface lists a reference counter and a built-in callback that decrements it whenever called. In addition, the class must expose all the properties of the interface. Here's some code:

```
public class CompositeAsyncResult : IAsyncResult
{
    AsyncCallback _cb;
    object _state;
    AsyncCallback _completionCallBack;
    int _pendingOperations;

    // The volatile modifier is usually used for a field that is
    // accessed by multiple threads without using the lock
    // statement to serialize access
    volatile bool _allCompletedSynchronously;

    // Ctor
    public CompositeAsyncResult(AsyncCallback cb, object state, int count)
    {
```

```
            _cb = cb;
            _state = state;
            _pendingOperations = count;
            _allCompletedSynchronously = true;
            _completionCallBack = new AsyncCallback(this.CompletionCallback);
        }


        // Returns the completion callback delegate
        public AsyncCallback Callback
        {
            get { return _completionCallBack; }
        }


        // The built-in callback function invoked when a task terminates
        public void CompletionCallback(IAsyncResult ar)
        {
            // If the current call is not terminated synchronously,
            // set state properly
            if (!ar.CompletedSynchronously)
                _allCompletedSynchronously = false;

            // Decrement and check if all tasks are complete
            if (Interlocked.Decrement(ref _pendingOperations) == 0)
            {
                // Done; call the ASP.NET callback
                _cb(this);
            }
        }


        // Returns the state object passed through the ctor
        object IAsyncResult.AsyncState
        {
            get { return _state; }
        }


        // Returns the wait-handle object we're using
        WaitHandle IAsyncResult.AsyncWaitHandle
        {
            get { return null; }
        }


        // Indicates whether all tasks terminated and terminated synchronously
        bool IAsyncResult.CompletedSynchronously
        {
            get { return (_pendingOperations == 0) &&
                        _allCompletedSynchronously; }
        }


        // Indicates whether the asynchronous operation has completed
        bool IAsyncResult.IsCompleted
        {
            get { return (_pendingOperations == 0); }
        }
    }
```

The class receives the ASP.NET callback to signal the page and stores it internally. It also implements a public completion callback to be used with all asynchronous tasks. In this way, when a task completes, the completion callback is invoked and decrements the counter. When the counter is zero, it is time to signal the ASP.NET page. The number of tasks to control is set through the constructor. The following page uses a single *Begin* handler to fire two feed requests simultaneously:

```
void Page_Load (object sender, EventArgs e)
{
    AddOnPreRenderCompleteAsync (
        new BeginEventHandler(BeginTask),
        new EndEventHandler(EndTask));
}

IAsyncResult BeginTask(object sender, EventArgs e,
    AsyncCallback cb, object state)
{
    // Create the custom AsyncResult object
    CompositeAsyncResult ar = new CompositeAsyncResult(cb, state, 2);

    // Fire the first request
    req1 = WebRequest.Create(RSSFEED1);
    ar1 = req1.BeginGetResponse(ar.Callback, state);

    // Fire the second request
    req2 = WebRequest.Create(RSSFEED2);
    ar2 = req2.BeginGetResponse(ar.Callback, state);
    return ar;
}

void EndTask(IAsyncResult ar)
{
    string text;
    WebResponse response;
    StreamReader reader;

    using (response = req1.EndGetResponse(ar1))
    {
        using (reader = new StreamReader(response.GetResponseStream())) {
            text = reader.ReadToEnd();
        }
        rssData += ProcessFeed(text);
    }

    using (response = req2.EndGetResponse(ar2))
    {
        using (reader = new StreamReader(response.GetResponseStream())) {
            text = reader.ReadToEnd();
        }
        rssData += ProcessFeed(text);
    }
}
```

There's a shorter path to execute multiple tasks simultaneously and even within a richer execution context—using the *RegisterAsyncTask* method. We'll return to this topic in just a moment.

Using Custom "Begin" Methods

In all the examples considered, the *IAsyncResult* object to return or to compose in a wrapper object is always generated by a method of a .NET Framework class such as *BeginGetResponse* on the *WebRequest* class. What if you need to execute asynchronously a method that doesn't support the asynchronous pattern? You build a generic asynchronous wrapper through the *BeginInvoke* and *EndInvoke* pair.

```
public partial class MultiTaskAsync : System.Web.UI.Page
{
    protected delegate void AsyncTaskDelegate();
    private AsyncTaskDelegate _func;

    void Page_Load(object sender, EventArgs e)
    {
        AddOnPreRenderCompleteAsync(
            new BeginEventHandler(BeginTask),
            new EndEventHandler(EndTask));
    }

    IAsyncResult BeginTask(object sender, EventArgs e,
                           AsyncCallback cb, object state)
    {
        _func = new AsyncTaskDelegate(DoTheAsyncTask);
        IAsyncResult result = _func.BeginInvoke(cb, state);
        return result;
    }

    public void DoTheAsyncTask()
    {
        // Perform any task
        // Your code goes here
        // For example: Thread.Sleep(10000);
    }
    void EndTask(IAsyncResult ar)
    {
        _func.EndInvoke(ar);
    }
}
```

Caution   If you take a deeper look at the programmer interface of the *Page* class, you might find that a writable Boolean property named *AsyncMode* exists. The property is protected, but it can be overridden in a code-behind class. The property is not intended to be used directly from user's code, and it's set by the parser based on the value of the *Async* attribute in the *@Page* directive. The current value of the property indicates whether the page is working asynchronously. This information is publicly exposed through the *IsAsync* read-only property. For a page to be asynchronous, the *IHttpAsyncHandler* interfaces are required; otherwise, the HTTP runtime will call the page synchronously no matter what. As you know, the implementation of an interface is not something that can be switched on and off programmatically.

Programmatically setting the *AsyncMode* property influences the value returned by *IsAsync*, but it doesn't change the behavior of the page, which is dependent only on the *Async* page attribute.

The *RegisterAsyncTask* Method

RegisterAsyncTask is an alternative way to execute tasks asynchronously in an ASP.NET page. *RegisterAsyncTask* is an API that is, to some extent, independent from asynchronous pages. In fact, it also works when the *Async* attribute of the *@Page* directive is set to *false*. Combined with asynchronous pages, though, it forms an extremely powerful programming model for lengthy operations.

You can use *RegisterAsyncTask* to register one or more asynchronous tasks. Tasks start when the page reaches the async point—that is, immediately after the *PreRender* event.

Setting Up an Asynchronous Task

The following code shows how to rework the sample page that reads some RSS feed and make it use the *RegisterAsyncTask* method:

```
void Page_Load (object sender, EventArgs e)
{
    PageAsyncTask task = new PageAsyncTask(
        new BeginEventHandler(BeginTask),
        new EndEventHandler(EndTask),
        null,
        null);

    RegisterAsyncTask(task);
}
```

To call *RegisterAsyncTask*, you need to first create an instance of the *PageAsyncTask* class. The constructor accepts up to five parameters, as shown in the following code:

```
public PageAsyncTask(
    BeginEventHandler beginHandler,
    EndEventHandler endHandler,
    EndEventHandler timeoutHandler,
    object state,
    bool executeInParallel)
```

The *beginHandler* and *endHandler* parameters have the same prototype as the corresponding handlers we use for the *AddOnPreRenderCompleteAsync* method. Compared to the *AddOnPreRenderCompleteAsync* method, *PageAsyncTask* lets you specify a timeout function and an optional flag to enable multiple registered tasks to execute in parallel.

The timeout delegate indicates the method that will get called if the task is not completed within the asynchronous timeout interval. By default, an asynchronous task times out if not completed within 45 seconds. You can indicate a different timeout in either the configuration file or the *@Page* directive. Here's what you need if you opt for the *web.config* file:

```
<system.web>
    <pages asyncTimeout="30" />
</system.web>
```

The *@Page* directive contains an integer *AsyncTimeout* attribute that you set to the desired number of seconds.

Just as with the *AddOnPreRenderCompleteAsync* method, you can pass some state to the delegates performing the task. The *state* parameter can be any object. Here's how to use the *state* parameter to reuse the same code seen earlier to read from two blogs:

```
void Page_Load (object sender, EventArgs e)
{
    PageAsyncTask task1 = new PageAsyncTask(
        new BeginEventHandler(BeginTask),
        new EndEventHandler(EndTask),
        null,
        RSSFEED1,
        true);
    PageAsyncTask task2 = new PageAsyncTask(
        new BeginEventHandler(BeginTask),
        new EndEventHandler(EndTask),
        null,
        RSSFEED2,
        true);

    RegisterAsyncTask(task1);
    RegisterAsyncTask(task2);
}
public IAsyncResult BeginTask(object sender, EventArgs e,
        AsyncCallback cb, object state)
{
    // Prepare to make a Web request
    string blog = (string) state;
    req = WebRequest.Create(blog);

    // Begins the operation
    IAsyncResult obj = req.BeginGetResponse(cb, state);
    return obj;
}
```

A cleaner approach to define tasks that execute asynchronously and perhaps in parallel entails the use of a wrapper class. Let's create an *RssFeedAsyncReader* class to contain the logic to read an RSS feed asynchronously:

```
public class RssFeedAsyncReader
{
    private WebRequest _req;
    private string _rssData;
    private string _blogUrl;

    public RssFeedAsyncReader(string blog)
    {
        _blogUrl = blog;
    }
```

```
    public IAsyncResult BeginRead(object sender, EventArgs e,
        AsyncCallback cb, object state)
    {
        // Prepare to make a Web request
        _req = WebRequest.Create(_blogUrl);

        // Begins the operation
        IAsyncResult obj = _req.BeginGetResponse(cb, state);
        return obj;
    }

    public void EndRead(IAsyncResult ar)
    {
        string text;
        using (WebResponse response = _req.EndGetResponse(ar))
        {
            StreamReader reader;
            using (reader = new StreamReader(response.GetResponseStream()))
            {
                text = reader.ReadToEnd();
            }

            // Process the RSS data
            _rssData = ProcessFeed(text);
        }
    }

    private string ProcessFeed(string feed)
    {
        ⋮
    }

    public string GetRssData()
    {
        return _rssData;
    }
}
```

The class contains two public methods to begin and end asynchronous operations. A third public method can be added to handle timeout exceptions. Now you can register as many of these tasks as you like and have them run in parallel, too. The following sample code (*RssAsync.aspx*) shows how to access my English and Italian blogs simultaneously:

```
public partial class RssAsync : System.Web.UI.Page
{
    const string RSSFEED1 = "http://weblogs.asp.net/despos/rss.aspx";
    const string RSSFEED2 = "http://blogs.ugidotnet.org/dinoes/rss.aspx";
    RssFeedAsyncReader rss1, rss2;
    public string rssData;

    void Page_Load (object sender, EventArgs e)
    {
        // Register a handler for PreRenderComplete
        PreRenderComplete += new EventHandler(RssAsync_PreRenderComplete);
```

```
// Create instances of the blog async reader class
rss1 = new RssFeedAsyncReader(RSSFEED1);
rss2 = new RssFeedAsyncReader(RSSFEED2);

// Create tasks
PageAsyncTask task1 = new PageAsyncTask(
    new BeginEventHandler(rss1.BeginRead),
    new EndEventHandler(rss1.EndRead),
    null,
    null,
    true);
PageAsyncTask task2 = new PageAsyncTask(
    new BeginEventHandler(rss2.BeginRead),
    new EndEventHandler(rss2.EndRead),
    null,
    null,
    true);

// Register tasks
RegisterAsyncTask(task1);
RegisterAsyncTask(task2);
}

void RssAsync_PreRenderComplete(object sender, EventArgs e)
{
    // Update the user interface with the feed
    rssData = rss1.GetRssData() + rss2.GetRssData();
}
}
```

Admittedly, this code is longer and richer. But can you honestly say it is obscure or quirky? To me, it looks much more professional. Figure 5-6 shows the output of the page.

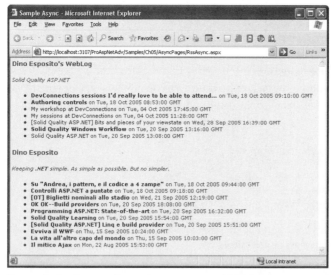

Figure 5-6   An asynchronous page to read RSS feed.

Explicit Execution of Asynchronous Tasks

The execution of all tasks registered with the *RegisterAsyncTask* method begins with a call to a method on the *Page* class—*ExecuteRegisteredAsyncTasks*. This method is automatically invoked by the Page code just before the async point is reached, as the following pseudo-code demonstrates:

```
// This pseudo-code runs inside the ProcessRequest
// method of the Page class

// Fires the PreRender event for the page and all of its child controls
this.PreRenderRecursiveInternal();

// Execute registered tasks
if (this._asyncInfo == null)
    this.ExecuteRegisteredAsyncTasks();

// This is the async point: stop if the second part
// of the request is not allowed
if (!includeStagesAfterAsyncPoint)
    return;

// This code fires when all async tasks are terminated
// Fires the PreRenderComplete event for the page and
// proceeds with the remainder of the page lifecycle
this.PerformPreRenderComplete();
⋮
```

The *ExecuteRegisteredAsyncTasks* method is declared public and can be called programmatically from any location you want to start tasks under your total control.

RegisterAsyncTask in Synchronous Pages

If you call *AddOnPreRenderCompleteAsync* on a page devoid of the *Async* attribute, the page throws an exception. If you do the same with *RegisterAsyncTask*, the page works just fine but is not optimal from a scalability point of view. Let's put tracepoints at the beginning of sensitive functions in the *RssAsync.aspx* page discussed earlier. In addition, let's set the *Async* attribute of the *@Page* directive to *false*. Here's what we get:

```
Page_Load(object, EventArgs), Thread: 0x230
BeginRead(object, EventArgs, AsyncCallback, object), Thread: 0x230
BeginRead(object, EventArgs, AsyncCallback, object), Thread: 0x230
EndRead(IAsyncResult), Thread: 0x1718
EndRead(IAsyncResult), Thread: 0x1228
RssAsync_PreRenderComplete(object, EventArgs), Thread: 0x230
```

As you can see, the thread 0x230 starts the two asynchronous tasks but remains blocked until the operations complete to finalize the page request. In an asynchronous page, the thread 0x230 would return to the pool immediately after the second call to *BeginRead* and another thread would take care of finalizing the request.

Choosing the Right Approach

When should you use *AddOnPreRenderCompleteAsync*, and when is *RegisterAsyncTask* a better option? Functionally speaking, the two approaches are nearly identical. In both cases, the execution of the request is split in two parts—before and after the async point. So where's the difference?

The first difference is logical. *RegisterAsyncTask* is an API designed to run tasks asynchronously from within a page—not just from asynchronous pages. *AddOnPreRenderCompleteAsync* is an API specifically designed for asynchronous pages. This said, a couple of further differences exist.

One is that *RegisterAsyncTask* executes the *End* handler on a thread with a richer context than *AddOnPreRenderCompleteAsync*. The thread context includes impersonation and HTTP context information that is missing in the thread serving the *End* handler of a classic asynchronous page. In addition, *RegisterAsyncTask* allows you to set a timeout to ensure that any task doesn't run for more than a given number of seconds.

The other difference is that *RegisterAsyncTask* makes the implementation of multiple calls to remote sources significantly easier. You can have parallel execution by simply setting a Boolean flag, and you don't need to create and manage your own *IAsyncResult* object.

The bottom line is that you can use either approach for a single task, but you should opt for *RegisterAsyncTask* when you have multiple tasks to execute simultaneously.

Building Custom Expressions

There are various flavors of expressions in ASP.NET, each serving a particular scenario and providing a specific missing capability. What's an expression, anyway? An ASP.NET expression is any executable piece of code you can write in the *.aspx* file wrapped by <% ... %> tags.

There are two different types of expressions in ASP.NET 1.x—code blocks similar to code blocks in classic ASP, and data-bound expressions. A third type of dynamic expression has been added in ASP.NET 2.0 to better address the needs of a fully declarative programming model.

ASP-Style Code Blocks

In classic ASP, code blocks are fragments of executable code delimitated by <% ... %> tags. Within those tags, you can put virtually everything that the ASP runtime engine can understand and parse, including variable assignments, loop statements, function declarations, and, of course, function calls. The internal architecture of classic ASP pages allows for this programming model that appears unstructured, loose, not very rigorous, and inelegant to software purists and to, well, not just them.

How Code Blocks Work in Classic ASP

The ASP runtime engine builds the page incrementally as it parses the contents of the source file. The final output is obtained by composing any literal expressions found along the way with the output of code blocks. A scripting environment is up and running all the time to process the contents of <% ... %> blocks statefully with respect to the current request.

> **Note**   In classic ASP, the surrounding scripting engine is the key to understanding why a function declared in one block can safely be invoked later in another block. This happens because the function body has been published and remains visible in the scripting context for the request lifetime. The lack of a similar engine in ASP.NET is the primary factor that resulted in the scaling down of features supported by code blocks in ASP.NET pages.

In classic ASP, there are two types of code blocks—inline code and inline expressions. Inline expressions are merely shortcuts for *Response.Write* and take the following well-known form:

```
<% x = 1 %>
<% = x %>
```

The first expression is an example of inline code; the second is an inline expression that outputs the contents of the *x* variable set earlier.

How Code Blocks Work in ASP.NET

To the extent that it was made possible by a brand new runtime environment, code blocks survived during the transition from classic ASP to ASP.NET. They lost some features along the way, but they are still a fully supported ASP.NET feature. The advent of ASP.NET 2.0 doesn't change anything in this regard.

In ASP.NET, code blocks can't any longer be used to declare functions. At the same time, any variables declared in code blocks are no longer given a global scope, whereas inline statements and expressions work as in ASP.

In ASP.NET, code blocks are processed at rendering time, not when the page loads up. This probably doesn't make a huge difference for old code, but it's always the sign of an underlying brand new runtime model. Let's consider the following sample page:

```
<form id="Form1" runat="server">
  <% for (int i=0; i<8; i++) %>
  <% { %>
      <font size="<%=i %>">
      I <b style="font-family:Webdings;color:Red">Y</b>
      this book!
      </font><br>
  <% } %>
</form>
```

To form an idea about the preceding code, take a look at Figure 5-7.

Figure 5-7 An ASP.NET page built using ASP-style code blocks.

Applying what we learned in Chapter 1 about the dynamically generated code for each served page, let's dig out the source code of this page after parsing.

The dynamically generated code for the page associates any code blocks with a server-side parent element. In the previous example, the parent is the *Form1* control. If there's no server-side form tag, it might be the *<head>* if that tag is marked with the *runat* attribute. If the page has no tag with the *runat=server* attribute, the code block is associated with the page. In any case, the code block is associated with a server-side object that inherits from *Control*. (The *Page* class does have the *Control* class in its list of ancestors.) Why *Control*? Because the *Control* class defines a little-used method named *SetRenderMethodDelegate*.

Any server controls that embed a code block have a rendering delegate added through a call to the *SetRenderMethodDelegate* method. Here's the code used to render the form. (The code is an edited version of the dynamic page code captured as mentioned in Chapter 1.)

```
HtmlForm BuildControlForm1()
{
    HtmlForm ctrl = new HtmlForm();
    form1 = ctrl;
    ctrl.ID = "Form1";

    // Add other child server controls to the page's tree
    :

    // Add the render delegate to handle code blocks
    ctrl.SetRenderMethodDelegate(new RenderMethod(RenderForm1));
    return ctrl;
}
```

```
void RenderForm1(HtmlTextWriter w, Control parameterContainer)
{
    for (int i=1; i<8; i++)
    {
        w.Write("<font size=\"");
        w.Write(i);
        w.Write("\">" +  I
                "<b style=\"font-family:Webdings;color:Red\">Y</b> " +
                "this book! </font><br>");
    }
}
```

The contents of all code blocks are incorporated in the form rendering procedure and inter-spersed with calls to the *RenderControl* method of declared server controls and literals. The output of the code block is used to create an ad hoc rendering function that completes the page.

Limitations of Code Blocks in ASP.NET

In ASP.NET, you can't use code blocks to dynamically set control properties. The following won't work:

```
<asp:Button runat=server id="Button1" Text=<% =GetText() %> />
```

If you wrap the code block in quotes, the text is output verbatim. If you don't use quotes, as in the preceding code, you get a compile error—server tags cannot contain <% ... %> con-structs. The model based on *SetRenderMethodDelegate* works for building the body of the page at rendering time, not for setting object properties at parse time.

In ASP, the building model of the page made it possible because all text was accumulated into a memory buffer and two successive writings could, in the end, compose an attribute assign-ment. The object model of ASP.NET prohibits this approach.

The original question of this section remains unanswered: how can you assign a control property declaratively? Enter data-binding expressions.

Data-Binding Expressions

To let developers assign values to control attributes in a declarative manner, the ASP.NET team introduced a new type of dynamic expression in version 1.x named *data-binding expressions*. Consider the following fragment:

```
<form id="form1" runat="server">
    <h2>Today is
        <asp:Label ID="Today" runat="server" Text="<%# DateTime.Now %>" />
    </h2>
</form>
```

The *Text* property of the *Label* control takes what results from the evaluation of the expression embedded in the code block tags. In terms of syntax, a data-binding expression is nearly identical to a code block, except that it is prefixed by a # symbol. (For brevity, I'll also refer to data-binding expressions as *#-expressions*.)

How Data-Binding Expressions Work

The simple insertion of a # symbol changes the perspective of the markup completely. The ASP.NET page parser recognizes the symbol and automatically creates an event handler for the *DataBinding* event of the control instance. Here's the code (edited for clarity) generated by the ASP.NET runtime:

```
Label BuildControlToday()
{
    Label ctrl = new Label();
    this.Today = ctrl;
    ctrl.ApplyStyleSheetSkin(this);
    ctrl.ID = "Today";
    ctrl.DataBinding += new EventHandler(DataBindingToday);
    return ctrl;
}
void DataBindingToday(object sender, EventArgs e)
{
    Label target = (Label) sender;
    Control container = (Control) target.BindingContainer;
    target.Text = Convert.ToString(DateTime.Now,
                                  CultureInfo.CurrentCulture);
}
```

The body of the *DataBindingToday* method—the handler of the *DataBinding* event—incorporates the evaluation of the expression and assigns it to the *Text* property.

The expression is copied verbatim. This means that any error or wrong syntax elements will be caught at compile time. If the code is badly written, proper exceptions will be thrown at run time. You can use any code snippet in a data-binding expression that returns a valid value (that is, any that is type compatible) for the property being bound. You can even use the return value of methods defined on the *Page* class or external components.

Important   Data-binding expressions are evaluated only after a call to *DataBind* is made. The *DataBind* method can be called on the page or specific control. If no call is made, no data-bound expressions are ever evaluated.

Limitations of Data-Binding Expressions

In ASP.NET 2.0, a new breed of controls make their debut—data source controls. Data source controls push an alternate model for data binding. When attached to a data-bound control, data source controls intelligently serve the needs of the control without firing events to the page to ask for data. Data source controls enable a scenario in which all settings are defined at design-time, including commands to execute, connection strings, data types to use, and so on.

> **More Info**   For more information on data source controls, refer to my book *Programming Microsoft ASP.NET 2.0: Core Reference* (Microsoft Press, 2005).

As champions of declarative programming, data source controls present the possibility of binding data to properties without an explicit call to *DataBind*. Data source controls *are not* data-bound controls, even though they work closely with data-bound controls—especially the new generation of data-bound controls such as *GridView* and *DetailsView*. Considering that data source controls are not data-bound controls, should we expect the *DataBind* event to be fired on data source controls to set properties declaratively?

The quick answer is that we should not expect *DataBind* to be called when data source controls bind their data because it breaks the declarative model. If *DataBind* were to be called, the control would not have its data declared at all—its data would be provided at run time just as with traditional data-bound controls. So data source controls are different beasts when it comes to rendering bound data. And because of this, #-expressions simply aren't an option when using data source controls.

However, the real problem with #-expressions and data source controls is not the additional call to *DataBind*. In some situations, even the call to *DataBind* is not sufficient to make data source controls work as expected. Let's see why.

Why Are #-Expressions Unfit to Serve Data Source Controls?

Because data-binding expressions attach a *DataBinding* event handler to the control, a call to *DataBind* is required to trigger the evaluation of bound expressions. Fine, but why not use data-binding expressions to set properties on data source controls? Let's try the following code:

```
<asp:SqlDataSource id="MySource" runat="server"
    ConnectionString=<% #ConfigurationManager.ConnectionStrings[...] %>
    ⋮
/>
<asp:GridView id="grid" runat="server" datasourceid="MySource" />
```

You place a call to *DataBind* in *Page_Load*, and the code just works. When *DataBind* is called, the *ConnectionString* property of the *SqlDataSource* control is set. Hence, when the *GridView* needs to fetch data, the data source control can promptly serve it.

Now invert the position of the two controls in the markup and make the *GridView* precede *SqlDataSource*. When *DataBind* is called, all controls are bound to their data in the order they appear in the page. When called to bind its data, the *GridView* finds out that it has to ask the *SqlDataSource* control to supply data. Unfortunately, at this time the connection string property of the *SqlDataSource* control is not set because the data-binding process for the *SqlDataSource* hasn't started yet. So you get an exception.

To fully support data source controls, therefore, a new type of expression is required. ASP.NET 2.0 calls them *dynamic expressions*. For brevity, I'll be referring to them as *$-expressions*.

> **Note** Expressions are not the only way to set properties on data source controls. You can use hard-coded strings or, better yet, set properties programmatically in the *Page_Load* event. A new breed of expressions is required to do some good declarative programming not just with data source controls but also with any other server control in ASP.NET pages.

Dynamic Expressions in ASP.NET 2.0

Dynamic expressions serve the purpose of setting control properties at parse time without relying on the data-binding mechanism. To get the gist of dynamic expressions, think back to the code generated when a #-expression is used. If a #-expression is used, the property assignment is made inside the *DataBinding* event handler. If you use a $-expression, the assignment is made in the method that builds the control.

All dynamic expressions are instances of a common class—*ExpressionBuilder*. The class defines an engine that parses the expression and returns a CodeDOM tree to represent the expression. A few predefined expression builders exist, as listed in Table 5-2.

Table 5-2   Custom Expression Builders

Syntax	Description
AppSettings:[Attribute]	Returns the value of the specified setting from the *<appSettings>* section of the configuration file
ConnectionStrings:[Entry].[Attribute]	Returns the value of the specified attribute of the given entry in the *<connectionStrings>* section of the configuration file
Resources:[ResourceFile], [ResourceName]	Returns the value of the specified global resource

To declaratively bind a control property to the value of the expression, you follow the schema below:

```
<%$ Prefix:Expression %>
```

The builder defines both the prefix and the exact syntax required for the expression. What follows the colon (:) is typically (but not necessarily) a comma-separated list of parameters.

The *$ConnectionStrings* Builder

The *$ConnectionStrings* builder retrieves a connection string entry from the configuration file. The prefix is *ConnectionStrings*; the syntax is a dot-separated list of two attributes—the name of the entry in *<connectionStrings>* section to process and the name of the attribute to read. Here's an example:

```
<%$ ConnectionStrings:LocalNWind.ConnectionString %>
```

The expression accesses the LocanNWind entry in the *<connectionStrings>* section and returns the value of the *ConnectionString* attribute. The part following the dot (.) is optional. If nothing is specified, it defaults to *ConnectionString*. The preceding code can be rewritten in the more compact format that follows:

```
<%$ ConnectionStrings:LocalNWind %>
```

Only two attributes are supported—*ConnectionString* and *ProviderName*. The following code shows a real-world usage of the expression to initialize a data source control:

```
<asp:SqlDataSource runat="server" id="MySource"
    ConnectionString="<%$ ConnectionStrings:LocalNWind %>"
    ProviderName="<%$ ConnectionStrings:LocalNWind.ProviderName %>"
    :
/>
```

The *$AppSettings* Builder

The *$AppSettings* builder provides a declarative way to access the contents of the *<appSettings>* section in the configuration file. The prefix is *AppSettings*; the syntax consists of a simple string. The parameter of the builder indicates the name of the entry from which you want to read the value. Consider the following *web.config* section:

```
<appSettings>
    <add key="AppVersionNumber" value="8.2.2001" />
</appSettings>
```

The expression *<% $AppSettings:AppVersionNumber %>* returns the contents of the *value* attribute.

```
<asp:Label runat="server" id="Label1"
    Text="<%$ AppSettings:AppVersionNumber %>"
    :
/>
```

The *$Resources* Builder

The *$Resources* builder retrieves global resources defined in the specified *.resx* file. The prefix is *Resources*; the syntax is a comma-separated string in which the first element indicates the name (without path and extension) of the *.resx* file to access. The second element specifies the name of the resource to retrieve. Both elements are required.

```
<asp:Label runat="server" id="Label1"
    Text="<%$ Resources:MyResources, AppTitle %>"
    :
/>
```

The blanks in the expressions are generally optional and don't influence the parser. (This mostly depends on the parser's implementation, so pay attention to this when using custom builders.)

The preceding code snippet retrieves the value of a resource named *AppTitle* from the *MyResources.resx* file. Be aware that the *$Resources* expression builder doesn't retrieve resources local to a page; it works only with *.resx* files located in the *App_GlobalResources* folder.

> **Note** As a page developer, you must pay due attention to using expressions with control properties of compatible types. If you bind a connection string where, say, a color is expected, you might cause an exception or run into a page anomaly.

Design-Time Capabilities

$-expressions can also be defined through the Visual Studio 2005 designer. You select the control of choice and click on the *Expressions* entry in the property grid. Once there, you select the property you want to set and the expression you need. Figure 5-8 shows the dialog box. Similar capabilities can also be built into custom expression builders, but it's not required. Check with the particular expression builder regarding its particular designer capabilities.

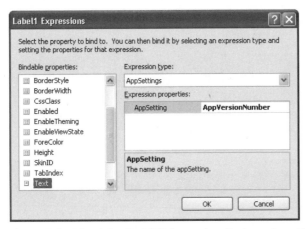

Figure 5-8 Visual Studio 2005 Expression Designer in action.

No-Compile Pages and Expressions

In ASP.NET 2.0, no-compile pages are special *.aspx* pages flagged with the *CompilationMode* attribute on the *@Page* directive. When *CompilationMode* is set to *Never*, the page is not compiled by ASP.NET, but it is still served correctly and quickly. (See Chapter 1 for more information on no-compile pages.)

A no-compile page contains no executable code—that is, no event handlers and no code file. These pages can still contain server controls and dynamic expressions. $-expressions can be used to add some simple customization to a no-compile page.

Writing a Custom Expression Builder

To create a custom expression, you have two tasks to perform. First, create a new class that inherits from *ExpressionBuilder* and register it in the *<compilation>* section of the configuration file. As an example, let's see how to create an expression that inserts in the page values from the *Profile* object.

Part of the HTTP context, the *Profile* object is an instance of a dynamically created class. The profile class inherits from the *ProfileBase* class and is enriched with as many properties as there are entries in the *<profile>* section of the configuration file. In other words, the *Profile* object is a user-defined object that is associated with each user—registered or anonymous. In Chapter 4, we discussed how to create a provider for this data. For more information on the user profiling API, refer to Chapter 5 of *Programming Microsoft ASP.NET 2.0: Core Reference* (Microsoft Press, 2005).

The *ProfileExpressionBuilder* Class

When inheriting from *ExpressionBuilder*, you have three methods to override and one property. For details, take a look at Table 5-3.

Table 5-3   Members of the *ExpressionBuilder* Class

Member	Description
EvaluateExpression	Returns an object that represents the evaluated expression. The method is called only if the expression is used from within no-compile pages and *SupportsEvaluate* returns *true*. The method is not abstract but returns *null* in the base class.
GetCodeExpression	Returns a CodeDOM expression object. The object is used to generate source code in the page class that returns the evaluated expression. The method is abstract and must be overridden.
ParseExpression	Returns an object that represents the parsed expression. The method is expected to parse the argument of the expression and return any object that makes that data usable by other methods in the class. The method is not abstract but returns *null* in the base class.
SupportsEvaluate	Boolean property, indicates whether an expression can be evaluated in a page that uses the no-compile feature. Set to *false* by default.

The *GetCodeExpression* method is the heart of the builder. It receives the object returned by *ParseExpression* with any useful information obtained from the string following the colon (:) symbol in the expression. *GetCodeExpression* is expected to return a CodeDOM object that describes the code that must be generated in lieu of the expression. For the *Profile* builder, we assume the following syntax:

```
<%$ Profile:PropertyName %>
```

The prefix is *Profile*, and *PropertyName* is intended to be the name of a property defined on the profile object. Let's start building the class.

```
[ExpressionPrefix("Profile")]
public class ProfileExpressionBuilder : ExpressionBuilder
{
    // Parse the expression's arguments
    public override object ParseExpression(string expression,
            Type propertyType, ExpressionBuilderContext context)
    {
        return expression;
    }
    ⋮
}
```

The *[ExpressionPrefix]* attribute sets the prefix of the builder. The prefix can also be set in the *web.config* file when you register the builder. Using the attribute is optional. The *ParseExpression* method receives the expression's arguments through the *expression* parameter. Arguments come in the form of a string, and the method is expected to parse the string and extract any useful information. In this particular case, the expression's argument is already the name of a profile property; so no parsing is necessary and the method just returns the string. In other situations, you might want to parse the string and fill a custom object (for example, an array) with ready-to-use information. The object returned by *ParseExpression* becomes the input of *GetCodeExpression*.

```
public override CodeExpression GetCodeExpression(
    BoundPropertyEntry entry,
    object parsedData,
    ExpressionBuilderContext context)
{
    // Grab the name of the profile property.
    // (I'm assuming parsedData is a string. You should check it.)
    string property = (string) parsedData;

    // Must generate code for the right-side part of an assignment.
    // We make it call into a static method of this class.

    // Define the CodeDOM object that represents the
    // parameter of the static method
    CodePrimitiveExpression prim = new CodePrimitiveExpression(property);
    CodeExpression[] args = new CodeExpression[1] { prim };

    // Define the CodeDOM object to represent the method invocation
    CodeTypeReferenceExpression refType;
    refType = new CodeTypeReferenceExpression(base.GetType());
    return new CodeMethodInvokeExpression(refType, "GetProperty", args);
}
```

GetCodeExpression gets the name of the profile property from the *parsedData* argument—just the object returned by *ParseExpression*. The method is expected to generate the CodeDOM representation of the right-side part of an assignment. In fact, the final assignment will be of the form

```
control.PropertyName = <result of the expression>;
```

A smart technique that built-in builders use extensively is making the CodeDOM tree reference a static method on the expression class. In this way, the burden of CodeDOM is minimal—just set up a method call—and most of the code is written in a programming language. The code just shown returns a CodeDOM tree that places a call to a static method named *GetProperty*. This method accepts a single parameter that is the name of the property. *GetProperty* is a static method you need to add to the *ProfileExpressionBuilder* class. This method is ultimately responsible for accessing data in the *Profile* object.

```
public static object GetProperty(string propertyName)
{
    return HttpContext.Current.Profile.GetPropertyValue(propertyName);
}
```

The second and third parameter passed to the constructor of the *CodeMethodInvokeExpression* class indicate the name of the method to call and the arguments to pass. The first parameter denotes the target object that exposes the method. Because the target object is ultimately a type, the method is intended to be static.

Supporting No-Compile Pages

At this point, the profile builder is pretty much done. If you want it to be used also in no-compile pages, there's a little more work to do. To start out, you must override the *Evaluate-Expression* method. The method is expected to return the value of the expression. Spot the difference: a no-compile page is merely interested in the results of the expression because no compilable code is going to be generated. A regular page, instead, is interested in a generic CodeDOM description of the code that will be internally translated to C# or Visual Basic .NET.

```
public override object EvaluateExpression(object target,
    BoundPropertyEntry entry,
    object parsedData,
    ExpressionBuilderContext context)
{
    // "parsedData" gets what ParseExpression returns
    string propName = (string) parsedData;
    return GetProperty(propName);
}
public override bool SupportsEvaluate
{
    get { return true; }
}
```

Finally, to enable no-compile pages, you must override the *SupportsEvaluate* property to make it return true.

Registering the *$Profile* Builder

You add a new expression builder to your application by creating a new entry under the
<expressionBuilders> element of the *<compilation>* section in the configuration file.

```
<compilation>
    <expressionBuilders>
        <add expressionPrefix="Profile"
             type="ProAspNet20.CS.Components.ProfileExpressionBuilder" />
    </expressionBuilders>
</compilation>
```

A new expression builder cannot be registered in a *web.config* file located in a child directory
of the application. It must go in the application's *web.config* or the site's *web.config*.

Using the *$Profile* Builder

The *$Profile* expression can be used in any ASP.NET page to assign a value to any control prop-
erty. Assume the following profile data model, as seen in Chapter 4:

```
<profile enabled="true">
    <properties>
        <add name="BackColor" type="string" allowAnonymous="true"/>
        <add name="ForeColor" type="string" allowAnonymous="true"/>
        <add name="Links"
             type="System.Collections.Specialized.StringCollection"
             allowAnonymous="true" serializeAs="Xml" />
    </properties>
</profile>
```

Here's a quick example that sets the background color of the *<body>* tag and the data source
for a drop-down list control:

```
<body runat="server" bgcolor="<%$ Profile:BackColor %>">
    <form id="form1" runat="server">
        <asp:DropDownList id="List1" runat="server"
                          DataSource="<%$ Profile:Links %>" />
    </form>
</body>
```

The *Links* property is a string collection and, as such, can be used to populate a drop-down list
control. However, to trigger the binding mechanism of the drop-down list, you must place a
call to *DataBind* in the page. (This has nothing to do with the expression builder—it's just a
requirement for any data-bound control.)

An expression builder is designed to be a property setter. If used to insert free-floating text
inside the page, it throws an exception.

```
<body>
    <%$ Profile:CopyrightText %>
</body>
```

If you want to use the expression builder feature to bring in your own parse-time macros, you have to resort to a little trick. You use a *Literal* control—the most lightweight of ASP.NET server controls—to wrap it, as shown here:

```
<asp:Literal runat="server" Text="<%$ Profile:CopyrightText %>" />
```

In any case, a server-side control with at least one public property is required to use an expression builder. This is by design.

Implementation Details

To top off our discussion of expression builders, let's take a look at the code that ASP.NET generates while processing the source code of a page that uses builders. It is remarkable that expression builders are a parse-time feature. The component interacts with the ASP.NET parser while this is in the process of creating the source code for the dynamic page class. Here's the code generated for the preceding sample drop-down list that has its *DataSource* property bound to a profile property:

```
DropDownList BuildControlList1()
{
    DropDownList ctl = new DropDownList();
    List1 = ctl;
    ctl.ApplyStyleSheetSkin(this);
    ctl.ID = "List1";
    ctl.DataSource = (object) ProfileExpressionBuilder.GetProperty("Links");
    return ctl;
}
```

On purpose, we added a *GetProperty* method to the *ProfileExpressionBuilder* class and declared it static. In the builder, the CodeDOM tree returned by *GetCodeExpression* describes a call to such a static method.

Building Parser Filters for ASP.NET Pages

Before being displayed to users, an ASP.NET page is parsed to a class and then compiled to an assembly. In ASP.NET 1.x, the page parser component—the *PageParser* class—is totally out of reach for the developer, except for a public static function that can be used to obtain an instance of the dynamic page class. This feature, though, is not very useful except, perhaps, for building ad hoc testing environments or developer-oriented tools. However, here's what we have:

```
public static IHttpHandler GetCompiledPageInstance(
        string virtualPath,
        string inputFile,
        HttpContext context)
```

The function takes the virtual and file paths of the page and the HTTP context, and it returns an instance of the *Page*-derived class to serve the markup of the *.aspx* resource. In addition, the *PageParser* class is sealed and most of its methods are marked as private or internal.

In ASP.NET 2.0, the programming interface of the *PageParser* class is nearly identical to ASP.NET 1.x, but a new feature comes up to let you create interesting applications—filtering the output of the page parser. The purpose of page parser filters is to provide a mechanism at parse time that filters control or code in a page. Aimed at creating an environment where some key Microsoft SharePoint features can easily be replicated, parser filters let you block certain control types, page base classes, script code, and references to user controls and master pages.

 Important   A parser filter does not generate code and is not allowed to alter the control tree created for the page. It is simply asked to say Yes or No to a given control type appearing in the page or other features that page code supports. You use parser filters to block things you don't want in the page, not to replace existing elements or alter the standard code being generated for the *.aspx* resource.

The *PageParserFilter* Class

By default, ASP.NET 2.0 doesn't use any parser filter. However, a base class is provided for you to create custom filters. This class is *PageParserFilter* and is located in the *System.Web.UI* namespace.

The class is marked as abstract, meaning that you can derive from it but not use the class directly. No members in the class, though, are left abstract. However, as we'll see in a moment, if you decide to build your own filter, you must override a number of members to make sure an application will compile.

The Programming Interface

Table 5-4 and Table 5-5 list methods and properties defined on the *PageParserFilter* class.

Table 5-4   Methods of the *PageParserFilter* Class

Member	Description
AllowBaseType	Indicates whether the page can be derived from the specified class type.
AllowControl	Indicates whether the specified control type is allowed inside the page. You use this method to build a SharePoint-like safe list of controls.
AllowServerSideInclude	Indicates whether the given server-side include is permitted on the page.
AllowVirtualReference	Indicates whether a virtual reference to a specific type of resource (such as user controls, master pages, or controls) is permitted on the page.

Table 5-4   Methods of the *PageParserFilter* Class

Member	Description
GetCompilationMode	Retrieves the compilation mode for the page.
ParseComplete	The page parser calls this method to notify when the parsing of the page is complete.
PreprocessDirective	Allows the page parser filter to preprocess page directives. Note that this method cannot be used to support custom directives in a page.

All methods are virtual and can be overridden in a derived class. Although not mandatory from a syntactical point of view, overrides are required in practice because most of these methods have an empty implementation.

Properties are overridable, too. Overriding properties is even more important because the default values they hold make it virtually impossible for ASP.NET to compile any page under the jurisdiction of a parser filter.

Table 5-5   Properties of the *PageParserFilter* Class

Member	Description
AllowCode	Indicates whether an ASP.NET parser permits code on the page. Set to *false* by default, the property raises a compile error if the page contains a *<script>* block or is bound to a code file.
NumberOfControlsAllowed	Indicates the maximum number of controls that the parser can parse for a single page. This is set to *0* by default.
NumberOfDirectDependenciesAllowed	Indicates the maximum number of direct file dependencies that the parser permits for a single page. This is set to *0* by default.
TotalNumberOfDependenciesAllowed	Indicates the maximum number of direct and indirect file dependencies that a parser permits for a single page. This is set to *0* by default.

A custom page parser filter looks like the one shown in the following code:

```
public class CustomPageFilter : PageParserFilter
{
    public override bool AllowCode {
        get { return true; }
    }

    public override int NumberOfControlsAllowed {
        get { return 20; }
    }

    public override int NumberOfDirectDependenciesAllowed {
        get { return 10; }
    }
```

```
public override int TotalNumberOfDependenciesAllowed {
    get { return 100; }
}
   ⋮
}
```

As mentioned, overriding the variables to make them return nonzero values is fundamental to avoid receiving tons of compile errors with respect to perfectly legitimate code that would work just fine without the parser filter around.

Registering a Parser Filter

The *PageParserFilter* class is not the filter that ASP.NET uses by default. More simply, it is a base class for you that you might want to use as the starting point for building your own. To enable your own parser filter, you need to add the following script to the *web.config* file:

```
<pages pageParserFilterType="ProAspNet20.CS.Components.YourPageFilter" />
```

The *<pages>* element goes underneath the *<system.web>* section. The effect of the parser is not visible at run time. The only signs of life you can get from a parser filter are compile-time errors that, as usual, appear in the Visual Studio 2005 Error pane window.

Real-World Scenarios

Let's review some concrete scenarios in which you can see the benefits of page parser filters. The main reason for these filters is to enable developers to build in their own applications a typical feature of Windows SharePoint Services—the safe control list.

Simply put, the safe control list enables a Web master to stop a specific set of controls from rendering to the client. ASP.NET doesn't implement a safe control list feature, but it provides developers with the necessary hooks to build a similar feature.

In addition, the hooks supplied by a custom parser filter class allow developers to implement a number of related checks and stop certain page base classes, virtual references, and includes.

Building a Safe Control List

In SharePoint, the safe control list is the list of server controls that are known to be safe for use in documents. In ASP.NET, there's no such filter, but you can easily build one through a parser filter component. Note, though, that in ASP.NET the filter is applied at parse time and results in compile errors.

You override the *AllowControl* method and compare the type of the control being parsed against the allowed types listed in an external source. The *AllowControl* method takes a couple of parameters, the first of which is the type of the control being currently parsed. The second parameter is the *ControlBuilder* object used to parse the tag of the control. You use this parameter if you need to investigate the source markup for the control before making your decision.

```
public class SafeListPageFilter : PageParserFilter
{
    private List<Type> _safeControlList;
    protected virtual List<Type> SafeControlList
    {
        get {
            if (_safeControlList == null) {
                _safeControlList = new List<Type>();
                LoadSafeControlList();
            }
            return _safeControlList;
        }
    }

    public override bool AllowControl(Type controlType,
                                      ControlBuilder builder)
    {
        return SafeControlList.Contains(controlType);
    }

    private void LoadSafeControlList()
    {
        // You typically read the list of types from an external source:
        // be it a database, an XML file or, better yet, a custom provider

        SafeControlList.Add(typeof(System.Web.UI.WebControls.TextBox));
        SafeControlList.Add(typeof(System.Web.UI.WebControls.Button));
        ⋮
    }
    ⋮
}
```

The sample code maintains a list of *Type* objects filled with all control types that are regarded as safe to use. You typically fill the list by reading from an external data source such as a database or an XML file. In light of what we saw in Chapter 4, this is also a nice feature to test custom providers. With the preceding code in place, only two controls are allowed in any ASP.NET page in the application—*TextBox* and *Button*. This means that any page using other controls is erroneous, as shown in Figure 5-9.

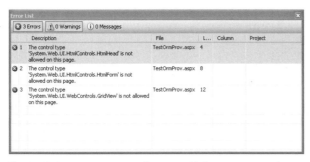

Figure 5-9   You get compile errors if the page contains unsafe controls.

Note that the safe control list is a typical SharePoint concept, for which ASP.NET provides some plugs to aid in its implementation. Nothing prevents you from building a similar feature from an opposite perspective—a block list of controls instead of a safe list.

The bottom line is, do all the checks you want. If *AllowControl* returns true, all is fine; if it returns false, a compile error is raised.

Blocking Base Classes

In much the same way you block controls in an ASP.NET page, you can prevent a page from rendering that inherits from an unsafe base class. You override the *AllowBaseType* method and make it return a Boolean value to denote whether the page base class is safe to use or not.

```
public virtual bool AllowBaseType(Type baseType)
{
    return IsSafeClass(baseType);
}
private bool IsSafeClass(Type classType)
{
    // Check the class type against a list of safe class types
    :
}
```

For example, by using this feature, you can enforce that each and every page in the application inherits from a given base class.

Note The *pageBaseType* attribute of the *<pages>* section in the configuration file lets you set a common base class for all pages in the application. In which way is this feature different from *AllowBaseType* in a parser filter? A parser filter is a way to enforce that certain coding requirements are fulfilled. The *pageBaseType* attribute is a way to write code that fulfills a particular requirement—using a base class reckoned safe.

Blocking Virtual References

The *AllowVirtualReference* method determines whether a virtual reference to a specific type of resource is permitted on a page. The method takes two parameters, as shown here:

```
public virtual bool AllowVirtualReference(
    string virtualPath,
    VirtualReferenceType referenceType
)
```

The former parameter indicates the virtual path to a resource, such as a master page, another ASP.NET page, or user control. The second parameter indicates the type of the referenced resource. *VirtualReferenceType* is an enumerated type.

Table 5-6   The *VirtualReferenceType* Enumeration

Member	Description
Master	The virtual path references a master page.
Page	The virtual path references an ASP.NET page.
SourceFile	The virtual path references a code file that is compiled using a specific language compiler.
UserControl	The virtual path references a user control.
Other	The virtual path references a resource that is none of the above.

With a single line of code, you can block all user controls. Here's how to do it:

```
public override bool AllowVirtualReference(string virtualPath,
                                    VirtualReferenceType refType)
{
    // Let everything pass except user controls
    return (refType != VirtualReferenceType.UserControl)
}
```

Adding a Literal String to All Pages

As mentioned, the page parser filter is not a feature intended to let developers alter the code generated by the standard parser—the *PageParser* class, which is sealed and internal. All the overridable methods we hitherto examined let you deny or accept—in a word, filter—elements in the page, but nothing more.

There is one exception to this, however. You can partially modify the output of the page. Admittedly, there's not much value in this, so I mention it mostly as a curiosity and for completeness. You can use the filter to append a literal string to all processed pages. Here's how to do it:

```
public override void ParseComplete(ControlBuilder rootBuilder)
{
    // Make sure this is a page and not another type of resource
    if (rootBuilder is FileLevelPageControlBuilder)
    rootBuilder.AppendLiteralString("<b>written by Dino Esposito</b>");
}
```

You override the *ParseComplete* and append the string to the builder object passed to the method. Before adding the literal, you should check that the resource being parsed is a page and not, say, a skin file or another resource. The risk is that with non-page resources, the literal might break the accepted syntax and, as a result, generate parse errors.

ParseComplete is invoked on the filter when the page has been fully parsed. The argument is a reference to the root builder. The root builder is the object that outputs the *BuildControlTree* method in the dynamically created page code. (See Chapter 1 for more details.) The *Build-ControlTree* method is ultimately responsible for the page markup. It contains calls to methods that build each and every server control in the page. Here is its structure when a literal is appended using the technique just shown (and, as usual, the real code has been edited for clarity):

```
private void BuildControlTree(YourPage_aspx ctrl)
{
    IParserAccessor parser = (IParserAccessor) ctrl;

    // Start writing the beginning of the markup
    parser.AddParsedSubObject(new LiteralControl("<html>"));

    // Create the <head> control if any
    HtmlHead ctrl1 = BuildControl__control1();
    parser.AddParsedSubObject(ctrl1);

    // Start writing the body
    parser.AddParsedSubObject(new LiteralControl("<body>"));

    // Create the form and all of its children
    HtmlForm ctrl2 = BuildControl__form1();
    parser.AddParsedSubObject(ctrl1);
    ⋮
    parser.AddParsedSubObject(new LiteralControl("</body></html>"));

    // Anything you add through the filter goes here
    parser.AddParsedSubObject(new LiteralControl(your-message-here));
}
```

The message is emitted verbatim and won't get parsed. You can use any HTML decoration if you want—things like bold, anchors, and images. Note that the text is appended to the markup *past* the closing *</html>* tag. However, most browsers won't complain about it.

Conclusion

The runtime environment for processing pages is significantly richer in ASP.NET 2.0 than in previous versions. New directives, additional attributes, and syntax enhancements let you build more complex and feature-rich pages more easily. Asynchronous pages are perhaps the tip of the iceberg, but other tools and resources are available to let you interact closely with the page-building process. The final goal is not just building more sophisticated pages, but building them more easily. To paraphrase a popular slogan, "Get rich pages with less effort."

In this chapter, I discussed three apparently unrelated topics such as asynchronous pages, dynamic expressions, and page parser filters. What do these features really have in common? They let you add—albeit in different ways—value and power to pages, and they let you enable interesting application scenarios. More importantly, they require only limited code.

Asynchronous pages let you execute multiple tasks asynchronously without thread blocking and without incurring scalability penalties. Dynamic expressions let you extend the basic set of expressions with a custom syntax. The ultimate goal of expressions is taking declarative programming to the next level—and declarative programming means more support from development tools and, in the end, less code to write. Finally, parser filters let you enforce what can be part of your pages as well as what is not allowed.

This chapter completes Part 1 of the book, which was dedicated to the ASP.NET machinery and extensibility. With the next chapter, I'll start taking a look at special features and capabilities of the ASP.NET runtime that can be leveraged to create added value in user applications. We'll start with script capabilities.

Just the Facts

- Asynchronous pages are ideal for implementing lengthy operations, such as long-running database transactions or Web service calls, without blocking any thread and getting some parallelism from the simultaneous execution of multiple tasks.

- ASP.NET 2.0 provides a tailormade API to build asynchronous pages more easily. ASP.NET 1.x does support the asynchronous pattern, but most of the code required must be built on your own and, worse yet, it is not exactly trivial code to write.

- In ASP.NET 2.0, you flag the page with the *Async* attribute and register tasks to execute asynchronously. A modified request-processing cycle splits the execution of the page in two parts served by different pooled threads. In the first part, the task is run and the thread returns to the pool. A callback mechanism is set up that queues the second part of the request when the task is complete. A new thread is scheduled, and the page finally renders out.

- ASP.NET 2.0 is endowed with three different types of expressions—code blocks, data-binding expressions, and dynamic expressions. Dynamic expressions operate at parse time and act as property setters.

- You can write custom expressions by deriving a new class from *ExpressionBuilder*.

- Page parser filters let you govern which controls and features are enabled at parse time in a page. For example, you can create a block list of controls and enforce that if any controls on the list are present in the page. In such cases, a compile error is raised.

- Page parser filters cannot be used to alter the code generated by ASP.NET.

Part II
Special Features

Chapter 6
Working with Script Code

In the early days of Web development, ten and more years ago, most people considered applications to be far too serious a thing to reduce to a handful of script and HTML markup code. At the time, tears, sweat, blood, and frustration were the cost of achieving the triumph of getting compiled code that actually ran. What was that childlike programming language that tried to mimic the language of adult programmers? That was script, and the languages were VBScript and JavaScript.

Today, while we put tears, sweat, and blood into building Web applications that compile to binary code, we are still bound to script code and primordial scripting languages to do something significant on the client. Web applications are particular because they require client and server code to interact. The demand for rich and powerful applications delivered over the Web has grown quickly and abundantly but, for a number of reasons, this brought new achievements and development only on the server side of the matter. In the past ten years, the disparity between the level of technology employed on the client and server enlarged quite a bit. Currently, a server environment that has grown richer and richer over the years corresponds to a client-side environment that is the same as ten years ago.

As a result, today we adopt powerful software technologies on the server to make up for the objective limitations we have to deal with on the client. The server tends to auto-generate client-side code and inject it into server pages so that users can have the best of two worlds—Web-deployed applications making server calls without the performance penalties of continual postbacks.

In this chapter, I'll explore the ASP.NET-based technologies and related techniques that can help you make good use of script code in client pages, at least when the browser allows for them. This approach reduces to just two features—overcoming the limitations of JavaScript by abstracting client-side code in server-side classes and executing remote calls without refreshing the page.

Adding Client-Side Script to Pages

Client-side script code is important because it lets users do some work without posting the page back to the server. With today's graphically richer and larger pages, the number of post-backs is definitely an issue regardless of the power of computers and the availability of broadband connections.

By design, a Web application works by posting stateless requests to the server, so the number of tasks that can really be accomplished on the client is limited to a few, such as validating data on the client, prefilling fields, showing or hiding parts of the page, dynamically modifying the page, and popping up page-related windows. For any of this to actually happen on the client, you have to inject script code in the page served to the user.

When you author a server-side ASP.NET page, how would you inject this code? There are several possible approaches—use hard-coded script, use client-side include files, or set up server-side generation of script code. The script code is expected to interact with the browser and the object model it uses to represent the current page and its settings. Checking the browser capabilities allows pages and controls to know in advance whether a certain piece of script will work on the actual browser. In this way, the script code that pages and controls emit can be fine-tuned to the actual device.

Checking Browser Capabilities

Browser information is packed in the *HttpCapabilitiesBase* object returned by the *Request.Browser* property. In the .NET Framework, two classes derive from *HttpCapabilitiesBase*. They are *HttpBrowserCapabilities* and *MobileCapabilities*. The former is specialized for desktop browsers; the latter works for mobile devices. Checking browser capabilities is a two-fold task.

The first scenario is when you simply need to detect the browser type and know, for example, whether it is Internet Explorer or Firefox. You use this approach when you *know* that the features your script relies on are supported on a particular browser.

The second scenario is when you just don't care about the actual browser type, and you focus instead on a given set of capabilities—such as support for cookies, script callback, or frames.

Getting to Know the Current Browser Type

Full information about the browser type is packed into the User-Agent header. You access the string through the *Request.UserAgent* property. For Internet Explorer (IE) 6.0, the user agent string looks like the following:

```
Mozilla/4.0 (compatible; MSIE 6.0; Windows NT 5.2; SV1; .NET CLR 1.1.4322;
 .NET CLR 2.0.50727; InfoPath.1)
```

For Mozilla Firefox 1.0, it is a string like the following one:

```
Mozilla/5.0 (Windows; U; Windows NT 5.2; en-US; rv:1.7.5) Gecko/20041107 Firefox/1.0
```

The user agent string is not limited to the browser's name but includes information such as the version, host operating system, language, and platforms supported. What if you simply want to know if the client is using Internet Explorer or Firefox? You use the *Browser* or *Type* property instead.

```
<h2>This browser is <% =Request.Browser.Browser %></h2>
<h2>This browser is <% =Request.Browser.Type %></h2>
<h2>This browser is <% =Request.UserAgent %></h2>
```

The *Browser* property returns the name of the browser, whereas the *Type* property adds some basic version information. Take a look at Table 6-1 for an example of the return values you get.

Table 6-1   Browser Names

Browser	*Browser* Property	*Type* Property
Internet Explorer 6.0	IE	IE6
Internet Explorer 5.5	IE	IE55
Mozilla Firefox 1.0	Mozilla	Mozilla1.7.5
Netscape 7.2	Netscape	Netscape72
Netscape Communicator 4.6	Netscape	Netscape4

Note that the *HttpCapabilitiesBase* class also makes available a Boolean function for quick tests–*IsBrowser*. This function takes a string representing a browser's name and returns true or false according to the browser's actual type. It is essential to know that the return value is decided based on the *Browser* property. For example, *IsBrowser("IE6")* and *IsBrowser("Internet Explorer")* will both return false on any version of Internet Explorer. To test Internet Explorer, you have to use the *IE* string.

```
<h2>This browser is IE: <% =Request.Browser.IsBrowser("IE") %></h2>
```

What if you want to check carefully the version of the browser and distinguish, say, between Internet Explorer 5.5 and Internet Explorer 4.0? You use two other properties of the *HttpCapabilitiesBase* class: *MajorVersion* and *MinorVersion*. The following code shows how to make sure that the browser is Internet Explorer version 4.0 or newer:

```
HttpBrowserCapabilities caps = Request.Browser;
if (caps.IsBrowser("IE") && caps.MajorVersion >3)
{
    ⋮
}
```

> **Note** Who's responsible for the ASP.NET codified browser's name? In other words, why is it IE instead of Internet Explorer? And why is it Mozilla, where perhaps Firefox would have been more natural? All information about a browser—both type and capabilities information—are read from a set of server-side files located in the installation folder of ASP.NET. Information about a fair number of popular browsers is set by the ASP.NET team (including the nickname of browsers), but this can be extended and/or modified by Web administrators.

Getting to Know About Browser Capabilities

Browser capabilities are determined statically by reading from a server-side database instead of querying the browser itself dynamically. The browser information that ASP.NET uses is hard-coded in the *Browsers* folder under the following installation path:

```
%WINDOWS%\Microsoft.NET\Framework\[version]\Config
```

The *Browsers* folder contains several *.browser* files, one for each recognized family of browser. The *.browser* file is an XML file that lists identity and capabilities information for each known version of the browser. It should be noted that this information represents the public knowledge ASP.NET has of the browser. When you check for a particular capability, the response is based on what's written in the files. However, the contents of the *.browser* files are not set in stone and can be updated as more browsers make their debut on the market or newer versions are released. If you find that a particular device is not listed, all you have to do is get (or write) the proper *.browser* file and install it in the ASP.NET browser folder.

HttpCapabilitiesBase is the base class that defines the capabilities that a given browser or handheld device might or might not have. *HttpCapabilitiesBase* offers a large number of read-only properties that provide type-safe access to the browser's set of capabilities. Table 6-2 lists some properties that express the capabilities of a browser. The properties are defined as public members of the *HttpCapabilitiesBase* class.

Table 6-2 Most Popular Browser Capabilities

Property	Description
ActiveXControls	Indicates whether the browser supports ActiveX controls
BackgroundSounds	Indicates whether the browser supports background sounds
Beta	Indicates whether the browser is a beta release
Browser	Gets the name of the browser
ClrVersion	Gets the *Version* object containing version information for the .NET common language runtime installed on the client
Cookies	Indicates whether the browser supports cookies
Crawler	Indicates whether the browser is a Web crawler search engine
EcmaScriptVersion	Gets the version number of ECMA script supported by the browser
Frames	Indicates whether the browser supports HTML frames

Table 6-2   Most Popular Browser Capabilities

Property	Description
Item	Indexer property; gets the value of the specified browser capability
JavaApplets	Indicates whether the client browser supports Java applets
JavaScript	Indicates whether the browser supports JavaScript
MajorVersion	Gets the integer number denoting the major version number of the browser
MinorVersion	Gets the decimal number denoting the minor version number of the browser
MSDomVersion	Indicates the version of the Microsoft HTML (MSHTML) document object model that the browser supports
SupportsCallback	Indicates whether the browser supports callback scripts
SupportsCss	Indicates whether the browser supports CSS
SupportsXmlHttp	Indicates whether the browser supports receiving XML over HTTP through the *XmlHttpRequest* object or a variation
Tables	Indicates whether the client browser supports HTML tables
Type	Gets a string made of the name and the major version number of the browser (for example, Internet Explorer 6 or Netscape 7)
VBScript	Indicates whether the browser supports VBScript
Version	Gets a string representing the full (integer and decimal) version number of the browser
W3CdomVersion	Gets the version of the World Wide Web Consortium (W3C) XML Document Object Model (DOM) supported by the browser

If you're writing a mobile application, you must cast the *Request.Browser* return value to the *MobileCapabilities* object and work with that. The mobile capabilities object is not supported by version 1.0 of the .NET Framework. However, a separate download is available to enable mobile controls support for version 1.0 of the .NET Framework.

Choosing Client Targets

By default, the *Request.Browser* property returns an *HttpCapabilitiesBase* object that reflects the capabilities of the actual browser. The actual browser is found by looking at the user agent string sent with the request. In ASP.NET, you can also configure pages to generate their output for a particular client target. In this case, browser detection is disabled, and the page will use the browser capabilities associated with the specified client target.

You can set the client target in either of two ways—programmatically through the *ClientTarget* property on the *Page* class or declaratively using the *ClientTarget* attribute on the @Page directives. The *ClientTarget* property is a string and accepts values that can be matched to registered client targets. As we saw in Chapter 3, the *<clientTarget>* section of the configuration file lists a number of possible client targets. In the end, a client target is an alias for a particular registered browser.

Device-Specific Output in ASP.NET 2.0

In most cases, you just need to detect the browser to change the value assigned to a property. If your goal is limited to this, you can delegate most of the work to ASP.NET 2.0 and specify browser-specific values for control properties. Here's a quick example:

```
<asp:Button ID="Button1" runat="server" Text="I'm a Button"
     ie:Text="IE Button"
     mozilla:Text="Firefox Button" />
```

The *Text* property of the button will contain "IE button" if the page is viewed through Internet Explorer and "Firefox button" if the page goes through Firefox. If another browser is used, the value of the unprefixed *Text* attribute is used. All properties you can insert in a tag declaration can be flagged with a browser ID. To identify the browser, you use the browser name as returned by the *Browser* property of the *HttpCapabilitiesBase* class.

> **Note**   Checking the browser's capabilities programmatically is also important for controls to decide how to implement certain features. For example, a control that has some information to show on demand (for example, a tree-view node) might want to check the browser's capabilities and implement the expand button as an ordinary submit button (causing a postback) or as a client-side button. In the latter case, the text to display must already be part of the page and will be shown/hidden with a click. We'll return to the topic of server controls' script capabilities in Chapter 13.

Registering Script Blocks

When you author an ASP.NET page, you build the markup for the browser one piece after the next. Just as you add and configure server controls, you retrieve and insert blocks of script code. Most of the time, though, the script code needs to interact with client-side elements generated on the server. For example, say you put a *TextBox* control on a page. A script function that validates the contents of the text box on the client needs to know the ID of the text box. What's the best way of coding this? You can write the script manually and emit it in verbatim *<script>* sections. Alternatively, you can import the script from external files and resources or build it programmatically. Let's review the various options.

Hard-Coded Script

In a classic HTML page, script code goes into a *<script>* section flagged with a language attribute. Any script code bound to HTML elements and events must be found in the page or linked to it. The simplest way to insert script code in ASP.NET pages, therefore, is just by hard-coding the script in one or more *<script>* tags, devoid of the *runat=server* attribute. Let's consider the simple script required to make the current page the home page for the current browser:

```
<script language="javascript" type="text/javascript">
function SetAsHomePage(obj) {
   obj.style.behavior="url(#default#homepage)";
```

```
    obj.setHomePage("http://www.contoso.com");
}
</script>
```

You place this code in the page and add a client-side button to invoke it when the button is clicked.

```
<input type="button" value="Set home page" onclick="SetAsHomePage(this)" />
```

If you use an ASP.NET *Button* control, the client receives a submit button, and the page posts back whenever you click it. This behavior wouldn't be wrong here—just unnecessary.

What's the problem with the preceding code? It uses a built-in Dynamic HTML behavior and requires Internet Explorer 5.5 or later. If you hard-code the script in the page, you can test the user agent string only inside the client script or add some further client-side code that checks the browser's capabilities first and emits the home page script only if the browser allows it. You can do this through the *document.write* function that most browsers support.

Hard-coded script is rarely functional, although it is definitely a resource for developers. Another issue you encounter when using hard-coded functions is that you are forced to know the ID of the HTML elements you're working with. This gets a bit complicated if different teams write pages and client script. Any change in the ID of the controls must be reflected in a timely manner by the script. Let's see how to rewrite the home page feature in an ASP.NET page to be browser-dependent. In doing so, we're going to make the server-side code smarter so that it generates a tailormade script when appropriate.

The *ClientScriptManager* Class

The *Page* class represents a running instance of the page. Whatever the page displays through the browser is described through literals or instances of server-side controls. Script code is no exception. If you want some JavaScript code to be emitted with the page markup, you have to make it part of the server-side page's object model. Hard-coded script is emitted as literal text. As mentioned, though, this is just one of the possible options.

The *Page* class has a number of members that declaratively emit script code based on run-time conditions. For example, you are allowed to conditionally register a JavaScript string to be emitted with the page. In ASP.NET 2.0, methods to emit script on demand are grouped under the *ClientScript* property of the *Page* class. In ASP.NET 1.x, on the other hand, the same methods are defined directly on the *Page* class. The *ClientScript* property is an instance of a helper class named *ClientScriptManager*. Table 6-3 lists the members of *ClientScriptManager*. You use these members to inject script code in client pages based on run-time conditions detected on the server.

Table 6-3 Members to Manipulate Script in ASP.NET Pages

Member	Description
GetCallbackEventReference	Returns the prototype of the client-side script function that causes, when invoked, a script callback invocation.
GetPostBackClientHyperlink	Appends *javascript:* to the beginning of the return string received from *GetPostBackEventReference*. `javascript:__doPostBack('CtlID','')`
GetPostBackEventReference	Returns the prototype of the client-side script function that causes, when invoked, a postback. It takes a *Control* and an argument and returns a string like this: `__doPostBack('CtlID','')`
GetWebResourceUrl	Returns the URL to invoke a resource stored in the page's assembly.
IsClientScriptBlockRegistered	Determines whether the specified client script is registered with the page.
IsClientScriptIncludeRegistered	Determines whether the specified script-include element is registered with the page.
IsOnSubmitStatementRegistered	Determines whether the specified client submit script is registered with the page.
IsStartupScriptRegistered	Determines whether the specified client startup script is registered with the page.
RegisterArrayDeclaration	Use this method to add an *ECMAScript* array to the client page. This method accepts the name of the array and a string that will be used verbatim as the body of the array. For example, if you call the method with arguments such as *theArray* and '*a*', '*b*', you get the following JavaScript code: `var theArray = new Array('a', 'b');`
RegisterClientScriptBlock	Emits client-side script blocks in the client page just after the opening tag of the HTML *<form>* element and before any server controls.
RegisterClientScriptInclude	Emits the markup to import an external script file through the *src* attribute of the *<script>* tag.
RegisterClientScriptResource	Calls into *RegisterClientScriptInclude* to register an external script file, except that in this case the external file is taken from the page's resources.
RegisterExpandoAttribute	Emits the markup to import a custom, nonstandard attribute.
RegisterHiddenField	Emits the markup required for a hidden field.
RegisterOnSubmitStatement	Emits client-side script associated with the form's *OnSubmit* event.
RegisterStartupScript	Emits client-side script at the end of the *<form>* tag so that it can be run at startup when all controls have been fully initialized.

As you can see, there are three types of members—*GetXXX*, *IsXXX*, and *RegisterXXX*. *GetXXX* methods return a standard piece of JavaScript code as a string. This refers to a string of script code that pages and controls use to implement native features such as script callback, postback, and hyperlinking. *RegisterXXX* methods register a piece of code with the page so that the script will be emitted in the response when the page renders out. All *IsXXX* methods check whether a given piece of script is already registered with the page to avoid duplication and, subsequently, client page errors.

On-Demand Script Blocks

To rewrite the home page feature to consider the underlying browser, you first check the browser's identity, compose the JavaScript code in a string, and finally register the script with the page. You use the *RegisterClientScriptBlock* method to associate the required script with the page. This executes only if explicitly invoked from within any *<script>* block in the page—for example, the event handler of a button click or the code that handles the change of selection in a drop-down list.

Any code registered with *RegisterClientScriptBlock* appears inside the *<form>* tag following the view-state hidden field and preceding any page form's literals and server controls. Here's how to modify the previous page to emit the home page script only if the browser is Internet Explorer version 5.5 or later. The page markup might be limited to the following:

```
<body>
   <form id="form1" runat="server">
   <div>
      <input runat="server" type="button" ID="HomePageButton"
             value="Set home page" />
   </div>
   </form>
</body>
```

The page includes a client-side, non-submit button with no event handler set yet. The attributes for the element are completed on the server before the markup for the page is generated. Let's dig out the code-behind class of the page.

```
protected void Page_Load(object sender, EventArgs e)
{
    string HOMEPAGE = "http://weblogs.asp.net/despos";

    // Must be IE55 or higher
    HttpBrowserCapabilities caps = Request.Browser;
    if (caps.IsBrowser("IE") && (caps.MajorVersion > 5 ||
        (caps.MajorVersion == 5 && caps.MinorVersion >= 5)))
    {
        // Enable the button and set the onclick handler
        HomePageButton.Disabled = false;
        HomePageButton.Attributes["onclick"] = "SetHomePage(this)";
```

```
        // Register needed script code
        Type t = this.GetType();
        if (!ClientScript.IsClientScriptBlockRegistered(t, "SetHomePage"))
        {
            // Compose and register the script
            string js = BuildScriptCode(HOMEPAGE);
            ClientScript.RegisterClientScriptBlock(t, "SetHomePage", js);
        }
    }
    else
        HomePageButton.Disabled = true;
}

private string BuildScriptCode(string url)
{
    StringBuilder sb = new StringBuilder();
    sb.AppendLine("function SetHomePage(obj) {");
    sb.AppendLine("  obj.style.behavior=\"url(#default#homepage)\";");
    sb.AppendFormat("  obj.setHomePage(\"{0}\");\r\n", url);
    sb.AppendLine("}");
    return sb.ToString();
}
```

In the *Page_Load* event handler, you check the characteristics of the browser and, if all is fine, proceed with configuring the button and composing the script. Once the script is ready, you register it with the page for inclusion in the page response.

The *Page* class maintains a number of hashtables to track all the scripts to be included in the response. The lifetime of the hashtables is limited to the request; however, you can use the *IsClientScriptBlockRegistered* method to check whether the script is already registered. A registered script is scoped with the type of the page or control that uses it and is given a unique name. Attempts to associate the same script multiple times with the same type and name are blocked, and the script is registered and emitted only once. If you register the same script with a different name or in association with a different type, the same script is emitted twice or more. As a result, a scripting error is raised on the client when the script is invoked.

Figure 6-1 shows the sample page viewed with Mozilla Firefox and Internet Explorer 6.0. The home page button is active and working only in Internet Explorer.

In ASP.NET 2.0, the *RegisterXXX* methods feature an overloaded version that accepts a final Boolean argument—false by default. If you set it to true, the script is emitted in its own *<script>* block. Otherwise, no *<script>* block is added and the developer is responsible for wrapping the code in a proper element.

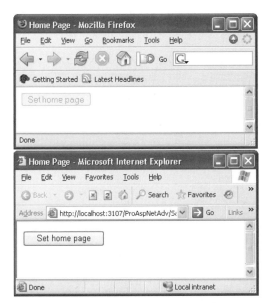

Figure 6-1 The script is emitted only if the browser is Internet Explorer 5.5 or later.

> **Caution**   An ASP.NET button (the *<asp:Button>* tag) is rendered to the client as an *<input type=submit>* element, meaning that the page will first execute the JavaScript code associated with the *onclick* attribute and then post back. In ASP.NET 2.0, the *Button* control features the *UseSubmitBehavior* Boolean property, set to true by default. If you set it to false, the type of the *<input>* element is *Button* but the *onclick* attribute is decorated with a standard postback script. As a result, the page still posts back but you can't use the *onclick* attribute to execute client code before the form is submitted. However, because the form post occurs through the page DOM's submit method, you can intercept the *OnSubmit* client event and execute some code before the post occurs. To register a submit script, you use the *RegisterOnSubmitStatement* method.

Startup Script Blocks

A startup script block is a piece of script code that executes when the page has been fully initialized but before it is displayed to the user. To register such code, you first ensure that the functions to call are available within page. The functions can be created on the fly, hard-coded, or linked from external files or resources. Next, you need to place a call to the function of choice.

For the code to execute at startup, you need to place the call through the *RegisterStartupScript* method. A startup *<script>* block is inserted immediately before the closing *</form>* tag. If the block contains only a function declaration, nothing happens. If the code contains a function call (or both a declaration and a function call), the code executes as the first thing in the client-side page life cycle. Accessing any HTML element is absolutely safe because the script is located at the bottom of the form and executes past all HTML elements.

> **Important**   Each browser has its own DOM, but most of them comply with the HTML 4.0 standards. To avoid problems with different browsers, it is recommended that you write your script code using standard DOM methods, regardless of the shortcuts that some browsers (well, mostly Internet Explorer) might offer. To access an HTML element, for example, use *document.getElementById*, or a similar method, and avoid other techniques based on the direct name of the element. Here's the safe way to access a text box:
>
> ```
> function ShowValue()
> {
>     var obj = document.getElementById("TextBox1");
>     alert(obj.value);
> }
> ```
>
> In Visual Studio 2005, you find full IntelliSense support for the *document* object.

Script Code on Submit

There might be situations in which you need to execute some script code just before the page posts back. How you do that mostly depends on what you want to achieve exactly. If the page posts back using a standard submit button (that is, the type of the *<input>* element is *submit*, *reset*, or *image*), you can only attach some script code to the *onclick* attribute of the corresponding elements. Period.

If you do so, the *onclick* function executes first and can even block the operation. For example, the following script aborts an ongoing postback if the user doesn't confirm (that is, it returns *false*):

```
function ConfirmDeletion(msg) {
    return confirm(msg);
}
```

It is important to know that submit buttons are *not* affected by on-submit scripts. According to W3C DOM standards, the page DOM should expose an *OnSubmit* script event. Writing a handler for such an event is not sufficient if the form submission occurs through a submit button. The *OnSubmit* event is fired only if the form is posted using the DOM's *submit* method.

From an ASP.NET perspective, this means that if you need to run script code on submit, you don't have to use plain *Button* controls. Instead, opt for the *LinkButton* class or use the *Button* control with the *UseSubmitBehavior* property set to false. In all these cases, the page is enriched with ad hoc script code to control the postback. In the end, the page uses the submit method to post and the *OnSubmit* event is raised and can be successfully executed as you would expect. Note that the aforementioned ad hoc script code to control the postback is the string returned by the *GetPostBackEventReference* method listed in Table 6-3. To register a submit handler, you use the *RegisterOnSubmitStatement* method.

```
ClientScript.RegisterOnSubmitStatement(this.GetType(), "MySubmit", js);
```

The effect of this code is the following. First, the form has added to it an *OnSubmit* attribute bound to a fixed function name—*WebForm_OnSubmit*. A *<script>* block is added with the prototype of this function. The body of this function is the code you pass to the *RegisterOnSubmit-Statement* method. As a result, the script code passed to *RegisterOnSubmitStatement* must be of executable code only and can't include the declaration of any helper functions. Here's what's in the page once you register an on-submit script:

```
<script type="text/javascript">
function WebForm_OnSubmit()
{
  // What you pass to RegisterOnSubmitStatement goes here
  ⋮

  // True to continue, False to abort
  return true;
}
</script>
```

The form is decorated with an *onsubmit* attribute, as follows:

```
<form id="form1" method="post" action="HomePage.aspx"
      onsubmit="javascript:return WebForm_OnSubmit();">
```

Handling the *OnSubmit* event is helpful in all situations in which the author of the script can't control how and when the page posts back. For example, if you're writing a page with one submit button, you might find it easier to write an *onclick* handler for the button instead of hooking the *OnSubmit* event. And it's quite the reverse if you're writing a custom control. A control is hosted on a page with other controls, one of which might cause the postback. Registering some on-submit code is the only chance the control has to do something before the postback starts. This said, bear in mind that no controls in the page will ever be able to catch the submit event if the page posts back through a submit, reset, or image *<input>* element.

Server-Side Include

In addition to being hard-coded or dynamically generated, the script code can also be linked to the page from an external file or from an embedded resource in the page assembly. To link a JavaScript file, you use the *RegisterClientScriptInclude* statement:

```
ClientScript.RegisterClientScriptInclude("MyScript",
    "http://www.foo.com/script.js");
```

The first argument is the script's nickname. Here is the resulting markup:

```
<script src="http://www.foo.com/script.js"
        type="text/javascript"></script>
```

Loading Script Code from Resources

You can also load a script file from the resources of the page assembly. You start by adding a script file to the project as an embedded resource. Next, you link the code to the page using the *RegisterClientScriptResource* method:

```
ClientScript.RegisterClientScriptResource(this.GetType(), "MyScript.js");
```

The markup of the page contains the following *<script>* element:

```
<script src="/ProAspNetAdv/WebResource.axd?d=...&t=..."
        type="text/javascript"></script>
```

The *WebResource.axd* HTTP handler is used to load the specified script from the resources of an assembly. The call to the *RegisterClientScriptResource* method is resolved in terms of a call to the *RegisterClientScriptInclude* method, where the URL to link is based on *WebResource.axd*. The following pseudo-code gives an idea of the internal implementation of *RegisterClientScriptResource*:

```
public void RegisterClientScriptResource(Type type, string resourceName)
{
    RegisterClientScriptInclude(type, resourceName,
        GetWebResourceUrl(type, resourceName));
}
```

GetWebResourceUrl is a method on the *ClientScriptManager* class that returns a URL for the specified resource. The URL refers to *WebResource.axd* and retrieves the requested resource from an assembly. *GetWebResourceUrl* requires a *Type* object, which will be used to locate the assembly that contains the resource. The assembly is identified with the assembly that contains the definition of the specified type in the current AppDomain. As its second argument, the *GetWebResourceUrl* method requires the name of the embedded resource.

Benefits of Loading Script Code from Resources

Where's the benefit of loading script from the resources of the assembly? Script from resources provides the best of two worlds. The script is easy to edit and share as a file and, to some extent, as a piece of hard-coded script. At the same time, it can be programmatically loaded in memory and preprocessed—for example, expanding placeholders and adding missing parts depending on run-time conditions.

To achieve this result, though, you have to take a slightly different route because all techniques based on *GetWebResourceUrl* work on the URL instead of the contents. The idea is that you load the contents of the resource directly from the assembly, transform it into a proper object (for example, a string or an array of bytes), and inject it in the page as appropriate.

```
Assembly current = Assembly.GetExecutingAssembly();
Stream stm = current.GetManifestResourceStream("MyScript.js");
StreamReader reader = new StreamReader(stm);
string contents = reader.ReadToEnd();
reader.Close();
stm.Close();

// Now process the contents of the embedded resource
```

The preceding code snippet shows how to access the resources of the current assembly as a stream and extract the contents of an embedded script file.

> **Note**   As mentioned, in ASP.NET 1.x there was no *ClientScript* property, and all script-related methods were defined directly on the *Page* class. In ASP.NET 2.0, it is recommended that you use the methods exposed by *ClientScript*. Old methods are still available but are marked as obsolete. Finally, note that *ClientScript* defines many more methods than the *Page* class in ASP.NET 1.x.

Adding Popup Windows

Some people love popup windows; some hate them. As a matter of fact, popup windows are quite popular these days and popup blockers are also a common presence on the vast majority of browser's toolbars. From a neutral developer's viewpoint, popup windows are not necessarily a bad thing. If there's something bad with popups, it likely has to do with the contents displayed through them. For popups, in fact, contents do matter!

Popup windows are good friends of Web developers who need to show relatively static and read-only data in response to a specific user's clicking. Popup windows don't affect the site navigation mechanism. This means that the caller page is still active underneath; the viewed page is not added to the history and, subsequently, is not subject to the Back button.

In ASP.NET 2.0, there's no specific support for injecting popup windows into a Web application and there's no *Register*-like method to generate the needed code programmatically. Far from being real rocket science, creating a popup window can be a bit boring because of the script code required and the string-based interface for styling the dialog box. Let's see how to wrap the basic API exposed by most browsers into a *Register*-like method to call programmatically.

> **Note**   There are countless articles on the Web to push or censure the use of popup windows. An interesting article that illustrates pros and cons in an unbiased way can be found at *http://www.accessify.com/tutorials/the-perfect-pop-up.asp*.

The Basic Popup API

The DOM of most browsers features the *window* object, which contains at least one method to create modal and modeless popup window—the *open* method. The prototype of the method is not standardized; in most cases, the following works:

```
window.open(url, title, [, style]);
```

The *url* parameter indicates the target URL to show in the window; the *title* parameter determines the title of the window, whereas the optional *style* argument sets the visual features of the window. This method works with both Internet Explorer and Mozilla browsers. Since version 4.0, Internet Explorer features two more specific methods named *showModalDialog* and *showModalessDialog*.

```
window.showModalDialog(url [, params] [, style]);
window.showModalessDialog(url [, params] [, style]);
```

Both methods take a URL and a couple of optional arguments. The URL indicates the page to display in the popup window. The *params* argument represents a JavaScript object that carries over external values for the page to process. Finally, the style argument is a semicolon-separated string that contains visual settings for the window-like scrollbars, resize grips, help button, status bar, and so forth.

To create a popup window from within ASP.NET pages, you inject some script code that makes a call to any of the preceding methods. The script code can be attached to any client-side buttons (that is, non-submit input fields) or invoked at startup.

```
<script language="javascript">
function ShowPopup(url)
{
    window.showModalDialog(url, "", "");
}
</script>
```

Instead of adding similar pieces of code whenever you need a popup window, you can create a custom routine that registers any popup-related script code with the current page. The effect is the same, but the final page is neater and more elegant.

> **Note**   The syntax to set window styles differs in the Internet Explorer and Mozilla DOMs. Refer to respective documentation for details. You will find full online documentation on the Mozilla DOM at *http://www.mozilla.org/docs/dom*. The Internet Explorer DOM is described starting at *http://msdn.microsoft.com/library/default.asp?url=/workshop/author/dom/domoverview.asp*.

Designing a Global Method

There are basically two approaches to designing a global component to inject popup code in a Web page—a new *RegisterXXX*-like method in the code-behind class, and a new custom control. We'll tackle custom controls only in Chapter 13; so for the time being, let's discuss a page method.

```
public void RegisterPopupWindow(Type t, string functionName,
       string targetUrl, bool modal, string style, bool addScriptTag)
{
   // Get the Javascript code
   string js = BuildScriptCode(targetUrl, functionName, modal, style);

   // Register the script with the page
   if (!ClientScript.IsClientScriptBlockRegistered(functionName))
       ClientScript.RegisterClientScriptBlock(t, functionName, js,
           addScriptTag);
}
```

The custom *RegisterPopupWindow* method mimics the prototype of other *RegisterXXX* methods. It takes a type, a moniker for the script, and a Boolean argument to denote whether or not an outermost <*script*> tag should be used. In addition, it takes a few additional parameters to configure the popup window being created—the URL for the contents, modal flag, and visual styles.

Armed with these arguments, the *RegisterPopupWindow* method builds the JavaScript code to emit and registers it with the current page using the *RegisterClientScriptBlock* method exposed by the *ClientScript* property. To top off things, you can also add a couple of overloads to the method as shown here:

```
public void RegisterPopupWindow(Type t, string functionName,
                                string targetUrl)
{
    RegisterPopupWindow(t, functionName, targetUrl, true, "", true);
}

public void RegisterPopupWindow(Type t, string functionName,
                                string targetUrl, bool modal)
{
    RegisterPopupWindow(t, functionName, targetUrl, modal, "", true);
}
```

The *RegisterPopupWindow* method should be added, or at least made available, to the code-behind class of every page that intends to use popup windows. For example, you could compile the method in an external library as a static method of a helper class. Alternatively, you can define the method on a parent page class and make actual code-behind classes derive from that one.

> **Note** Under Mozilla-powered browsers, a modal popup is created by adding the *Modal=yes* attribute to the string of window settings. However, this flag requires the *Universal-BrowserWrite* privilege. Without this privilege set, the window created is modeless and the actual behavior is equivalent to setting *dependent=true*. The *dependent* attribute makes the new window a child of the parent.

Putting It All Together

Binding the popup window to a client-side event handler is as easy as binding any other piece of script code. The *functionName* parameter indicates both the moniker to identify the script in the page's internal hashtables and the name of the client function that actually displays the popup. Here's some sample code that shows how to click a button and navigate to a given page inside a popup window:

```
protected void Page_Load(object sender, EventArgs e)
{
    string URL = "http://weblogs.asp.net/despos";

    // Register needed script code
    Type t = this.GetType();
    if (!Page.ClientScript.IsClientScriptBlockRegistered(t, "ShowPopup"))
    {
```

```
    // Configure the button
    PopupButton.Attributes["onclick"] = "ShowPopup()";
    PopupButton.Disabled = false;

    // Compose and register the script
    RegisterPopupWindow(t, "ShowPopup", URL, true);
  }
  else
    PopupButton.Disabled = true;
}
```

During the *Page_Load* event, the sample button is bound to the *ShowPopup* JavaScript function. The script behind the function is created with a call to *RegisterPopupWindow*. When the client clicks the button, he or she will be rewarded with a popup displaying the Web page associated with the URL used during our popup registration, as shown in Figure 6-2.

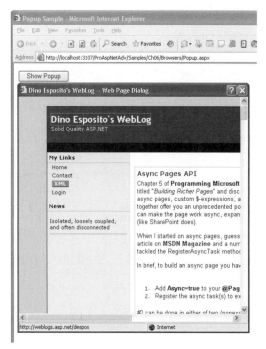

Figure 6-2 A sample page using a popup window in Internet Explorer.

Script Callbacks

All Web developers would heartily welcome a programmatic and programmable tool to avoid page refresh. Imagine the following, fairly common, scenario. You add a grid control to an ASP.NET page and make it show a navigation bar for users to page through. Whenever the user clicks to display a new set of rows, the page posts back, performs some work on the server, and then redisplays content identical to what was there prior to the post back, except for the new set of grid rows. Especially for large and complex pages, this is a significant performance hit and a possible source of frustration for end users. Why should you accept that, say, 50 KB of markup and view state is downloaded for each user action (not to mention that a large part of it is also uploaded with the same frequency)?

Designed to favor stateless requests to a Web server from tiny and lightweight clients, the HTTP protocol, and therefore the Web as a whole, has never paid sufficient attention to this issue. This need to update data without refreshing the entire page was overlooked for some good reason, I'd say, almost as if the "update without refresh" concept appeared to pollute the request-response nature of the Web and spoil the purity of the original stateless Web concept. However, updating client-side data without refreshing the entire page is a long-time dream of many Web developers. To turn this dream into reality, you need the browser to operate a silent connection to a remote URL, pass some client-side data, do some work on the server, and finally return a value to the client. Once the browser has collected any return values, it updates the page using the Dynamic HTML object model.

As you can see, quite a few requirements and prerequisites must be met. First and foremost, the browser must provide an internal component that can govern the operation. Next, a well-known and widely agreed-upon programming model must be established so that server resources can receive and interpret client data and send return values back. Finally, how can the browser update the client page? A JavaScript function should be used and, more importantly, the browser must support Dynamic HTML—that is, the browser must provide a page object model that running scripts can use to modify both the structure and content of the displayed page dynamically. Let's see what ASP.NET has to offer in this regard.

The ASP.NET Raw API

With the current browser technology, server calls that do not resubmit the whole page are possible only if you embed in the page an ad hoc component capable of issuing a parallel, out-of-band call to a server resource. This component acts like an intermediary and can take various forms—an ActiveX control, a Java applet, or perhaps an object defined in the browser's object model.

The intermediary receives calls from the client's script code and sets up a background connection to a server resource—typically, an ASP.NET page or handler. The server resource gets some input and returns some output. The output returned is processed on the client and used to update the page via the Dynamic HTML object model. Once the intermediary is known, implementing this pattern doesn't require much effort and can be easily coded also in ASP.NET 1.x and even in classic ASP.

ASP.NET 2.0 doesn't change the terms of the problems; however, it adds some system code that is a further abstraction of the details of the out-of-band call and the data exchange. In ASP.NET 2.0, script callbacks offer an out-of-the-box mechanism that greatly simplifies the whole procedure. More importantly, it hides a lot of the implementation details and also shields you from a bunch of browser issues.

The *XmlHttpRequest* Object

Back in 1999, Internet Explorer 5.0 introduced a simple but effective object to send XML strings over the HTTP protocol—the *XmlHttpRequest* object. All in all, I believe that the name is sort of a misnomer. The *XmlHttpRequest* object is simply a component that opens a socket and sends an HTTP request. It is nothing different than an object model built on top of the HTTP protocol. The role of XML in the *XmlHttpRequest* is purely fictitious—sure, the object allows you to send XML over HTTP, but only if it's packed in a regular HTTP payload.

In Internet Explorer, the *XmlHttpRequest* object is implemented as a COM object and its progID is *Microsoft.XmlHttp*. This component is the key to arrange out-of-band calls without leaving the current page. The following code snippet shows a piece of JavaScript code that connects to a remote URL and returns the response:

```
function DoPost(url)
{
    var http = new ActiveXObject("Microsoft.XmlHttp");
    http.open("POST", url, false);
    http.setRequestHeader("Content-Type",
                          "application/x-www-form-urlencoded");
    http.send(null);
    return http.responseText;
}
```

The *open* method takes three parameters—an HTTP verb (for example, GET or POST), a target URL, and a Boolean flag to indicate whether the call should be asynchronous (*false* means synchronous). The *open* method prepares the call, but nothing really happens until the *send* method is invoked. Meanwhile, you can set any number of request headers. The argument to the *send* method is the body of the HTTP request. When send is invoked, the packet is prepared and sent. The Web server receives and serves the request. The response is returned to the *XmlHttpRequest* object and exposed to callers in a number of formats, including raw text and XML DOM. The *responseText* property stores the response as text. The *responseXml* property attempts to expose the response as an XML DOM object, if possible. Note, though, that the COM interfaces of the MSXML library are used to represent the DOM. The *XmlHttpRequest* object has no notion of the .NET platform.

In ASP.NET 2.0, the implementation of script callbacks passes through the use of this object. The abstraction layer, though, hides it entirely.

> **Note** The *XmlHttpRequest* is a victim of the emphasis that XML and COM received in the past few years, before the advent of the .NET Framework. XML was supposed to be everywhere, and declaring open support for XML was seen as a plus for any technology. Created at a time when COM was considered the only possible future for components, *XmlHttpRequest* was implemented as a reusable COM object, which is today its major limitation. I'll return to this later.

Implementation Details

When you enable script callbacks in your ASP.NET pages, a JavaScript script file is linked to the page. This file is referenced from the resources of the system.web assembly; its URL begins with WebResource.axd, in case you want to take a look at the source code from the Internet Explorer temporary files folder.

This script file defines a function named *WebForm_DoCallback*, which takes care of preparing and issuing the out-of-band call. *WebForm_DoCallback* takes various parameters, including the JavaScript function to update the page and input data for the server code. The URL is not passed as an argument to the function, but it is defined in the script as a global variable. As far as ASP.NET script callbacks are concerned, the target URL is always the current page.

Inside the *WebForm_DoCallback* function, a new instance of the *XmlHttpRequest* object is created, and the response is processed and passed to the JavaScript callback that updates the page in the browser.

In the end, a script callback is a special type of postback—a request made to the same page that goes through the usual cycle of events of each page request. Additional information is appended to the request to qualify it as a callback operation so that it enjoys special treatment from the *ProcessRequest* method of the *Page* class. In particular, a couple of extra hidden fields—CALLBACKPARAM and CALLBACKID—are added. The former carries the input data for the page method to process the request; the latter indicates the ID of the page (or server control) that will handle the request. When these fields are set, the *IsCallback* Boolean property on the *Page* class returns *true*.

> **Note**   When a script callback is made, the server page or control receives the original view-state and input field values. In other words, the post data string is created when the page loads and doesn't account for the changes the user might enter before starting the out-of-band call. To make sure that the server receives what's currently selected in a drop-down list, you should pass it as an explicit argument. Likewise, the view state is not updated when a callback operation returns. In the end, a callback request is handled just like a postback, but it goes through an incomplete cycle.

Cross-Browser Support

The Internet Explorer *XmlHttpRequest* object inspired the Mozilla team and brought them to create an equivalent *XMLHttpRequest* object integrated with the browser's DOM. The ASP.NET script callback abstraction layer—read, the *WebForm_DoCallback* function—detects the underlying browser and uses the *new* operator or *ActiveXObject* as appropriate. Here's an excerpt from the code of the linked script file:

```
__nonMSDOMBrowser = (window.navigator.appName.indexOf('explorer') == -1);
function WebForm_DoCallback(eventTarget, eventArgument, eventCallback,
                           context, errorCallback)
```

```
{
    if (__nonMSDOMBrowser) {
        var xmlRequest = new XMLHttpRequest();
        ⋮
    }
    else
    {
        var xmlRequest = new ActiveXObject("Microsoft.XmlHttp");
        ⋮
    }
}
```

As a result, the ASP.NET script callback code works with Internet Explorer– and Mozilla-based browsers—Firefox, Netscape 6.x, Safari 1.2, and even the latest version of Opera. Altogether, these browsers reach over 95 percent of the market. So, why not use scripting all the way?

> **Caution**   As mentioned, Internet Explorer implements the *XmlHttpRequest* object as a COM component. This means that for ASP.NET callbacks to work on Internet Explorer browsers, users need to lower their security settings to enable at the very minimum the use of ActiveX controls marked safe for scripting. No security changes are required to take advantage of script callbacks with other browsers.

Executing an Out-of-Band Call

At its core, an out-of-band ASP.NET call is not much different from a programmatic postback ordered by some JavaScript code. A roundtrip to the server occurs, and the target is the same URL that originated the current page. ASP.NET callbacks are based on two distinct and interoperable blocks of code—one on the client that triggers and controls the whole operation and one on the server that serves the request and generates return values.

The callback mechanism leaves the current page unaffected and gives users the illusion that everything is taking place on the client like in a classic desktop application. When the callback is actually invoked, it receives the return value of the server operation and might update the page dynamically if the browser supports Dynamic HTML.

Let's start our exploration of the ASP.NET script callback feature with an attentive look at the code on the client side.

> **Note**   In the Microsoft world, the first implementation of script callbacks was Remote Scripting and dates back to the late 1990s. Remote Scripting leverages a Java applet to open a background connection to the Web server and requires a classic-ASP page to serve the request. In addition, the ASP page has to provide a made-to-measure object model—a sort of public and common interface—for the interaction to take place. The client-side code calls into a public object with a known name exposed by the ASP page. Input parameters and return values are serialized to strings. Remote Scripting provides synchronous and asynchronous remote procedure calls and works with Netscape 4.x and Internet Explorer 4 and later, but only on Windows platforms. For more information, take a look at *http://msdn.microsoft.com/library/en-us/rmscpt/Html/rmscpt.asp*.

The Client-Side Code

An ASP.NET out-of-band call begins with the execution of a system-provided JavaScript function. This function is generally bound to the handler of a page-level event such as a client button click or a change event in a drop-down list. To exemplify, let's consider a page with a button that retrieves additional information about the selected employee.

Imagine a Web page with a button labeled "More Info," which is to be clicked by users to request additional information regarding a specific employee. For our out-of-band mechanism to work, we'll first make sure that the button is not a submit button; otherwise, a regular postback occurs with full refresh of the page—just what remote scripting and ASP.NET callbacks are here to avoid. Let's work with the following markup:

```
<asp:dropdownlist id="cboEmployees" runat="server"
    DataTextField="lastname" DataValueField="employeeid" />
<input type="button" runat="server" id="buttonTrigger"
    value="More Info">
```

The code-behind class of the page fills the drop-down list with the results of a query. The user picks up an element from the list and clicks the button to get more details. The button's *onclick* event handler is added dynamically as the page is processed on the server. The *Page_Load* event is the right place for all this to happen.

```
private IEnumerable GetListOfNames()
{
    // Retrieve the list of records to fill the drop-down list
    :
}
protected void Page_Load(object sender, EventArgs e)
{
    if (!IsPostBack)
    {
        // Populate the drop-down list
        cboEmployees.DataSource = GetListOfNames();
        cboEmployees.DataBind();

        // Prepare the Javascript function to call
        string rpc = ClientScript.GetCallbackEventReference(
            this,
            "document.forms[0].elements['cboEmployees'].value",
            "UpdateEmployeeViewHandler",
            "null",
            "null",
            false);

        // Bind it to a button
        string js = String.Format("javascript:{0}", rpc);
        buttonTrigger.Attributes["onclick"] = js;
    }
}
```

GetCallbackEventReference returns a JavaScript command that is bound to the *onclick* attribute of the client button. When the page is served to the user, the button contains the following script:

```
<input name="buttonTrigger" type="button" id="buttonTrigger"
    value="More Info"
    onclick="javascript:WebForm_DoCallback('__Page',
                        document.forms[0].elements['cboEmployees'].value,
                        UpdateEmployeeViewHandler,
                        null, null, false)" />
```

Where's *WebForm_DoCallback* defined? The script is stored in the resources of the system.web assembly and is linked to the page through a dynamically generated script-include statement—to be more precise, a script-include statement loading code from resources.

```
<script src="/ProAspNetAdv/WebResource.axd?d=...&t=..."
        type="text/javascript"></script>
```

In the page served to the user, the preceding element appears immediately after the opening *<form>* tag. The changes to the client page don't end here—a startup script is also registered to initialize the callback environment. The following script appears immediately before the closing *</form>* tag.

```
<script type="text/javascript">
  var pageUrl = '/ProAspNetAdv/Samples/Ch06/Callback/ShowInfo.aspx';
  WebForm_InitCallback();
</script>
```

The global *pageUrl* variable is set to the URL of the current page. Also defined in the linked script, *WebForm_InitCallback* caches the current contents of all input fields (including view state) so that the same data can be posted with each callback fired from the page.

The Callback Starter Code

The script loaded from the ASP.NET resources and the contents of the script functions called from within the JavaScript code embedded in the page are considered private implementation details, and they can vary in the future without compromising existing applications. As a developer, you should uniquely focus on the programming interface of the *GetCallbackEvent-Reference* method of the *ClientScript* object. The arguments passed to this method determine how the underlying callback machinery is invoked and works.

```
public string GetCallbackEventReference(
    Control target,
    string argument,
    string clientCallback,
    string context,
    string clientErrorCallback,
    bool useAsync)
```

The role of each parameter is detailed in Table 6-4. The method has several overloads where some of the following parameters take default values. Note that in one of these overloads, the *target* argument takes the form of a string and denotes the unique ID of the control target of the call. If the target is the page, you can use the *__Page* predefined ID.

Table 6-4   Parameters of *GetCallbackEventReference*

Parameter	Description
target	Indicates the server-side object that will handle the call. The object can be the page or any of the contained controls provided that implement the *ICallbackEventHandler* interface. If the target object doesn't implement the required interface, an exception is thrown.
argument	Indicates the input parameters for the method to be invoked on the server in response to the call. If multiple values are to be passed, it is up to developers to pack all of them into a single string. The contents of this parameter are passed verbatim to the server method serving the request.
clientCallback	Indicates the name of the client-side JavaScript function that will receive the return value of the server call. Whatever the server method returns—even a string—is passed verbatim to this JavaScript function. If this function is not defined or available on the client page, a script error occurs. The JavaScript function will typically use the passed data to update the page dynamically.
context	Client-side script that is evaluated on the client prior to initiating the callback. The result of the script is passed back to the client-side event handler.
clientErrorCallback	The name of the client-side JavaScript function that receives the result when an error occurs in the server-side method. In this case, the *clientCallback* is not called.
useAsync	If set to *true*, the server call is performed asynchronously; otherwise, it occurs synchronously. It is *false* by default.

Armed with this background information, let's return to the code that we briefly looked at earlier:

```
// Called from within Page_Load
string rpc = ClientScript.GetCallbackEventReference(
    this,
    "document.forms[0].elements['cboEmployees'].value",
    "UpdateEmployeeViewHandler",
    "null",
    "null",
    false);
```

The target of this call is the page, meaning that the code-behind class of the page must implement *ICallbackEventHandler*. If this is not the case, the *GetCallbackEventReference* method throws an exception. Internally, the method checks whether the *target* argument (set to *this* in the code snippet) implements the required interface. (If the *target* argument is an ID, it is first mapped to a control and then the check on the interface is made.)

The argument passed to the server method is the result of the specified JavaScript expression:

```
document.forms[0].elements['cboEmployees'].value
```

Note that this is the only safe way to pass up-to-date values to the server callback. As mentioned, server control properties are not guaranteed to contain fresh values. When the page posts back—and a server callback is just a regular postback with a shorter life cycle—the state of control properties is generally retrieved from the view state and updated with posted values. In case of script callbacks, though, both the view state and posted input fields don't reflect the latest version of the form at the moment in which the callback was made. As a result, if you access any properties on a drop-down list, you see the initial state of the control when the page was created and not the current state as the client user modified it.

> **Note**   When the ASP.NET run time receives a callback invocation, it restores the state of the page as it was during the last postback. This is by design, but why is it so? In other words, why isn't the current client state used? The answer is that the state of the last postback is the last good and consistent page state known. The actual state of the form at the time the callback is made might be inconsistent because some of the fields might contain invalid data. In addition, if the latest version of the form were sent, server change events would fire on every single callback. This is not desirable because it could have side effects. For example, what if one of the controls in the page uses a hidden field to track its own client-side state? (This is what the *Tree-View* control does, but similarly rich controls can do the same.) This state would be posted and raise change events on every callback, which might be quite heavy because of the involved operations (say, database updates) and the fact that all changes since the last postback will be replayed for every callback.
>
> The bottom line is that fresh values, and not just state data, can be transmitted to the server only as parameters of your specific callback operation.

When you resort to JavaScript code to retrieve and post form values, make sure you use a syntax that most browsers understand. For example, to access the currently selected item on a drop-down list, you can use either of the following:

```
document.forms[0].elements["yourDropDown"].value
document.all["yourDropDown"].value
```

Both work with Internet Explorer, but only the first works with Mozilla browsers, too. In addition, the former expression complies with current DOM standards; the latter is Internet Explorer–specific.

The Server-Side Code

The target of the callback operation—be it the page or one of its controls—must implement *ICallbackEventHandler* interface. The interface counts two methods— *RaiseCallbackEvent* and *GetCallbackResult*. The former method should contain the code you want to execute on the server in response to a callback operation. Any result generated should be cached in an internal method that the latter method–*GetCallbackResult*–returns. Here's an example:

```
public partial class ShowInfo : Page, ICallbackEventHandler
{
    private string _results;
    void ICallbackEventHandler.RaiseCallbackEvent(string eventArgument)
    {
        // Get more info about the specified employee
        int empID = -1;
        bool success = Int32.TryParse(eventArgument, out empID);
        EmployeeInfo emp = GetEmployeeDetails(empID);

        // Prepare the response for the client: a comma-separated string.
        // The format of the return string is up to you. This format must
        // be known to the Javascript callback
        string[] buf = new string[6];
        buf[0] = emp.ID.ToString();
        buf[1] = emp.FirstName;
        buf[2] = emp.LastName;
        buf[3] = emp.Title;
        buf[4] = emp.Country;
        buf[5] = emp.Notes;
        _results = String.Join(",", buf);
    }

    string ICallbackEventHandler.GetCallbackResult()
    {
        return _results;
    }
    ⋮
}
```

If the target is the page, you can implement the *ICallbackEventHandler* interface in the code file class; if you're not using a code file, use the *@Implements* directive and place the code inline. If the target is a control, you simply add the interface to the list of base classes.

The input of the *RaiseCallbackEvent* method is the *argument* parameter of Table 6-4. The output of *GetCallbackResult* is the string that will be passed to the *clientCallback* JavaScript function in charge of finalizing the operation showing the results through the page.

As mentioned, the content and format of the strings that the *RaiseCallbackEvent* method receives and *GetCallbackResult* returns is completely up to you. Exchanged strings can be plain text, or perhaps an array of strings separated by a given character, and even the serialization of an object. In this case, though, it can only be a JavaScript object because the final link of the chain, where the data will be actually consumed, is a JavaScript function.

Note   The supported formats of the return value is one point used to ascertain the superiority of one callback technology over another. Today, the Ajax.NET framework allows you to return a variety of .NET classes, and it takes care of serializing them to a JavaScript object automatically. Atlas—the technology preview of future ASP.NET platforms—does something similar. I'll return to this topic later on.

The sample code receives the ID of the employee and uses an internal method to query for more information. All the data is packed into an *EmployeeInfo* object. As long as you use the raw script callback API, you can't return this object as is. You need to streamline its contents to a string—the actual format is up to you and is arbitrary. In the sample code, I create a comma-separated string where the position determines the field—the first position is ID, the second is first name, the third is last name, and so on.

> **Note**   The *ICallbackEventHandler* interface can also be implemented by a custom control. In this case, the control emits client script code in the host page and handles the client request.

Updating the Page

The client JavaScript callback must be linked to or embedded in the page. Furthermore, the function must be aware of the format used to return the server response. The Ajax.NET and Atlas platforms perform some magic to let the page contain all the helper scripts that are needed to let the callback work with objects that have, to the extent possible, the same interface as server objects. If you work with the raw API, you have to go through your own deserialization stage and transform the received string into something usable and useful.

```
<script language="javascript">
    function UpdateEmployeeViewHandler(response, context)
    {
        // Deserialize the response to an array of strings
        var o = response.split(',');

        // Get references to page elements to update
        var e_ID = document.getElementById("e_ID");
        var e_FName = document.getElementById("e_FName");
        var e_LName = document.getElementById("e_LName");
        var e_Title = document.getElementById("e_Title");
        var e_Country = document.getElementById("e_Country");
        var e_Notes = document.getElementById("e_Notes");

        // Update the page elements with data from the server
        e_ID.innerHTML = o[0];
        e_FName.innerHTML = o[1];
        e_LName.innerHTML = o[2];
        e_Title.innerHTML = o[3];
        e_Country.innerHTML = o[4];
        e_Notes.innerHTML = o[5];
    }
</script>
```

Figure 6-3 shows the same page working with Internet Explorer 6.0 and Firefox.

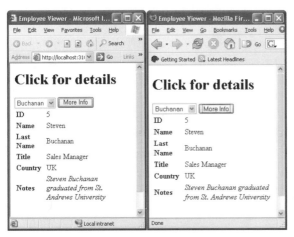

Figure 6-3 A sample page using ASP.NET script callbacks in action in Internet Explorer and Firefox.

The Importance of the DOM

The underlying implementation of ASP.NET script callbacks shields you from the details of cross-browser script programming. The code you import from the ASP.NET core assemblies is guaranteed to work with Internet Explorer and all Mozilla-compliant browsers. Unfortunately, this is only half the work. The ASP.NET platform ensures that each compliant browser can complete the roundtrip and deliver a server-generated response to a local JavaScript function. What happens next, like it or not, depends on you and the client browser.

If the client browser doesn't support dynamic updates to the page, there's not much you can do—other than perhaps resorting to frames, popups, or lots of *document.write* calls. Thankfully, today the vast majority of browsers that support callbacks also implement a page DOM that supports dynamic updates.

It is essential that you write your JavaScript client callback having the standard object model in mind and that you code it right. If the page update code takes advantage of some Internet Explorer–specific features, it won't work on Firefox or Netscape Navigator. Here's the description of a common mistake. Imagine you have a *<span>* tag in your page named *e_ID*. The following code will work with Internet Explorer but not with Firefox or other Mozilla browsers:

```
var userID = ...;
e_ID.innerHTML = userID;
```

There's no *e_ID* element in the Mozilla's DOM, even though the DOM inspector shows an element with that name. The difference lies in what Internet Explorer does beyond the standards. Internet Explorer, in fact, automatically defines a property named after each page element. This behavior is not a ratified standard and should be avoided. The correct version of the code would use the W3C standard *document.getElementById* method.

```
var userID = ...;
var e_ID = document.getElementById("e_ID");
e_ID.innerHTML = userID;
```

To stay on the safe side, write your script code in strict adherence to the W3C DOM standards. (I understand that if you have an Internet Explorer scripting background, this might be a bit painful at first.)

> **Note** Neither the raw ASP.NET API nor Ajax.NET provides a more abstract object model to hide the differences between browsers' document object models. The answer is that a ratified standard does exist. There's no reason to bother yourself further; just use it. With Atlas, on the other hand, Microsoft seems to be taking a new and much more promising and ambitious route—a control object model that spans the client and the server and gives you a way to set a property programmatically on both. The control's browser adapter will take care of rendering the requested update in terms of script code that the underlying browser can understand. However, this is just a glimpse of the (brilliant) future of ASP.NET.

A Master/Detail Example

Script callbacks are extensively used by some of the new ASP.NET controls such as the *TreeView* and *GridView*. The *TreeView*, in particular, uses callbacks to retrieve the contents of expanded nodes. The *GridView* optionally employs callbacks to page and sort its data.

Script callbacks are useful in a number of real-world situations, especially in master/detail pages and where hierarchical data is involved. Let's tackle one of these scenarios. Imagine a page with a parent list and a child list. When the user selects an element on the parent, the child is updated to show related contents. For example, suppose the parent list contains employee names while the child list is filled with all orders issued.

You can use script callbacks to retrieve the data, display it in the child list, and populate the list in the JavaScript callback. The remote call begins when the user changes the selection in the parent list. Here's the code of the page:

```
<asp:SqlDataSource runat="server" ID="EmpSource"
    ConnectionString="<%$ ConnectionStrings:LocalNWind %>"
    SelectCommand="SELECT employeeid, lastname FROM employees" />
<asp:DropDownList ID="listEmployees" runat="server"
    DataSourceID="EmpSource"
    DataTextField="lastname" DataValueField="employeeid"
    onchange="ShowOrders(this.options[this.selectedIndex].value);" />
<asp:DropDownList runat="server" ID="listOrders"
    style="visibility:hidden" />
```

The *listEmployees* drop-down list is filled by the *SqlDataSource* control, and it lists the last name of all employees in the Northwind database. The *onchange* attribute of the control captures the client-side event fired when the user selects a new item. The *onchange* attribute points to a JavaScript function that wraps the callback trigger. The *ShowOrders* function is generated in the *Page_Load* event:

```
void Page_Load(object source, EventArgs e)
{
    string rpc = ClientScript.GetCallbackEventReference(this,
        "arg", "UpdateOrders", "null", "ShowError", false);
    string func = "function ShowOrders(arg) { " + rpc + "; }";
    ClientScript.RegisterClientScriptBlock(this.GetType(),
        "ShowOrders", func, true);
}
```

The code in *Page_Load* adds the following script in the page:

```
<script type="text/javascript">
    function ShowOrders(arg) {
        WebForm_DoCallback('__Page', arg, UpdateOrders,
                            null, ShowError, false);
    }
</script>
```

Note that *GetCallbackEventReference* is not passed an explicit expression to use as the parameter for the server method. It is passed the name of a formal parameter—*arg*—whose value is more comfortably coded in the *.aspx* source file.

```
this.options[this.selectedIndex].value
```

Set to the preceding expression, the *arg* parameter carries the value of the currently selected item in the drop-down list. This syntax is equivalent to the one we used in the previous example to retrieve the current selection in a drop-down list.

On the server, the callback method receives an employee ID and runs a query to fetch all orders related to the specified employee. All order IDs are packed into a comma-separated string and returned. The string is then passed to a JavaScript function named *UpdateOrders*.

```
function UpdateOrders(result)
{
    if (!result)  return;
    var childDropDown = document.forms[0].elements['listOrders'];
    if (!childDropDown)  return;

    childDropDown.length = 0;
    var listOrders = document.getElementById("listOrders");
    var rows = result.split('|');
    for (var i = 0; i < rows.length; ++i)
    {
        var option = document.createElement("OPTION");
        option.value = rows[i];
        option.innerHTML = rows[i];
        listOrders.appendChild(option);
    }
    listOrders.style.visibility = "visible";
}
```

The child drop-down list is emptied and repopulated dynamically based on the fetched order IDs. The child drop-down list is invisible by default; when filled, its visibility flag is turned on. Note the use of the *visibility* style instead of *display*. When *visibility* is used, the element retains its own real estate in the page. When *display* is used, the control is not inserted in the page DOM. Figure 6-4 shows the page in action.

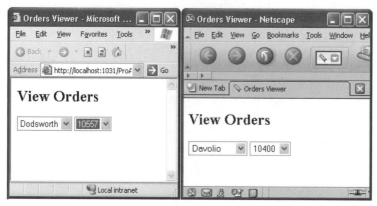

Figure 6-4   Master/detail page using ASP.NET script callbacks in Internet Explorer 6.0 and Netscape 7.2.

Are Out-of-Band Technologies Worth the Cost?

Out-of-band calls are a loudly requested feature that most browsers provide today and that contribute to the availability of richer client pages. ASP.NET Script Callback is just one possible API that can be used to implement out-of-band calls. More sophisticated libraries are in the works, including the open-source project Ajax.NET (which we'll cover in a moment) and the "Atlas" framework created from the same ASP.NET team and destined to be a sneak preview of the future ASP.NET. In brief, out-of-band technologies reduce the need for the browser to completely redraw the page every time that additional data is required and downloaded.

The payoff of an out-of-band call is clear—it makes the page run faster and transmits a sense of continuity to the user because everything appears to work locally. Although from the point of view of Web usability, out-of-band calls are an excellent feature, from an architectural perspective, some doubts about them are legitimate. The adoption of out-of-band calls might break the principle of separation that should exist between presentation and business layers. When data is downloaded on the client, the JavaScript code is expected to *do* something with it and, more importantly, to *know* about it. Depending on which kind of client code you write—and which services you get from the surrounding framework—the violation of the layer boundaries might or might not be an issue. In any case, this aspect is definitely worth a review.

The Ajax.NET Library

The ASP.NET Script Callback API represents the hard way of performing a common task—dispatching requests to the server and getting responses, without leaving the current page. Such out-of-band calls would just be impossible to implement without some browser support—specifically, an embedded broker component to send and receive requests to and from the Web server. Internet Explorer allows you to do this through the *XmlHttpRequest* COM object; Mozilla-powered browsers and Opera use a DOM object with the same name. The availability of such a component is a prerequisite.

What happens next, then, depends on the API that a given framework provides you with. The ASP.NET Script Callback API is a low-level API with no significant abstraction except, perhaps, a method to auto-generate the script code required to trigger the call.

Other ASP.NET libraries exist to implement out-of-band calls. The trait that makes them different from ASP.NET Script Callbacks is the abstraction they provide of the raw engine. A popular library is Ajax.NET.

Using the Library

The name *Ajax* is an acronym for Asynchronous JavaScript And XML. It doesn't refer to a new, specific technology, but rather to a bunch of existing technologies (such as JavaScript, a browser's DOM, XmlHttpRequest, and CSS) combined to create more interactive Web applications. By using Ajax-style products, you build pages that get updated rather than entirely redrawn at each postback. An Ajax-style Web application works by sending individual requests to get data instead of submitting forms to get a brand-new page to display.

Today, an Ajax-style approach is used in several Google applications—such as Google Maps, Google Suggest, and Gmail—which greatly contributed to the explosion of the related programming model. Several free and commercial libraries propound the Ajax approach to Web applications, each trying to simplify the development and provide the tightest possible integration between the client and the server environment.

The Ajax.NET library, available for both ASP.NET 1.x and 2.0, is an open-source project aimed at the creation of an Ajax-style library for the ASP.NET platform.

Note   To download the Ajax.NET library, and for more information and walkthroughs, make sure you visit the page at *http://ajax.schwarz-interactive.de/csharpsample/default.aspx*. For an overview on the Ajax programming style, the best place to go is *http://en.wikipedia.org/wiki/ajax*.

Setting Up the Ajax Library

To use the Ajax.NET library, you need the *ajax.dll* assembly, which is available in the global assembly cache (GAC) or in the *Bin* folder of the application. Next, you need to add an HTTP handler entry in the *web.config* file.

```
<httpHandlers>
   <add verb="POST,GET" path="ajax/*.ashx"
        type="Ajax.PageHandlerFactory, Ajax" />
</httpHandlers>
```

The goal of the entry is to make sure all requests for URLs that match the pattern *ajax/*.ashx* are forwarded to an Ajax component. Note that you don't need to create an *ajax* subdirectory in the application. As we saw in Chapter 2, a custom HTTP handler is used to hook up requests of resources with a given name. The existence of a real file with that name is instrumental to what the particular handler is expected to do. In this case, no files or directories are required. The Ajax handler simply needs to get involved when the page is loaded in the browser to emit some ad hoc script code.

At this point, you're ready to start practicing with the Ajax.NET library. Let's see how to build a page that is representative of the actual capabilities of the library.

Building a Sample Page

The following page is named *TestAjax.aspx* and contains an inline JavaScript function plus some client and server tags. In particular, the page contains a client button (labeled *Find*) bound to the *GetCustomerDetail* JavaScript function, embedded in the page. When the user clicks the *Find* button, the *GetCustomerDetail* code runs.

```
<%@ Page Language="C#" CodeFile="TestAjax.aspx.cs" Inherits="TestAjax" %>
   <script type="text/javascript">
      function GetCustomerDetail()
      {
          var customerID = document.getElementById("customerID");
          var response = TestAjax.GetCustomerByID(customerID.value);
          var oCustomer = response.value;

          if (oCustomer.Type == "UnknownCustomer")
          {
              alert("Customer not found");
          }
          else
          {
              var fn = document.getElementById("firstName");
              var ln = document.getElementById("lastName");
              fn.innerHTML = oCustomer.FirstName;
              ln.innerHTML = oCustomer.LastName;
          }
      }
   </script>
```

```
<html>
<head runat="server">
    <title>Testing Ajax</title>
</head>
<body>
    <form id="form1" runat="server">
        <h2>Enter a Customer ID (1, 2, 3, ...)</h2>
        <asp:textbox id="customerID" runat="server" text="1" />
        <input onclick="GetCustomerDetail()" type="button" value="Find">
        <hr />
        <asp:label id="firstName" runat="server" /> 
        <asp:label id="lastName" runat="server" /> <br />
    </form>
</body>
</html>
```

Figure 6-5 shows the page in action in yet another browser—Opera 8.5.

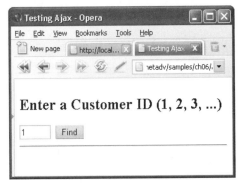

Figure 6-5   The Ajax sample page as it displays in the Opera 8.5 browser.

What's the deal with this page? The markup contains no special elements. The inline JavaScript function, on the other hand, is worth some attention. Two things, in particular, catch the eye. A call is made to an apparently missing object, and a JavaScript object is used to process the return value of the call:

```
var response = TestAjax.GetCustomerByID(customerID.value);
var oCustomer = response.value;
if (oCustomer.Type == "UnknownCustomer") {
    ⋮
} else {
    ⋮
}
```

Where's the *TestAjax.GetCustomerByID* method defined? And where is the prototype of *oCustomer* variable defined? To find the answer, let's take a look at the page's code file:

```
using System;
using System.Web;
using System.Web.UI;
```

```
using System.Web.UI.WebControls;
using Ajax;
using ProAspNet20;

public partial class TestAjax : System.Web.UI.Page
{
    protected void Page_Load(object sender, EventArgs e)
    {
        Utility.RegisterTypeForAjax(typeof(TestAjax));
        Utility.RegisterTypeForAjax(typeof(ProAspNet20.Customer));
        Utility.RegisterTypeForAjax(typeof(ProAspNet20.UnknownCustomer));
    }

    [AjaxMethod()]
    public Customer GetCustomerByID(string customerID)
    {
        // Place here any code to retrieve customer
        // information from a database
        switch (customerID)
        {
            case "1":
                return new Customer("John", "Doe");
            case "3":
                return new Customer("Jim", "Idontknowthisguy");
            default:
                return new UnknownCustomer();
        }
    }
}
```

As you can see, *GetCustomerByID* is the method on the server class flagged with the
[AjaxMethod] attribute. In addition, three types–*ProAspNet20.Customer, ProAspNet20.Unknown-
Customer,* and *TestAjax*–are registered with the Ajax infrastructure in the *Page_Load* event.
What's the purpose of this?

The server page is rendered on the client through a JavaScript object having the same name as
the page class–*TestAjax,* in this case. Any server method flagged with the *[AjaxMethod]*
attribute is defined as a method on this JavaScript object. The body of this method is automatically generated to place an out-of-band call to the corresponding server method using
XmlHttpRequest.

The server method can return any object that is registered with the Ajax infrastructure and is
in no way limited to returning strings as in ASP.NET Script Callback. Each object registered
with Ajax is rendered as a JavaScript object whose definition is then linked to the client page.
(See Figure 6-6.)

As a result, you can make remote calls to as many server-side methods as you want and use
your own objects too on both the client and the server.

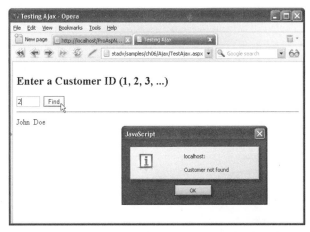

Figure 6-6   The Ajax sample page in action in the Opera 8.5 browser.

Implementation Details

When an Ajax-powered page displays in the browser, you find the following *<script>* tags:

```
<script type="text/javascript"
        src="/ProAspNetAdv/ajax/common.ashx" />
<script type="text/javascript"
        src="/ProAspNetAdv/ajax/TestAjax, [assembly].ashx" />
<script type="text/javascript"
        src="/ProAspNetAdv/ajax/ProAspNet20.Customer,
             [assembly].ashx" />
<script type="text/javascript"
        src="/ProAspNetAdv/ajax/ProAspNet20.UnknownCustomer,
             [assembly].ashx" />
```

As mentioned, none of the *.ashx* resources points to a real file that you need to deploy to the Web server. All *.ashx* resources are just symbolic endpoints for requests made to have the Ajax HTTP handler generate some ad hoc script code.

For example, the *common.ashx* endpoint injects the following code for the *TestAjax.aspx* page:

```
var TestAjax =
{
    GetCustomerByID:function(customerID,callback,context)
    {
        return new ajax_request(this.url +
                                '?_method=GetCustomerByID&_session=no',
                                'customerID=' + enc(customerID),
                                callback,
                                context);
    },
    url:'/ProAspNetAdv/ajax/TestAjax,App_Web_3obyp7mk.ashx'
}
```

The *TestAjax* JavaScript object contains two members—the *GetCustomerByID* function and the *url* property. Generally, the object will contain as many functions as there are methods on the *TestAjax* code file class decorated with the *[AjaxMethod]* attribute. The internal *ajax_request* method is also defined in the same script and represents the core API to trigger the remote call. In a certain way, *ajax_request* is the Ajax counterpart of *WebForm_DoCallback*.

> **Note**   The page-specific JavaScript object closely resembles a Web service proxy class. Like a proxy class, the JavaScript object mirrors a remote interface on the client and attaches some predefined code to each method to place a remote call to the target.

While *common.ashx* injects the core Ajax.NET API into the page, the other *.ashx* endpoints insert the JavaScript code that renders registered .NET types as JavaScript objects. Serializable .NET classes originate a JavaScript object that mirrors the same set of properties and fields. Simple types (for example, strings, dates, and numbers) are rendered through native Java-Script types. Each .NET class can be associated with a tailormade converter, and the Ajax library does provide some of them natively for *DataSet*, *DataTable*, *DataView*, *DataRow*, *Image*, and collections. You can create and register custom converters, too. An Ajax converter is a class that implements the *IAjaxObjectConverter* interface.

Ajax.NET vs. Script Callbacks

ASP.NET Script Callbacks and Ajax.NET are equivalent tools that use the same underlying infrastructure—*XmlHttpRequest*—to accomplish their tasks. In spite of this, they provide quite a different API and, to a large extent, a diametrically opposed vision of the out-of-band call.

Step-by-Step Analysis

Table 6-5 details the steps required to set up an out-of-band call with both ASP.NET Script Callbacks and Ajax.NET.

Table 6-5   Step-by-Step Guide to Script Callbacks and Ajax.NET

ASP.NET Script Callbacks	Ajax.NET
Add script code to a client element to start the remote call. This requires a call to *GetCallback-EventReference* and is typically done in the *Page_Load* event of the code file class.	Add script code to a client element to execute the remote call. The script code consists of a call to a dynamically created client object acting as a proxy. The same script code bound to the trigger element acts as the starter and the client callback.
Make the code file class implement *ICallback-EventHandler* and write the server-side code to invoke it. The method receives and returns strings.	Register .NET types that must be known to the client code. At a minimum, this includes the type of the code file class. This call occurs typically in the *Page_Load* event.
Write the JavaScript client callback to be invoked when the out-of-band call returns. This function receives the response as a string.	Decorate page methods that should be callable from the client with the *[AjaxMethod]* attribute.

All in all, the programming model of Ajax.NET is simpler and more intuitive. It also has a couple of technical advantages. First, it doesn't force you to concentrate all the callable server-side actions in a single method. Second, you can return virtually any (serializable) .NET object to the client script code.

Aside from the aforementioned practical differences, script callbacks and Ajax.NET are also different architecturally.

Chunky vs. Chatty

The option of calling any server method defined on the page class makes the Ajax.NET library inherently more "chatty." You can write a single JavaScript function that begins the call, collects its data, and updates the page. Writing complex applications, or simply adding several remote calls to a page, is much easier in this way. Be aware that each Ajax call requires a roundtrip—so the more you get chatty, the more you pay in terms of performance. Pay attention to reduce the number of remote calls to a reasonable number or, even better, use them only when strictly necessary.

The Script Callback approach is inherently more "chunky." It forces you to write less specialized server methods and to concentrate all the server logic in one method. In this way, you are brought to design your pages around a single call that returns as much information as possible.

The Ajax.NET approach is significantly more flexible and elegant. Offering a more spartan API, the Script Callback approach lets you do (nearly) the same with less.

Remote Procedure Call vs. Postback

Architecturally speaking, the two technologies envision the out-of-band call differently. For Ajax.NET, it is a plain remote procedure call, and you have full liberty of choosing the method you want and passing the parameter types you need. For Script Callbacks, it is a special, shrinkwrapped postback. The request is made to the same page (as in a regular postback) and the last known good state of the page is sent back. In other words, the view state travels back to the server with every callback.

The request is processed as usual until the *LoadComplete* event is fired. The callback unwind point is set exactly before the *PreRender* event. When the processing reaches this point, the callback method is invoked and the results are written back to the client. The following pseudo-code shows what happens at the callback unwind point:

```
ICallbackEventHandler handler;
handler = FindControl(target) as ICallbackEventHandler;
if (handler != null)
{
    handler.RaiseCallbackEvent(arguments);
    string results = handler.GetCallbackResult();
    Response.Write(results);
    return;
}
```

The postback approach is less direct than a simple remote procedure call, and it has the usual overhead of postbacks, including the view state. Note, though, that the view state is transmitted to the server, but it is not updated and returned to the client.

The key point to consider is, do you really need the view state during a callback? More to the point, do you really need state during a callback? As I see it, most of the time you just want to execute a perfectly stateless remote call. If so, ASP.NET Script Callbacks are unnecessarily heavy. On the other hand, the chatty programming style that is naturally pushed by Ajax.NET might lead to a bad page design in which multiple unnecessary remote calls occur.

The "Atlas" Framework

The "Atlas" framework is a bundle of Web development technologies that altogether enable you to create applications that can update pages by making direct calls to a Web server—without needing to roundtrip the whole page. Atlas is the Microsoft response to the Ajax programming model. At its core, Atlas consists of a client and server infrastructure. The client script libraries provide an object-oriented API and cross-browser compatibility. In addition, they let you code asynchronous calls to Web services and consume Dynamic HTML behaviors and other components for creating a fully featured user interface. The server code consists of updated server controls that provide a declarative way to emit markup and client script to match Atlas features.

To create effective Ajax applications, developers need to have extensive knowledge of client script and master the often subtle differences between the DOMs of the various browsers. Thus, Atlas is not simply another Ajax-style library. Instead, it attempts to extend the Ajax approach in two ways—by simplifying the client development and by integrating client and server development through a set of rich server controls and Web services. Atlas comes with an extended JavaScript library that allows you to work with software elements such as classes and namespaces that are not natively provided by JavaScript.

As originally presented at the Professional Developer's Conference 2005, the Atlas Framework contains the first preview of a new generation of server controls planned for future versions of ASP.NET. A unique trait of these controls is their ability to work (and be programmable) on the client as well as on the server and always through a true object-oriented API. For more information and sample code, take a look at *http://atlas.asp.net*.

Conclusion

Since the beginning, Web applications have posted forms to the Web server and displayed the markup that the server returns in response. There are many advantages to this model. Each request is independent from the next, and no state must be maintained to serve requests. The communication between browser and server consists of forms sent and pages received. Whenever the currently displayed page needs some additional data to be retrieved from the server, a form is posted and a brand new page is returned. With particularly rich pages that might contain a lot of graphics and content, a continual refresh and redraw results in a relevant performance drop.

Most attentive developers in the community have been developing around interactive Web technologies since the late 1990s. Various technologies followed without forming a critical mass of acceptance and use. Or perhaps the mass was big enough already, but we were all waiting for the spark of a killer application. Google Maps gave the start to what appears to be a real revolution in the Web world: no more, or not just, forms posted in a change of pages, but individual requests for data and dynamic updates to displayed pages. This is the future of Web pages.

As a server technology aimed at the creation of Web pages, ASP.NET couldn't let the opportunity pass unnoticed. Script callbacks have been the first attempt to offer an API for building interactive pages. Modeled after the classic postback event, callbacks are sometimes unnecessarily heavy and inflexible, but they promote a super-optimized model for data exchange—do as much as you can in each call. Ajax.NET is an even better try, but it's based on an opposite vision of the interaction. Ajax.NET is chatty, whereas script callbacks are chunky. Ajax.NET is also much more flexible, lightweight, and direct in its programming model. Both technologies have two main drawbacks—the lack of a rich client object model to blur the distinction between the DOM of the various browsers, and the neat separation between the client and server aspects of programming. The Atlas framework, introduced at the 2005 Professional Developer's Cconference and distributed as an add-on for the ASP.NET 2.0 platform, encapsulates the key technology for the Web pages of future applications. When ready, Atlas will take the form of a new family of server controls that, taking advantage of new runtime services, can be programmed on the client and the server in a totally integrated way. Atlas is available as a technology preview today, but it will be at the heart of the next generation of ASP.NET. Keep Atlas in mind for tomorrow, but use Ajax.NET today.

Just the Facts

- There are three ways to incorporate script code in ASP.NET pages—with inline code, server-side script generation, and links.

- The *Page* class contains methods to register blocks of script code to be injected at well-known locations in the page code—for example, on-submit event and form startup.

- The markup of an ASP.NET page can statically target a given browser or be dynamically emitted to meet the capabilities of the detected device.

- Script callbacks allow you to post a request to the server programmatically and receive a string value in response. The response string is parsed and consumed on the client via JavaScript to update the page.

- Script callbacks execute as a regular postback up until the unwind point is reached—before *PreRender*. The view state of the original page is posted with each callback, and no current client value is posted. The callback executes in the last known good page state—the state when the page was generated.

- Ajax.NET is an open-source library that allows you to call a server-side method using a script proxy class and serializing .NET types to JavaScript objects.

Chapter 7

Composing Pages with Web Parts

Getting the information you need in a timely manner and in the right format is essential to save time, and time—as you know—is money. Today's Web sites make a point of showing large amounts of content. At first this can be a feast for users, but in the long run it often becomes the perfect source of confusion. Modular page layouts and personalized contents are the key to increasing user satisfaction and productivity. If a manager needs to review a given set of data each and every morning, you should be able to serve her just those data with no frills and in an-easy-to-access way.

How would you build such a personalizable, content-rich, portal-like Web site? Admittedly, displaying rich content is not a programmatic issue, but being able to handle a wide range of content is a crucial design issue. As a page developer, you are responsible for building a modular site and making it personalizable. Web Parts are the tools in Microsoft ASP.NET 2.0 that make building modular and customizable Web sites easier, and even pleasant.

In this chapter, we'll take a tour of the ASP.NET 2.0 Web Parts framework and build a small but highly personalizable Web site.

Web Parts at a Glance

The ASP.NET Web Parts Framework provides an infrastructure for creating Web applications that can handle rich content as well as large amounts of it. Using Web Parts, you can build sites that enable users to select and receive only the content they want. Web Parts are container components that aggregate different types of content. As such, they are particularly useful for creating portal pages.

What Are Web Parts, Anyway?

Figure 7-1 is taken from the My MSN Web site. The page is an aggregation of different blocks, each presenting a particular type of information.

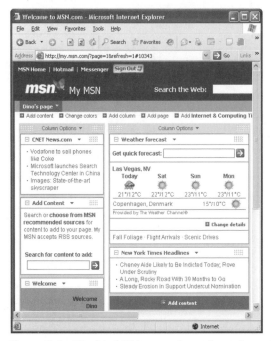

Figure 7-1   The My MSN page of a registered user is composed of all the blocks of information the user selected.

No block displayed on the page is there by chance. By using the *Add Content* and *Change Details* links, the user can select which blocks to display and their graphical layout.

Pages with a similar personalizable structure can be built in ASP.NET by combining an array of Web Parts components.

Content of a Web Part

You can think of a Web Part as a window of information available within the page. Users can close, minimize, or restore that window. The Web Part is essentially a container filled with the usual HTML stuff—static text, links, images, and other controls, including user controls and custom controls. By combining Web Parts and the user profile application programming interface (API), page developers can easily create pages and controls tailored to the individual user's needs.

The content of a Web Part can be any information that is useful to all users, a subset of users, or one user in particular. Most commonly, the content of a Web Part is provided by external Web sites—for example, financial, weather, and sports news. The content of a Web Part can range from a list of favorite links to a gallery of photos to the results of a search.

Layout of a Web Part

From the developer's perspective, a Web Part component is a sort of smart *Panel* control. Like a panel, a Web Part can contain any valid ASP.NET content. What makes the Web Part more powerful than a simple panel is the support it gets from the Web Part manager and the extra visual elements it renders. The layout of a Web Part mimics that of a desktop window. It has a caption bar with a title, as well as links to common verbs such as minimize, close, and restore.

Although the Web Part can act as a container for information from external sites and pages, it is quite different from a frame. A frame points to a URL, and the browser is responsible for filling the area with the content downloaded from the URL. A Web Part, on the other hand, is a server-side control that is served to the browser as plain HTML. You can still populate a Web Part with the content grabbed from external sites, but you are responsible for retrieving that content, either by using HTML scraping or, better yet (when available), Web services.

ASP.NET Web Parts and Microsoft SharePoint

In the Microsoft Windows world, SharePoint products and technologies simplify various forms of collaboration between partners within a company or an organization. The pages of a Web site based on SharePoint can contain special components named Web Parts, which are specifically designed to provide personalized and customizable windows of information to users.

SharePoint technologies and ASP.NET are different things with a common and overlapping area. SharePoint products and related technologies are aimed at empowering collaboration within an organization, between members and their partners and customers. In this context, a portal is just one possible practical application of the term *collaboration*. ASP.NET supplies a run-time environment that can host a SharePoint application. In addition, ASP.NET 2.0 comes with a framework that developers can use to build portal-like solutions without resorting to SharePoint products and the related set of technologies.

Are there any points of contact between SharePoint and the ASP.NET portal framework? Sure, Web Parts components. In the end, today's SharePoint Web Parts are ASP.NET controls with an extra layer of code that make them interact with the SharePoint framework. ASP.NET 2.0 Web Parts are server controls that interact with the ASP.NET Web Parts framework to provide a behavior that mimics that of SharePoint documents.

Note SharePoint and ASP.NET are destined to converge in the future, even though the level of the convergence is not clear just yet. What's certain is that the next version of SharePoint will be entirely based on ASP.NET 2.0 and that ASP.NET Web Parts will be fully supported by Share-Point. To a large extent, this already happens now when you install the SharePoint Service Pack 2. Some new features in the ASP.NET compilation model (such as no-compile pages, parser filters, and virtual path providers) have been introduced just to facilitate—and, in some cases, to make happen—the porting of the SharePoint engine to ASP.NET 2.0. Web Parts are the next due step. In the future, with the next major release of SharePoint, SharePoint Web Parts and ASP.NET Web Parts will be the same thing. This is not entirely true today.

Introducing the Web Parts Framework

A page employing Web Parts uses several components from the Web Parts Framework, each performing a particular function. The *WebPart* control is the central element in the Web Parts infrastructure, but it is not the only one. Table 7-1 details these components.

Table 7-1   Components of the Web Parts Framework

Component	Description
WebPartManager	The component that manages all Web Parts on a page. It has no user interface and is invisible at run time.
WebPart	Contains the content presented to the user through moveable windows. Note that *WebPart* is an abstract class; you have to create your own *WebPart* controls to display actual contents either through inheritance or via user controls.
WebPartZone	A page-level container for *WebPart* controls.
CatalogPart	The base class for Catalog Part controls. A Catalog Part control presents to users a list of available Web Parts for dynamic inclusion in the page. Derived classes you actually use in applications are *ImportCatalogPart*, *PageCatalogPart*, and *DeclarativeCatalogPart*.
CatalogZone	A page-level container for *CatalogPart* controls.
ConnectionsZone	A page-level container for the connections defined between any pair of Web Parts found in the page.
EditorPart	The base class for all editor controls that allow modifications to Web Parts. An Editor Part presents its own user interface to let users set properties.
EditorZone	A page-level container for *EditorPart* controls.

Aside from the *WebPartManager* class, the Web Parts infrastructure is made up of three types of components, known as *parts*: Web Parts, Catalog Parts, and Editor Parts. The screen real estate of a page is partitioned among zones, and each zone contains homogeneous parts.

Parts and Zones

The zone is a container for parts and provides additional user-interface elements and functionality for all parts it contains. An ASP.NET page can contain multiple zones, and each zone can contain one or more parts. A zone is responsible for rendering common user-interface elements around the parts it contains, such as titles, borders, and verb buttons, as well as a header and footer.

A Web Part defines the content to show through page windows, whereas an Editor Part lets users edit the structure and settings of a particular Web Part. For example, suppose you have a weather Web Part that shows forecasts for a few selected cities. An Editor Part for this Web Part would provide a friendly user interface for users to add or remove cities and decide whether to see the temperature in Celsius or Fahrenheit. Based on the weather applet in the My MSN Web site, you enter Edit mode by clicking either the Select Your Cities button on the page or the Edit button in the caption bar (shown in Figure 7-2). The properties you can edit are specific to the Web Part type. In general, you end up editing the contents of the displayed *WebPart* control.

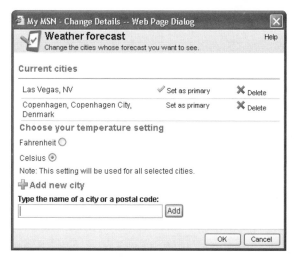

Figure 7-2 Editing the weather content block of the My MSN Web site.

The Web Parts infrastructure enables users to choose a personalized set of parts to display on a page and specify their position. The list of available parts is provided by a Catalog Part control. In this way, users can add parts dynamically. The catalog also acts as a store for the parts that the user has removed from the page by acting on the standard and system-provided user interface. Removed parts can be restored if a catalog is specified for the page. We'll cover Catalog Parts and Editor Parts in greater depth later in the chapter.

Web Parts are ultimately server controls. *WebPart* is the base class of all contents-enabled parts controls used in ASP.NET pages. It derives from an abstract base class named *Part*. Likewise, *EditorPart* and *CatalogPart* are the base classes for Web Part editors and catalogs. All part classes inherit from *Part*, which in turn inherits from one of the native ASP.NET server controls—*Panel*. All parts, therefore, are implemented as ASP.NET-specific containers of other controls. Figure 7-3 shows the entire hierarchy.

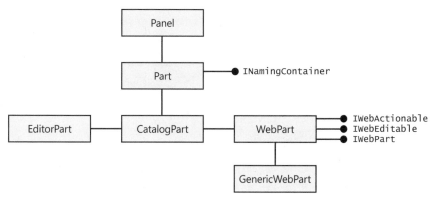

Figure 7-3 Hierarchy of part classes.

> **Note**   In ASP.NET 2.0, the *Panel* control has been enriched with the capability of scrolling its contents. The effect is obtained by adding the corresponding cascading style sheet (CSS) style—*overflow*. You can obtain the same results in ASP.NET 1.x by applying the same CSS style manually in the *.aspx* markup.

The *WebPartManager* Class

The *WebPartManager* is a nonvisual control that manages the many kinds of elements on a Web Parts–enabled page. In particular, the manager maintains a collection of zones and parts, and it tracks which parts are contained in each zone. Only one *WebPartManager* can be contained in a Web form. In the simplest cases, your interaction with the manager control is limited to adding it to a page:

```
<asp:WebPartManager runat="server" id="MyWebMan" />
```

However, the Web Part manager is responsible for more advanced functions that require a bit of coding. For example, it tracks the display mode of the page and notifies zones and parts of any change in the display mode. Depending on the Display mode, parts and zones render differently. The default display mode is Normal, which means that catalog and editor zones are hidden and only Web Parts are displayed with their own titles and borders. You can access the list of zones via the *Zones* collection.

The *WebPartManager* allows end users to move parts to different zones or to different locations within the same zone. It also enables the views in which users can edit the appearance, properties, and behavior of controls; and it raises Web Parts life-cycle events, such as when parts are being added, moved, connected, or deleted.

Finally, the *WebPartManager* is responsible for initiating communication between two part-connected controls and for programmatically moving, closing, and importing Web Parts.

Two part controls within the same page can communicate and exchange information using a special channel represented by a *WebPartConnection* object. Communication between parts is possible if both parts implement ad hoc interfaces. A Web Part that is intended to provide some information to others would implement the provider's set of interfaces. In this way, a consumer Web Part can access properties and methods in a consistent fashion. A made-to-measure connection zone allows end users to define connections dynamically by visually selecting connectable Web Parts from a list and designating which is the consumer and which is the provider. We'll return to how connection objects connect to Web Parts later in the chapter.

Zones of Web Parts

Each type of part requires its own zone object. The *WebPartZone* is the container for *WebPart* generic controls. It hosts all the Web Part contents and tracks them all through a collection property named *WebParts*. In addition, it provides free drag-and-drop functionality when the

Web Parts are switched to Design mode. The Design mode is one of the display modes supported by the Web Part manager, and it applies to all Web Parts in the page. When working in Design mode, end users can modify the layout of the page by moving Web Parts around. The drag-and-drop facility is provided by the zone component. The *WebPartZone* control allows you to define quite a few style properties, such as *PartStyle* (the style of the contents), *PartTitleStyle* (the style of the caption bar), and *MenuVerbStyle* (the style of the menu elements attached to each Web Part in a zone). We'll return to the supported styles a bit later.

The other zone types are more specialized. The *EditorZone* is used to contain editor controls to configure existing Web Parts. The *CatalogZone* is used to display the catalog of available Web Parts the user can choose from. The *ConnectionsZone* groups elements that represent links between pairs of Web Parts to communicate and form master/detail views.

Building Pages with Web Parts

You probably can't wait to see some markup code to illustrate pages composed with Web Parts. Here's a quick example:

```
<%@ Page Language="C#" CodeFile="Parts.aspx.cs" Inherits="Parts" %>
<%@ Register TagPrefix="x" TagName="News" Src="News.ascx" %>
<%@ Register TagPrefix="y" TagName="Favorites" Src="Favorites.ascx" %>

<html>
<head><title>Simple Web Parts</title></head>
<body>
   <form id="form1" runat="server">
      <h1>Demonstrating WebParts zones</h1>

      <asp:WebPartManager ID="WebMan" runat="server" />

      <asp:WebPartZone ID="WebPartZone1" runat="server"
            HeaderText="This is Zone #1"
            PartChromeType="TitleAndBorder" BorderColor="#CCCCCC">
         <PartStyle Font-Size="0.8em" ForeColor="#333333" />
         <PartTitleStyle Font-Size="0.8em" Font-Names="verdana"
            BackColor="#507CD1" ForeColor="White" />
         <PartChromeStyle BackColor="#EFF3FB" BorderColor="#D1DDF1"
            Font-Names="Verdana" ForeColor="#333333" />
         <ZoneTemplate>
            <x:News runat="server" id="News" />
            <y:Favorites runat="server" id="Favs" />
         </ZoneTemplate>
      </asp:WebPartZone>

   </form>
</body>
</html>
```

Let's focus on the body of the page. The form contains a *WebPartManager* control that governs the execution and rendering of all child parts. The form also contains one Web zone richly styled and containing a couple of parts. The Web Part zone is configured to show a title and a border around its content. The <*ZoneTemplate*> tag includes all the Web Parts defined for the zone. Figure 7-4 shows the page in action.

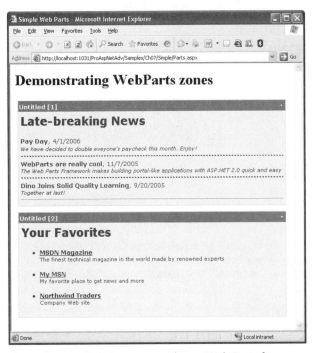

Figure 7-4   A Web Part zone with two Web Parts for news and useful links.

The content of each Web Part is shown through a user control—an *.ascx* source file. User controls are composite controls made of controls, literals, and markup declared and persisted through source files compiled on the fly like pages. (We'll fully cover user controls in Chapter 12.) To be used within a page, user controls must first be registered through the *@Register* directive. The *@Register* directive creates a mapping between a tag name and prefix pair and a source file.

The Role of User Controls

There are two ways to define content Web Parts. One approach entails creating a custom server control that inherits from *WebPart* and implements some of the interfaces shown earlier in Figure 7-3. This approach is the most flexible and powerful, but it requires you to master the most common techniques for creating custom ASP.NET controls. The second approach is simpler, faster, and, in most cases, equally effective. It entails the use of a user control.

What's the relationship between Web Parts and user controls? Web Parts display contents expressed through markup. Similarly, user controls are also a way of expressing contents through markup. By creating custom Web Parts, you can implement more interfaces, add conditional rendering, and simplify deployment and sharing across different applications.

However, as long as you just need to display some relatively static contents with relatively little processing logic, user controls are fast to write and effective. Joining the two is a powerful combination.

Chrome, Verbs, and Menu

The Web Parts in Figure 7-4 show a button in the caption bar. If you click the button, a drop-down menu appears, as depicted in Figure 7-5.

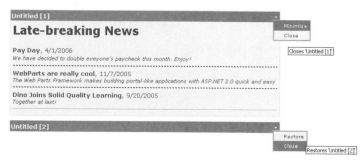

Figure 7-5   When a Web Part is minimized, a Restore button becomes available to let you restore the original panel later.

The verbs in the system menu are customizable to some extent. By default, you find the *Minimize* (or *Restore*) and *Close* items. If you click the *Close* button, the Web Part is hidden from view. It is not destroyed, though. If the page includes a Catalog Part, all closed Web Parts are listed in the catalog so that users can restore them later.

The menu can be styled at will and natively supports mouse hover effects. The "chrome" of a part indicates the structure of the caption and border that surrounds a part. In the preceding example, the chrome includes the title and border. You can choose to display the border only or title only. In general, the chrome is defined on the zone and inherited by all contained parts.

> **Note**   As you can see in Figure 7-5, the title of the Web Parts is unspecified. The Web Parts in the sample are implemented as plain user controls. How can you specify the title of a Web Part? The title and other settings of a Web Part can be defined through the members of several ASP.NET-defined ad hoc interfaces—for example, *IWebPart*. Implementing the interface is more natural if you create the part as a server control; however, user controls can also implement interfaces, as you'll see demonstrated later.

Role-Based Web Parts

When a Web Part is added to a page, it must be checked to see whether run-time conditions exist to add it. Web Parts are given a filter property that, if set, can be checked at run time to validate the expected role of the Web Part. You can create an event handler for the *AuthorizeWebPart* event on the manager object and provide filtering for Web Parts. In this way, you can show and hide Web Parts based on the user's role. We'll return to this topic later.

Building Web Parts

Let's build a sample Web Part and experiment with its properties. As mentioned, a Web Part is a pseudo-window nested in the Web page that contains some sort of information your users want to see. Like a window, it can be moved around, and its content can be configured to some extent. The Web Parts infrastructure provides drag-and-drop facilities for moving the control around and changing the page layout. The programmer is responsible for building any logic and user-interface elements for editing and cataloging the contents.

The primary goal of a Web Part control is to deliver information to users. The information can be retrieved in a variety of ways, depending on the characteristics of both the Web Part and the hosting application. In a portal scenario, the Web Part shows, through the user's personalized page, some content grabbed over the internal network (reports, documents, announcements) or provided by external Web sites (blogs, news, stock quotes).

A Web Part control inherits either explicitly or implicitly from the *WebPart* abstract class. So let's start our tour of Web Parts from here.

The *WebPart* Class

You have two basic options to create the markup for a Web Part component. You can create a custom control that derives from *WebPart*, or you can use other server controls, including custom controls and user controls (*.ascx* files). Existing server and user controls that do not inherit from *WebPart* automatically share full Web Parts functionality when declared in, or programmatically added to, a Web Part zone. In this case, the controls are wrapped by a *GenericWebPart* object at run time and exposed to the Web Part manager as true Web Part controls.

As shown in Figure 7-3, the *GenericWebPart* class derives from *WebPart*. You cannot use *GenericWebPart* directly in the page markup. In addition, note that a single instance of the *GenericWebPart* class can wrap only one server control at a time.

Note   Thanks to *GenericWebPart*, you could also define a valid zone template as shown here:

```
<ZoneTemplate>
    <asp:Button runat="server" ID="Button1" Text="Hello" />
</ZoneTemplate>
```

When more than one control is specified as a direct child of the *<ZoneTemplate>* tag, only the first one is considered. You cannot use literals unless you make them server-side controls.

```
<ZoneTemplate>
    <h1 runat="server" ID="H1">Hello</h1>
</ZoneTemplate>
```

If you omit the *runat=server* attribute, the preceding contents are ignored.

Using existing controls to compose Web Parts is definitely a good option and one that can save you from quite a bit of coding. The drawback is that you can put only one control in each zone. To work around this limitation, you can use custom composite controls only or, better yet, aggregate and link more controls together by creating a user control. However, creating a new specific control that derives from the *WebPart* class gives you the maximum programmatic control over the behavior of the Web Part.

> **Important**   Building Web Part components through user controls gives you the opportunity to build your control visually thanks to the excellent support from the Microsoft Visual Studio 2005 environment. In terms of functionality, creating custom controls or user controls is nearly identical; as a matter of fact, you can build fully featured Web Parts as user controls. In other words, user controls are not merely a secondary option for building Web Parts. They can implement interfaces and actions just as regular server controls derived from WebPart can be. The difference is mostly a matter of preference. This said, though, user controls and server controls have different characteristics that remain whether they are used in context with WebParts or not. One significant limitation to user controls you should be aware of is that user controls are not inheritable and can't be added to the Visual Studio 2005 toolbox. We'll cover user controls in Chapter 12.

Members of the *WebPart* Class

The Table 7-2 lists the main properties of the *WebPart* class, and it should give you an idea of the programming power of the Web Part controls. Notice that the class indirectly inherits *WebControl* and *Panel*, so it also features quite a few extra visual properties—such as *BackColor*, *BackImageUrl*, and *ScrollBars*—that are not listed here.

Table 7-2   Properties of the *WebPart* Class

Property	Description
AllowClose	Indicates whether end users can close the Web Part.
AllowConnect	Indicates whether the Web Part control allows other controls to connect to it.
AllowEdit	Indicates whether end users can modify a Web Part through the user interface of an Editor Part control.
AllowHide	Indicates whether end users can hide the Web Part.
AllowMinimize	Indicates whether end users can minimize the Web Part.
AllowZoneChange	Indicates whether end users can move the Web Part between zones.
AuthorizationFilter	An arbitrary string that the Web Part manager uses to determine whether the Web Part can be added to a page.
CatalogIconImageUrl	The URL to an image that represents the Web Part in a catalog of Web Parts.
ChromeState	Indicates the state of the Web Part: normal or minimized.
ChromeType	Indicates the type of the frame for the Web Part: border, title, title and border, or none.

Table 7-2   Properties of the *WebPart* Class

Property	Description
ConnectErrorMessage	Gets an error message for end users if any errors occur during the connection process.
Description	The description used in Web Part catalogs and as a ToolTip in the title bar.
Direction	The direction of the text: left-to-right or right-to-left.
DisplayTitle	The full title text actually displayed in the title bar of the Web Part.
ExportMode	Indicates whether all, some, or none of the Web Part properties can be exported. By default, no properties are exported.
HasSharedData	Indicates whether a Web Part has any shared personalization data associated with it.
HasUserData	Indicates whether a Web Part has any user personalization data associated with it.
HelpMode	Indicates the type of user interface selected to display help content for the Web Part.
HelpUrl	The URL to a topic in the Web Part's help content.
Hidden	Indicates whether the Web Part is displayed.
ImportErrorMessage	An error message used if errors occur when the Web Part is imported.
IsClosed	Indicates whether the Web Part is currently closed.
IsShared	Indicates whether multiple users share the Web Part.
IsStandalone	Indicates whether the Web Part is not contained within a Web Parts zone.
IsStatic	Indicates whether the Web Part is declared in the markup and not added to the page programmatically.
Subtitle	String concatenated with *Title* to form a complete caption for the Web Part.
Title	The title of the Web Part.
TitleIconImageUrl	The URL to an image that appears in the title bar.
TitleUrl	The URL to additional information about the Web Part. If it is specified, the URL appears in the title bar.
Verbs	The set of verbs associated with the Web Part. A verb is an action that users can take on the Web Part.
WebBrowsableObject	Gets a reference to the Web Part when the part can be edited by a custom Editor Part control.
Zone	The zone object that currently contains the Web Part.
ZoneIndex	The index of the Web Part in the zone it lives in.

The programming interface of the *WebPart* class is mostly in the properties listed in the table. The class has one method and no events, aside from those inherited from base server controls. The public method is *CreateEditorParts*. It returns a collection of custom Editor Part objects that can be used to edit the Web Part when it is in Edit mode.

Given the abstract nature of the *WebPart* class, it might be interesting to take a look at protected properties. Aside from those inherited from parent controls, The *WebPart* class has just one property—*WebPartManager*—which returns a reference to the corresponding Web Part manager. As for protected methods, have a look at Table 7-3.

Table 7-3   Protected Overridable Methods of the *WebPart* Class

Method	Description
OnClosing	Invoked when a Web Part is closed on a page
OnConnectModeChanged	Invoked when a Web Part control is beginning or ending the process of connecting to other controls
OnDeleting	Invoked when a Web Part is permanently deleted from a page
OnEditModeChanged	Invoked when a Web Part is entering or leaving Edit mode

By overriding any of the methods in Table 7-3, a class derived from *WebPart* can provide custom handling of some events in the life of a Web Part. All these events are triggered by user actions or methods invoked on the Web Part manager class.

Web Parts Interfaces

As you recall from Figure 7-3, the *WebPart* class derives from *Part* and implements a few interfaces—*IWebPart*, *IwebActionable*, and *IWebEditable*. These interfaces define common user-interface (UI) properties used to enhance the user experience when working with Web Parts. These interfaces represent the main difference between writing Web Parts through the base class *WebPart* or simple user controls.

When you inherit from *WebPart*, these interfaces are already implemented in the base class, but you can decide if and how to override some of the members. When you create a *WebPart* through a user control, you have to implement these interfaces manually if you require their functionality. Implementing these interfaces is optional, but omitting them does cause side effects. For example, omitting an *IWebPart* implementation causes the untitled captions you see in Figure 7-4. Collectively, members of each interface are described in Table 7-2, as you can see by this review of the structure of the various Web Parts interfaces:

```
public interface IWebPart
{
    string CatalogIconImageUrl { get; set; }
    string Description { get; set; }
    string Subtitle { get; }
    string Title { get; set; }
    string TitleIconImageUrl { get; set; }
    string TitleUrl { get; set; }
}
public interface IWebEditable
{
    EditorPartCollection CreateEditorParts();
    object WebBrowsableObject { get; }
}
```

```
public interface IWebActionable
{
    WebPartVerbCollection Verbs { get; }
}
```

In the default implementation, *WebBrowsableObject* returns *this* (or *Me* when using Microsoft Visual Basic .NET), and the *Verbs* collection is empty. As far as *IWebPart* is concerned, *Title* and *Description* fall back to the implementation of analogous properties on the *Part* class. These properties store their values in the view state. By default, *Subtitle* and other string properties on *IWebPart* return an empty string.

The Authorization Filter

The Web Part manager controls the process of adding Web Parts to a page. It is essential to note that not all Web Parts can be added to a given page by any user. When a Web Part is added—either at startup time or programmatically—the Web Part manager fires the *Authorize-WebPart* event to determine whether the part can be added to the page. By writing a page-level event handler, developers can check the *AuthorizationFilter* property of the Web Part and determine whether run-time conditions exist to add the Web Part.

The *AuthorizationFilter* is similar to roles, but a bit more general. In other words, you can use role information to fill the property, but that's not the only possibility available to you. For example, you can use other arbitrary information or simulate roles in a system where roles are not supported as an authentication feature.

```
<asp:WebPartManager runat="server" OnAuthorizeWebPart="AuthorizeWebPart" />
```

The preceding code executes the following event handler whenever a Web Part is added to the page under the jurisdiction of the manager:

```
void AuthorizeWebPart(object sender, WebPartAuthorizationEventArgs e)
{
    if (!String.IsNullOrEmpty(e.AuthorizationFilter))
    {
        if (e.AuthorizationFilter == "Admin")
            e.IsAuthorized = true;
        else
            e.IsAuthorized = false;
    }
}
```

The *WebPartAuthorizationEventArgs* structure includes a property named *AuthorizationFilter* that just mirrors the corresponding property on the Web Part. You assess the value of the filter string and set the *IsAuthorized* property accordingly. If not authorized, the Web Part won't be added to the page.

Note that by default—that is, unless you handle the *AuthorizeWebPart* event in the page— setting the *AuthorizationFilter* property to the empty string means that the Web Part is authorized.

> **Important**   A Web Part is ultimately a custom server control. In addition to providing the features covered here, it can provide control and view-state management and access ASP.NET intrinsics, the request context, and authentication information.

The *StockViewer* Web Part

The structure of a realistic Web Part is usually not much more complicated than this:

```
public class StockViewerWebPart : WebPart
{
   // Public properties, if any, are defined here...

   public override string Title
   {
      ⋮
   }

   protected override void RenderContents (HtmlTextWriter writer)
   {
      ⋮
   }
}
```

It defines some public properties that affect the behavior of the component, optionally overrides the *Title* property to display a representative caption on the title bar, and overrides the *RenderContents* method to generate the output.

This code gives you an idea of the minimum amount of work required to set up a custom Web Part. However, the sample component I'm going to build—named *StockViewer*—will be a bit more sophisticated because of some extra features. As the name suggests, the *StockViewer* Web Part is expected to list current quotes of some stocks and refresh them automatically at prefixed intervals.

The Public Interface

The *StockViewer* Web Part overrides the *Title* and *Subtitle* properties to control what's displayed in the title bar of each part that contains the component. Here's the standard way of overriding properties defined on the *WebPart*'s base class:

```
public override string Title
{
   get
   {
      if (String.IsNullOrEmpty(base.Title))
         return "Stock Viewer";
      return base.Title;
   }
   set
   {
      base.Title = value;
   }
}
```

Unlike *Title*, the *Subtitle* property is read-only. Here's how to override it in the *StockViewer* code:

```
public override string Subtitle
{
   get
   {
      if (String.IsNullOrEmpty(base.Subtitle))
         return "Random quotes";
      return base.Subtitle;
   }
}
```

A custom Web Part should generally expose some public properties so that users can customize, to the extent that your Web Part makes it possible, the contents being displayed. The *StockViewer* Web Part sports two properties—*Stocks* and *RefreshRate*. The former indicates the stocks currently being monitored; the latter sets the interval in seconds after which the stock quotes will automatically be refreshed. *Stocks* is expected to be a comma-separated string of stock names.

```
[Personalizable]
[WebBrowsable]
public string Stocks
{
   get { return _stocks; }
   set { _stocks = value; }
}

[Personalizable]
[WebBrowsable]
public int RefreshRate
{
   get { return _refreshRate; }
   set { _refreshRate = value; }
}
```

Both properties store their value in a stateless private member. Values of public properties don't change during page postbacks (unless explicitly changed through editors), so there's no need to pack them into the view state. The values are somewhat static and can be more effectively set every time the Web Part is loaded in the page.

What's the role of the two attributes used here?

Attributes for Web Part Properties

Assigned to a public control property, the *[Personalizable]* attribute indicates that the property needs to persist its value to the underlying data store if the control is used in a Web Part zone or inside a composite control wrapped in a Web Part. As discussed in Chapter 4, Web Parts automatically save their state through the currently selected personalization provider. By default, personalization data flows into one of the tables in the *aspnetdb.mdf* file. If you omit the attribute, the value for the property simply won't be persisted and will be lost when the request ends.

Not all properties can be decorated with such an attribute. In particular, the property must be public, read/write (that is, both get and set accessors are required), and not indexed (that is, it can't be a collection property, such as *Item*). A property lacking this attribute won't be persisted unless the control implements the *IPersonalizable* interface and manually persists in code the property value.

The *[WebBrowsable]* attribute indicates that the property can be edited through the user interface of the Editor Part. The Editor Part provides some user interface features to enable users to change the value of the property. The UI is based on the type of the property. Properties marked as Web-browsable must be read/write and public. A control property that lacks the *[WebBrowsable]* attribute can't be edited by users and relies on executing code alone to change values.

Typically, a Web-browsable property is a property that configures the behavior of the control or Web Part, and this is just what *Stocks* and *RefreshRate* do for the sample *StockViewer* Web Part.

In addition to supporting *[Personalizable]* and *[WebBrowsable]*, a Web Part property can support two more attributes—*[WebDescription]* and *[WebDisplayName]*—which will be used when the Web Part is in Edit mode. The former defines the string to use as a ToolTip for a Web Part property. The latter allows you to specify the text for the label that appears to describe the property in the editing UI.

The Rendering Engine

If no stocks are listed, the Web Part control renders a simple message, as you see in Figure 7-6. However, if there are stocks to quote, *StockViewer* creates a table and adds one row for each monitored stock. (This is shown in Figure 7-7.)

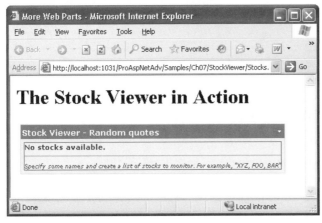

Figure 7-6   The *StockViewer* Web Part with empty data.

The output is created by overriding the *RenderContents* method of the *WebPart* class. Here's the code for *StockViewer*'s *RenderContents* method:

```
protected override void RenderContents (HtmlTextWriter writer)
{
    if ((_stocks == null) || (_stocks.Length == 0))
    {
        writer.Write("<b>No stocks available.</b><hr>" +
                "<i style=\"font-size:85%\">Specify some names
                    and create a list of stocks to monitor. " +
                "For example, \"XYZ, FOO, BAR\"</i>");
    }
    else
    {
        CreateTableOfStocks(writer);
        string msg = "No auto refresh";
        if (RefreshRate >0)
            msg = String.Format("{0} seconds delay", RefreshRate);
        string text = String.Format(
                "<br><div style=\"margin:5\">" +
                "<span style=\"font-size:80%\">" +
                "<span id=\"LastUpdated\">{0}</span> - " +
                "Quotes supplied by <b>RandomQuotes Inc</b>, {1}. " +
                "</span></div><br>",
                DateTime.Now.ToString("hh:mm:ss"),
                msg);
        writer.Write(text);
    }
}
```

Aside from creating the message to be displayed at the bottom of the part, the heart of the method is in the *CreateTableOfStocks* helper method. This method is implemented by the following code:

```
void CreateTableOfStocks(HtmlTextWriter writer)
{
    Table t = new Table();

    // Header
    CreateTableHeader(t);

    // Rows
    string[] list = _stocks.Split(new char[] { ',' });
    for (int i = 0; i < list.Length; i++)
    {
        string stockID = list[i];

        TableRow row = new TableRow();
        c1 = new TableCell();
        c1.Text = stockID;
        row.Cells.Add(c1);

        // The ID will be used to update the client-side
        // control through an ASP.NET remote script call.
        c2 = new TableCell();
```

```
        c2.ID = "StockValue" + i.ToString();
        c2.Text = GetCurrentValue(stockID);
        row.Cells.Add(c2);

        t.Rows.Add(row);
    }
    t.RenderControl(writer);
}
```

Each table row is formed by two cells—one for the stock name and one for the current value. The number of rows equals the number of monitored stocks. As mentioned, the *Stocks* property is a comma-separated string whose contents are split into a string array for easier processing. Figure 7-7 shows the final output of the Web Part.

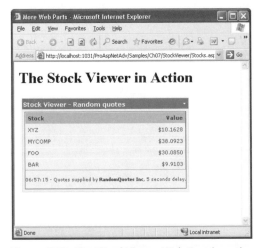

Figure 7-7   The *StockViewer* Web Part in action.

Automatic Updates

A control designed to display stock quotes can't just be static. At the very minimum, it has to provide a way (that is, a clickable button) for users to refresh the quotes periodically. It would be much better if the control could automatically update the quotes at fixed intervals. The *RefreshRate* property indicates the period; let's see how to use the property.

The idea is to have the Web Part control emit some script callback code to regularly go to the server, grab values, and update the control. The ASP.NET Script Callback technology, or the Ajax.NET library, can be successfully employed to arrange some code that collects fresh quotes and updates the page. Let's add the following code at the bottom of the *CreateTableOf-Stocks* method:

```
if (RefreshRate > 0)
{
    if (!Page.ClientScript.IsStartupScriptRegistered(
        this.GetType(), "RefreshQuotes"))
    {
```

```
        string js = GetRefreshScript();
        Page.ClientScript.RegisterStartupScript(
            this.GetType(), "RefreshQuotes", js, true);
    }
}
```

The code registers a piece of Javascript code at the page startup. This code creates a timer and periodically executes an out-of-band call to the server to pick up current stock values:

```
private string GetRefreshScript()
{
    StringBuilder sb;
    sb = new StringBuilder("\r\nfunction RefreshQuotes() {\r\n");
    sb.AppendLine(Page.ClientScript.GetCallbackEventReference(
        this, "null", "UpdateQuotes", "null"));
    sb.AppendFormat("  window.setTimeout(\"RefreshQuotes()\", {0});",
        RefreshRate*1000);
    sb.AppendLine("\r\n}");
    sb.AppendLine(GetUpdateQuotesScript());
    sb.AppendLine("RefreshQuotes();");

    return sb.ToString();
}
```

The preceding code generates the following Javascript script:

```
function RefreshQuotes()
{
    WebForm_DoCallback('WebMan$MyStocks', null, UpdateQuotes,
                        null, null, false);
    window.setTimeout("RefreshQuotes()", 5000);
}
```

As a result, a server call is made every five seconds to the Web Part control on the server.

The technology used for the out-of-band call is ASP.NET Script Callback This *StockViewer* control is a good example of a custom control that implements script callbacks. The *StockViewer* control retrieves up-to-date quotes, and it returns and displays their values. Here's the server-side code that implements the callback mechanism. In this case, the quotes are just random numbers.

```
private string results;
void ICallbackEventHandler.RaiseCallbackEvent(string argument)
{
    string buf = "," + _stocks;
    string[] list = buf.Split(new char[] { ',' });
    list[0] = DateTime.Now.ToString("hh:mm:ss");
    for (int i=1; i<list.Length; i++)
    {
        list[i] = GetCurrentValue(list[i]);
    }
    results = String.Join(",", list);
    return;
}
```

```
string ICallbackEventHandler.GetCallbackResult()
{
    return results;
}
```

As we saw in Chapter 6, when an ASP.NET Script Callback method returns, a Javascript call-back runs to update the page. In this case, the Javascript callback looks like the following code:

```
function UpdateQuotes(response, context) {
    var quotes = response.split(',');
    for(i=1; i<quotes.length; i++)
    {
        var elem = document.getElementById("StockValue" +
            (i-1).toString());
        elem.innerHTML = quotes[i];
    }
    var now = document.getElementById("LastUpdated");
    now.innerHTML = quotes[0];
}
```

The string the remote script callback function receives from the server method has the following schema:

```
currentTime, quote1, ..., quoteN
```

The values are extracted and used to update the cells in the table that show stock quotes and the label that displays the current time.

> **Note**   The full source code of this example, as well as all other examples discussed in the book, is available at *http://www.microsoft.com/mspress/companion/0-7356-2177-2/*.

To use the *StockViewer* Web Part control in a sample page, the following markup is required. Needless to say, you can just drag and drop necessary controls from the Visual Studio 2005 toolbox.

```
<asp:WebPartManager ID="WebMan" runat="server" />
<asp:WebPartZone ID="WebPartZone1" runat="server"
    HeaderText="This is Zone #1"
    PartChromeType="TitleAndBorder">
  <ZoneTemplate>
    <x:StockViewerWebPart runat="server" id="MyStocks"
        RefreshRate="5" Stocks="XYZ,MYCOMP,FOO,BAR"
        Title="Stock Viewer" />
  </ZoneTemplate>
</asp:WebPartZone>
```

If the *RefreshRate* property is set to a value greater than 0, a client timer is created to fire an out-of-band call each time the specified number of seconds has elapsed. If you didn't do this, the list of stock quotes would remain immutable all the time unless you were to modify the Web

Part's user interface and add a button that refreshes the contents on demand. Figure 7-8 demonstrates an auto-updatable version of the Web Part.

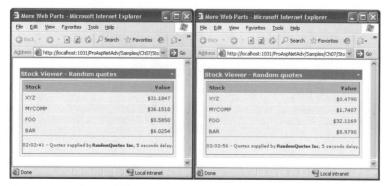

Figure 7-8 The *StockViewer* Web Part retrieves stock quotes at regular intervals based on the value of its *RefreshRate* property.

> **Note** In the preceding example, stock names are fictitious and quotes are just randomly generated numbers. However, the code responsible for retrieving the current value for a given stock name is insulated in a helper method named *GetCurrentValue*. By simply modifying this method to point to a (Web) service that can return real values for real stocks, you upgrade the *StockViewer* Web Part from the rank of a nice toy to that of a useful component.

Other Ways of Building Web Parts

As mentioned, inheriting from the *WebPart* base class is just one way of building Web Parts—even though it is perhaps the most flexible and powerful approach. Let's review other quicker and no less effective ways to build Web Parts.

Web Parts as User Controls

In Figure 7-4, you see a sample page made of two user control–based Web Parts. Once user controls have been registered with the page, you use them in a zone as follows:

```
<ZoneTemplate>
    <x:News runat="server" id="News" />
    <x:Favorites runat="server" id="Favs" />
</ZoneTemplate>
```

What does the source code for each of them look like? The two user controls share a nearly identical internal architecture. They retrieve their data from a linked XML file and repeat a layout for each bound item. The difference lies in the different XML nodes that each accesses and, of course, in the different HTML tree each generates. Here's the source code for the Favorites user control.

```
<%@ Control Language="C#" ClassName="MyFavorites"%>

<asp:XmlDataSource ID="XmlData" runat="server"
     DataFile="/App_Data/webpartsdata.xml"
     XPath="WebPartsData/Favorite" />

<asp:Repeater ID="Repeater1" DataSourceID="XmlData" runat="server">
    <HeaderTemplate>
        <h2>Your Favorites</h2>
        <ul>
    </HeaderTemplate>
    <SeparatorTemplate>
        <br /><br />
    </SeparatorTemplate>
    <ItemTemplate>
        <li>
        <a href='<%# XPath("url")%>'><b><%# XPath("title")%></b></a>
        <br />
        <span style="font-size:85%">
            <%# XPath("description") %>
            </span>
            </li>
    </ItemTemplate>
    <FooterTemplate>
        </ul>
    </FooterTemplate>
</asp:Repeater>
```

When a user control is used in a Web Part zone, it gets wrapped by an instance of the *GenericWebPart* class. This wrapper class derives from *WebPart* and thus provides a generic implementation for *IWebPart* as well as other Web Parts–related interfaces. As a result, to set the title, subtitle, and other visual properties on a user control Web Part you have two routes from which to choose: roll your own implementation of the interfaces, or rely on the default implementation provided by *GenericWebPart*.

To implement an interface in a user control, you resort to the *@Implements* directive as shown below for the *IWebPart* interface in the *Favorites* Web Part.

```
<%@ Control Language="C#" ClassName="MyFavorites"%>
<%@ Implements Interface="System.Web.UI.WebControls.WebParts.IWebPart" %>

<script runat="server">
private string _title = "Favorite Links";
string IWebPart.Title {
   get { return _title; }
   set { _title = value; }
}
// Implement all other members of the IWebPart interface
   ⋮
</script>
   ⋮
```

If the user control relies on a code-behind file, you simply implement the interface in the code-behind class.

If the user control doesn't implement any of the Web Part interfaces itself, you can still use corresponding properties in the markup. Those properties will be recognized because the wrapper *GenericWebPart* class implemented them for you.

```
<x:News runat="server" id="News" Title="News of the day" />
<x:Favorites runat="server" id="Favs" />
```

Now both Web Parts have a custom title. The *News* Web Part sets it explicitly through the *GenericWebPart* wrapper; the *Favorites* Web Part sets it implicitly through the internal implementation of *IWebPart*. Figure 7-9 shows the same user controls of Figure 7-4 properly titled.

Figure 7-9   User control Web Parts properly titled.

Web Parts as Plain Server Controls

As mentioned, you can use individual controls to create Web Parts. It suffices that you drop a server control into the *<ZoneTemplate>* segment of a Web Part zone and pay attention to have just one control in the template. Literals are ignored, and if multiple server controls are found, multiple Web Parts will be created.

```
<ZoneTemplate>
    <asp:Calendar ID="Calendar1" runat="server" Title="Today" >
        <TodayDayStyle BackColor="#FF8000" />
    </asp:Calendar>
    <asp:Wizard ID="Wizard1" runat="server" ActiveStepIndex="0">
        <WizardSteps>
            <asp:WizardStep ID="WizardStep1" runat="server" Title="Step 1" />
            <asp:WizardStep ID="WizardStep2" runat="server" Title="Step 2" />
        </WizardSteps>
    </asp:Wizard>
</ZoneTemplate>
```

The preceding markup originates the page in Figure 7-10.

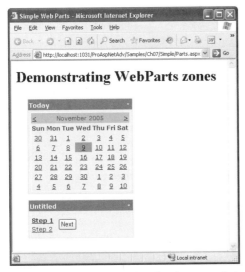

Figure 7-10   *Wizard* and *Calendar* controls in distinct Web Parts.

Note that you can use the *Title* attribute on server controls even though the server control itself has no notion of the *Title* property. This is again an artifact of the *GenericWebPart* wrapper class.

Styling the Web Zone

Just like any other server control, a Web Part can embellish its output through styles and visual properties. Note, though, once it is deployed to a zone, a Web Part is automatically themed according to the visual settings of the zone. A Web Part automatically inherits font, color, and border settings in use in the zone, thus gaining a look and feel that is similar to other Web Parts in the zone. The Web Part's visual appearance would change as soon as you move the Web Part to another zone if the theming differs in that other zone.

This said, each Web Part is free to control its appearance through a homemade set of properties and styles. In this case, the look of the part won't change as you move it around zones. It is a common practice to have the Web Part styled automatically by the system based on the settings in use in the current zone. Put another way, it's more common to allow the zone theme to dictate the visual appearance than it is to force a specific appearance by using custom visual properties and styles. This allows for more flexible user customization using the built-in tools ASP.NET provides.

Zone Style Properties

The Web zone supports quite a few style properties for customizing the look and feel of the zone and its constituent parts. Table 7-4 lists the supported zone styles.

Table 7-4   Style Properties of the Web Zone

Style	Description
EmptyZoneTextStyle	Style of an empty zone during the change-layout phase.
ErrorStyle	Style for rendering the error message that is displayed if a Web Part cannot be loaded or created. Note that in this case, an *ErrorWebPart* control is displayed in lieu of the originally requested Web Part.
FooterStyle	Style of the zone's footer.
HeaderStyle	Style of the zone's header.
MenuCheckImageStyle	Style applied to the check mark image that appears on a verb's menu next to the selected verb text.
MenuLabelHoverStyle	Style applied to the label of a verb's menu in the title bar when the user moves the mouse ready to open the menu.
MenuLabelStyle	Style of the label that indicates the verb's menu.
MenuPopupStyle	Style of the verb's drop-down menu.
MenuVerbHoverStyle	Style applied to a menu item in the verb's menu when the user moves the mouse over it.
MenuVerbStyle	Style applied to a label that represents a verb menu item.
PartChromeStyle	Style applied to the borders of Web Part controls contained by the zone.
PartStyle	Style applied to the border and contents of each Web Parts control contained by the zone.
PartTitleStyle	Style applied to the title bar of each Web Part in the zone.
SelectedPartChromeStyle	Style applied to selected WebPart control in a zone when the page is in Edit mode.
TitleBarVerbStyle	Style of the verbs in the zone's title bar.

In Visual Studio 2005, the AutoFormat feature of the *WebPartZone* control (see Figure 7-11) provides considerable help when it comes to styling a zone. In most cases, you just use it and don't bother setting these style properties yourself.

Figure 7-11   The AutoFormat feature of Visual Studio 2005 to style Web Part zones.

Zone Behavioral Properties

In addition to the style properties listed in Table 7-4, the Web Part zone control also supports quite a few other more behavioral properties. They are detailed in Table 7-5.

Table 7-5 Other Properties of the Web Zone

Property	Description
AllowLayoutChange	True by default, indicates whether Web Parts can be added to, removed from, or moved within the zone.
DragHighlightColor	Color of the zone's border when a Web Part is being dragged over the zone in Design mode.
EmptyZoneText	Text shown when the zone is empty in Design mode.
LayoutOrientation	Specifies how Web Parts are arranged within the zone— horizontally or vertically. It's vertical by default.
Padding	Space, in pixels, between Web Parts in the zone.
ShowTitleIcons	Indicates whether the icon of each Web Part (if any) should be displayed in the title bar.
WebPartVerbRenderMode	Indicates how the verbs associated with the Web Parts should be rendered. Options are menu or title bar. Verbs go to a drop-down menu by default.

Verbs play a fundamental role in Web Parts and Web zones. A verb indicates an action that the Web Part can execute. Available verbs should be made visible in some way. By default, they are grouped in the title bar of each Web Part either through a drop-down menu (as in all the examples considered so far) or through a series of links on the right side of the title bar. (See Figure 7-12 for an example of a linked-verb arrangement.)

Figure 7-12   Verbs listed on the Web Part's title bar in a linked arrangement.

The Web Part zone control features a few properties to let you configure system-provided verbs and enable or disable them as appropriate. Web Part controls, on the other hand, can individually override the verb's settings defined at the zone level. Let's dig into this a bit more.

Web Part Verbs

Verbs identify actions that users can take on the Web Part as a whole—for example, minimizing, restoring, editing, or closing the component. Verbs are configured in the zone, but each Web Part can disable (or enable) them individually through the various *AllowXXX* properties that we considered earlier in Table 7-2. System-defined verbs are listed in Table 7-6.

Table 7-6   Web Part System-Provided Verbs

Verb	Description
Close	Closes the Web Part and hides it from view. A closed Web Part can be re-added to a zone later through the Catalog Part. (More later.)
Connect	Connects two Web Parts that are configured to act as provider/consumer of information according to the same contract. (More later.)
Delete	Deletes the Web Part from the page. A deleted Web Part is lost and can't be re-added to the page later.
Edit	Displays an Editor Part for the current Web Part so that Web-browsable properties that it might have can be edited.
Export	Enables end users to export an XML definition file for a Web Part. For the verb to appear on the menu, though, the Web Part must have its *ExportMode* property not set to *WebPartExportMode.None*.
Help	Displays help for the Web Part by either navigating to the page or showing a modal/modeless window. For the verb to appear on the menu, though, the Web Part must have its *HelpUrl* property set.
Minimize	Minimizes the Web Part.
Restore	Restores a minimized Web Part.

Note that verb properties belong to the zone, not to the individual Web Part. This means that all Web Parts in a given zone share the same verb settings, even though the Web Part can disallow some verb-related actions.

In the zone, you can disable the Close verb through the following code:

```
<CloseVerb Enabled="false" />
```

A verb disabled in the zone can't be enabled at the Web Part level through the corresponding *AllowXXX* property. For example, the statement in the previous code cannot be reverted by setting *AllowClose* to *true* in the Web Part. The reverse is possible, though. A verb enabled in the zone can be disallowed in the Web Part.

```
<MinimizeVerb Enabled="true" />
```

For example, you can set *AllowMinimize* to *false* and prevent the Web Part from ever being minimized.

Verbs are represented by *WebPartVerb* objects and feature a few properties, including *Description* (the ToolTip to be displayed), *Text* (the text or alternate text if an image is used), and *ImageUrl* (the image to render). The list of members is completed by the addition of a couple of Boolean properties—*Enabled* and *Visible*—which toggle the availability and visibility of the verb in the menu.

Defining a Custom Verb

In addition to the standard verbs, each Web Part can define its own verbs. You do this through the *IWebActionable* interface, which consists of the sole property *Verbs*. If you're writing the Web Part as a classic server control, you must override the *Verbs* property, as it is already part of the class inherited from the base *Part* class. If you're writing the Web Part as a user control, you implement the *IWebActionable* interface in your user control. Here's how to proceed to add a custom *Refresh* verb to the *StockViewer* Web Part:

```
private WebPartVerbCollection _verbs;
⋮
public override WebPartVerbCollection Verbs
{
    get
    {
        if (_verbs == null)
        {
            ArrayList a = new ArrayList();
            WebPartVerb verb = new WebPartVerb("Refresh",
                new WebPartEventHandler(RefreshQuotesFromMenu));
            verb.Text = "Refresh";
            a.Add(verb);
            _verbs = new WebPartVerbCollection(base.Verbs, a);
        }
        return _verbs;
    }
}
```

You store the verbs in a private member of type *WebPartVerbCollection*. The *Verbs* collection will contain only new verbs. However, it is a good practice to merge custom verbs (if any) defined on the base class with the verbs you're defining in the current class. (This is accomplished for us when we create the new instance of *WebPartVerbCollection* in the preceeding code snippet.) Each verb is represented with an instance of the *WebPartVerb* class. In addition to the properties that we briefly mentioned in the previous section, a verb can have two click handlers—one for the client and one for the server. You can specify one or both through the constructor. Based on the preceding code snippet, when the *Refresh* verb is clicked, the Web Part page posts back and executes any code set in the *RefreshQuotesFromMenu* method. There is no corresponding client-side code in this case. Figure 7-13 shows the custom *Refresh* verb in the title bar of the *StockViewer* Web Part.

Figure 7-13   Custom verbs in the *StockViewer*'s title bar.

Note that like standard verbs, a custom verb will be shown as a link on the title bar or in the drop-down menu, depending on the settings in the zone.

Persistence of Web Part Personalization Data

A typical Web Part–powered page is inherently user specific. So if the user changes the layout of the zones or edits the part's attributes, the new layout must be stored and used whenever that page is visited again. In ASP.NET 2.0, this doesn't require any coding work on your part. All you have to do is configure the application so that it has a valid personalization provider to work with. In general, this simply means that you have to ensure that a valid aspnetdb.mdf file exists in the App_Data folder or that an equivalent SQL Server table exists and is reachable through the settings in the *web.config* file. (We covered Web Parts personalization providers in Chapter 4.)

Personalization allows the properties or state of Web Parts controls to be saved in long-term storage. Personalization data differs from both view state and user profiles. It is different from view state because the data is not request specific and tied to a browser session. It is different from user-profile information because it is tied to a specific page. User profiles, in fact, change on a per-user basis but remain the same across different pages in the same application. Web Parts personalization data is user and page specific.

Personalization information can have two possible scopes: User (default) or Shared. Based on the scope, the information is stored in a distinct data store. In the case of the default SQL Server personalization provider, for example, User and Shared data go to distinct tables.

When a page is running in *User* personalization scope, the Web Part manager loads and saves personalization data for each control based on the current user. This means that Web Part properties marked as user-specific will be loaded and saved, whereas Web Part shared properties will be loaded but not saved. A Web Part property is declared with a *User* or *Shared* scope through the *[Personalizable]* attribute that we met earlier. The *[Personalizable]* attribute has a few overloads.

```
[Personalizable(PersonalizationScope scope)]
[Personalizable(PersonalizationScope scope, bool isSensitive)]
```

In the first case, you specify the required scope of the property—User or Shared. In the second case, you also specify whether the property data should be considered sensitive. When you use the parameterless attribute (as we did in the *StockViewer* example), it defaults to *User* and not sensitive.

When a page is running in *Shared* personalization scope, the Web Part manager loads only the properties marked as *Shared*—that is, properties whose contents are applicable to all users viewing the control. Depending on the currently executing user's rights, this broadly applicable data can also be modified and saved back to the data store.

You can set the personalization scope for a page either statically in the *<asp:WebPartManager>* markup element or programmatically in the page's *PreInit* event.

```
WebPartManager1.Personalization.InitialScope = PersonalizationScope.Shared;
```

By default, a Web Part–powered page runs in *User* scope. The *Personalization* property has other interesting members—such as *ToggleScope*, to toggle the current page scope from user to shared and vice versa, and *Provider*, which returns the current instance of the personalization provider. (See Chapter 4.)

> **Tip**   The Web Part personalization data is persistent and never expires. What if you need to reset it? If you know the details of the provider's data store (the *aspnetdb.mdf* database in the default case), you can clear any persisted data at the source. If you don't know these details, or as a developer you don't have permissions to access the data store, you can clear the personalization data programmatically:
>
> ```
> WebPartManager1.Personalization.ResetPersonalizationState();
> ```
>
> The *ResetPersonalizationState* method clears any user/shared persisted state for the current page.

In summary, personalization scope refers to how personalization data is applicable to different users. *User* personalization data is applicable to only a specific user and control on a specific page. *Shared* personalization data is applicable to all users who view any page in the site. As a rule of thumb, when you create a Web Part with public properties, most of the time properties represent *User* data. *User* data indicates a property value that is specific to the user viewing that Web Part control on that page. To get this behavior, simply use the *[Personalizable]* attribute with no parameters.

> **Caution**   It should be noted that when the current user is not authenticated, the personalization scope defaults to *Shared*, no matter what. In addition, the current user is not given the permission to modify personalization state. The typical consequence of this situation is that when you move parts around zones or change property values, you get an exception upon saving.

Editing and Listing Web Parts

Among other things, the Web Part manager is responsible for setting the current display mode of the Web Parts. The display mode dictates how Web Parts are actually rendered inside their zones and whether any additional user interface and functionality are required. Changing the display mode enables advanced operations such as moving Web Parts around zones, editing properties on individual Web Parts, adding or removing Web Parts, and connecting two existing Web Parts.

Changing the Display Mode

To switch the display mode, you need to assign a new value to the *DisplayMode* property of the Web Part manager, as shown here:

```
WebPartManager1.DisplayMode = mode;
```

There's no predefined user interface block (that is, menu or other similar control) to enable the change of the display mode. You have to build your own user interface around the preceding statement. Typical options entail the use of the *Menu* control, a list of radio buttons, or perhaps a drop-down list showing all available modes. Let's first examine the various display modes and their characteristics.

Available Display Modes

Table 7-7 lists and details all supported display modes for ASP.NET Web Parts. The default display mode is Browse, meaning that no additional user-interface elements are displayed except the contents of the Web Parts.

Table 7-7   Display Modes

Mode	Description
Browse	Web Parts display their own contents; no additional user interface is shown, and no extra functions are available.
Catalog	All Catalog Parts associated with the page are displayed for users to add new Web Parts from available catalogs or import existing Web Parts serialized to disk files.
Connect	Enables the user to connect two existing Web Parts so that one can automatically consume any data the other is publishing.
Design	Enables the user to move Web Parts around within the same zone or across different zones in the page.
Edit	All Editor Parts associated with the page are displayed for users to modify attributes of individual Web Parts. Distinct editors are available for different families of properties—appearance, behavior, and custom properties.

When activated, the Design mode allows end users to move Web Parts around using a drag-and-drop operation. All necessary script code is automatically injected in the client page care of the Web Part manager. Like Browse, the Design mode is available to all users and in all cases.

The Edit, Catalog, and Connect modes are available only if the page contains an editor zone, catalog zone, or connections zone, respectively. To know which modes are available at a given time, you check the *SupportedDisplayModes* collection property on the Web Part Manager class.

Creating a Mode-Switcher User Control

My favorite way of letting users change the display mode of a Web Part–powered page consists of presenting all currently available modes through a drop-down list control, as shown in Figure 7-14.

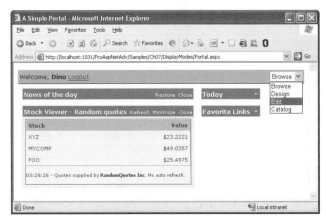

Figure 7-14 A sample mode-switcher drop-down control.

The structure of the mode-switcher control is fairly simple. Upon loading, the drop-down list control is filled with all the modes returned by the *SupportedDisplayModes* collection property of the Web Part manager. In addition, the drop-down list is configured for auto-postback, meaning that it originates a post to the server whenever the user changes the selection. Once on the server, the *DisplayMode* property of the Web Part manager is updated accordingly, and the page displays back to the user with a new style. The following code shows the full implementation of a mode-switcher user control named *modeswitcher.ascx*.

```
<%@ Control Language="C#" ClassName="ModeSwitcher" %>

<script runat="server">
WebPartManager wpm;

void Page_Load(object sender, EventArgs e)
{
    wpm = WebPartManager.GetCurrentWebPartManager(Page);
    if (!IsPostBack)
    {
        foreach (WebPartDisplayMode mode in wpm.SupportedDisplayModes)
        {
            if (mode.IsEnabled(wpm))
                SupportedModes.Items.Add(mode.Name);
        }
    }
}
```

```
public void SelectedIndexChanged(object sender, EventArgs e)
{
    string selectedMode = SupportedModes.SelectedValue;
    WebPartDisplayMode mode = wpm.SupportedDisplayModes[selectedMode];
    if (mode != null)
        wpm.DisplayMode = mode;
}
</script>

<asp:DropDownList ID="SupportedModes" runat="server"
    AutoPostBack="true"
    OnSelectedIndexChanged="SelectedIndexChanged" />
```

It goes without saying that you could also write a similar component using a classic server control. However, this is just one of the situations where user controls show their true power—they're quick to write, easy to learn and, more importantly, effective. (As promised, we'll return to user controls in Chapter 12.)

To use the mode-switcher control in a sample page, you first need to register it as follows:

```
<%@ Page Language="C#" CodeFile="Portal.aspx.cs" Inherits="Portal" %>
<%@ Register tagprefix="x" tagname="Mode" src="ModeSwitcher.ascx" %>
⋮
<x:Mode runat="server" id="Switcher" />
```

Let's see how the user interface of Web Part zones changes according to the various display modes.

Changing the Zones Layout

Before we go any further, we need a sample page that is representative of capabilities of the Web Parts framework so that display modes can be tested and understood appropriately. The sample page I'm going to use includes a couple of zones and various Web Parts.

Building a Sample Portal Page

The core code you need for a Web Part zone is shown next. However, to catch the user's eye you might want to add some colorful styles. The easiest way of doing this is through the AutoFormat menu of the Visual Studio 2005 page designer. (See Figure 7-11.) For simplicity, I'm not showing styles here.

```
<asp:WebPartZone ID="WebPartZone1" runat="server" HeaderText="Zone #1">
    <ZoneTemplate>
        <x:News runat="server" id="News" Title="News of the day" />
        <x:Favorites runat="server" id="Favs" />
    </ZoneTemplate>
</asp:WebPartZone>
<asp:WebPartZone ID="WebPartZone2" runat="server" HeaderText="Zone #2">
    <ZoneTemplate>
        <asp:Calendar ID="Calendar1" runat="server" Title="Today" />
        <asp:Wizard ID="Wizard1" runat="server" ActiveStepIndex="0" />
```

```
        <WizardSteps>
            <asp:WizardStep ID="WizStep1" runat="server" Title="Step 1" />
            <asp:WizardStep ID="WizStep2" runat="server" Title="Step 2" />
        </WizardSteps>
    </asp:Wizard>
    <x:StockViewerWebPart runat="server" id="MyStocks"
        Title="Stock Viewer"
        RefreshRate="5"
        Stocks="XYZ,MYCOMP,FOO,BAR" />
    </ZoneTemplate>
</asp:WebPartZone>
```

As you can see, the second zone contains three Web Parts, two of which are plain server controls—a *Calendar* and a (simplistic) *Wizard*.

Note that the two zones can have different settings for verbs, as well as being able to apply different styles to change the chrome and overall appearance.

As I've often mentioned in this chapter, Web Parts are designed to be user-specific and are the main tool in the Web Parts framework to deliver personalized contents to a particular user. So it is a natural assumption that a Web Part–powered page requires authentication and is to be viewed by authenticated users.

In light of this, it might be good to design such a page so that it displays the name of the connected user and provides a link to log out. In ASP.NET 2.0, a couple of new security controls make generating this user interface incredibly easy.

```
<table width="100%" bgcolor="cyan">
    <tr>
        <td align="left">
            <asp:LoginName runat="server" ID="LoginName1"
                FormatString="Welcome, <b>{0}</b>" />
            <asp:LoginStatus runat="server" id="LoginStatus1" />
        </td>
        <td align="right">
            <x:ModeSwitcher runat="server" id="Switcher" />
        </td>
    </tr>
</table>
```

The following markup creates a horizontal bar that shows the user's name (the *LoginName* control), a link to log out (the *LoginStatus* control) and, on the right edge of the screen, the mode-switcher control. (See Figure 7-14 earlier in the chapter.)

Moving Web Parts Around

Users can interactively move Web Parts up or down in the same zone or to another zone. To enable this scenario, though, they must first switch the display mode to Design. When in Design mode, drag-and-drop facilities are automatically active to let you move Web Parts around. Once dropped onto a new zone, the Web Part inherits the currently active graphical settings, including the title bar and verb settings. Figure 7-15 shows the *Today* Web Part being moved from Zone #2 to Zone #1. The horizontal line in between the two Web Parts in Zone #1 provides visual feedback as to the location of the available insertion point. (If there were more Web Parts in Zone #1, more insertion points would be indicated.)

Figure 7-15   In Design mode, users can move Web Parts around zones using drag-and-drop operations.

In Design mode, each zone sports a border and displays its title text so that users can easily spot which Web Parts are available for moving. When users finish moving Web Parts around, they can click the Browse mode to return to the standard view.

> **Note**   Drag-and-drop operations are implemented through client-side script and require ad hoc support from the browser's DOM. When a Web Part is released to its new position, an automatic postback occurs to persist the new zone layout to the personalization data store. If at the end of the drag-and-drop operation the position of the Web Part isn't changed (that is, you dropped it in the same position), no postback is made. Drag-and-drop operations are supported only on Internet Explorer browsers. Keep this in mind when you allow users to shift into Design mode—you might want to check the browser type to disable the Design mode if the user is not using Internet Explorer.

Creating an Editor Zone

The first step in enabling dynamic editing on your Web Part–driven page is defining an editor zone. The control to use is *EditorZone*. You need one editor zone per page that can contain multiple editors. ASP.NET supports quite a few types of editors, each designed to edit a particular aspect of Web Parts. There are editors to change the values of public and Web-browsable properties, the overall behavior of the part, and its layout and appearance.

The Edit Mode

To add an editor zone to a Web Part page, you need the following code. As usual, for illustration purposes, the style information has been stripped off. The zone template lists the editors you want to make available for use:

```
<asp:EditorZone runat="server">
    <ZoneTemplate>
        <asp:AppearanceEditorPart runat="server" />
        <asp:LayoutEditorPart runat="server" />
        <asp:PropertyGridEditorPart runat="server" />
    </ZoneTemplate>
</asp:EditorZone>
```

The editor zone shows up only in Edit mode and appears at the exact position you defined for it in the page. For this reason, you should choose an appropriate placement that doesn't obstruct the editing process.

> **Tip**   A common practice entails creating a table structure in the page and assigning each cell to a different type of zone—Web Part, editor, catalog, or connections. The typical table layout consists of horizontal cells where editor, catalog, and connections zones take the rightmost positions.

When the page enters in Edit mode, all Web Parts in the page are embellished with a new verb–Edit. How this verb is represented depends on the zone settings; it might be a link on each Web Part title bar or a new item in the drop-down menu of the Web Part. From a purely graphical perspective, the Edit mode looks a lot like the Design mode. And, in fact, when in Edit mode, users can do whatever they're allowed to do in Design mode (keep in mind the browser type).

To start editing the properties of a particular Web Part, you have to click the Edit verb on the Web Part. As you do this, all registered editors appear, as in Figure 7-16.

As you can see, the Web Part being currently edited–*StockViewer* in this case–loses the Edit verb. All other Web Parts show off the Edit verb in the title bar or the menu.

Figure 7-16   The user interface to change settings for the selected Web Part.

The Editor Part Components

Table 7-8 details the Editor Part components. You can select more than one editor in the same zone. Editors are displayed in the specified order within the editor zone.

Table 7-8   Editor Parts

Editor	Description
AppearanceEditorPart	Lets you edit visual settings such as width, title, direction of the text, and border type.
BehaviorEditorPart	Lets you modify some behavioral settings, such as whether the Web Part supports editing, and minimization. The Editor Part also lets you edit help and title links.
LayoutEditorPart	Lets you edit the frame style (normal or minimized) and the zone the part belongs to. You can also modify the index of the part within the selected zone.
PropertyGridEditorPart	Lets you edit the custom properties of the Web Part component. A custom property is a public property defined on a *WebPart*-derived class marked with the *[Personalizable]* and *[WebBrowsable]* attributes.

The footer of the editor zone has a standard toolbar with buttons for saving and exiting (the OK button), saving and continuing (the Apply button), and exiting without saving (the Cancel button). Any change applied during the edit phase is stored in the personalization data store. This feature is automatically provided by the ASP.NET 2.0 framework and requires no additional coding.

> **Important**   For the property grid editor to show up, the Web Part must have publicly browsable and personalizable properties. Also controls and user controls can have their properties listed as long as these are properly decorated with *[WebBrowsable]* and *[Personalizable]* attributes. Fields are not accepted.

Creating a Catalog Zone

The catalog zone groups components that enable users to add Web Parts to the page at run time. A catalog contains the list of Web Parts you want to offer to users for optional inclusion. At a minimum, though, the catalog acts as a store for Web Parts that the user has removed from the page since the last time the personalization state was reset. Put another way, in addition to listing optional parts, the catalog zone guarantees that no inadvertently closed Web Part is lost. You bring up the catalog for a page by selecting the Catalog display mode.

The Catalog Mode

The following code shows how to add a catalog zone to a Web Part page. Note that, as with the other examples, the style information has been stripped for clarity. The catalog zone template lists the specific catalogs you want to use.

```
<asp:CatalogZone ID="CatalogZone1" runat="server">
    <ZoneTemplate>
        <asp:PageCatalogPart ID="PageCatPart1" runat="server" />
        <asp:DeclarativeCatalogPart ID="DeclCatPart1" runat="server">
            ⋮
        </asp:DeclarativeCatalogPart>
        <asp:ImportCatalogPart ID="ImportCatalogPart1" runat="server" />
    </ZoneTemplate>
</asp:CatalogZone>
```

As you can see, a few types of catalogs exist, each with different characteristics and functionality, as described in Table 7-9.

Table 7-9   Catalog Parts

Editor	Description
DeclarativeCatalogPart	Lists the Web Parts that don't participate to the initial layout of the page, but that each user can optionally add.
ImportCatalogPart	Allows users to import a Web Part that another page might have exported to a disk file.
PageCatalogPart	Lists the Web Parts that were originally part of the page and that the user might have closed.

Figure 7-17 demonstrates the page catalog part. The catalog lists all Web Parts that have been closed, and it gives users a chance to check and add them to one of the existing zones.

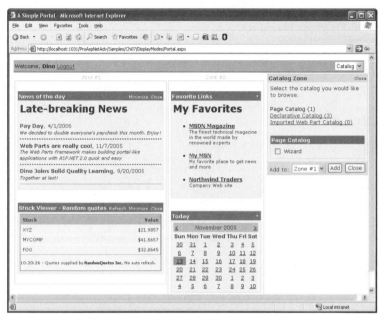

Figure 7-17   The page catalog in action.

Catalog parts appear in the page in the order they are declared in the *CatalogZone*. The catalog zone provides a list of links to display the user interface of each catalog. The user interface of the first catalog in the list is displayed automatically.

The Declarative Catalog Part

The *DeclarativeCatalogPart* control contains the list of Web Parts that users can optionally add to the page. The Web Parts are statically declared in the *.aspx* source file in the child *WebPartsTemplate* section, as shown here:

```
<asp:DeclarativeCatalogPart runat="server">
   <WebPartsTemplate>
      <x:WeatherWebPart runat="server" zipcode="00015" />
      <x:BookFinder runat="server" author="Dino Esposito" />
   </WebPartsTemplate>
</asp:DeclarativeCatalogPart>
```

The Web Parts managed by the *DeclarativeCatalogPart* are not instantiated and managed until they are explicitly added to the page by the user.

To review the list of available Web Parts, you first click the corresponding link in the catalog zone. Figure 7-18 shows the typical user interface of the declarative catalog.

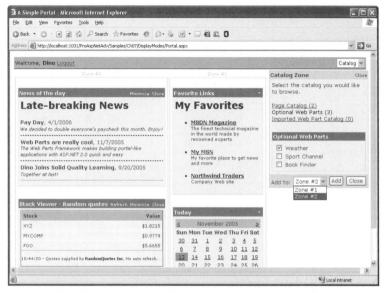

Figure 7-18 The catalog zone lists the optional Web Parts for the page.

To add a Web Part, users need to check it and select the zone where they want it to be added. Note that once an optional Web Part has been added, it becomes an integral part of the page. If closed later, its name will appear in the page catalog part.

Important You can change the titles of the Catalog Parts and Editor Parts that appear in the Edit and Catalog modes by setting the *Title* property of part controls. In Figure 7-18, the Declarative Part Catalog panel has been labeled "Optional Web Parts".

Importing and Exporting Web Parts

The import catalog part provides a user interface for users to import a Web Part from another application through a *.webpart* file. A *.webpart* file is created when a Web Part is exported from a page. (See Figure 7-19.)

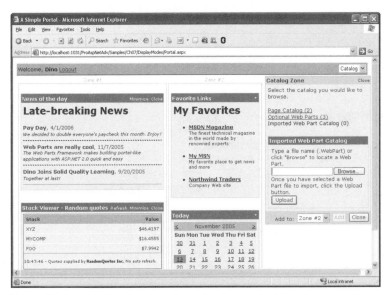

Figure 7-19   The user interface that allows users to import previously exported Web Parts.

By default, a Web Part control cannot be exported unless its *ExportMode* property is set to a value other than *None*.

```
<asp:StockViewerWebPart runat="server" ExportMode="All" ... />
```

To enable exporting all properties for the control, set the *ExportMode* value to *All*. To export only properties that do not contain sensitive data, you set the property value to *NonSensitiveData*. (Remember that the sensitivity of the property data is set through the *[Personalizable]* attribute.) When a Web Part can be exported, a new verb appears in the title bar or the verb menu—Export. When you click to export, a message box appears to warn about the risks of inadvertently exporting sensitive data. (See Figure 7-20.)

Figure 7-20   A message warning of the risks of exporting sensitive data.

Regardless of any Web Part's export settings, the host application must explicitly enable Web Parts to be exported. You enable Web Parts to be exported from the current application by setting the *enableExport* attribute in the *web.config*'s *<webParts>* section.

```
<webParts enableExport="true" />
```

Only properties marked with the *[Personalizable]* attribute are exported. As mentioned earlier, only through the *[Personalizable]* attribute can you specify whether or not the property contains sensitive data.

The *.webpart* file is downloaded on the client in the folder that the user interactively indicates. Its contents consist of pure XML, as shown here:

```xml
<?xml version="1.0" encoding="utf-8"?>
<webParts>
  <webPart>
    <metaData>
      <type name="ProAspNet20.StockViewerWebPart, ProAspCompLib" />
      <importErrorMessage>Cannot import this Web Part.</importErrorMessage>
    </metaData>
    <data>
      <properties>
        <property name="AllowClose" type="bool">True</property>
        <property name="ExportMode" type="exportmode">All</property>
        ⋮
      </properties>
    </data>
  </webPart>
</webParts>
```

The *.webpart* file can be copied to another machine and imported into another application. Once imported, the Web Part will look like it did when it was in the original application.

Connecting Web Parts

Web Part controls can communicate with other Web Parts on the same Web page and exchange data. For this feature to work, each Web Part must implement the appropriate interfaces. The communication is one-way and relies on the services of a connection object. The Web Part connection object establishes a channel between a Web Part control that acts as a provider and a Web Part that acts as a consumer.

Two connected Web Parts operate in a publisher/subscriber fashion. Any change in the values exposed by the provider are immediately reflected by the consumer. As you can imagine, this model lends itself well to representing master/detail models of data.

The Connection Model

The Web Part connection model consists of two interoperating entities: a connection and a connection point. A connection connects two points, one from the provider control and one from the consumer. The connections available in the page are managed by the Web Part manager. Web Part controls can communicate with more than one other part.

Connectable Web Parts

Connections can be defined in two nonexclusive ways: statically and dynamically. Static connections are declaratively listed in the body of the Web Part manager; dynamic connections are managed by the user through the connections zone. While discussing Web Part connections, we'll be using the following Web Parts as examples:

```
<ZoneTemplate>
    <x:EmployeesWebPart runat="server" id="emp" Title="Employee Info" />
    <x:OrdersWebPart runat="server" id="ord" Title="Orders 1997" />
</ZoneTemplate>
```

Let's assume for a moment that the two Web Parts I've identified are contained somewhere in a Web zone and are to be made connectable. Connectable Web Parts are required to have a particular internal structure—either consumer or provider. Let's tackle static connections first.

Enabling Static Connections Between Web Parts

You define static connections by adding a *<StaticConnections>* node to the Web Part manager, as shown here:

```
<asp:WebPartManager runat="server" id="WebPartManager1">
    <StaticConnections>
        <asp:WebPartConnection ID="Conn1"
            ProviderID="emp"
            ProviderConnectionPointID="EmployeeIDProvider"
            ConsumerID="ord"
            ConsumerConnectionPointID="EmployeeIDConsumer" />
    </StaticConnections>
</asp:WebPartManager>
```

A connection is identified by a provider object and a consumer object. For both objects, you specify an ID and the name of the corresponding connection point. The *ProviderID* and *ConsumerID* properties must match the ID of existing connectable Web Parts. The *Consumer-ConnectionPointID* and *ProviderConnectionPointID* properties must match the name of a connection point defined within the Web Parts.

Static connections don't require a connections zone and are available to users as soon as they open the page.

Enabling Dynamic Connections Between Web Parts

Dynamic connections enable users to connect and disconnect two Web Parts interactively. For this to happen, a proper connections zone must exist in the page.

```
<asp:ConnectionsZone ID="ConnectionsZone1" runat="server" />
```

The connections zone doesn't contain child text or nodes except style nodes. If a connections zone is defined within the page, the Web Part manager adds a new Connect display mode to the list of available modes. When in Connect mode, the Web Parts menu of any connectable Web Parts around is automatically provided with an extra Connect verb.

By clicking the Connect verb on a Web Part, users cause the connections zone to display some user interface. The user interface differs slightly depending on the publisher/subscriber role of the Web Part. Figure 7-21 shows the user interface when a user attempts to link a provider Web Part to a compatible consumer.

Figure 7-21   Setting up a connection between a provider Web Part and a consumer.

The screen shot on the right displays what a user sees once he or she clicks the link in the left-most screen shot. A similar user interface attempts to link a provider to a consumer Web Part.

> **Note**   If one of two connected Web Parts is closed and then reopened, the link is lost and must be re-created.

Connection Points and Interfaces

Let's delve a bit deeper into what makes two Web Parts connectable. As mentioned previously, a link between compatible Web Parts is obtained through a connection point and an explicit communication contract.

A connection point defines a possible connection for a *WebPart* control. A connection point doesn't guarantee communication—it simply provides a way for the *WebPartManager* object to establish a communication channel between two Web Parts. A connection point can act as a provider or as a consumer. In the former case, the Web Part exposes information through the connection channel that other registered Web Parts consume. A consumer connection point, on the other hand, receives incoming data exposed by a provider.

The communication between providers and consumers is defined by a communication contract. The contract set between a provider and a consumer consists of an interface implemented in the provider that the consumer needs to interact with. The interface could contain properties, events, or methods that the consumer can use once the communication is established. The consumer doesn't need to implement any interface, but it must be aware of the interfaces that its provider supports.

Building a Master/Detail Schema

Let's apply the aforementioned connection model to a couple of custom Web Parts that inherit from the *WebPart* base class. The provider Web Part is named *EmployeesWebPart* and displays some information about a selected employee. A simple input form allows users to type in the ID of a particular employee and get his personal notes. In addition, the Web Part will export the ID of the selected employee through the communication contract.

The consumer component is the *OrdersWebPart* control; it binds to the employee ID of any Web Part that implements the given communication contract and displays all the orders issued by that employee in a given year.

This link ends up creating a master/detail relationship between the involved Web Parts.

The Provider Web Part

When creating a provider Web Part, the first thing a developer defines is the communication contract for the connection point. The contract is defined as an interface:

```
interface IEmployeeInfo
{
    int EmployeeID { get; set; }
}
```

The sample *EmployeesWebPart* component is a custom ASP.NET control derived from *WebPart*, which implements the contract interface:

```
public class EmployeesWebPart : WebPart, IEmployeeInfo
{
    private int _empID;
    public int EmployeeID
    {
        get { return _empID; }
        set { _empID = value; }
    }
    :
}
```

To make *EmployeeID* show up in the property grid editor, you mark it as browsable and personalizable.

```
[Personalizable(true)]
[WebBrowsable(true)]
public int EmployeeID
{
    get { return _empID; }
    set { _empID = value; }
}
```

The next step entails creating a provider connection point. You define a function that returns an instance of the current class and mark it with the *[ConnectionProvider]* attribute. This function creates the connection point for the data based on the *IEmployeeInfo* interface.

```
[ConnectionProvider("EmployeeIDProvider", "EmployeeIDProvider")]
public IEmployeeInfo GetEmployeeInfo()
{
    return this;
}
```

Notice that the name of the connection point must match the *ProviderName* or the *Consumer-Name* property of the *<asp:WebPartConnection>* tag, depending on whether the connection point is for a provider or a consumer.

> **Note** When the *WebPart* provider control implements just one provider interface, as in this case, there's no need to explicitly mention the interface in the connection provider attribute. When multiple interfaces are supported, you must add a third parameter to the *[Connection-Provider]* attribute to indicate the contract on which the connection is based.
>
> ```
> [ConnectionProvider["Prov", "Prov", typeof(IMyInterface)]
> ```

The Consumer Web Part

A Web Part that acts as a consumer is even simpler to write than a provider. Besides generating its own user interface, the Web Part has only one duty—that of creating a consumer connection point for the specified interface.

```
[ConnectionConsumer("EmployeeIDConsumer", "EmployeeIDConsumer")]
private void GetEmployeeInfo(IEmployeeInfo empInfo)
{
   if (empInfo != null)
   {
      _empID = empInfo.EmployeeID;
      FindEmployeeInfo();
   }
   else
      throw new Exception("No connection data found.");
}
```

A consumer connection point is automatically created by the ASP.NET runtime in correspondence with a method marked with the *[ConnectionConsumer]* attribute. The method marked with the attribute is taken as the callback to invoke when anything on the specified interface changes.

The user interface is composed of a *DataGrid* control. The grid is filled with the results of a query run against the Orders table in the Northwind database.

Putting It All Together

Let's briefly review the markup code that defines a static Web Part connection object within the page. (For a dynamic connection, you won't see any code in either the markup or in the code-behind source file, as the connection is created via the user interface of the connections zone.)

```
<StaticConnections>
    <asp:WebPartConnection
        ProviderID="emp" ProviderConnectionPointID="EmployeeIDProvider"
        ConsumerID="ord" ConsumerConnectionPointID="EmployeeIDConsumer" />
</StaticConnections>
```

This declaration can be read as a connection set between a Web Part with an ID of *emp* and a Web Part named *ord*. The former acts as the provider through a connection point of name *EmployeeIDProvider*. The latter plays the role of the consumer through a connection point named *EmployeeIDConsumer*.

As a result, any change in any of the properties exposed by provider results in an internal field-changed event that is resolved by invoking the consumer's callback. The consumer retrieves and displays the orders for the specified employee. The two Web Parts work perfectly in sync, as Figure 7-22 shows.

Figure 7-22   A master/detail relationship set using two independent but communicating Web Parts.

The provider Web Part also defines a public and browsable *EmployeeID* property. If you set the *EmployeeID* property on the *EmployeesWebPart* control (the provider), the change is immediately reflected by the consumer after a postback.

Conclusion

The Web Parts framework provides a simple and familiar way for ASP.NET developers to create modular Web applications that support end user personalization. A Web Part is a panel-like server control that displays some user-interface elements. Like any other server control, it is configurable through properties, methods, and events.

Web Parts are integrated into a framework aimed at composing pages with components that are smarter and richer than traditional controls. The surrounding Web Parts framework provides all the magic (or difficult-to-write infrastructural code, if you will) that keeps developers and users happy. In particular, you can partition the surface of your Web page into zones and bind one or more parts to each zone. Each Web Part is automatically given a frame, a title bar, and some verbs (such as Minimize, Edit, and Close). Overall, a Web Part looks like a traditional window of a desktop application.

The Web Parts framework supports a variety of working modes, including Design, Edit, and Catalog. In Design mode, users can use drag-and-drop operations and move Web Parts around, changing the layout of the page. In Edit mode, users can also change visual and behavioral properties. The user interface of the editors is provided, free of programming charge, by the Web Parts framework. Finally, in Catalog mode the framework lists all available Web Parts, including those that the user might have previously closed.

When a user reconfigures the Web Parts on a page, the user's settings are automatically persisted. The next time the user visits the page, the last Web Parts configuration is restored. No code is required to store the user settings, but the page personalization engine must be configured off line.

Just the Facts

- ASP.NET pages can be built using Web Parts, which are SharePoint-like components that mimic the behavior of desktop windows.

- Web Parts frames show some content and can look like frames. However, Web Parts are an integral part of the host page, and if clicked they cause the whole page to post back.

- Web Parts belong to zones, and a Web Part–powered page can have several distinct zones such as for editors, catalogs, and connections.

- A Web Part is a server control and can be implemented with any of the following: a composite control, user control, or custom server control that derives from *WebPart*. Although it's much less interesting from an application's perspective, a Web Part can also be implemented by a single server control—be it a native ASP.NET control or custom server control.

- Each Web Part is given a number of verbs. Each verb indicates a system action that is allowed on that Web Part—either Edit, Export, Minimize, Close, or Connect.

- Two Web Parts can be connected according to the publisher/subscriber model. In this way, when the public interface of the publisher (that is, the provider) changes, the subscriber (that is, the consumer) has its own user interface automatically updated.

Chapter 8
Programming for Mobility

ASP.NET mobile controls enable you to build Web applications for wireless devices using the same rich application model that characterizes development for desktop browsers. Mobile controls target a variety of devices, such as cell phones, pagers, Pocket PCs, and other personal digital assistants (PDA) such as Palm and BlackBerry devices. ASP.NET mobile controls extend the Web Forms model of ASP.NET in two ways—devices and ad hoc controls. All supported devices are listed in a new section of the *machine.config* file. It's an extensible list open to the contribution of third parties, which can register new devices as well as new controls.

You write mobile applications using the ASP.NET mobile controls and the ASP.NET object model. Based on the configuration information, Mobile Web Forms detect the underlying device and adaptively render the output of controls using specific markup language and logic. ASP.NET mobile controls abstract a subset of ASP.NET server controls and intelligently render your application on the target device. In addition, several mobile-specific controls are provided, such as the *PhoneCall* control.

In this chapter, I'll provide an overview of the ASP.NET mobile controls, discuss the basics of the mobile technology, and take a quick tour of the Microsoft Visual Studio 2005 mobile features.

Overview of Mobile Controls

ASP.NET mobile controls are server controls and thus require their *runat* attribute to be set to *server*. They execute on the server, and for this reason, they can take advantage of the potential of the .NET Framework despite the modest amount of memory typically available on wireless devices. All mobile controls inherit from the *MobileControl* base class, which, in turn, inherits from *Control*. Both server and mobile controls share a common set of properties, methods, and events. Mobile Web forms, on the other hand, inherit from the *MobilePage* class.

Architecture of Mobile Controls

ASP.NET mobile controls are an extension of ASP.NET server controls. Another way of characterizing mobile controls is to say that they are the twin brother of server controls, which are usually served to desktop browsers. Mobile controls add the capability of adapting to the device that is making the request. Automatic browser detection is a key aspect of mobile applications and controls, and it's probably a bit more important for them than for classic server controls.

Mobile Controls vs. Classic Server Controls

Classic server controls are rendered in different modes to accommodate a few client targets (the set of known desktop browsers). Although the final output can vary greatly from one target to the next, the area of markup most affected is style. Validation controls in particular are controls whose output varies significantly from one target desktop browser to another.

Classic server controls always generate HTML or perhaps XHTML code. Although differences exist between the HTML 3.2 and HTML 4.0 standards and between standards and the implementations of individual browsers, we're still far from the untangled mess of dialects and syntaxes that characterize the markup in the mobile world. For this reason, browser detection in mobile controls is automatically implemented at the system level rather than as optional detection code you may or may not have included in your own pages destined for desktop clients. Basically, the ASP.NET mobile runtime evaluates the browser's user agent and selects the appropriate device adapter object to use for any task that involves the request. As a result, mobile controls adhere to the capabilities of the particular device making the request.

The set of supported wireless devices is rather heterogeneous and ranges from full-featured browsers found on PDAs to small cell phone displays. As a result, not just the markup output but also the design of the application might significantly change from one device to the next. In general, a multiauthoring tool for mobile controls must abstract a number of aspects of the application: different markup languages (described as follows), vendor-specific implementations of the same markup, and different form factors, such as display size and programmable buttons. ASP.NET mobile controls internally handle much of the boring device-specific rendering and let you focus on the Web-application logic.

Multiple Markup Languages

ASP.NET mobile controls support a few types of markup languages, which are listed in Table 8-1. Acceptable values don't include all possible wireless markup languages, but they certainly include the most popular ones.

Table 8-1   Markup Languages in ASP.NET Mobile Controls

Markup	Description
Compact HTML 1.0	Subset of HTML 3.2 that has been specifically designed for mobile phones and in general for battery-powered, low-memory devices. Abbreviated as cHTML. The language is widely used in Japanese I-Mode devices.
HTML 3.2	Relatively old version of HTML that is supported by high-end PDAs such as Pocket PC 2002, Palm, and BlackBerry devices.
WML 1.x	The Wireless Markup Language (WML) is probably the most popular wireless language. It has been developed as a part of a larger initiative aimed at defining an application protocol for wireless devices—the Wireless Application Protocol (WAP). WML lets you program the keys of a mobile phone, such as softkeys and the numeric pad.
XHTML	XHTML is the XML reformulation of HTML and a key element of the WAP 2.0 standard.

Mobile Controls Hierarchy

ASP.NET mobile controls can be logically grouped into five categories: container, text, validation, list, and miscellaneous controls. Table 8-2 lists them all in alphabetical order. Some controls work in much the same way as do ASP.NET Web Forms controls. However, mobile controls also provide adaptive rendering for mobile devices. We'll discuss adaptive rendering more later in the "Adaptive Rendering" section.

Table 8-2   ASP.NET Mobile Controls

Mobile Control	Description
AdRotator	Provides advertisement rotation in the same way that the ASP.NET *AdRotator* control does.
Calendar	Provides date-picking functionality, mimicking the behavior of the ASP.NET *Calendar* control.
Command	Similar to the ASP.NET *Button* control, causes a postback event after users click.
CompareValidator	Identical to the ASP.NET *CompareValidator* control.
CustomValidator	Identical to the ASP.NET *CustomValidator* control.
DeviceSpecific	Provides a way to target the appearance of *Form* and *Panel* controls to specific types of hardware devices.
Form	The control is similar to the *HtmlForm* control of ASP.NET pages. However, multiple form controls are admitted on mobile pages.
Image	Identical to the ASP.NET *Image* control.
Label	Identical to the ASP.NET *Label* control.

Table 8-2   ASP.NET Mobile Controls

Mobile Control	Description
Link	Represents a hyperlink to another form on a mobile page or an arbitrary URL. Similar to the ASP.NET *HyperLink* control.
List	Similar to the ASP.NET *Repeater* and *DataList* controls, applies templates to bound data. Supports device-specific templates.
ObjectList	Similar to the ASP.NET *DataGrid* control, displays multiple fields for each data item and supports multiple commands.
Panel	Provides grouping mechanism for organizing controls in much the same way as the ASP.NET *Panel* control does.
PhoneCall	For devices that support phone calls, the control represents a link to a phone number to call. Similar to the *mailto* tag of HTML hyperlinks.
RangeValidator	Identical to the ASP.NET *RangeValidator* control.
RegularExpressionValidator	Identical to the ASP.NET *RegularExpressionValidator* control.
RequiredFieldValidator	Identical to the ASP.NET *RequiredFieldValidator* control.
SelectionList	Displays a list of data-bound items with different styles. It can be configured to behave like a drop-down or check-box list. Selection, however, does not automatically cause the control to post back. The change of selection, though, will fire a server event with the next postback.
StyleSheet	Invisible control, can be used to organize styles to apply to other controls. Can contain multiple style definitions.
TextBox	Represents a single-line text-box control. Does not support read-only and multiline.
TextView	Used to display large blocks of text, supports basic text formatting and pagination.
ValidationSummary	Similar to the *ValidationSummary* control of ASP.NET, displays the results of the validation in a separate form.

Almost all mobile controls have a counterpart in the family of ASP.NET server controls or, at a minimum, a control that looks the same. *PhoneCall* and *TextView* are the only two without an equivalent control. Other controls, such as *SelectionList* and *Command*, group the functionality of multiple ASP.NET controls. The programming interface of validation controls, on the other hand, is nearly identical to ASP.NET; a key difference here is that not all devices support client-side validation. Figure 8-1 shows graphically the relationships between controls. Controls with a white background are abstract classes.

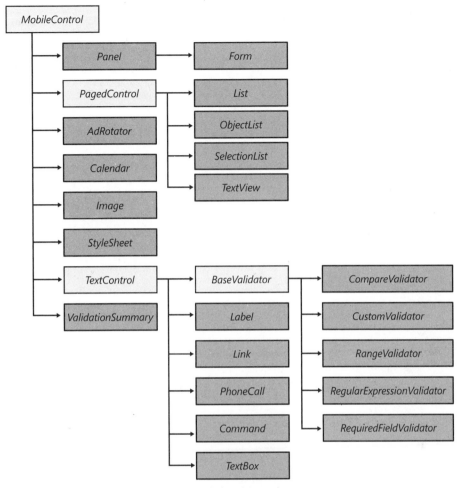

Figure 8-1   The ASP.NET mobile control class hierarchy.

Before taking a closer look at the characteristics of each group of controls, let's learn more about the structure of an ASP.NET mobile page.

ASP.NET Mobile Pages

The *MobilePage* class is the base class for all ASP.NET mobile Web pages, and it inherits from the ASP.NET *Page* class. The code-behind class of a mobile page inherits from *MobilePage* or from a class that, in turn, derives from *MobilePage*. In addition, all mobile controls are perceived as custom controls and must be explicitly registered in all pages. Let's examine the source code of a simple mobile page.

A Sample Mobile Page

The following listing shows a simple page that displays the name of the wireless language being used by the device:

```
<%@ Page Language="C#" CodeFile="Hello.aspx.cs" Inherits="Hello" %>
<%@ Register TagPrefix="mobile" Namespace="System.Web.UI.MobileControls"
            Assembly="System.Web.Mobile" %>
<%@ Import Namespace="System.Web.Mobile" %>

<html xmlns="http://www.w3.org/1999/xhtml" >
<body>
    <mobile:Form ID="Form1" runat="server">
        Language is
        <mobile:Label runat="server" font-bold="true" id="theBrowser" />
    </mobile:Form>
</body>
</html>
```

The page contains a *Label* control that renders with bold typeface and some literal text. During the page *Load* event, the code retrieves the preferred rendering type from the requesting device, reads related settings from the configuration file, and displays it. The *MobileCapabilities* class is defined in the *System.Web.Mobile* namespace; the controls, on the other hand, are all defined in the *System.Web.UI.MobileControls* namespace.

```
public partial class Hello : System.Web.UI.MobileControls.MobilePage
{
    protected void Page_Load(object sender, EventArgs e)
    {
        MobileCapabilities mobCaps = (MobileCapabilities) Request.Browser;
        theBrowser.Text = mobCaps.PreferredRenderingType;
    }
}
```

When viewed through a device that incorporates the Openwave browser 7.0 (more information for which can be found at *http://odn.openwave.com*), the page looks like the one shown in Figure 8-2.

The mobile page detected the device capabilities and generated the following WML 1.1 output:

```
<wml>
  <head>
    <meta http-equiv="Cache-Control" content="max-age=0" />
  </head>
  <card>
    <do type="accept"><noop /></do><p>
        Language is <b>wml11</b></p>
  </card>
</wml>
```

Figure 8-2   A mobile application in action as seen through the Openwave emulator.

Interestingly, the same page is also viewable through Internet Explorer. In this case, the target language is HTML 3.2. Figure 8-3 shows the Internet Explorer version of the page.

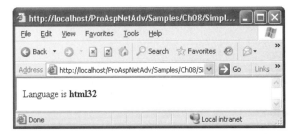

Figure 8-3   The same mobile application rendered by Internet Explorer.

In this case, the output sent to the device is completely different:

```
<html><body>
<form id="Form1" name="Form1" method="post"
      action="Hello.aspx?__ufps=149742">
  <input type="hidden" name="__VIEWSTATE"
         value="/wEXA ... CVL">
  <input type="hidden" name="__EVENTTARGET" value="">
  <input type="hidden" name="__EVENTARGUMENT" value="">
  <script language=javascript><!--
    function __doPostBack(target, argument){
      var theform = document.Form1
      theform.__EVENTTARGET.value = target
      theform.__EVENTARGUMENT.value = argument
     theform.submit()
    }
    // -->
  </script>
```

```
Language is <b>html32</b>
</form>
</body></html>
```

> **Note**   A variety of emulators exist to test the interface of a mobile application at develop-
> ment time. Although you should never ship a wireless application without first extensively test-
> ing it on real devices, emulators are indeed extremely helpful to prototype the user interface.
> Phone emulators are available from most vendors.

A *MobilePage* object can contain only a *Form* or *StyleSheet* control. Literal text placed outside a
form is ignored. If other controls are used outside the boundaries of a form, a compiler error
is raised. All desired text and controls must always be placed within a form. A mobile page
must contain at least one form; multiple forms are supported, but only one is visible at a time.
A style sheet is not required for a mobile page. In addition, you can't indicate more than one
style sheet per page.

Pagination in Mobile Pages

ASP.NET mobile controls provide a mechanism for automatically partitioning the form's contents into smaller portions of markup code. This mechanism is known as *pagination*. When
you use pagination, these segments of content are automatically formatted to fit the target
device. The final output is also completed with common user-interface elements that you can
use to browse to other pages.

By default, pagination is not activated for a form. To activate pagination, you must set the
Paginate property of the *Form* to *true*. You should note that although pagination can be enabled
on individual controls, the setting has no effect if the *Paginate* property of the containing form
is set to *false*. The *Form* control also provides other properties—such as *PageCount*, *CurrentPage*,
and *PagerStyle*—that allow you to control pagination behavior. You can also specify pagination
for a particular control on a form using the *ControlToPaginate* property of the form with the ID
of the control.

The main motivation for pagination is to not exceed the memory capabilities of the device
with a page that is too large. Pagination is particularly effective for controls that display large
amounts of data; it's often redundant for forms that display interactive and input controls. The
pagination is implemented by sectioning the structure of the form or the control into pieces.
Some controls (for example, the *List* control) handle pagination internally and decide for
themselves how to break their output. Other controls are managed by the container controls;
to be effectively pageable, they must contain child controls or fit entirely in a single page.

Figure 8-4 shows how the final output of a paginated form might look compared with the output of a nonpaginated form. The screen shot on the left shows the effect when pagination is
disabled; the screen shot on the right gives an idea of the final user interface when pagination
is on.

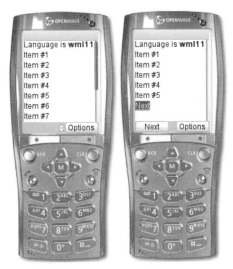

Figure 8-4   The effect of pagination on mobile forms.

> **Warning**   If you run the sample page that produces the output shown in Figure 8-4, don't be surprised to get an exception when you click the Next link on the mobile device. To fix it, disable cookies in the Web application.

The Life Cycle of a Mobile Page

The life cycle of an ASP.NET mobile page is nearly identical to the life cycle of a conventional Web Forms page. The events are the same, even though the system's behaviors before and after the various events are different. The phases in the cycle are summarized as follows. For more information on the page life cycle, refer to Chapter 3 of my book *Programming Microsoft ASP.NET 2.0: Core Reference* (Microsoft Press, 2005).

- **Page initialization**   At this phase, the page determines the device adapter to use and sets the *Adapter* property on the *MobilePage* class. The search for the adapter begins with the *machine.config* file and then proceeds to the root *web.config* and any innermost *web.config* that might have been defined. The adapter is picked up based on the detected characteristics of the underlying device. Note that the adapter is cached for performance so that the search is conducted only once per user agent.

- **Loading the view state**   During this phase, any saved state for the page is restored. There is no event associated with this phase.

- **Loading postback data**   The page loads all incoming *<form>* data cached in *Request* and updates the page properties accordingly. No user event is associated with this phase.

- **Loading the user code**   The page is ready to execute any initialization code related to the logic and behavior of the page. The page fires the *Load* event and performs device adapter–specific loading of information. To control this phase, you can handle the *Load* event both on the page and the adapter.

- **Send postback change notifications**   Controls in the page raise change events in response to state changes between the current and previous postbacks. A control must implement the *IPostBackDataHandler* interface to get a chance from the page to fire a state change event during this phase. No user event is provided.

- **Handle postback events**   The page executes the code associated with the event that caused the postback.

- **Prerendering**   The code can perform its last updates before the output is rendered. The event that developers can hook up from a mobile page or the device adapter at this phase is *PreRender*. Pagination occurs at this time. During this phase, the output of the page is determined based on the pagination settings.

- **Saving the view state**   During this phase, the page serializes its state to a string, which will then be persisted—typically, through a hidden field. No user event is associated with this phase.

- **Page rendering**   The page generates the output to be rendered to the client. The adapter is responsible for accessing and rendering child controls in the appropriate order.

- **Page unload**   This phase performs the device adapter–specific cleanup and unloading. The event is *Unload*, and it's available on both the page object and the device adapter.

If you compare mobile and desktop ASP.NET pages in ASP.NET 1.x, they differ because of the initialization step. At that phase, in fact, mobile pages and controls have to determine the device adapter to use from the list of registered objects. The adapter is exposed through the *Adapter* property, and pages and controls refer to it for rendering. In ASP.NET 2.0, any differences tend to blur as desktop ASP.NET pages also support adaptive rendering.

Device Adapters

Although the programmer writes ASP.NET mobile applications in a device-independent fashion, a set of device adapters take care of translating the high-level description of a user interface into the device-specific presentation layer. Interesting analogies exist between device drivers in Microsoft Windows and device adapters in ASP.NET mobile controls. Both control a device by generating device-specific command text; device adapters just generate that in the form of markup languages. Device adapters are the bridge between individual mobile controls and target devices. For any given device, each mobile control can have a unique adapter and each instance of a control is bound to a corresponding instance of an adapter. The availability of an adapter is critical for the appropriate rendering of mobile controls. In general, for each supported device, the following classes can be defined:

- **Page adapter**   Associated with the page, this class provides view-state and postback functionality, as well as methods that save and load device-specific control-state information, such as pagination information and the currently active form. The page adapter is also responsible for preparing the response to the client and for rendering the skeleton of the page. In the mobile API, the page adapter class implements the *IPageAdapter* interface.

- **Form adapter**   Associated with the form control, this adapter provides methods that handle device-specific form-based interactivity. In addition, it should supply methods that adapt a generic form to the particular device. For example, the fields of the forms could be paginated or grouped into a menu. Finally, the form adapter must be able to render the skeleton of the form.

- **Control adapter**   This is the base class for control adapters and also the base class for page and form adapters. It provides methods for rendering control postback events and style properties.

- **Text writer**   The text writer class is not an adapter class, but it works in conjunction with adapters. The text writer class inherits from the *HtmlTextWriter* class and performs all rendering for a control. An instance of the text writer class is created and passed through every adapter for rendering purposes. The text writer usually contains helper methods to perform tasks such as encoding of data.

The ASP.NET 2.0 framework contains a few device adapters, one for each supported markup language—cHTML, XHTML, HTML, and WML.

Container Controls

ASP.NET mobile controls include a couple of controls—*Panel* and *Form*—that act as containers of other controls. The *Form* control differs from *Panel* in that it supports posting of data, whereas the *Panel* represents a simple static group of related controls. Multiple panels can be nested and included in forms; forms, on the other hand, cannot be nested.

The *Panel* Control

The following code demonstrates a couple of panels containing plain text with minimal formatting. Note that not all attributes are supported on all devices. For example, background and foreground colors are ignored by cell phones.

```
<mobile:Form runat="server">
    <mobile:Panel runat="server" Font-Bold="true" Alignment="Right">
        <mobile:Label runat="server">Programming ASP.NET 2.0</mobile:Label>
    </mobile:Panel>
    <mobile:Panel runat="server" BackColor="yellow">
        <mobile:Label runat="server">Dino Esposito</mobile:Label>
    </mobile:Panel>
</mobile:Form>
```

A panel can contain any ASP.NET mobile control other than *MobilePage*, *Form*, or *StyleSheet* controls. Panel controls do not have a visual representation and cascade any style properties down to the individual controls. Both the layout and style of the child controls are mediated by the device adapter.

Note that a *Panel* control can also work as a sort of placeholder to contain dynamically generated child controls.

The *Form* Control

The *Form* control represents the outermost container of controls within a mobile page. The *Form* control features common-use properties such as *Action* and *Method*. In particular, *Action* defaults to the empty string, which causes a postback to the same URL. A form fires events when activated and deactivated.

A page can contain multiple forms, but only one form is rendered to the browser at a time. The currently active form can be set and retrieved through the *ActiveForm* property. When multiple forms are active on the same page, you can move from one to the other by using a *Link* control.

```
<mobile:Form id="Form2" runat="server">
    <mobile:Label runat="server"
        text="Second page of information" />
    <mobile:Link runat="server" NavigateURL="#Form1" text="Back" />
</mobile:Form>
```

To make a *Link* control point to an internal form, you set the *NavigateURL* property to the ID of the form prefixed with a # (hash) symbol.

List Controls

The *List*, *ObjectList*, and *SelectionList* controls are the mobile counterparts of ASP.NET list-bound and iterative controls. The *List* control looks like the *Repeater* and the *DataList*, and it displays a static or bound list of items. The *SelectionList* is helpful if you need the user to pick one or more items from a list. Finally, you should use the *ObjectList* control if you need to display database information in a tabular format. Note that the *ObjectList* control is strictly data-bound, while the other two can also display a list of items set either statically or programmatically.

The *List* Control

As mentioned, a *List* control renders a sequence of items to a device. The control can work in static or interactive mode. In static mode, the control generates a static list in which each item is plain text. In interactive mode, all items are rendered as clickable elements that generate an event if clicked. If an event handler for the *ItemCommand* event is present, the control works interactively; otherwise, it appears as a static option list. When set to *true*, the *ItemsAsLinks* property transforms the list items into hyperlinks. In this case, no *ItemCommand* event will ever be fired, as the click is resolved by jumping to a new URL. You indicate the URL through the *DataValueField* property and the hyperlink text using *DataTextField*.

The following listing shows a sample application that displays a list of cities and lets users pick one. The page consists of two forms, one with the list of cities and one that shows the result of the choice.

```
<mobile:Form id="IntroForm" runat="server">
    <b>Where do you want to go today?</b>
    <mobile:List runat="server" id="Cities" OnItemCommand="List_Click" >
```

```
            <item Text="Rome" Value="€10" />
            <item Text="New York" Value="$500" />
            <item Text="London" Value="€200" />
            <item Text="Paris" Value="€350" />
            <item Text="Sydney" Value="$1200" />
        </mobile:List>
    </mobile:Form>
    <mobile:Form runat="server" id="ResultsForm">
        <mobile:Label runat="server" id="Info"/>
    </mobile:Form>
```

The code-behind class injects the code to switch to the results form.

```
protected void List_Click(object sender, ListCommandEventArgs e)
{
    string msg = String.Format("Going to {0} for {1}.",
    e.ListItem.Text, e.ListItem.Value);
    Info.Text = msg;
    ActiveForm = ResultsForm;
}
```

Figure 8-5 shows the application in action.

Figure 8-5   The list of cities as generated by the *List* control. The presence of the *ItemCommand* handler makes each item selectable.

> **Warning**   Pay attention when you use the $ symbol with mobile applications. In WML, the $ symbol has a special meaning and is used to identify variables. However, ASP.NET mobile controls automatically process occurrences of $ symbols in the source code and render them correctly using a double $$ symbol.

A *List* control can be bound to a data source only through the *DataSource* property and *IEnumerable*-based objects. Mobile controls don't support data source controls and don't define the *DataSourceID* property. For more information on the ASP.NET data-binding model, refer to Chapter 9 of *Programming Microsoft ASP.NET 2.0: Core Reference* (Microsoft Press, 2005).

You should note that the *List* control can bind only to two columns on the specified data source—one for the *Text* property of the list item and one for the *Value* property. These values are set through the *DataTextField* and *DataValueField* properties of the *List* control. By defining a handler for the *ItemDataBind*, you can also set the text of a list item as the combination of more source fields.

```
void OnItemDataBind(object sender, ListDataBindEventArgs e) {
    e.ListItem.Text = String.Format ("{0} - ${1}",
        DataBinder.Eval(e.DataItem, "city"),
        DataBinder.Eval(e.DataItem, "price"));
}
```

On devices that support richer rendering, you can specify templates to customize the view of data items. In templated mode, the *List* control functions similarly to the *Repeater* ASP.NET server control.

The *ObjectList* Control

The *ObjectList* is the mobile counterpart of the ASP.NET *DataGrid* server control. In particular, the *ObjectList* can have two views—list and details. In list view, the control displays a sort of menu made of the values of a single field. This has been done to accommodate devices with small screens. The *LabelField* property lets you choose which bound field is to be used to populate the quick menu. Each displayed item is clickable and generates a detail view in which all the fields in the current data row are displayed. The way in which the item is made clickable is device specific.

The detail view can include a toolbar with all the commands specified using the *<command>* tag plus the back command, whose text is set through the *BackCommandText* property. Finally, the *AutoGenerateField* property (which is *true* by default) along with the *<fields>* elements let you decide which bound fields are to be actually displayed.

The *ObjectList* differs from the *List* control in some respects. One is that the *ObjectList* allows you to associate multiple commands with each item. The set of commands for an item can be either shared among all items or unique to the item. Other differences are that the *ObjectList* supports multiple views and doesn't support static items. Later on in this chapter, when building a sample application, we'll use an *ObjectList* control to display some data.

The *List* and *ObjectList* controls fully support internal pagination and fire the *LoadItems* event when they display a new portion of the user interface. Developers specify the total number of items in the *ItemCount* property. Changing the value of the *ItemCount* property from its default value of zero to the total number of items indicates that the control is to be custom paginated. The *LoadItems* event handler is expected to retrieve the appropriate data and bind it to the control.

The *SelectionList* Control

In the gallery of mobile list-bound controls, the *SelectionList* control is unique in that it provides UI selection capability for a list of items. Like a drop-down list or a check-box list, it shows a list of items and can allow users to select one or more items. When an item is selected, no server-side event is automatically generated, as it happens in certain Web list controls when the *AutoPostBack* property is set to *true*. The *SelectedIndexChanged* event is generated for the change of selection.

The *SelectionList* control can be rendered in five different selection types: drop-down (default), radio button, check box, list box, and multiselection list box. You choose the selection type by using the *SelectType* property. Not all devices support all these selection types. Typically, a cell phone will recognize only check-box and multiselection types, so radio button, list box, and drop-down are rendered with a pick list.

The following listing shows how to display a list of selectable items and how to retrieve all the selected items:

```
<mobile:Form runat="server" id="Form1">
    Your skills? <br />
    <mobile:SelectionList runat="server" id="list"
SelectType="checkbox" />
    <mobile:Command runat="server" OnClick="Button_Click" Text="Go" />
</mobile:Form>
<mobile:Form runat="server" id="ResultsForm">
    <mobile:Label runat="server" id="Results" />
</mobile:Form>
```

The code behind this form fills the *SelectionList* control with bound data.

```
public partial class Select : System.Web.UI.MobileControls.MobilePage
{
    protected void Page_Load(object sender, EventArgs e)
    {
        if (!IsPostBack) {
            ArrayList values = new ArrayList();
            values.Add("ASP.NET");
            values.Add("ADO.NET");
            values.Add("SQL Server");
            values.Add("XML");
            list.DataSource = values;
            list.DataBind();
        }
    }
    protected void Button_Click(object sender, EventArgs e)
    {
        string buf = "";
        foreach (MobileListItem item in list.Items)
            buf += (item.Selected ? item.Text + ", " : "");
```

```
        buf = buf.TrimEnd();
        if (buf.EndsWith(","))
            buf = buf.TrimEnd(',');
        Results.Text = buf;
        ActiveForm = ResultsForm;
    }
}
```

Figure 8-6 shows the application in action. The left-most image shows the populated *Selection-List*, and you see the results of the selection in the right-hand image. The center image shows the command button rendered at the top of the screen.

Figure 8-6   A checkbox *SelectionList* control in action on a cell phone.

Text Controls

The *TextControl* class is an abstract class from which some navigation and input controls derive. All text-based controls have a *Text* property, which can be programmatically set and is usually used to render the output of the control. *Link*, *TextBox*, and *Label* are examples of controls derived from the *TextControl* class. The *Label* mobile control is similar to the ASP.NET *Label* control and the *Link* mobile control looks a lot like the ASP.NET *HyperLink* control. Other text controls are the *Command* control, which logically represents a command button, and the *PhoneCall* control.

The *TextBox* Control

The *TextBox* control generates a single-line text box and stores in the *Text* property the text that a user enters. The control can work in password or numeric mode, but it doesn't support multiline editing or the read-only attribute. Alignment and maximum length are other advanced characteristics of the control.

```
<mobile:TextBox runat="server" id="theUser" OnTextChanged="Alert" />
```

The *TextBox* control also supports the *OnTextChanged* server-side event, which executes the specified handler if the text changes between two successive postbacks of the same page.

The *Command* Control

The *Command* control sums up most of the characteristics of the ASP.NET *Button* and *LinkButton* controls. It can be rendered as a submit button (default) or as a hyperlink. It can also be rendered as an image. The *Format* property lets you choose between *Button* or *Link*; if the output format is *Link*, you can also choose an image to display as a clickable element. The image is set through the *ImageUrl* property. If the device supports softkeys, the output of the *Command* control can just be the label of one of the softkeys. (A *softkey* is a programmable button available on many cell phones.)

Any click on a *Command* control causes a postback event. You can set the server-side code in either of two ways—the *ItemCommand* or *OnClick* event handler. With the *ItemCommand* event handler, you must also give the control a command name and optionally a command argument. When the control is clicked, the *CausesValidation* Boolean property determines whether the control has to perform validation on all other controls in the same form.

The following listing shows how to use a *TextBox* and *Command* control.

```
<mobile:Form runat="server">
    Search for:
    <mobile:TextBox runat="server" font-bold="true" id="theSubject" />
    <mobile:Command runat="server" Text="GO" OnClick="OnSearch" />
</mobile:Form>

<mobile:Form runat="server" id="ResultsForm">
    <mobile:Label runat="server" id="theResults" />
</mobile:Form>
```

When the user clicks on the command button, the following code is executed on the server:

```
protected void OnSearch(object sender, EventArgs e)
{
    string msg = "Results for '{0}'";
    msg = String.Format(msg, theSubject.Text);
    theResults.Text = msg;

    ActiveForm = ResultsForm;
}
```

The *ActiveForm* property on a *Form* object programmatically gets or sets the form's currently active form. Figure 8-7 shows the application in action.

Figure 8-7 *TextBox* and *Command* controls in action.

The *PhoneCall* Control

The *PhoneCall* control is an output-only control that is used to represent a phone number to call. For devices that support placing phone calls (for example, cell phones), the control looks like an interactive element that makes a call when clicked. On other nonvoice devices, the phone number is displayed as a link to a URL or, optionally, as plain text.

```
<mobile:Form runat="server">
Phone numbers found for Joe:
    <mobile:PhoneCall runat="server"
        AlternateFormat="{0} at {1}"
        AlternateURL="http://www.acme.com"
        PhoneNumber="111-222-0000"
        Text="ACME Corp" />
    <mobile:PhoneCall runat="server"
        AlternateFormat="{0} at {1}"
        PhoneNumber="111-333-0000"
        Text="Home" />
</mobile:Form>
```

The *AlternateFormat* property can be any string and is used to represent the control on devices without telephony capabilities. It can accept two parameters, one having the value of *Text* and the other having the value of *PhoneNumber*. The alternate text is rendered as plain text unless the *AlternateURL* property is specified. In this case, the control generates a hyperlink that points to the specified URL. If the *Text* property is unspecified, the phone number is also used for display. Figure 8-8 shows the output of the *PhoneCall* control on an Openwave-equipped cell phone.

Figure 8-8   The *PhoneCall* control in action.

Validation Controls

All validation mobile controls inherit from an abstract class named *BaseValidator*, which, in turn, descends from the *TextControl* base class. All controls share a *Text* and *ErrorMessage* property. The *Text* property becomes the output of the control in case of an invalid entry. If the *Text* property is not set, the validator displays the value of the *ErrorMessage* property instead. The value stored in *ErrorMessage* is also the text that gets displayed in the *ValidationSummary* control. Mobile controls include the following five validators:

- **CompareValidator**   This control compares the values of two controls using the specified comparison operator. The *ControlToValidate* property indicates the ID of the control to validate. The value against which the validation should occur can be indicated either explicitly—through the property *ValueToCompare*—or indirectly through the *ControlToCompare* property. This latter property contains the ID of the control to compare against the current ID. While setting up the validator, you can also indicate the type of the data being compared (for example, date, string, or integer) and the required operator (for example, greater-than or not-equal-to).

- **CustomValidator**   This control allows you to validate the value of a control using your own method. You use the *ControlToValidate* property to indicate the control being verified and write your own validation code handling the server-side *ServerValidate* event. To inform the run time about the outcomes of the process, you set the *IsValid* property of the event data structure to *true* or *false*, as appropriate.

- **RangeValidator**   This control ensures that the values of another control fall within the specified range. The *MinimumValue* and *MaximumValue* properties set the bounds of the range. You can also indicate the type of the values being compared. You do this through the *Type* property. The range must include both bounds. If you need to check values without an upper or lower bound, use the *CompareValidator* instead.

- **RegularExpressionValidator**   This control verifies that the value of a given control matches the specified regular expression. *ControlToValidate* indicates the control to keep under observation, and *ValidationExpression* sets the pattern to match.

- **RequiredFieldValidator**   This control makes an input control a required field. You should note, though, that a required field isn't necessarily an empty field. The concept of requirement applies to any value that is different from the contents of *InitialValue*. The validation is successful only if the value of the control is different from the initial value upon losing focus.

When validators are used within a page, ASP.NET can display a summary of the validation errors, if any. This task is accomplished by the *ValidationSummary* control. The control collects all the error messages set for the various validators, organizes them in an all-encompassing string, and displays the resulting text in a secondary form. The *BackLabel* property lets you set the text for the Back button that restores the failed form.

The *Command* control is the only mobile control that causes validation of input data in the form. *TextBox* and *SelectionList* are, on the other hand, the only mobile controls whose value can be validated. In particular, *Text* is the validation property of the *TextBox* control and *SelectedIndex* is the validation property of the *SelectionList* control. However, other controls (for example, custom and user controls) can participate in the validation process with their own properties. To do so, they need to be marked by the *[ValidationProperty]* attribute. (See Chapter 4 of *Programming Microsoft ASP.NET 2.0–Core Reference.*)

The following listing shows how to set up a page that validates the user input. The page contains a *SelectionList* control that enumerates possible skills to communicate to the company. At least one skill must be specified, though. We use a *RequiredFieldValidator* control associated with the *SelectionList*. In this case, the *InitialValue* is automatically set to –1 by ASP.NET.

```
<mobile:Form runat="server" id="Main">
    <mobile:RequiredFieldValidator runat="server"
        ErrorMessage="Must indicate a skill!"
        ControlToValidate="skills" />

    <b>Indicate your skills</b><br>
    <mobile:SelectionList runat="server" id="skills"
        SelectType="checkbox" />
    <mobile:Command runat="server" OnClick="Submit" Text="Send" />
</mobile:Form>

<mobile:Form runat="server" id="ResultsForm">
    <b>Recognized skills</b>
    <mobile:Label runat="server" id="Results" />
</mobile:Form>
```

When the user clicks to submit data, the page interrogates all the contained validators to see whether they have valid data.

```
protected void Page_Load(object sender, EventArgs e)
{
    if (!IsPostBack) {
        ArrayList values = new ArrayList();
        values.Add("ASP.NET");
        values.Add("ADO.NET");
        values.Add("XML");
        values.Add("Windows Forms");
        values.Add("SQL Server");
        skills.DataSource = values;
        skills.DataBind();
    }
}
protected void Submit(object sender, EventArgs e)
{
    if (!Page.IsValid) return;

    string buf = "";
    foreach (MobileListItem item in skills.Items)
        buf += (item.Selected ? item.Text + ", " : "");
    buf = buf.TrimEnd();
    if (buf.EndsWith(","))
        buf = buf.TrimEnd(',');

    Results.Text = buf;
    ActiveForm = ResultsForm;
}
```

If the *IsValid* property of the *MobilePage* is set to *false*, the procedure aborts and the same form is rendered back to the client with the validator that now displays its error message. If needed, you can use a *ValidationSummary* control in a secondary form that can be activated on demand. Figure 8-9 shows the previous code in action.

Figure 8-9   Validating the user input through mobile validation controls.

Developing Mobile Applications

To wrap up what we've learned so far about mobile controls and mobile pages, let's build an application that is representative of a typical wireless scenario. Depending on the capabilities of the device, you normally build a mobile application to cache information that will later be transmitted to a back-end system, or to interact in real-time with the back-end system. The former scenario is more common for rich and smart devices such as the Pocket PC family of products. For their modest processing power and RAM, cell phones are typically used for interacting with systems. However, the limited hardware and software capabilities of such devices makes it challenging for developers to build effective and usable wireless applications. A typical scenario for mobile applications is the search of information. I've chosen to focus on this category of programs because of the repercussions it has on a critical aspect of wireless applications—usability.

Our goal in this section is building a mobile application that lets users retrieve information about a customer and perhaps place a call. Of course, the subject of the search—customers—is totally arbitrary. The pattern applies with any large database to be navigated through. The term *large* is used here in a relative sense—that is, the databases in question are large in the context of the display capabilities of mobile devices. If displaying 20 records at a time makes sense for conventional Web applications, you should never exceed a few compact units of data for an application that is used through a small-screen cell phone.

Another key point to consider is the input capabilities of the device. Again, while letting the user type a matching string to narrow the set of customers being retrieved is sensible in the Web world, in a wireless context such an action has to be reckoned with the (normally very limited) input capabilities of the device and, subsequently, with the high level of frustration the poor user might soon reach.

The CustomerFinder Application

Our goal is to build a customer finder application—that is, an application that lets you retrieve personal information about a particular customer you would like to call or visit if only you could remember their darn phone number. The rub, though, is that you can't afford keeping hundreds of addresses and phone numbers in your cell phone. If you're using a smarter device, well, then imagine that you simply forgot to synchronize it with the database before you left the office!

Devising the Application for Usability

Many Web and desktop applications let you perform searches in an incremental way. You enter a string that is a partial key and the system soon prompts you with all the keys that match. Next, you further narrow the list by using a less partial key or simply picking the right one from the displayed list. This way of working makes perfect sense as long as you have enough screen space and memory. But there's an extra, often unnoticed, asset that you normally have if you're working at your desk—the keyboard. In general, with mobile devices you can easily enter numbers but not free text. So using a text box to type the key and a button to access the server is a rather unfair approach—easy for you as a developer, but annoying for the poor user who could be trying to use that application with only one hand while walking or eating.

A general guideline for wireless applications can be summarized in the following slogan: one additional click is a more enjoyable torture than having to type text. In a wireless application, especially if you know it will be used through cell phones, data entry should be avoided altogether or, at least, limited only to when it's absolutely necessary. You should use any information you might have about the user (for example, name, e-mail address, profile, and even global position) to personalize the screen and present options in a way that is optimized for the specific user.

The structure of a form must be as terse as possible, with short but effective descriptions and just one way of accomplishing tasks. Data should be downloaded in small chunks for bandwidth reasons, and using the application should be as easy as scrolling and clicking softkeys or numbers in the keypad.

A good design pattern for mobile applications that require input from the user is that of wizards. A tree-based representation of the tasks and the data to obtain is the key, as it makes it easier for you to submit a list of options to simply click or leave. With this in mind, let's move on and build a serious mobile application.

Mobile Applications in Visual Studio 2005

Visual Studio 2005 supplies ready-made project templates only if you're building against a specific rich device such as Pocket PC 2003, SmartPhone 2003, or Windows CE 5.0. In all other cases, you simply create a regular Web site project and add mobile Web Forms instead of classic Web Forms. It is also important that you choose the mobile version of the *web.config* file to automatically import some predefined device filters.

An ad hoc designer module shows up to help you create mobile forms and fill them with controls and code. Controls cannot be resized, as resizing is handled by ASP.NET when it generates the actual markup code for a particular device. You should try to organize the user interface of the application in forms and provide commands to move from one form to the next.

Working with Emulators

By default, Visual Studio 2005 uses Internet Explorer to test and debug mobile applications. However, you can also install your own device emulator and use it to browse the application. Once the emulator has been downloaded and installed on the machine, you register it with Visual Studio through the *Browse With* item in the page's context menu. You locate the emulator executable, give it a friendly name, and you're done. (See Figure 8-10.)

By selecting an emulator, you can browse the current application using a particular device without leaving the development environment. If you set an emulator as the default browser, Visual Studio .NET will launch it whenever you debug an application.

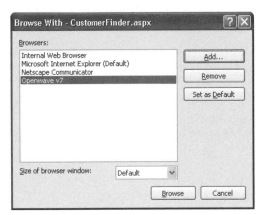

Figure 8-10 The dialog box used to install a browser emulator within Visual Studio .NET.

> **Note** Although ASP.NET does a fantastic job of abstracting the various wireless markup languages and fusing them to the .NET Framework, a lot remains for developers to do. In particular, you should be aware that ASP.NET alone is not enough to build real-world mobile applications that work great on a wide range of devices. This is not because of flaws and shortcomings in the ASP.NET implementation, however. It's more the result of the deep differences, in both hardware and software, existing between devices. For this reason, you should carefully consider the possibility of extending the ASP.NET mobile code with device-specific extensions.

The Navigation Model of the Application

The CustomerFinder application is composed of three forms. The first two forms let you narrow the set of customers to be displayed. When a reasonably small number of customers has been reached, the data is passed on to an *ObjectList* component for a more detailed display.

If you look at this strategy from a pure Web perspective, you might find it questionable, to say the least. However, designed this way, a mobile application is easier to use because it requires the user only to push buttons to proceed. The overall set of data is seen as a tree, and it is traversed by making a logical choice at each step. Only small chunks of information need be downloaded at any stage. Because the Customers table is likely to be used by all sessions, it needs to be created only once and stored in the ASP.NET *Cache* for better performance.

The Main Form

The first form to display employs a *List* control to display four options that, when combined, cover the 26 letters of the alphabet. The *Text* property of the *ListItem* object indicates the range, while the *Value* property contains all letters included separated by a comma.

```
<mobile:form id="MainForm" runat="server">
    <mobile:List id="Menu" runat="server" OnItemCommand="Menu_ItemCommand">
        <Item Value="A,B,C,D,E,F" Text="A-F" />
        <Item Value="G,H,I,J,K,L,M" Text="G-M" />
        <Item Value="N,O,P,Q,R,S" Text="N-S" />
        <Item Value="T,U,V,W,X,Y,Z" Text="T-Z" />
    </mobile:List>

    <mobile:Label id="Desc" runat="server" Text="Select Customers" />
    <mobile:TextBox id="Initials" runat="server" Size="5" />
    <mobile:Command id="FindButton" runat="server"
            OnClick="FindButton_Click">Find</mobile:Command>
</mobile:form>
```

The main form is completed with a text box and a command button. If the button is clicked, the text in the input field is used to select and display, in the customer form, a subset of customers. If you click on one of the list items, the following code executes:

```
void Menu_ItemCommand(object sender, ListCommandEventArgs e)
{
    string[] menuItems = e.ListItem.Value.Split(",".ToCharArray());
    Session["AvailableInitials"] = menuItems;
    LetterList.DataSource = menuItems;
    LetterList.DataBind();

    // Move to the second form
    ActiveForm = SecondMenuForm;
}
```

The comma-separated list of letters is split into a string array and temporarily parked in the session cache. We might need to retrieve it later to validate any text the user should enter in the Find text box for a more direct search. The same array of strings is used to fill another *List* object. In this case, the instance of the *List* control is bound to dynamically generated data rather than to static data.

To make a selection, the user might simply push buttons in the numeric keypad. However, if the user feels comfortable with typing, he or she can use the text box and make a more precise search for a substring. Figure 8-11 shows the succession of screens for the user who doesn't like typing.

Figure 8-11   The expanded sequence of letters to narrow the list of customers.

The *ActiveForm* property gets and sets the currently active form in a mobile page class. When a page is initially rendered, the first form in the page is automatically activated and displayed. On subsequent postbacks, another form might be brought to the foreground, either program-matically or as the result of user navigation. The *ActiveForm* property is a fundamental element for the implementation of wizard-like mobile user interfaces. In this case, the *ActiveForm* property is set to the second menu form.

The Second Menu Form

The second menu form shows all the letters that were listed in the *Value* property of the selected *ListItem* object. The code for the second menu form is shown here:

```
<mobile:form id="SecondMenuForm" runat="server">
    <mobile:List id="LetterList" runat="server" />
    <mobile:Label id="Desc" runat="server" Text="Select Customers" />
    <mobile:TextBox id="CustName" runat="server" />
    <mobile:Command id="FindCustomerButton" runat="server" text="Find" />
</mobile:form>
```

When the user clicks on any of the individual letters displayed, the code prepares a sort of in-memory query and returns an ADO.NET *DataView* object with all customers whose name begins with the selected letters. The customers are listed using an *ObjectList* control.

If the user wants to type a string to restrict the search, there's a text box available at the bottom of the second menu form. The text you can type is subject to validation; only strings that start with any of the listed letters are acceptable. (See Figure 8-12.)

Figure 8-12   The user types some text to identify more precisely the desired customer.

The Customer Form

As the final step in the application, let's display customers. We'll use an *ObjectList* control and bind it to the collection of rows selected by the following code:

```
DataView SelectCustomers(string filterString)
{
    // Get data
    DataTable data = GetData();
    DataView view = new DataView(data);

    // Filter data
    string cmdText = "";
    string[] initials = filterString.Split(",".ToCharArray());
    string opOR = "";
    foreach(string s in initials) {
        cmdText += String.Format("{0} {2} LIKE '{1}%' ",
            opOR, s, "companyname");
        opOR = " OR ";
    }

    // Return the filtered view
    view.RowFilter = cmdText;
    return view;
}
```

The code sets up a view on top of the global table of customers that was downloaded upon startup. The filtered view is then assigned to the *DataSource* property of *ObjectList* control.

```
void LetterList_ItemCommand(object sender, ListCommandEventArgs e) {
    DataView view = SelectCustomers(e.ListItem.Value);
    CustomerList.DataSource = view;
    CustomerList.DataBind();

    ActiveForm = CustomerForm;
}
```

Here is the structure of the customer form:

```
<mobile:form id="CustomerForm" runat="server" paginate="true">
    <mobile:ObjectList id="CustomerList" runat="server"
        Wrapping="nowrap" AutoGenerateFields="False"
        LabelField="Company">
        <Field Name="Company" DataField="companyname" Visible="False" />
        <Field Name="Address" DataField="address" />
        <Field Name="City" DataField="city" />
        <Field Name="Country" DataField="country" />
        <Field Name="Phone" DataField="phone" />
    </mobile:ObjectList>
    <mobile:Command id="BackMenuCommand" runat="server" text="Back" />
</mobile:form>
```

The *ObjectList* control first displays a list of the values bound through the *LabelField* column. When you click on any of these items, a detail view is provided that includes all the rows for which a *<field>* element exists. The collection of displayed fields must include the label field—*Company*, in the preceding example. If you don't want it to be displayed, set the *Visible* attribute to *false*. The *Name* attribute allows you to alias the physical data field. (See Figure 8-13.)

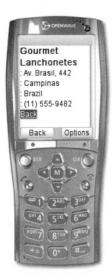

Figure 8-13   The long-awaited information about the customer.

The detail view provided by the *ObjectList* control, as well as the *List* control, can be customized to some extent using templates.

> **Caution**   In WML, a Web page is typically referred to as a *card*. A group of cards is called a deck. Most WML-based browsers have a limitation on the size of the deck they can receive. This is known as the deck size limit, and it can vary according to the individual device. Because the limit applies to content compiled at the WAP gateway, it's difficult to determine whether a WML deck is too large for a device. Exceeding the size limit could easily lead to a deck overflow error. This is particularly a risk for dynamic, data-bound pages.
>
> You should note that ASP.NET doesn't truncate pages to make decks fit within the deck size limit of a device. To be on the safe side, programmers should either use pagination within the form or consider approximately 1200 characters as a realistic threshold for decks.

Adaptive Rendering

Mobile applications can adapt the appearance of controls to specific devices or to categories of devices. Because they are based on known device capabilities, you can vary the style of the controls as well as make the rendering of the control more or less rich to accommodate the device characteristics. Adaptive rendering is performed using device filters. A device filter is represented with a *<DeviceSpecific>* tag in the controls layout.

Understanding Device Filters

The ASP.NET runtime abstracts the *.aspx* code and generates appropriate markup for rendering on a variety of device types. However, when you need different code to be generated for the same control on a device-by-device basis, you should define a set of device filters for the application and then specify the code to generate for each filter. You express a device filter using the *<DeviceSpecific>* and *<Choice>* elements.

The *<DeviceSpecific>* element is merely a container that holds a number of choices. Choices represent pairs made from a device characteristic and the corresponding value. The device filters are defined in the *web.config* file. A choice is selected if the filter is verified—that is, if the attribute of the device and the value match. The following listing demonstrates some filters that are defined in the mobile *web.config* file:

```
<deviceFilters>
    <filter name="isHTML32"
        compare="PreferredRenderingType"
        argument="html32" />
    <filter name="isWML11"
        compare="PreferredRenderingType"
        argument="wml11" />
    <filter name="prefersGIF"
        compare="PreferredImageMIME"
        argument="image/gif" />
    ⋮
</deviceFilters>
```

The *<filter>* element has a name that is used to bind to the *<choice>* element. The *compare* attribute defines the capability of the device you want to test. The *argument* property is the value to match. For example, if you want a label to render in italic on WML 1.1 devices and as normal text elsewhere, do the following:

```
<mobile:Form runat="server">
    <mobile:Label runat="server" text="Some text">
        <DeviceSpecific>
            <choice filter="isWML11" font-italic="true" />
        </DeviceSpecific>
    </mobile:Label>
</mobile:Form>
```

Note that this technique works as long as you have the filter defined in the *web.config* file. Choices are evaluated in the order they appear in the *<DeviceSpecific>* construct. In practice, a device filter is a declarative way to test some capabilities of the device and configure the control properly.

Creating Control Templates

Device filters can also be used to change the default template used by list controls. For instance, in the example just discussed, we end up displaying the phone number of the selected customer. Wouldn't it be nice if we could automatically associate it with a *PhoneCall* control? In this way, in fact, our user could click and place a call. Both the *List* and *ObjectList* controls let you change the structure of the default template.

The following code shows how to change the template used to render all the items of a *List* object using a *PhoneCall* control:

```
<mobile:List id="CustomerList" runat="server" OnItemCommand="ItemCommand">
    <DeviceSpecific>
    <Choice>
    <ItemTemplate>
        <mobile:PhoneCall runat="server"
            Text='<%# Eval("companyname") %>'
            PhoneNumber='<%# Eval("phone") %>'>
        </mobile:PhoneCall>
    </ItemTemplate>
    </Choice>
    </DeviceSpecific>
</mobile:List>
```

If the *Filter* property is omitted, the choice is picked by default, and this allows you to modify the output of some built-in controls using templates.

State Management

Most Web applications need state to be persisted between requests, and mobile applications are no exception. ASP.NET provides several services and facilities for state management, among which view state and session state play a primary role. View state is a page-level cache that is saved and loaded for each request of the page. This trick makes possible the development of stateful applications on top of a stateless protocol.

The View State

On ASP.NET pages, the view state is packed as a hidden variable in the unique server-side form object that is submitted. The view state is sent back and forth as part of every response and request being exchanged. The way in which applications interact with the view state is the same in ASP.NET mobile applications. The internal implementation is different, however.

To reduce bandwidth, ASP.NET does not send the view state of a mobile page to the client. Instead, the view state remains on the server and is saved as part of the user's session. Because the view state is kept on the server, it's possible for the currently cached state and the currently displayed page to be out of sync. For example, suppose the user navigates to a given page and then moves back to another page by using the Back button. At this point, the current page doesn't match the view state on the server.

For this reason, ASP.NET maintains for mobile pages a history of view states on the server. Each page is assigned a numeric ID that corresponds to the position in the view-state history where information about that page is held. The size of the history array is set to 6 by default, but it can be changed in the *web.config* file, as shown in the following code. Of course, too high a value might lead to unnecessary consumption of server memory.

```
<configuration>
    <system.web>
        <mobileControls sessionStateHistorySize="15" />
    </system.web>
</configuration>
```

Because the view state of mobile pages and controls is stored in *Session*, chances are that this information will get lost if the session expires or the process is recycled. When the view state can't be restored for a mobile page, the *ViewStateExpire* event is fired. The event normally results in an exception being thrown; however, if there's a way for the application to restore a consistent state on a view-state failure, you should override the method *OnViewStateExpire* on the *MobilePage* class and execute your recovery code there.

> **Note** Just as for ASP.NET Web Forms, the use of the view state can be minimized and completely disabled if it's not really needed. You can disable the view state by using the *Enable-ViewState* attribute on the *@Page* directive; if you want to disable the view state for an individual control, use the *EnableViewState* property on the control's programming interface.

The Private View State

You should note, though, that even when view state is disabled, mobile controls might save state information in a hidden field on the client. For example, a *MobilePage* control saves the index of the currently active form in a hidden field implemented in a way that closely resembles the Web Forms view state. The view-state history identifier is also saved in this sort of private view state.

The *ClientViewState* property returns a string that represents the serialized version of the private view state. Applications cannot add custom information to this table. The private view state should be used only for general state information, is always saved to the client, and cannot be disabled.

> **Note**   The *HiddenVariables* collection of the *MobilePage* class provides a way to create hidden variables in the output. Although this feature has nothing to do with the private view state, it represents an easier-to-use alternative to the private view state. Mobile controls do not support control state in the way it works for server controls.

The Session State

The session state is tied to an identifier that uniquely identifies the session within the application. By default, this identifier is stored in a client-side cookie and is retrieved across roundtrips. Using cookies in mobile applications can be problematic because some devices and gateways do not support cookies.

ASP.NET supports cookieless sessions. A cookieless session relies on a special format of the URL to retrieve the identifier. When working in cookieless mode, ASP.NET redirects the browser to another page whose URL embeds the identifier, which is then parsed out of the actual URL. In this case, though, you should pay attention to devices that might experience difficulty if passed a URL with special formatting, such as the URL of a cookieless application.

Hidden variables are a fair alternative to using the session state in the unfortunate case that you can't avoid keeping some session information handy.

Conclusion

Developing mobile applications can be quite a complex task because of differences in browser presentation models and gateways. Like it or not, the market for wireless devices is fragmented, although this fragmentation is possibly stronger in Europe than in other parts of the world. So, to be on the safe side and deploy effective applications, you should multi-author your application for each relevant class of devices. Writing multiple applications is not usually an attractive prospect to developers and managers, who are understandably reluctant to give the green light on such costly projects.

In the wireless world, though, the difference between devices is too large to be effectively addressed in all cases even by a well-written library such the ASP.NET mobile controls. The need to deal with radically different sets of capabilities forces developers to implement navigation models, data-entry capabilities, and strictly device-specific commands. If you're going to build mobile applications for multiple devices, your best bet is to endow yourself with a server-side programming library that abstracts the presentation of content from the underlying platform. ASP.NET mobile controls do just this and much more.

Just the Facts

- ASP.NET mobile controls are an extension of ASP.NET server controls.

- A mobile page must contain at least one form, but multiple forms are supported as long as only one is visible at a time.

- Pagination is a mechanism for automatically partitioning the form's contents into smaller portions of markup code. The final output is also completed with common user-interface elements so that users can move around.

- The *List*, *ObjectList*, and *SelectionList* controls are the mobile counterpart of ASP.NET list-bound and iterative controls.

- In mobile applications, the use of the keyboard has to be reckoned with the usually limited input capabilities of the device.

- In general, for mobile users, one more click is a more enjoyable torture than having to type text.

- Deep differences in both hardware and software exist between mobile devices. Although ASP.NET does a fantastic job in abstracting differences, you should *never* deploy an application without carefully testing it on the widest possible number of real devices.

- Device filters are the tool you need to declaratively differentiate the markup on a per-device basis.

Chapter 9
Working with Images

As dramatic as it may seem, the World Wide Web wouldn't have been the same without the images. Effective browser support for images, in fact, is one of the keys to the rapid success of the Web because it sanctioned the Web platform as a new multimedia channel. Any page we get from the Web today is topped with so many images and is so well conceived and designed that the overall page looks more like a magazine advertisement than an HTML page. Looking at the current pages displayed by portals, it's rather hard to imagine there was a time—and it was only seven or eight years ago—when one could create a Web site by using only a text editor and some assistance from a friend who had some familiarity with Adobe PhotoShop.

These days, images are a common presence in Web pages, but their use is still mostly limited to art designers and other specialized professional figures. Programmers, for example, are rarely involved with images because although many images are the fruit of intense work and planning, they are nearly always deployed as static files. When static JPEG or GIF images are involved, a programmer can't do much to add more spice to the final page served to the user.

Over the Web, images are not merely and not always used as a publishing tool. In many applications, images play a much more active role and are as significant as data. Examples of this include image data banks, photographic galleries, museums, and financial and business analysis applications. In all these cases, the application might need to work with dynamically generated images (for example, charts) or images that must undergo special treatment before display (for example, adding a watermark or copyright message).

Several third-party vendors provide powerful and professional tools to perform charting and image processing over the Web. Prior to the release of the .NET Framework, the need to resort to these tools was a foregone conclusion. Thanks to GDI+, ASP.NET applications can sometimes accomplish a variety of tasks in-house without requiring additional tools and libraries. You'll be surprised to see how many tasks can be accomplished with the wise use of GDI+ and other .NET Framework facilities.

Accessing Images from Web Pages

There is just one way in which Web pages can reference an image—by using the HTML *<img>* tag. By design, this tag points to a URL. As a result, to be displayable within a Web page, an image must be identifiable through a URL, and its bits should be contained in the output stream returned by the Web server for that URL. In many cases, the URL points to a static resource such as a GIF or JPEG file. In this case, the Web server takes the request upon itself and serves it without invoking external components.

That many *<img>* tags on the Web are bound to a static file does not mean there's no other way to include images in Web pages. Let's start with a few basic points on this topic and briefly recall the main points of Web image access.

The *<img>* Element

The HTML *<img>* element is used to display an image within an HTML page. It supports a few attributes such as width, height, and alternate text to display if the image is not available. The HTML definition of the element is as follows:

```
<img id="control ID"
    alt="alternate text"
    align="top | middle | bottom | left | right"
    border="border width"
    height="image height"
    src="URL"
    width="image width" />
```

In ASP.NET, the *<img>* tag is rendered through the *HtmlImage* class. The ASP.NET *Image* control represents another way of generating the *<img>* tag. *HtmlImage* belongs to the *System.Web.UI.HtmlControls* namespace, whereas *Image* is a member of the *System.Web .UI.WebControls* namespace and provides a more abstract programming interface but no extra features.

Showing Images Without Server Controls

Although it's good that two controls are provided to create a server-side representation of the *<img>* tag, a highly optimized ASP.NET application will not use any. Even though server controls are extremely easy to use, they're not always the best choice for a relatively simple task such as showing an image because they consume server resources without really needing to. In many cases, a simple rendering or data-binding substitution will nicely and more efficiently do the job of showing an image.

The following code snippet successfully displays an image but doesn't require the creation of a server-side *Image* control:

```
<img src='<%# expression that evaluates to the image URL %>' />
```

How can the preceding expression work without the *runat=server* attribute? Shouldn't the expression be rendered verbatim? The trick lies in the fact that ASP.NET 2.0 transforms the whole expression in a *DataBoundLiteralControl* control instance with both static and dynamic text. As long as there's a *DataBind* method called that reaches the #-expression, the expression is correctly evaluated and used to complete the *<img>* tag.

When the *<img>* tag is configured on the server, you should pay careful attention to the URL you output, especially if the URL is in some way a function of the user input. The URL associated with the *<img>* element can be tampered with by a malicious user and result in undesired script code that runs on the client. Also, to validate the URL, you don't necessarily have to resort to a server control. A call to a local function within the data-bound expression can also do the job.

Beyond Static Image Files

Although the *<img>* element is mostly used with static files, it can easily display images stored on other storage media—for example, a database, assembly resources, or even the Web server's memory. The key structure of the element doesn't change to support this feature. What changes, instead, is just the extension of the URL and the content type of the HTTP response. If you make the *<img>* tag point to an *.aspx* page, the Web server will run the specified page and send the resultant output to the tag. As long as the output can be recognized as a valid image format, it is displayed. Let's see how.

Referencing Nonfile Images

From the browser's perspective, a Web page is nothing more than a long strip of characters to be processed sequentially. The browser displays some characters and interprets some others, such as *<b>*, according to special rules. When an *<img>* tag is found, the browser knows that it has to open another download channel and request the specified URL. To the browser's eyes, the type of the URL and the protocol have no importance. What matters is that the expected output matches a given format—the MIME type.

The browser requests the image URL and processes the returned output as the expected MIME type dictates. If the bytes form an image of the correct type, the picture is displayed with the attributes set in the *<img>* tag; otherwise, an error is raised and a standard picture-missing bitmap is displayed. For a better understanding of the whole process, let's see the steps needed to send an image to the browser from within an *.aspx* page.

Important   To serve users' images stored in the file system, you set the *<img>* tag to the URL of the file. If the image bytes are stored in other storage media (for example, databases or memory) or if you need to do some work on the bytes before you serve them, you need to bind the *<img>* tag to a server-side HTTP handler that in the end returns the bytes for the image.

Setting the Content Type

All the response packets that reach the browser contain a *Content-Type* header that provides information about the type and, subsequently, the format of the incoming data. The browser looks at that value and decides how to process the data. The following snippet shows the Internet Information Services (IIS) response to a browser that requested a JPEG image:

```
HTTP/1.1 200 OK
Server: Microsoft-IIS/6.0
Date: Thu, 24 Nov 2005 14:30:12 GMT
X-Powered-By: ASP.NET
X-AspNet-Version: 2.0.50727
Cache-Control: private
 Content-Type: image/jpeg
Content-Length: 28521
```

In ASP.NET, the *HttpResponse* object is responsible for setting the *Content-Type* header in the response packet. By default, the *ContentType* property of the *HttpResponse* object is set to *text/html*. Accepted values for the property are all HTTP MIME types. Of course, for the download to succeed, the content type must be set only once in the page and before the page has sent some data to the output stream.

```
Response.ContentType = "image/jpeg";
```

The preceding code illustrates how to set the *ContentType* property of a page that returns a JPEG image.

Flushing to the Output Stream

The following code demonstrates a simple page that displays an image obtained through another ASP.NET page:

```
<%@ Page Language="C#" %>
<html>
<body>
<form runat="server">
    <img src="image.aspx" />
</form>
</body>
</html>
```

The *image.aspx* page will first gain access to the bytes of the image and then serialize them all to the output stream.

```
protected void Page_Load(object sender, EventArgs e)
{
    string fileName = Server.MapPath(@"/proaspnet/images/slotmachine.jpg");
    Response.ContentType = "image/jpeg";
    Response.WriteFile(fileName);
}
```

If you need to do some work on the file stream, you can explicitly read the bytes, do whatever is needed, and then write the final array of bytes to the output stream.

In their overall simplicity, this pair of pages illustrates well the pattern necessary to obtain and manipulate images dynamically. The client page sets the *src* attribute of the *<img>* tag to an *.aspx* resource. The server page, in turn, will retrieve or generate the bytes of the image and write them to the output stream along with the proper content type.

> **Important**   Serving images dynamically through an ASP.NET page is fine, but it's not particularly effective. What you really need is not an ASP.NET page, but a simpler HTTP handler. An ASP.NET page is certainly an HTTP handler, but it performs a number of extra tasks that are unnecessary to serve an image. We'll return to this key point later.

Loading Images from Resources

Managed assemblies can optionally contain resources. Resources are images, localizable text, script, and other auxiliary files packed with the compiled code to form a unique deliverable—the assembly file. For example, *system.web*—the assembly that is the heart of ASP.NET—embeds as resources all script code that the various rich controls can insert in user pages. (See Chapter 6.) The same assembly incorporates a lot of images that are mostly used to decorate server controls when they show up in the Microsoft Visual Studio 2005 toolbox.

Adding Images as Resources

To add a file as an embedded resource, you just add the file to the project and set the build action attribute to *Embedded Resource*. Note that you can use this technique only with projects that return a dynamic-link library (DLL). If you add a resource to the project that builds a Web application, you won't find any additional properties box for setting the build action. The build action, in fact, makes sense only for the files included in projects in which a classic compiler is run on the development machine to generate deployable binaries.

In ASP.NET 1.x, any Visual Studio 2003 project generates an all-encompassing assembly where pages and resources are joined together. In ASP.NET 2.0, no binaries are generated during the build process on the client to be deployed on the server. As we saw in Chapter 1, either you precompile your application and deploy it as a set of binaries or you deploy it as source code and files that are compiled on demand on the server. In both cases, the Visual Studio build action makes no sense any longer. For projects expected to generate a helper DLL, it's a different story, as Figure 9-1 documents.

The name of the resource is determined according to the following convention: Namespace.FileName.Extension. The *Namespace* token matches the default namespace of the assembly, whereas *FileName* and *Extension* tokens correspond to the name and extension of the embedded file. For the file added in Figure 9-1, the name of the resource in the assembly is *ProAspCompLib.SlotMachine.jpg*. (See Figure 9-2.)

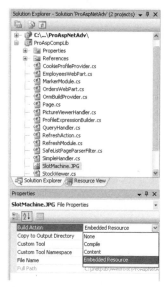

Figure 9-1   Adding an image as an embedded resource to an assembly.

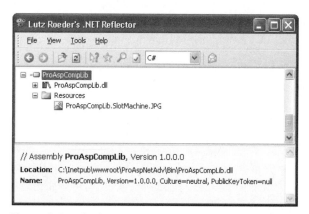

Figure 9-2   Viewing resources in an assembly through .NET Reflector.

Referencing Embedded Resources

Any file embedded in the resource of an assembly can be accessed programmatically and consumed just as any other file of the same type available to the application. For example, this means that you could embed small bitmaps in the assembly that defines a custom control, thus making the control self-contained and still based on rich graphics. How would you reference an embedded resource? There are two main, nonexclusive approaches. Which one is preferable depends on the characteristics of the resource file.

Embedded images can be consumed only through a URL bound to the <img> tag. So you need an HTTP handler to extract the bits of the image from a given assembly and serve it to the browser. Suppose you have such a handler named, say, *image.axd*. The *<img>* tag, then, might look like this:

```
<img src="image.axd?asm=...&res=..." />
```

The *src* attribute points to the URL of the handler padded with query string arguments to identify the assembly and resource. Internally, the sample *image.axd* assembly will take the resource name and retrieve its contents from the assembly file.

Writing such an HTTP handler is not a hard task, and I'll demonstrate it later in the context of a broader example. For now, let's discuss the core code that should be placed in this HTTP handler—code that specifies how to access the resource stream inside a given assembly.

Accessing the Resource Stream

Images are just one of the resource types you can embed in an assembly. You can also embed script files, strings, and XSLT files. In some cases, you only need to package up these resource files with the assembly and serve them as stored; in other cases, you need to extract the contents, perform some manipulation, and then serve them to the client user. How do you read resource contents from any assembly?

The *Assembly* class (found in the *System.Reflection* namespace) features two methods that are slick to use here. They are *GetManifestResourceNames* and *GetManifestResourceStream*. The former returns an array of strings in which each element represents a contained resource. The latter takes one of these names and retrieves the stream to the corresponding embedded resource.

The following code snippet shows how to fill a drop-down list named *ResourceNames* with all the names of all resources contained in the *system.web* assembly:

```
Assembly dll = Assembly.LoadWithPartialName("system.web");
string[] resources = dll.GetManifestResourceNames();
ResourceNames.DataSource = resources;
ResourceNames.DataBind();
```

The output is shown in Figure 9-3.

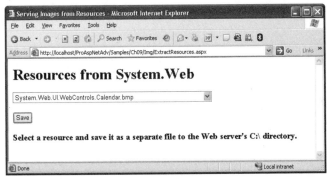

Figure 9-3   The list of resources embedded in the ASP.NET *system.web* assembly.

To read the bytes of a given resource, you use the *GetManifestResourceStream* method, as shown here:

```
private System.Drawing.Image LoadImageFromResources(string imageID)
{
    Assembly dll = Assembly.LoadWithPartialName("system.web");
    Bitmap img = new Bitmap(dll.GetManifestResourceStream(imageID));
    return img;
}
protected void buttonSave_Click(object sender, EventArgs e)
{
    string resourceName = ResourceNames.SelectedValue;
    System.Drawing.Image img = LoadImageFromResources(resourceName);
    if (img != null)
    {
        string path = string.Format(@"c:\{0}", resourceName);
        StreamWriter bin = new StreamWriter(path);
        MemoryStream ms = new MemoryStream();
        img.Save(ms, ImageFormat.Jpeg);
        img.Dispose();
        ms.WriteTo(bin.BaseStream);
        ms.Close();
        bin.Close();

        // Inject a bit of script code to notify users
        string js = "alert('Done.');";
        ClientScript.RegisterStartupScript(this.GetType(),
            "Alert", js, true);
    }
}
```

The *GetManifestResourceStream* method returns a stream that represents the contents of the specified resource. Hence, by using the .NET Framework API for file I/O, you save that content to a disk file. (The preceding code works if the ASP.NET process does have writing permission on the target folder, which is always the case for *C:* as long as you don't change the default process account.)

> **Important**   In ASP.NET 2.0, new facilities have been added to automate, to the extent that it is possible, the display of images embedded as resources in compiled assemblies. This feature, expressed by the *GetWebResourceUrl* method on the *ClientScriptManager* class and the *[WebResource]* attribute, is specifically targeted to custom controls or custom page classes explicitly compiled to distinct assemblies. I'll return to this topic in Chapter 13, when I discuss custom server controls.

Accessing Database Images

The use of a database as the storage medium for images is controversial. Some people have good reasons to push it as a solution; others tell you bluntly they would never do it and that you shouldn't either. Some people could tell you wonderful stories of how storing images in a properly equipped database was the best experience of their professional life. Other people, no matter what argument you might make to the contrary, would confess that they would never use a database for such a task.

The facts say that all database management systems (DBMS) of a certain reputation and volume have supported binary large objects (BLOB) for quite some time. A BLOB field doesn't necessarily contain an image, but it can contain a multimedia file or a long text file. There must be a good reason for having this BLOB support in Microsoft SQL Server, Oracle, and similar popular DBMS systems!

Working with Binary Fields

To read a binary database field, you use ADO.NET classes as you would for any other database query. At the end of the day, in fact, a BLOB field is only a database column of a special type and of a reasonably large size. If you know that the size of the object is not excessive (say, tens of kilobytes), you can go for a single-step read; otherwise, you might want to opt for sequential access and read one chunk of information at a time.

The ADO.NET data reader is the tool that proves most useful for reading information out of a BLOB field. This doesn't mean you can't store large binary content in a *DataSet*. It's only that the *DataSet* is an in-memory cache of data, and caching data of that size in the memory of the Web server is rarely a great solution. BLOB fields are the type of data that should be read, consumed, and disposed of as soon as possible, without the programmer being tempted by the siren's song of caching techniques.

For now, assume we'll store BLOB fields in SQL Server; later on, I'll share some thoughts about Oracle.

Reading Images from BLOB Fields

To read an image from a BLOB field with ADO.NET, you execute a SELECT statement on the column and use the *ExecuteScalar* method to catch the result and save it in an array of bytes. Next, you send this array down to the client through a binary write to the response stream. Let's write an HTTP handler to serve the image in a more efficient way than from plain ASP.NET pages.

```
public class DbImageHandler : IHttpHandler
{
    public void ProcessRequest(HttpContext ctx)
    {
        // Ensure the URL contains an ID argument being a number
        int id = -1;
        bool result = Int32.TryParse(ctx.Request.QueryString["id"], out id);
        if (!result)
            ctx.Response.End();

        string connString = "...";
        string cmdText = "SELECT photo FROM employees WHERE employeeid=@id";

        // Get an array of bytes from the BLOB field
        byte[] img = null;
```

```
SqlConnection conn = new SqlConnection(connString);
using (conn)
{
    SqlCommand cmd = new SqlCommand(cmdText, conn);
    cmd.Parameters.AddWithValue("@id", id);
    conn.Open();
    img = (byte[])cmd.ExecuteScalar();
    conn.Close();
}

// Prepare the response for the browser
if (img != null)
{
    ctx.Response.ContentType = "image/jpeg";
    ctx.Response.BinaryWrite(img);
}
}

public bool IsReusable
{
    get { return true; }
}
}
```

There are quite a few assumptions made in this code. First, we assume that the field named *photo* contains image bits and that the format of the image is JPEG. Second, we assume that images are to be retrieved from a fixed table of a given database through a predefined connection string. Finally, we're assuming that the URL to invoke this handler includes a query string parameter named *id*.

Notice the attempt to convert the value of the *id* query parameter to an integer before proceeding. This simple check significantly reduces the surface attack for malicious users by verifying that what is going to be used as a numeric ID is really a numeric ID. Especially when you're inoculating user input into SQL query commands, filtering out extra characters and wrong data types is a fundamental measure for preventing attacks.

The *BinaryWrite* method of the *HttpResponse* object writes an array of bytes to the output stream.

Warning   If the database you're using is Northwind (as in the preceding example), an extra step might be required to ensure that the images are correctly managed. For some reason, the SQL Server 2000 version of the Northwind database stores the images in the *photo* column of the Employees table as OLE objects. This is probably because of the conversion that occurred when the database was upgraded from the Microsoft Access version. As a matter of fact, the array of bytes you receive contains a 78-byte prefix that has nothing to do with the image. Those bytes are just the header created when the image was added as an OLE object to the first version of Access. Although the preceding code would work like a champ with regular BLOB fields, it must undergo the following modification to work with the *photo* field of the Northwind.Employees database:

```
Response.OutputStream.Write(img, 78, img.Length);
```

Instead of using the *BinaryWrite* call, which doesn't let you specify the starting position, use the code shown here.

A sample page to test BLOB field access is shown in Figure 9-4. The page lets users select an employee ID and post back. When the page renders, the ID is used to complete the URL for the ASP.NET *Image* control.

```
string url = String.Format("dbimage.axd?id={0}", EmpList.SelectedValue);
Image1.ImageUrl = url;
```

Figure 9-4 Downloading images stored within the BLOB field of a database.

As discussed in Chapter 2, an HTTP handler must be registered in the *web.config* file and bound to a public endpoint. In this case, the endpoint is *dbimage.axd*, and the script to enter in the configuration file is shown next:

```
<httpHandlers>
    <add path="dbimage.axd" verb="*"
         type="ProAspNet20.Components.DbImageHandler,ProAspCompLib"/>
</httpHandlers>
```

Uploading Images to BLOB Fields

Uploading an image to a database is simply a matter of preparing and executing an *INSERT* or *UPDATE* statement with the right set of parameters. You can use a single SQL statement or even a stored procedure. If the BLOB field is a column of type *Text*, you can pass the value as a string parameter. If the BLOB is expected to contain an image—the SQL Server type *Image*—you set the specific parameter by using an array of bytes.

In Figure 9-5, you can see a sample page that lets you upload a local file to the Web server and from there into a SQL Server database.

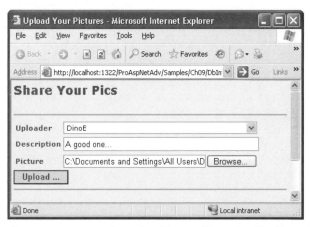

Figure 9-5 Users select a local image file and upload it to the Web server, where the image is further processed and copied into a SQL Server database.

The structure of the database table is described in Table 9-1.

Table 9-1   The Schema of the Sample Table

Column	Type
ImageID	Represent the unique ID of the image; integer and auto-increment
Bits	BLOB field of type *Image* contains the bits of the image
Description	Contains a short description of the image
ImageSize	Size in bytes of the image
MIME	String that represents the MIME type of the image
Uploader	Foreign-key reference to the user who uploaded the image
UploadTime	Time at which the upload occurred

The sample page contains a *FileUpload* control that is normally used to upload files. The *FileUpload* control is a new control of ASP.NET 2.0 that is functionally equivalent to the *HtmlInputFile* control you can use in ASP.NET 1.x. For the file upload to work, the containing form must have its *EncType* attribute set to *multipart/form-data*. In ASP.NET 2.0, both *FileUpload* and *HtmlInputFile* controls ensure that the *EncType* attribute is set before proceeding, so you don't have to worry about it any longer in ASP.NET 2.0.

```
<asp:FileUpload ID="theFile" runat="server" />
```

The uploaded file is made available on the server through the *PostedFile* property of the upload control. The *PostedFile* property is an object of type *HttpPostedFile* and features interesting properties such as *ContentLength*, *ContentType*, and *InputStream*. The first two properties indicate the length and MIME type of the posted file; the third property exposes the posted file as a stream object, making it easy for the application to transform it into an array of bytes.

The following code shows how to upload an image directly into the *MyPics* table of a SQL Server named *MyBlobs*:

```
protected void UploadButton_Click(object sender, EventArgs e)
{
....// "theFile" is the ID associated with the FileUpload object
....// in the markup.
    int sizeOfFile = theFile.PostedFile.ContentLength;
    int recordsAffected = -1;

    // Prepare for the SQL command
    string connString =
        ConfigurationManager.ConnectionStrings["MyBlobs"].ConnectionString;
    SqlConnection conn = new SqlConnection(connString);
    using (conn)
    {
        string cmdText = "INSERT INTO MyPics " +
            "(bits, description, uploader, uploadtime, imagesize, mime) " +
            "VALUES (@imageBits, @description, @uploader, @uploadTime, " +
            "@imageSize, @mimeType)";
        SqlCommand cmd = new SqlCommand(cmdText, conn);

        // Set parameters
        cmd.Parameters.AddWithValue("@imageBits",
            GetImageBits(theFile.PostedFile.InputStream, sizeOfFile));
        cmd.Parameters.AddWithValue("@description",
            theDesc.Text);
        cmd.Parameters.AddWithValue("@uploader",
            theUploader.SelectedItem.Value);
        cmd.Parameters.AddWithValue("@uploadTime",
            DateTime.Now);
        cmd.Parameters.AddWithValue("@imageSize",
            sizeOfFile);
        cmd.Parameters.AddWithValue("@mimeType",
            theFile.PostedFile.ContentType);

        // Copy the bits into the table
        conn.Open();
        recordsAffected = cmd.ExecuteNonQuery();
        conn.Close();
    }

    // Feedback to users
    string msg = (recordsAffected != -1
            ? "Successfully done!" : "Something went wrong...");
    string js = String.Format("alert('{0}');", msg);
    ClientScript.RegisterStartupScript(this.GetType(), "Alert", js, true);
    return;
}

private byte[] GetImageBits(Stream fs, int size)
{
    byte[] img = new byte[size];
    fs.Read(img, 0, size);
    return img;
}
```

The content of the posted file is accessed through the *InputStream* property of the *HttpPosted-File* class. The stream is read into an array of bytes, and the array is used as the value for the command parameter that will fill the BLOB field. Information about the content type and the length of the posted file are inferred from the file itself. Other information (description, uploader) is retrieved from input controls in the form.

> **Note** Prior to ASP.NET, a server-side process was required to run in the background to handle a file upload to the server. The background application—the posting acceptor—is called to handle submissions. IIS *multipart/form-data* and ASP applications use the Microsoft Posting Acceptor, but other tools (mostly CGI applications) are available over the Web. In ASP.NET, the role of the posting acceptor is no longer necessary because it is carried out by the ASP.NET runtime.

Real-World Scenarios

More often than not, you need to retrieve information about a certain entity defined in the domain of the problem. The information might include both text and binary fields. As we architect the solution, distinct database access is necessary to retrieve the BLOB and no special countermeasures are taken to minimize the memory footprint if the images are particularly large.

Optimizing the Database Query

It's clear that images, because of their potentially large size, need to be handled with care and should be cached sparingly. However, be aware that an *.aspx* or *.axd* resource like those discussed earlier, bound to an *<img>* tag, generates a distinct and extra call to the database. In practice, you make one call to retrieve all the text-based information and one call to fill each image bound to a Web page.

If you decide this model is not what you want, consider the following alternatives to optimize database access. First, you could create copies of the image in a temporary directory and look for local files before you embark into a database query. Especially if the size of the image is considerable, at a minimum you save a segment of the bandwidth to reach the database. Because database fields are global resources shared by all sessions, figuring out an effective naming convention for these images shouldn't be an issue. In addition, you can also modify the source code of the calling page so that it points to an existing image file rather than to a server-side page. In this case, you also gain faster access because IIS will resolve the call to the image without posting the request to ASP.NET.

If the size and number of images allow for it, a second alternative to optimize database access is to use caching. This entails making a full query of all fields and caching the BLOB field temporarily, just long enough for the successive request for the image to be served. To make sure the object is not maintained in memory for long, you can store it in *Cache* and define a short-term expiration policy.

Optimizing Memory Usage

The *ExecuteScalar* method we used to read BLOB contents works by loading the incoming data as soon as it becomes available. In other words, the BLOB is read in a single shot, along with the rest of the data row, potentially consuming a lot of memory. Such large objects should be treated in a different way—particularly when you know they might contain hundreds of megabytes of data. For this reason, neither *ExecuteScalar* nor the default data reader is probably the best approach to take. Let's look at a better alternative.

The behavior of ADO.NET command objects can be controlled through an additional parameter passed to the *ExecuteReader* method. This parameter is a value taken from the *CommandBehavior* enumeration. Of particular interest here is the *SequentialAccess* value. When specified in a call to *ExecuteReader*, the sequential access attribute changes the standard behavior of the reader and makes it return data as it is received instead of one complete row at a time. In other words, it streams column data as the data is available instead of waiting for all of the data from all of the columns in the row to be made available.

If you configure the reader for sequential reading, the order in which you access fields is important. The data reader, in fact, is a forward-only cursor and can't move back to consider bytes it has read past. For example, once you have accessed the third field, it's too late to access the first and second fields.

When accessing the data in the BLOB field, you should use the *GetBytes* method of the data reader and fill an array with data.

```
bytesRead = reader.GetBytes(colIndex, startPos, buf, 0, bufSize);
while (bytesRead == bufSize)
{
    // Process the bytes
    ProcessBytes(buf);

    // Reposition the start index
    startPos += bufSize;
    bytesRead = reader.GetBytes(colIndex, startPos, buf, 0, bufSize);
}

// Process the remaining buffer
ProcessBytes(buf);
```

GetBytes accepts a starting position and buffer size, and it returns the number of bytes effectively read. Using sequential access and *GetBytes* for reading allows you to conserve system resources, which could be compromised by too large of a BLOB value.

What About SQL Server?

SQL Server stores images in a field of type *Image*, which should be used for any binary content exceeding 8 kilobytes (KB) and up to 2 gigabytes (GB). It goes without saying that regardless of the availability of smart and to-the-point T-SQL commands—such as UPDATETEXT, READTEXT, and WRITETEXT—working with large images (several megabytes each) is complex and difficult.

If you find the preceding discussion too generic and rather ineffectual and still need to decide what to do with your images, use the following rule of thumb: Use the file system if you are manipulating images larger than 1 MB. Use the file system also if you have several hundred thousand images—up to about one million images. If your images are less than 1MB in size or fewer in number than several hundred thousand, accessing the images from a SQL Server database is a consideration. If your numbers are close to these, either file system or database storage might be OK. Just be sure to test your application's performance and tune as necessary.

An additional parameter to consider is the topology of the network. For Web farms, a single central location—that is, SQL Server—might be better than using the file system. SQL Server, in turn, can get bytes off the disk pretty quickly and implements an excellent caching layer, but the Tabular Data Stream (TDS)—that is, the protocol it uses to transmit data over the wire—certainly wasn't designed with BLOBs in mind.

What About Oracle?

Oracle supplies two different data types to deal with large binary objects—the BFILE and LOB data types. Both reference binary data with a maximum size of 4 GB. A BFILE differs from a LOB data type in that its data is stored in a physical file in the operating system instead of within the database. Other characteristics distinguish BFILEs from LOBs. In particular, the BFILE uses reference copy semantics, meaning that if you perform a copy operation on a BFILE, only the reference to the file is copied, not the data in the file.

The BFILE data type should be used for referencing binary objects that are very large and, therefore, not practical to store in the database. On the other hand, using a BFILE introduces a slight increase in overhead because of the extra communication necessary to synchronize the database engine, file, and client application. In general, it's more efficient to access a BFILE if you need to obtain only a small amount of data. It's preferable to access a database-resident LOB if you need to obtain all the data.

Should You Really Store Images in the Database?

About ten years ago, I started one of the first Internet projects—an image data bank. We were supposed to deliver images of various sizes and resolution to registered users. Each image was designed as a collection of images, from the thumbnail to the highest resolution. The largest image available was about 4 MB. Each image stored in the archive took up a total of 6 MB of space.

The back-end database was not running on a Microsoft platform but provided support for BLOB fields. Without much debate, we decided to store descriptions and other catalog information in the database and to store images as individual files under a well-known path. We also stored in the database enough information for the software to retrieve the file. Being designed for a relatively small number of registered users, the application never showed scalability problems and at no time did anyone on the team, or any users, complain about performance.

Can this brief experience—especially an experience from a relatively old age of software and database technologies—be used as an example of the superiority of file-based storage over database storage? Certainly not, but reading between the lines of how modern DBMS systems implement BLOB fields, I've used this experience to formulate an idea about image storage and databases.

In short, should you consider storing images in a database? If you need to edit the images frequently, I suggest storing the images as separate files on the server's hard drive. If the size of the images are very large (for example, hundreds of megabytes), I suggest storing the images as separate files in the file system. If your images are essentially read-only and relatively static, and if you measure the size in kilobytes, you can consider storing your images in the database.

Generating Images Dynamically

Some Web sites offer a nice feature: you ask for something, and they return your request graphically. A lot of financial Web sites do this to satisfy their users. Isn't it true that an image is worth dozens of words? Web-deployed charts are often dynamically generated on the server and served to the browser as a stream of bytes traveling over the classic response output stream.

So far, we've returned images read from a file or database. In the end, the key thing with dynamically generated images is not so much the ability to return pictures from the Web server—that is nothing new and can be accomplished with almost all languages and over almost all platforms. The real issue is how easily you can create and manipulate server-side images. For these tasks, Web applications normally rely on ad hoc libraries or the graphic engine of other applications (for example, Microsoft Office applications).

ASP.NET applications are different and, to some extent, luckier. ASP.NET applications, in fact, can rely on a powerful and integrated graphic engine capable of providing an object model for image generation. This back-end system is GDI+.

A Quick Tour of GDI+ Classes

GDI+ is the graphic engine of Microsoft Windows XP, which is also made available for other 32-bit and 64-bit platforms such as Windows 2000 and Windows 2003. As its name suggests, GDI+ is the successor of GDI, the Graphics Device Interface included with earlier versions of the Windows operating system. The .NET Framework encapsulates the key GDI+ functionalities in a handful of managed classes and makes those functions available to Web, Windows Forms, and Web service applications.

Most of the GDI+ services belong to the following categories: 2D vector graphics and imaging. 2D vector graphics involve drawing simple figures such as lines, curves, and polygons. Under the umbrella of imaging are functions to display, manipulate, save, and convert bitmap and vector images. Finally, a third category of functions can be identified—typography, which includes the display of text in a variety of fonts, sizes, and styles.

Having the goal of creating images dynamically, we are most interested in drawing figures and text and in saving the work as JPEGs or GIFs.

The *Graphics* Class

The central element in the Win32 GDI programming model is the *device context*. The device context is a data structure that stores information about the capabilities of a particular display device. A device context is associated with a drawing surface such as a window, printer, or block of memory. Win32 programs obtain a handle to a device context and pass that handle to all GDI functions they call. A device context also maintains a list of the graphics attributes that are set—background and foreground color, pen, brush, and font. The device context is the connecting link between the high-level front-end API and the underlying device drivers.

GDI+ replaces the concept of a device context and its child handle–based programming style with a truly object-oriented approach. In GDI+, the role of the central console for drawing is played by the *Graphics* object. A big step forward is that graphics surfaces (such as the window and the printer) and graphics objects (such as the pen or the brush) are independent entities. GDI+ drawing methods take graphics objects only as an argument, whereas in Win32, you have to select those objects in the device context.

The first step for a GDI+ application is creating, or obtaining, a new graphics context. The *Graphics* class has no constructor. A new *Graphics* object can be obtained in various ways, however. Of all of the other mechanisms for creating a new *Graphics* object, the method *Graphics.FromImage* is the only creator method that makes sense in the context of ASP.NET applications. It creates a *Graphics* object based on an instance of a .NET graphic object that you provide. Any operation performed on the *Graphics* is recorded in the associated image.

> **Important**   No matter how you obtained it, when a *Graphics* object is no longer needed, it must be explicitly disposed of through a call to the *Dispose* method. The garbage collector, in fact, doesn't work with managed GDI+ objects because they are mere wrappers around unmanaged GDI+ objects.

The *Bitmap* Class

The *Bitmap* class encapsulates a GDI+ bitmap, which consists of the pixel data for a graphics image plus some attributes. A bitmap object is an object used to work with images defined by pixel data. In GDI+, there are three types of images—bitmaps, icons, and metafiles. All three classes derive from a common abstract class named *Image*. Note that an instance of the *Bitmap* class doesn't necessarily represent a *.bmp* file. It is, instead, a generic container of pixel data that could be saved as a *.bmp* or *.jpg* image, as required.

When you create a *Graphics* object, you associate it with a particular canvas. As mentioned, for a Web application, an in-memory bitmap is the only viable option. The following code shows how to instantiate a *Bitmap* object of the desired size and creates a drawing context from it:

```
Bitmap bmp = new Bitmap(100, 100);
Graphics g = Graphics.FromImage(bmp);
```

From now on, any graphics primitives called to operate on the *Graphics* object will affect the underlying *Bitmap* object. Once you're done with the graphics work, a *Bitmap* object can be saved to a number of formats, including PNG, JPEG, BMP, and GIF. Note also that the *Bitmap* class supplies methods to rotate and flip the image and that you can also instantiate a bitmap from an existing file.

Filling Rectangles

To fill a rectangle, you need only a brush and the dimensions of the rectangle to paint. The method to use is *FillRectangle*, and the area to work on can be indicated using coordinates or a *RectangleF* structure.

```
g.FillRectangle(brush, area);
```

The brush is the object you use to paint the rectangle. GDI+ supports different types of brushes, including solid, gradient, and textured brushes. A solid brush fills the region with a uniform color; a gradient brush uses a dithered combination of two or more colors. Finally, a textured brush tiles the rectangle with the specified image. The following code snippet shows how to draw and fill a rectangle:

```
// Draw the border
Pen p = new Pen(Color.Black);
g.DrawRectangle(p, 0, 0, width, height);

// Fill the interior
Brush brInterior = new SolidBrush(Color.SkyBlue);
g.FillRectangle(brInterior, 1, 1, width-2, height-2);
```

GDI+ also provides a tailor-made method to draw the border of a rectangle. Instead of a brush, the *DrawRectangle* method takes a pen object.

A gradient is a special brush you use to fill a shape with a gradually changing color. GDI+ supports two breeds of gradients: linear and path gradients. A linear gradient is fully identified with two colors and two points. The actual filling varies from the starting color to the final color as you move from the initial point to the final point. The *LinearGradientBrush* class implements the functionality of a linear gradient. The following code snippet shows how to create and fill a rectangle with a linear and horizontal gradient:

```
// Fill the interior using a gradient
Rectangle area = new Rectangle(0, 0, width, height);
LinearGradientBrush brInterior;
```

```
brInterior = new LinearGradientBrush(area, Color.SkyBlue,
    Color.AntiqueWhite, LinearGradientMode.Horizontal);
g.FillRectangle(brInterior, area);
brInterior.Dispose();
```

In a linear gradient, the color changes linearly, but you can adjust how the color intensity varies from one edge of the gradient to the next. To do that, you use the *Blend* property to set arrays of color intensities and corresponding positions in a 0 through 1 range.

```
// Set intensities and relative positions
float[] relativeIntensities = {0.0f, 0.6f, 1.0f};
float[] relativePositions   = {0.0f, 0.1f, 1.0f};

// Create a Blend object and assign it to the brush
Blend blend = new Blend();
blend.Factors = relativeIntensities;
blend.Positions = relativePositions;
brInterior.Blend = blend;
```

The gradient will have three key intensity points, two of which are clearly the starting and the ending points of filling. The default blending for a linear gradient is expressed by the following code:

```
float[] relativeIntensities = {0.0f, 1.0f};
float[] relativePositions   = {0.0f, 1.0f};
```

The code just shown indicates that the minimum and maximum intensities are reached at the beginning and end of the filling. The code we looked at prior to this states that 60 percent (the value 0.6 in a 0 through 1 range) of the color transition must be accomplished within the first 10 percent of the area to cover (the value 0.1 in a 0 through 1 range).

The third type of brush is the textured brush. A textured brush lets you fill a shape with a pattern stored in a bitmap. You can use a textured brush to draw lines, draw figures, and even write text.

```
// Fill the interior using a "texture" (image)
Image img = Image.FromFile("pattern.bmp");
TextureBrush brInterior = new TextureBrush(img);
g.FillRectangle(brInterior, area);
brInterior.Dispose();
```

Drawing Text

The *DrawString* method on the *Graphics* object accepts the string to write, the font object, and the brush to color the text. Another block of arguments you can pass on to *DrawString* allows specifying the rectangle within which the text should fit. You can decide the vertical and horizontal alignment and whether the text can exceed the assigned area or whether it must be trimmed if too long. The *StringFormat* structure lets you set all these parameters in a single shot.

```
StringFormat sf = new StringFormat();
sf.Alignment = StringAlignment.Center;
sf.LineAlignment = StringAlignment.Center;

// Draw the text
Font f = new Font("Tahoma", 16);
g.DrawString("Hello, world", f, new SolidBrush(Color.White),
    new Rectangle(0, 0, width, height), sf);
```

GDI+ is much more than just these simple operations. Covering all the capabilities of GDI+ is beyond the goal of this book.

Writing Images to Memory

In ASP.NET, writing images—that is, creating disk files—might require some security adjustments. Normally, the ASP.NET worker process runs under the aegis of the user ASPNET or NETWORK SERVICE account. In case of anonymous access with impersonation disabled—which are the default settings in ASP.NET—the worker process lends its own identity and security token to the thread that executes the user request of creating the file. With regard to the default scenario, an access-denied exception might be thrown if ASPNET or NETWORK SERVICE lack writing permissions on virtual directories.

So to implement a file-based cache of images, you can create a new folder and give the ASP.NET account full control over that folder. In this way, files can be created seamlessly. However, ASP.NET and GDI+ provide an interesting alternative to writing files on disk—in-memory generation of images. In other words, the dynamically generated image can be saved directly to the output stream in the needed image format or in a memory stream.

Supported Image Formats

GDI+ supports quite a few image formats, including JPEG, GIF, BMP, and PNG. The whole collection of image formats is in the *ImageFormat* structure. You can save a memory-resident *Bitmap* object to any of the supported formats by using one of the overloads of the *Save* method.

```
bmp.Save(outputStream, ImageFormat.Gif);
```

When you attempt to save an image to a stream or disk file, the system attempts to locate an encoder for the requested format. The encoder is a GDI+ module that converts from the native format to the specified format. Note that the encoder is a piece of unmanaged code that lives in the underlying Win32 platform. For each save format, the *Save* method looks up the right encoder and proceeds.

Getting the encoder for a particular image type is important because it can allow you to change settings for that type. For example, if you want to control the compression ratio of a dynamically created JPEG image, you must obtain the GDI+ encoder for the JPEGs. We'll return to the subject of encoders later.

Writing Copyright Notes on Images

The next example wraps up all the points we touched on. This example shows how to load an existing image, add some copyright notes, and serve the modified version to the user. In doing so, we'll load an image into a *Bitmap* object, obtain a *Graphics* for that bitmap, and use graphics primitives to write. When finished, we'll save the result to the page's output stream and indicate a particular MIME type.

The sample page that triggers the example is easily created, as shown in the following listing:

```
<html>
<body>
    <img id="picture" src="dynimage.ashx?url=images/pic1.jpg" />
</body>
</html>
```

The page contains no ASP.NET code and displays an image through an HTML *<img>* tag. The source of the image, though, is an HTTP handler that manipulates the image passed through the query string. Here's the source code for the *ProcessRequest* method of the HTTP handler. (We create the handler as an *.ashx* resource in this case.)

```
public void ProcessRequest (HttpContext context)
{
    object o = context.Request["url"];
    if (o == null)
    {
        context.Response.Write("No image found.");
        context.Response.End();
        return;
    }

    string file = context.Server.MapPath((string)o);
    string msg = "Courtesy of 'Programming Microsoft ASP.NET 2.0
                Applications--Advanced Topics'";

    if (File.Exists(file))
    {
        Bitmap bmp = AddCopyright(file, msg);
        context.Response.ContentType = "image/jpeg";
        bmp.Save(context.Response.OutputStream, ImageFormat.Jpeg);
        bmp.Dispose();
    }
    else
    {
        context.Response.Write("No image found.");
        context.Response.End();
    }
}
```

Note that the server-side page performs two different tasks indeed. First, it writes copyright text on the image canvas; next, it converts whatever the original format was to JPEG.

```
Bitmap AddCopyright(string file, string msg)
{
    // Load the file and create the graphics
    Bitmap bmp = new Bitmap(file);
    Graphics g = Graphics.FromImage(bmp);

    // Define text alignment
    StringFormat strFmt = new StringFormat();
    strFmt.Alignment = StringAlignment.Center;

    // Create brushes for the bottom writing
    // (green text on black background)
    SolidBrush btmForeColor = new SolidBrush(Color.PaleGreen);
    SolidBrush btmBackColor = new SolidBrush(Color.Black);

    // To calculate writing coordinates, obtain the size of the text
    // given font typeface and size
    Font btmFont = new Font("Verdana", 7);
    SizeF textSize = new SizeF();
    textSize = g.MeasureString(msg, btmFont);

    // Calculate the output rectangle and fill
    float x = ((float) bmp.Width-textSize.Width-3);
    float y = ((float) bmp.Height-textSize.Height-3);
    float w = ((float) x + textSize.Width);
    float h = ((float) y + textSize.Height);
    RectangleF textArea = new RectangleF(x, y, w, h);
    g.FillRectangle(btmBackColor, textArea);

    // Draw the text and free resources
    g.DrawString(msg, btmFont, btmForeColor, textArea);
    btmForeColor.Dispose();
    btmBackColor.Dispose();
    btmFont.Dispose();
    g.Dispose();

    return bmp;
}
```

Figure 9-6 shows the final results.

Note that the additional text is part of the image the user receives. If the user saves the picture by using the Save Picture As menu from the browser, the text (in this case, the copyright note) will be saved with the image.

Figure 9-6   A server-resident image has been modified before being displayed.

Generating Thumbnails

GDI+ also provides other handy facilities, such as the ability to generate thumbnails. Although browsers have no particular problem stretching and shrinking images to make them fit into the assigned space, if a small image is needed there's no reason to return a big one. In doing so, you pay a double price: first, you consume more bandwidth, and, second, you require the browser to do extra work to shape up the image.

A Web site that makes its bread and butter from images will probably conserve predefined thumbnails for each displayable image. In other circumstances, a thumbnail can be generated on the fly using the *GetThumbnailImage* method on the *Bitmap* class.

```
Bitmap GetThumbnail(string file)
{
    Bitmap bmp = new Bitmap(file);
    Bitmap newImg = (Bitmap) bmp.GetThumbnailImage(
        bmp.Width/3, bmp.Height/3, null, IntPtr.Zero);
    return newImg;
}
```

You decide the scale factor to use, and you can also indicate fixed measures. Pay attention, though, that your width and height values are taken as absolute values, meaning that no aspect ratio is guaranteed if your parameters don't ensure that.

Figure 9-7 shows the final results.

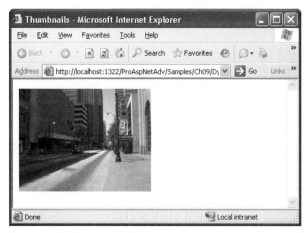

Figure 9-7   The image is properly shrunk before being displayed.

Controlling the Compression Ratio of JPEG Images

JPEG images are the result of a compression algorithm that breaks the original image into 8 × 8 pixel blocks and then adjusts ("smoothes") the colors of those 8 × 8 pixel blocks to minimize the number of colors to be compressed. In this process, some of the actual color values are irretrievably lost. The pixel blocks are then compressed in a manner very similar to "zip" compression. A decompressed image, therefore, is different from the original because of this color adjustment prior to compression. However, because the JPEG format is mostly used to store photographic images, the effective loss often passes unnoticed to the human eye. JPEGs store 24 bits per pixel and are capable of displaying 16 million colors, but they don't support transparency or animation. The level of compression in JPEG images is configurable. You should note that higher compression levels result in smaller files, but only because more data is discarded as the color smoothing process becomes more aggressive and, therefore, more information is lost. Subsequently, the quality of the decompressed image might be bad. It's hard to indicate a compression ratio that fits every scenario. In general, a 15-to-1 ratio is acceptable and generates an imperceptible loss of data. This doesn't mean you can't compress at 30 to 1 with good results, depending upon the original image.

Choosing the compression ratio for a JPEG image using GDI+ is a bit tricky because you need to deal with the JPEG encoder, which is not easily found. To find the encoder for a particular image format, you must loop through the collection of supported encoders and find one whose *MimeType* property matches that of the type you're interested in.

```
// Search for the JPEG encoder
string mimeType = "image/jpeg";
ImageCodecInfo[] encoders;
ImageCodecInfo jpegEncoder = null;

// Loop through all GDI+ encoders
encoders = ImageCodecInfo.GetImageEncoders();
```

```
for(int j=0; j < encoders.Length; j++) {
    if(encoders[j].MimeType == mimeType)
        jpegEncoder = encoders[j];
}
```

Once the encoder has been found, you set some of its parameters. In particular, you create an encoder parameter that affects the quality of the final image.

```
// Create an encoding parameter for the expected quality
EncoderParameter paramRatio;
paramRatio = new EncoderParameter(Encoder.Quality, ratio);
```

The ratio value you pass to the constructor indicates the quality you want for the image. It is not a mere compression ratio. The higher the value, the better the quality and the larger the size of the image.

```
// Add the just created encoding param to the collection of
// parameters for the encoder
EncoderParameters jpegParams;
jpegParams = new EncoderParameters(1); // only one param
jpegParams.Param[0] = paramRatio;

// Send the image
Response.ContentType = "image/jpeg";
bmp.Save(Response.OutputStream, jpegEncoder, jpegParams);
bmp.Dispose();
```

Caching Images

To serve images dynamically, you need to use an HTTP handler. How this handler retrieves the bits of the image to serve depends on its internal implementation. There are typically three approaches—the bits of the image are stored in a database, stored in the ASP.NET cache, or generated dynamically through GDI+.

Opting for the ASP.NET cache also means that the image must first be retrieved from a file or database or, alternately, created on the fly. An image stored in the *Cache* doesn't take space on disk and, more importantly, doesn't require reading bytes off the disk. On the down side, it takes up memory in the ASP.NET worker process.

Building Chart Generator Pages

Let's put the various pieces of the puzzle together and build a sample page that exploits the aforementioned techniques to generate and display dynamic graphics charts. To start, build a page that contains a couple of child *<img>* tags, and make each tag point to an ASP.NET handler that returns a chart image.

```
<table>
    <tr><td><img runat="server" id="bar"></td></tr>
    <tr><td><img runat="server" id="pie"></td></tr>
</table>
```

The *<img>* tags are configured during the page loading to point to a particular URL. Dynamic binding is needed to pass required arguments to the page. The following code snippet shows how the image controls are actually initialized:

```
void Page_Load(object sender, EventArgs e)
{
    bar.Src = "chart.ashx?Type=bar&Data=Sales";
    pie.Src = "chart.ashx?Type=pie&Data=Sales";
}
```

The chart generator handler includes all the logic necessary to create the chart. Data is fetched using an external and pluggable provider. The type name of the provider to use is written in the *web.config* file under the *<appSettings>* section.

Fetching Chart Data

The *chart.ashx* HTTP handler supports two query string parameters—*Type* to indicate whether a pie or bar chart is required and *Data* to specify the entry under the *<appSettings>* section where the type of chart data provider object is stored.

The chart handler implements a relatively simple provider model (which is discussed in Chapter 4) where the data is fetched by code in a provider component. The base provider class defines the contract that defines the rules for data exchange between the provider and the chart generator. Here's the definition of the base provider class:

```
public abstract class ChartDataProvider
{
    public abstract DataTable GetData();
    public abstract string DataLabelField { get; }
    public abstract string DataField { get; }
}
```

The provider class is expected to return a *DataTable* with at least two fields—data and label. The data column will be used to render the chart's bars or pie wedges, whereas the label column will be used to label chart items. Imagine you have created a custom *SalesChartDataProvider* class to return a *DataTable* with two columns named *Employee* and *Sales*. The *Employee* column contains the last name of the employee; the *Sales* column contains the amount sold by the employee in a given year.

The default chart data provider is registered in the *<appSettings>* section of the configuration file.

```
<appSettings>
    <add key="Sales" value="SalesChartDataProvider,ProAspCompLib" />
</appSettings>
```

The name of the key is referenced by the *Data* parameter of the chart handler.

> **Note**   When you get to designing a custom service based on the provider model, you'll be better off creating custom configuration sections to store any required data. You might want to define a service-specific section with a child section to list all available providers and one attribute on the main node to specify the default provider. Each provider, then, will feature as many custom attributes as needed.

Architecture of a Chart Generator

As mentioned, our sample chart generator is implemented as an HTTP handler named *chart.ashx*. Here's its *ProcessRequest* method:

```
public void ProcessRequest(HttpContext context)
{
    // Process arguments
    string type = "bar";
    string dataProvider = String.Empty;
    object arg1 = context.Request["Type"];
    object arg2 = context.Request["Data"];
    if (arg1 != null)
        type = (string) arg1;
    if (arg2 == null)
        context.Response.End();
    else
        dataProvider = (string) arg2;

    // Retrieve the data provider
    string info = ConfigurationManager.AppSettings[dataProvider];
    string[] typeInfo = info.Split(',');
    string cls = typeInfo[0];
    string asm = typeInfo[1];
    ObjectHandle handle = Activator.CreateInstance(asm, cls);
    ChartDataProvider prov = (ChartDataProvider)handle.Unwrap();

    // Draw the chart
    Bitmap bmp;
    Graphics g;

    if (type == "bar")
    {
        bmp = new Bitmap(700, 200);
        g = Graphics.FromImage(bmp);
        DrawBarChart(g, prov);
    }
    else
    {
        bmp = new Bitmap(300, 300);
        g = Graphics.FromImage(bmp);
        DrawPieChart(g, prov);
    }
```

```
    // Send bits
    context.Response.ContentType = "image/png";
    MemoryStream ms = new MemoryStream();
    bmp.Save(ms, ImageFormat.Png);
    ms.WriteTo(context.Response.OutputStream);
    bmp.Dispose();
    g.Dispose();
}
```

Initially, the method processes query string arguments and determines the type of chart to be created (bar or pie). Given the type, we know which *<appSettings>* entry contains the information we need to create the appropriate chart data provider. The data provider is expressed through a comma-separated string formed by type and assembly name. An instance of the provider is created using *Activator.CreateInstance*.

> **Warning**   When using the *Activator.CreateInstance* overload that accepts type and assembly names, you won't get back a direct instance of the newly created type. Instead, you get an *ObjectHandle* object—that is, an object that wraps marshal-by-value object references. *ObjectHandle* is designed to pass an object between multiple AppDomains without loading the metadata for the wrapped object in each AppDomain. In our example, we're not moving any objects through AppDomains, yet we're using the method overload that specifically addresses that scenario in the context of .NET Remoting applications. You extract the wrapped object by calling the *Unwrap* method.

Next, you create the *Graphics* object to contain the chart and invoke the code that actually creates the graph. When done, you save the image as in the PNG format to the output stream.

Drawing a Pie Chart

Once you have the data to create the chart, drawing a pie chart is a matter of running a couple of loops. To draw a wedge, you need the sweep angle, the color, and the whole area of the pie. The loop begins with a sweep angle of zero and is increased, at any step, by the angle that is proportional to the value to represent.

```
// Get the total of sales from the DataTable ("data")
float total = Convert.ToSingle(data.Compute("Sum(sales)", ""));

// Calculate the sweep angle for the value to represent in the wedge
float sweep = Convert.ToSingle(value) / total * 360;
```

To draw the wedge, you use the *FillPie* method, whereas the *DrawEllipse* method can be used to give it a border. Both methods are exposed by the *Graphics* object.

```
g.FillPie(new SolidBrush(wedgeColor), rectChart, angle, sweep);
g.DrawEllipse(new Pen(Color.DarkGray, 1), rectChart);
```

If you want to make things look finer, add a shadow. Because of the lack of specific support from the graphics system, the shadow can be obtained only by drawing the wedge many times with a different offset. To improve the graphics result, we also use a hatch brush. The following listing shows the source code that draws a pie chart with a 3D shadow:

```
for(int j=ShadowDepth; j>0; j--)
{
    for(int i=0; i<data.Rows.Count; i++)
    {
        // Angle for the value
        float sweep = Convert.ToSingle(data.Rows[i]["Sales"])/total*360;

        // Pick up a color
        wedgeColor = colors[i];

        // Draw the shadow
        Rectangle shadowArea = new Rectangle(area.Location, area.Size);
        shadowArea.Offset(j, j);
        g.FillPie(new HatchBrush(HatchStyle.Percent50, wedgeColor),
            shadowArea, angle, sweep);

        // Draw the wedge
        g.FillPie(new SolidBrush(wedgeColor), area, angle, sweep);
        g.DrawEllipse(new Pen(Color.DarkGray, 1), area);

        // Calculate the center of the wedge to use later to draw labels
        Point center = GetPoint(angle + sweep/2, area.Width, area.Height);
        center.X = (int) ((area.Right - area.Left) / 2 + center.X) / 2;
        center.Y = (int) ((area.Bottom - area.Top) / 2 + center.Y) / 2;
        centers[i] = center;

        // Increase the sweep angle for the next iteration
        angle += sweep;
    }
}
```

For pie charts, choosing the wedge color and drawing a descriptive label are two nontrivial problems. Choosing the color, in particular, is a relatively simple instance of a complex problem—the map coloring problem. It's been proven that you never need more than four colors to fill a map so that adjacent regions have different colors. In this case, two colors might be enough, but not if the total number of wedges is odd. Three colors would suffice, but that amount doesn't ensure a good graphical result. A better approach is defining a relatively large subset of colors, say 10 colors, and iterating through them, paying attention to pick up a color that has not been used for the previous wedge or the first wedge. In case of conflict, you resort to an extra color not included in the list or just pick up a nonconflicting color from the same list.

To draw the label within the wedge, you need to know the point at the center of the area. This requires just a little bit of trigonometry. Assuming that the pie is a circle, you obtain the coordinates of the point using the following formulas:

```
// width is the width of the smallest rectangle that contains the pie
int radius = width / 2;

// Get the radiant. The variable angle is angle of wedge
double rad = Math.PI * 2 * angle / 360;
```

```
// Get the coordinates of the point, including an offset
Point pt = new Point();
pt.X = (int) (radius * Math.Cos(rad)) + radius;
pt.Y = (int) (radius * Math.Sin(rad)) + radius;
```

The point you obtain in this way is located on the arc that represents the pie wedge. To move it to the center of the wedge, do the following:

```
pt.X = (int) ((rcChart.Right - rcChart.Left) / 2 + pt.X) / 2;
pt.Y = (int) ((rcChart.Bottom - rcChart.Top) / 2 + pt.Y) / 2;
centers[i] = pt;
```

The center is calculated during the generation of the pie, but no label is drawn at this time. The points are stored in an array and used to render text later. Because labels could likely exceed the space of the wedge, drawing them within the loop would truncate the text. For this reason, we draw the labels only when the pie has been created.

```
for(int i=0; i<dt.Rows.Count; i++)
{
    g.DrawString(data.Rows[i]["Employee"].ToString(),
        new Font("Tahoma", 8),
        new SolidBrush(Color.Black),
        centers[i].X, centers[i].Y);
}
```

Figure 9-8 shows the final results.

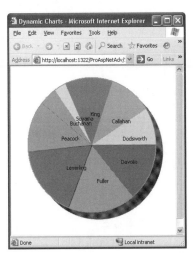

Figure 9-8 A dynamically generated 3D pie chart with inside labels.

Drawing a Bar Chart

Drawing a bar chart is slightly simpler than drawing a pie chart because you don't have to deal with sweep angles, radius, and other trigonometric tidbits. A bar chart is made of two labels and a rectangle to fill. The top label represents the value; the bottom label shows the legend for the chart.

Assuming that all the *x,y* coordinates for the various elements have been set up, the following code demonstrates how to create a 3D-like bar chart with a shadow effect. (Find the sample code for this book at *http://www.microsoft.com/mspress/companion/0-7356-2177-2/.*)

```
)
// Draw the top label with the value
g.DrawString(String.Format("{0:c}", data.Rows[i]["Sales"]),
    new Font("Tahoma", 8), new SolidBrush(Color.Blue),
    xBarPos, yCaptionPos);

// Calculate the bar
Rectangle rcBar = new Rectangle(xBarPos, yBarPos, barWidth, barHeight);

// Draw the shadow
Rectangle rcShadow = new Rectangle(rectBar.Location, rectBar.Size);
rectShadow.Offset(j, -j);
g.FillRectangle(new HatchBrush(HatchStyle.Percent50, Color.Orange),
    rectShadow);

// Draw the bar
g.FillRectangle(new LinearGradientBrush(rectBar, Color.Orange, Color.Yellow,
    LinearGradientMode.Horizontal), rectBar);

// Draw the bottom bar
Font fnt = new Font("Tahoma", 8, FontStyle.Bold);
g.DrawString(dt.Rows[i]["Employee"].ToString(), fnt,
    new SolidBrush(Color.Blue), xBarPos, yBarBottom);
```

The final result is shown in Figure 9-9.

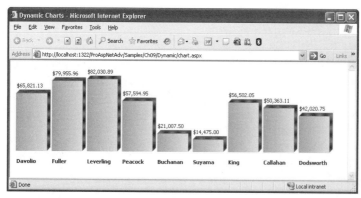

Figure 9-9   A dynamically generated 3D bar chart with top and bottom labels.

> **Note**   In this chapter, we used HTTP handlers to demonstrate the capabilities of ASP.NET to generate images and charts dynamically. Note, though, that HTTP handlers are not the right tool to produce advanced charts. HTTP handlers are great for displaying images selected under run-time conditions, but for dynamic charts, you are better off using server controls built around the *<img>* element. This is also the approach taken by a quite a few commercial charting libraries.

Conclusion

These days, it's unquestionably true that images are fundamental elements of the Web. They aren't part of the infrastructure and don't contribute to the functionality of sites, yet they are a critical element that has contributed to the emergence of the Web as an extremely powerful and expressive medium. In spite of the key role images play, the HTML language doesn't provide support that goes beyond the <img> tag. The <img> tag can be bound only to a URL and requires an extra roundtrip for the download.

If you bind the <img> tag to an .aspx page or, better yet, to an HTTP handler, you can gain some level of flexibility and use any needed logic to generate the image dynamically or to read it out of a database. To generate an image dynamically, you simply set the content type of the HTTP response and flush the bits of the image to the output stream. In ASP.NET, the process of generating images is extremely simplified and empowered with the addition of GDI+.

GDI+ is the graphics library of Windows XP and has been made available for other 32-bit and 64-bit Windows platforms. In the .NET Framework, GDI+ is offered as a set of managed wrapper classes that define drawing surfaces and tools for you to create images algorithmically.

In this chapter, we demonstrated various techniques to edit and create images and serve them to a Web browser. In particular, we discussed how to add copyright notes on existing images, how to extract images out of the BLOB fields of a database, and how to create images dynamically. The typical example of a dynamically generated image is the chart. We created a couple of charts—3D pie charts and bar charts—using a component that reads data out of custom data providers, in full accordance with the provider model infrastructure pushed by ASP.NET 2.0.

Just the Facts

- Web pages can display images only through the <img> tag, and the <img> tag requires a URL to locate and download the image.

- To manipulate the image before displaying it, or to read it from sources other than the file system, you need to bind the <img> tag to a resource that is not a picture file. You typically use an .aspx page or an HTTP handler.

- When it comes to defining resources for serving images dynamically, HTTP handlers should be preferred to ASP.NET pages because an HTTP handler normally goes through a much longer number of processing steps.

- Requests for images are served by setting the content-type of the response to the proper MIME type and writing the bits of the image to the output stream.

- Images can be read off the disk and programmatically modified before being displayed.

- Images can be read off BLOB fields of databases.

- Images can be manipulated or even generated dynamically using GDI+ primitives.

Chapter 10
Site Navigation

Real-world Web sites have a complex structure made of hundreds of pages, grouped and filtered according to business and membership rules. Having a detailed map of the site helps in two ways. First, you can show users where the current page is logically located in the site, thus simplifying search operations. Second, you can bind the overall user interface of the home page to the structure of the site, thus reflecting any structural changes in a rather effortless way.

In ASP.NET 2.0, the new site navigation API allows you to define the map of the site and provide a declarative description of how it is laid out. By using the site navigation API, you define the hierarchy of pages and group them to form sections and subsections of the site. ASP.NET caches this information and makes it programmatically accessible at run time. With site navigation, you store links to pages in a central location and can optionally bind those links to navigation controls such as the *TreeView* and *Menu* controls.

ASP.NET site navigation offers a number of features, including site maps to describe the logical structure of the site, site-map providers to physically store the contents of a map and optional security access rules, and a bunch of controls to display site map information through navigation components. In this chapter, we discuss how to define, configure, and consume site map information.

Defining Site Map Information

To use ASP.NET site navigation, you must first describe the structure of the site in terms of constituent pages and relationships between them. Exposed in a standard way, this information then will be easily consumed by site navigation controls and reflected by page output.

By default, the site map is expressed through an XML file that defines the site hierarchy. However, you can also configure the site navigation system to use alternative data sources.

Creating the Map of a Site

A site map file serves one key purpose—making it easy and automatic to construct a navigation system in Web sites larger than just several pages. Building a navigation system for large sites without a centralized map of pages and their links would soon become a painful task because it would require continual changes and updates to keep hyperlinks in sync with page URLs.

The internal layout of a site map is application specific and subject to the implementation of a special component—the site map provider. This component is registered with the ASP.NET runtime and is responsible for providing site map information by reading the contents from a given durable medium. As mentioned, the default site map provider reads site map information from an XML file with a well-known and fixed name—*web.sitemap*.

The Default Site Map Provider

The default site map provider is registered in the root configuration files and is an instance of the *XmlSiteMapProvider* class.

```
<siteMap>
    <providers>
        <add name="AspNetXmlSiteMapProvider"
             siteMapFile="web.sitemap"
             type="System.Web.XmlSiteMapProvider, System.Web, ... " />
    </providers>
</siteMap>
```

As the preceding code snippet shows, the site map provider contains a *siteMapFile* attribute that indicates the name of the source file where site map information can be read from. In spite of the extension, the file must be an XML file validated against a given schema. Note that the *XmlSiteMapProvider* class doesn't handle files with an extension other than *.sitemap*. Finally, note that the *XmlSiteMapProvider* class detects changes to the site map file and dynamically updates the site map to reflect changes.

The *web.sitemap* File

Located in the application's root directory, the *web.sitemap* file organizes the pages in the site hierarchically. It can reference other site map providers or other site map files in other directories in the same application. Here's a sample site map file that attempts to describe a Web site to navigate through the contents of the book:

```
<siteMap>
    <siteMapNode title="My Book" url="default.aspx">
        <siteMapNode title="Introduction" url="intro.aspx" />
        <siteMapNode title="Acknowledgements" url="ack.aspx">
            <siteMapNode title="References" url="ref.aspx" />
        </siteMapNode>
```

```
      <siteMapNode title="Chapters" url="toc.aspx">
         <siteMapNode title="The Compilation Model" url="ch01.aspx" />
         <siteMapNode title="HTTP Handlers and Modules" url="ch02.aspx" />
         ⋮
      </siteMapNode>
      <siteMapNode title="Appendix" url="appendix.aspx">
      <siteMapNode title="Sample Code" url="samples.aspx">
         ⋮
      </siteMapNode>
   </siteMapNode>
</siteMap>
```

A site map XML file is composed of a collection of *<siteMapNode>* elements rooted in a
<siteMap> node. Each page in the Web site is represented with a *<siteMapNode>* element. Hier-
archies can be created by nesting *<siteMapNode>* elements, as in the preceding code snippets.
In most cases, the root *<siteMap>* node contains just one child *<siteMapNode>* element, even
though this is not a strict rule hard-coded in the schema of the XML file. All URLs linked from
the site map file should belong to the same application using the file. Also in this case, though,
exceptions are acceptable. In other words, you are allowed to specify links to pages in other
applications, but the site navigation API won't check these links. As long as links belong to the
same application, the API can verify them and return design-time errors in case of broken
links.

Table 10-1 lists the feasible attributes of the *<siteMapNode>* element.

Table 10-1   Attributes of the *<siteMapNode>* Element

Attribute	Description
description	Defines the text used to describe the page. This text is used to add a ToolTip to the page link in a *SiteMapPath* control (discussed later) and as documentation.
provider	String that indicates the site map provider to use to fill the current node.
resourceKey	Indicates the name of the resource key used to localize a given node of the site map.
roles	String that indicates the roles that users must have to view this page.
siteMapFile	Indicates the name of the site map file to use to fill the current node.
title	Defines the text used as the text of the link to the page.
url	Defines the URL of the page.

The *roles* attribute is key to implementing a feature known as *security trimming*. Security trimming essentially refers to the site map API capability of preventing unauthorized users from
viewing pages that require a particular role.

In addition to using the attributes listed in Table 10-1, you can use custom attributes too. You
cannot use custom nodes. A *.sitemap* file can contain only *<siteMapNode>* elements and a
<siteMap> root node.

Site Navigation Providers

The site navigation subsystem is provider based, meaning that you can use custom providers to define some site map contents. A custom site map provider reads information from a different storage medium, be it another XML file with a distinct schema, a text file or, perhaps, a database. As we've seen in Chapter 4, a custom site map provider is a class that inherits from *SiteMapProvider* or, better yet, from *StaticSiteMapProvider*.

It is interesting to notice that you can optionally use multiple providers at the same time. For example, by setting the *provider* attribute on a *<siteMapNode>* node, you instruct the site map subsystem to use that site map provider to retrieve nodes to insert at that point of the hierarchy.

```
<siteMap>
    <siteMapNode title="Intro" url="intro.aspx" >
        <siteMapNode title="Acknowledgements" url="ack.aspx" />
        <siteMapNode title="References" url="ref.aspx" />
    </siteMapNode>
    <siteMapNode provider="SimpleTextSiteMapProvider" />
        ⋮
</siteMap>
```

The additional provider must be registered in the configuration file and feature all information needed to connect to its own data source. Here's an example for the sample text file provider:

```
<system.web>
    <siteMap defaultProvider="XmlSiteMapProvider">
        <providers>
            <add name="SimpleTextSiteMapProvider"
                type="SimpleTextSiteMapProvider, Samples"
                siteMapFile="MySiteMap.txt" />
        </providers>
    </siteMap>
</system.web>
```

The *<siteMapNode>* linked to the *SimpleTextSiteMapProvider* component will contain all the nodes defined in the *MySiteMap.txt* file. As a result, you have a site map file that uses two providers at the same time—the default *XmlSiteMapProvider* and the custom *SimpleTextSiteMap-Provider*.

Configuring the Site Map

There are various ways to further configure the site map file to address specific real-world scenarios. For example, you can tie together distinct site map files, localize the title and description of pages, and serve each user a site map that complies with his or her roles in the application's security infrastructure. Let's tackle each of these situations.

Using Multiple Site Map Files

As mentioned, the default site map provider reads its information from the *web.sitemap* file located in the application's root directory. Additional *.sitemap* files written according to the same XML schema can be used to to describe portions of the site.

The idea is that each *<siteMapNode>* element can define its subtree either explicitly by listing all child nodes or implicitly by referencing an external *.sitemap* file, as shown here:

```
<siteMap>
    <siteMapNode title="My Book" url="default.aspx">
        <siteMapNode siteMapFile="introduction.sitemap" />
        <siteMapNode siteMapFile="chapters.sitemap" />
        <siteMapNode siteMapFile="appendix.sitemap" />
    </siteMapNode>
</siteMap>
```

The content of each of the child site map files is injected into the final tree representation of the data at the exact point where the link appears in the root *web.sitemap* file. Child site map files can be located in child directories if you desire. The value assigned to the *siteMapFile* attribute is the virtual path of the file in the context of the current application.

Note that in this case all site map files are processed by the same site map provider component—the default *XmlSiteMapProvider* component. In the previous section, we examined a scenario in which different providers were used to process distinct sections of the site map. The two features are not mutually exclusive and, in the end, you can have a default site map file that spans over multiple *.sitemap* files with portions of it provided by a different provider. In this case, as you've seen, all settings for the custom provider must be set in the *web.config* file.

User-Specific Views of the Site

Most Web sites require that only certain members be allowed to see certain pages. How should you specify that in a site map? The most effective and efficient approach is using roles. Basically, you associate each node in the site map with a list of authorized roles and the ASP.NET infrastructure guarantees that no unauthorized users will ever view that page through the site map. This approach is advantageous because you define roles and map them to users once—for security purposes and membership—and use them also for site maps.

A feature known as *site map security trimming* provides a way to hide navigational links in a site map based on security roles. Enabled on the site map provider and individual nodes, security trimming serves user-specific views of a site. It does only that, though. It hides links from view whenever the content of the site map is displayed through user interface controls. (We'll return to this topic in greater detail later.) However, it doesn't block users from accessing pages by typing the URL in the address bar of the browser or following links from other pages. For ensuring that unauthorized users don't access pages, you need to configure roles and bind them to the identity of the connected user. (For more information, see Chapter 15 of my other recent book *Programming Microsoft ASP.NET 2.0: Core Reference*, published by Microsoft Press.)

Securing ASP.NET Site Maps

By default, nonprogrammatic access to *.sitemap* files is protected and results in a forbidden-resource ASP.NET exception. Be aware of this if you plan to replace the default site map configuration and use files with a custom extension. In this case, make sure you explicitly prohibit access to these files through IIS. To further improve security, grant NETWORK SERVICE or ASPNET—the ASP.NET runtime accounts—read-only access to these custom site map files. If you store site maps in a database, configure any involved tables to make them accessible to the smallest number of accounts with the least possible set of privileges.

> **Note**   An excessively large site map file can use a lot of memory and CPU. Aside from a possible performance hit, this situation constitutes a potential security risk in a hosted environment. By restricting the size of site maps for a Web site, you better protect your site against denial-of-service attacks.

Localizing Site Map Information

There are a few properties that you can localize in a site map. They are *Title*, *Description*, and all custom properties. You can use an explicit or implicit expression to localize the property. First of all, though, you should enable localization by adding a Boolean attribute to the *<siteMap>* node.

```
<siteMap enableLocalization="true">
    ⋮
</siteMap>
```

Localizing site map properties consists of binding properties with resource expressions. (For more information on resource $-expressions, look at Chapter 5.) You can explicitly bind the attribute to a global resource or have it implicitly associated with a value that results from a local resource key. Here's an example of explicit expressions:

```
<siteMap enableLocalization="true">
    <siteMapNode
        url="~/homepage.aspx"
        title="$Resources:MyLocalizations,HomePage" />
    ⋮
</siteMap>
```

An explicit expression is a *$Resources* expression that points to a global *.resx* file and extracts a value by name from there. If the *MyLocalizations.resx* file contains an entry named Home-Page, the value will be read and assigned to the attribute. If it isn't there, an implicit expression takes over.

An implicit expression takes values out of a local resource file. The localizable *<siteMapNode>* is associated with a resource key and all of its localizable properties are defined in the *.resx* file as entries named after the following pattern:

```
[resourceKey].[Attribute]
```

The following site map snippet shows how to use implicit expressions:

```
<siteMap enableLocalization="true">
    <siteMapNode
        resourceKey="Home"
        url="~/homepage.aspx"
        description=" default "
        title=" default " />
    ⋮
</siteMap>
```

In this case, the resource file has the same name of the *.sitemap* file plus the *.resx* extension. In the default case, it will be *web.sitemap.resx*. This file is expected to contain entries named *Home.description* and *Home.title*. If these exist, their values will be used to determine the value of *title* and *description* attributes. In the case of implicit expressions, the values that localizable attributes may have in the *.sitemap* file are considered default values to be used in case of trouble with the localized resource files.

> **Note**   A *.resx* file contains resource values for the default culture. To specify resources for a particular language and culture (say, French), you have to change the extension to *fr.resx* because *fr* is the identifier of the French culture. Similar prefixes exist for most of the languages and cultures.

Localizing the Site Navigation Structure

What if you want to adapt the navigation structure to a given locale? Unfortunately, the *Url* property cannot be localized in a site map in the same way as the *Title* and *Description* properties. If you want to change URLs, or perhaps change the structure of the site, you create a distinct site map for each supported culture and register all of them in the configuration file.

```
<siteMap defaultProvider="XmlSiteMapProvider">
    <providers>
        <add name="DefaultSiteMap"
            type="System.Web.XmlSiteMapProvider"
            siteMapFile="default.sitemap" />
        <add name="FrenchSiteMap"
            type="System.Web.XmlSiteMapProvider"
            siteMapFile="fr.sitemap" />
        ⋮
        <add name="ItalianSiteMap"
            type="System.Web.XmlSiteMapProvider"
            siteMapFile="it.sitemap" />
    </providers>
</siteMap>
```

Essentially, you have multiple providers of the same type—*XmlSiteMapProvider*—but working on distinct site map files. When you access site map information programmatically, you can specify which site map you want to use. (I'll say more about this in a moment.)

> **Important**   You use *.resx* files as previously discussed to localize site maps as long as you're using the default provider and the XML *.sitemap* provider. If you use a custom provider, say a database-driven provider, you're totally responsible for setting up a localization mechanism.

Accessing Site Map Information

Creating the map of a site is only the first step. Once created, in fact, this information must be easily and programmatically accessible. Although most of the time, you consume site information through a bunch of ad hoc controls, it's useful to take a look at the class that acts as the official container of site map information—the *SiteMap* class. When an ASP.NET application runs, the site map structure is exposed through a global instance of the *SiteMap* class.

The *SiteMap* Class

Defined in the *System.Web* assembly and namespace, the *SiteMap* class has only static members. It exposes a collection of node objects that contain properties for each node in the map. The class is instantiated and populated when the application starts up; the data loaded is cached and refreshed care of the provider. In particular, the XML site map provider monitors the site map file for changes and refreshes itself accordingly.

Properties of the *SiteMap* Class

Table 10-2 shows and describes syntax and behavior of the members featured by the *SiteMap* class.

Table 10-2   Members of the *SiteMap* Class

Member	Description
CurrentNode	A property that returns the *SiteMapNode* object that represents the currently requested page.
Enabled	A property that indicates whether a site map provider is enabled.
Provider	A property that returns the *SiteMapProvider* object that indicates the provider being used for the current site map.
Providers	A property that returns a read-only collection of *SiteMapProvider* objects that are available to the application.
RootNode	A property that returns a *SiteMapNode* object that represents the root page of the navigation structure built for the site.
SiteMapResolve	An event that occurs when the *CurrentNode* property is accessed. Whether this event is really raised or not depends on the particular provider being used. It does fire for the default site map provider.

The *SiteMap* class retrieves the *CurrentNode* property by making a request to the provider. A null value is returned if no node exists for the requested page in the site map or if role information for the current user doesn't match the role enabled on the node.

Members of the *SiteMapNode* Class

The *SiteMapNode* class represents a node in the site map structure. The class includes quite a few properties to describe a single page in a Web site plus a bunch of methods to retrieve and manage child nodes. Table 10-3 details the properties of the *SiteMapNode* class.

Table 10-3   Properties of the *SiteMapNode* Class

Property	Description
ChildNodes	Gets or sets all the child nodes of the current node from the associated site map provider
Description	Gets or sets a description for the current node
HasChildNodes	Indicates whether the current node has any children
Item	Gets or sets a custom attribute for the current node
Key	Gets a string representing a lookup key for a site map node
NextSibling	Gets the next node on the same nesting level as the current node, if any
ParentNode	Gets or sets the node that is the parent of the current node
PreviousSibling	Gets the previous node on the same nesting level as the current one, if any
Provider	Gets the provider that is responsible for the current node
ReadOnly	Indicates whether the site map node can be modified
ResourceKey	Gets or sets the resource key that is used to localize the node
Roles	Gets or sets the collection of roles associated with the node
RootNode	Returns the root node of the hierarchy the node belongs to
Title	Gets or sets the title of the current node
Url	Gets or sets the URL of the page that the node represents

Most of these properties find a corresponding attribute in the *<siteMapNode>* element of *.sitemap* files, as listed in Table 10-1.

Methods of the *SiteMapNode* Class

Table 10-4 lists the methods supported by the *SiteMapNode* class.

Table 10-4   Methods of the *SiteMapNode* Class

Method	Description
Clone	Makes a copy of the current node
GetAllNodes	Returns the read-only collection of nodes that are descendants of the current node
GetDataSourceView	Returns the data source view object associated with the current node

Table 10-4   Methods of the *SiteMapNode* Class

Method	Description
GetHierarchicalDataSourceView	Retrieves the hierarchical data source view object associated with the current node
IsAccessibleToUser	Returns a value to indicate whether the node can be viewed by the specified user
IsDescendantOf	Returns a value to indicate whether the current node is a child or a direct descendant of the specified node

As you can see, the *SiteMapNode* class provides quite a rich programming interface around the object that represents a site map node.

Navigating to a Node

Programmatic access to the current node of a site map hierarchy is mostly obtained through the *CurrentNode* property of the *SiteMap* class. The following code snippet, for example, shows how to navigate through the children of a given site map node:

```
if (SiteMap.CurrentNode.HasChildNodes)
{
    foreach(SiteMapNode node in SiteMap.CurrentNode.ChildNodes)
    {
        // Process the node information here
    }
}
```

Each time the *CurrentNode* property is accessed, the *SiteMap* class fires the *SiteMapResolve* event. By handling the event, a page or a control can implement some logic to build a custom representation of the site map without creating a custom site map provider.

Programmatically Modify Site Map Nodes in Memory

The site map is designed to be a relatively static hierarchy of node information even though it doesn't mean that dynamic changes are not allowed. At the same time, a site map structure should not change too often to accommodate dynamically created URLs.

Consider a Web site where pages are added dynamically based on a user action. The canonical example is a Web site that implements a newsgroup or a forum, where each new post originates a new page with a bunch of parameters passed on the query string. How should you represent the tree of this page—that is, the path from the home page of the Web site up to the displayed page? (In a moment, we'll see which controls are available in ASP.NET 2.0 to render the path of a page in a site.)

The page created to contain the thread of a user's post is not found in the static site map file, if any such file exists. Should you regularly modify the site map for each post? Keep in mind that the site map file is hard to modify programmatically because ASP.NET provides no ready-made API for this. If you roll your own site map provider, you'll have to do so at your own expense.

A better approach entails repeatedly using a single page to show posts—say, the *showpost.aspx* page that you might have seen in various ASP.NET-powered forum applications. The idea is to write a *SiteMapResolve* event handler in the page and return a temporary node that incorporates information about the right URL. Here's some code:

```
void Page_Load(object sender, EventArgs e)
{
   SiteMap.SiteMapResolve += new SiteMapResolveEventHandler(ResolveNode);
}

SiteMapNode ResolveNode(object sender, SiteMapResolveEventArgs e)
{
   // Make a copy of the current node, including parent nodes
   SiteMapNode tempNode = SiteMap.CurrentNode.Clone(true);

   // Get the post ID
   int postID = GetPostID();

   // Build a node to represent correctly the path to the requested page
   tempNode.Url += "?ID=" + postID;
   return tempNode;
}

string GetPostID()
{
   return HttpContext.Current.QueryString["ID"].ToString();
}
```

In this way, the URL bound to the *showpost.aspx* page is updated with dynamically specified query string parameters. We'll return to this example in a moment, just after introducing the *SiteMapPath* control.

The *SiteMapPath* Control

Even though the expression "site map path" may sound a bit unfamiliar, the concept behind it is something you know very well—as a Web user, if not as a Web developer. A site map path is the overall combination of text and links that appears in some pages to indicate the path from the home page to the displayed resource, as shown in Figure 10-1.

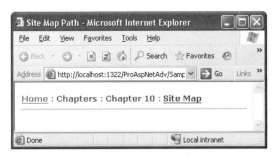

Figure 10-1   A sequence of links that renders a site map path.

To get a similar rendering in earlier versions of ASP.NET, you had to do it manually, typically by tracking all URLs on the way and building a sequence of links. ASP.NET 2.0 includes a made-to-measure navigation path control—the *SiteMapPath* control—that produces the output of Figure 10-1. That type of output is also known as a *breadcrumb* or *eyebrow*. The control provides many options for customizing the appearance of the links.

Members of the *SiteMapPath* Control

SiteMapPath is a composite control that reflects node data supplied by the *SiteMap* object. The control takes limited space in the page and makes parent pages of the current page only one click away. Table 10-5 shows the properties supported by the *SiteMapPath* control.

Table 10-5   Properties of the *SiteMapPath* Control

Method	Description
CurrentNodeStyle	The style used to render the display text of the current node
CurrentNodeTemplate	The template to use to represent the current node in the site navigation path
NodeStyle	The style used to render the display text for all nodes in the site navigation path
NodeTemplate	The template used to represent all the functional nodes in the site navigation path
ParentLevelsDisplayed	The number of levels of parent nodes displayed, relative to the current node
PathDirection	Gets or sets the order for rendering the nodes in the navigation path
PathSeparator	The string used to delimit nodes in the rendered navigation path
PathSeparatorStyle	The style used for the *PathSeparator* string
PathSeparatorTemplate	The template used to render the delimiter of a site navigation path
Provider	The site map provider object associated with the control
RenderCurrentNodeAsLink	If set, causes the control to render the current node as a hyperlink
RootNodeStyle	The style for the display text of the root node
RootNodeTemplate	The template used for the root node of a site navigation path
ShowToolTips	If set, displays a ToolTip when the mouse hovers over a hyperlinked node
SiteMapProvider	Gets or sets the name of the site map provider object used to render the site navigation control
SkipLinkText	Gets or sets the value used to render alternate text for screen readers to skip the control's content

Each node displayed by a *SiteMapPath* control is wrapped by an instance of a container class named *SiteMapNodeItem*. Whenever such an item is created, the control fires an *ItemCreated* event. The *ItemDataBound* event, on the other hand, occurs once data has been bound to the node item.

Displaying the Location of the Current Page

The *SiteMapPath* control works by taking the URL of the current page and populating an instance of the *SiteMapNode* class with information obtained from the site map. Retrieved information includes the URL, title, description, and location of the page in the navigation hierarchy. The node is then rendered out as a sequence of templates—mostly hyperlinks—styled as appropriate.

No code is required to use a *SiteMapPath* control. All that you have to do is place the following markup in the *.aspx* source file:

```
<asp:SiteMapPath ID="SiteMapPath1" runat="server"
    RenderCurrentNodeAsLink="True" PathSeparator=" : " >
  <PathSeparatorStyle Font-Bold="True" />
  <NodeStyle Font-Bold="True" />
  <RootNodeStyle Font-Bold="True" />
</asp:SiteMapPath>
```

As you can guess, style properties in the preceding markup are not essential to make the control work and can be omitted for brevity. The final output you get matches that of Figure 10-1.

The *SiteMapPath* control interrogates the *SiteMap* object about the current node. A page that registers a *SiteMapResolve* event handler can intercept the action and return a node different from the one that would otherwise be returned from the site map file. This is exactly what we demonstrated earlier in the "Programmatically Modify Site Map Nodes in Memory" section. Let's go one step further and build a custom site map path component.

Designing a Custom Site Map Path Component

The most useful and reasonable way of displaying a site map path is through a sequence of links or, at least, readable elements. The *SiteMapPath* control does just that and, most of the time, it even does it in a codeless manner. Could you ask for more? Honestly, I don't think so. However, for purely educational purposes, let's briefly stop to consider what would be needed to build a custom site map path renderer. Consider the following code:

```
void Page_Load(object sender, EventArgs e)
{
    RenderCustomSiteMapPath(TreeView1);
}

void RenderCustomSiteMapPath(TreeView tv)
{
    for (SiteMapNode node=SiteMap.CurrentNode;
        node != null;
        node=node.ParentNode)
    {
        TreeNode tn = new TreeNode(node.Title, node.Title,
                "", node.Url, "");
        tv.Nodes.AddAt(0, tn);
    }
}
```

Whenever it is time to render the component, you set up a loop from the current URL up the hierarchy until the root node is found. In C#, you can use the *for* operator and an iterator variable of type *SiteMapNode*. The step consists of assigning the *ParentNode* property to the iterator. The ending condition is the nullness of the iterator, which indicates no parent *SiteMapNode* (or in other words, the root URL). Each node found represents a piece of information to write out to the rendered stream. In the preceding sample code, we just add a new node to a sample *TreeView* control. Each new node is added at the top so that the top-down direction of nodes is maintained in the result. Figure 10-2 shows what you get when you render your site map in this way.

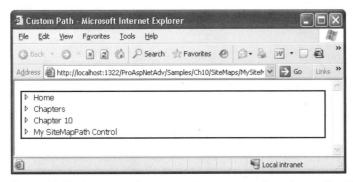

Figure 10-2   A custom site map path component based on a *TreeView* control.

The *SiteMapDataSource* Control

The *SiteMapPath* control has full access to site map information but is limited to displaying the list of URLs that form the logical path from the home page down to the currently displayed page. The main advantage of a *SiteMapPath* control is that it gives users a fast way to click to see parent pages of the current one. Overall, a site map path to a page is just one possible path from the site map root to one leaf. What about the rest of the site information? Enter data source controls.

In ASP.NET 2.0, a data source component is a server control designed to interact with data-bound controls and hide the complexity of the manual data-binding pattern. Data source components have no visual rendering and support data-bound controls in the data display and execution of other common operations such as insertions, deletions, sorting, and updates. Each data source component wraps a particular data provider—relational databases, custom data stores, or perhaps XML documents. Data source controls come in two flavors—tabular and hierarchical—based on their capability of handling flat or nested data. In Chapter 9 of *Programming Microsoft ASP.NET 2.0: Core Reference*, you find in-depth coverage of data source controls with a focus on tabular controls.

In this chapter, we're mainly interested in the capabilities of the *SiteMapDataSource* control—a hierarchical data source control that exposes any information contained in a site map data store. You typically bind an instance of the *SiteMapDataSource* class to hierarchical controls such as *TreeView* and *Menu* to have the interface of these controls automatically populated with the contents of the site map.

Members of the *SiteMapDataSource* Control

As a hierarchical data source control, the *SiteMapDataSource* control inherits from the *HierarchicalDataSourceControl* class and implements the *IDataSource* interface to expose internal views of data. Table 10-6 details the properties defined by the class.

Table 10-6   Properties of the *SiteMapDataSource* Control

Property	Description
Provider	References the site map provider object that is associated with the control. You use this property to get or set the provider of choice.
ShowStartingNode	Indicates whether the map should include the node that represents the current page. It is *True* by default.
SiteMapProvider	Gets or sets the name of the site map provider that the control is currently bound to.
StartFromCurrentNode	Indicates whether the root of the displayed map should be the node that represents the current page. It is *False* by default.
StartingNodeOffset	Indicates a positive or negative offset from the starting node that determines the root of the hierarchy exposed by the data source control. It is set to 0 by default.
StartingNodeUrl	Indicates whether the map should be displayed starting from the node with specified URL.

The site map provider used by the control is the default provider because it results from the configuration file of the application. You can switch to another registered provider by setting *SiteMapProvider*—a *string* property—to the name of the provider of choice. In this way, the control will automatically update the reference stored in the *Provider* property to reflect the change.

Using the *SiteMapDataSource* Control

The *SiteMapDataSource* control is cataloged in the Microsoft Visual Studio 2005 toolbox under the *Data* tab. More often than not, you just drop it to the Web form and go. The default settings, in fact, work most of the time without reconfiguration on your part.

```
<asp:SiteMapDataSource ID="SiteMapDataSource1" runat="server" />
```

To bind the data source to a particular provider, you set the *SiteMapProvider* attribute to the name of the provider. To bind the data source to a hierarchical control, say a *TreeView*, you set the *DataSourceID* property of the *TreeView* to the ID of the data source, as shown in the following code:

```
<asp:TreeView ID="TreeView1" runat="server"
    DataSourceID="SiteMapDataSource1" ImageSet="WindowsHelp">
    :
</asp:TreeView>
```

A nearly identical markup is required to display site map information through a *Menu* control. The view of the site provided by *SiteMapDataSource* is based on a specified starting node. By default, this node is the root node of the map hierarchy—that is, the home page, but it can also be any node within the hierarchy.

Determining the Starting Node

You can narrow the returned set of nodes by combining the values of three properties—*StartFromCurrentNode*, *StartingNodeOffset*, and *StartingNodeUrl*. It is essential to note that the *StartFromCurrentNode* and *StartingNodeUrl* properties are mutually exclusive. You can set the *StartingNodeUrl* property only if the *StartFromCurrentNode* property is *false*; otherwise, you'll get an exception. You can choose to start either by position (the current node only) or by URL. In both cases, you can further control the root of the displayed hierarchy by setting an offset.

The offset can be either a positive or negative integer. It indicates how many levels should be traversed up or down the hierarchy from the current starting node to find the node you really want to see at the root. For example, consider the following markup:

```
<asp:SiteMapDataSource ID="SiteMapDataSource1" runat="server"
    StartFromCurrentNode="true"
    StartingNodeOffset="-1" />
```

In this case, the map will be rooted in the parent of the node that represents the currently requested page. The *ShowStartingNode* property simply determines whether or not the map tree should include the starting node. The starting node is included by default.

> **Tip**   You typically don't want to change the default settings of the *SiteMapDataSource* control if you're using the map to build the navigation system in the sole home page. You might want to use URL or name-based positioning and offsets if you're showing the map in each page.

SiteMap vs. *SiteMapDataSource*

So far, we have examined two possible approaches to site map data access—the *SiteMap* object and the *SiteMapDataSource* control. Although in both cases you put your hands on the site map, each object serves a particular purpose. The *SiteMap* class is designed as the public API to query for map information. The *SiteMapPath* control internally uses the *SiteMap* object to access site map information. The *SiteMapPath* control is a simple but effective way to display to users where the current page fits in the site hierarchy.

The *SiteMapDataSource* control is a highly specific API designed to deliver map information to hierarchical data source controls such as *TreeView* and *Menu*. You can't use a specialized control such as *SiteMapDataSource* to display portions of site map data through a nonhierarchical control such as a drop-down list. If displaying inherently hierarchical information through tabular controls is a must for your application, you should use the *SiteMap* class to navigate the map and manually extract all the information you need.

Displaying Site Map Information

The primary reason for having a site map is to break any dependencies between the dynamically changing structure of the site and the links from the home and other intermediate pages. With a manually built menu with hard-coded links, you introduce a regression each and every time you rename or move a page. This is in addition to the work required if you want only to filter clickable links based on roles.

In ASP.NET 2.0, the site map serves the purpose of letting you store in a centralized place all information that relates to the structure of the site. This file, though, would be useless without a pair of server controls capable of displaying hierarchical data—the *TreeView* and *Menu* controls. Placed in the home page, these two controls—and all custom hierarchical controls you might build yourself—would take the site map as input and automatically fill the user interface. No changes to the code would be required if you rename or move a site page. All that you have to do is update the site map file.

The connection between hierarchical controls (for example, *TreeView* or *Menu*) and site map data is established through the *SiteMapDataSource* control. To get an idea of how tree-view controls work, take a look at Figure 10-3.

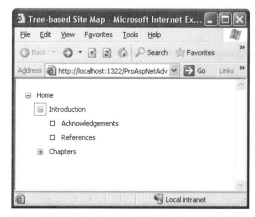

Figure 10-3 A site map shown through a *TreeView* control.

Each node of the *TreeView* control is associated with a node in the bound site map. Thanks to the *SiteMapDataSource* control, the binding is automatic.

> **Important** In ASP.NET 2.0, hierarchical binding done through hierarchical data source controls is read-only.

The *TreeView* Control

The *TreeView* control is a hot new entry in the ASP.NET 2.0 toolbox. Used to display hierarchical data—such as a table of contents or a site map—in a tree structure, the *TreeView* control sports a broad set of features including full support for data binding, client-side node population, themes, node customization and, of course, site navigation.

The output of the *TreeView* control is made up of nodes, and it includes the logic required to expand and collapse these nodes either through a postback or via client script. Each node is represented by a *TreeNode* object and can optionally have a parent and child nodes.

Members of the *TreeView* Control

The *TreeView* control has several properties in addition to those inherited from base classes. I've catalogued control properties in three groups—visual, behavioral, and style properties. Table 10-7 details visual properties through which you control the appearance of the *TreeView*.

Table 10-7   Visual Properties of the *TreeView* Control

Property	Description
CollapseImageToolTip	Indicates the ToolTip for the image that is displayed for a collapsible node indicator.
CollapseImageUrl	Indicates the URL to a custom image used to render a collapsible node indicator.
ExpandImageToolTip	Indicates the ToolTip for the image that is displayed for an expandable node indicator.
ExpandImageUrl	Indicates the URL to a custom image used to render an expandable node indicator.
ImageSet	Indicates the group of images used to render the user interface of the control.
NoExpandImageUrl	Indicates the URL to a custom image used to render a nonexpandable node indicator.
NodeIndent	Indicates how many pixels of indentation are required for child nodes.
NodeWrap	Indicates whether text wraps in a node when there's not enough space to render.
ShowCheckBoxes	Indicates which node types will display a check box in the control. Node types are leaf, parent, and root.
ShowExpandCollapse	Indicates whether expansion node indicators are displayed.
ShowLines	Indicates whether lines connecting child nodes to parent nodes are displayed.

Various configurable elements form a node in a *TreeView* control. First, you will find the small image used to expand or collapse the node. (Distinct images can be used when the node is expanded or collapsed.) Next, there's the node text that you can choose to render as a hyperlink or as static text. Child nodes are usually indented with respect to their parents, and optional connecting lines can be rendered to make the dependency clearer.

Table 10-8 lists another set of properties in the *TreeView* control—the properties that express or control a behavior and the control's object model.

Table 10-8   Behavior Properties of the *TreeView* Control

Property	Description
AutoGenerateDataBindings	Indicates whether the control automatically generates tree node bindings.
CheckedNodes	Returns a collection of *TreeNode* objects that represent the nodes in the control that display a selected check box.
DataBindings	Returns a collection of *TreeNodeBinding* objects that define the relationship between a data-bound item and a control's node.
EnableClientScript	Indicates whether the control renders client-side script to handle expanding and collapsing events. It is *True* by default.
ExpandDepth	Indicates the number of levels that are expanded when a *TreeView* control is displayed for the first time.
MaxDataBindDepth	Indicates the maximum number of tree levels to bind.
Nodes	Returns a collection of *TreeNode* objects that represents the nodes in the control.
PathSeparator	Indicates the character to be used to separate elements in the path of each node. Set to the slash (/) by default.
PopulateNodesFromClient	Indicates whether node data is populated on demand from the client. It is *True* by default.
SelectedNode	Returns a *TreeNode* object that represents the selected node in the control.
SelectedValue	Returns the value of the selected node.

The *TreeView* control is commonly used to display a large quantity of data. How and when do you bind this data to the control? Should you opt for a one-time binding upon loading? Or are you better off opting for an on-demand approach? Should you post back to the server, or are script callback options available?

The *TreeView* is a data-bound control that can be attached to data through either the *DataSourceID* or *DataSource* property. In both cases, though, the bound data source must preferably be a hierarchical source such as an XML document or a site map. (You can't bind an *IEnumerable* object to a *TreeView*, anyway.) The *TreeView* can also be bound to its data declaratively or programmatically by filling the *DataBindings* collection through node/data bindings. A node/data binding is expressed by the class *TreeNodeBinding* or the *<asp:TreeNodeBinding>* markup element. Yet another form of data population involves the *Nodes* collection that can be used to add nodes with explicit, non-data-bound values. A node is expressed through an instance of the *TreeNode* class or the *<asp:TreeNode>* markup element.

In the case of binding with a data source, by default the node population occurs on demand using some client-side script and ASP.NET script callbacks. (See Chapter 6.)

Table 10-9 details the style properties supported by the *TreeView* control.

Table 10-9   Styles of the *TreeView* Control

Style	Description
HoverNodeStyle	The style to set the appearance of a node when the mouse hovers over it
LeafNodeStyle	The style to set the appearance of leaf nodes
LevelStyles	Returns a collection of *Style* objects containing style settings applied to nodes based on their level in the tree
NodeStyle	The style to set the default appearance of all nodes
ParentNodeStyle	The style to set the appearance of parent nodes
RootNodeStyle	The style to set the appearance of the root node
SelectedNodeStyle	The style to set the appearance of the selected node

The style of a node is an object of type *TreeNodeStyle*. This class inherits from *Style* and extends it with a bunch of attributes to control node spacing and padding. Styles are applied in a given order of precedence. The first style applied is *NodeStyle* followed by *RootNodeStyle* and *ParentNodeStyle* or *LeafNodeStyle*, depending on the node type. If defined, any *LevelStyles* styles are applied at this time, thus overriding other node style properties. The node style is then completed by applying *SelectedNodeStyle* and *HoverNodeStyle*.

> **Note**   The *TreeView* control also features a couple of methods—*ExpandAll* and *FindNode*. The former renders the *TreeView* with all nodes expanded. The latter searches for the node object that matches the given path and returns a *TreeNode* object. Both methods are designed for use in server-side code.

Tree-Based View of the Site

Binding a *TreeView* control to a site map data source control couldn't be easier. Once you have dropped a *TreeView* and a *SiteMapDataSource* control onto the form, you are pretty much done. If you love a rather spartan user interface, or if you are extensively using themes, you just save and test the page.

The association between a *TreeView* and *SiteMapDataSource* control makes it easy to build pages in which the left edge is reserved for the navigation area and the rest of the screen real estate is for the contents. You can style the *TreeView* at will, but no other changes are required to set up binding when the source is a site map. All that might be needed is provided by the site map. If you happen to write a custom site map format, you build a custom site map provider to normalize any differences and make your data show correctly through a hierarchical control.

An interesting property of *TreeView* controls is *ImageSet*. The property gets or sets the group of images to use for nodes of the *TreeView* control. The property values can come only from the *TreeViewImageSet* enumerated type and basically point to a group of related images embedded as resources in the *system.web* assembly. For example, the tree view in Figure 10-3 uses the *Simple2* image set. Figure 10-4 shows a sample page that demonstrates a few other sets of images. (Note that you can pick up the preferred image set at design time through an AutoFormat wizard.)

Figure 10-4   A TOC-like tree-based view of a site map.

Here's the code that allows you to bind the values of an enumerated type to a drop-down list and change the image set of the tree view on selection change:

```
void Page_Load(object sender, EventArgs e)
{
    if (!IsPostBack)
    {
        Type t = typeof(TreeViewImageSet);
        DropDownList1.DataSource = Enum.GetValues(t);
        DropDownList1.DataBind();
    }
}
void DropDownList1_SelectedIndexChanged(object sender, EventArgs e)
{
    Type t = typeof(TreeViewImageSet);
    string imageSet = DropDownList1.SelectedValue;

    TreeView1.ImageSet = (TreeViewImageSet) Enum.Parse(t, imageSet);
}
```

> **Caution**   When you use site map information in a page—and especially when you employ the *SiteMapDataSource* component—make sure that the page is defined in the site map. This should be a nonissue for a deployed application, but it can create quite a bit of confusion and hassle at development time.

The *Menu* Control

The menu is one of the most typical UI elements of any Windows application. Before the advent of ASP.NET 2.0, a number of third-party vendors and a countless number of individual developers put effort and money into building a reusable component that behaved like the typical drop-down menus of desktop Windows applications. Finally, in ASP.NET 2.0 a dazzling new *Menu* control makes its debut.

The *Menu* control allows you to arrange a strip of clickable elements to invoke pages and execute code. Appearance, orientation, and contents of the *Menu* control can be specified both declaratively and through data binding, and they can be hard-coded in the *.aspx* source or determined dynamically. A *Menu* is made of items, each of which is represented with a *MenuItem* object.

When the user clicks a menu item, the control can either navigate to a linked page or simply post back to the Web server. What happens depends on how the menu item is configured. By default, a linked page is displayed in the same window or frame as the parent *Menu*.

ASP.NET 2.0 supports two types of menus: static and dynamic. A static menu is an integral part of the page and is always displayed whenever the page is shown. Conversely, a dynamic menu appears only when the user positions the mouse over a menu item that contains a dynamic submenu. Dynamic menus disappear after a certain duration.

Members of the *Menu* Control

The *Menu* control has several properties, listed in Table 10-10, which are in addition to those inherited from base classes. Most of these properties refer to the appearance of static and dynamic menu items.

Table 10-10   Visual Properties of the *Menu* Control

Properties	Description
DynamicBottomSeparatorImageUrl	The URL to an image to display at the bottom of each dynamic menu item to separate it from other menu items
DynamicEnableDefaultPopOutImage	Indicates whether the built-in image that indicates that a dynamic menu item has a submenu is displayed
DynamicHorizontalOffset	The number of pixels to shift a dynamic menu horizontally from its parent menu item

Table 10-10   Visual Properties of the *Menu* Control

Properties	Description
DynamicItemFormatString	Text to format menu items that are dynamically displayed
DynamicPopOutImageTextFormatString	Alternate text to indicate that a dynamic menu item has a submenu
DynamicPopOutImageUrl	URL to an image to display in a dynamic menu item when a submenu is found
DynamicItemTemplate	The template that contains the custom content to render for a dynamic menu
DynamicTopSeparatorImageUrl	URL to the image to display at the top of each dynamic menu item to separate it from others
DynamicVerticalOffset	Number of pixels to shift a dynamic menu vertically relative to its parent menu item
ScrollDownImageUrl	URL to the image that dynamic menus display to indicate that the user can scroll down for additional menu items
ScrollDownText	Alternate text for the image assigned to the *ScrollDownImageUrl* property
ScrollUpImageUrl	URL to the image that dynamic menus display to indicate that the user can scroll up for additional menu items
ScrollUpText	Alternate text for the image assigned to the *ScrollUpImageUrl* property
StaticBottomSeparatorImageUrl	URL to the image displayed to separate at the bottom each static menu item
StaticDisplayLevels	Number of menu levels to display in a static menu
StaticEnableDefaultPopOutImage	Indicates whether the built-in image is displayed to indicate that a static menu item has a submenu
StaticItemFormatString	Text to format menu items that are statically displayed
StaticItemTemplate	Indicates the template that contains the custom content to render for a static menu
StaticPopOutImageTextFormatString	Alternate text for the pop-out image used to indicate that a static menu item has a submenu
StaticPopOutImageUrl	URL to an image displayed to indicate that a static menu item has a submenu
StaticSubMenuIndent	Number of pixels to indent submenus within a static menu
StaticTopSeparatorImageUrl	URL to the image displayed to separate at the top each static menu item

A menu item mainly consists of a text and an optional navigation URL. Items in static and dynamic menus can be embellished with images or alternate text to denote the presence of more items to scroll or a submenu. The structure of both static and dynamic menu items can be extensively customized using templates.

Table 10-11 lists the *Menu* properties that, with their values, affect the behavior of the control.

Table 10-11   Behavior Properties of the *Menu* Control

Properties	Description
DataBindings	Returns a collection of *MenuItemBinding* objects that define the relationship between a data item and a menu item
DisappearAfter	Indicates the duration in milliseconds for which a dynamic menu is displayed after the mouse pointer is moved away from the menu
Items	Returns a *MenuItemCollection* object that contains all menu items in the menu
ItemWrap	Indicates whether the text for menu items should wrap in case of limited space
MaximumDynamicDisplayLevels	Number of menu levels to render for a dynamic menu
Orientation	Indicates the direction in which to render the *Menu* control
PathSeparator	Indicates the character used to delimit the path of a menu item
SelectedItem	Gets the selected menu item
SelectedValue	Gets the value of the selected menu item

The simplest way to build a menu in an ASP.NET page is through static items. You populate the *Items* collection of the *Menu* control, declaratively or programmatically, by creating instances of the *MenuItem* class or adding *<asp:MenuItem>* tags to the *<Items>* container. To create submenu items, you just nest additional *<asp:MenuItem>* elements inside existing menu items.

The *Menu* control fully supports data binding, in particular through the site map data source component because menus are, by nature, heirarchical. You can bind the *Menu* control to data source controls through the *DataSourceID* property or to hierarchical objects via the *Data-Source* property. The *DataBindings* collection allows you to add bindings programmatically or declaratively between a menu item and a data item.

> **Note**   As you can see, the programming interface and the internal mechanics of *TreeView* and *Menu* controls are pretty much the same, especially as far as data binding is concerned. Although both controls can be bound to data in a variety of ways, the most common and effective approach remains binding the controls to a site map through the *SiteMapDataSource* control. In this way, you use a centralized data store decoupled from the page that hosts the navigation control. In addition, you have free support for security trimming and roles. I'll say more about security trimming in a moment.

The appearance of a menu is highly customizable through themes, images, user-defined templates and, of course, styles. Table 10-12 lists the style properties supported by the *Menu* control.

Table 10-12   Style Properties of the *Menu* Control

Style	Description
DynamicHoverStyle	The style to set the appearance of a dynamic menu item when the mouse pointer is positioned over it
DynamicMenuItemStyle	The style to set the appearance of the menu items within a dynamic menu
DynamicMenuStyle	The style to set the appearance of a dynamic menu
DynamicSelectedStyle	The style to set the appearance of the dynamic menu item selected by the user
LevelMenuItemStyles	Returns a collection of *Style* objects containing style settings applied to menu items based on their level in the menu
LevelSelectedStyles	Returns a collection of *Style* objects containing style settings applied to the selected menu item based on its level in the menu
LevelSubMenuStyles	Returns a collection of *Style* objects containing style settings applied to the submenu items in the static menu based on their level
StaticHoverStyle	The style to set the appearance of a static menu item when the mouse pointer is positioned over it
StaticMenuItemStyle	The style to set the appearance of the menu items in a static menu
StaticMenuStyle	The style to set the appearance of a static menu
StaticSelectedStyle	The style to set the appearance of the menu item selected by the user in a static menu

The style of a menu item is an object of type *MenuItemStyle*. This class inherits from *Style* and extends it with a bunch of attributes to control menu item spacing and padding. Styles are applied in a given order of precedence. The first style applied is *StaticMenuStyle* followed by *StaticMenuItemStyle*. If defined, any styles contained in the *LevelMenuItemStyles* or *LevelSubMenuStyles* collections are applied at this time, thus overriding other style properties. The node style then has the settings in the *StaticSelectedStyle* property applied. If the *LevelSelectedStyles* collection is defined, it is applied at this time. Finally, the style properties defined in *HoverNodeStyle* are processed.

> **Note**   The *Menu* control also features one method—*FindItem*—and a couple of interesting events. The *FindItem* method searches for the menu item that matches the given menu path and returns a *MenuItem* object. The menu path is a string of delimited values that form the path from a root menu item to the current menu item. The delimiter character is set through the *PathSeparator* property. The *Menu* control features events such as *MenuItemClick* and *MenuItemDataBound*. The former occurs when the user clicks on a menu item; the latter event is fired whenever a menu item is bound to data.

Menu-Oriented View of the Site

Binding a site map data source to a *Menu* control is nearly identical to binding to a *TreeView* control.

```
<asp:SiteMapDataSource ID="SiteMapDataSource1" runat="server" />
<asp:Menu ID="Menu1" runat="server" DataSourceID="SiteMapDataSource1"
        DynamicHorizontalOffset="2" StaticSubMenuIndent="10px">
    ⋮
</asp:Menu>
```

Figure 10-5 shows the menu in action on the sample site map.

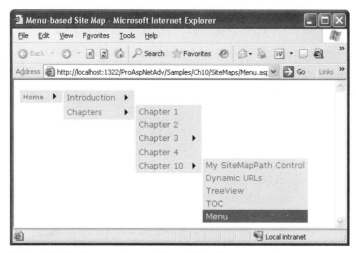

Figure 10-5   A menu-based view of the site.

Note that *Menu* and *TreeView* controls generate an HTML markup and script that works just fine with both Internet Explorer and Mozilla-powered browsers.

Tip   Choosing a tree-based or menu-based view for your site is merely a matter of prefer-ence. A nice thing you can do is create two distinct master pages for your site, one with a *Tree-View* and one with a *Menu* control, and then let users choose the one they like best. You save the user preferences in the *Profile* object and restore them whenever a page is required. To make sure that each page in the site dynamically sets the master of choice, you could create a custom *Page* class that overrides the *PreInit* event (which is the only time you can program-matically set the master) and derive all your site pages from there. This approach is the first step toward building *skinned pages*—that is, pages where components can be themed and rearranged by the end user. You can refer to Chapter 3 and Chapter 5 of *Programming Microsoft ASP.NET 2.0: Core Reference* for more information on pages, master pages, and user profiles in ASP.NET 2.0.

Role-Based Display

Most realistic Web applications implement role-based security. Role-based security revolves around the idea of associating each registered user with one or more strings that describe the role the user plays in the context of the application. In ASP.NET 2.0, role information is automatically associated with the identity object and made available to code through the *User* object. In ASP.NET 1.x, on the other hand, the same association must be manually coded, but the *User* object still exposes methods to test if a given user belongs to a certain role. For more information on roles, check out Chapter 15 in *Programming Microsoft ASP.NET 2.0: Core Reference*.

Assuming that your application has a few registered users grouped by roles, let's see how to filter the site map to serve each user just the right set of pages and links.

Interestingly enough, you need no changes on the site map data source nor on the view control, be it a *TreeView* or a *Menu*. View controls blissfully render what they receive from the site map data source, and the site map data source control blissfully passes on what it receives from the current site map provider.

The capability of filtering the site map based on user roles is known as *security trimming*. Security trimming must be enabled on the site map provider in the *web.config* file. Needless to say, security trimming works only if the site map provider supports that.

```
<siteMap defaultProvider="XmlSiteMapProvider" enabled="true">
   <providers>
      <add name="XmlSiteMapProvider"
           description="Default SiteMap provider."
           type="System.Web.XmlSiteMapProvider "
           siteMapFile="Web.sitemap"
           securityTrimmingEnabled="true" />
   </providers>
</siteMap>
```

In the site map file, you use the *roles* attribute of the *<siteMapNode>* element to list which roles are enabled to view that node. The *roles* attribute is assigned a comma-separated string in which each token indicates a valid role. The following code snippet defines a node that is accessible only to users belonging to the *Editor* role:

```
<siteMapNode title="Introduction" roles="Editor">
   ⋮
</siteMapNode>
```

TreeView and *Menu* controls automatically reflect the value of the *roles* attribute in the nodes, if any. Figure 10-6 and Figure 10-7 show the same page viewed by users with different roles.

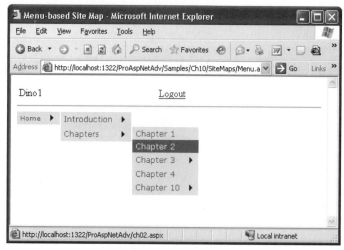

Figure 10-6 The site map when viewed by a user of role Editor.

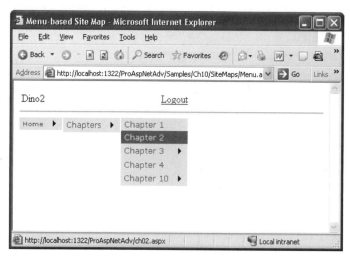

Figure 10-7 The site map when viewed by a user of role Reader. The node Introduction is now missing.

> **Note** When security trimming is enabled on the site map provider, site map nodes that lack the *roles* attribute are automatically removed from view. To display nodes, you must explicitly add a role property to them. If the node is not subject to role-based security, set the roles attribute to '*'.

Conclusion

When the size of the Web site grows beyond a certain threshold, and the relationships between constituent pages become increasingly difficult to navigate, you probably need to introduce a site map document. A site map describes the pages found in a Web site and groups them logically. What's the purpose of this? Pure documentation? Well, not just that.

In ASP.NET 2.0, the site map provides the common ground for a number of site navigation controls—*SiteMapPath*, *TreeView*, and *Menu*. If the site map is the abstract data source, the site map provider is the physical component that takes care of binding navigation controls to the contents of the site map. The default site map provider reads map information from an XML file, but other solutions can be easily architected and implemented—for example, storing the site map in a tabular database table.

You typically use the site map to describe how a *TreeView* or *Menu* control will render your home page and its main menu of choices. This apparently simple feature allows you to endow your sites with a rich user interface, and it gives you the greatest flexibility to manage and rename pages.

> **Just the Facts**
>
> - A site map is a document that describes the structure of the Web site and the links that correlate constituent pages.
>
> - By default, the site map is stored in an XML file named *web.sitemap* and located in the root folder. The content of the site map file is read by a site map provider component.
>
> - By defining a new custom site map provider, you can read site map information from any other source, including files with a different XML schema or even a database.
>
> - When a site map is defined, each page has a path to it that starts from the root of the map. This path can be graphically displayed through the *SiteMapPath* control.
>
> - The content of the site map is loaded into memory at the start of the application, and it's made programmatically accessible through the static members of the class *SiteMap*.
>
> - *SiteMapDataSource* is a hierarchical data source control designed to display the contents of a site map through ad hoc hierarchical controls such as *TreeView* and *Menu*.
>
> - If the site map provider supports role-based security, and the site map includes role information in the nodes, the *TreeView* and *Menu* controls can easily display views of the site filtered on the currently logged-on user.

Part III
ASP.NET Controls

Chapter 11
ASP.NET Iterative Controls

Data binding and data-bound controls were two of the greatest surprises that developers found out of the box in ASP.NET 1.0. The data-binding mechanism has been significantly improved in ASP.NET 2.0, with the primary goal being to simplify the development of relatively common scenarios. I covered data binding and core data-bound controls in Chapter 9 of *Programming Microsoft ASP.NET 2.0: Core Reference* (Microsoft Press, 2005), and devoted Chapter 10 and Chapter 11 of the same book to delving deep into the capabilities of ASP.NET 2.0 view controls—*GridView*, *DetailsView*, and *FormView*. One topic was left uncovered, though—ASP.NET iterative controls—and I'll cover it here to open the section dedicated to the various flavors of ASP.NET controls.

Iterative controls are special types of controls that combine two key capabilities. They support ASP.NET-compliant data sources and supply template-based mechanisms to create free-form user interfaces. You use iterative controls to create an advanced and highly customized data-driven front-end for your Web applications. Iterative controls are supported by all versions of ASP.NET.

What Is an Iterative Control, Anyway?

An ASP.NET data-bound control is said to be *iterative* if it provides the ability to loop over a set of data items to apply an ASP.NET template to each of them. Each loop iteration generates a control-specific item that incorporates information from the bound data item as well as layout information from the parent control. The control item object is exposed as a customizable and configurable stand-alone object that holds its own set of properties, methods, and events. As of version 2.0, ASP.NET provides two iterative controls—*Repeater* and *DataList*.

To identify the ideal scenarios where *Repeater* and *DataList* fit, let's briefly compare these controls with other categories of data-bound controls available to ASP.NET developers—list controls and view controls.

Iterative Controls vs. List Controls

List controls are controls that show a list of items through a fixed and immutable user interface. Typical list controls are *DropDownList*, *ListBox*, *CheckBoxList*, *BulletedList*, and the like. With the notable exception of *DataList*, we could reasonably conclude that all server controls with the string *List* in the name are list controls.

The Rendering Engine

The big difference between, say, a *DropDownList* control, and what we recognize here as iterative controls—that is, the *Repeater* and *DataList*—is all in how each control shows its contents.

The *DropDownList* control uses a drop-down list and doesn't provide relevant facilities for you to change the user interface of each displayed item, except perhaps for some cascading HTML styles.

Similarly, the *CheckBoxList* control displays a list of selectable options whose values and displayed text can be bound to a data source. With this list control, you can apply some relatively simple HTML formatting to each item. However, you have no way to access the properties of the item being rendered unless you completely replace the rendering engine of the control.

If you want to render, say, some items of the check-box list in boldface type, you can only modify the text of the single item being displayed and wrap it in a *<b>* element. While this is (much) better than nothing, it's still too little for complex applications that need more advanced display features.

In summary, iterative controls differ from list controls because of their greater rendering flexibility. An iterative control lets you apply an ASP.NET template to each row in the bound data source. A list control, on the other hand, provides a fixed and built-in template for each data item. List controls are customizable to some extent, but you can't change anything other than the text displayed. No changes to layout are supported.

The Programming Interface

Using a list control is considerably easier than setting up an iterative control. A list control only needs data binding, meaning that once you have a data source control or an *IEnumerable* object to bind, you're pretty much done.

Iterative controls require the definitions of one or more templates. An ASP.NET template is a piece of markup code—a kind of embedded form with data placeholders—to be merged with the overall layout of the *Repeater* or *DataList* control. Defining a template requires quite a bit of declarative code, and if accomplished programmatically, it requires that you write a class that implements the *ITemplate* interface or load the template from an external user control file. We'll cover ASP.NET user controls (**.ascx* files) in the next chapter.

Reusing a list control is straightforward, as a list control is a self-contained component that has little dependency on the pages, limited only to the code necessary to bind data. If you then use data source controls for binding in ASP.NET 2.0, any page dependency fades away. Reusing a solution based on an iterative control is harder, as the template information (which is key to the control) is usually inserted into the host page. To avoid this form of dependency, you have to introduce dependencies on external files (user controls), or write quite a bit of code to define the template programmatically through the *ITemplate* interface. (We'll describe this technique later on.)

Iterative Controls vs. View Controls

View controls are *GridView*, *DetailsView*, *FormView*, and our old acquaintance, *DataGrid* control. All these controls work iteratively by repeating templates that are customizable to some extent. However, they also can be considered types of list controls because the customization facilities they provide don't allow you to break the rigid scheme of a tabular, multicolumn representation of data.

Grid-Based Controls

DataGrid and *GridView* controls have more advanced features than the *Repeater* and *DataList*—such as paging and sorting. On the other hand, they don't offer the same level of flexibility as iterative controls when it comes to rendering. In a certain sense, grid controls are a sort of highly specialized, off-the-shelf version of iterative controls.

When using a *Repeater* control, you can build a grid of data, and you can do so even more easily when using a *DataList*. Note also that you can't always use a grid control to reproduce the same output as you can with either a *Repeater* or *DataList*. Table 11-1 summarizes the differences among grid, iterative, and list controls.

Table 11-1   Outlining Iterative and List Controls

	Rendering	Usage
Grid Controls	Loop over data and create a tabular representation of data allowing for column-specific templates.	Use when you have tabular data to display. If the data is not naturally tabular but can be rendered as such, consider using iterative controls.
Iterative Controls	Loop over data-bound items and apply a user-defined template.	Use when you have data to render as a free-form monolithic structure.
List Controls	Loop over data-bound items and apply an immutable, control-specific template.	Use when you don't need item-specific customization and you like the standard user interface.

Record-Based Controls

DetailsView and *FormView* fill a gap in the controls toolbox of ASP.NET 1.x. They provide a way to display all fields of a record, whereas grid controls let you display all records in a query. The layout of the *DetailsView* control is a rigid two-column table—one column for the label of the field, and one column for the value. This structure is hard to alter.

The *FormView*, conversely, is a kind of exception. It's a fully iterative control that gives you full freedom when it comes to defining the final user interface. However, the *FormView* control is limited to displaying one record at a time and works like a specialized version of the *Repeater* control that only iterates through the fields of a data item.

The *Repeater* Control

The *Repeater* is a data-bound control that displays data using a custom layout. It works by repeating a specified ASP.NET template for each item displayed in the list. The *Repeater* is a rather basic templated data-bound control. It has no built-in layout or styling capabilities. All formatting and layout information must be explicitly declared and coded using HTML tags and ASP.NET classes.

Programming Interface of the *Repeater* Control

The *Repeater* class inherits from *Control* and acts as a naming container by implementing the marker interface *INamingContainer*. Table 11-2 lists the properties exposed by the control, not counting those inherited from the base class *Control*.

Table 11-2   Properties of the *Repeater* Control

Property	Description
AlternatingItemTemplate	The template used to render every other item.
DataMember	Gets or sets the specific table in the *DataSource* that is to be bound to the control.
DataSource	Gets or sets the *IEnumerable* data source that provides any data for populating the list.
DataSourceID	Gets or sets the name of the data source control that provides any data for populating the list.
FooterTemplate	The template that defines how the footer is rendered.
HeaderTemplate	The template that defines how the header is rendered.
Items	Returns a *RepeaterItemCollection* object—that is, a collection of *RepeaterItem* objects. Each element of the collection represents a displayed data row in the *Repeater*.
ItemTemplate	The template that defines how items are rendered.
SeparatorTemplate	The template that renders separators between items.

For the most part, properties are the template elements that form the control's user interface. Aside from that, the *Items* property contains the list of child items that are associated with each displayed data row. The *Repeater* populates the *Items* collection by enumerating all the data objects in the bound data source. All objects contained in the data source are mapped onto a *RepeaterItem* object and inserted in the collection.

The *RepeaterItem* class is used to represent any type of constituent item (header, footer, separator) and is not limited to representing only data items. A few properties characterize the programming interface of the *RepeaterItem* class, as listed in Table 11-3.

Table 11-3   Properties of the *RepeaterItem* Control

Property	Description
DataItem	Returns the data object from the bound data source that corresponds to the item being rendered. This property is null on non-data-bound *Repeater* items such as the header and footer.
ItemIndex	Returns the 0-based index of the item being rendered.
ItemType	Returns a value from the *ListItemType* enumeration to denote the type of the item being rendered. Feasible values are *Header*, *Footer*, *Item*, *AlternatingItem*, and *Separator*.

Note that the *ListItemType* enumeration is shared by various iterative and list controls and is not specific to the *Repeater* control. The *ListItemType* type is defined in the following code snippet. As you can see, not all values defined apply to *RepeaterItem* objects.

```
public enum ListItemType
{
    Header,
    Footer,
    Item,
    AlternatingItem,
    SelectedItem,
    EditItem,
    Separator,
    Pager
}
```

It is important to note that the *DataItem* property of the *RepeaterItem* class is not set at all times for data-bound items. The *DataItem* property returns null if accessed before the repeater's item is physically bound to its data. We'll visit this point again when I discuss the *Repeater*'s events, later in the chapter.

Binding a *Repeater* to Data

Just like any other data-bound ASP.NET control, the *Repeater* generates its user interface only when a call to its *DataBind* method is made or when, in ASP.NET 2.0, it is bound to a data source control. *DataBind* is the only method in the control's interface aside from those directly inherited from parent classes. A call to *DataBind* causes the control to rebuild its control hierarchy.

> **Note**   Like all data-bound controls existing in earlier versions of ASP.NET, the *Repeater* control supports binding through data source controls. However, the binding is limited to the SELECT operation. In other words, the *Repeater* control doesn't include any ad hoc logic to work with a data source control to update or delete records on the data source.

The call to *DataBind* is necessary for generating the HTML code for the control and adding it to the output stream. In addition to the events defined by the parent class, the *Repeater* exposes three additional events—*ItemCreated*, *ItemCommand*, and *ItemDataBound* (as described in Table 11-4). Note that the *DataBinding* event defined by the parent *Control* class precedes all events listed in Table 11-4.

Table 11-4   Events of the *Repeater* Control

Event	Description
ItemCommand	Fires when a button is clicked within the *Repeater* control.
ItemCreated	Fires when a repeater item is being created. At this time, the *DataItem* property always returns null.
ItemDataBound	Fires after an item in the *Repeater* has been bound to underlying data. At this time, for bindable items like items and alternating items, the *DataItem* property is not null.

Handlers for the *ItemCreated* and *ItemDataBound* events receive an argument that contains a reference to the *RepeaterItem* object being created. Any change you make to this object is reflected in the final output of the *Repeater* control.

How the *Repeater* Builds the Output

The final output generated by a *Repeater* control results from the composition of various templates. The logic applied is contained in a protected overridable method named *CreateControl-Hierarchy*. If you want to customize the *Repeater* control and derive a new class from it that renders differently, this is the method to override.

The *CreateControlHierarchy* method connects to the data source and iterates over the items in the bound collection. The following pseudocode illustrates the process that leads to the creation of the *Repeater* output.

```
// Create the header item
if (headerTemplate != null)
    CreateItem(ListItemType.Header);

int _counter = 0;
RepeaterItem _repItem;
```

```
// Create items and alternating items
foreach(object _dataItem in DataSource)
{
    if (useSeparator && _counter > 0)
        CreateItem(ListItemType.Separator);
    if (_counter % 2)
        _repItem = CreateItem(_counter, ListItemType.Item, _dataItem);
    else
        _repItem = CreateItem(_counter, ListItemType.AlternatingItem,
            _dataItem);
    Items.Add(_repItem);

    _counter ++;
}

// Create the footer item
if (footerTemplate != null)
    CreateItem(ListItemType.Footer);
```

The *Repeater* first applies the header's template, if any. Next, it walks its way through the collection of bound objects and applies the *ItemTemplate* or the *AlternatingItemTemplate*, as appropriate. Each item template might be interspersed with a separator template, if any has been provided. Finally, at the end of the loop, the footer's template is applied, but only once.

Within the *CreateItem* placeholder, a new *RepeaterItem* object is created and initialized to default values. Next, the *ItemCreated* event fires and the object is added to the *Items* collection. Finally, data is associated with the item and the *ItemDataBound* event occurs.

Templates of the *Repeater* Control

Speaking abstractly, a template is a block of server controls, literals, and HTML text that is used as a monolithic output element. To some extent, you can think of a template as a dynamically defined ASP.NET control with a composite interface that can be either defined declaratively using client and server tags, or programmatically via ad hoc classes.

At a minimum, the *Repeater* must provide the *ItemTemplate* template. Unspecified (null) templates are simply ignored; however, if you also omit the *ItemTemplate* template, the *Repeater* will have blank output.

A Sample Item Template

In most cases, you define a template by using declarative code. For example, the following code shows how to generate output that looks like that of a *DataGrid*:

```
<asp:Repeater ID="Repeater1" runat="server" DataSourceID="SqlDataSource1">
    <HeaderTemplate>
        <table>
            <thead>
                <td> <b>ID</b> </td>
```

```
                       <td> <b>First Name</b> </td>
                       <td> <b>Last Name</b> </td>
                  </thead>
          </HeaderTemplate>

          <ItemTemplate>
             <tr>
                 <td bgcolor="white">
                     <%# Eval("EmployeeID") %></td>
                 <td bgcolor="white">
                     <%# Eval("FirstName")%></td>
                 <td bgcolor="white">
                     <%# Eval("LastName") %></td>
             </tr>
          </ItemTemplate>

          <AlternatingItemTemplate>
             <tr>
                 <td bgcolor="#eeeeee">
                     <%# Eval("EmployeeID") %></td>
                 <td bgcolor="#eeeeee">
                     <%# Eval("FirstName")%></td>
                 <td bgcolor="#eeeeee">
                     <%# Eval("LastName") %></td>
             </tr>
          </AlternatingItemTemplate>

          <FooterTemplate>
              </table>
          </FooterTemplate>
</asp:Repeater>
```

Figure 11-1 shows what this *Repeater* control looks like.

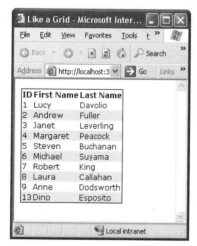

Figure 11-1   The *Repeater* control can do whatever a *DataGrid* can do, even though it might require a lot of coding. The opposite is not true.

In this case, the data source of the *Repeater* control is a *SqlDataSource* control.

```
<asp:SqlDataSource ID="SqlDataSource1" runat="server"
    ConnectionString="<%$ ConnectionStrings:LocalNWind %>"
    SelectCommand="SELECT employeeid, firstname, lastname FROM employees">
</asp:SqlDataSource>
```

The final output of the *Repeater* is simply the summation of the HTML generated by each involved template. As illustrated in the aforementioned example, the *Repeater* control allows you to split HTML tags across the various templates. For example, the *<table>* tag is opened in the header and closed in the footer.

The *ITemplate* Interface

The *Repeater* class references a template through the *ITemplate* interface, meaning that any template property can be programmatically set only to an instance of any class that implements the *ITemplate* interface. In spite of this, you are allowed to specify a template using server-side tags and HTML tags. How is this possible?

When the page is compiled, all the fragments defined within a template block are compiled into an internal object that implements the *ITemplate* interface. What if you want to create templates programmatically? Before I get to that, let's review the definition of the *ITemplate* interface.

The *ITemplate* interface consists of a single method, named *InstantiateIn*.

```
void InstantiateIn(Control container);
```

The expected behavior of *InstantiateIn* is intuitive: it programmatically creates all the child controls to be used in the template. All the controls are then added to the container's *Controls* collection. If needed, the newly created controls can also be bound to the data source by giving them a handler for the *DataBinding* event.

Loading Templates from User Controls

There are basically two ways to set template properties programmatically. The simplest way is by using the *LoadTemplate* method of the *Page* class. *LoadTemplate* takes only one argument, that being the name of the user control file that describes the template. The file name must have an *.ascx* extension, where *.ascx* is the typical extension of Web user control files. (We'll cover Web user controls in the next chapter.) You create a file-based template using the following code:

```
Repeater1.ItemTemplate = Page.LoadTemplate("item_template.ascx");
```

The template file can be written in any .NET language and doesn't necessarily have to be written in the language of the page. The *LoadTemplate* method can be used to load the layout code for any template property, including *HeaderTemplate* and *FooterTemplate*. The following code shows how to write an *.ascx* control to emulate the behavior of the repeater data items for the page shown in Figure 11-1.

```
<%@ Control Language="C#" %>
<tr>
    <td bgcolor="white">
    <%# Eval("EmployeeID")%>
    </td>
    <td bgcolor="white">
    <%# Eval("FirstName") %>
    </td>
    <td bgcolor="white">
    <%# Eval("LastName") %>
    </td>
</tr>
```

Note that, in ASP.NET 2.0, the use of *Eval* greatly simplifies coding. The preceding syntax doesn't work for ASP.NET 1.x, so you have to resort to a slightly different approach:

```
<%# DataBinder.Eval((RepeaterItem) Container.DataItem, "LastName") %>
```

The cast to *RepeaterItem* is required from within a user control, but not if you use the same code from within the host page.

Creating Templates Programmatically

The second way to set template properties programmatically is by using a class that implements the *ITemplate* interface. Using a class that implements *ITemplate* achieves the same effect as using *LoadTemplate* and an *.ascx* file. Here is an example of such a class:

```
public class MyItemTemplate : ITemplate
{
    public void InstantiateIn(Control container)
    {
        // Create the <tr> element
        TableRow row = new TableRow();

        // Add the employeeID <td>
        TableCell empID = new TableCell();
        empID.DataBinding += new EventHandler(BindEmpID);
        row.Cells.Add(_empID);

        // Add the lastname <td>
        TableCell lname = new TableCell();
        lname.DataBinding += new EventHandler(BindLastName);
        row.Cells.Add(_lname);

        // Add the firstname <td>
        TableCell fname = new TableCell();
        fname.DataBinding += new EventHandler(BindFirstName);
        row.Cells.Add(fname);
```

```
      // Add the row to the container
      container.Controls.Add(row);
  }

  public void BindEmpID(object sender, EventArgs e)
  {
      TableCell cell = (TableCell) sender;
      RepeaterItem container = (RepeaterItem) cell.NamingContainer;
      object data = DataBinder.GetPropertyValue(container.DataItem,
                      "EmployeeID");
      cell.Text = data.ToString();
  }

  public void BindLastName(object sender, EventArgs e)
  {
      TableCell cell = (TableCell) sender;
      RepeaterItem container = (RepeaterItem) cell.NamingContainer;
      object data = DataBinder.GetPropertyValue(container.DataItem,
                      "LastName");
      cell.Text = data.ToString();
  }

  public void BindFirstName(object sender, EventArgs e)
  {
      TableCell cell = (TableCell) sender;
      RepeaterItem container = (RepeaterItem) cell.NamingContainer;
      object data = DataBinder.GetPropertyValue(container.DataItem,
                      "FirstName");
      cell.Text = data.ToString();
  }
}
```

Note that the actual type of the data item depends on the data source that has been bound to the *Repeater*. The *sender* argument in the preceding code refers to the control that is being bound to the data—the *TableCell*. The *NamingContainer* property is only a shortcut to obtain a reference to the parent *Repeater*. In this case, the *Repeater* is the naming container of the cell.

> **Note**   In ASP.NET 2.0, data-bound controls can be associated with data source controls or any object that implements, at a minimum, the *IEnumerable* interface. The *IEnumerable* interface, though, only exposes methods to scroll through collection members and doesn't include methods to read values. How can iterative controls distinguish between such disparate enumerable objects as *DataTable*, *DataSet*, *DataView*, and custom collections? As in the preceding code snippet, you can use the *DataBinder.GetPropertyValue* method to extract the value stored in the specified property on a given object. For the method to work, though, the property must be public and feature at least the *get* accessor. The method won't work if the property is implemented as a field.

Working with the *Repeater* Control

The output that a *Repeater* control can generate for you is any HTML code that can be obtained by repeating ASP.NET templates for all rows in a data source. The overall output can be bound within a table as well as flow as plain HTML text. The *Repeater* control doesn't provide any facility for formatting or styling the output, so whatever effect you need must be manually coded.

Let's build a page that lists some customer information stored in the Microsoft SQL Server Northwind database. Showing this information through a grid control would be child's play, but the user interface is established by the grid control. However, the *Repeater* adds a lot of user-interface flexibility and allows us to create a sort of Web form for each customer. In particular, our goal will be to initially list some minimal customer information along with a check box. When the page is refreshed, all checked items will display with different colors and with more detailed information associated with each checked customer.

For a realistic *Repeater* control, the item template is a fundamental tool for showing the actual data. The *Repeater* also needs to have the header template, which is normally used to introduce the user to the information displayed below. The separator template is effective to graphically separate one item from the next. It's especially needed if you use the alternating item template. In this example, we provide a simple implementation of the separator, making it include only a thin horizontal ruler—an <hr> element. However, keep in mind that a more complex separator template might be the ideal tool to use when you need to display summary rows or subtotals.

Building the Page

The following listing illustrates the underpinnings of the page shown in Figure 11-2. It contains a few templates for the header, data items, and separator.

```
<asp:repeater runat="server" id="Repeater1">
   <HeaderTemplate>
      <div style="background-color:yellow;">Customers</div>
   </HeaderTemplate>

   <ItemTemplate>
      <span style="display:none;">
         <%# m_checkBox = (CheckBox) FindCheckBox(Container) %>
      </span>
      <asp:checkbox runat="server" id="ExpandButton" />
      <%# ShowHeader(Container.DataItem) %><br>
      <%# ShowInfoBar(Container.DataItem) %>
      <%# ShowAddressBar(Container.DataItem) %>
   </ItemTemplate>

   <SeparatorTemplate>
      <hr style="border:dashed 1px black;height:1px;" />
   </SeparatorTemplate>
</asp:repeater>
```

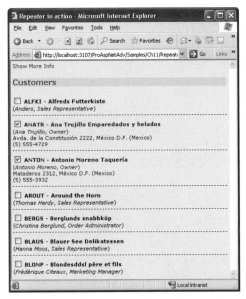

Figure 11-2   The *Repeater* in action showing Northwind customer information.

The header template is applied only once, whereas the separator is applied before every displayed item except the first. We modified the default style of the *<hr>* element to thin it to one pixel. The core of the page is in the *<ItemTemplate>* section. Let's examine its constituent pieces.

Building the Item Template

You see that the item's template begins with a rather odd, hidden *<span>* tag that I'll return to in a moment. Next, it includes a check box and three additional functions, each to run within a data-bound code block, *<%# ... %>*. As is clearly visible in Figure 11-2, address information is displayed for checked customers and all checked customer information appears in blue, even though this last effect is not clear from a grayscale picture.

The *ShowHeader*, *ShowInfoBar*, and *ShowAddressBar* methods output the various blocks of information that make up the customer's form. *ShowHeader* outputs the boldface line with the customer code and name. *ShowInfoBar* generates the italicized line with contact details. Finally, *ShowAddressBar* shows the address of the customer and other personal information such as the phone number. All these functions take the data item and return the HTML-formatted string to add to the page's output stream.

```
protected string ShowHeader(object dataItem)
{
    // Determine the color to use
    string color = (m_checkBox.Checked ? "blue" : "black");

    // Set up the pattern of the final HTML string
    string output = "<b style='color:{0};'>{1} - {2}</b>";
```

```
    // Fill in the placeholders
    output = String.Format(output, color,
        DataBinder.GetPropertyValue(dataItem, "customerid"),
        DataBinder.GetPropertyValue(dataItem, "companyname"));

    // Return the output string
    return output;
}
```

The other helper routines have a similar structure. (See this book's sample code for those details.) The key here is how the function determines the color to use. The color to use is determined based on the status—checked or unchecked—of the check box.

Retrieving Child Controls

Each item template runs its own copy of the check box; all check boxes have the same ID but belong to different naming containers. To retrieve the correct instance of the check box, you need to hold a reference to the correct container. The *FindCheckBox* method does just that. The global *m_checkBox* variable simply caches the reference to the check box through all the calls to methods in the same template.

```
<ItemTemplate>
    <span style="display:none;">
        <%# m_checkBox = (CheckBox) FindCheckBox(Container) %>
    </span>
        ⋮
</ItemTemplate>
```

Because the *<span>* tag where *m_checkBox* is set is invisible, no additional output is generated.

```
private CheckBox FindCheckBox(Control container)
{
    // Retrieve the item-specific instance of the checkbox
    CheckBox ctl = (CheckBox) container.FindControl("ExpandButton");
    if (ctl == null)
        return null;

    // Update the state of the control
    ctl.Checked = (Page.Request[ctl.UniqueID]=="on");

    // Return the instance of the control
    return ctl;
}
```

When we need to know whether the check box is checked or not, the most reliable way to get the information is to read the value directly from the *Request* object. To do this, we need to know the unique ID of the check box.

Note that calling the *FindControl* method exposed by the *Page* class won't work because *Find-Control* explores only the subtree rooted in the naming container.

Handling Postback Events

If the item template contains a button or any other control that can post back, how should you intercept postback events? The *ItemCommand* event comes to the rescue. Let's consider a slightly reworked version of the previous example:

```
<ItemTemplate>
    <asp:Button runat="server" id="ExpandButton" CommandName="Expand" />

    <%# ShowHeader(Container.DataItem) %><br>
    <asp:panel runat="server" id="ExtraInfo" visible="false">
        <%# ShowInfoBar(Container.DataItem) %>
        <%# ShowAddressBar(Container.DataItem) %>
    </asp:panel>
</ItemTemplate>
```

The button is optionally given a *CommandName* attribute to distinguish it from other buttons in the same template. Optional information such as the information and address bar is initially hidden in an invisible panel. When the user clicks, the page posts back and the *ItemCommand* event handler runs:

```
void Repeater1_ItemCommand(object source, RepeaterCommandEventArgs e)
{
    Panel p = (Panel) e.Item.FindControl("ExtraInfo");
    p.Visible = !p.Visible;
}
```

FindControl helps you to retrieve the exact instance of the *Panel* the user clicked. Once you locate the panel instance, you toggle the *Visible* property and obtain the well-known expand/collapse effect for additional information. (See Figure 11-3.)

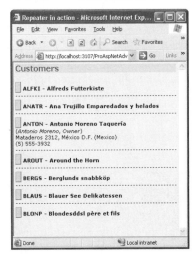

Figure 11-3 Showing and hiding additional information.

The *DataList* Control

Functionally speaking, the *DataList* is a data-bound control that begins where the *Repeater* ends and terminates a little before the starting point of grid controls. In some unrealistically simple cases, you can even take some code that uses a *Repeater*, replace the *DataList* control, and not notice any difference. If you are looking at the programming interface, though, the *DataList* is much more similar to a rich grid control than to the more simplistic *Repeater* programming interface.

In spite of such deep similarities to the *Repeater* control, the *DataList* is a control with its own personality and set of features that makes it unique and ideal in a number of situations. Compared to the *Repeater*, the *DataList* control comes with a full bag of goodies and new features, mostly in the area of graphical layout. The control is superior to the *Repeater* in several respects. For example, it supports directional rendering, meaning that items can flow horizontally or vertically to match a specified number of columns.

Furthermore, just as with the *DataGrid*, it provides facilities to retrieve a key value associated with the current data row, and has built-in support for selection and in-place editing. In addition, the *DataList* control supports more templates and can fire some extra events beyond those of the *Repeater*. Data binding and the overall behavior are nearly identical for the *Repeater* and *DataList* controls.

Programming Interface of the *DataList* Control

The *DataList* is smarter than the *Repeater* and works by making some assumptions about the expected results. This is both good and bad news for you as a programmer. It means that, in some cases, much less code is needed to accomplish the same effect; on the other hand, it also indicates that you should know the behavior of the control very well if you want to govern it. For example, the *DataList* assumes that no HTML tag is split across templates. This fact isn't a problem per se, but it can result in badly formed or totally unexpected HTML output. In addition, by default, the *DataList* renders its entire output as an HTML table, meaning that, if this is exactly what you want, there's no need for you to deal with individual *<table>* or *<td>* elements. If this isn't the behavior you want, the *DataList* control just doesn't work for you.

The *DataList* control is declared as follows:

```
public class DataList : BaseDataList, INamingContainer, IRepeatInfoUser
```

It inherits from *BaseDataList* and implements the *INamingContainer* interface. In addition, the *DataList* class implements the *IRepeatInfoUser* interface. The *IRepeatInfoUser* interface defines the properties and methods that must be implemented by any list control that repeats a list of items. This interface is also supported by the *CheckBoxList* and *RadioButton-List* controls.

Properties of the *DataList* Control

Table 11-5 lists the properties of the *DataList* control. The table doesn't include properties inherited from *Control* and *WebControl*.

Table 11-5   Properties of the *DataList*

Property	Description
AlternatingItemStyle	Gets the style properties for alternating rows.
AlternatingItemTemplate	Gets or sets the template for alternating items.
CellPadding	Gets or sets the space (in pixels) between the cell's border and the embedded text.
CellSpacing	Gets or sets the space (in pixels) between two consecutive cells, both horizontally and vertically.
Controls	Gets the collection of all the child controls in the list.
DataKeyField	Gets or sets the key field in the bound data source.
DataKeys	Gets a collection that stores the key values of all the records displayed in the list. The column used as the key is the one stored in the *DataKeyField* property.
DataMember	Gets or sets a string that indicates the specific table in a multimember data source to bind. The property works in conjunction with *DataSource*. If *DataSource* is a *DataSet* object, *DataMember* contains the name of a child table to bind.
DataSource	Gets or sets the data source object that contains the values to populate the control.
DataSourceID	Gets or sets the name of the data source control that provides any data for populating the list.
EditItemIndex	Gets or sets the 0-based index of the item to edit.
EditItemStyle	Gets the style properties for the item being edited.
EditItemTemplate	Gets or sets the template for the item selected for editing.
ExtractTemplateRows	Gets or sets a value that instructs the *DataList* to extract the constituent rows from any HTML table in the templates. The extracted rows are then combined to create a single, all-encompassing HTML table. The rows are then set to *false* by default.
FooterStyle	Gets the style properties for the footer section.
FooterTemplate	Gets or sets the template for the footer section.
GridLines	Gets or sets a value that indicates whether all cells must have the border drawn. The property is ignored if the *RepeatLayout* property is set to *RepeatLayout.Flow*.
HeaderStyle	Gets the style properties for the heading section.
HeaderTemplate	Gets or sets the template for the heading section.
HorizontalAlign	Gets or sets the horizontal alignment of the text in the list.
Items	Gets the collection of the currently displayed items.
ItemStyle	Gets the style properties for the items in the list.

Table 11-5   Properties of the *DataList*

Property	Description
ItemTemplate	Gets or sets the template for the items in the *DataList*.
RepeatColumns	Gets or sets the number of columns to display.
RepeatDirection	Gets or sets a value that indicates whether the *DataList* control displays its items vertically or horizontally.
RepeatLayout	Gets or sets a value that indicates whether the output of the control is displayed within an automatically created table or by using a flow layout. In a flow layout, text is output in free form.
SelectedIndex	Gets or sets the index of the currently selected item.
SelectedItem	Gets the *DataListItem* object that represents the currently selected item.
SelectedItemStyle	Gets the style properties for the selected item.
SelectedItemTemplate	Gets or sets the template for the currently selected item.
SeparatorStyle	Gets the style properties of the separator used to break text between consecutive items.
SeparatorTemplate	Gets or sets the template for the separator.
ShowFooter	Gets or sets a value that indicates whether the footer section is to be displayed.
ShowHeader	Gets or sets a value that indicates whether the heading section is to be displayed.

The *ShowFooter* and *ShowHeader* properties are both set to *true* by default, but they're considered only if the *FooterTemplate* and *HeaderTemplate* properties, respectively, are non-null.

The data-binding process of the *DataList* control is nearly identical to that of the *Repeater*, and the generation of the output also takes place according to the same rules. However, the *DataList* control has a richer programming interface that lets you handle two additional states—selected and editing. The currently selected item is tracked through the *SelectedIndex* and *SelectedItem* properties. The same process occurs for the item being edited. In this case, the property is *EditItemIndex*.

Events of the *DataList* Control

Table 11-6 lists the events that, under various circumstances, the *DataList* control can fire. The list doesn't include the base events (for example, *Load* and *DataBinding*) the class inherits from *Control* and *WebControl*.

Table 11-6   Events Fired by the *DataList*

Event	Description
CancelCommand	Fires when a button with a command name of *Cancel* is clicked for a displayed item.
DeleteCommand	Fires when a button with a command name of *Delete* is clicked for a displayed item.

Table 11-6   Events Fired by the *DataList*

Event	Description
EditCommand	Fires when a button with a command name of *Edit* is clicked for a displayed item.
ItemCommand	Fires when a button is clicked within the *DataList* control.
ItemCreated	Fires when a *DataList* item is being created.
ItemDataBound	Fires after an item in the *DataList* has been bound to its underlying data. (Note that only items and alternating items are bindable.)
SelectedIndexChanged	Fires when a new item is selected in the *DataList*.
UpdateCommand	Fires when a button with a command name of *Update* is clicked for a displayed item.

With the exception of *ItemCreated* and *ItemDataBound*, all the events relate to the execution of some sort of command. *ItemCommand* is the base command event and always fires before the more specific event, such as *EditCommand* or *DeleteCommand*. Finally, *SelectedIndexChanged* also is a command event that fires when a button with the reserved command name of *Select* is clicked.

> **Note**   Command buttons don't necessarily have to be item specific. Any button within the user interface of the *DataList* control can be given a special command name such as *Edit* or *Delete*. The effect is always that of firing the related event. Of course, if the button is not item specific, the logic of the application must determine the effect on the item and decide the proper action.

The *Update* and *Cancel* command buttons are normally generated by the *DataList* itself when a particular item enters into edit mode. Finally, note that the *DataList* class provides constants to identify special command names in a parametric way. The constants are *CancelCommand-Name*, *DeleteCommandName*, *EditCommandName*, *SelectCommandName*, and *UpdateCommand-Name*.

Formatting Capabilities

As mentioned earlier, the *Repeater* control is a general-purpose iterator and is limited to generating templated text without applying any extra formatting rules. The *DataList* control, on the other hand, provides additional features specifically for controlling the layout of the list. In particular, the *DataList* can render surrounding table rows and cells around its template-defined elements. This allows you to build more advanced and user-friendly layouts with less code. Key elements for taking advantage of this enhanced set of capabilities are the *Repeat-Columns*, *RepeatDirection*, and *RepeatLayout* properties. They let you specify the number of columns the output will span and the direction (vertical or horizontal) in which to render the data items.

Table and Flow Layout

The *RepeatLayout* property takes its values from the *RepeatLayout* enumeration, which consists of two possibilities—*Table* and *Flow*. The default is *Table*. If the layout is set to *Flow*, the *DataList* wraps any template element within a *<span>* tag. Next, it automatically adds a *
* element if the rendering direction is vertical. You should note that vertical is the default direction. If the direction is horizontal, the output text simply flows in a concatenated HTML string. The following *DataList* output is for a vertical *Flow* layout:

```
<span id="DataList1">
   <span> header template </span>
   <br>
   <span> item template </span>
   <br>
   <span> separator template </span>
   ⋮
   <span> footer template </span>
</span>
```

The *Table* mode saves you from a lot of HTML coding if you're just going to build an HTML table. The following *DataList* output is for a vertical *Table* layout:

```
<table id="DataList1">
   <tr>
      <td> header template </td>
   </tr>
   <tr>
      <td> item template </td>
   </tr>
   <tr>
      <td> separator template </td>
   </tr>
       ⋮
   <tr>
      <td> footer template </td>
   </tr>
</table>
```

If the direction is horizontal, the layout of the table is slightly different and is composed of only three table rows—the header, one row for all the items, and the footer.

```
<table id="DataList1">
   <tr>
       <td> header template </td>
   </tr>
   <tr>
      <td> item template </td>
      <td> separator template </td>
      ⋮
   </tr>
   <tr>
      <td> footer template </td>
   </tr>
</table>
```

When the *ExtractTemplateRows* property is set to *true*, the *DataList* control extracts table rows out of all declared templates and merges them into an all-encompassing table. The *Extract-TemplateRows* property allows you to create a single table from other smaller tables defined for each *DataList* template. The use of the property is subject to a few restrictions. In particular, you must provide a well-formed *Table* control (the *<asp:Table>* tag) for each template you want to include in the output. An exception would be thrown if you were to specify the table using the HTML *<table>* element or the ASP.NET *HtmlTable* control—the *<table runat="server">* element. Note also that *all* templates must be expressed using the *Table* control and that only the rows of the tables will be displayed. All other content in the templates will be ignored. The following code shows how to define a table in an item template:

```
<ItemTemplate>
   <asp:table runat="server">
      <asp:tablerow runat="server">
         <asp:tablecell runat="server">
            <%# Eval("Name") %>
         </asp:tablecell>
      </asp:tablerow>
   </asp:table>
</ItemTemplate>
```

The *ExtractTemplateRows* property is really helpful only when you're going to create a complex structure in which tables with different templates are to be merged together. You can use the *ColumnSpan* and *RowSpan* properties of the *TableCell* object to control the number of columns and rows the cell spans.

> **Note**   When the *ExtractTemplateRows* property is set to *true*, the *RepeatColumns*, *Repeat-Direction*, and *RepeatLayout* properties are ignored and do not affect the appearance of the *DataList* control.

Extracting Template Rows

Let's drill down into a common scenario in which *ExtractTemplateRows* proves extremely useful. Suppose that you need to create a report in which multiple rows for each data item should be displayed. Assuming that you want it to work with a table of customers, let's say that you want to display the customer IDs and names on the first rows and the addresses on the second.

With a *Repeater*, you could accomplish this by defining a table in the header template and then add a couple of rows for each item. If you don't mind using a *Repeater*, this is just fine. However, the *DataList* control has styling and formatting capabilities that one wouldn't normally sacrifice. The *DataList*, though, doesn't let you break HTML elements across templates. In other words, this means that you cannot place the opening tag of a table in the header and close it in the footer.

The *DataList* control requires that you express the layout of each template using stand-alone tables. You can use, for instance, a table for the header and a table for the item template. However, if you set the *ExtractTemplateRows* property to *true*, all the rows of the various tables will automatically converge into one unique, all-encompassing table.

```
<asp:datalist runat="server" id="list" extracttemplaterows="true">
    <AlternatingItemStyle backcolor="palegoldenrod" />
    <headerstyle backcolor="brown" forecolor="white"
        font-size="larger" font-bold="true" horizontalalign="center" />

    <HeaderTemplate>
    <asp:table runat="server">
        <asp:tablerow runat="server">
            <asp:tablecell runat="server">Customer</asp:TableCell>
            <asp:tablecell runat="server">Contact</asp:TableCell>
        </asp:tablerow>
    </asp:table>
    </HeaderTemplate>

    <ItemTemplate>
        <asp:table runat="server">
            <asp:tablerow runat="server" font-bold="true">
                <asp:tablecell runat="server">
                    <%# Eval("CustomerID") %>
                </asp:tablecell>
                <asp:tablecell runat="server">
                    <%# Eval("ContactName") %>
                </asp:tablecell>
            </asp:tablerow>

            <asp:tablerow runat="server">
                <asp:tablecell runat="server" columnspan="2">
                    <%# Eval("Address") + " - " +
                        Eval("City")   %>
                </asp:tablecell>
            </asp:tablerow>
        </asp:table>
    </ItemTemplate>
</asp:datalist>
```

At display time, the *DataList* merges the two *Table* objects and removes any table element that is not an instance of the *TableRow* class. The final table contains two columns, and each record displays on two different rows, the second of which contains a single cell spanning two columns. The *DataList* control is smart enough to consistently manage visual settings (for example, the alternating item styles) for all table rows that actually participate in a data item row. The results are shown in Figure 11-4.

Figure 11-4   The *DataList* shows a data table in which all records display in two table rows.

> **Note**   The need to merge multiple tables explains the strict requirement set on the use of the *<asp:table>* tag, which corresponds to the *Table* object. The *DataList* builds the resulting table object in memory. If you use a *<table>* tag with no *runat* attribute, it will be emitted verbatim and not processed by ASP.NET at all. If you use a *<table>* tag with the *runat* attribute set, other (lesser) ASP.NET objects are involved (the *HtmlTable* object specifically) and the trick just can't work because the proper ASP.NET processing isn't invoked.

Multicolumn Rendering

The output of a *DataList* control can be rendered over multiple columns, whose number you specify by using the *RepeatColumns* property. By default, the text displays in one column. You can create multicolumn output by using either a flow or a table layout. However, the ideal way of repeating items over multiple columns is within a fixed table layout. Figure 11-5 shows the effect of the *RepeatColumns* property along with some possible shortcomings. For example, the text isn't aligned between columns and there's nothing you can do about it. In a table where you have full control of the options, you could give all cells in a row the same vertical alignment.

```
<asp:datalist runat="server" id="list" RepeatColumns="3">
    ⋮
</asp:datalist>
```

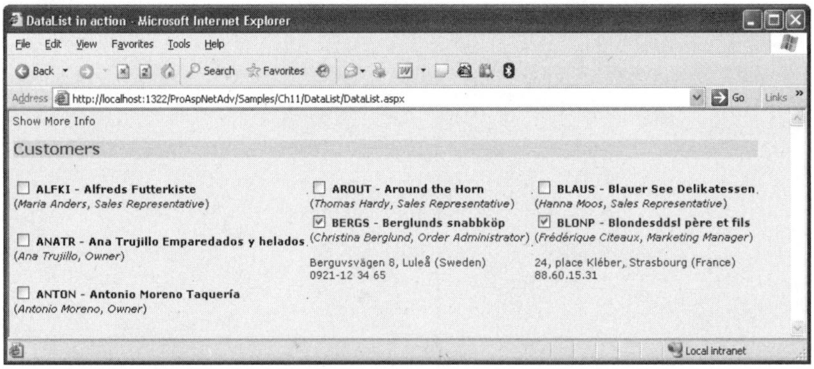

Figure 11-5 A *DataList* control that renders its output over three columns.

Templates of the *DataList* Control

In addition to all the templates supported by the *Repeater* control, the *DataList* control supports two new templates—*SelectedItemTemplate* and *EditItemTemplate*. The *SelectedItemTemplate* template lets you control the contents and functionality of the selected item. The *EditItemTemplate* template takes care of in-place editing, which is the user interface displayed to edit in-place the contents of the current data item.

The *SelectedItemTemplate* Template

The selection process is triggered when the user clicks on a command button labeled with the *Select* command name. If you want to do more when an item is selected, such as adding more information or controls to the current interface, you can replace the default template with a new one. You specify a template for the selected item through the <*SelectedItemTemplate*> tag. If you need to programmatically access the currently selected item, you use the *SelectedItem* property. It returns the instance of the *DataListItem* object that corresponds to the specified index. For each displayed row, the *DataKeys* collection contains the source values stored in the column that the *DataKeyField* column specifies.

When the page posts back because of a selection, the *SelectedIndexChanged* event occurs. The following code first retrieves the key that uniquely identifies the selected element, and then uses the key to obtain the additional data to display for the selected record. The key field retrieved through *DataKeys* is set to the *DataKeyField* property. Needless to say, the field has to be the name of one of the fields in the bound data source.

```
// Get the key of the currently selected record and
// drill down into the available data
int key = (int) list.DataKeys[list.SelectedIndex];
GetChildData(key);
```

Items can be selected programmatically by setting the *SelectedIndex* property to a 0-based value. A value of −1 means that no item is currently selected. Note that the value stored in the *SelectedIndex* property is persisted in the view state and survives across consecutive page requests. For this reason, you should reset it whenever a new page of data is displayed.

The *EditItemTemplate* Template

You use the *EditItemTemplate* property to control the contents of the item selected for editing in a *DataList* control. The look and feel of the item selected for editing is controlled by the *EditItemStyle* property. The *EditItemIndex* property contains the 0-based index of the item being edited. Also, this value is cached in the view state, so you should reset it whenever your data set is bound to the control changes.

The *DataList* fires the *EditCommand* event when the user clicks a button with the *Edit* command. However, the control enters into edit mode only if the associated event handler sets the *EditItem-Index* to a 0-based value (remember—it's initially set to {−}1). When in edit mode, the *DataList* shows the contents of the *EditItemTemplate* for the selected element. When the user clicks to commit the changes, the *UpdateCommand* event fires. You retrieve the current values from input fields using the *FindControl* method and then proceed to persist those changes.

Working with the *DataList* Control

Let's delve into the details of some operations you might want to accomplish using *DataList* controls in some common situations.

Making an Item Selectable

To add support for item selection, you first need to add a command button labeled with the special keyword *Select*. You can use any name for the command button, but the name *Select* is recognized by the control and causes the automatic execution of some built-in code. In particular, the *SelectedItemStyle* attributes are applied to the *DataList* element, and the *Selected-Index* property is updated. If, for some reason, you need more control over the whole process of selection, you could give the clickable element any command name. Then, when *Item-Command* fires, you intercept the command and activate the selection yourself by setting the *SelectedIndex* property to a correct index.

Imagine a scenario in which you have a list of clickable buttons, each of which represents a letter. By using a *DataList*, you can create a button for each distinct letter in the *companyname* column of the Customers table.

```
SELECT DISTINCT substring(companyname, 1, 1) AS Initial FROM customers
```

The following markup creates a data-bound list of buttons. The background color of buttons changes for the latest button the user has clicked. Each button has a unique command name that corresponds to the letter it represents.

```
<asp:datalist runat="server" id="Picker"
repeatlayout="flow" repeatdirection="horizontal"
OnItemCommand="ItemCommand">
```

```
        <ItemTemplate>
          <asp:button ID="Button1" runat="server"
              backcolor='<%# GetBackColor(Container.DataItem) %>'
              forecolor='<%# GetForeColor(Container.DataItem) %>'
              text='<%# Eval("Initial")%>'
              commandname='<%# Eval("Initial")%>' />
        </ItemTemplate>
</asp:datalist>
```

The *ItemCommand* handler uses the caption of the clicked button to run a second query that selects and displays all customers whose names begin with that letter. Figure 11-6 shows the expected results.

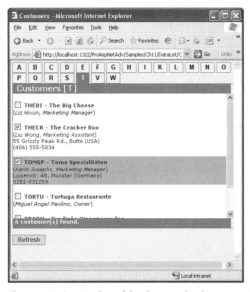

Figure 11-6   A selectable element in the output of a *DataList* control.

The list of customers is displayed using a second *DataList* control, as shown in the following code:

```
<asp:datalist runat="server" id="Customers"
    RepeatLayout="flow"
    DataKeyField="customerid">
  <SelectedItemStyle backcolor="cyan" width="100%" />

  <HeaderTemplate>
     <div><big><b><%# SetHeader() %></b></big></div>
  </HeaderTemplate>

  <ItemTemplate>
     <span id='<%# Eval("customerid") %>'>
        <span style="display:none;">
           <%# m_checkBox = (CheckBox) FindCheckBox(Container) %>
        </span>
```

```
            <asp:checkbox runat="server" id="ExpandButton" />
            <asp:linkbutton ID="Link1" runat="server"
                commandname="select"
                text='<%# Eval("companyname") %>' />
            <br>
             ⋮
        </span>
    </ItemTemplate>

    <FooterTemplate>
        </div>
    </FooterTemplate>
</asp:datalist>
```

The code in the *DataList* is the same code we examined earlier for the *Repeater*. A link button
with the name of the customer's company is displayed as the *Select* button. When clicked,
the background color of the entire row that contains the particular *Select* button turns to the
specified color (cyan):

```
<SelectedItemStyle backcolor="cyan" width="100%" />
```

At this point, we have a fully functional infrastructure for handling the item selection event.
To take a particular action on the selected item, just register a handler for the *SelectedIndex-
Changed* and update the user interface.

Adding Support for Paging

The *DataList* control has a user interface that is more free form than the grid controls interface. This consideration alone makes the *DataList* control particularly compelling to many
developers who have the need to create interactive reports outside the relatively standard visu-
alization pattern employed by grids. For example, no matter how powerful and customizable
a grid can be, you can hardly force it to use multiple rows of the grid to display a data item. The
schema represented in Figure 11-4 cannot be easily obtained with a grid. By contrast, you can
easily obtain all the flexibility you need using *DataList* controls. However, the *DataList* control
doesn't support pagination.

Pagination is the control's ability to display equally sized blocks of data according to an internal index the user can modify through links. Both *DataGrid* and *GridView* controls incorporate a pager bar element, which is nothing more than a table row with links to internal pieces
of code that handle the page movements. The *DataList* user interface does not provide any
predefined link bar for pagination, meaning that the host page can define, anywhere in the
body, a couple of links to move the data source back and forth.

Rendering Pages of Data

To handle pagination on a *DataList*, you need a page-level variable to track the page index.
In addition, a couple of buttons will give users a way to move backward and forward.

The following code snippets illustrate some sample code that sets the index and contents of the requested page:

```
private void OnPreviousPage(object sender, EventArgs e)
{
    CurrentPageIndex -= 1;
    RefreshPage();
}

private void OnNextPage(object sender, EventArgs e)
{
    CurrentPageIndex += 1;
    RefreshPage();
}
```

The code adjusts the page index—a variable named *CurrentPageIndex*—and binds the data to the *DataList* control. *RefreshPage* is a page-level helper routine that extracts the data to bind from the database or, more logically, from a server-side cache. *CurrentPageIndex* should persist its value across consecutive requests. Whether you add paging to a *DataList* by extending the code file of the page or by writing a custom control, the member that tracks the page index must be persisted to the view state.

In this sample implementation, the *RefreshPage* method assumes it is working with a *DataTable* container:

```
private void RefreshPage()
{
    DataTable data = GetData();
    AdjustPageIndex(data.Rows.Count);

    CurrentPage.Text = (CurrentPageIndex +1).ToString();
    list.DataSource = GetPage(data, CurrentPageIndex);
    list.DataBind();
}
private DataTable GetData()
{
    // Try to get the data from the session cache
    DataTable data = (DataTable) Session["MyData"];

    // If no data is available, read from the database
    if (data == null)
        data = LoadData();

    return data;
}
```

The *GetPage* method is responsible for extracting the right subset of rows that fit into the current page. The page of data is returned as a *DataTable* object and is bound to the *DataList*.

```
private DataTable GetPage(DataTable dt, int pageIndex)
{
    if (dt==null)
```

```
    {
        CurrentPageIndex = 0;
        dt = LoadData();
    }

    int firstIndexInPage = (CurrentPageIndex*PageSize);
    DataRowCollection rows = dt.Rows;

    DataTable target = dt.Clone();
    for (int i=0; i<PageSize; i++)
    {
        int index = i+firstIndexInPage;
        if (index < rows.Count)
            target.ImportRow(rows[i+firstIndexInPage]);
        else
            break;
    }

    return target;
}
```

The function clones the original table of data and creates a new, smaller table with only the rows that fit into the specified page index. The *Clone* method creates a new empty object with the same structure as the sample. The *ImportRow* method duplicates and copies a new row from one *DataTable* object to another. Note that a deep copy of the row is necessary because an ADO.NET object can't be contained in more than one parent object at the same time.

In ASP.NET 2.0, if you bind the *DataList* control to an *ObjectDataSource* control, you can leverage paging capabilities implemented in the data access layer (DAL), if any. Chapter 9 of *Programming Microsoft ASP.NET 2.0: Core Reference* (Microsoft Press, 2005) details the *Object-DataSource* control.

Conclusion

In this chapter we examined the characteristics of two iterative controls available with the ASP.NET programming platform. The two controls are the *Repeater* and *DataList* controls. Iterative controls differ from list controls because of their native support for templates and their extremely flexible rendering engines. Iterative and list controls also have some points in common. Both can be bound to a data source and display a list of items. The key point is in the algorithm and the templates that each control, and the category of controls each employs.

In an ideal scale, the *Repeater* is the simplest of all controls, but it's also the most flexible; grid controls have the richest sets of features but are also the ones that tie the developers to multi-column, tabular views. The *DataList* control falls somewhere in the middle, but is logically closer to grid controls. Just like the *Repeater*, the *DataList* displays the contents of a data-bound list through ASP.NET templates. But just like grid controls, it supports selecting and in-place editing and can have its look and feel customized using style properties.

Compared to the *Repeater* control, the *DataList* also shows off predefined layouts and more advanced formatting capabilities. On the other hand, when compared to grid controls, it lacks a key functionality: the ability to inherently page through bound data. You can provide this functionality yourself, however.

In this chapter, I mentioned Web user controls more than once. In the next chapter, we'll unveil their most important facts and features.

Just the Facts

- An ASP.NET data-bound control is said to be iterative if it provides the ability to loop over a set of data items in order to apply a template.

- ASP.NET provides two iterative controls—*Repeater* and *DataList*.

- List controls differ from iterative controls because they show a list of items through fixed and immutable user interfaces.

- View controls such as *GridView*, *DetailsView*, *FormView*, and *DataGrid* work iteratively by repeating templates. However, they also can be considered kinds of list controls because the customization facilities they provide don't allow you to break the rigid scheme of a tabular, multicolumn representation of data.

- The *Repeater* control is a rather basic templated data-bound control and has no built-in layout or styling capabilities.

- Templates can be added programmatically by loading them from a Web user control file or a class that implements the *ITemplate* interface.

- *DataList* supports directional rendering, meaning that items can flow horizontally or vertically to match a specified number of columns.

- *DataList* also supports the concept of a "selected item" and provides you with the ability to edit row data.

Chapter 12
ASP.NET Web User Controls

At the highest level of abstraction, ASP.NET provides two types of component-based extensibility—custom controls and user controls. With custom controls, you create a new control inheriting from a base class (for example, *Control* or *WebControl*) or extend an existing control class. A custom control is primarily a class built to be hosted in a page or parent control and to provide a set of functionalities that no built-in controls provide. The user interface of a custom control is created programmatically either by concatenating HTML text in the response or composing child controls. (I'll devote the next two chapters to custom controls.)

With Web user controls, you take a different and, to a large extent, opposite route. You take a mix of controls, HTML markup, and literals and group them under the umbrella of a new monolithic component—a sort of embeddable child Web form that shows a composite user interface while hiding any details about its constituent elements. Although user controls can appear to be not particularly object-oriented at first, the actual class you come up with is built on top of a base ASP.NET class—the *UserControl* class.

What's a User Control, Anyway?

A user control is primarily a Web form made of any combination of server and client controls sewn together with literals, server code, and client script code. A typical user control has a rich user interface, but it can also optionally expose an object model to facilitate programmatic access to some or all of its encapsulated components. As with Microsoft Visual Basic ActiveX controls, all the constituent controls are protected and inaccessible if not made available through a public programming interface you put together.

My favorite definition to describe a user control is that it's an *embeddable Web form*—that is, a kind of ASP.NET page that can be nested inside other container pages. The similarity between user controls and pages is not coincidental. (By the way, one of the first names assigned to this technology in the very early days of ASP.NET 1.0 was *pagelets*.) You create a user control in much the same way you create a Web form. When you're done with code and layout, you give the resulting file a mandatory *.ascx* extension. Then, you can use the control with any ASP.NET page. Pages see the new control as a unique, monolithic component and work with it as with any other built-in Web control. Creating a Web user control is normally simpler and faster than creating a custom control, and it requires fewer advanced skills.

In the end, though, Web user controls and custom controls are two distinct and seldom overlapping ways to extend ASP.NET, and each is targeted to a particular scenario.

The *UserControl* Class

User controls are server files with an *.ascx* extension that are referenced from within ASP.NET pages. They offer Web developers an easy and effective way to capture and reuse common pieces of the user interface with some optional code attached. Like ASP.NET pages and controls, Web user controls are compiled when first requested, and the generated assemblies are cached to quickly serve successive requests. As with a page, you can develop user controls using code-behind classes as well as inline code. (*Inline code* means that you place all control-relevant code in an embedded *<script runat="server">* tag.)

Unlike pages, though, user controls cannot be requested independently through the browser's address bar or programmatically. Internet Information Services (IIS), in fact, is configured to block and deny any requests directed at URLs that include the *.ascx* extension when you install ASP.NET. As a result, user controls can be requested only from *.aspx* pages or other user controls that contain them.

> **Note**   In their simplest form, user controls can be seen as a much more flexible alternative to server-side includes (SSI). However, thinking of user controls only as a smarter form of SSI misses the point. User controls can expose their own object model instead of copying a piece of static HTML text. They're live objects and can be used just like any other ASP.NET server control.

UserControl is the .NET Framework class that represents an *.ascx* file when called from within an ASP.NET page. It inherits from *TemplateControl*, which is the base abstract class that provides a base set of functionality to both *Page* and *UserControl*. (This set of relationships is another element that marks the structural affinity between Web pages and user controls.)

```
public class UserControl : TemplateControl
```

The *UserControl* class implements a bunch of internal interfaces, the most important of which is *INamingContainer*. This interface marks a control as a naming container for all its contained controls, meaning that the actual ID of contained controls will be prefixed with the ID of the parent.

UserControl adds to the programming interface of the *Control* class a few methods, such as *LoadControl*, *LoadTemplate*, and *ParseControl*. The first two methods load a user control and a template, respectively, from an external *.ascx* file. The *ParseControl* method parses an input string into an instance of a control or user control as appropriate.

Base Properties of User Controls

Table 12-1 lists the properties of the *UserControl* class, but it doesn't include those inherited from *TemplateControl*.

Table 12-1 Properties of the *UserControl* Class

Property	Description
Application	Gets the *HttpApplicationState* object for the current request.
Attributes	Gets the collection of all attributes declared in the user control tag.
Cache	Gets the *Cache* object associated with the current application.
CachePolicy	Gets the *ControlCachePolicy* object that defines the cache parameters for the control. The property is read-only, but parameters can be configured programmatically by setting properties on the referenced *ControlCachePolicy* object. *Not available in ASP.NET 1.x.*
IsPostBack	Determines whether the user control is being loaded for the first time or in response to a postback event.
Request	Gets the *HttpRequest* object for the current request.
Response	Gets the *HttpResponse* object for the current request.
Server	Gets the *HttpServerUtility* object for the current request.
Session	Gets the *HttpSessionState* object for the current request.
Trace	Gets the *TraceContext* object for the current request.

As you can see, the class provides properties to access all the intrinsic objects of an ASP.NET application plus the *IsPostBack* value, which is critical information to all ASP.NET components. A user control features all the various flavors of ID properties (*ID*, *ClientID*, and *UniqueID*) and acts as a naming container for all of its child controls. As usual, the list of child controls is accessible via the *Controls* collection.

Base Methods of User Controls

The *UserControl* class features only a few methods in addition to those inherited from base classes. Inherited methods include commonly used functions such as *DataBind*, *FindControl*, and *LoadTemplate*. The methods of the *UserControl* class appear in Table 12-2.

Table 12-2 Methods of the *UserControl* Class

Property	Description
DesignerInitialize	Performs any initialization steps on the user control that are required by rapid application development (RAD) designers.
InitializeAsUserControl	Completes the initialization of the *UserControl* object that has been created declaratively.
MapPath	Returns the physical file path that corresponds to the given virtual path. Note that the method maps the path from the *.ascx* file's location, not the page's location.

The *DesignerInitialize* and the *InitializeAsUserControl* methods are rarely used in normal pages and are there mostly for internal use by the .NET Framework. In particular, the *InitializeAsUserControl* method ensures that the user control is initialized properly. The most important thing it does is hook up automatic event handlers. In other words, this method ensures methods named *Page_Load* or *Page_Init*, if present, are invoked during the control's *Load* and *Init* events. Table 12-3 shows the list of automatic event handlers that are supported.

Table 12-3 Automatic Event Handlers Hooked by the *UserControl* Class

Event Handler	Description
OnTransactionAbort, *Page_AbortTransaction*	Event *AbortTransaction*, occurs when a user aborts a transaction.
OnTransactionCommit, *Page_CommitTransaction*	Event *CommitTransaction*, occurs when a user commits a transaction in a transacted page.
Page_DataBinding	Event *DataBinding*, occurs when the control binds to a data source.
Page_Error	Event *Error*, occurs when an unhandled exception is thrown.
Page_PreInit	Event *PreInit*, occurs before the control is initialized. *Not available in ASP.NET 1.x.*
Page_Init	Event *Init*, occurs when the control is initialized.
Page_InitComplete	Event *InitComplete*, occurs after the control has been fully initialized. *Not available in ASP.NET 1.x.*
Page_PreLoad	Event *PreLoad*, occurs before the control is loaded into the page. *Not available in ASP.NET 1.x.*
Page_Load	Event *Load*, occurs when the control is loaded into the page.
Page_LoadComplete	Event *LoadComplete*, occurs when the control has been fully loaded into the page. *Not available in ASP.NET 1.x.*
Page_PreRender	Event *PreRender*, occurs when the control enters the pre-rendering stage.
Page_PreRenderComplete	Event *PreRenderComplete*, occurs when the control has finished with the pre-rendering stage and is about to render the contents.
Page_SaveStateComplete	Event *SaveStateComplete*, occurs when the control finished saving its view state.
Page_Unload	Event *Unload*, occurs when the control is going to be unloaded from memory.

The events listed in this table are also the events supported by all user controls. It is important to note that the preceding events are raised as the host page goes through its life cycle. As discussed in Chapter 1, some page operations originate events on hosted controls and user controls. A user control recognizes the automatic event handlers listed in the table.

Converting Pages into User Controls

User controls and pages have so much in common that transforming each into the other is no big deal. However, in most cases, you need to convert a page into a user control. As we'll see in a moment, it's a simple operation that takes only a few steps.

To start, make sure the user control does not contain any of the following tags: *<html>*, *<body>*, or *<form>*. Eliminating such tags will help to avoid conflicts because the layout of the control will be merged with the layout of the hosting page and tags such as *<html>* and *<body>* must be unique in the final page. As for the *<form>* tag, you can have as many form elements as needed, but only one can be marked with the *runat* attribute. So remove from the original page any reference you might have to a *<form runat="server">* element. If you have HTML forms, on the other hand, there is no need to remove them. (An HTML form is the *<form>* tag without the *runat* attribute.)

Once any offending HTML tags have been removed, rename the file with an *.ascx* extension. This is the key that will enable special treatment of the file. Furthermore, if the page you're converting contains a *@Page* directive, change it to a *@Control* directive.

The *@Control* Directive

The *@Control* and *@Page* directives share several attributes. The list of attributes supported by user controls is shown in Table 12-4.

Table 12-4   Attributes of the *@Control* Directive

Attribute	Description
AutoEventWireup	Indicates whether the control's events are automatically bound to methods with a particular name. The default is *true*.
ClassName	Indicates an alias for the name of the class that will be created to render the user control. This value can be any valid class name but should not include a namespace.
CodeBehind	Included only for compatibility with ASP.NET 1.x. It indicates the name of the compiled file that contains the class associated with the control.
CodeFile	In ASP.NET 2.0, it indicates the name of the compiled file that contains the class associated with the control. *Not available in ASP.NET 1.x.*
CodeFileBaseClass	Indicates an optional base class for the code-behind class of a control. If used, the *CodeFile* attribute must be set, too. *Not available in ASP.NET 1.x.*

Table 12-4   Attributes of the @*Control* Directive

Attribute	Description
CompilationMode	Indicates whether the control should be compiled. *Not available in ASP.NET 1.x.*
CompilerOptions	A sequence of compiler command-line switches used to compile the control's class.
Debug	Indicates whether the control should be compiled with debug symbols. If *true*, the source code of the class is not deleted and can be retrieved as discussed in Chapter 1.
Description	Provides a text description of the control.
EnableTheming	Indicates whether themes are used on the control. *Not available in ASP.NET 1.x.*
EnableViewState	Indicates whether view state for the user control is maintained across page requests. The default is *true*.
Explicit	Determines whether the page is compiled using the Visual Basic *Option Explicit* mode. Ignored by languages other than Visual Basic .NET. *False* by default.
Inherits	Defines a code-behind class for the user control to inherit. The class can be any class derived from *UserControl*.
Language	Specifies the language used throughout the control.
Strict	Determines whether the page is compiled using the Visual Basic *Option Strict* mode. It's ignored by languages other than Visual Basic .NET. *False* by default.
Src	Specifies the source file name of the code-behind class to dynamically compile when the user control is requested.
TargetSchema	Specifies the name of a schema that validates content on the control. This serves only a descriptive purpose; the attribute is ignored by the parser. *Not available in ASP.NET 1.x.*
WarningLevel	Indicates the compiler warning level at which you want the compiler to abort compilation for the user control.

From within a control, you cannot set any property that affects the overall behavior of the page. For example, you cannot enable or disable tracing, nor can you enable or disable session-state management. You can only change properties that affect the operation of the control itself.

Note   The @*Control* directive makes it possible to use different languages for the user control and the page. For example, you can use Visual Basic .NET in the user control and C# in the calling page. The interaction between the two occurs at the level of compiled classes and therefore uses the common intermediate language (IL).

Finally, note that giving a user control an alias using the *ClassName* attribute is not strictly necessary but is highly recommended. The *ClassName* attribute allows the user control to be strongly typed when it is added to a container programmatically.

Fragment Output Caching

User controls also provide an optimized version of a performance-related feature specific to Web Forms pages—output caching. *Output caching* is an ASP.NET system feature that caches the response of a page so that subsequent requests to the same URL can be satisfied without executing the page but simply by returning the cached output. By the way, note that IIS 6.0 supports this feature at the Web-server level, thus supporting all types of Web applications. For more information, refer to Chapter 14 of *Programming Microsoft ASP.NET 2.0: Core Reference* (Microsoft Press 2005).

Output caching can take place at two levels—for the entire page or for a portion of a page. User controls are the smallest unit of a page whose output is cacheable. To make the entire page cacheable, you place an *@OutputCache* directive within the *.aspx* file. As a result, the whole output of the page will be cached according to the parameters you specify. To cache only a portion of the page, you first isolate that portion in a user control and then declare the *@OutputCache* directive in the *.ascx* file.

When caching the output of a user control, you must set at least a couple of attributes—*Duration* and *VaryByParam*. The following code snippet caches the output of the user control for 60 seconds:

```
<% @OutputCache Duration="60" VaryByParam="None" %>
```

Page and control output caching is smart enough to let you save distinct output, even output based on the parameters in a *GET* query string.

Important Custom controls and user controls are two different and distinct ways to create user-defined controls for ASP.NET applications. Both have pros and cons, and each have advantages in particular scenarios. User controls are ideal if you have to encapsulate a rich and complex user interface and keep it separate from the page. A user control can also be separated into two files—the *.ascx* file representing the layout, and the file with the code (either a source file or an assembly).

Custom controls are implemented in an assembly and expose both the user interface and the object model programmatically. Unlike user controls, custom controls better leverage the power of object-oriented programming (OOP) in the sense that they can be built from existing classes and new classes can be derived from them. Although user controls could technically be derived from existing controls, the presence of a distinct layout file makes inheritance a bit more problematic.

Developing User Controls

The structure of a user control is not much different than that of a regular Web page. It is composed of a directive section, inline code, and the graphical layout of the control. The inline code—that is, the *<script runat="server">* block—can be omitted if you use a code-behind file. Although nothing prevents you from writing user-interface-less user controls, the user interface is the most important part of the control and typically the most compelling reason for writing one. The typical structure of an *.ascx* file is shown as follows:

```
<%@ Control Language="C#" %>
<script runat="server">

    // Insert user control code here
    // or in a code file

</script>
<!-- Insert content here -->
```

Many Web sites have pieces of user interface that must be repeated in a large number of pages. Typical examples are headers and footers, login and search forms, and menus and panels. A login form doesn't need a really complex object model and often doesn't need one at all. In other situations, you need to add a layer of logic on top of the control and make it programmable from within the host page. To start out with user controls, let's see how to build a *Tab-Strip* control with a relatively simple object model.

Building a *TabStrip* User Control

A typical *TabStrip* control is made of a series of buttons laid out in a single row. When users click on a tab, the control selects the particular tab and fires an event to the host page. The page will in turn update and refresh its own user interface. Figure 12-1 shows the final form.

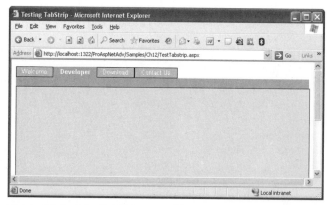

Figure 12-1   The *TabStrip* control in action within a sample page.

The user interface of the control is generated using a *Repeater* control and consists of a single-row HTML table in which each cell contains a button. Just below the table, an empty, tiny panel separates the tab strip from the rest of the page. The control acts as a simple selector and doesn't include any smart code to process the click event. Whenever the user clicks on any of the tabs, a postback event is generated back to the page. The page is also responsible for creating the tabs to display. In this example, we represent a tab with a simple string. In real-world scenarios, you might want to use an ad hoc class to describe a tab and include a key value, a ToolTip, a Boolean state (enabled/disabled), or maybe a URL.

```
<%@ Control Language="C#" CodeFile="Tabstrip.ascx.cs" %>
<asp:Repeater runat="server" id="__theTabStrip">
    <headertemplate>
        <table cellpadding="0" cellspacing="0" border="0" ><tr>
    </headertemplate>

    <itemtemplate>
        <td>
            <asp:button runat="server" id="__theTab"
                text='<%# Container.DataItem %>' />
        </td>
    </itemtemplate>

    <footertemplate>
        </tr></table>
    </footertemplate>
</asp:Repeater>
<asp:panel runat="server" id="__theSep" width="100%" backcolor="gray" />
```

The code file class includes a few properties and methods as shown in the following code:

```
public ArrayList Tabs = new ArrayList();
protected void Page_Load(object sender, EventArgs e)
{
    if (!IsPostBack)
        BindData();
}
private void BindData()
{
    __theTabStrip.DataSource = Tabs;
    __theTabStrip.DataBind();
}
```

The *Tabs* array contains the string to display as the caption of each tab. The object is initialized together with the user control and consumed during the rendering phase of the control. The caller page typically populates the *Tabs* collection in its *Page_Load* event.

```
protected void Page_Load(object sender, EventArgs e)
{
    menu.Tabs.Add("Welcome");
    menu.Tabs.Add("Developer");
    menu.Tabs.Add("Download");
    menu.Tabs.Add("Contact Us");
}
```

Before taking the *TabStrip* user control to the next level, let's see what's needed to include a user control in a Web page.

Including a User Control in a Page

A user control is inserted in a Web page using a custom tag marked with the *runat* attribute. The control instance has an ID and can be programmed using that name. The server tag is divided in two parts—a tag prefix and a tag name. In the following code snippet, the tag prefix is *expo* and the tag name is *tabstrip*. (Note that for user controls, the tag name doesn't have to match the name of the user control class.)

```
<expo:tabstrip runat="server" id="menu" />
```

If you give the control the *asp* prefix, or no prefix at all, the ASP.NET runtime will look for the needed class only in the *system.web* assembly. Because the user control is not implemented there, an exception is thrown. How do you register a tag name and prefix for a user control? And how do you bind both with an *.ascx* file?

The *@Register* Directive

The *@Register* directive associates aliases with namespaces and class names to provide a concise notation to reference custom and user controls within Web pages. Table 12-5 details the attributes of the directive.

Table 12-5   Attributes of the *@Register* Directive

Attribute	Description
Assembly	The assembly in which the namespace associated with the tag prefix resides. The assembly name does not include a file extension.
Namespace	The namespace to associate with the tag prefix.
Src	The relative or absolute location of the user control file to associate with the tag prefix and name. The file name must include the *.ascx* extension.
TagName	A tag name to alias the custom or user control. It is *tabstrip* in the code snippet just shown, and it can be set to an arbitrary string.
TagPrefix	A tag prefix to alias the namespace of the control, if any. It is *expo* in the code snippet above, and it can be set to an arbitrary string.

You use the *@Register* directive in one of two ways. The first way is to register a custom control—that is, a server control that you write as a class, as we'll see in the next two chapters. In this case, you use the following syntax:

```
<%@ Register tagprefix="..." namespace="..." assembly="..." %>
```

The second way is to register a user control by using the following syntax:

```
<%@ Register tagprefix="..." tagname="..." src="..." %>
```

The tag prefix is a custom string that points to a namespace and subsequently the assembly in which the code for the control is located. For user controls, the namespace defaults to *ASP* and the class name is the value of the control's *ClassName* attribute, if any. If the *ClassName* attribute is omitted, the class name defaults to the name of the control file with the dot (.) replaced with an underscore character (_). For example, it is *ASP.TabStrip* if you set *ClassName* to *TabStrip*; it is *ASP.tabstrip_ascx* if you miss setting the *ClassName* attribute in the *tabstrip.ascx* user control file.

The assembly is dynamically created the first time the ASP.NET runtime accesses the resource. The tag name is any unique name you use to refer to the user control within a client page. Different pages can use different tag names for the same user control.

For a custom control, you indicate the namespace and assembly and specify any namespace prefix you like better. The tag name, on the other hand, is fixed and must match the custom control class name.

Setting Up a User Control

Although absolute path names can be used to register a user control, you should always use relative names. However, you should be aware that any code within a user control is always executed taking the URL of the control as the base URL. This means that if the user control needs to access an image in the application's Images folder, you can't just use a relative path like the following one:

```
<img src="images/logo.gif" />
```

To address the right location, you could either move one or more folders back or, better yet, indicate a relative path that begins from the root. In the former case, you use .. to move one level up in the virtual Web space; in the latter case, you use the tilde (~) character to indirectly refer to the root directory of the application.

```
<img src="~/images/logo.gif" />
```

To register the *TabStrip* control, you use the following registration directive:

```
<%@ Register TagPrefix="expo" TagName="TabStrip" Src="tabstrip.ascx" %>
```

An instance of the user control is created upon page loading. Just as for Web pages, a class that represents the control is created on the fly and cached in the ASP.NET temporary folders. Any updates to the source code of the *.ascx* file (or the code-behind class) are immediately detected and invalidate the existing assembly. In no case do you need to compile the user control to make it available to the page. (To sum it up, there's just one case in which you need to compile it first—when the control is included in code-behind pages. I'll say more about this later in the chapter in the section "Getting Serious About User Controls.")

Registering Controls in the *web.config* File

In ASP.NET 1.x, you can register controls only on a per-page basis. In ASP.NET 2.0, you can also register user and custom controls for all pages in an application. You do this by adding a *<controls>* section to the *web.config* file at any possible level where you can place this file—site level, application level, or child folders.

```
<controls>
    <add tagPrefix="expo" tagName="Tabstrip" src="tabstrip.ascx" />
</controls>
```

Note that the *<controls>* section is a child of the *<pages>* section. As we saw in Chapter 3, the *<pages>* section defines page-specific configuration settings globally, including registered user and custom controls and namespaces to import.

Building a User-Control Object Model

For a user control, as well as for Web pages, every property or method that is marked as public is externally callable and, as such, part of the control's object model. The following code snippet declares a couple of read/write properties that represent the background and foreground color of the unselected tabs:

```
public Color BackColor
{
    get
    {
        object o = ViewState["BackColor"];
        if (o == null)
            return Color.Silver;
        return (Color)o;
    }
    set { ViewState["BackColor"] = value; }
}
public Color ForeColor
{
    get
    {
        object o = ViewState["ForeColor"];
        if (o == null)
            return Color.White;
        return (Color)o;
    }
    set { ViewState["ForeColor"] = value; }
}
```

The qualifier *public* is essential to make the property (or the method) externally visible and callable—for example, from within a host page. Note the use of the *ViewState* collection as the store for the value of the properties.

> **Note**   For a .NET Framework class, a *property* is a name by means of which a value is retrieved and/or set. The property is an abstraction for a pair of optional *get* and *set* methods. If the property references a value (and most of the time, it does just that), the value must be stored somewhere. Unlike a *field*, a *property* is not a variable per se and requires a helper data structure to store its referenced value. You commonly use a private field to store the value of a property. However, when the property is defined on a server or Web user control, a local variable is no longer sufficient. To make sure the value referenced by a property can be retrieved when the page posts back, you should store it in a persistent container such as *Cache*, *Session*, or the control's *ViewState* collection. The *ViewState* collection is appropriate for control properties because they don't charge the Web server memory.

If you're simply exposing at the user-control level the property of an embedded control—say, the *Text* property of a child *Button*—you don't need to resort to the view state.

```
public string Caption
{
    get { return TextBox1.Text; }
    set { TextBox1.Text = value; }
}
```

In this case, in fact, the embedded control takes care of the variable persistence. In the preceding code, the *Caption* name is used to reference the *Text* property of the *TextBox1* control from the host environment of the user control. Child controls of a Web user control are protected from access from outside the Web user control itself. By leveraging this approach, you can expose selected bits and pieces of the user control's internal structure to callers.

Adding Properties

At a minimum, the *TabStrip* control should expose properties to let you add tabs and track the current index. The *Tabs* collection shown earlier serves just this purpose. The *CurrentTabIndex* property, shown in the following code snippet, tracks the index of the currently selected tab:

```
public int CurrentTabIndex
{
    get
    {
        object o = ViewState["CurrentTabIndex"];
        if (o == null)
            return 0;
        return (int) o;
    }
}
```

When defining a property, you can indicate a *get* accessor, *set* mutator, or both. A *get* accessor (also known as the property *getter*) is a special subroutine that retrieves and returns the value of the property. Likewise, the *set* mutator (also known as the property *setter*) is a method that receives and sets the value of the property. The value passed to the property setter is exactly the value the caller assigned to the property. The lack of an accessor/mutator automatically disables the corresponding function, thus making the property read-only (no *set* mutator) or write-only (no *get* accessor). In the preceding code, for example, the *CurrentTabIndex* property is read-only.

> **Important**   Note the pattern used to define the *getter* of the *CurrentTabIndex* property. The value is first retrieved and then checked for nullness. If null, the default value for the property is returned. If not null, the object representing the value is cast to the expected type. This pattern is commonly used by all built-in ASP.NET controls.

In addition to the aforementioned *BackColor* and *ForeColor* properties, the *TabStrip* user control should also feature *SelectedBackColor* and *SelectedForeColor* properties with a nearly identical implementation.

User control properties can be set both declaratively and programmatically. If you opt for a declarative approach, the name of the property is used as a tag attribute.

```
<expo:tabstrip runat="server" id="menu" selectedbackcolor="cyan" />
```

In this case, you can use only strings to specify the value. To set the background color, you use a string that represents the desired color. ASP.NET will attempt to convert the assigned string into a valid value of the expected type. On the other hand, if you set a property programmatically, you must pass values of the correct type.

```
void Page_Load(object sender, EventArgs e)
{
    // Since the Tabs collection is not stored in the view state,
    // you must populate it each time the page posts back. This code
    // must be placed outside the IsPostBack branch.
    menu.Tabs.Add("Welcome");
    menu.Tabs.Add("Developer");
    menu.Tabs.Add("Download");
    menu.Tabs.Add("Contact Us");

    if (!IsPostBack)
    {
        // Do here all the things that need to be done only the
        // first time the control is loaded in the page.
        // For example, select here the tab to be displayed
        // by default.
        :
    }
```

```
    // Set colors programmatically
    menu.SelectedBackColor = Color.Green;
    menu.SelectedForeColor = Color.White;
    menu.BackColor = Color.LightGray;
    menu.ForeColor = Color.Black;
}
```

The instance of the user control is identified using the ID of the control. If you're handling properties that do not rely on the view state, you should configure them each time the page posts back, without distinguishing between the first load and postbacks.

The selected tab is rendered with different colors, which are applied through data-bound expressions, as shown here. (We covered data-bound expressions in Chapter 5.)

```
<itemtemplate>
    <td>
        <asp:button runat="server" id="__theTab"
            BorderWidth="1px"
            BorderStyle="solid"
            BorderColor='<%# GetBorderColor(Container) %>'
            text='<%# Container.DataItem %>'
            font-bold='<%# (Container.ItemIndex == CurrentTabIndex) %>'
            backcolor='<%# GetBackColor(Container) %>'
            forecolor='<%# GetForeColor(Container) %>' />
    </td>
</itemtemplate>
```

The *SetXXX* functions are internal members of the *TabStrip* that compare the current tab index with the index of the item being created and decide which color to apply.

```
protected Color GetBackColor(object elem)
{
    RepeaterItem item = (RepeaterItem)elem;
    if (item.ItemIndex == CurrentTabIndex)
        return SelectedBackColor;
    return BackColor;
}
protected Color GetForeColor(object elem)
{
    RepeaterItem item = (RepeaterItem)elem;
    if (item.ItemIndex == CurrentTabIndex)
        return SelectedForeColor;
    return ForeColor;
}
protected Color GetBorderColor(object elem)
{
    RepeaterItem item = (RepeaterItem)elem;
    if (item.ItemIndex == CurrentTabIndex)
        return SelectedBackColor;
    return Color.Black;
}
```

> **Note** All the properties in the *TabStrip* user control except *Tabs* use accessors/mutators and persist their value to the control's view state. To be precise, the *Tabs* property doesn't have an accessor/mutator pair because it is actually implemented as a field. The point is that in this way, the contents of the *Tabs* collection are lost and must be rebuilt whenever the page is served—be it a postback or the first request. Note that nothing would prevent you from storing the *Tabs* collections in the view state as you do with other properties. You can store any object you want in the view state as long as it is serializable or provides a state manager behavior. (More on state managers can be found in the next chapter.) The real point here is another—should you do this? If you can keep the collection out of the view state, you have in general shorter download and upload times for the page that hosts the control. Consider also that several built-in controls use and persist collections. By not saving properties to the view state, you're forcing developers to remember to comply with this behavior. Most people just expect controls to be self-contained and persistable. Whatever your final decision is, you should document it very well.
>
> Built-in controls set the serialization code in the collection class itself and don't delegate the serialization to the view state infrastructure. This trick guarantees a more compact view state. I'll return to this point in Chapter 13 and Chapter 14 while discussing custom server controls.

Adding Methods

The next step in the process of building a functional and reusable *TabStrip* control is adding a method to programmatically select a particular tab. So far, in fact, the selection can be triggered only by the user when she clicks on a button. The *Select* method we'll add will do that programmatically. Here is the prototype of the *Select* method:

```
public void Select(int index)
```

The method takes an integer argument, which is the 0-based index of the tab to select. Internally, it sets the current tab index and rebinds the data.

```
public void Select(int index)
{
    // Ensure the index is a valid value, otherwise select the first
    if (index <0 || index >Tabs.Count)
        index = 0;

    // Updates the current index. Must write to the view state
    // because the CurrentTabIndex property is read-only
    ViewState["CurrentTabIndex"] = index;

    // Ensure the bottom panel is of the selected color
    __theSep.BackColor = SelectedBackColor;

    // Refresh the user interface
    BindData();
}
```

A method on a user control is simply a public method defined either as inline code or in the code-behind class. Note that the *Select* method can't set the current tab index using the public property *CurrentTabIndex*. The reason is that the *CurrentTabIndex* property is marked as read-only (that is, it lacks a *set* mutator), and subsequently no code within the class can set it explicitly. The workaround is to directly access the *ViewState*, where the values of the property are actually stored.

The sample page can now offer some user interface elements to let users select tabs programmatically. The following code snippet shows a text box in which you can type the index of the tab to select and a link button to execute the code:

```
<asp:textbox runat="server" id="tabIndex" />
<asp:linkbutton runat="server" text="Select tab" onclick="OnSelectTab" />
```

The *OnSelectTab* event handler simply calls the *Select* method on the user control, as Figure 12-2 demonstrates.

```
void OnSelectTab(object sender, EventArgs e)
{
    int index = -1;
    Int32.TryParse(tabIndex.Text, out index);
    menu.Select(index);
}
```

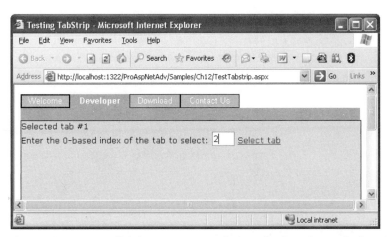

Figure 12-2   A new link button commands the selection of a particular tab.

The *Select* method acts as the *set* mutator of the *CurrentTabIndex* property. If you want to read the index of the current tab, you use the property; if you want to programmatically set a particular tab, you use the method.

Handling User-Control Events

So far, we've built a user control that displays its own user interface and allows users to select tabs. For a control such as the *TabStrip*, though, a key feature has not been implemented yet. How can a page that hosts the control be notified of a user's tab clicks? A *TabStrip* makes sense only if the page can detect the fact that a tab was clicked and properly refresh to activate the tab's contents. For example, the page could generate different content according to the selected tab; alternatively, it can redirect the user to a child page within a frame or simply jump to a new URL. To let the page know about the selection, we must add an event to the user control.

Adding the *SelectionChanged* Event

Within the *TabStrip* control, the selection changes whenever the user clicks on the buttons or when the page calls the *Select* method. Let's define an event named *SelectionChanged* to handle these situations.

```
public event SelectionChangedEventHandler SelectionChanged;
```

An event is a special property bound to a delegate. A delegate is a reference to a method signature. An instance of a delegate is actually a pointer to a function with a well-known signature so that the event invocations are type safe. (Without this, event invocations, or "callbacks," could cause crashes if they received parameters they didn't expect or didn't receive parameters they required.) The .NET Framework provides a general-purpose delegate for event handlers—the *EventHandler* class. Here is the prototype of such event handlers:

```
public delegate void EventHandler(object sender, EventArgs e);
```

The *EventHandler* delegate represents all methods that take an *object* and an *EventArgs* argument and return *void*. This predefined delegate is good as long as you don't need to pass custom data back to the caller. You should use it only for events that work as simple notifications of some server-side event.

In this case, however, we need to pass at least the index of the selected tab back to the server for processing. Therefore, the *EventHandler* delegate doesn't suit our needs—it's not a simple notification because we're passing data back. No problem. We'll simply define a custom delegate and a custom event data structure that will allow us to pass the selected tab index into the event handler for processing.

```
public delegate void SelectionChangedEventHandler(
    object sender, SelectionChangedEventArgs e);
```

A custom delegate for the event differs from *EventHandler* because a custom data structure will be used to carry event arguments. The common naming convention for events entails using the name of the event (*SelectionChanged* in this case) to prefix both the delegate and the data structure name.

```
public class SelectionChangedEventArgs : EventArgs
{
    public int SelectedIndex // 0-based index of the selected tab
}
```

The *SelectionChangedEventArgs* structure inherits from *EventArgs* and adds an integer property that represents the 0-based index of the selected tab. An instance of this data structure will be created and initialized when the event occurs within the user control.

Thanks to the introduction of generic types in the .NET Framework 2.0, in ASP.NET 2.0 you can save yourself the definition of a delegate for custom events. You can resort to the generic version of the *EventHandler* type—*EventHandler<T>*.

```
public event EventHandler<SelectionChangedEventArgs> SelectionChanged;
```

The generic type is the type of the second parameter taken by the event handler. In ASP.NET 2.0, the two definitions for events are absolutely equivalent. I find the one based on generics to be cleaner.

Firing a Custom Event

To better handle custom events, you might want to define a helper routine like the one shown at the end of this paragraph. The name you choose for this routine is unimportant. Likewise, the method qualifiers (*protected*, *virtual*) are subject to your personal preferences and object-oriented design considerations. However, declaring such a helper routine as protected and overrideable is considered a best programming practice that is widely employed in the .NET Framework itself. My suggestion is that either you declare it as protected and virtual, following the model used by the .NET Framework itself, or that you don't declare it at all.

```
// Helper function that fires the event by executing user-defined code
protected virtual void OnSelectionChanged(SelectionChangedEventArgs e)
{
    // SelectionChanged is the event property. Check if the user defined it
    if (SelectionChanged != null)
        SelectionChanged(this, e);
}
```

The routine doesn't do much—it just ensures the event property is not null and makes the call. However, it adds an extra layer of code that, if made overrideable, can help derived classes to customize the behavior more easily and effectively.

> **Note**   The helper function simply ensures that any code for the event is defined and then raises the event. In C#, you typically create this function to better encapsulate the event call. You don't strictly need to create such a helper function in Visual Basic .NET, as the language natively provides you with the *RaiseEvent* statement that employs the same test and raises the event. However, it is important to note that an *OnEventName* method flagged to be protected and overrideable makes your code more flexible; so you might want to add it regardless of the language you're using.

At this point, firing the event becomes simply a matter of initializing the data structure and calling the helper function. The event is fired by the *Select* method.

```
public void Select(int index)
{
    // Ensure the index is a valid value
    if (index <0 || index >Tabs.Count)
        index = 0;
```

```
    // Updates the current index. Must write to the view state
    // because the CurrentTabIndex property is read-only
    ViewState["CurrentTabIndex"] = index;

    // Ensure the bottom panel is of the selected color
    _theSep.BackColor = SelectedBackColor;

    // Refresh the UI
    BindData();

    // Fire the event to the client
    SelectionChangedEventArgs ev = new SelectionChangedEventArgs();
    ev.SelectedIndex CurrentTabIndex;
    OnSelectionChanged(ev);
}
```

When the user clicks on the tabs, the underlying *Repeater* control that we used to create the control's user interface fires an *ItemCommand* event. The embedded handler for the *Item-Command* event just forwards a call to *Select*.

```
private void ItemCommand(object sender, RepeaterCommandEventArgs e)
{
    // Select the tab that corresponds to the clicked button
    Select(e.Item.ItemIndex);
}
```

Now that the user control fires an event, let's see what's needed on the enclosing page to detect and handle it.

Handling a Custom Event

A .NET component that wants to sink events emitted by controls must write a handler whose prototype matches that of the event delegate. How you bind the handler with the event on a particular instance of the component is language specific. For example, in C#, you create a new instance of the event handler class and add it to the component's event property.

```
// YourHandler is the actual name of the handler in your code
menu.SelectionChanged += new SelectionChangedEventHandler(YourHandler);
```

In Visual Basic .NET, you can use the *AddHandler* keyword as shown here:

```
' YourHandler is the actual name of the handler in your code
AddHandler menu.SelectionChanged, AddressOf YourHandler
```

This technique is not always necessary in ASP.NET applications. In ASP.NET, in fact, you can also register event handlers declaratively using the *OnXXX* attribute, where *XXX* stands for the actual name of the event property.

```
<expo:TabStrip runat="server" id="menu"
    SelectedBackColor="cyan"
    OnSelectionChanged="SelectionChanged" />
```

Here is the *SelectionChanged* event handler:

```
void SelectionChanged(object sender, SelectionChangedEventArgs e)
{
    msg.Text = "Selected tab #" + e.Position.ToString();
}
```

> **Note**   In ASP.NET 2.0, the new *MultiView* control can be used to implement a custom *Tab-Strip* control. The *MultiView* control allows you to specify any number of views, where a view is an ASP.NET template. The *MultiView* control natively provides a settable index property and automatically switches the selected template into view. The *MultiView* control, though, doesn't provide a user interface to list available views and let users select one. You could rewrite this *TabStrip* control to employ a *MultiView* control internally.

Getting Serious About User Controls

Most custom and Web user controls need data binding to operate in the real world. A data-bound version of the *TabStrip* user control would use the results of a SQL query to automatically generate the tabs.

Building Data-Bound User Controls

In most cases, a data-bound user control is not really different than a data-free control. The only relevant difference is that a data-bound control features a few properties that bind it to an *IEnumerable*-based data source object—mostly, but not necessarily, an ADO.NET object. Let's build a variation of *TabStrip* that creates tabs from a data source. I'll call the new Web user control *ButtonList*.

The *ButtonList* User Control

The layout of the *ButtonList* control is fairly simple and contains a *Repeater* control to enumerate all the bound items and create a push button for each. In addition, a thin one-row table is placed below the *Repeater* for a better graphical effect.

```
<%@ Control Language="C#" AutoEventWireup="true"
        CodeFile="ButtonList.ascx.cs" Inherits="ButtonList" %>

<asp:repeater runat="server" id="__theMenu">
    <HeaderTemplate>
        <table border="0" cellspacing="0" cellpadding="0"><tr>
    </HeaderTemplate>

    <ItemTemplate>
        <td valign="bottom">
            <asp:button runat="server" id="TheButton"
                style="border:solid 1px gray" />
        </td>
    </ItemTemplate>
```

```
<FooterTemplate>
    </tr></table>
  </FooterTemplate>
</asp:repeater>
<asp:panel runat="server" id="__theSep" width="100%" />
```

The .ascx file contains only the skeleton of the control's user interface. As you can see, there's no data-binding expression and no event handlers.

The Programming Interface of the *ButtonList* Control

The *ButtonList* control exposes a few properties, as listed in Table 12-6. These properties are primarily related to the data-binding mechanism, which leverages the data binding of the underlying *Repeater* control.

Table 12-6   Properties of the *ButtonList* Control

Property	Description
ButtonWidth	Integer that indicates the width in pixels of the buttons
CurrentButtonIndex	Gets the 0-based index of the currently selected button
DataSource	Indicates the data source used to populate the control
DataTextField	Indicates the name of the data source column used to render the caption of the buttons
DataValueField	Indicates the name of the data-source column used to express the command associated with the buttons

The *DataSource* property plays the same role as in other data-bound controls. It provides a collection of data items the control will use to populate its own user interface. A couple of columns from this data source are used to render the caption and the command name of each button. The command name of a *Button* object is a string that uniquely identifies that button and is used to detect events. When binding data to this control, you should set *DataValueField* to a column with unique values. Note that the value will be converted into a string, so be sure you choose a column that maintains unique values after being converted into a string. All the properties except *DataSource* are cached in the view state.

The contents of the *DataSource* are cached internally in the ASP.NET *Cache* object. This shouldn't be a big issue because the number of records bound to the *ButtonList* user control is not expected to be high.

```
public object DataSource
{
    get
    {
        object o = Cache[ID];
        if (o == null)
        {
            RefreshDataEventArgs ev = new RefreshDataEventArgs();
            OnRefreshData(ev);
```

```
        o = ev.DataSource;
      }
      return o;
    }
    set { Cache[ID] = value; }
}
```

The data source is cached in a slot with a unique name—the ID of the user control. This guarantees that multiple instances of the user control in the same page work correctly and without conflicts.

Generally, data-bound ASP.NET server controls don't cache their data source but force host pages to bind fresh data every time a postback event occurs that makes it necessary. In this case, I decided to make the user control a bit smarter and had it autonomously cache the data source. However, data stored in the *Cache* (as well as in the session state) is not guaranteed to remain valid and available all the time—memory constraints or application recycles can, in fact, destroy it. For this reason, the *DataSource* getter checks the data slot for nullness, and if it finds the data is not there, it raises an event to the host page asking for fresh data.

```
public event EventHandler<RefreshDataEventArgs> RefreshData;
```

The *RefreshDataEventArgs* structure is defined as follows:

```
public class RefreshDataEventArgs : EventArgs
{
    public object DataSource;
}
```

As mentioned, all the other properties are cached in the control's view state, which, in turn, is flushed in the page's view state. Here's the implementation of a sample property— *DataTextField*:

```
public string DataTextField
{
    get
    {
        object o = ViewState["DataTextField"];
        if (o == null)
            return String.Empty;
        return (string) o;
    }
    set { ViewState["DataTextField"] = value; }
}
```

The view state is specific to the individual control, so there's no need to devise a scheme for unique names. When writing a *get* accessor for a property, you should always make sure that the value you read is not null (that is, the value was not previously stored in the view state).

The overall data-binding mechanism of the *ButtonList* control mirrors the data-binding engine of the *Repeater* control. In particular, the *BindData* method used to populate the user interface of the *ButtonList* control with data is nothing more than a wrapper.

```
private void BindData() {
    __theMenu.DataSource = DataSource;
    __theMenu.DataBind();
}
```

The *BindData* method is invoked twice—in *Page_Load* the first time the user control is set up and to update the user interface whenever a new button is clicked.

```
protected void Page_Load(object sender, EventArgs e)
{
    if (!IsPostBack)
        BindData();
}
```

The *ButtonClicked* event completes the programming interface of the control. The event fires whenever the user clicks a button. The client page receives a custom structure containing the index and the command of the button. Let's explore this aspect in more detail.

Generating the Output

When the control is initialized—that is, after the constructor is called—it hooks up its own set of events. In this case, we need to register handlers for some events fired by the embedded *Repeater* control.

```
private void HookUpEvents() {
    __theMenu.ItemCommand += new RepeaterCommandEventHandler(ItemCommand);
    __theMenu.ItemCreated += new RepeaterItemEventHandler(ItemCreated);
    __theMenu.ItemDataBound += new RepeaterItemEventHandler(ItemBound);
}
```

During the *ItemCreated* event, we take care of the appearance of each button and decide about colors, borders, and sizes. In particular, the selected button is larger than others and highlighted.

```
protected void ItemCreated(object sender, RepeaterItemEventArgs e)
{
    if (e.Item.ItemType != ListItemType.Item &&
        e.Item.ItemType != ListItemType.AlternatingItem)
        return;

    // Retrieve the item being created
    RepeaterItem item = e.Item;
    bool isSelected = IsSelectedItem(item);
    Button btn = (Button) item.FindControl("TheButton");

    // Customize the appearance
    if (isSelected) {
        btn.BackColor = SelectedBackColor;
```

```
        btn.ForeColor = SelectedForeColor;
        btn.Height = Unit.Pixel(SELECTEDBUTTONHEIGHT);
        btn.Width = Unit.Pixel(ButtonWidth*150/100);
    }
    else
    {
        btn.BackColor = BackColor;
        btn.ForeColor = ForeColor;
        btn.Height = Unit.Pixel(BUTTONHEIGHT);
        btn.Width = Unit.Pixel(ButtonWidth);
    }
}
```

Note that although the colors are not exposed as public properties, they are used as if they were. (If you want to enhance the *ButtonList* control, this feature shouldn't be too hard to add, especially in light of your previous experience with the *TabStrip* control.) Pay attention to the type of the item being created, and exit the *ItemCreated* event handler if the *Repeater* is not creating an item of type *Item* or *AlternatingItem*.

When *ItemCreated* fires, the item has not yet been bound to data. So to adjust the caption and the command name for the button, we need to wait for the *ItemDataBound* event.

```
protected void ItemBound(object sender, RepeaterItemEventArgs e)
{
    if (e.Item.ItemType != ListItemType.Item &&
        e.Item.ItemType != ListItemType.AlternatingItem)
        return;

    // Retrieve the item being bound to data
    RepeaterItem item = e.Item;
    Button btn = (Button) item.FindControl("TheButton");

    // Bind to data
    btn.Text = DataBinder.GetPropertyValue(item.DataItem,
        DataTextField).ToString();
    btn.CommandName = DataBinder.GetPropertyValue(item.DataItem,
        DataValueField).ToString();
}
```

The *DataBinder* class is used to bind properties with data. Note that the code-behind class (from which all of this code is excerpted) doesn't know anything about ADO.NET and enumerable collections of data. Instead, *DataBinder* handles this for us. We just pass in the values for *DataTextField* and *DataValueField* and retrieve the corresponding bound data.

Finally, when the user clicks one of the buttons, the *Repeater* fires the *ItemCommand* event.

```
protected void ItemCommand(object sender, RepeaterCommandEventArgs e)
{
    // Update the internal state
    CurrentButtonIndex = e.Item.ItemIndex;
```

```
    // Fire the ButtonClicked event to the client
    ButtonClickedEventArgs ev = new ButtonClickedEventArgs();
    ev.ButtonCommand = e.CommandName;
    ev.ButtonIndex = CurrentButtonIndex;
    OnButtonClicked(ev);

    // Refresh the UI
    BindData();
}
```

The *RepeaterCommandEventArgs* class contains both the index of the clicked item and its command name. These two pieces of information are packed into a *ButtonClickedEventArgs* structure and passed to the client's handler, if any. Basically, the *ButtonList* control captures an internal event and re-throws it with another name.

Setting Up a Client Page

Now that we have the *ButtonList* control ready to go, let's see how to set up a client page that intends to use the control. The following directive registers the control for use within the page:

```
<%@ Register TagPrefix="expo"
    TagName="ButtonList" Src="buttonlist.ascx" %>
```

Once more, note that you can change at will the content of the *TagName* and *TagPrefix* attributes. The following code declares a couple of *ButtonList* controls sharing the same handler for the *ButtonClicked* event:

```
<expo:buttonlist runat="server" id="initialStrip"
    onbuttonclicked="ButtonClicked" />
<expo:buttonlist runat="server" id="yearStrip"
    onbuttonclicked="ButtonClicked" />
```

The page is responsible for downloading data from a data source and binding it to the controls.

```
void Page_Load(object sender, EventArgs e)
{
    if (!IsPostBack)
    {
        BindInitials();
        BindYears();
    }
}
private void BindInitials()
{
    DataTable data = GetData_Initials();
    initialStrip.DataSource = data;
    initialStrip.DataTextField = "Initial";
    initialStrip.DataValueField = "Initial";
    initialStrip.DataBind();
}
private void BindYears()
{
    DataTable data = GetData_Years();
    yearStrip.DataSource = data;
```

```
        yearStrip.DataTextField = "Year";
        yearStrip.DataValueField = "Year";
        yearStrip.DataBind();
}
private DataTable GetData_Years()
{
        DataTable data = new DataTable();
        SqlDataAdapter adapter = new SqlDataAdapter(m_cmdYears,
                                         m_connString);

        adapter.Fill(data);
        return data;
}
private DataTable GetData_Initials()
{
        DataTable data = new DataTable();
        SqlDataAdapter adapter = new SqlDataAdapter(m_cmdInitial,
                                         m_connString);

        adapter.Fill(data);
        return data;
}
```

In the sample code we're considering, *BindInitials* and *BindYears* execute the following queries (made against the *NorthWind* database):

```
-- Get the first letter of all customer names
SELECT DISTINCT substring(companyname, 1, 1) AS Initial FROM customers

-- Get the years for which at least an order exists
SELECT DISTINCT year(orderdate) AS Year FROM orders
```

The following code shows how to initialize the *initialStrip* control. The code to initialize the *yearStrip* control is similar.

```
initialStrip.DataSource = data;
initialStrip.DataTextField = "Initial";
initialStrip.DataValueField = "Initial";
initialStrip.DataBind();
```

Figure 12-3 shows the final results.

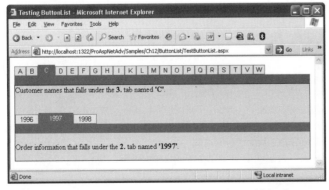

Figure 12-3   Two *ButtonList* controls in action within the same page.

The code that handles the *ButtonClicked* event for both controls is as follows:

```
// Namespace "ProAspNet.CS.Ch10" imported
void ButtonClicked(object sender, ButtonClickedEventArgs e)
{
    string t1 = "Customer names that fall under the <b>{0}.</b> " +
                "tab named <b>'{1}'</b>.";
    string t2 = "Order information that falls under the <b>{0}.</b> " +
                "tab named <b>'{1}'</b>."

    // Recognize the sender and update a label control.
    // If you use distinct event handlers, one for each ButtonList
    // control, you don't need to check for the sender here
    if (sender.Equals(initialStrip))
        msg1.Text = String.Format(t1, 1 + e.ButtonIndex, e.ButtonCommand);
    else
        msg2.Text = String.Format(t2, 1 + e.ButtonIndex, e.ButtonCommand);
}
```

Because we implemented *DataSource* through the *Cache* object, it is essential that the host page defines a proper handler for the *RefreshData* event that the user control fires when it can't find any data to bind. Here's an implementation that fits in the scenario depicted by the sample page of Figure 12-3.

```
protected void RefreshData(object sender, RefreshDataEventArgs e)
{
    if (sender.Equals(initialStrip))
        e.DataSource = GetData_Initials();
    else
        e.DataSource = GetData_Years();
}
```

Loading Controls Dynamically

Just like any other ASP.NET server controls, user controls can be created programmatically. Unlike server controls, though, you normally don't use the *new* operator to instantiate user controls but resort to the *LoadControl* method on the containing page.

The *LoadControl* Method

Defined on the *TemplateControl* base class, the *LoadControl* method loads a *Control* object from a file based on a specified virtual path.

```
Control ctl = LoadControl("ButtonList.ascx");
```

LoadControl returns a generic reference to a *Control* object; so you need to cast the reference to the appropriate strong type to be able to set individual properties and use the control at its fullest. The *ClassName* attribute in the *@Control* directive represents the only means you have to name the user control class in a way that is both easy to remember and consistent with the expected behavior.

To cast an object to a user-control strong type, you need to have a reference to the assembly that contains the compiled code of the control. This is exactly the role of the *@Reference* directive.

> **Note**   If the control supports caching, the object returned by *LoadControl* is not actually of type *Control*; rather, it is a *PartialCachingControl* object.

The *@Reference* Directive

When you create the user control programmatically, the strong type for the user control is available to the page only after you have created a reference to it. The following code creates a reference to the *ButtonList* user control created in the *buttonlist.ascx* file:

```
<%@ Reference Control="buttonlist.ascx" %>
```

The net effect of this directive is to make available in the context of the Web Forms page a reference to a type that represents the specified control. The type is named *ASP.buttonlist_ascx* if the user control doesn't contain a *ClassName* attribute; otherwise, it is named *ASP.XXX*, where *XXX* is the content of the *ClassName* attribute.

The *@Reference* directive declaratively indicates that another user control or page should be dynamically compiled and linked against the current page or control. The directive supports only two, mutually exclusive, attributes—*Page* and *Control*. Both point to a URL and identify the Web element to bind to the current page or control. Once you hold a reference to the *.ascx* file, you can create instances of the user control programmatically.

```
ButtonList btn = (ButtonList) LoadControl("buttonlist.ascx");
```

In general, you use the *@Register* directive to register user controls that are declared in the page layout and instantiated by the system. You use the *@Reference* directive if you create the controls programmatically.

Conclusion

User controls are a type of ASP.NET server control that you can easily create by using the same techniques you've learned for common Web pages. Little code is normally required for building a user control, and in some cases Web Forms user controls can even be codeless. However, there's no technical limitation to what a user control can do, and the amount and complexity of the embedded code depends only on the functionality you want to obtain.

User controls offer an easy way to partition and reuse common user-interface elements across applications. They are ideal whenever the reuse of layout and graphical functionality is critical. You can top off this component with some code that gets compiled on the fly like a Web page; however, quick and effective reuse of user-interface functionality is the primary objective of

Web Forms user controls. Like pages, user controls can be developed with inline code as well as with code-behind classes. User controls are not the ideal tool to leverage if you need to build a hierarchy of controls according to a pure object-oriented model. Although not impossible to obtain, inheritance is not the goal of user controls. Just the presence of a fair quantity of layout code makes user-control inheritance harder. You can stuff the code of a user control into a class and reuse it, but the associated layout information remains a separate entity that's a bit harder to manage programmatically. If you're going to build a control others can inherit from, you should drop user controls in favor of more flexible custom controls. We'll cover custom controls in the next two chapters.

We started this chapter by building an interactive control just to emphasize how the user control technology can help you to reuse common pieces of a Web site. Next, we built an object model on top of it. The summation of an advanced user interface with a layer of business logic constitutes a powerful model that can be helpful in any scenario in which you need rich and reusable components.

Just the Facts

- A user control is primarily a Web form made of any combination of server and client controls sewn together with literals, server code, and client script code.

- User controls are server files with an *.ascx* extension that are referenced from within ASP.NET pages or other user controls.

- Like ASP.NET pages and controls, Web user controls are compiled when first requested, and the generated assemblies are cached to quickly serve successive requests.

- Any ASP.NET page can be converted into a user control with little effort—you need to remove *<html>*, *<body>*, and *<form>* tags and replace the *@Page* directive with *@Control*.

- User controls are the smallest unit of a page whose output is cacheable. To output-cache a portion of a page, save that portion as a user control.

Chapter 13
Creating Custom ASP.NET Controls

Microsoft ASP.NET custom controls are compiled, server-side components that encapsulate user-interface and other functionality into reusable packages. Custom controls are no different than standard ASP.NET server controls except that they are bound to a different tag prefix and must be registered and deployed explicitly. Aside from that, custom controls can have their own object model, fire events, and support all the design-time features of Microsoft Visual Studio 2005, such as the Properties window, the visual designer, property builders, and the Toolbox.

Custom controls are not to be confused with Web user controls, which we covered in the previous chapter. Web user controls are dynamic-compile components and cannot be added to the Toolbox. For the same reason, their design-time support is limited, and so is their visual feedback when added to a page, where they simply display with a placeholder glyph. In addition, user controls should be deployed as source code unless the application that incorporates them is precompiled. (See Chapter 1.) In this case, you can extract the dynamic assembly that contains the user control and share it between applications.

ASP.NET custom controls are compiled code. Once you have compiled the control, you can add it to the Toolbox and take advantage of the rich visual environment of Visual Studio 2005. Because of their compiled nature, custom controls can be installed in a single copy in the global assembly cache (GAC), making them available to all applications, or they can simply be deployed to the *Bin* directory for use by a single application.

A custom control is a class and inherits from a base control class. The logic already available in the base class determines how much, and what, code you have to write. There are basically two ways of creating custom controls. If you find that an existing control meets your requirements only partially and lacks some key features, the simplest thing you can do is extend the control by deriving a new class from it. You can override specific properties, methods, and events as well as add new features. If none of the existing Web server controls meet your requirements, consider creating a custom control from scratch by deriving from one of the base control classes—*Control* and *WebControl*. These classes provide only the basic functionality of ASP.NET server controls, and they require that you take care of some of the control's operational aspects yourself, such as rendering, styling, view state, and state management.

Another derived approach that we'll also extensively examine in this chapter entails the creation of *composite controls*. A composite control is a new control created by combining other existing controls. Actually, composite controls and derived controls differ mostly in the structure of their rendering engine.

> **Important**   ASP.NET controls are limited in their overall functionality by the target markup language. For Web pages, the HTML language and HTML object model of the browser delimit the upper bound of implementable functionality. When you need a certain functionality that no existing control provides, you should first ask whether that functionality can be obtained from an HTML environment at all and what support it expects from the browser. For example, there's no standard ASP.NET control that provides an editable drop-down menu à la Windows Forms; however, while this feature can be implemented—and, indeed, several third-party vendors do it—it requires a rich dynamic HTML (DHTML) object model on the client.

Extending Existing Controls

When you realize you need a custom control to accomplish a certain task, first pause and make sure the feature you devised can really be obtained with HTML, literals, and JavaScript code. If you know how to do that in pure HTML, you can start planning an ASP.NET control and then architect and engineer the feature for the best reusability and efficiency.

Choosing a Base Class

A custom server control is a Microsoft .NET Framework class that inherits—either directly or indirectly—from *Control*. *Control* is the root class for all server controls in ASP.NET applications. It should be noted, though, that very few controls that you commonly use in ASP.NET applications really inherit directly from *Control*. For the most part, ASP.NET controls inherit from intermediate classes that encapsulate a given predefined behavior.

Inheriting from a Base Class

Each ASP.NET server control that is not marked as sealed can be further inherited and specialized. Table 13-1 lists all the classes that in ASP.NET represent some sort of base functionality. Each class in the list represents the root of a family of controls.

Table 13-1   Base Control Classes Available in ASP.NET 2.0

Class	Version	Description
BaseDataBoundControl	2.0	Incorporates the basic mechanism and object model for data binding. Inherits from *WebControl*.
BaseDataList	1.x	Adds grid capabilities such as advanced rendering, templates, and paging. Inherits from *WebControl*.
CompositeControl	2.0	Incorporates the mechanics of composite controls with regard to the building of the control's tree. Inherits from *WebControl*.
CompositeDataBoundControl	2.0	Incorporates the mechanics of composite data-bound controls with regard to view-state management and building of the control's tree. Inherits from *DataBoundControl*.
DataBoundControl	2.0	Adds support for data source controls and overrides some methods marked as abstract in the parent class. Inherits from *BaseDataBoundControl*.
HierarchicalDataBoundControl	2.0	Adds support for data hierarchical data source controls and overrides some methods marked as abstract in the parent class. Inherits from *BaseDataBoundControl*.
ListControl	1.x	Adds support and an object model tailor-made for list controls such as *CheckBoxList* and *DropDownList*. Introduced in ASP.NET 1.x, this class was refactored in ASP.NET 2.0. Inherits from *DataBoundControl*.
WebControl	1.x	Adds an array of user-interface (UI) properties such as style settings, colors, font, and borders. Inherits from *Control*.

Among the commonly used controls that inherit directly from *Control*, you find *Repeater*, *Substitution*, *MultiView*, *Placeholder*, and *LiteralControl*. All other controls in ASP.NET inherit from one of these classes.

Extending a Base Class

The base *Control* class incorporates a number of features and makes them available to all child controls. A quick list includes view-state management, control identification, naming container capabilities, design-time support, and, in ASP.NET 2.0, theming, control state, and adaptive rendering. If you choose to inherit from any of the classes in Table 13-1, be prepared to write quite a bit of code, as the control you get in the beginning is not particularly rich with concrete functionalities.

You typically inherit from any of those classes if you're going to write a control that provides unique capabilities that are hard to find in other ASP.NET controls. Inheriting from any of the classes in Table 13-1 is more like building a custom control from scratch, where the effective starting point is determined by the selected base class. Note that most of the classes in Table 13-1 refer to data-bound controls, which we'll cover in detail in the next chapter.

If you opt for inheritance from a concrete control class—that is, a control that provides an observable behavior and user interface—you should strive to add new features or override existing capabilities without altering too much the structure and the personality of the control itself.

A Richer *HyperLink* Control

Let's start with a sample custom control that extends the standard behavior of the *HyperLink* built-in control. By default, the ASP.NET *HyperLink* control outputs an anchor <a> tag that points to a URL. By design, any click on an anchor tag is served directly by the browser, which navigates to the specified page. No postback occurs to the page that originally displayed the anchor. Put another way, if you want to track that the user clicked on a given anchor, you need to extend the behavior of the *HyperLink* control.

Designing a Usage Scenario

Let's further develop the idea of a control that drives users to a different page but gives the page author a way to track the event. The canonical example used to illustrate the importance of this feature is the page hit counter. Monitoring the visitor activity is an important task that each administrator of a Web site should consider to improve the quality and content of the site. A *click-through* is the name commonly used to indicate the user's clicking to see particular content, and it's an important parameter for evaluating how the visitors of a site receive advertising. How would you implement a counter service that counts click-throughs in a page?

You could associate each button control in a page (*Button*, *HyperLink*, *ImageButton*, *LinkButton*, *AdRotator*) with an extra layer of code that first tracks the click and then proceeds with the expected behavior. Getting this with controls that entail a postback is not difficult. Take the *LinkButton* class, for example. You could derive a new control and override the *OnClick* protected member as follows:

```
protected virtual void OnClick(EventArgs e)
{
    // Track the event
    ⋮

    // Proceed with the default behavior
    base.OnClick(e);
}
```

What about the *HyperLink* control, though? The *HyperLink* control doesn't post back, as the click on the resulting <a> tag is handled directly by the browser rather than your ASP.NET code. It's this capability we need to add.

A Redirector for the *HyperLink* Control

The idea is that you force the *HyperLink* control to adopt a navigation URL that is different from the one set by the programmer. In other words, you divert the *HyperLink* control to a custom page on your site, where you first accomplish any requested tasks (such as tracking) and then redirect to the originally requested page. The code for such a modified version of the *HyperLink* control doesn't look particularly scary:

```
using System;
using System.Web.UI.WebControls;

namespace ProAspNet20.Advanced.CS.Components
{
    public class Hyperlink : System.Web.UI.WebControls.HyperLink
    {
        public string RedirectPage
        {
            get
            {
                object o = ViewState["RedirectPage"];
                if (o == null)
                    return "redir.aspx";
                else
                    return (string)o;
            }
            set { ViewState["RedirectPage"] = value; }
        }

        public new string NavigateUrl
        {
            get { return base.NavigateUrl; }
            set
            {
                string url = "{0}?page={1}";
                url = String.Format(url, RedirectPage, value);
                base.NavigateUrl = url;
            }
        }
    }
}
```

As you can see, the new control has a brand new property—*RedirectPage*—and overrides an existing property—*NavigateUrl*. *RedirectPage* indicates the URL of the intermediate page where the user is temporarily redirected so that any custom tasks such as click-through tracking can be accomplished. Here's an example of the code file of such a page:

```
public partial class Redir : System.Web.UI.Page
{
    protected void Page_Load(object sender, EventArgs e)
    {
        // Capture the originally requested page
        string url = String.Empty;
        object o = Request["Page"];
        if (o != null)
        {
            url = (string) o;
            if (String.IsNullOrEmpty(url))
                return;
        }
```

```
        // Do something here such as updating a counter
        ⋮

        // Redirect the user to the originally requested page
        Response.Redirect(url);
    }
}
```

We are assuming that the custom *HyperLink* control calls the redirector page, passing a *Page* parameter on the query string set to the original URL. Of course, this trick is arbitrary, and you can find better workarounds if you want.

The navigation URL for a hyperlink is set through the *NavigateUrl* property. We need to ensure that whenever a new value is assigned to the *NavigateUrl* property (say, *http://www.asp.net*), it gets overridden by something like the following:

```
redir.aspx?page=http://www.asp.net
```

In this way, the user first reaches *redir.aspx*, where his action is tracked and then is directed to his final destination.

To override the *setter* (or the *getter*) of a control property, you need the property to be marked as *virtual* at some point in the control's inheritance chain. The *HyperLink* control has a virtual property—*Text*—and a couple of public, but not virtual, properties such as *Target* and *Navigate-Url*. If the property is not marked virtual (namely, it is overridable), you can't override it; however, you can replace its implementation altogether. You do this through the *new* modifier in C# and the *Shadows* modifier in Microsoft Visual Basic .NET.

```csharp
public new string NavigateUrl
{
    get { return base.NavigateUrl; }
    set
    {
        string url = "{0}?page={1}";
        url = String.Format(url, RedirectPage, value);
        base.NavigateUrl = url;
    }
}
```

The *new* modifier applied to a property instructs the compiler that the current implementation for the member replaces any other implementation available on base classes. If you redefine the *NavigateUrl* property without using the *new* keyword, you simply receive a warning from the compiler. The warning informs you that you are hiding an existing member and just recommends the use of the *new* modifier if hiding the member was intentional.

Building Controls from Scratch

There are two main situations in which ASP.NET developers feel the need to create custom controls. At times, developers need a control that simply doesn't exist in the ASP.NET built-in toolbox. And occasionally, developers need a control that is similar to one of the native controls but not close enough to justify using one. In this case, developers typically derive a new control from an existing one and add or override members as appropriate. Let's discuss techniques and tricks to design and code completely new ASP.NET controls that address functionalities that ASP.NET doesn't provide out of the box.

Base Class and Interfaces

Several programming aspects support the development of a custom control in ASP.NET. First, there are base classes such as *Control* and *WebControl*. Each class provides a common set of base properties that address and fit into a particular use case. In addition to base classes, interfaces help you to better characterize the behavior and programming model of the control. A few interfaces are worth mentioning. They are *INamingContainer*, *IPostBackDataHandler*, *IPostBackEventHandler* and, only in ASP.NET 2.0, *ICallbackEventHandler*.

In Table 13-1, you see listed all base classes for controls and data-bound controls. I'll leave data-binding issues for the next chapter, so as far as base classes are concerned, in this chapter I'll focus on *Control* and *WebControl*.

Control vs. WebControl

The *Control* class defines the properties, methods, and events common to all ASP.NET server controls. These include the methods and events that determine and govern the life cycle of the control plus a few properties such as *ID*, *UniqueID*, *Parent*, *ViewState*, and the collection of child controls named *Controls*.

The *WebControl* class derives from *Control* and adds extra properties and methods, mostly regarding control styles that affect rendering. These properties include *ForeColor*, *BackColor*, *Font*, *Height*, and *Width*. *WebControl*, in particular, is the base class for the family of Web server controls in ASP.NET.

When developing a new ASP.NET control, there's just one guideline to follow. If your control renders a user interface, you should derive it from *WebControl*. If you're authoring a component that doesn't provide specific user-interface features, you're better off using *Control* as your base class. Although these rules are effective in most cases, there might be exceptional situations in which you would reasonably do otherwise. For example, you can derive from *Control* if you want to provide a subset of the user-interface features.

When building composite controls—that is, controls designed by aggregating multiple controls together—you might want to use *CompositeControl* as the base class in ASP.NET 2.0 and stick to *Control* in ASP.NET 1.x, where the new class is not available. You should never use *UserControl*, on the other hand, as a base class for a custom control.

Related Interfaces

Depending on the functionality of your control, you might have to implement additional interfaces. Typically, a server control will implement some of the following four interfaces:

- **INamingContainer**   This interface, also referred to as a marker interface, doesn't contain methods—it simply notifies the ASP.NET runtime that the control that exposes it should be treated as a naming container. Child controls contained within a naming container control have their *UniqueID* property prefixed with the ID of the container. The naming container, therefore, acts as a namespace and guarantees the uniqueness of the control IDs within the specified naming scope. The use of the *INamingContainer* interface is essential if you're writing composite controls or controls that include templates. (We'll discuss templates in the next chapter.)

- **IPostBackDataHandler**   The *IPostBackDataHandler* interface is needed whenever your control has to examine postback data. If the user can execute actions that affect the state of the control, you need to look into the postback data. For example, a *TextBox* control stores its configuration in the view state but also needs to read what the user typed in through the browser. This scenario is just where the *IPostBackDataHandler* interface fits in. The method *LoadPostData* lets controls examine posted values. The interface is also helpful if you need to raise events on the server based on changes to the data (method *RaisePostDataChanged*). Again, the *TextBox* control is the perfect sample control; if the data changed between postbacks, the *TextChanged* event is also raised.

- **IPostBackEventHandler**   The *IPostBackEventHandler* interface serves to capture a client-side postback event (for example, a click). Upon postback, after raising data change events, the ASP.NET runtime looks for a server control whose *UniqueID* property matches the name of a posted value (for example, the name of the clicked button). If a match is found and the control implements *IPostBackEventHandler*, ASP.NET invokes the *RaisePostBackEvent* method on the control. *RaisePostBackEvent* is the only method defined on the *IPostBackEventHandler* interface. What a particular control does within the *RaisePostBackEvent* method can vary quite a bit. The *Button* control—a simple control that implements this interface—fires its *Click* event when ASP.NET invokes the *RaisePostBackEvent* method.

- **ICallbackEventHandler**   The *ICallbackEventHandler* interface allows a control to be used as the target of a client script call, as described in Chapter 6. In Chapter 7, we also demonstrated a Web Part control that implements callbacks using the *ICallbackEventHandler* interface, although I didn't specifically mention the interface at that time.

Choosing a Rendering Style

For an ASP.NET server control, the sole purpose in life is outputting markup text. The control's object model and the system infrastructure it leverages serve to determine the contents to output, but the whole life cycle of controls (and host pages) inevitably ends with the rendering step. There are various ways for a server control to render out.

The *Render* Method

Typically, an ASP.NET control renders out through the *Render* method. To take total control of the control's rendering, you therefore override the *Render* method and write markup code to the specified HTML text writer object.

```
protected override void Render(HtmlTextWriter writer)
```

The HTML text writer object is a sort of buffer where you can accumulate all the text to be output. You can compose markup using the methods of the *HtmlTextWriter* object or building plain strings. Writing to the text writer is indeed the fastest way for controls to generate their markup, but unfortunately it doesn't result in as much readable code. If you take this route for a reasonably complex control, your final code will look like an intricate mess of nested if-then-else statements. Your code will be hard to read and maintain.

There's another aspect to consider about direct markup output. Consider the following code snippet:

```
protected override void Render(HtmlTextWriter writer)
{
    writer.Write("<input type=text id=\"TextBox1\" />");
}
```

The final page contains an input field of type text with an ID of *TextBox1*. The server environment, though, doesn't know anything about this element and might not be able to process server events for this element correctly. In other words, you should render the markup directly only for controls that output raw HTML, that don't match ASP.NET controls, and that don't need to raise or handle server events such as postbacks or post-data-changed events. If you're going to write a server control that renders an HTML marquee or a table of data, writing to the control's text writer buffer is fine. If you're building a control that results from the composition of other controls, you're better off taking another approach—building the control tree programmatically.

Building the Control Tree

When your control embeds constituent child controls, you have a *composite control*. In this case, it is recommended that you build the final tree of controls programmatically by overriding the *CreateChildControls* method defined on the *Control* class. You do this by adding all constituent controls to the *Controls* collection of the control being developed. Here's an example:

```
protected override void CreateChildControls()
{
    // Clears child controls
    Controls.Clear();

    // Build the control tree
    CreateControlHierarchy();

    // Clear the viewstate of child controls
    ClearChildViewState();
}
```

ClearChildViewState is a method on the *Control* class that deletes the view-state information for all the server child controls. *CreateControlHierarchy*, on the other hand, is an arbitrary name and represents a user-defined method that builds the control's tree. You should feel free to replace that function with your own function or plain code. As a matter of fact, though, most ASP.NET built-in composite controls define a protected, overridable method with just that name. Here's a possible implementation for *CreateControlHierarchy* that creates a text box with a leading label. Note that not only is the name of *CreateControlHierarchy* arbitrary, but so is its prototype.

```
protected void CreateControlHierarchy()
{
    // Add the label
    Label lbl = new Label();
    lbl.Text = "Some text";
    Controls.Add(lbl);

    // Add a blank literal control for spacing
    Controls.Add(new LiteralControl("  "));

    // Add the textbox
    TextBox txt = new TextBox();
    txt.Text = String.Empty;
    Controls.Add(txt);

    // Sets that child controls have been created
    ChildControlsCreated = true;
}
```

The ultimate goal of *CreateControlHierarchy* is populating the *Controls* collection of the current control with all child controls in the proper position in the final hierarchy. The *ChildControls-Created* Boolean property is defined on the *Control* class and indicates whether all child controls have been created or not.

For a composite control, you don't need to override the *Render* method, but it is recommended that you implement the marker interface *INamingContainer* to facilitate the ability of ASP.NET to recognize postback events caused by any child control.

> **Tip**   In ASP.NET 2.0, make sure you always inherit a composite control from the base class *CompositeControl*. This will save you a good deal of effort with the Visual Studio 2005 designer and ensure that the control renders correctly at run time and displays a valid preview at design time. Without that base class, the control will still work as expected at run time but won't show up at design time in the Web form. In ASP.NET 1.x, you can work around the issue by overriding the *Render* method and explicitly rebuilding the control hierarchy if in design mode.

Finally, a method that is worth mentioning regarding composite controls is *EnsureChildControls*. This method checks whether all child controls have been created, and, if not, it re-creates them. How can the control know about that? It simply reads the value of the *ChildControlsCreated* Boolean property and calls *CreateChildControls* if all child controls haven't been created. The following code snippet illustrates the behavior of *EnsureChildControls*:

```
protected virtual void EnsureChildControls()
{
    if (!ChildControlsCreated)
    {
        try {
            CreateChildControls();
        }
        finally {
            ChildControlsCreated = true;
        }
    }
}
```

The *SimpleGaugeBar* Control

To get a grip on building new ASP.NET controls, let's create a control with a limited state but significant rendering engine. The control, named *SimpleGaugeBar*, is a simple, non-data-bound gauge bar that you can use to implement a rating system that represents the progress made for certain tasks. Generally, it could be used to give a friendly user interface to measurable quantities.

Defining the Object Model

A gauge control needs to have at least two properties—one to indicate the value being rendered, and one that provides the scale. In addition, we also give users a chance to control the ruler and the descriptive text for the gauge. Table 13-2 lists the properties of a *SimpleGaugeBar* control.

Table 13-2   Properties of the *SimpleGaugeBar* Control

Property	Description
FormatString	Formats the string that the control will render alongside the control. The string can contain up to two placeholders. The first placeholder is set with the value; the second placeholder is set with the scale. The default string has the following form: {0} / {1}.
GridLines	Indicates whether vertical delimiters should be displayed to mark notches.
Maximum	Indicates the maximum value the gauge can represent. Set to 100 by default.
Segments	Indicates the number of notches to draw on the gauge ruler. Set to 4 by default.
Value	Indicates the value to represent. Set to 0 by default, and cannot be higher than the scale.

The *set* mutator of the *Value* properties adjusts any value provided that exceeds the current *Maximum*. The value stored in *Maximum* is the highest value you can assign to *Value*. The format string should be formed using two parameters in a fixed order—*Value* and *Maximum*. In the format string, you can use any HTML formatting and even reference the parameters in the reverse order. The following code snippet shows possible ways of setting the format string:

```
GaugeBar1.FormatString = "{0} ({1})";
GaugeBar2.FormatString = "Maximum is {1}. Value is <b>{0}</b>";
```

The *SimpleGaugeBar* control has no methods and doesn't fire any events.

Implementing the Object Model

Internally, the control renders the gauge using an HTML table. The *Value* and *Maximum* pair are translated in percentages, and the ruler is drawn using table cells. Figure 13-1 shows the control within the Visual Studio 2005 designer.

Figure 13-1 The *SimpleGaugeBar* control in action in the Visual Studio designer.

The notches on the ruler are obtained simply by adding as many cells to the underlying table as there are units in the *Segments* property. The following listing shows the implementation of the control properties:

```
public class SimpleGaugeBar : CompositeControl
{
    private int _dividerCell;

    public SimpleGaugeBar()
    {
    }

    // Gets and sets the value to represent in the gauge bar
    public float Value
    {
        get
        {
            object o = ViewState["Value"];
            if (o == null)
                return 0;
            return (float) o;
        }
        set
        {
            ViewState["Value"] = value;
```

```
            if (value > Maximum)
                ViewState["Value"] = Maximum;
    }
}

// Gets and sets the maximum value representable in the gauge bar
public float Maximum
{
    get
    {
        object o = ViewState["Maximum"];
        if (o == null)
            return 100;
        return (float) o;
    }
    set { ViewState["Maximum"] = value; }
}

// Number of segments to divide the bar into
public int Segments
{
    get
    {
        object o = ViewState["Segments"];
        if (o == null)
            return 4;
        return (int) o;
    }
    set
    {
        ViewState["Segments"] = value;
        if( value < 1)
            ViewState["Segments"] = 1;
    }
}

// Gets and sets the pattern to format the value in the gauge bar
public string FormatString
{
    get
    {
        object o = ViewState["FormatString"];
        if (o == null)
            return "<b>{0}</b> / <b>{1}</b>";
        return (string) o;
    }
    set { ViewState["FormatString"] = value; }
}

// Gets and sets whether the gaugebar has grid lines
public bool GridLines
{
    get
    {
        object o = ViewState["GridLines"];
```

```
            if (o == null)
                return true;
            return (bool) o;
        }
        set { ViewState["GridLines"] = value; }
    }
    :
}
```

The control maintains some state by using the view-state collection. All the properties, in fact, are persisted using *ViewState*. Because all the persisted properties are marked as public, you can disable the view state altogether and still keep the control fully functional by explicitly setting properties upon page loading.

> **Caution**   A page can disable the view state for all embedded controls or for individual controls. Note, though, that disabling the view state for a control results in a loss of functionality if the control stores in the view state private or protected properties. Unlike public properties, in fact, private or protected properties cannot be programmatically set from within a host page.

Setting Up the Ruler

The ruler divides the area of the control into segments, which are filled proportionally based on the current value of the gauge. Each segment of the ruler corresponds to a cell in the underlying table. All cells but one are entirely filled or entirely empty. Filled cells are rendered using the current foreground color; empty cells are rendered using the current background color. One cell, named the divider cell, contains a child table with exactly one row and two cells. The first cell is rendered with the foreground color; the second cell is colored as the control's background. The two cells have a width, measured in percent, whose total amounts to 100. The latter cell denotes how much is still left to do to reach the maximum. The following HTML code snippet shows the final HTML markup to render a value of 52 out of 100 using a ruler with four notches or segments:

```
<table><tr>
    <td bgcolor=orange width=25%></td>
    <td bgcolor=orange width=25%></td>
    <td>
      <table><tr>
        <td bgcolor=orange width=2%></td>
        <td bgcolor=white width=98%></td>
      </tr></table>
    </td>
    <td bgcolor=white width=25%></td>
</tr></table>
```

Figure 13-2 shows how this gauge will look (four segments displaying a value of 52 out of 100). Figure 13-2 also shows gauges with different ruler settings.

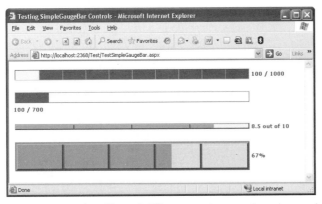

Figure 13-2   The effect of different settings on the gauge ruler.

Setting Up the Control's Site

As you might have guessed already from the preceding figures, other properties get into the game in addition to those discussed in Table 13-2. Admittedly, the grayscale rendering used in this book doesn't do justice to the actual capabilities of the *SimpleGaugeBar* control in terms of color support. However, the control exploits a few color-related properties defined on the base class. These properties are *BackColor*, *ForeColor*, *Width*, and *Height*.

Width and *Height* are used to delimit the control's site—that is, the area within the container the control is assigned for rendering. The control is assigned a default size that can be changed either programmatically or through the Visual Studio Properties window.

The value of the *ForeColor* property is used to render the text of the label that accompanies the gauge. The value of the *BackColor* property determines the color to be used for the progress bar. Note that the implementation we just discussed assumes that only known colors can be used.

Rendering the *SimpleGaugeBar* Control

The user interface of a Web control is pure HTML, sometimes topped off with a bit of client script. As mentioned, there are basically two ways in which this HTML can be generated. You can compose the HTML code in the supplied writer, or you can build an in-memory representation of the output using existing HTML and Web server controls and then have them recursively render their contents to the writer. Let's discuss these two options in more detail.

Generating the HTML for a Custom Control

From a pure performance standpoint, writing out the control's markup to a HTML text writer object is the preferred approach. No server control is ever instantiated, and the final and correct markup is sent to the browser. There a few downsides to this approach you should consider, however. One is that you end up making several calls to the writer. And, aside from some negligible repercussions in terms of the performance (repercussions that are negligible when compared to control instantiation), the size of the code grows considerably, making your source code on the whole much less readable and harder to maintain. Let's consider a quick but significant example.

To write the content of a string in a table cell, you would need the following code if you decide to opt for the rich interface of the writer:

```
output.WriteFullBeginTag("table");
output.WriteFullBeginTag("tr");
output.WriteFullBeginTag("td");
output.Write(text);
output.WriteEndTag("td");
output.WriteEndTag("tr");
output.WriteEndTag("table");
```

However, as long as you don't have a full bag of attributes to render, or a really complex structure to build, the following code is equally effective and even slightly faster:

```
output.Write("<table><tr><td>");
output.Write(text);
output.Write("</td></tr></table>");
```

In general, neither of these two approaches is always the best possible approach. A good compromise between the two is recommended to optimize performance while producing compact code. Taking the first approach to its natural limit, you end up with many more lines of code than is necessary. Taking the second approach further, you resort to building the control using strings, which is indeed not the best thing you can do mainly from a maintenance point of view.

In ASP.NET, every piece of HTML code can be managed on the server as an instance of a class. This pattern results in extreme flexibility and ease of development. However, it doesn't come free of problems, either. The rub lies in the fact that you instantiate lots of controls, which always affects performance. Let's take a look at this in more detail.

Note   In general, in ASP.NET, using controls is the first option. You shouldn't use them, though, in situations in which the control is just overkill. If you need to output constant text, there's no reasonable justification for using a *Label* control instead of a simpler call to the text writer.

Using Child Controls for Rendering

Sometimes the custom control needs to build up a complex infrastructure with nested tables and elements. In this case, it makes sense to build an in-memory representation of the overall tree and then render everything to HTML using the *RenderContents* method of the root control. Typically, for controls with a relatively complex hierarchy of child controls and rich styles, you override the *Render* method as follows:

```
protected override void Render(HtmlTextWriter output)
{
    // This is a custom method that you normally use
    // to ensure that all elements are styled properly.
    // We'll show an implementation of this method later.
    PrepareControlForRendering();

    // Render the contents of the control
    base.RenderContents(output);
}
```

The *SimpleGaugeBar* control renders a nontrivial table structure that is much more manageable through a control tree.

```
protected override void CreateChildControls()
{
    Controls.Clear();
    CreateControlHierarchy();
    ClearChildViewState();
}

protected virtual void CreateControlHierarchy()
{
    // Build the outermost container table
    Table outer = new Table();
    TableRow outerRow = new TableRow();
    outer.Rows.Add(outerRow);

    // Ruler cell
    TableCell rulerCell = new TableCell();
    outerRow.Cells.Add(rulerCell);
    BuildGaugeBar(rulerCell);

    // Text cell
    TableCell textCell = new TableCell();
    if (!_textStyle.DisplayTextAtBottom)
    {
        outerRow.Cells.Add(textCell);
        BuildLabel(textCell);
    }

    // Save the control tree-add the table as a child of the gauge
    Controls.Add(outer);

    // Build the label
    if (!_textStyle.RenderInsideTable && _textStyle.DisplayTextAtBottom)
        BuildLabel(null);
}
```

```
void BuildGaugeBar(TableCell container)
{
    // Create the table with one or two rows: ruler (and label)
    Table t = new Table();
    TableRow ruler = new TableRow();
    t.Rows.Add(ruler);

    // Build the ruler row
    BuildRuler(ruler);

    // Build the label
    if (_textStyle.RenderInsideTable)
        BuildLabelIntoTable(t);

    // Save the control tree
    container.Controls.Add(t);
}
```

The output of the *SimpleGaugeBar* control consists of an outermost table that has one row and two cells. The first cell contains the gauge bar; the second cell optionally contains the text, when the companion text has to be displayed on the side of the gauge. (See Figure 13-2.) If the text goes below the gauge, it can either be part of the table (a second row) or just an additional *Label* control. You control rendering styles of the text through a custom style property—the *TextStyle* property—that I'll say more about in a moment. Let's first focus on the ruler.

The ruler is a sequence of table cells. Each cell corresponds to a notch you want to see on the final gauge. The number of notches is determined by the *Segments* property. The *Value* property is scaled as a percentage of the *Maximum* value, and the resulting value is used to determine the color of the various cells. If the value to represent is larger than the value represented by the current notch, a cell is added with the average width given by 100 divided by the number of notches. The same happens if the value is smaller and the divider cell has been rendered already. (In this case, *finished* is true.)

```
void BuildRuler(TableRow ruler)
{
    // Calculate the value to represent
    float val = GetValueToRepresent();
    float valueToRepresent = 100f * val / Maximum;
    int numOfSegments = GetNumOfSegments();

    int segmentWidth = 100 / numOfSegments;
    bool finished = false;

    for (int i = 1; i <= numOfSegments; i++)
    {
        if (valueToRepresent < i * segmentWidth)
        {
            if (finished)
            {
                // Still-To-Do
                TableCell stillToDo = new TableCell();
```

```
                ruler.Cells.Add(stillToDo);
                stillToDo.Width = Unit.Percentage(segmentWidth);
        }
        else
        {
                // Cell to divide
                _dividerCell = i - 1;   // need a 0-based index
                TableCell cell = new TableCell();
                ruler.Cells.Add(cell);
                cell.Width = Unit.Percentage(segmentWidth);
                cell.Height = Unit.Percentage(100);

                // Add a child table to the cell
                Table child = new Table();
                child.Width = Unit.Percentage(100);
                child.Height = Unit.Percentage(100);
                cell.Controls.Add(child);
                child.CellPadding = 0;
                child.CellSpacing = 0;
                TableRow childRow = new TableRow();
                child.Rows.Add(childRow);

                float fx = (100 *
                            (valueToRepresent - segmentWidth *
                            (i - 1)) / segmentWidth);
                if (valueToRepresent > (i - 1) * segmentWidth)
                {
                    TableCell left = new TableCell();
                    childRow.Cells.Add(left);
                    left.Width = Unit.Percentage(fx);
                }
                TableCell right = new TableCell();
                childRow.Cells.Add(right);
                right.Width = Unit.Percentage(100 - fx);
                finished = true;
        }
    }
    else
    {
        // Done
        TableCell done = new TableCell();
        ruler.Cells.Add(done);
        done.Width = Unit.Percentage(segmentWidth);
    }
    }
    }
}
```

The divider cell is the cell that is split in two to represent the remaining value, as shown in Figure 13-3.

The divider cell is the first cell where the value of the corresponding notch is larger than the value to represent. The divider cell is rendered through an embedded table with one row and two cells. The index of the divider cell is cached for further use. It'll be of great help to style the control, as we'll see in a moment.

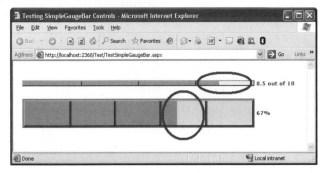

Figure 13-3 The divider cell in sample *SimpleGaugeBar* controls.

The companion text of the gauge can be displayed to the right of the gauge or below it. When rendered below it, the text can either be incorporated in the table or added as an extra control. *BuildLabel* can either add the text as an additional control or place it in the rightmost cell. *BuildLabelIntoTable* writes the text in an additional table row below the gauge. In this case, the text inherits most of the gauge graphical settings.

```
void BuildLabel(TableCell container)
{
    // Calculate the value to represent
    float buf = GetValueToRepresent();

    // Get the string to display on the label
    string msg = GetTextToRepresent();

    Label lbl = new Label();
    if (container is TableCell)
        container.Controls.Add(lbl);
    else
        Controls.Add(lbl);
    lbl.Text = String.Format(msg, buf, Maximum);
}

// Build the control tree for the label
void BuildLabelIntoTable(Table t)
{
    // Calculate the value to represent
    float buf = GetValueToRepresent();
    int numOfSegments = GetNumOfSegments();

    // Get the string to display on the label
    string msg = GetTextToRepresent();

    if (_textStyle.DisplayTextAtBottom)
    {
        // Add a bottom row
        TableRow label = new TableRow();
        t.Rows.Add(label);
```

```
        TableCell lblCell = new TableCell();
        label.Cells.Add(lblCell);

        lblCell.ColumnSpan = numOfSegments;
        lblCell.Text = String.Format(msg, buf, Maximum);
    }
}
```

> **Note** In the code shown thus far for the *SimpleGaugeBar* control, there are a pair of unex-
> plained methods—*GetValueToRepresent* and *GetTextToRepresent*. In this simple control, the
> methods return, respectively, the value of the *Value* and *FormatString* properties. In the next
> chapter, though, we'll extend the *SimpleGaugeBar* control with data-binding capabilities. Most
> of the changes will consist of extending the *GetValueToRepresent* and *GetTextToRepresent*
> methods.

There's no functional difference between the two approaches—it's purely a matter of appearance and preference. But how can you control the rendering and the styles of the companion
text? You do that through a new style property.

Styling the Control

The *SimpleGaugeBar* control indirectly inherits from *WebControl* and features a number of
graphical properties such as *BackColor*, *Font*, and *BorderStyle*. What if you want to render the
text using a different set of colors and borders? You have no other choice than to add a new
set of color and border properties. Instead of adding and managing several new properties,
though, you can instead add a single style property that encompasses a bunch of related,
visual properties.

Style is the base class for style properties. *TableItemStyle* is another commonly used style base
class. You derive from any of these classes if you want to come up with a style object that
includes custom properties. The *SimpleGaugeBar* control features a *TextStyle* property, implemented as follows:

```
private TextItemStyle _textStyle;
⋮
[PersistenceMode(PersistenceMode.InnerProperty)]
public TextItemStyle TextStyle
{
    get
    {
        if (_textStyle == null)
            _textStyle = new TextItemStyle();
        if (IsTrackingViewState)
            ((IStateManager)_textStyle).TrackViewState();

        return _textStyle;
    }
}
```

The *TextStyle* property persists its value through a private member named *_textStyle*. Looking at the preceding code, though, you can't figure out how style persistence is ensured across two postbacks. This is a good point we should examine in a bit more detail.

Note that the *[PersistenceMode]* attribute has nothing to do with this, regardless of the name. The attribute simply instructs Visual Studio 2005 to persist the contents of the style object using a nested tag in the .aspx source file. The style persistence is coded in the source of the style class—*TextItemStyle*.

```
public class TextItemStyle : TableItemStyle, IStateManager
{
    private bool _renderInsideTable;
    private bool _displayTextAtBottom;

    public TextItemStyle()
    {
        _displayTextAtBottom = true;
        _renderInsideTable = false;
    }

    // Public Members
    public bool RenderInsideTable
    {
        get { return _renderInsideTable; }
        set { _renderInsideTable = value; }
    }

    public bool DisplayTextAtBottom
    {
        get { return _displayTextAtBottom; }
        set { _displayTextAtBottom = value; }
    }
    ⋮
}
```

By implementing the *IStateManager* interface, a class tells the view-state machinery how to store its values to the view state. In other words, *IStateManager* acts as a sort of view-state custom serializer for a class. Without *IStateManager*, a class would be stored in the view state only if it were serializable and using the services of the *BinaryFormatter* class. Designed to address other scenarios, *BinaryFormatter* is sort of overkill and certainly not the best fit here. Here's the *IStateManager* implementation for *TextItemStyle*:

```
bool IStateManager.IsTrackingViewState
{
    get { return base.IsTrackingViewState; }
}

void IStateManager.TrackViewState()
{
    base.TrackViewState();
}
```

```
object IStateManager.SaveViewState()
{
    object[] state = new object[2];
    state[0] = base.SaveViewState();

    object[] extraData = new object[2];
    extraData[0] = _renderInsideTable;
    extraData[1] = _displayTextAtBottom;
    state[1] = (object)extraData;

    return state;
}

void IStateManager.LoadViewState(object state)
{
    if (state == null)
        return;
    object[] myState = (object[])state;
    base.LoadViewState(myState[0]);

    object[] extraData = (object[])myState[1];
    _renderInsideTable = (bool)extraData[0];
    _displayTextAtBottom = (bool)extraData[1];
}
```

The *IStateManager* interface counts four members, as in Table 13-3.

Table 13-3   Members of *IStateManager*

Member	Description
IsTrackingViewState	Indicates whether the class is currently tracking the view state for changes.
LoadViewState	Populates a new instance of the class with the data stored in the view state.
SaveViewState	Saves the current state of the class to the view state. This value will then be passed to *LoadViewState* on the next postback.
TrackViewState	Begins tracking the view state for changes.

In *SaveViewState*, you typically create an array with two elements. The first element is filled with the return value of *SaveViewState* called on the base class. The second element is an array (or a similar object, such as a combination of *Pair* and *Triplet* objects). The array contains the class data to persist. *LoadViewState* receives just this object and does the reverse.

You set style properties through the Visual Studio 2005 interface, as shown in Figure 13-4. Public properties on the *TextItemStyle* class show up in the Properties window of Visual Studio 2005.

Figure 13-4   Setting style properties in Visual Studio 2005.

Any values you assign in this way are persisted in the *.aspx* source file in a child *<TextStyle>* element.

Applying Styles

When you build a composite control, make sure you create the hierarchy without style information. Style information is better added just before rendering to all constituent controls.

```
protected override void Render(HtmlTextWriter output)
{
    PrepareControlForRendering();
    base.RenderContents(output);
}
```

PrepareControlForRendering is a user-defined method whose structure and prototype are totally arbitrary.

```
protected virtual void PrepareControlForRendering()
{
    if (Controls.Count < 1)
        return;

    // Get the table
    Table outer = (Table)Controls[0];
    Table t = (Table)outer.Rows[0].Cells[0].Controls[0];

    // Apply the base style attributes
    t.CopyBaseAttributes(this);

    // Configure additional properties on the overall table
    t.CellPadding = 0;
    t.CellSpacing = 0;
```

```
// Set colors on the cells
for (int i = 0; i < Segments; i++)
{
    TableCell cell = t.Rows[0].Cells[i];
    if (GridLines)
    {
        cell.BorderColor = BorderColor;
        cell.BorderStyle = BorderStyle;
        cell.BorderWidth = BorderWidth;
    }

    if (i < _dividerCell)
        cell.BackColor = ForeColor;
    if (i >= _dividerCell)
        cell.BackColor = BackColor;
    if (i == _dividerCell)
    {
        Table inner = (Table)cell.Controls[0];
        if (inner.Rows[0].Cells.Count > 1)
        {
            inner.Rows[0].Cells[0].BackColor = ForeColor;
            inner.Rows[0].Cells[1].BackColor = BackColor;
        }
        else
            inner.Rows[0].Cells[0].BackColor = BackColor;
    }
}

// Style the gauge bar text style
if (!_textStyle.DisplayTextAtBottom)
    outer.Rows[0].Cells[1].ApplyStyle(TextStyle);
else if (_textStyle.RenderInsideTable &&
        _textStyle.DisplayTextAtBottom)
{
    // bottom row
    TableRow row = t.Rows[1];
    row.ApplyStyle(TextStyle);
}
else
{
    // text below
    Label lbl = (Label)Controls[1];
    lbl.ApplyStyle(TextStyle);
}
}
```

The bottom line is that in *PrepareControlForRendering*, you locate each constituent control that needs styling and apply style properties. To locate a control, you walk your way through the control hierarchy.

The Gauge in Action

Once compiled, the *SimpleGaugeBar* control can be installed in the Visual Studio 2005 Toolbox and dragged onto any Web Forms page you're developing. The control is automatically registered and provides a preview of its final output.

```
<expo:SimpleGaugeBar id="GaugeBar1" runat="server"
    Width="500px" Height="15px"
    FormatString="<b>{0}</b> out of <b>{1}</b>"
    Segments="10"
    Value="65">
    <TextStyle Font-Bold="True" Font-Names="Verdana" Font-Size="8pt" />
</expo:SimpleGaugeBar>
```

The properties of the control that feature simple types can be set using the Properties window; for complex types, such as classes, you need to write a type converter and configure the property for the design-time environment of Visual Studio. The following code shows how to set properties on the gauge control programmatically:

```
private void Button1_Click(object sender, EventArgs e)
{
    GaugeBar1.Maximum = 200;
    GaugeBar1.Value = 55;
}
```

You should try to set the *Maximum* property first because, in this way, the control automatically validates the value. *Maximum* and *Value* are stored in the view state and are automatically restored when the page posts back. If the host page disables the view state, you should modify the code that relates to the control so that the needed properties are set on each request.

Building Rich Controls

In ASP.NET 1.x, the *Panel* control is a mere server-side abstraction for the *<div>* tag. It works as a container for server controls and HTML elements and literals that are graphically grouped in a common page section. In ASP.NET 2.0, the *Panel* control has added support for scrollbars and, in addition, can render out as a field set with a fixed legend text.

An advanced feature that the *Panel* control lacks is the ability to show its contents on demand. The idea, therefore, is to wrap the contents of the *Panel* control in a surrounding structure with a caption and a collapse/expand button. By clicking the button, a user can show or hide the contents of the panel in much the same way the items in a drop-down list control are displayed or hidden as the user clicks on the drop-down button.

There are quite a few issues related to building such a drop-down *Panel* control—graphics, state, clicking, and especially rendering.

The Drop-Down *Panel* Control

The new *Panel* control inherits from the built-in *Panel* control, and it adds a few properties to enable and govern the drop-down functionality. When working in drop-down mode, the control will render out a table with two rows. The top row contains the caption and a button to show or hide the contents. The bottom row incorporates the standard output of the base *Panel* control. Here's a sample:

```
<table>
   <tr>
      <td>Caption</td>
      <td>Drop-down button</td>
   </tr>
   <tr>
      <td colspan="2">Standard contents</td>
   </tr>
</table>
```

The base *Panel* server control is defined as a bunch of child controls grouped under a parent tag.

```
<asp:Panel runat="server">
   <!-- child controls -->
</asp:Panel>
```

All child controls are automatically parsed and added as sub-objects to the *Controls* collection of the *Panel*. The *Panel* is not a composite control, and while we'll override *CreateChildControls* to build our own control tree, the code to do so won't be terribly complex. The ASP.NET standard rendering machinery ensures that when *Render* is called on the *Panel*, the *Controls* collection is filled with an instance of each child control.

Rendering, however, is a different story. To pursue our own purposes—adding a clicking mechanism to show/hide contents—we need to override the rendering engine quite a bit. To start, though, let's review the set of new properties.

The Programming Interface

The new control derives from *System.Web.UI.WebControls.Panel* and features the same control name but in a different namespace. The definition is shown here:

```
namespace ProAspNet20.Advanced.CS.Components
{
    public class Panel : System.Web.UI.WebControls.Panel, INamingContainer
    {
        ⋮
    }
}
```

Table 13-4 lists the additional properties defined on the control.

Table 13-4   Properties of the Drop-Down *Panel* Control

Property	Description
Caption	The text that surrounds the child controls.
CaptionBackColor	Background color of the caption bar.
CaptionForeColor	Foreground color of text displayed in the caption bar.
EnableClientScript	Indicates whether the drop-down functionality should be implemented using client-side script code. Set to *false* by default.
EnableDropDown	Indicates whether the *Panel* should work in drop-down mode. Set to *false* by default.
ShowExpanded	Indicates whether the drop-down *Panel* should initially display expanded or collapsed. Set to *true* by default.

The key property is *EnableDropDown*—a Boolean member set to *false* by default. If the property is false, the custom *Panel* control behaves exactly like its parent control. In this case, you can use this control and the parent interchangeably. When *EnableDropDown* is set to *true*, the rendering mechanism of the new control kicks in and generates a table-based structure with a button to show/hide the contents.

The button can either raise a postback event or resolve any clicking on the client side through an ad hoc piece of script code. The property that selects either behavior is *EnableClientScript*. By default, the property is *false*, meaning that the drop-down button is a submit button that originates a classic server roundtrip.

To provide a nicer user interface, the button is rendered as an image. The image is embedded as a resource in the same assembly that contains the control. This trick eliminates at the root any potential deployment issue related to the images. In this way, the image is part of the control binaries and is installed along with the control. Figure 13-5 shows the new *Panel* control in action.

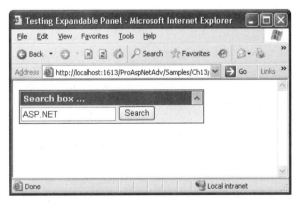

Figure 13-5   The new *Panel* control in action.

You can extend the programming interface of the control and provide for, say, a *ButtonUrl* property that would allow users to set the image programmatically.

The *Caption* property indicates the text to show in the title bar. *CaptionBackColor* and *CaptionForeColor* indicate background and foreground colors for the title bar. Other graphical properties could be added as well.

Control State

All properties in the drop-down *Panel* control use the control view state for storage, as shown next for the *EnableDropDown* property:

```
public bool EnableDropDown
{
    get
    {
        object o = ViewState["EnableDropDown"];
        if (o == null)
            return false;
        return (bool) o;
    }
    set { ViewState["EnableDropDown"] = value; }
}
```

What do you expect to be the control's behavior when the page that contains the control posts back or is refreshed? Should the drop-down state be maintained or reset to the initial mode set through the *ShowExpanded* property? Quite obviously, you want the control to maintain its drop-down state—expanded or collapsed—across postbacks. For this to happen, the state must be persisted in some nonpublic member. Is the view state appropriate for persistence? While you could use *ViewState* for this, the control state, in fact, is a better option.

Introduced in ASP.NET 2.0, the control state looks like a subset of the view state designed to remain in place regardless of the settings in the host page. The view state persists the state of controls across postbacks, but it can be disabled on a per-page or per-control basis by page authors for performance reasons. This is not necessarily an issue for public properties that can be explicitly reconfigured on postback. But what about internal properties that represent (and persist) state information that is critical for the working of the control?

Control state represents state information that is stored and processed like view state except that it cannot be disabled programmatically. For this reason, you should store in it only sensitive information that the control can't work without. A Boolean flag that indicates whether the panel is expanded or closed is the canonical example of information that should be stored in the control state.

View-state information is stored in a public collection object—the *ViewState* property. Unlike view state, the control state can be maintained in a strongly typed manner through a bunch of private and protected members whose names and types are totally arbitrary, as shown in the following code:

```
private bool _panelDisplayed;
protected override object SaveControlState()
{
    Pair p = new Pair();
    p.First = base.SaveControlState();
    p.Second = _panelDisplayed;
    return p;
}
protected override void LoadControlState(object savedState)
{
    if (savedState == null)
        return;
    Pair p = (Pair) savedState;
    base.LoadControlState(p.First);
    _panelDisplayed = (bool)p.Second;
}
```

For the *Panel* control, the control state consists of a single Boolean value that indicates whether the panel's contents are visible or hidden. Control state information is saved to the same hidden field as the view state, but it requires a couple of specific methods to save and restore. In a control that manages its state, you override the *SaveControlState* and *LoadControlState* methods.

SaveControlState returns an object that incorporates any state you want to persist. *LoadControlState* receives that object as an argument, unpacks it, and initializes private members with stored data. To pack data more efficiently, you might want to use *Pair* or *Triplet* collections, or, if you need more than two or three entries, you resort to arrays of *Object*. A typical implementation of *SaveControlState* creates a *Pair* object and saves the return value of the base method in the first slot. The second slot is filled with an object that groups in a single object all control state data. The data format you choose is arbitrary. *LoadControlState* simply extracts data from the previously returned object and sets internal members accordingly.

Unlike view state, control state support is optional. For this reason, a control that makes use of control state needs to let the host page know about it. In this way, the page will call *LoadControlState* and *SaveControlState* during its life cycle.

```
protected override void OnInit(EventArgs e)
{
    base.OnInit(e);
    Page.RegisterRequiresControlState(this);
}
protected override void OnLoad(EventArgs e)
{
    if (!Page.IsPostBack)
        _panelDisplayed = ShowExpanded;
}
```

A control registers for control state management in the *Init* event by calling the *Register-RequiresControlState* method on the *Page* class. Note that the drop-down *Panel* control also needs to initialize the internal member for control state—the *_panelDisplayed* private member. The initialization occurs the first time the control is loaded in the page, and you do that in the *Load* event when *IsPostBack* is *false*. During the postbacks that follow, the value of *_panelDisplayed* is set from the control state.

Adding Theme Support

ASP.NET 2.0 adds support for themes in pages and controls. Themes are application-wide files that determine the appearance of HTML elements and server controls. Themes are a superset of cascading style sheets (CSS) and basically work by extending the same styling approach of CSS to control properties. We covered themes in Chapter 5 of my related book, *Programming Microsoft ASP.NET 2.0: Core Reference*.

ASP.NET themes consist of two main files—CSS files and skins. A skin is a collection of default settings for a variety of server controls. These settings are automatically applied to all controls of that type within the page or application. Predefined settings can be defined for custom controls too. Here's a sample script that defines a skin for the drop-down *Panel* control:

```
<%@ Register TagPrefix="expo" Namespace="ProAspNet20.CS.Components"
          Assembly="ProAspCompLib" %>
⋮
<expo:Panel runat="server" Width="300px" BorderWidth="1px"
    Font-Bold="True" Font-Names="Verdana" Font-Size="Small"
    HorizontalAlign="Left" BackColor="#FFFF80"
    CaptionBackColor="Teal">
</expo:Panel>
```

Not all properties are themeable. An empirical rule dictates that you should theme only properties that are relevant to the user interface of the control. Any behavioral properties should be made themeable. How can you flag a property to be themeable or not? You use the *[Themeable]* attribute. By default, all properties are themeable. To keep a property off any skin files, you proceed as follows:

```
[Themeable(false)]
public bool EnableDropDown
{
    ⋮
}
```

EnableDropDown, *EnableClientScript*, and *ShowExpanded* are properties that you typically don't want to theme.

> **Note**   What's the preferred way to define graphical properties on a custom control? Should you opt for individual properties such as *CaptionBackColor*? Or are you better off grouping a bunch of properties in a style object? It is mostly a matter of preference. Personally, I'd go for style properties and even for custom style properties as we did earlier for the *SimpleGaugeBar* control. However, a style property is generally persisted as a child element of the control, and this might pose an issue if the control has other child elements. This is exactly the case for the drop-down *Panel* control. There are ways to work around this issue by configuring the serialization format of the style property. In this case, when the number of individual properties is limited to just a few, I don't mind using properties instead of styles.

The Rendering Engine

As mentioned, you can create the markup for a control in either of two ways—by writing the code that renders out markup as plain text, or by building a control tree. In the latter case, the ASP.NET rendering engine will take care of transforming the control tree into all-encompassing markup. Using text writer objects is generally faster; using a control tree to compose the markup programmatically is a more flexible approach that is especially important if the control posts back and interacts with the ASP.NET runtime infrastructure.

The base *Panel* control simply writes out a *<div>* tag and its attributes and leaves each contained control free to render itself using its own algorithm. For the drop-down *Panel* control, we need to build a control tree dynamically that contains a caption bar and a clickable button and that includes all child controls. Building the desired output through text writers is definitely possible, but to handle postback events correctly we need a full control tree. Let's start by overriding the *CreateChildControls* method.

Enhancing the Standard Markup

The rendering engine of the base *Panel* control is based on the standard implementation of the *Render* method. The method loops through all the child controls and renders the markup for each. When the *Render* method is invoked, the *Controls* collection of the *Panel* control is filled with as many instances as there are child controls under the *<asp:panel>* tag. This same behavior is maintained when you inherit the new drop-down *Panel* class.

To add a surrounding table and build a structure like that in Figure 13-5, you need to create a control tree. The *CreateChildControls* method is ultimately responsible for populating the *Controls* collection of each server control. Here's how to override the method for the drop-down *Panel* control:

```
protected override void CreateChildControls()
{
    if (EnableDropDown)
    {
        base.CreateChildControls();
        CreateControlHierarchy();
    }
}
```

```
        else
            base.CreateChildControls();
}
```

If *EnableDropDown* is *false*, the control behaves ordinarily and there's no difference between the derived and the base *Panel* control. Otherwise, the base method is invoked followed by a custom method—*CreateControlHierarchy*.

CreateControlHierarchy is the internal method that adds elements to the *Controls* collection to reproduce the expected structure. The name and signature of this method are arbitrary; however, most ASP.NET built-in composite controls feature a method with this name and behavior. Moreover, in some cases, the method is even flagged as protected and virtual.

Building a Control Tree

CreateControlHierarchy creates a table with two rows. The second row includes all child controls found in the *Controls* collection when the method is called. Here's some sample code:

```
protected virtual void CreateControlHierarchy()
{
    // Create a container table control
    Table t = new Table();

    // Create the title bar row
    TableRow row1 = new TableRow();
    t.Rows.Add(row1);

    // Create the title cell
    TableCell cell1 = new TableCell();
    row1.Cells.Add(cell1);
    cell1.Text = Caption;

    // Create the button cell (the image will be added later)
    TableCell cell2 = new TableCell();
    row1.Cells.Add(cell2);
    cell2.HorizontalAlign = HorizontalAlign.Right;

    // Create the content row
    TableRow row2 = new TableRow();
    t.Rows.Add(row2);

    // Create the contents cell
    TableCell body = new TableCell();
    body.ID = "Body";
    row2.Cells.Add(body);
    body.ColumnSpan = 2;

    // Add existing child controls to the cell
    Control[] children = new Control[Controls.Count];
    Controls.CopyTo(children, 0);
    foreach (Control ctl in children)
        body.Controls.Add(ctl);
```

```
// Replace the panel's Controls collection
Controls.Clear();
Controls.Add(t);
    ⋮
}
```

When this method is invoked, the *Controls* collection contains references to the child controls of the panel. These references are temporarily parked in an array of *Control* objects and then incorporated in the table being built. When done, the *Controls* collection is cleared and replaced with the newly created table. Figure 13-6 shows the new control tree as rendered by the ASP.NET trace utility.

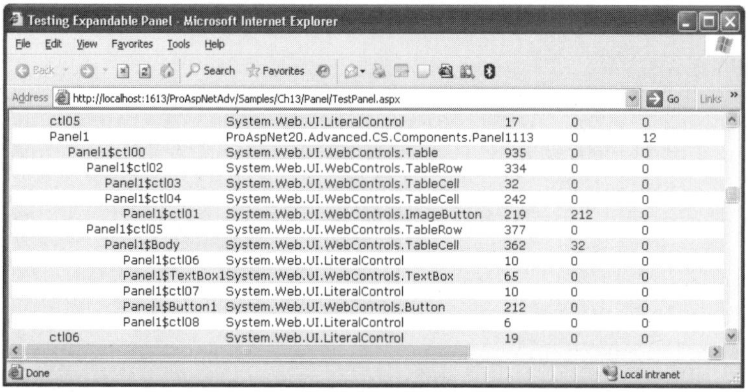

Figure 13-6   The control tree of the drop-down *Panel* control.

There's one main reason for building a control tree. In this way, any component in the final structure has a server-side counterpart and can handle events through the ASP.NET page life cycle. If the control you're building has no need to handle server events, you can build it through HTML text writers and save yourself and ASP.NET the burden of instantiating a bunch of controls for each request. If the control does need to interact with ASP.NET (for example, it contains a clickable element that raises a server event), you must guarantee that ASP.NET can find a server control with a matching ID. This happens only if such a control is added to the *Controls* collection. We'll return to this point in a moment.

The source code for the *CreateControlHierarchy* method that we showed earlier is incomplete. In particular, it lacks the code that adds a clickable image to the top row. This clickable image will be an *ImageButton* control if postbacks are supported or a plain *Image* control if the show/hide function requires a pure client-side implementation. The value of the *EnableClient-Script* property determines which route we're going to take.

Using Embedded Images

The second cell of the top row contains a clickable element. The following code shows how it gets created:

```
WebControl img;
if (!EnableClientScript)
{
```

```
        img = new ImageButton();
        ((ImageButton)img).Click += new ImageClickEventHandler(OnClick);
    }
    else
    {
        img = new System.Web.UI.WebControls.Image();

        // Add script code here to handle the user's clicking
        :
    }

    // cell2 is the second cell of the top row (see previous listing)
    cell2.Controls.Add(img);

    // Show/hide child controls
    ShowChildControls(_panelDisplayed);

    // Change the image according to the drop-down state
    ShowImageButton(_panelDisplayed);
```

In the default case, the expand/collapse button is an *ImageButton* object with a predefined *Click* event handler. *OnClick* is an internal member that fires whenever the control posts back because the user clicks on the image.

Where is the image URL set? The *ShowImageButton* internal member takes the current value of the drop-down state and updates the *ImageUrl* property of either *ImageButton* or *Image*. Note that *ImageButton* inherits from *Image*, meaning that a polymorphic approach is perfectly legal and in this case is highly effective.

```
void ShowImageButton(bool display)
{
    // Make sure there are controls to work with
    if (Controls.Count != 1)
        return;

    // Retrieve the button cell
    Table t = (Table)Controls[0];
    TableRow r = t.Rows[0];
    TableCell icon = r.Cells[1];

    // Can be Image or ImageButton depending on EnableClientScript.
    // (ImageButton derives from Image.)
    Image img =(Image) icon.Controls[0];
    string imageName = "ProAspNet20.Advanced.CS.Components.Expand.bmp";
    if (display)
        imageName = "ProAspNet20.Advanced.CS.Components.Collapse.bmp";
    img.ImageUrl = Page.ClientScript.GetWebResourceUrl(
                        this.GetType(), imageName);
}
```

ShowImageButton first retrieves the table cell where the image object is defined and then determines the name of the image to show. The images are embedded as resources in the control's assembly. (See Chapter 9.)

To embed an image as a resource, you first add the image to the Visual Studio 2005 project you're using to build the control. Then you set the build action to Embedded Resources. Note that the image name will be prefixed by the default assembly namespace. Next, you export the resource as a Web resource from the assembly. In the *assemblyinfo.cs* file (or *assemblyinfo.vb*), you add the following attributes:

```
[assembly: WebResource("ProAspNet20.Advanced.CS.Components.Expand.bmp",
                       "image/jpg")]
[assembly: WebResource("ProAspNet20.Advanced.CS.Components.Collapse.bmp",
                       "image/jpg")]
```

To retrieve the image programmatically, you call the *GetWebResourceUrl* method on the page's *ClientScript* object. You pass to the *GetWebResourceUrl* method the type of the control and the exported name of the resource. The method returns to you a URL that can be used to set the *ImageUrl* property of an image control and ultimately the *src* property of an *<img>* element. As discussed in Chapter 6, the URL is based on the *WebResource.axd* system HTTP handler. The handler reads the bytes of the resource from the assembly manifest stream and returns them using the Multipurpose Internet Mail Extensions (MIME) type specified in the *[WebResource]* attribute.

> **Note**   In ASP.NET 2.0, you can create a custom control by simply placing the source code in the *App_Code* folder of the Web site project where the control is being used. In this case, Visual Studio 2005 doesn't let you add embedded images to the control. To be able to add embedded images, you need to create the control in its own project or class library type.

The assembly that contains the drop-down *Panel* control includes a couple of images that look like the combo-box button in the Microsoft Windows XP system theme. Figure 13-7 shows how the button picture changes based on the drop-down state of the control.

Figure 13-7   The button image varies with the drop-down state of the control.

The biggest advantage you get out of embedded images in ASP.NET 2.0 is that you can now deploy self-contained custom controls that have appealing graphics, rich with images and resources. In ASP.NET 1.x, UI-rich controls are possible, but you have to take care of the deployment of any auxiliary resource file.

Adding Styles

The visible structure of the drop-down *Panel* control is almost complete now. Before we start looking at its behavior, let's talk a bit about the application of style attributes. When you build a control by composition—that is, whenever you end up overriding *CreateChildControls*—you should avoid applying styles and graphical properties directly in the hierarchy. To the extent that it is possible, you should try to keep hierarchy and styles separated.

In the *CreateControlHierarchy* method, you simply build the hierarchy of constituent controls and limit yourself to defining parent/child relationships. Next, you override the *Render* method as follows and apply styles just before rendering:

```
protected override void Render(HtmlTextWriter writer)
{
    PrepareControlForRendering();
    base.Render(writer);
}
protected virtual void PrepareControlForRendering()
{
    // Make sure there are controls to work with
    if (Controls.Count != 1)
        return;

    // Apply the table style
    if (!EnableDropDown)
        return;
    Table t = (Table) Controls[0];
    t.CopyBaseAttributes(this);
    if (ControlStyleCreated)
        t.ApplyStyle(ControlStyle);

    // cell spacing/padding set on title work for the whole table
    t.CellPadding = 1;
    t.CellSpacing = 0;

    // Style the title row
    TableRow row1 = t.Rows[0];
    row1.BackColor = CaptionBackColor;
    row1.ForeColor = CaptionForeColor;
}
```

PrepareControlForRendering is an internal member whose name and signature are totally arbitrary. Likewise, the *protected* and *virtual* modifiers used here can be changed at will in a custom implementation. The goal of the method is retrieving key elements in the *Controls* collection and applying to each its own set of styles and graphical properties. In this case, the first control in the collection is the surrounding *Table*.

The table inherits all the base attributes defined on the control through Visual Studio 2005. For example, if you set the *BackColor* property of the drop-down *Panel* control, that setting will be transferred to the *Table* that surrounds the HTML markup for the *Panel* control. In addition, you can style each constituent control with the values collected through style properties or individual graphical properties.

The *PrepareControlForRendering* method doesn't add new features to a control; it simply factors out the control's code in a more rational and neater way.

Raising Postback Events

The main benefit of the drop-down *Panel* control over the classic *Panel* control is that users can click on the side button and hide or show at will the contents of the panel. The state of child controls is maintained across postbacks, and so it is also for the drop-down state of the control. In other words, if a user expands the panel and then clicks on any other element in the page that posts back, the *Panel* will remain expanded also in the new served page.

In general, clicking a button causes a page postback. However, the decision between a server event or a client event should be made based on the expected results of the click. In this case, the user's click should hide or show the second row in the overall table that represents the output of the drop-down *Panel* control. Toggling the visibility state of an HTML element is an operation that can be accomplished both on the client and the server. As a control developer, the best thing you can do is provide both options and leave page authors with the final decision.

Handling User Clicks

By default, the drop-down *Panel* control renders the button through an *ImageButton* control. The *ImageButton* control inherits from *Image* and includes all the typical capabilities of a button—submit behavior, validation, postback data, and postback event handling. The *ImageButton* control emits proper script code to capture the user's click on the displayed image and submit a postback event.

When the page posts back, you need to modify the control's internal state so that the generated markup can reflect the new state of the control—be it collapsed or expanded. For this reason, the *ImageButton* control must be associated with an internal *OnClick* handler.

```
ImageButton img = new ImageButton();
img.Click += new ImageClickEventHandler(OnClick);
```

Here's the source code for the *OnClick* method:

```
void OnClick(object sender, ImageClickEventArgs e)
{
    // Change the drop-down state
    _panelDisplayed = !_panelDisplayed;

    // Make the UI reflect the change in the drop-down state
    ShowChildControls(_panelDisplayed);
    ShowImageButton(_panelDisplayed);
}
```

It is important to note that this server event will never be handled by ASP.NET if you omit the *INamingContainer* interface in the control class declaration and if the *ImageButton* control is not added to the *Controls* collection. If you simply render out the equivalent markup code for the *ImageButton* control, ASP.NET won't be able to match the postback data with a server control, and the *Click* server event will be lost.

The internal *Click* handler toggles the drop-down state of the control, changes the image to display for the button, and shows or hides the second row of the table where all child controls of the panel are listed. The *ShowChildControls* method takes care of this task.

```
void ShowChildControls(bool display)
{
    // Make sure there are controls to work with
    if (Controls.Count != 1)
        return;

    // Apply the table style
    Table t = (Table)Controls[0];
    TableRow r = t.Rows[1];
    TableCell body = r.Cells[0];
    body.Style["display"] = (display ? "" : "none");
}
```

Note that all controls always generate their markup and populate the view state as usual. This guarantees that the state will be maintained correctly. The visibility of elements in the client page is controlled through the browser's page document object model (DOM).

In the standard DOM, the *style* object features a *display* attribute to indicate whether or not a given element should be included in the page. If you set *display* to *none*, the browser ignores the element and doesn't render it to the user. If you set *display* to the empty string, the element is displayed correctly. This feature works on most browsers today, including Firefox and Netscape 6.0 and later versions.

> **Note**   In the standard DOM, two similar style attributes exist—*display* and *visibility*. Both can be used to toggle the visibility state of HTML elements. The difference is that when you use *visibility* to hide an element, the browser doesn't reuse the space occupied by the element. In other words, *visibility* lets you choose between displaying the element or leaving its space blank. With *display*, you choose to display or ignore the element entirely.

The *PanelClick* Public Event

In addition to properly modifying the internal state of the *Panel* control, you can also bubble the *Click* event to the outer level (for example, the host page). Or you can swallow the original event and expose it to the outside world through a brand new and custom interface. Let's tackle this scenario first and explore how to add a custom public event to the drop-down *Panel* control.

The *PanelClick* event fires when the user clicks on the drop-down panel and causes the host page to post back. The event is declared as follows:

```
public event EventHandler<PanelClickEventArgs> PanelClick;
```

The event carries some information to the handler packed in the *PanelClickEventArgs* class:

```
public class PanelClickEventArgs : EventArgs
{
    public bool BeingClosed;
}
```

The *PanelClickEventArgs* class derives from *EventArgs*—the base class for most event data structures—and extends it by adding a Boolean member. *BeingClosed* indicates whether the panel is being closed or expanded.

Any registered handler for the *PanelClick* event is invoked from within the internal handler associated with the *Click* event of the *ImageButton* control.

```
void OnClick(object sender, ImageClickEventArgs e)
{
    PanelClickEventArgs args = new PanelClickEventArgs();
    args.BeingClosed = _panelDisplayed;
    OnPanelClick(args);

    // Change the drop-down state.
    // (Same code shown above.)
    :
}
protected virtual void OnPanelClick(PanelClickEventArgs args)
{
    if (PanelClick != null)
        PanelClick(this, args);
}
```

The net effect of this code is that the host component (the page or any other container control that embeds the *Panel*) receives a *PanelClick* event whenever the *Panel* receives a *Click* event from the internal *ImageButton* control.

Custom Events vs. Event Bubbling

Wouldn't it be possible to let the original *Click* event flow outside the *Panel* control and reach the host component? Yes, it would, and the associated technique is known as *event bubbling*.

When an ASP.NET control is built as a hierarchy of constituent controls, its overall behavior results from some processing made on the events fired by internal controls. Event bubbling is the key technique that allows child controls to propagate their events up the containment hierarchy so that events physically fired by internal controls can be made visible at a more convenient level.

A control that wants to bubble up one of its original events simply adds a call to *RaiseBubble-Event* in the method used to fire the event, as shown here:

```
protected virtual void OnPanelClick(PanelClickEventArgs args)
{
    if (PanelClick != null)
        PanelClick(this, args);
    base.RaiseBubbleEvent(this, args);
}
```

RaiseBubbleEvent is a method defined on the *Control* class and inherited by all ASP.NET server controls.

A bubbled event is not visible in its native form to upper levels of the containment hierarchy. A host component that wants to handle an event bubbled from a child control must override the *OnBubbleEvent* method.

```
protected override bool OnBubbleEvent(object source, EventArgs e)
{
    bool handled = false;
    if (e is PanelClickEventArgs)
    {
        PanelClickEventArgs args = (PanelClickEventArgs) e;
        if (args.BeingClosed)
        {
            // Handle the event at this level
            // TO DO

            // Determine whether we're done with the event handling.
            // If we return true, the event propagation ends here.
            handled = true;
        }
    }
    return handled;
}
```

The *EventArgs* argument is the event data object for the specific event. You cast it to the expected type and handle the event as appropriate. The value you return from *OnBubbleEvent* plays an essential role in the event propagation. If you return true, the event propagation ends immediately, and upper levels in the hierarchy won't receive the event. If you return false, it means that event handling is not done yet and propagation should continue.

All in all, event bubbling is not a technique for everyday use, and, most of the time, you find that custom events are more useful and appropriate. Event bubbling is an excellent technique when you know that certain events might be fired but don't know in advance from which controls. What would be such a situation? When you work with templated controls, you can't know in advance what the template will actually contain. Here, event bubbling shows off its added value. We'll cover templated controls in the next chapter.

Adding Script Code

The drop-down *Panel* control doesn't require a deep interaction between the client and server environments. The postback event to show or hide the panel is not, therefore, strictly necessary. You can obtain the same effect with a bit of client-side script code. You can still show or hide the panel at will and save yourself a postback. To get this, you can't use an *ImageButton* control, as the *ImageButton* control automatically posts back.

To display the button, you use an *Image* control and add script code to display the hand cursor and to manage the visibility state of the panel.

Showing the Drop-Down Image

When the *EnableClientScript* property is *true*, the drop-down button is rendered as a plain image topped with some script code.

```
// Create the Image control
Image img = new Image();
img.Attributes["onmouseover"] = "this.style.cursor = \"hand\";";
img.Attributes["onmouseout"] = "this.style.cursor = \"\";";
img.Attributes["onclick"] = "__toggle()";

// cell2 is the second cell of the top row (see previous listing)
cell2.Controls.Add(img);
```

The *Image* control is given a couple of client-side style attributes—*onmouseover* and *onmouseout*—to show the hand cursor when the mouse hovers over the element. In addition, client clicks on the image are associated with a JavaScript function arbitrarily named *__toggle*.

The *ShowImageButton* method (see previous listing) is called from within the *CreateControl-Hierarchy* method to set the URL of the image to display. To change the URL programmatically as the user clicks, you need to know the URL of both images to use when the panel is expanded or collapsed. For simplicity, I'm not swapping images when the drop-down *Panel* supports client script.

```
// Use the same image for both expanded and collapsed state
string imageName = "ProAspNet20.Advanced.CS.Components.Expand.bmp";
img.ImageUrl = Page.ClientScript.GetWebResourceUrl(
        this.GetType(), imageName);
```

Emitting Script Code

The *__toggle* JavaScript function contains the code that shows or hides the contents of the panel as the user clicks. The source code of this function must be available in some way in the host page. For example, you can import it from the control's assembly or from an external file. As an alternative, you can have the control generate and emit the source code.

```
if (!Page.ClientScript.IsClientScriptBlockRegistered("__toggle"))
{
    string js = BuildScript(body);
    Page.ClientScript.RegisterClientScriptBlock(
          this.GetType(), "__toggle", js, true);
}
```

Any client script block that must be emitted with the host page must be registered with the page and named. You use a pair of methods. With the *IsClientScriptBlockRegistered* method, you check whether a given piece of code is already registered. With the *RegisterClientScript-Block* method, you register a new block of script code. A block of script code corresponds to a client-side *<script>* block.

In ASP.NET 2.0, each block of script code must have a unique name and be associated with a type. In ASP.NET 1.x, all blocks are associated with the host page type, and there's no need for you to indicate a type explicitly. You typically set the type to the control's type and use the name of the JavaScript function as the nickname of the script block.

The JavaScript source code is specified as a string, and the optional Boolean argument in the call to the *RegisterClientScriptBlock* method indicates whether you want a surrounding *<script>* tag to be automatically created for you. By passing *false*, you are responsible for adding that (required) tag yourself.

Generating Script Code

The source of the JavaScript script block can be created in any way; what matters is that you get a string that evaluates to a JavaScript function. Here's some sample code that uses a *String-Builder* object to accumulate some text. Note that in the .NET Framework, the *StringBuilder* object is the recommended tool for concatenating strings and is much more efficient than just composing individual strings through the plus (+) operator.

```
private string BuildScript(TableCell body)
{
    StringBuilder sb = new StringBuilder();
    sb.AppendLine("function __toggle() {");
    sb.AppendFormat("var body = document.getElementById(\"{0}\");\r\n",
              body.ClientID);
    sb.AppendLine("var display = body.style.display;");
    sb.AppendLine("if (display == \"\") {");
    sb.AppendLine("body.style.display = \"none\";");
    sb.AppendLine("} else {");
    sb.AppendLine("body.style.display = \"\";");
    sb.AppendLine("}");
    sb.AppendLine("}");

    return sb.ToString();
}
```

The final JavaScript code emitted in the page looks like the following:

```
<script type="text/javascript">
<!--
function __toggle() {
   var body = document.getElementById("Panel1_Body");
   var display = body.style.display;
   if (display == "") {
      body.style.display = "none";
   } else {
      body.style.display = "";
   }
}
// -->
</script>
```

Basically, the code retrieves the table cell element that represents the contents of the panel and toggles its display state. It uses the *document.getElementById* expression from the standard page DOM to find a reference to the HTML element that represents the table cell hosting the panel contents.

To generate the script code that does this, the *BuildScript* helper function needs to get a reference to the server-side *TableCell* object. This reference is passed to *BuildScript* as an argument. If you take a closer look at the full source code of the drop-down *Panel* control, you won't fail to notice that the server-side ID of the table cell is *Body* while the corresponding client-side ID is *Panel1_Body*. Why is that so? And, more importantly, how can you match the two strings?

Element Identification

One of the essential rules of composite controls is that the ID of any child control must be scoped in the ID of the parent control. In other words, you need a namespace-like mechanism to ensure that a table cell named *Body* in a *Panel* control named *Panel1* is different from an analogous table cell in a *Panel* control named *Panel2*. As a page developer, you have no control over the ID of the internal table cell, which is invisible to you. You name two instances of the same control differently, but this is not enough to guarantee that in the page DOM the table cells of both controls are also named differently and can be identified without ambiguity.

By implementing the marker interface *INamingContainer*, you ensure that on the server each constituent control is given an ID scoped in the ID of the parent. For example, consider the following code:

```
cell.ID = "Body";
```

If this code is run in the context of a *Panel* control named *Panel1*, the unique ID of the cell will be *Panel1$Body*. The *ID* property is still set to *Body*, but the *UniqueID* property returns *Panel1$Body*. When the markup for the cell is generated, neither of the two ID properties is used. The *ClientID* property is used instead. *ClientID* is like *UniqueID* except that it replaces the $ symbol with the underscore (_) symbol.

The bottom line is that to script the HTML counterpart of a server-side control, you need to reference it through the name returned by the *ClientID* property of the server control.

> **Important**   The value of the *ClientID* property is updated to reflect naming containment rules only when the control is added to the *Controls* collection of its container. Looking at the preceding code, if you call *BuildScript* before the table cell object is added to *Controls*, the *ClientID* property returns *Body* instead of *Panel1_Body*, and the script will fail on the client because no object is found with that name.

Conclusion

ASP.NET provides a wealth of server controls from which you can likely choose exactly the control you are looking for. If this is not the case, and the control simply doesn't exist, you can create your own control from the ground up or by extending an existing control and obtain incredibly powerful results. Writing a control is a matter of defining an appropriate object model and providing an effective rendering algorithm. Aside from these two points, other equally important aspects of control development are containment, naming, and integration with the engine that supplies state management.

In this chapter, we've built three controls and learned how to design a rendering engine by choosing between the pure HTML approach and the control-based approach. The HTML approach provides speed but sacrifices a bit of readability and ease of code maintenance. The control-based approach applies different priorities and chooses code modularity over the raw speed of rendering.

Composite controls are a special case of new controls. They exploit the principle of aggregation rather than inheritance. You create a composite control by assembling multiple, distinct controls and synthesizing a new object model on top of them. The resulting object model can be the summation of all elements or, more simply, can be built by taking what is really needed out of constituent elements. For composite controls, being a naming container is a critical point.

In the next chapter, we'll take a look at even more complex types of controls—data-bound and templated controls.

Just the Facts

- You can create a custom server control by inheriting from an existing control and adding new properties and methods to it.

- You can create a custom server control by inheriting from a base control class and implementing a number of built-in behaviors such as control state, themes, rendering, and state management.

- You can create the markup for a control in either of two ways—by writing the code that renders out markup as plain text or by building a control tree. In the latter case, you create a composite control.

- When many graphical properties need to be managed, you might want to consider using a style object instead. Style properties should be applied before rendering and not during the creation of the control hierarchy.

- Various interfaces can enrich the way a control behaves. Through additional interfaces, you can handle postback events, manage postback data, and also manage client requests through script callbacks.

Chapter 14
Data-Bound and Templated Controls

All sample custom controls we have built thus far are effective and functional but lack a few key features. More often than not, real-world controls need to be data-bindable and support templates. The importance of a control being data-bindable surfaced clearly in Chapter 11, in which we thoroughly discussed and explored the *Repeater* and *DataList* controls. The topic was covered even more extensively in Part 2 of *Programming Microsoft ASP.NET 2.0: Core Reference* (Microsoft Press 2005), the companion book to this one.

For an ASP.NET programmer, a control that can be bound to a collection of data is an essential aid that smooths development and significantly increases both personal and team productivity. Similarly helpful is built-in support for templates, which makes the control much more flexible and reduces by an order of magnitude the need for further customization. Often when you buy a third-party feature-rich control, you're not completely satisfied with its user interface and overall set of capabilities and functions. Many software houses buy only components that come with full (and commented) source code, primarily so that they can solve any issues that derive from the integration between the component and the core application. Templates provide a way to customize controls. Templates don't ensure that you'll never want something more or different from a component; however, templates have been introduced mainly as a way to make portions of the user interface as generic and parametric as possible.

In this chapter, we'll take the gauge control introduced in Chapter 13 to the next level by adding data-binding capabilities. We'll also design and implement a couple more sample controls to provide a broader view of data-bound controls. In particular, we'll discuss list controls and composite data-bound controls with template support.

Designing a Data-Bound Control

A data-bound control is mainly characterized by a data source property and a bunch of string properties to define mappings between fields in the bound data source and parts of the control's user interface. In ASP.NET 1.x, the data source property can point only to an object of type *IEnumerable* (or any derived type) or *IListSource*. ASP.NET 2.0 adds a new data source model. It consists of a bunch of new user interface–less controls that bridge the gap between visual parts of data-bound controls and data containers. Basically, the vast majority of code that developers were required to write in ASP.NET 1.x, properly factored and authored, is now embedded in a new family of controls–data source controls. Data source controls are covered in great detail in Chapter 9 of *Programming Microsoft ASP.NET 2.0: Core Reference* (Microsoft Press 2005).

There are many benefits to using data source controls in ASP.NET pages. First and foremost, we have the possibility of a fully declarative data-binding model. The new model reduces the loose code inserted inline in *.aspx* files or scattered through code-behind classes. The new data-binding architecture forces developers to play by strict rules. Moreover, it inherently changes the quality of the code to be written. Long blocks of code attached to events tend to disappear and are replaced by components that just plug into the existing framework. These components (for example, data source controls) derive from abstract classes, implement well-known interfaces, and overall signify a higher level of reusability.

How does this affect control developers? In ASP.NET 2.0, any data-bound control must be able to support both forms of binding–against enumerable objects and data source controls. With ASP.NET 2.0, you get a completely redesigned graph of classes that add more specific data-binding capabilities as you scroll the tree from base to leaf classes. The new hierarchy of data-bound controls makes it easier for everybody to pick up the right class to inherit from for building their own custom data-bound control.

Types of Data-Bound Controls

Any server control can be designed to automatically retrieve some of its data from an external data source. Based on the interaction between the data source and the control, you can identify three distinct forms of data binding and, subsequently, data-bound controls–simple binding, list controls, and complex binding.

Simple Data Binding

Simple data binding consists of binding an object and one or more control properties. The data source binds to an individual item as opposed to a list of items. The internal structure of a control that uses simple binding is nearly identical to that of a complex bound control–only simpler.

The *SimpleGaugeBar* control that we discussed in the previous chapter is a good example of a simple data-bound control. Later, we'll extend the *SimpleGaugeBar* control to make the *Value* and *FormatString* properties bindable to a field on a data source object or data source control.

List Controls

List controls are controls that display a list of data items through a fixed and immutable user interface. Popular examples of list controls are *RadioButtonList*, *CheckBoxList* and, new in ASP.NET 2.0, *BulletedList*. The main trait of list controls is the strict association between data items and child controls—such as a radio button, check box, or bullet point.

As we'll see later in the chapter, a custom list control can be built by defining a control to repeat and initialize the control with the data contained in each bound data item. Most list controls also feature advanced layout capabilities such as rendering data in a given number of columns or rows. We'll see how to add that capability to custom controls, too.

Complex Data Binding

Complex data-bound controls are typically composite controls that display a list of items with no limitation at all on the rendering mechanism. A good example of complex data-bound control is the *DataGrid* control.

In this chapter, we'll design and implement a *BarChart* control as a real-world example of complex binding and template support. The *BarChart* control renders as an HTML table where each row represents a horizontal bar in a chart. Needless to say, information for the chart comes from a bound data source.

> **Important**   In ASP.NET 1.x, data binding works only in one direction, meaning that the control has typically no way to update the data source. Each data-bound control generally reads data from the data source and fires events when something happens that requires updates on the bound source. In ASP.NET 2.0, data source controls form the underlying machinery for two-way data binding. In the whole ASP.NET 2.0 control toolbox, only three controls support two-way binding—*GridView*, *FormView*, and *DetailsView*. Two-way data binding requires additional logic in the control code to invoke proper methods on the bound data source, which has to be a data source control. All examples in this book refer to the most common scenario—one-way data binding.

The Data-Binding Mechanism

Figure 14-1 presents the list of data-bound controls available in ASP.NET 2.0. As you can see, all classes derive from *BaseDataBoundControl*—the root class for ASP.NET 2.0 data-bound controls.

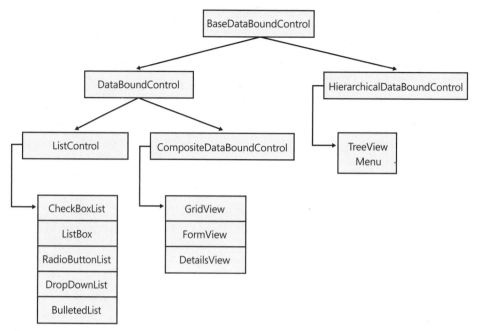

Figure 14-1 The hierarchy of data-bound controls in ASP.NET 2.0.

The *BaseDataBoundControl* class defines the machinery through which the data binding occurs and validates any bound data. Common data source properties are defined on this class—*DataSource* for enumerable data, and *DataSourceID* for data source controls.

```
public virtual object DataSource { get; set; }
public virtual string DataSourceID { get; set; }
```

Each property activates a distinct binding mechanism. The two properties are mutually exclusive; if both are set simultaneously, you run into an exception. Because *DataSource* and *DataSourceID* refer to distinct mechanisms, as a control developer, should you be ready to incorporate both in your code? To find an effective answer to this central question, we need to delve deeper in the internals of *BaseDataBoundControl* and its derivatives.

Binding to a Data Source

The *DataSource* property accepts objects that implement the *IEnumerable* (for example, collections) or *IListSource* (for example, *DataTable*) interface. The assignment occurs just as in ASP.NET 1.x.

```
ctl.DataSource = dataTable;
ctl.DataBind();
```

In addition to setting the *DataSource* property, you have to call the *DataBind* method on the control (or on the control's container object—say, the page). Only when *DataBind* is invoked is the data physically loaded into the runtime image of the control.

The *DataSourceID* property is a string and refers to the ID of a bound data source control. Once a control is bound to a data source, any further interaction between the two (in both reading and writing) is out of your control and hidden from view. This is good and bad news at the same time. It is good (actually, it is great) news because you cut a large quantity of code from your pages. The ASP.NET framework guarantees that correct code executes and is written against recognized best practices. You're more productive because you author pages faster with the inherent certainty of having no subtle bugs in the middle. If you don't like this situation, you can stick to the ASP.NET 1.x programming style.

The internal architecture of data-bound controls changed quite a bit in the transition to ASP.NET 2.0. Most of the changes are incorporated in the *BaseDataBoundControl* class. Let's start looking at what happens when you set *DataSource* and *DataSourceID* on any data-bound controls. The following code shows the *setter* of *DataSource*:

```
// Pseudo-code for setting DataSource
set (object value)
{
    if (value != null)
        ValidateDataSource(value);
    _dataSource = value;
    OnDataPropertyChanged();
}
```

The passed data source object is first validated to check whether it is of an acceptable type and then cached in a private member. Finally, the internal *OnDataPropertyChanged* method is invoked. Let's look at the *setter* of *DataSourceID* also:

```
// Pseudo-code for setting DataSourceID
set (string value)
{
    ViewState["DataSourceID"] = value;
    OnDataPropertyChanged();
}
```

The value of *DataSourceID* is cached in the view state, and then a call to *OnDataProperty-Changed* is made. What happens within the *OnDataPropertyChanged* method? The method sets a protected Boolean variable named *RequiresDataBinding*. The protected member is defined on *BaseDataBoundControl* and inherited by all derived controls—it is set to *true* whenever the control requires binding to data.

Let's take a deeper look at some key members of the *BaseDataBoundControl* class.

The *BaseDataBoundControl* Class

Most of the behavior of the *BaseDataBoundControl* class revolves around a few built-in event handlers, the override of *DataBind* (a method originally defined on *Control*), and a pair of virtual methods.

The class handles the *Init* and *PreRender* events. In the *OnInit* method, it automatically sets *RequiresDataBinding* to *true* if the host page is posting back. This trick guarantees that data-bound controls are correctly refreshed even when bound to data source controls. In the *OnPreRender* method, the class ensures that data binding is executed if required. Another internal method—named *EnsureDataBound*—takes care of this task. It checks *RequiresDataBinding* and calls *DataBind* if the property returns *true*.

As mentioned, the *DataBind* method is defined on the *Control* class and gets overridden in *BaseDataBoundControl*. Here's the pseudo-code:

```
public override void DataBind()
{
    PerformSelect();
}
```

Interestingly enough, *PerformSelect* is marked as abstract on *BaseDataBoundControl* so its implementation is left to derived classes. The ultimate goal of the method, though, is quite unequivocal—performing any operation aimed at retrieving the bound data. The second abstract method is *ValidateDataSource*, which is invoked when you set the *DataSource* property.

The *DataBoundControl* Class

ValidateDataSource is overridden, care of the *DataBoundControl* class. Here's the related pseudo-code:

```
protected override void ValidateDataSource(object dataSource)
{
    if (dataSource != null)
    {
        if (!(dataSource is IListSource) &&
            !(dataSource is IEnumerable) &&
            !(dataSource is IDataSource))
        throw new InvalidOperationException(...);
    }
}
```

As you can see, the *DataSource* object can either be null or one of the following types—*IListSource*, *IEnumerable*, or *IDataSource*. *IDataSource* is the interface that characterizes data source controls. In other words, you can bind a control to a data source control in two ways—declaratively using the *DataSourceID* property, or programmatically by setting the *DataSource* property with the instance of the data source control.

DataBoundControl also overrides the *PerformSelect* method. Here's how:

```
protected override void PerformSelect()
{
    // Get the data-source-view object associated to the control
    DataSourceView view = GetData();
```

```
    // Invoke the SELECT operation on the bound data source control
    // _arguments is an internal member that references a data
    // structure filled with arguments for the SELECT operation
    _arguments = CreateDataSourceSelectArguments();
    view.Select(_arguments, OnDataSourceViewSelectCallback);

    // bound data is processed through the internal callback function
}
```

It connects to the data source object and obtains the default view. Next, it prepares a *SELECT* command to execute on the data source control, such as *SqlDataSource* or *ObjectDataSource*.

Even though control developers are offered two distinct ways of binding (*DataSource* vs. *DataSourceID*), under the hood of data-bound controls data retrieval occurs in just one way—through data source view objects. If the control is bound to a data source control, the incorporated data source view object is retrieved via the members of the *IDataSource* interface. If the control is bound to an enumerable object, a data source view object is dynamically built and returned by *GetData*. If the *DataSource* is non-empty, the bound object is wrapped in a dynamically created data source view object of type *ReadOnlyDataSource*—an internal and undocumented class.

By design, a *DataSourceView* object features the *Select* method and returns the bound data through it. As shown in the preceding pseudo-code, the *Select* method accepts some input arguments and a callback function. The callback function receives an enumerable collection of data—the items to bind to the control.

The bottom line is that whatever data source object you bind to the control, a data source view object is created. A data source view object is a class that can perform SELECT, INSERT, DELETE, and UPDATE operations on a bound object. *DataBoundControl* performs a SELECT operation on the data source view and obtains an enumerable collection of data. This collection contains the data to show in the control's user interface regardless of whether *DataSource* or *DataSourceID* was used.

As a control developer, how can you access this bindable collection of data?

> **Note**   The *HierarchicalDataBoundControl* class has an internal structure that is nearly identical to *DataBoundControl* except that data source view objects are used with a hierarchical nature.

The *PerformDataBinding* Overridable Method

The callback function that gets to process the results of the SELECT operation on the data source view ends up calling a protected overridable method—*PerformDataBinding*.

```
protected virtual void PerformDataBinding(IEnumerable data)
{
    // data is the collection of data to show in the data-bound
    // control's user interface
}
```

The *PerformDataBinding* method defined on *DataBoundControl* contains no executable code. In derived classes, you override this method and load the bound data in internal structures as necessary.

In summary, data-bound controls support a larger set of features in ASP.NET 2.0 than in any previous versions. Building custom data-bound controls, though, has never been easier. In most cases, all that you have to do is create a new class from *DataBoundControl* and override the *PerformDataBinding* method.

Armed with this knowledge, let's see how to build a few typical custom data-bound controls. Along the way, we'll explore in more depth other data-bound control classes that appear in Figure 14-1.

> **Note**   *DataMember* was a pretty popular property for data-bound controls in ASP.NET 1.x and was often used in conjunction with *DataSource*. *DataMember* is a string property that selects a data member in the specified source. In ASP.NET 2.0, the two properties have been separated. *DataSource* is defined on *BaseDataBoundControl*, whereas *DataMember* is defined on *DataBoundControl*.

Building a Simple Data-Bound Control

In the previous chapter, we created the *SimpleGaugeBar* control as a composite control to display a notched indicator of a given quantity. By setting the *Value* and *Maximum* properties on the control, you can graphically represent a value on the proper scale. The *SimpleGaugeBar* control is not data bound, meaning that no elements in its programming interface can be automatically and declaratively bound to external data. Derived from *CompositeControl*, the *SimpleGaugeBar* control doesn't incorporate any of the features listed previously regarding data-bound controls.

The goal of this section is to extend the *SimpleGaugeBar* control to make it support data binding through enumerable objects and data source controls.

Key Features

A data-bound version of *SimpleGaugeBar* is a form of simple binding. A couple of existing properties—*Value* and *FormatString*—can be automatically filled with external data according to the classic data-binding pattern of ASP.NET. A data source object specified through either *DataSource* or *DataSourceID* and with bindable properties is mapped to public fields on the data source object through mapper properties. In simple binding, the bound data source object is an individual object that contains just one logical piece of information—no items, no lists.

The key features of a data-bound control can be summarized as follows:

- Additional properties to represent mappings between control properties and data source fields

- An additional property to represent and persist the data source object

- Additional view-state management to persist the data source object

- Modified rendering to take bound data into account

Let's dig out more.

Adding Data-Bound Properties

When you bind data to, say, a *DropDownList* control, you first set the data source and then specify which fields on the data source should be used to display the text and the value of the resulting list. The *DropDownList* control features a pair of *DataTextField* and *DataValueField* string properties.

The former is set to the name of the public field on the data source that will render the text of displayed list items. The latter is set to the name of the field on the bound data source object that will render the unique value associated with each displayed list item.

On a brand new data-bound control, you need to define similar properties to specify any required mapping between data source fields and bindable control properties. All these properties are usually string properties stored in the view state; the name is arbitrary, but it generally follows the pattern *DataXxxField*, where *Xxx* indicates the role of the bindable control property.

Adding a Data Item Property

By design, the bound data source object must be an object that implements any of the following interfaces: *IEnumerable* (collections), *IListSource* (ADO.NET objects), or *IDataSource* (data source controls). Let's suppose you bind a control to one row of a *DataTable*. Do you really need to persist the whole data row? If yes, what if the data row contains a couple of large binary object (BLOB) fields?

The recommended approach entails that you extract a subset of information from the originally bound data source object and copy that to a control-specific data item object. This object is an instance of a custom class that typically has as many public properties as there are bindable properties on the control. For example, the *DropDownList* control has two bindable properties—*Text* and *Value*. Subsequently, the data item object—named *ListItem*—has two properties—*Text* and *Value*. (Naming is arbitrary, though.)

In a brand new data-bound control, you define a data item class that will be filled with any necessary information contained in the bound data source. This data item object must be persisted through the view state to guarantee that the control refreshes properly across post-backs. For performance reasons, the data item class must be able to serialize itself to the view state without resorting to the binary formatter. Put another way, it means that the data item class must implement *IStateManager* just like style classes do.

> **Note**   The data item class will be a collection of single data item classes if the data binding involves the association of a list of elements to a control.

Extra View-State Management

A custom data-bound control that supports data items must also provide extra view-state management code to ensure that the data item class is saved and restored. The data-bound control must override its *LoadViewState* and *SaveViewState* methods to persist any useful objects that implement *IStateManager*, such as styles and data items.

Note that in the *SimpleGaugeBar* control (discussed in Chapter 13), we haven't overridden *LoadViewState* and *SaveViewState* methods for the custom style object. That was an arguable implementation choice. To stay on the safe side of development, you must override *LoadView-State* and *SaveViewState* whenever you have a custom control that works with *IStateManager* objects. If you omit this, as we did in Chapter 13, the risk is that any dynamically modified style attributes (or attributes on *IStateManager* objects) are lost across postbacks. Consider the following code snippet:

```
protected void Page_Load(object sender, EventArgs e)
{
    if (!IsPostBack)
        SimpleGaugeBar1.TextStyle.BackColor = Color.Yellow;
}
```

The *BackColor* attribute is set only the first time the page displays. If the *TextStyle* property is not explicitly persisted to the view state (as in the *SimpleGaugeBar* control of Chapter 13), the color yellow will be irreversibly lost the first time the page posts back.

```
protected void Page_Load(object sender, EventArgs e)
{
    // The style is dynamically changed any time the page
    // is invoked. In this case, there's no need to persist the style
    // object to the viewstate.
    SimpleGaugeBar1.TextStyle.BackColor = Color.Yellow;
}
```

If you can assume that users of your control will always set styles at design time or don't check the *IsPostBack* property, you should save extra view-state management for styles as a safeguard.

Overriding the *PerformDataBinding* Method

The final key feature for a custom data-bound control—that is, a control that inherits from *DataBoundControl*— is overriding the *PerformDataBinding* method. The method receives the contents of the bound data source object in the form of an enumerable object. As a control developer, you must read any required data from the source and cache it in the data item object.

Finally, you modify the rendering engine of the control to display bound data.

> **Note**   Unless you need a data-bound control that behaves in a particular way (for example, a list control or a composite data-bound control), deriving your control from *DataBound-Control* is the most reasonable thing to do most of the time. If you need to start from a lower level, though, you can inherit from *BaseDataBoundControl* and override *PerformSelect* and *ValidateDataSource*. Needless to say, you might want to take this route only if you need to change the way a data source is validated and/or retrieved.

The *GaugeBar* Control

Let's apply all the steps outlined so far to a new version of the *SimpleGaugeBar* control, aptly named *GaugeBar*. The new control will still be a composite control, but it will inherit from *DataBoundControl* to gain standard data-binding capabilities.

```
public class GaugeBar : DataBoundControl
{
    :
}
```

To be precise, ASP.NET 2.0 features a class that incorporates both composition and data binding—*CompositeDataBoundControl*. We'll tackle that in the next example.

Mapping Data Source Fields to Control Properties

The new *GaugeBar* control uses the same code of *SimpleGaugeBar* that we carefully examined in Chapter 13 and extends it in the way we discuss here. You need to have a string property for each bindable property on the control's programming interface. The *GaugeBar* control has two bindable properties—*Value* and *FormatString*. This choice of bindable properties is arbitrary. You define a pair of *DataXxxField* properties—one for *Value* and one for *FormatString*. These string properties contain the name of the data source fields mapped to the *Value* and *FormatString*. In particular, *DataValueField* indicates that the field mapped to *Value* and *DataTextField* specifies the field linked to *FormatString*. Once again, note that the names used here are arbitrary.

```
public virtual string DataValueField
{
    get
    {
        object o = ViewState["DataValueField"];
```

```
        if (o == null)
            return String.Empty;
        return (string) o;
    }
    set { ViewState["DataValueField"] = value; }
}

public virtual string DataTextField
{
    get
    {
        object o = ViewState["DataTextField"];
        if (o == null)
            return String.Empty;
        return (string) o;
    }
    set { ViewState["DataTextField"] = value; }
}
```

As you can see, both properties use the *ViewState* as the storage medium and are set to the empty string by default. Other popular data-bound properties available on the *GaugeBar* class are *DataSource*, *DataSourceID*, and *DataMember*, all of which are inherited from parent classes.

The *GaugeBar* Data Item Object

Once the *GaugeBar* control is bound to some external data, you need to track and cache any bound data. For this purpose, you need a data item object. As mentioned, a data item object is a custom class with as many public properties as there are bindable properties in the control's interface. The data item class for the *GaugeBar* control is named *GaugeBarDataItem* (again, an arbitrary name) and is defined as follows:

```
public class GaugeBarDataItem : IStateManager
{
    private string _text;
    private float _value;
    private bool _marked;

    public GaugeBarDataItem()
    {
    }
    public GaugeBarDataItem(float value, string text)
    {
        _text = text;
        _value = value;
    }
    public string Text
    {
        get { return _text; }
        set { _text = value; }
    }
    public float Value
    {
```

```
        get { return _value; }
        set { _value = value; }
    }
    public bool IsTrackingViewState
    {
        get { return _marked; }
    }
    public void LoadViewState(object state)
    {
        if (state != null)
        {
            Pair p = (Pair)state;
            _value = (float)p.First;
            _text = (string)p.Second;
        }
    }
    public object SaveViewState()
    {
        return new Pair(_value, _text);
    }
    public void TrackViewState()
    {
        _marked = true;
    }
}
```

The class has two public properties—*Text* and *Value*—persisted through local members, and it implements the *IStateManager* interface to save its contents to the view state across postbacks.

The *SaveViewState* method returns a *Pair* object (a sort of simplified array of two elements) filled with the current values of *Text* and *Value* properties. The *Pair* object returned by *SaveViewState* becomes the input argument of *LoadViewState*, which unpacks the *Pair* object and initializes the *Text* and *Value* properties.

The *GaugeBar* control will need to expose a read-only property of type *GaugeBarDataItem*. You can use any name for this variable—I'm using *DataItem* here. The name of the property is not as important as its implementation. Take a look at the following code:

```
private GaugeBarDataItem _dataItem;
    :
private GaugeBarDataItem DataItem
{
    get
    {
        if (_dataItem == null)
        {
            _dataItem = new GaugeBarDataItem();
            if (base.IsTrackingViewState)
                _dataItem.TrackViewState();
        }
        return _dataItem;
    }
}
```

Unlike other control properties that are persisted directly in the *ViewState* collection object, the *DataItem* property uses a private member (*_dataItem*) to persist its value. A private member, though, is not persistent and doesn't survive postbacks. For this reason, in the *get* accessor of the property you need to check *_dataItem* for nullness and create a new instance if it is null.

The code contained in the *get* accessor of a property runs whenever that property is invoked. As we'll see in a moment, the preceding code ensures that no access to *DataItem* results in a null object exception, and that the state of the object is restored correctly after each postback.

Data Item and View State

Most of the control properties we've considered thus far use the *ViewState* container to persist the values. Why should we not store *DataItem* or style properties in the same way? Is there anything wrong with the following code?

```
// NB: for this code to work, GaugeBarDataItem must be
// a serializable type
public virtual GaugeBarDataItem DataItem
{
    get
    {
        object o = ViewState["DataItem"];
        if (o == null)
            return new GaugeBarDataItem();
        return (string) o;
    }
    set { ViewState["DataItem"] = value; }
}
```

Actually, nothing is "wrong" with the code per se—but consider for a moment view-state size and performance. Saving a class type directly in the *ViewState* container results in the object being serialized using the binary formatter. The *BinaryFormatter* class—the standard way to serialize managed objects in .NET applications—is not particularly fast and is designed to save the entire state of the object, including both public *and* private members, both simple and complex. The use of the *BinaryFormatter* increases the response time for each request and generates a larger view-state output. By customizing the view-state serialization, you obtain much faster code and save exactly the information you need to save.

As a rule of thumb, you should use the *ViewState* container to store property values if the type of the property is primitive—string, numbers, Boolean values, colors, dates, bytes, and arrays of any of these types. Reference types (for example, custom classes) should be serialized by implementing *IStateManager* and exposing the property via a get accessor like the one shown previously. As far as control development is concerned, this is commonly required for styles and data item properties.

Ad Hoc View-State Management

A control that has properties that take advantage of custom view-state serialization must override the *SaveViewState* and *LoadViewState* protected methods. These methods are defined on the *Control* class, and they indicate how to save and restore the state of the control to and from the view state. The default implementation of both methods takes care only of the contents of the *ViewState* container object.

```
protected override object SaveViewState()
{
    // Get the standard state object-ViewState container
    object baseState = base.SaveViewState();

    // Get the state object for the DataItem property
    object itemState = DataItem.SaveViewState();

    // Get the state object for the TextStyle object
    object styleState = TextStyle.SaveViewState();

    // Pack everything into a unique object
    return new Triplet(baseState, itemState, styleState);
}
```

The *SaveViewState* method of the *GaugeBar* control needs to save three objects—the standard view state, the *DataItem* property, and the *TextStyle* property. You get the standard view-state output by calling *SaveViewState* on the base class, and other state objects by calling *SaveViewState* on the *IStateManager* implementation of *DataItem* and *TextStyle*. The *SaveViewState* method on the control needs to return a single object, so you just group all data to return in a single object—typically an array or a combination of *Pair* and *Triplet* objects.

The object returned by *SaveViewState* is received by *LoadViewState*, which extracts and assigns data back to the original objects.

```
protected override void LoadViewState(object savedState)
{
    if (savedState != null)
    {
        Triplet t = (Triplet) savedState;
        base.LoadViewState(t.First);
        DataItem.LoadViewState(t.Second);
        TextStyle.LoadViewState(t.Third);
    }
    else
    {
        base.LoadViewState(null);
    }
}
```

The *IStateManager* implementation of *LoadViewState* on the serialized objects determines how each object (for example, styles or data items) restores its own data.

Note that when *DataItem.LoadViewState* is called, the *get* accessor of *DataItem* is invoked and initializes the internal *_dataItem* member on the first call.

Getting Bound Data

In ASP.NET 2.0, a bound control obtains bound data through the *PerformDataBinding* method. Overriding this method is mandatory for any data-bound control, as the standard implementation of the method does nothing. It is important to recall that the *IEnumerable* argument passed to *PerformDataBinding* represents the collection of bound data regardless of the format of the originally bound data source—whether it is an ADO.NET object, a collection, or a data source control.

Here's the implementation of *PerformDataBinding* for the *GaugeBar* control:

```
protected override void PerformDataBinding(IEnumerable data)
{
    // Argument data is a single object, not a list to enumerate.
    // Need to get an enumerator and call MoveNext once to get to data
    if (data == null)
        return;
    IEnumerator e = data.GetEnumerator();
    e.MoveNext();

    // Set default values for bindable properties
    float displayValue = 0;
    string displayText = String.Empty;

    // Read the value for the Value property
    if (!String.IsNullOrEmpty(DataValueField))
        displayValue = (float) DataBinder.GetPropertyValue(
                e.Current, DataValueField);

    // Read the value for the FormatString property
    if (!String.IsNullOrEmpty(DataTextField))
        displayText = (string) DataBinder.GetPropertyValue(
                e.Current, DataTextField);

    // Fill the DataItem property
    DataItem.Value = displayValue;
    DataItem.Text = displayText;
}
```

In this particular case, the *IEnumerable* object passed to *PerformDataBinding* contains just one element. The *IEnumerable* interface, though, doesn't distinguish between a single element and a list of elements. In other words, to get the data object, you need to get the enumerator and move to the first item.

```
// data is of type IEnumerable
IEnumerator e = data.GetEnumerator();
e.MoveNext();
// Use e.Current to get the physical data object
```

The *e.Current* expression returns the data object bound to the control—that is, the container from which you extract the fields mapped to bindable properties. If you know the control is bound to, say, a *DataRow* object, you could retrieve the value for the *Value* property through the following code:

```
displayValue = ((DataRow) e.Current)[DataValueField];
```

Using the *DataBinder* class adds greater flexibility to your code and makes your code independent from the type of the bound data source. The *GetPropertyValue* method on the *DataBinder* class uses reflection to query the object to see whether it contains a public property with the specified name:

```
displayText = (string) DataBinder.GetPropertyValue(
        e.Current, DataTextField);
```

GetPropertyValue returns an object and requires a cast to the proper type.

The remaining step is updating the rendering engine so that it accesses the *DataItem* object whenever it requires bound data. The *BuildLabel* method shown next displays the descriptive text around the gauge. (See Chapter 13 for a full explanation of the logic behind this method.)

```
void BuildLabel(TableCell container)
{
    // Calculate the value to represent
    float buf = GetValueToRepresent();

    // Get the string to display on the label
    string msg = GetTextToRepresent();

    Label lbl = new Label();
    if (container is TableCell)
        container.Controls.Add(lbl);
    else
        Controls.Add(lbl);
    lbl.Text = String.Format(msg, buf, Maximum);
}
```

The *BuildLabel* method adds a *Label* control to the control hierarchy under construction. The text displayed through the label is composed using the value and the format string of the gauge. Both *Value* and *FormatString* can be either data-bound or statically assigned. For this reason, you should use a *get* function that checks the current binding, if any, and returns the bound value or the assigned value. Note that the bound value is returned in favor of an assigned value, if both are present.

```
float GetValueToRepresent()
{
    float f = 0;
    if (DataItem.Value >=0)
        f = DataItem.Value;
```

```
    else
        f = Value;
    return f;
}
string GetTextToRepresent()
{
    string msg = "";
    if (!String.IsNullOrEmpty(DataItem.Text))
        msg = DataItem.Text;
    else
        msg = FormatString;
    return msg;
}
```

No other changes are required to enhance the *SimpleGaugeBar* control of Chapter 13 and make it data-bound.

The following code shows the *Load* handler of a sample page that uses the *GaugeBar* control and binds it to a dynamically generated *DataTable* object:

```
protected void Page_Load(object sender, EventArgs e)
{
    // Uses a random number as the value of the GaugeBar.
    // The value is stored in a DataTable object
    Random rnd = new Random();
    DataTable dt = new DataTable();
    dt.Columns.Add("Numbers", typeof(float));
    dt.Columns.Add("Label", typeof(string));
    DataRow row = dt.NewRow();
    row[0] = rnd.Next(0,100);
    row[1] = "{0} out of {1}";
    dt.Rows.Add(row);
    dt.AcceptChanges();

    // Binds the DataTable to the GaugeBar
    GaugeBar1.DataValueField = "Numbers";
    GaugeBar1.DataTextField = "Label";
    GaugeBar1.DataSource = dt;
    GaugeBar1.DataBind();
}
```

The *DataTable* has two columns—*Numbers* and *Label*—of type float and string, respectively. The table contains one data row. If the table contained multiple rows, only the first would be taken into account according to the code in *PerformDataBinding*.

Note that you can also use the *DataItem* property to bind data to the *GaugeBar* control.

```
GaugeBar1.DataItem.Value = 12;
GaugeBar1.DataItem.Text = "{0} %";
```

Note that no call to *DataBind* is required to trigger the process and update the control's user interface.

Building a List Data-Bound Control

Data-bound controls are often list controls. A list control builds its own user interface by repeating a fixed template for each bound data item within the boundaries of the control's mainframe. For example, a *CheckBoxList* control just repeats a *CheckBox* control for each bound data item. Likewise, a *DropDownList* control iterates through its data source and creates a new *<option>* element within a parent *<select>* tag.

In ASP.NET 2.0, all list controls inherit from *ListControl*—the only class in Figure 14-1 to be defined already in ASP.NET 1.x. *ListControl* adds quite a few new members to the interface of its parent class—*DataBoundControl*. In addition, list controls often also feature some layout capabilities such as vertical or horizontal rendering.

Generalities of List Controls

As shown in Figure 14-1, five frequently used controls inherit from *ListControl*. They are *DropDownList*, *CheckBoxList*, *RadioButtonList*, *ListBox*, and *BulletedList*. *BulletedList* exists only in ASP.NET 2.0. All these controls have a common programming interface that goes significantly beyond the programming interface of *DataBoundControl*. Let's review the new members.

Additional Members of *ListControl*

Table 14-1 lists properties and methods that are specific to the *ListControl* class and all derived list controls.

Table 14-1   Properties Specific to List Controls

Member	Description
AppendDataBoundItems	Indicates whether the *Items* collection can be populated both programmatically and through data binding.
AutoPostBack	Indicates whether the control has to post back automatically when a change in the selection occurs.
CausesValidation	Indicates whether validation should occur before the control posts back.
DataTextField	Name of the data source field to use as the display text of each bound item.
DataTextFormatString	Format string for the display text.
DataValueField	Name of the data source field to use as the value of each bound item.
Items	Collection of bound items. Depending on the value of *Append-DataBoundItems*, the collection also can be filled programmatically. Elements in the *Items* collection are of type *ListItem*.
SelectedIndex	Returns the index of the currently selected item.
SelectedItem	Returns the *ListItem* object that corresponds to the currently selected item.

Table 14-1 Properties Specific to List Controls

Member	Description
SelectedValue	Returns the value of the currently selected item.
Text	String property that indicates the text of all list items.
ValidationGroup	Indicates the name of the validation group this control belongs to.

Some properties—such as *AutoPostBack*, *CausesValidation* and *ValidationGroup*—clearly have little to do with the data-binding process.

For all list controls, the data item type is *ListItem*. Because list controls display a list of items, instead of using a *DataItem* property (discussed in the previous section) that points to a single object, you need a collection object in this case. The *Items* property is just what you need, and it is of type *ListItemCollection*. When you bind a list control to its data, the *Items* collection gets filled, typically within the *PerformDataBinding* method. However, if *AppendDataBoundItems* returns true (the default value), you can add *ListItem* elements to *Items* programmatically.

A Very Simple List Control

When it comes to building a custom list control, you have two possible routes to take. In the simplest one, you derive your class directly from *ListControl*. As we'll see in a moment, the amount of code to write is minimal, but there are a few limitations to be aware of. Let's suppose we need to create a list of hyperlinks. The control to repeat is the *HyperLink* control, and we want to specify both the URL and the text of each link through bindable properties.

```
public class SimpleHyperLinkList : ListControl
{
    private HyperLink _controlToRepeat;
    private HyperLink ControlToRepeat
    {
    get
    {
        if (_controlToRepeat == null)
            _controlToRepeat = new HyperLink();
        return _controlToRepeat;
    }
    }

    protected override void Render(HtmlTextWriter writer)
    {
        for (int i=0; i<Items.Count; i++)
        {
            HyperLink ctl = ControlToRepeat;
            ctl.ApplyStyle(ControlStyle);
            ctl.Text = Items[i].Text;
            ctl.NavigateUrl = Items[i].Value;
            ctl.RenderControl(writer);
            writer.Write("<br />");
        }
    }
}
```

The *SimpleHyperLinkList* control revolves around the private *ControlToRepeat* property and the *Render* method. *ControlToRepeat* indicates the control tree that will be repeated for each bound item. You instantiate it the first time the control is used in the request and reuse it all the way through.

The *Render* method is based on a loop that renders out a *HyperLink* control for each bound item. The *Text* and *NavigateUrl* properties are set with bound fields. *RenderControl* generates the markup for the *HyperLink* control; the markup is accumulated in the text writer object and output as shown in Figure 14-2.

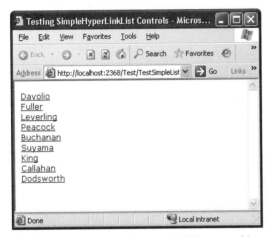

Figure 14-2 The *SimpleHyperLinkList* control in action.

What's wrong with this custom list control? Functionally speaking, there's nothing wrong, but there are some limitations of which you should be aware. Deriving your control from *ListControl* forces you to adopt *ListItem* as the data item object (you can't build your own) and *ListItemCollection* as the data item collection type. The names of the existing mapping properties cannot be changed, though new mapping properties can be added.

To further illustrate data-bound list controls, let's write an enhanced version of the *Simple-HyperLinkList* control that uses a made-to-measure data item collection and a bunch of custom mapping properties.

The *HyperLinkList* Control

The expected behavior of the new *HyperLinkList* control is nearly the same as the behavior we obtained by inheriting a control from *ListControl*. The new class declaration is as follows:

```
public class HyperLinkList : DataBoundControl, IRepeatInfoUser
{
    ⋮
}
```

The methods of the *IRepeatInfoUser* interface serve to express the layout capabilities of the new control and render the hyperlinks on a fixed number of rows and columns. We'll return to this topic later.

Mapping Data Source Fields to Control Properties

The *HyperLinkList* control has the following three field-mapping properties: *DataTextField*, *DataTooltipField*, and *DataUrlField*.

```
public virtual string DataTextField
{
    get
    {
        object o = ViewState["DataTextField"];
        if (o == null)
            return String.Empty;
        return (string) o;
    }
    set { ViewState["DataTextField"] = value; }
}

public virtual string DataTooltipField
{
    get
    {
        object o = ViewState["DataTooltipField"];
        if (o == null)
            return String.Empty;
        return (string) o;
    }
    set { ViewState["DataTooltipField"] = value; }
}

public virtual string DataUrlField
{
    get
    {
        object o = ViewState["DataUrlField"];
        if (o == null)
            return String.Empty;
        return (string) o;
    }
    set { ViewState["DataUrlField"] = value; }
}
```

The properties map three key attributes of a hyperlink to fields on a data source object—display text, ToolTip and, of course, the URL. The choice of these properties affects the structure of the data item object.

The *HyperLinkList* Data Item Object

The data item object is a class that represents a bound item. In this case, it will be the instance of a class that contains link information—URL, text, and ToolTip.

```
public class HyperLinkItem
{
    private string _text;
    private string _url;
    private string _tooltip;

    public HyperLinkItem()
    {
    }
    public HyperLinkItem(string url, string text, string tooltip)
    {
        _text = text;
        _url = url;
        _tooltip = tooltip;
    }
    public string Text
    {
        get { return _text; }
        set { _text = value; }
    }
    public string Tooltip
    {
        get { return _tooltip; }
        set { _tooltip = value; }
    }
    public string Url
    {
        get { return _url; }
        set { _url = value; }
    }
}
```

The class defines three public members—*Url*, *Tooltip*, and *Text*—stored in local variables and a couple of constructors. The *HyperLinkItem* class represents the nth bound item; to represent the whole data set bound to a list control, you need a collection of *HyperLinkItem* objects.

To build a collection in ASP.NET 2.0, you use generics. The use of generics normally reduces the amount of necessary collection code you have to write to nearly zero. However, in this case, you also need to provide an implementation for the *IStateManager* interface.

```
class HyperLinkItemCollection : Collection<HyperLinkItem>, IStateManager
{
    private bool _marked;

    public HyperLinkItemCollection()
    {
        _marked = false;
    }

    public bool IsTrackingViewState
    {
        get { return _marked; }
    }
```

```
public void TrackViewState()
{
    _marked = true;
}

public void LoadViewState(object state)
{
    if (state != null)
    {
    Triplet t = (Triplet) state;

    // This is required to ensure that the collection
    // we're going to fill is empty
    Clear();

    string[] rgUrl = (string[])t.First;
    string[] rgText = (string[])t.Second;
    string[] rgTooltip = (string[])t.Third;

    for (int i = 0; i < rgUrl.Length; i++)
        Add(new HyperLinkItem(rgUrl[i], rgText[i], rgTooltip[i]));
    }
}

public object SaveViewState()
{
    int numOfItems = Count;
    object[] rgTooltip = new string[numOfItems];
    object[] rgText = new string[numOfItems];
    object[] rgUrl = new string[numOfItems];

    for (int i = 0; i < numOfItems; i++)
    {
        rgTooltip[i] = this[i].Tooltip;
        rgText[i] = this[i].Text;
        rgUrl[i] = this[i].Url;
    }

    return new Triplet(rgUrl, rgText, rgTooltip);
    }
}
```

The real data item public property that matches the *DataItem* property of the *GaugeBar* control is a collection named *Items*. (The name is arbitrary.)

```
private HyperLinkItemCollection _items;
⋮
public virtual HyperLinkItemCollection Items
{
    get
    {
        if (_items == null)
        {
            _items = new HyperLinkItemCollection();
```

```
            if (base.IsTrackingViewState)
                _items.TrackViewState();
        }
        return _items;
    }
}
```

It is now interesting to take a look at the code of *SaveViewState*. The object returned by this method must contain a URL, text, and a ToolTip for each bound item. I opted for a triplet of arrays. Each array contains all URLs, text, and ToolTips for items listed by the control. Once filled, each array is added to a *Triplet* and returned. *LoadViewState* unpacks this information and refills the collection.

In this way, *HyperLinkItemCollection* is endowed with the capabilities of saving to, and restoring from, the view state. This code alone is not sufficient, though, to persist the collection through the view state. You also need, in fact, ad hoc view-state management code:

```
protected override object SaveViewState()
{
    object baseState = base.SaveViewState();
    object itemState = Items.SaveViewState();
    return new Pair(baseState, itemState);
}
protected override void LoadViewState(object savedState)
{
    if (savedState != null)
    {
        Pair p = (Pair) savedState;
        base.LoadViewState(p.First);
        Items.LoadViewState(p.Second);
    }
}
```

The *SaveViewState* and *LoadViewState* methods on the *HyperLinkList* control are invoked when the control is going to save itself to the view state and restore from it. The call to the same pair of methods on the *Items* property ensures that the collection is persisted and restored correctly.

Getting Bound Data

A data-bound control receives its data within the *PerformDataBinding* method. The data bound control is a collection that represents the data source. The goal of the *PerformDataBinding* method is to extract information from the data source and cache it in an intermediate data structure that is more lightweight for persisting across postbacks.

```
protected override void PerformDataBinding(IEnumerable dataSource)
{
    base.PerformDataBinding(dataSource);
```

```
          string urlField = DataUrlField;
          string textField = DataTextField;
          string tooltipField = DataTooltipField;

          if (dataSource != null)
          {
            foreach (object o in dataSource)
              {
              HyperLinkItem item = new HyperLinkItem();
              item.Url = DataBinder.GetPropertyValue(o, urlField, null);
              item.Text = DataBinder.GetPropertyValue(o, textField, null);
              item.Tooltip = DataBinder.GetPropertyValue(o, tooltipField, null);
              Items.Add(item);
              }
          }
      }
}
```

As you can see, for each item in the bound data source, the code creates a new *HyperLinkItem* object, fills it with the value of mapped fields, and finally adds it to the *Items* collection.

The *IRepeatInfoUser* Interface

So far the *HyperLinkList* control is not much different from its *SimpleHyperLinkList* predecessor, which we created in the previous section, except for a slightly different set of members. Let's add a brand new feature—the ability to render items in a given direction and within a fixed row/column scheme. If you ever used the ASP.NET built-in *CheckBoxList* control, you perhaps know about the *RepeatDirection*, *RepeatLayout*, and *RepeatColumns* properties. When set, these properties determine the way the output of the list control is laid out. Table 14-2 details the role of each property.

Table 14-2 *IRepeatInfoUser* **Specific Properties**

Property	Description
RepeatColumns	Gets or sets the number of columns to display in the control.
RepeatDirection	Gets or sets a value that indicates whether the control displays vertically or horizontally.
RepeatLayout	Gets or sets the layout of the check boxes (table or flow).

By using a combination of these properties, a page author can decide the number of rows and columns that must be used to render the hyperlinks. Let's see how to code this feature.

The first step consists of adding public properties to *HyperLinkList* to let page developers specify the desired layout.

```
public virtual RepeatDirection RepeatDirection
{
    get
    {
        object o = ViewState["RepeatDirection"];
```

```
         if (o != null)
            return (RepeatDirection) o;
         return RepeatDirection.Vertical;
      }
      set { ViewState["RepeatDirection"] = value; }
}
public virtual int RepeatColumns
{
   get
   {
      object o = ViewState["RepeatColumns"];
      if (o != null)
         return (int) o;
      return 0;
   }
   set { ViewState["RepeatColumns"] = value; }
}
public virtual RepeatLayout RepeatLayout
{
   get
   {
      object o = ViewState["RepeatLayout"];
      if (o != null)
         return (RepeatLayout) o;
      return RepeatLayout.Table;
   }
   set { ViewState["RepeatLayout"] = value; }
}
```

A control that intends to support special layout capabilities needs a special code fragment in the *Render* method. Here's an example:

```
protected override void Render(HtmlTextWriter writer)
{
   if (Items.Count > 0)
   {
      RepeatInfo ri = new RepeatInfo();
      Style controlStyle = (base.ControlStyleCreated
                            ? base.ControlStyle : null);
      ri.RepeatColumns = RepeatColumns;
      ri.RepeatDirection = RepeatDirection;
      ri.RepeatLayout = RepeatLayout;
      ri.RenderRepeater(writer, this, controlStyle, this);
   }
}
```

The *RepeatInfo* structure exists since ASP.NET 1.x just to allow controls to output their contents according to different rendering rules. The second parameter of the *RenderRepeater* method references the object (*this*, in the preceding code snippet) that implements the *IRepeatInfoUser* interface. The interface implementation is required for the feature to work on a given control. The interface members are presented in Table 14-3.

Table 14-3 *IRepeatInfoUser* Members

Member	Description
HasFooter	Indicates whether the control has a footer
HasHeader	Indicates whether the control has a header
HasSeparators	Indicates whether the control has a separator between items
RepeatedItemCount	Indicates the number of items to render

In addition, the interface has a couple of methods—*GetItemStyle* and *RenderItem*. The former returns the style object for each rendered item. The latter generates the markup. The following code snippet shows how we might implement this interface for our hyperlink control:

```
bool IRepeatInfoUser.HasFooter
{
    get { return false; }
}
bool IRepeatInfoUser.HasHeader
{
    get { return false; }
}
bool IRepeatInfoUser.HasSeparators
{
    get { return false; }
}
int IRepeatInfoUser.RepeatedItemCount
{
    get { return this.Items.Count; }
}
Style IRepeatInfoUser.GetItemStyle(ListItemType itemType, int repeatIndex)
{
    return null;
}
void IRepeatInfoUser.RenderItem(ListItemType itemType,
        int repeatIndex, RepeatInfo repeatInfo, HtmlTextWriter writer)
{
    HyperLink ctl = ControlToRepeat;
    int i = repeatIndex;
    ctl.ID = i.ToString();
    ctl.Text = Items[i].Text;
    ctl.NavigateUrl = Items[i].Url;
    ctl.ToolTip = Items[i].Tooltip;
    ctl.RenderControl(writer);
}
```

The *RenderItem* method is automatically invoked for each bound item—precisely once for each item in the *Items* collection—and is expected to render the output for the control to repeat. The control to repeat can be an instance of an individual control (for example, as in this case, a *HyperLink*) as well as the root of a control tree. The public properties of the control being repeated can be set using bound data. The control is then rendered out using the *Render-Control* method. Figure 14-3 shows the control in action.

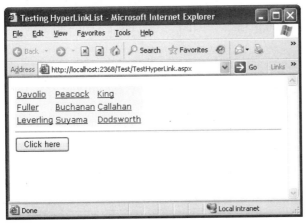

Figure 14-3   The *HyperLinkList* control in action when *RepeatColumns* is set to 3.

Building a Composite Templated Control

The *CompositeDataBoundControl* class is the starting point for building rich, complex, and data-bound composite controls. A composite data-bound control must do the following:

- Act as a naming container.
- Create its own user interface through the *CreateChildControls* method.
- Implement the necessary logic to restore its hierarchy of child elements after postback.

The last point is a subtle one that many developers cut their teeth on in ASP.NET 1.x. If you don't fully understand the third point yet, the good news is that you can now forget about it entirely. Everything that is needed is now hard-coded in the *CompositeDataBoundControl* class.

Generalities of Composite Data-Bound Controls

In ASP.NET 2.0, the main aspect you care about when building a composite data-bound control is designing the internal hierarchy of your control. The method to override for this purpose is an overloaded version of *CreateChildControls*. In addition, you typically add styles and templates.

In a real-world composite control, the internal control tree is usually quite complex. The outermost container is often a multirow HTML table, but what's in the various cells and rows can vary quite a bit and result in a pretty sophisticated combination of child controls and literals.

Creating a Hierarchy of Child Controls

You should know by now that composite controls build their own interface by composing controls in the override of the *CreateChildControls* method. Defined on the *Control* class, the method has the following prototype:

```
protected override void CreateChildControls()
```

In the *CompositeDataBoundControl* class, the method is overridden and overloaded. In particular, the overridden version accomplishes a few interesting tasks. Here's its pseudo-code:

```
protected override void CreateChildControls()
{
    Controls.Clear();
    object o = ViewState["_!ItemCount"];
    if ((o == null) && RequiresDataBinding)
        EnsureDataBound();
    else
    {
        int numOfItems = (int) o;
        object[] rg = new object[numOfItems];
        CreateChildControls(rg, false);
        base.ClearChildViewState();
    }
}
```

The method first empties the *Controls* collection so that no pending child controls are left around. Next, it retrieves a value from a particular (and internally managed) view-state entry named *_!ItemCount*. The view-state entry caches the number of items that form the composite control. The code that actually builds the control tree is responsible for storing this value in the view state.

It is important to know the number of items that form the control hierarchy if you want to optimize the data-binding process. In ASP.NET, complex controls showing a long list of data items are implemented as composite data-bound controls. In what way is this different from list and simple-bound controls?

List controls and simple-bound controls like the *GaugeBar* we considered earlier cache the data item or items in the view state. In addition, they can receive data either from the data-binding process or programmatically through the *Items* collection and the *DataItem* property, respectively. Composite data-bound controls (such as *DataGrid*, *DataList*, and *GridView*) work on the assumption that they receive data exclusively from data binding and, for this reason, don't persist bound data in any form. Consider now the following scenario.

Imagine a page that contains a rich control such as the *GridView* and some button controls. One of the button controls, when clicked, executes no code that involves the *GridView* but still refreshes the page. Without some special tricks in the control's code, you can be sure that the composite data-bound control would be empty upon postback. Why is it so? If the postback event handler doesn't bind data back to the composite control, the control has no way to figure it out and refresh properly. In ASP.NET, by design, composite data-bound controls take their data only from data binding and don't cache any bound data. Therefore, a special workaround is required to handle postback events.

For composite data-bound controls, the *CreateChildControls* method works in either of two modes—binding or nonbinding. When working in binding mode, the control tree is created as usual. When working in nonbinding mode, the control calls an overloaded version of

CreateChildControls. The method is defined as abstract on the *CompositeDataBoundControl* and must be overridden in any derived class.

The Overloaded *CreateChildControls*

The overloaded version of *CreateChildControls* that is defined on the *CompositeDataBound-Control* class is shown here:

```
protected abstract int CreateChildControls(
    IEnumerable dataSource, bool dataBinding);
```

The first parameter is the collection of bound data. The second parameter indicates whether the control is being bound to fresh data (that is, it is working in binding mode) or is being refreshed after a postback. The return value indicates the number of items added to the control tree. This value will then be stored in the view state during the call to *PerformDataBinding*. The following code snippet shows the pseudo-code of *PerformDataBinding* on the *Composite-DataBoundControl* class:

```
protected internal override void PerformDataBinding(IEnumerable data)
{
    base.PerformDataBinding(data);
    Controls.Clear();
    base.ClearChildViewState();
    TrackViewState();
    int numOfItems = CreateChildControls(data, true);
    base.ChildControlsCreated = true;
    ViewState["_!ItemCount"] = numOfItems;
}
```

Note that *PerformDataBinding* calls into the new overload of *CreateChildControls* and passes it *true* as the second argument, indicating that a binding operation is taking place. This makes sense, because executing *PerformDataBinding*, by definition, means we are performing a binding operation.

What kind of code should you place in the overloaded *CreateChildControls*? Basically, you'd choose your own control builder method (typically, *CreateControlHierarchy*) and return its return value. We'll return to this point later when discussing the sample *BarChart* control.

The overloaded *CreateChildControls* method is invoked in binding mode from within *Perform-DataBinding*, and it's invoked in nonbinding mode from within the other *CreateChildControls* method:

```
// o is the value read from ViewState
int numOfItems = (int) o;
object[] rg = new object[numOfItems];
CreateChildControls(rg, false);
```

In this case, the bound data passed to the method is an empty array of objects of a well-known size. The goal of this array is to force the control builder method (typically, *CreateControl-Hierarchy*) to loop the right number of times and build an outermost container with the right configuration—for example, a table with the right number of rows and columns. As we'll see in detail for the sample *BarChart* control, a composite data-bound control neatly separates hierarchy from data. If the Boolean parameter of *CreateChildControls* is *false*, no data is added to the hierarchy. How can the control show up as it did the last time? The ASP.NET postback mechanism guarantees that child controls are restored with all their values. In other words, if a composite data-bound control displays bound data through, say, a *Label* control, after a postback, the composite control doesn't restore its bound data directly. However, it asks any child control, including the *Label*, to restore itself from the view state. In doing so, the *Label* restores the bound data from its *Text* property.

The bottom line is that the amount of extra data that flows in the view state for a composite control is limited to the number of constituent items, and the control refreshes correctly after a postback. (Of course, child controls put the usual amount of data in the view state.)

The Control Item

It should be clear from the previous discussion that the ASP.NET team had excellent arguments to dictate that composite data-bound controls get their data exclusively from the data-binding process. This fact eliminates the need of having a kind of *Items* property on composite data-bound controls that works like the *Items* property of list controls. This said, feel free to add support for data item objects and collections to your composite controls if you need to.

Most composite controls feature a collection of items, but not a collection of data items. Each item represents a control item—that is, a logical building block of the control's user interface. For a *DataGrid*, it is a *DataGridItem* object that represents a table row. For a sample *BarChart* control that displays a bar chart, the control item will be a class derived from *TableRow* that contains all the information needed to handle a single bar. The number of items that composite controls store in the view state is exactly the number of "control" items.

Let's see how these concepts apply to a sample composite data-bound control such as *BarChart*.

The *BarChart* Control

The *BarChart* control inherits from *CompositeDataBoundControl* and defines the properties in Table 14-4.

Table 14-4 *BarChart* Properties

Property	Description
DataTextField	Name of the data field to use as the label of each bar.
DataTextFormatString	Format string for the display text.
DataValueField	Name of the data field to use as the value of each bar.

Table 14-4   *BarChart* **Properties**

Property	Description
DataValueFormatString	Format string for the value to display on top of each bar.
Items	Collection of *BarChart* items. Each element represents a bar in the chart. Elements in the *Items* collection are of type *BarChartItem*.
Maximum	Gets and sets the maximum value that can be represented in the chart.
SubTitle	Gets and sets the subtitle of the final chart.
Title	Gets and sets the title of the bar chart.

The final markup for the control is a horizontal bar chart such as the one illustrated in Figure 14-4.

Figure 14-4   The *BarChart* control in action.

Each bar is fully represented by an element in the *Items* collection. In addition, the *BarChart* control features a few style properties, as Table 14-5 details.

Table 14-5   *BarChart* **Style Properties**

Property	Description
BarStyle	The style of the whole row that contains the bar
LabelStyle	The style of the label
SubTitleStyle	The style of the subtitle in the control's header
TitleStyle	The style of the title in the control's header
ValueStyle	The style of the element displaying the value rendered

The attributes of all style properties are applied in the *Render* method, as in other data-bound controls.

The *BarChart* Item Object

The user interface of the *BarChart* control is created in the overloaded version of the *Create-ChildControls.*

```
protected override int CreateChildControls(
    IEnumerable dataSource, bool dataBinding)
{
    return CreateControlHierarchy(dataSource, dataBinding);
}
```

Both input arguments are passed down to an internal *CreateControlHierarchy* method, which is ultimately responsible for the creation of the bar chart.

```
int CreateControlHierarchy(IEnumerable dataSource, bool dataBinding)
{
    // Get the data to display (either from data source or viewstate)
    if (dataSource == null)
    {
        RenderEmptyControl();
        return 0;
    }

    // Start building the hierarchy of controls
    Table t = new Table();
    Controls.Add(t);

    // Add the header row with the caption
    CreateTitle(t);

    // Add the subtitle row
    CreateSubTitle(t);

    // Add bars
    int totalItems = CreateAllItems(t, dataSource, dataBinding);
    return totalItems;
}
```

The control hierarchy is a table with two rows for the title and subtitle and other rows for the bars of the chart. *CreateAllItems* adds bar chart items and counts their number. This number is then returned and ends up in the view state.

```
int CreateAllItems(Table t, IEnumerable data, bool useDataSource)
{
    // Count how many items we add
    int itemCount = 0;

    // Clears the Items collection (creates it, if null)
    Items.Clear();
```

```
    // Scroll data items and create table items
    foreach (object o in data)
    {
        // Create the match item object
        BarChartItemType itemType = BarChartItemType.Item;
        BarChartItem item = CreateBarChartItem(t,
                itemType, o, useDataSource);

        // Add the newly created object to the Items collection
        _items.Add(item);

        // Increase the counter
        itemCount++;
    }

    // Return how many items we have into the viewstate (for postbacks)
    return itemCount;
}
```

For each bound item, the method creates a *BarChartItem* object and adds it to the *Items* collection. We'll discuss the *BarChartItem* class in a moment.

Note that we use *Items.Clear* to clear the collection and *_items.Add* to add a new bar chart item to the collection. The *Items* property is implemented as follows:

```
private BarChartItemCollection _items;
⋮
public virtual BarChartItemCollection Items
{
    get
    {
        if (_items == null)
            _items = new BarChartItemCollection();

        return _items;
    }
}
```

The property *Items* uses the *_items* variable as its storage medium. The first call to *Items.Clear* ensures that the collection is properly initialized. The second call to the same collection can go through the local variable to save a call to the *get* accessor of the *Items* property.

The *BarChartItem* class represents a bar in the chart and is defined as follows:

```
public class BarChartItem : TableRow
{
    private object _dataItem;
    private BarChartItemType _itemType;

    public BarChartItem(BarChartItemType itemType)
    {
        _itemType = itemType;
    }
```

```
    public object DataItem
    {
        get {return _dataItem;}
        set {_dataItem = value;}
    }

    public BarChartItemType ItemType
    {
        get {return _itemType;}
    }
}
```

The class inherits from *TableRow* (actually, a bar in the chart is a table row) and defines a couple of properties—*DataItem* and *ItemType*. The *DataItem* property references the data item in the bound data source associated with the corresponding item. For example, if the *BarChart* is bound to a *DataTable*, *DataItem* is bound to the *DataRow* that corresponds to a given bar. *ItemType*, on the other hand, indicates the type of table row—title, subtitle, item. The item types are defined through an enumerated type:

```
public enum BarChartItemType
{
    Title,
    SubTitle,
    Item
}
```

The *Items* property groups a bunch of *BarChartItem* objects in a collection. The collection type is *BarChartItemCollection*:

```
public class BarChartItemCollection : Collection<BarChartItem>
{
}
```

Because bar chart item objects don't go to the view state, there's no need to implement *IState-Manager* and add extra view-state management methods as we did previously for the hyperlink control.

Adding Bound Data

With a composite data-bound control, you don't need to override the *PerformDataBinding* method. However, you should pay some attention to keeping the code that builds the structure of the control and the code that adds data neatly separated.

The *CreateBarChartItem* method creates a new table row and enriches it with a *DataItem* property. What's the content of the row? Looking at Figure 14-4, you can see that each table row has a cell for the label and a cell for the progress bar.

```
BarChartItem CreateBarChartItem(Table t, BarChartItemType itemType,
        object dataItem, bool useDataSource)
{
```

```
    // Create a new row for the outermost table
    BarChartItem item = new BarChartItem(itemType);

    // Create cells for label and value
    TableCell labelCell = CreateLabelCell(item);
    TableCell valueCell = CreateValueCell(item);

    // Add the row to the table
    t.Rows.Add(item);

    // Handle the data object binding
    if (useDataSource)
    {
        // Get the data source object
        item.DataItem = dataItem;

        // Data bind the team labels
        BindLabelCell(labelCell, dataItem);
        BindValueCell(valueCell, dataItem);
    }

    // Return the fully configured row item
    return item;
}
```

CreateLabelCell and *CreateValueCell* add cells to the table row. Here is their implementation:

```
private TableCell CreateLabelCell(BarChartItem item)
{
    // Create and add the cell
    TableCell cell = new TableCell();
    item.Cells.Add(cell);
    return cell;
}
private TableCell CreateValueCell(BarChartItem item)
{
    // Create and add the cell
    TableCell cell = new TableCell();
    item.Cells.Add(cell);

    // Add the internal labels
    Label lblGraph = new Label();
    Label lblText = new Label();

    cell.Controls.Add(lblGraph);
    cell.Controls.Add(new LiteralControl("<br>"));
    cell.Controls.Add(lblText);
    return cell;
}
```

The colored bar is represented with a label whose width is a percentage of the maximum value possible on the chart.

As you can see in the code of *CreateBarChartItem*, an *if* statement separates the creation of required child controls from the data binding. If the method is working in binding mode, the *DataItem* property is set on each bar chart item and the following two methods are called to add data to the child controls of the *BarChart* control:

```
private void BindLabelCell(TableCell cell, object dataItem)
{
    if (!String.IsNullOrEmpty(DataTextField))
    {
        string txt = DataBinder.GetPropertyValue(
                dataItem, DataTextField, DataTextFormatString);
        cell.Text = txt;
    }
}
private void BindValueCell(TableCell cell, object dataItem)
{
    // Bind the label for the graph
    Label lblGraph = (Label) cell.Controls[0];
    object o = null;
    if (!String.IsNullOrEmpty(DataValueField))
        o = DataBinder.GetPropertyValue(dataItem, DataValueField);
    else
        return;
    float val = Convert.ToSingle(o);
    float valueToRepresent = 100 * val / Maximum;
    lblGraph.Width = Unit.Percentage(valueToRepresent);

    // Bind the label for the text
    Label lblText = (Label) cell.Controls[2];
    lblText.Text = DataBinder.GetPropertyValue(
            dataItem, DataValueField, DataValueFormatString);
}
```

The data-binding process works in a way that is no different from what we've seen earlier for other types of data-bound controls. The trickiest part here is the calculation of the width of the label that, when properly styled, generates the horizontal bar.

> **Note** As you can see, no style properties are assigned when the control hierarchy is being built. Just as for other data-bound controls, style attributes are applied later in the control life cycle in the *Render* method, immediately before generating the control's markup.

Events of the *BarChart* Control

The *BarChart* control also features a couple of events—*BarChartCreated* and *BarChartDataBound*. It is not coincidental that these two events mimic analogous events on the *DataGrid* control. Although far simpler, the *BarChart* is a control designed along the same guidelines that inspired the creation of the *DataGrid* control.

```
public event EventHandler<BarChartItemEventArgs> BarChartItemCreated;
public event EventHandler<BarChartItemEventArgs> BarChartItemDataBound;
protected virtual void OnBarChartCreated(BarChartItemEventArgs e)
```

```
{
    if (BarChartItemCreated != null)
        BarChartItemCreated(this, e);
}
protected virtual void OnBarChartItemDataBound(BarChartItemEventArgs e)
{
    if (BarChartItemDataBound != null)
        BarChartItemDataBound(this, e);
}
```

The *BarChartItemCreated* event is fired whenever a new table row is added to represent a bar. The *BarChartItemDataBound* event fires when a newly added table row is bound to its data. The former event fires regardless of the working mode of the control. The latter fires only when the control is created in binding mode.

The data carried out with the event is grouped in the *BarChartItemEventArgs* class:

```
public class BarChartItemEventArgs : EventArgs
{
    private BarChartItem _item;
    public BarChartItemEventArgs(BarChartItem item)
    {
        _item = item;
    }

    // Properties
    public BarChartItem Item
    {
        get { return _item; }
    }
}
```

Both events are fired from within the *CreateBarChartItem* method.

```
BarChartItem CreateBarChartItem(Table t, BarChartItemType itemType,
        object dataItem, bool useDataSource)
{
    // Create a new row for the outermost table
    BarChartItem item = new BarChartItem(itemType);

    // Create cells for label and value
    TableCell labelCell = CreateLabelCell(item);
    TableCell valueCell = CreateValueCell(item);

    BarChartItemEventArgs argsCreated = new BarChartItemEventArgs(item);
    OnBarChartItemCreated(argsCreated);
    :
    if (useDataSource)
    {
        :
        BarChartItemEventArgs argsData = new BarChartItemEventArgs(item);
        OnBarChartItemDataBound(argsData);
    }
}
```

Using the *BarChart* Control

Let's see how to consume these events from within a host page. The following markup enables a *BarChart* control in an ASP.NET page:

```
<expo:BarChart runat="server" id="BarChart1"
    Maximum="100" SubTitle="Subtitle" Title="Title"
    OnBarChartDataBound="BarChart1_BarChartDataBound" >
    ⋮
</expo:BarChart>
```

Nothing in the preceding markup indicates the data source. In the *Page_Load* event, the control is bound to its data—a SQL Server query that returns a resultset with two columns that show the amount of sales for an employee in 1997 and the name of that employee. The source of the data is the Northwind database in SQL Server 2000.

```
protected void Button1_Click(object sender, EventArgs e)
{
    DataTable data = ExecuteQuery(1997);
    BarChart1.Maximum = 150000;
    BarChart1.Title = "Northwind Sales";
    BarChart1.SubTitle = "(Year 1997)";
    BarChart1.DataSource = data;
    BarChart1.DataTextField = "Employee";
    BarChart1.DataValueField = "Sales";
    BarChart1.DataBind();
}
```

The bar chart shown in Figure 14-4 is obtained by running the preceding code.

The sample page handles the *BarChartDataBound* event through the following code:

```
void BarChart1_BarChartDataBound(object sender,
            ProAspNet20.Advanced.BarChartItemEventArgs e)
{
    // Get the amount of sales for the current bar
    Decimal sales = (Decimal) DataBinder.GetPropertyValue(
                    e.Item.DataItem, "sales");

    // Add a tooltip
    string tip = sales.ToString();
    e.Item.Attributes["title"] = tip;

    // Highlight bar where sales > 50000
    if (sales > 50000)
        e.Item.Cells[1].BackColor = Color.LightGreen;
}
```

The amount of sales for the current employee is retrieved and added to the row as a ToolTip. In addition, if the sales are larger than $50,000, the cell is highlighted by using a different background color. (See Figure 14-5.)

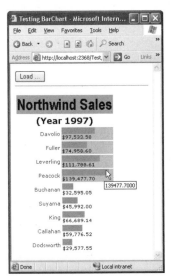

Figure 14-5   The output of a *BarChart* control modified by page-level event handlers.

Note   All data-bound controls feature a couple of common events—*DataBinding* and *DataBound*. Also supported by ASP.NET 1.x, the former event fires before the data-binding process begins. The *DataBound* event has been introduced in ASP.NET 2.0 and signals that the data-binding phase has terminated.

Adding Templates Support

The *BarChart* control accepts two strings to display as the title and subtitle of the chart. Likewise, you could define a third similar property for the footer. Title, subtitle, and footer are just distinct items in the *BarChart* control hierarchy. What are you allowed to display in these items? As long as the properties are implemented as plain strings, there's not much more than static text that can show up through the items.

A bit more flexibility can be added with format strings. A format string is a string that contains a predefined number of placeholders that the control machinery fills with internal data. For example, the *FormatString* property of the *GaugeBar* defaults to *{0}/{1}*—namely, a format string with two placeholders. The string is resolved as follows:

```
// First placeholder gets the Value to represent
// Second placeholder gets the Maximum value that can be represented
String.Format(FormatString, Value, Maximum);
```

You can enrich the format string with HTML tags to obtain more appealing results but, in the long run, this approach would result in unmanageable code. A much better route to deep customizations of the user interface of controls would be to use templates.

Templates and User Controls

In ASP.NET, you can import templates in two ways—through properties of type *ITemplate* or by dynamically loading user controls. As we saw in Chapter 12, a Web user control is a custom component that can be used wherever a server control is valid. You can import such a user-defined control into the layout of the main control and make the interface more flexible and generic. You put a *PlaceHolder* control in the location in which you want custom contents to be injected, and then at run time, you create an instance of the user control and add it to the *Controls* collection of the placeholder.

```
placeHolder.Controls.Add(Page.LoadControl("usercontrol.ascx"));
```

The right time to call this code is early in the control life cycle—that is, in an *Init* event handler. Using the *LoadControl* method, the code of the template is insulated in a separate file. This can be a good thing or a bad thing, depending on the context. If the template you want to implement is complex, keeping it off the main page is positive. Otherwise, it would certainly add a layer of unnecessary complexity. Having the template directly available in the source code of the page makes authoring the page much more intuitive and fast because you don't have to follow code into a separate file. There's a sort of compromise between the two approaches. You could define an *ITemplate* property in the control and leave the page author free to decide how to set it—with statically defined markup or using the contents of an *.ascx* file.

Defining a Template Property

A template property represents a collection of text and controls that is hosted within a container. The container is also responsible for exposing properties that page authors can use to create data-bound expressions. The following code snippet shows how to define a template property named *TitleTemplate*:

```
[PersistenceMode(PersistenceMode.InnerProperty)]
[TemplateContainer(typeof(TitleTemplateContainer))]
public ITemplate TitleTemplate
{
    get { return _titleTemplate; }
    set { _titleTemplate = value; }
}
```

The storage of the template is guaranteed by the private member *_titleTemplate*, defined as follows:

```
private ITemplate _titleTemplate = null;
```

A template property is characterized by a couple of attributes—*PersistenceMode* and *TemplateContainer*.

The *PersistenceMode* attribute indicates how a control property is persisted declaratively in a host page. Table 14-6 lists possible modes of persistence.

Table 14-6   Persistence Modes for Control Properties

Property	Description
Attribute	The property persists as an encoded HTML attribute in the final markup.
EncodedInnerDefaultProperty	The property persists as the only inner text of the control. The property value is HTML encoded. Only a string can be given this designation.
InnerDefaultProperty	The property persists in the control as inner text and is the element's default property. Only one property can be designated the default property.
InnerProperty	The property persists in the control as a nested tag. This is commonly used for complex objects with templates and styles.

The most common setting is *InnerProperty*, which instructs Microsoft Visual Studio 2005 to save the contents of the template as a nested tag named after the property.

```
<expo:BarChart runat="server" ID="BarChart1" ... >
    <TitleTemplate>
        ⋮
    </TitleTemplate>
</expo:BarChart>
```

If you choose *InnerDefaultProperty*, you can have only one nested tag; by opting for *InnerProperty*, you can have as many nested tags as needed. This is good for rich controls with multiple templates and styles.

The *TemplateContainer* attribute declares the type of the naming container that will contain the template once it is created. As mentioned, a template is hosted by a container that, in turn, is appended to the control's *Controls* collection. The *TemplateContainer* attribute references a type that, as a control developer, you're responsible for declaring.

Defining a Template Container

A template container type is a simple Web control decorated with the *INamingContainer* interface. This control can be given any public members you like. However, it will typically expose the host control as a whole with a bunch of quick-access properties. Here's a sample container type for the *TitleTemplate* property:

```
public class TitleTemplateContainer : WebControl, INamingContainer
{
    private BarChart _parent;
    public TitleTemplateContainer(BarChart parent)
    {
        _parent = parent;
    }
    public string Title
    {
        get { return _parent.Title; }
    }
```

```
public string SubTitle
{
    get { return _parent.SubTitle; }
}
public BarChart BarChart
{
    get { return _parent; }
}
```
}

Once again, it is important to note that there are no constraints or special guidelines to influence the set of members of the class. The class needs to have a reference to the parent control—the *BarChart*, in this case. Normally, you create this class for a particular control (or set of controls) and don't reuse it beyond that. It is up to you to expose the parent control through a direct property (*BarChart* in the preceding code) or to filter the control's programming interface with a subset of properties (for example, *Title* and *SubTitle*). You can also do both things.

The programming interface of the template container class is important because it defines the information that page authors have access to when creating a template for the property. The template container is made accessible through the *Container* property.

Setting a Template Property

Figure 14-6 shows the templated version of the *BarChart* control in action in Visual Studio 2005. The *TitleTemplate* property shows up through Microsoft IntelliSense and greatly simplifies the assignment of a template property.

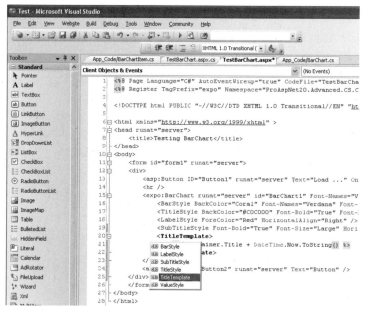

Figure 14-6   Visual Studio 2005 recognizes and supports a template property.

You can use any combination of controls and literals to populate a template. To access external information, though, you will need to use data-bound expressions. Here's an example:

```
<TitleTemplate>
    <img src="Title.gif" />
    <%# Container.Title %>
</TitleTemplate>
```

The code snippet demonstrates a *BarChart* title that displays an image in addition to the text set through the *Title* property. Here's another example:

```
<TitleTemplate>
    <%# Container.Title %>
    <small>(<%# DateTime.Now.ToString() %>)</small>
</TitleTemplate>
```

Figure 14-7 shows a templated title item where the originally set *Title* property is displayed side by side with the current time. The current time is rendered with a smaller font and within parentheses.

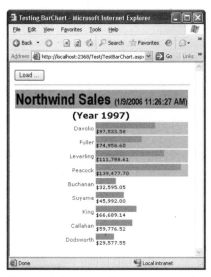

Figure 14-7 A *BarChart* control with a templated title.

Note that any style attributes set through the *TitleStyle* property are maintained in the template.

The *Container* keyword references an instance of the template container type. You use the *Container* keyword to access any control properties exposed through the template container class. Nonstatic information requires a <%# ... %> data-bound expression, just like in the templates of ASP.NET built-in controls.

Rendering a Template

So far we've seen how to define a template property in a server control. But what other changes to the code are required to host a template? In summary, to define a template property, you need to do the following:

- Define a property of type *ITemplate*, and use a private variable as its storage medium.
- Decorate the property with the *PersistenceMode* attribute.
- Define a template container class.
- Decorate the property with the *TemplateContainer* attribute.

These steps only define the public interface of the template; more is needed to embed the template in the control's hierarchy. In particular, you need to tweak the code that creates the portion of the control tree where you want the template to display. For example, the *TitleTemplate* property refers to the title item, so the internal method to modify is *CreateTitle*. Here's the updated version:

```
private void CreateTitle(Table t)
{
    // Create the table row
    BarChartItem item = new BarChartItem(BarChartItemType.Title);
    t.Rows.Add(item);

    // Add the title cell
    TableCell cell = new TableCell();
    cell.ColumnSpan = BarChart.ColumnsCount;
    item.Cells.Add(cell);

    // Decide between plain string and template
    if (TitleTemplate != null)
    {
        _titleTemplateContainer = new TitleTemplateContainer(this);
        TitleTemplate.InstantiateIn(_titleTemplateContainer);
        cell.Controls.Add(_titleTemplateContainer);
    }
    else
        cell.Text = Title;

    // Must call DataBind to enable #-expression on templates
    item.DataBind();
}
```

You must check whether a template for the title item is defined; if it is not, you just set the *Text* property of the title cell with the contents of the *Title* property. Otherwise, you get an instance of the template container type and use it as the input argument of the *InstantiateIn* method—the only method on the *ITemplate* interface. When done, you add the template container to the control hierarchy—in this case, to the *Controls* collection of the title cell.

A fundamental further step is required to enable the template to successfully process data-bound expressions. You must place a call to *DataBind* on the title item. Data-bound expressions, in fact, are evaluated only after a call to *DataBind* is made that involves the parent control that hosts the expression. Without the *DataBind* call, templates will work correctly but won't display any <%# ... %> expression.

How Data-Bound Controls Resolve Data Sources

Control developers using ASP.NET 1.x have an additional issue to solve. They need to figure out a way to normalize the data source to *IEnumerable*. Array, collection, and *DataView* objects implement *IEnumerable*, but the same isn't true for popular ADO.NET objects such as *DataTable* and *DataSet*. These two classes, in fact, implement *IListSource*. Things get even more complicated if the control supports the *DataMember* property. This piece of code is required by virtually any data-bound control, including built-in ASP.NET controls. And, in fact, built-in ASP.NET controls use an internal method to do the job. Unfortunately, this method is defined on an internal class that is not accessible outside the *system.web* assembly. The class is named *DataSourceHelper* and is defined in the *System.Web.UI* namespace. The class features just one static method named *GetResolvedDataSource*.

```
static IEnumerable GetResolvedDataSource(
                object dataSource, string dataMember);
```

If you're writing an ASP.NET 1.x data-bound control, you might want to consider taking a look at this code. There are two possible ways to view it. One entails that you use a bit of reflection to call it into the method. The other is that you use a decompiler tool to snoop into the source code of the method, grab its logic, and rewrite it into your own project.

Thankfully, this is no longer a problem in ASP.NET 2.0. Data-bound controls are designed to override *PerformDataBinding*, and this method receives a ready-to-use *IEnumerable* collection, no matter what the originally bound data source was.

Conclusion

Like it or not, real-world controls result from the composition of child controls and are data-bound. In addition, controls must be flexible enough to let people customize the user interface. When you resort to visual properties, a rich set of properties, styles, and perhaps themes can do the job. Another, and deeper, level of customization can be achieved through templates.

In this chapter, we've analyzed the ASP.NET support for building data-bound controls. In ASP.NET 1.x, developers first needed to learn about best practices and then code their way to excellence. Books and articles were the only help; no support came from the framework itself. For example, you had to experience on your own the pain of having pages post back and having data-bound controls disappear or render almost empty. Once you'd figured out the whys and the wherefores, you had to update the control properly in a sort of trial-and-error scheme.

In ASP.NET 2.0, things go much better because a number of well-designed intermediate classes have been introduced to incorporate best practices and to let you choose exactly the level of support you want from the framework. As a result, you have a number of classes to build data-bound controls with minimal or richer base capabilities. We discussed the internal implementation of all these classes—*BaseDataBoundControl*, *DataBoundControl*, *ListControl*, and *CompositeDataBoundControl*. If you ever endured the pain of developing custom controls with ASP.NET 1.x, with these classes it might look like child's play in ASP.NET 2.0

We recognized and thoroughly examined three types of data-bound controls—simple binding, list controls, and complex binding. Along the way, we got into styles, rendering, composition, view-state management, data items, persistence, and templates.

Once you learn about data-bound and templated controls, you realize that all the powerful programmatic features you might cook into the control count for little if there's no decent support from the Visual Studio design-time environment. Setting up a control for declarative programming is the next (and final) step in server control development and is the topic of the next chapter.

Just the Facts

- A data-bound control is characterized by a data source property and a bunch of string properties to define mappings between fields in the data source and parts of the control's user interface.

- A data-bound control can be bound through either *DataSource* or *DataSourceID* properties. The former points to an *IEnumerable* object; the latter references a data source control.

- A simple data-bound control typically inherits from *DataBoundControl* and overrides *PerformDataBinding*.

- *PerformDataBinding* passes your code a ready-to-use enumerable collection of bound data, no matter what the bound data source was.

- The collection of bound data must be shrunk to a collection of data item objects and persisted to the view state to survive page postbacks. You create a data item class (and a collection of data item objects if your control binds to a list) and make it capable of serializing efficiently to the view state.

- To persist data items to the view state, you also override methods on the control class that save and restore the state to and from the view state.

- *ListControl* is a ready-to-use class that can be easily extended to "repeat" any control or tree of controls. To build a completely custom list control, though, you follow the steps outlined in this chapter and inherit from *DataBoundControl*.

- To extend list controls with advanced layout capabilities, you implement the *IRepeatInfoUser* interface and modify the rendering engine accordingly.

- *CompositeDataBoundControl* is the base class to use for building complex controls that result from the composition of child data-bound controls.

- Templated properties let page authors modify the standard user interface of a control by adding additional markup.

Chapter 15
Design-Time Support for Custom Controls

A server control has two distinct sets of functionality—run-time and design-time capabilities. Run-time capabilities show up when the control is embedded in a page and served to the browser. Design-time capabilities integrate with a visual designer such as Microsoft Visual Studio 2005 and allow the programmer to configure the appearance and behavior of the control in a declarative and WYSIWYG (what-you-see-is-what-you-get) manner. Like standard and built-in controls, Microsoft ASP.NET custom controls can be architected to integrate with the host designer.

All controls inherit some basic design-time capabilities from the base class *Control*. For example, all controls can be dragged from the toolbox and dropped onto a Web Form, and all controls, when selected within the designer, cause their properties to display in the Properties window. The design-time behavior of a control can be enhanced in three ways: setting predefined attributes, defining custom editors for properties, and adding a made-to-measure designer. We'll review the characteristics and the caveats of these three types of extensions in the context of the sample controls developed in the previous chapters.

Before going any further, though, it's important to know that adding design-time features to a server control is optional. The *Control* class, from which all controls inherit directly or indirectly, already provides a base set of capabilities. These features are enough to make controls usable within a visual designer, but they're not necessarily enough to provide a rich (or even a decent) user experience and to make the controls look like professional components.

The Design-Time Architecture in .NET

In the Microsoft .NET Framework, a designable component is a class that implements the *IComponent* interface—for example, the *Control* class. The *IComponent* interface has just one property—named *Site*—which corresponds to an object that implements the *ISite* interface. Sites bind a component to a container and enable communication between them. In addition, a site allows the container to manage its components and acts as a repository for container-specific, per-component information, such as the component name and attributes.

> **Note**   Strictly related to the *IComponent* interface is the *Component* class. The *Component* class in the *System.ComponentModel* namespace implements the *IComponent* interface and acts as the base for all managed components. Generally speaking, a component is a reusable, black-box object that can interact and communicate with other objects. The definition has been extended a bit in the .NET Framework. A .NET Framework component can also control the life cycle of external resources and provide design-time support.
>
> ASP.NET controls, though, don't inherit from *Component* but simply provide a custom implementation of the *IComponent* interface.

Sites, Containers, and Controls

The *IComponent* interface extends the *IDisposable* interface and includes the *Dispose* method. So the *Dispose* method is available to components for releasing external resources explicitly. Note that the *Dispose* method represents a deterministic way to free resources, in contrast to the default nondeterministic cleanup performed by the garbage collector. Design-time support for classes that implement the *IComponent* interface is built into the .NET Framework and makes it possible for the classes to be manipulated on a design surface.

The design-time support basically consists of the component's ability to be hosted in a container. When hosted in a site, the component interacts with the container through the methods of the *ISite* interface. The component can access the services that the container publishes through the site. Table 15-1 lists the members of the *ISite* interface.

Table 15-1   Members of the *ISite* Interface

Property	Description
Component	Gets the component associated with the class that implements the *ISite* interface.
Container	Gets the *IContainer* object associated with the class that implements the *ISite* interface.
DesignMode	Determines whether the component is in design mode.
Name	Gets or sets the name of the component associated with the site.

A control is a designable component that provides its own user interface. This definition applies to both Microsoft Windows Forms and ASP.NET server controls. As mentioned, the ASP.NET *Control* class implements *IComponent* and provides the infrastructure on top of which the user interface is added. Note that a control is always a component; a component, on the other hand, is not necessarily a control.

The container for ASP.NET server controls is the visual designer. At design time, the designer offers services to controls and controls consume these services through the site's interface.

> **Note**   The *ISite* interface derives from the *IServiceProvider* interface, which provides the *GetService* method to let hosted controls access public services available on the host.

Controls and Designers

The Visual Studio 2005 design-time architecture is designed according to a guideline that establishes an important difference from earlier environments. In the .NET Framework, the design-time capabilities of a control are not implemented within the control but in separate classes. Design-time classes and controls are then declaratively linked using attributes.

Keeping run-time and design-time code separate has two advantages. First, the code that makes the control has a smaller footprint and makes the control itself more manageable at run time. Second, insulating design-time functionality in external classes results in a much more flexible and easily extensible architecture.

> **Note**   The control has a smaller memory footprint only if the design-time code is compiled to a distinct assembly. There's virtually no difference if the same assembly includes both run-time and design-time code. This difference, though, exists for built-in ASP.NET controls that are installed through distinct sets of assemblies. This might also be the case for large libraries of controls (for example, third-party frameworks); it's rarely the case for individual custom controls. Design-time assemblies are not required on the server and should not be deployed. They are only required by Visual Studio 2005.

You can extend the base design-time support for controls in several ways, the simplest of which is mostly declarative and consists of setting a few metadata attributes to control properties and a class declaration. To add any kind of design-time support to a control, you start by importing the *System.ComponentModel* namespace.

More advanced design-time support requires additional work such as the design and implementation of extra classes. You need to include the creation of components such as type converters, UI type editors, designers, and component designers. The various types of design-time functionality are summarized in Table 15-2.

Table 15-2   Design-Time Functionalities for a Control

Function	Description
Designer	Class that takes care of the appearance and behavior of the control when hosted in a .NET visual designer. The set of features you can code in a designer has been significantly improved and enlarged in ASP.NET 2.0.
Editor	Class that provides a convenient way of editing the properties of the associated control.
Type Converter	Class that performs conversions to represent values of arbitrary (and complex) types as strings. Used by the Properties window.

The design-time mechanism we'll discuss here for ASP.NET server controls is merely an instance of the more general design-time mechanism available in the .NET Framework.

In ASP.NET, the designable components are classes that inherit from *Control* hosted in the designer by a class that, in turn, derives from *ControlDesigner*. Generally, the container is a class that implements *IDesigner* and the designable component is any class that implements *IComponent*.

Design-Time Attributes

Generally speaking, metadata attributes are additional descriptive elements that decorate types and members. The attribute doesn't generally run code, and it is limited to exposing additional information about the type or member to any components that might be interested. Other code, outside the particular type, might check the value, or simply the presence, of a given attribute on a type member. Next, based on attributes, the external code might change its way of working with the decorated component accordingly.

Note   Attributes do not change the behavior of the decorated component. However, a component decorated with some attributes might look different to external programs and be ignored or processed in an attribute-specific way.

For ASP.NET server controls, the information contained in metadata attributes is checked and queried by design-time tools such as Visual Studio 2005. Metadata attributes are used to drive the representation and programmability of controls when sited in visual designers.

By convention, the name of a class that represents an attribute ends with the word *Attribute*, such as *BrowsableAttribute* and *DefaultValueAttribute*. When declaring an attribute in the control's source code, the suffix *Attribute* is normally omitted.

As we discuss attributes for controls, we should distinguish between design-time and run-time attributes. Both types of attributes can be applied to ASP.NET server controls—and should be used in real-world scenarios—but with different goals and outcomes. Run-time attributes affect how the control works within the ASP.NET environment and, in particular, can modify the request/response cycle. (In this case, the external code checking attributes is the ASP.NET worker process.) Design-time attributes have no impact on the run-time behavior of the control but simplify the control configuration in Visual Studio 2005. (In this case, the external code interested in attributes is just Visual Studio 2005.)

Using Design-Time Attributes

Table 15-3 details the most popular design-time attributes for a control. In most cases, attributes can be assigned to properties, events, or both. Some attributes, though, are specific to the control class.

Table 15-3   Common Design-Time Attributes for Server Controls

Attribute	Description
Bindable	Indicates whether and how a property can be bound to data.
Browsable	Indicates whether a property or an event should be displayed in the Properties window.
Category	Provides the name of the category in which a property or an event belongs. This allows for logical grouping of properties and events in the Properties window.
DefaultEvent	Indicates the default event for the control. This is the event that is handled when users double-click the control in the designer. *This attribute is valid only on the control class declaration.*
DefaultProperty	Indicates the default property for the control. The default property is selected in the Properties window when users click the control in the designer. *This attribute is valid only on the control class declaration.*
DefaultValue	Used to indicate the default value for a control property. If the property doesn't have a simple type, a type converter is needed.
Description	Provides a description of a property or an event. The text is displayed at the bottom of the Properties window when the user selects a property or event.
Editor	Specifies the editor to use for modifying a property in a visual designer.
Themeable	Indicates whether the property can be added to a control skin in a theme. *Not supported in ASP.NET 1.x.*
ToolboxData	Used to indicate the default markup that Visual Studio adds to the *.aspx* page when you drop the control onto the Web Form. *This attribute is valid only on the control class declaration.*
TypeConverter	Indicates the type converter class to use to convert the type of the property to text.

Most of the attributes affect how the control properties appear in the Visual Studio 2005 Properties window. The Properties window is shown in Figure 15-1. The window is often docked below the Solution box on the right edge of the Visual Studio 2005 window.

Figure 15-1   The Properties window in Visual Studio 2005.

Before we plunge into the details of the various attributes, a warning about Visual Studio 2005 is in order. When you open an ASP.NET page in the designer that contains a given control, Visual Studio 2005 loads the assembly that currently powers that control. The assembly is neither unloaded nor replaced automatically if you recompile the control—a typical scenario if you're developing the control and have a test page displayed and running. For Visual Studio 2005 to reflect design-time changes in the control, you must close and reopen all the pages that use the control.

Setting Attributes

An attribute is wrapped by square brackets in C# but requires angle brackets in Microsoft Visual Basic. Here's a C# example:

```
[Bindable(true)]
public int Count
{
    ⋮
}
```

And here is a Visual Basic example:

```
<Bindable(True)> _
Public Property Count As Integer
    ⋮
End Property
```

Note that in Visual Basic, the attribute is recognized as a set of keywords that precedes the statement; for this reason, you should either write everything on the same line or use the underscore (_) symbol to indicate that the statement wraps to the next line.

Multiple attributes can be assigned by repeating the declaration. Here's how:

```
[Bindable(true)]
[Browsable(true)]
public int Count
{
    ⋮
}
```

Alternatively, you can also group multiple attributes in the same pair of brackets:

```
[Bindable(true), Browsable(true)]
public int Count
{
    ⋮
}
```

The *Bindable* Attribute

The *Bindable* attribute tells the designer whether the property can be bound to data at design time. Note that the attribute, which usually takes a Boolean value, doesn't really control the data-binding capabilities of the property but simply marks it for display in the *DataBindings* dialog box. This is the behavior of the attribute in Visual Studio 2003. Properties with the *Bindable* attribute set to *false* can still be associated with data sources programmatically using data-bound expressions.

No *DataBindings* entry appears in the Properties window in Visual Studio 2005. You will find, instead, an *Expressions* entry that lists bindable properties. However, the value of the *Bindable* attribute doesn't seem to affect the properties listed in this dialog box. The *Bindable* attribute defaults to *false*.

The *Browsable* Attribute

All properties are browsable in the Properties window until you explicitly disable the feature by setting the *Browsable* attribute to *false*. Unless you have good reasons not to permit design-time editing of a property, you shouldn't touch the *Browsable* attribute. You might want to set it to *false* for read-only properties and for properties that are designed for programmatic access only.

This is the case for the *DataItem* public property of the *GaugeBar* control we examined in Chapter 14.

```
[Browsable(false)]
public GaugeBarDataItem DataItem
{
    ⋮
}
```

Note that read-only properties not explicitly made unbrowsable are grayed out in the Properties window.

The *Category* and *Description* Attributes

Category and *Description* are other attributes you normally set for each property or event. The *Category* attribute indicates the category to which the property logically belongs in the Properties window. The *Description* attribute provides short descriptive text to display at the bottom of the Properties window.

The category information is used only if the user selects a categorized view in the Properties window (as shown in Figure 15-1). By default, you get an alphabetical view. You use the buttons in the Properties window toolbar to switch between views.

Default categories are *Accessibility, Appearance, Behavior, Data, Layout,* and *Misc.* If you indicate a different name, a new category is created. By default, custom properties go under the *Misc* category.

```
[Category("Appearance")]
[Description("Gets and sets whether notches should be displayed")]
public bool GridLines
{
    :
}
```

The text assigned to *Category* and *Description* attributes can be localized by creating custom attributes, as shown here:

```
[LocalizableDescription("Local_GridLines_Desc")]
public bool GridLines
{
    :
}
```

The text assigned to custom *Category* and/or *Description* attributes will be used as the key to retrieve the real, and culture-specific, text from the assembly's resources using custom attribute code that you must write.

The *DefaultValue* Attribute

The *DefaultValue* attribute indicates the default value of a property. This value in no way influences the value that the property is assigned at run time. When a control is dropped onto a Web Form, Visual Studio 2005 creates an instance of that control and queries the instance for current values of properties while filling in the Properties window. Then Visual Studio 2005 compares the value read from the property with the value of the *DefaultValue* attribute. If it is different than what is indicated as the default value, the Properties window displays the actual value in a bold font. In this way, you have visual feedback that any given property is non-default valued.

The *Themeable* Attribute

ASP.NET 2.0 introduces the use of themes as a quick and effective way to define and apply a block of visual settings to controls. A theme consists of cascading style sheet (CSS) files and skins. A skin is a collection of control declarations where each control is assigned a bunch of default visual attributes. When a control is hosted in a themed ASP.NET page, the settings for that control type found in the selected theme are automatically applied.

The guideline is that only visual properties should be themed. Properties that affect the run-time behavior of the control should not be themed. However, compilers can't enforce this rule and will raise an exception unless you explicitly declare a property as not themeable.

```
[Themeable(false)]
public float Maximum
{
    ⋮
}
```

The *Maximum* property of the *GaugeBar* control clearly indicates a behavioral property and is not limited to modifying the visual appearance of the control. To prevent using this property in a theme, you mark it as unthemeable. By default, all properties are themeable.

The *Editor* Attribute

The *Editor* attribute specifies the editor to use to change the value of a control property. When editing the value of a property decorated with the *Editor* attribute, the designer creates a new instance of the editor type and displays it through a popup dialog box or drop-down window.

The idea is that the user selects the value through the provided user interface and returns it to the Properties window. An editor class must derive from the *UITypeEditor* base class. We'll explore an example later.

The *TypeConverter* Attribute

The *TypeConverter* attribute indicates a class that acts as a converter between data types. The type converter provides text-to-value conversion or a drop-down list of values to select from. A type converter lies behind the apparent magic that enables Visual Studio 2005 to display a drop-down list for each property of an enumerated type or a color palette for a color property. We'll explore a sample type converter later.

Class Attributes

Each control class declaration should be decorated with at least the following three attributes: *DefaultEvent*, *DefaultProperty*, and *ToolboxData*.

The *DefaultProperty* attribute, in particular, refers to the property that gets selected in the Properties window when the user clicks to select the control in the design surface. Likewise, the *DefaultEvent* attribute indicates the event that is handled when users double-click the control in the designer, as shown in Figure 15-2.

```
[ToolboxData("<{0}:BarChart runat=\"server\"></{0}:BarChart>")]
[DefaultProperty("Title")]
[DefaultEvent("BarChartCreated")]
public class BarChart : CompositeDataBoundControl
{
    ⋮
}
```

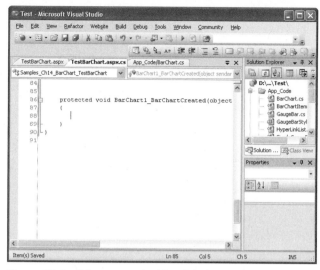

Figure 15-2 When users double-click the control in the designer, a handler for the default event is created.

The *ToolboxData* attribute specifies the default tag generated for a custom control when it is dragged from a toolbox in a tool such as Visual Studio. The text you pass to the attribute can contain any valid markup that contributes to giving the control instance the default aspect. The designer will replace all occurrences of {0} with the tag prefix associated with the control.

Enumeration and Color Types

The design-time environment provides special support for a few types, including colors and enumerations. For example, a property of type *Color* automatically supports using a color palette. (See Figure 15-3.)

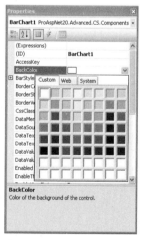

Figure 15-3 Properties of type *Color* can be edited using a color palette window.

Likewise, properties whose type is an enumeration are typically edited using a drop-down list with all possible enumeration values. To achieve this capability, you don't have to make any extra effort. Everything is built into the visual designer. Figure 15-4 shows how to edit the *BorderStyle* enumeration property of the *BarChart* control we created in Chapter 14.

Figure 15-4   The values for the *BorderStyle* property are available in a drop-down list.

You will obtain the same behavior from Visual Studio 2005 if the property is bound to a custom enumeration type.

Attributes That Affect Run-Time Behavior

When developing a server control, you normally use attributes to indicate design-time functionality. However, there are a few attributes that, although used like design-time attributes, affect the run-time behavior of the control. These attributes instruct the page parser how to proceed during the examination of the *.aspx* source code. These attributes are listed in the Table 15-4.

Table 15-4   Attributes that Affect Run-Time Behavior

Attribute	Description
ControlBuilder	Indicates the control builder class for a given control.
ParseChildren	Tells the ASP.NET runtime how to parse the nested content of a control. The attributes takes a Boolean value that indicates whether the nested content should be parsed as properties or child controls.
TemplateContainer	Indicates the container class that wraps a given template. (See Chapter 14.)

Control builders deserve more of an introduction. By default, every control on a page is associated with a control-builder class. A control builder works side by side with the page parser and helps to analyze the markup for the control and to build all the necessary child controls.

The control-builder class is responsible for handling any child markup element that the main tag of a control contains. The base class for control builders is *ControlBuilder*.

The default *ControlBuilder* class adds a child control to the *Controls* collection for every nested element it encounters within the control's tags. In addition, it creates literal controls for the text located between nested control tags. Custom controls are processed by the default control builder. If you don't like the way the *ControlBuilder* class works, replace the default control builder with a custom one. In most cases, you'll use a custom control builder if the control has a complex layout or contains child tags that require ad hoc parsing.

Rendering Types

Any information you enter in the Properties window is persisted to disk as attributes of the control. This serialization mechanism works seamlessly as long as strings and primitive types (dates, numbers, colors) are involved. However, not all information persisted in a block of markup code is actually a string. Let's consider the *Width* property of a control.

```
<expo:GaugeBar runat="server" ID="GaugeBar1" width="200px" />
```

The value of the *width* attribute looks like a string—*200px*—but the type of the underlying control property—the *Width* property—is not of type *String*. The *Width* property, in fact, is declared as type *Unit*. So what happens to make the string *200px* understandable by the control?

The page parser makes use of special modules—known as *type converters*—to convert to and from other types into a given type. In this case, the *UnitConverter* class transforms strings into *Unit* values and serializes *Unit* values into a string.

Implementing a Type Converter

To see the importance of type converters, let's extend the *GaugeBar* control we built in Chapter 14 with a complex property named *Filter*. The *Filter* property groups some attributes that relate to advanced rendering capabilities, such as alpha and glow filters.

> **Note**   Alpha and glow filters require proprietary components and are supported only by Microsoft Internet Explorer 5.0 and newer versions. To apply these filters, though, you simply add custom tags to the standard *Style* attribute. As a result, additional rendering filters are recognized and processed by Internet Explorer and blissfully ignored by other browsers.

In particular, we want to give *GaugeBar* controls the ability to apply a radial alpha filter with a settable level of opacity or, alternatively, a glow filter that renders a sort of faded frame around the control. You can control programmatically both the thickness and color of the frame.

Adding a *Filter* Property to the *GaugeBar* Control

The filter capabilities of the *GaugeBar* control are expressed through a new *Filter* property that is defined as follows:

```
private FilterSettings _gaugeFilters = null;
[Category("Appearance")]
[DesignerSerializationVisibility(DesignerSerializationVisibility.Content)]
[Description("Defines the filter settings of the gauge")]
public FilterSettings Filter
{
    get
    {
        if (_gaugeFilters == null)
            _gaugeFilters = new FilterSettings();
        return _gaugeFilters;
    }
}
```

As is typical with custom types, the new property is not persisted in the view state and is characterized by a new attribute–*DesignerSerializationVisibility*–which we'll discuss soon. The type of the *Filter* property is not a primitive, simple type such as string or *Color*. The type is a complex object with multiple properties defined as follows:

```
public class FilterSettings
{
    private GaugeFilterType _type;
    private Color _glowColor;
    private int _glowStrength;
    private int _alphaOpacity;

    public FilterSettings()
    {
        _type = GaugeFilterType.None;
        _glowStrength = 5;
        _alphaOpacity = 25;
    }

    [Description("Gets and sets the type of the filter to use")]
    [NotifyParentProperty(true)]
    public GaugeFilterType FilterType
    {
        get { return _type; }
        set { _type = value; }
    }

    [Description("Gets and sets the color of the border")]
    [NotifyParentProperty(true)]
    public Color GlowColor
    {
        get { return _glowColor; }
        set { _glowColor = value; }
```

```
        }

        [Description("Indicates the width of the border")]
        [NotifyParentProperty(true)]
        public int GlowStrength
        {
            get { return _glowStrength; }
            set { _glowStrength = value; }
        }

        [Description("Indicates the percentage of opacity desired")]
        [NotifyParentProperty(true)]
        public int AlphaOpacity
        {
            get { return _alphaOpacity; }
            set { _alphaOpacity = value; }
        }
    }
}
```

These properties are not persisted to the view state. Because these attributes are created to be set at design time, you give them default values that don't change programmatically. So, in this context, not using the view state just represents a possible form of optimization. There are no technical reasons for not using the view state, however.

What happens when you get to edit this property at design-time? Figure 15-5 shows how Visual Studio 2005 renders the contents of the property in the default case.

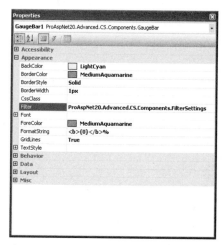

Figure 15-5   Visual Studio 2005 editing the contents of a custom and complex object.

As you can see, the Properties window is limited to displaying the type of the property. More precisely, it shows what the *ToString* method on the *FilterSettings* type returns. You can easily modify the text displayed, but how can you make the contents editable?

You have two basic options: adding a type converter or defining a type editor. Let's tackle the type converter option first.

What's a Type Converter?

A type converter is an object that implements some logic to convert one type into another. Many .NET Framework objects—for example, integers, colors, fonts, and the aforementioned *Unit* type just to name a few—are associated with a type converter. Type converters come in handy when serializing the value of nonprimitive types to a string format to be saved to an *.aspx* file. At the same time, type converters read a string description of a value and return it to its original type. Type converters are at work behind the scenes when you specify, for example, some font properties through text attributes at design time and retrieve a *Font* object ready to use at run time.

To edit the properties of a *FilterSettings* object conveniently in Visual Studio 2005, we need a type converter that reduces a complex object into small pieces that can be more easily set and persisted. To build a type converter, you create a class that inherits from *TypeConverter* and overrides a few members of its base class.

Creating a Type Converter

The converter for a given type must declare whether the conversion is permitted to and from a given type (for example, *string*). The members you override for this goal are *CanConvertTo* and *CanConvertFrom*. These methods simply check the destination and the source type with the list of types the converter supports. The list of supported types must include at least the type *String*, but other conversions can be made depending on the implementation of the converter. (Integers, for example, could be converted into byte arrays or decimal values, if such conversion serves your purpose.) Both methods return a Boolean value indicating their ability to perform the conversion.

Other members to override are *ConvertTo* and *ConvertFrom*. As the names suggest, the methods perform the actual transformation to and from *FilterSettings*. Typically, the serialization process consists of creating a comma-separated string in which the value of each property is rendered as a string. The way in which each property is serialized is completely up to the programmer.

The following listing shows the full implementation of the type converter for the *FilterSettings* class:

```
public class GaugeFilterSettingsConverter : TypeConverter
{
    private const int NumOfMembers = 4;

    public GaugeFilterSettingsConverter()
    {
    }

    // Conversion from String is possible
    public override bool CanConvertFrom(ITypeDescriptorContext context,
        Type sourceType)
```

```
    {
        if (sourceType == typeof(string))
            return true;

        return base.CanConvertFrom(context, sourceType);
    }

    // Conversion to String is possible and new instances can be created
    public override bool CanConvertTo(ITypeDescriptorContext context,
            Type destinationType)
    {
        if (destinationType == typeof(string))
            return true;

        if (destinationType == typeof(InstanceDescriptor))
            return true;

        return base.CanConvertTo(context, destinationType);
    }

    // Convert a FilterSettings to a string
    public override object ConvertTo(ITypeDescriptorContext context,
            CultureInfo culture, object value, Type destinationType)
    {
        // Ensure the value is a FilterSettings object
        if (value != null)
        {
            if (!(value is FilterSettings))
                throw new ArgumentException(
                        "Invalid FilterSettings object", "value");
        }

        // If null, return the empty string
        if (destinationType == typeof(string))
        {
            if (value == null)
                return String.Empty;

            // Get the object to serialize and necessary converters
            FilterSettings filter = (FilterSettings) value;
            TypeConverter cvInt;
            cvInt = TypeDescriptor.GetConverter(typeof(int));
            TypeConverter cvColor;
            cvColor = TypeDescriptor.GetConverter(typeof(Color));

            // Create the string
            string[] parts = new string[NumOfMembers];
            parts[0] = filter.FilterType.ToString();
            parts[1] = cvInt.ConvertTo(filter.AlphaOpacity, typeof(int));
            parts[2] = cvInt.ConvertTo(filter.GlowStrength, typeof(int));
            parts[3] = cvColor.ConvertTo(filter.GlowColor, typeof(string));
            return String.Join(culture.TextInfo.ListSeparator, parts);
        }

        return base.ConvertTo(context, culture, value, destinationType);
    }
```

```csharp
// Convert the specified value to FilterSettings
public override object ConvertFrom(ITypeDescriptorContext context,
        CultureInfo culture, object value)
{
    // Default instance
    if (value == null)
        return new FilterSettings();

    // Deserialize from a string representation
    if (value is string)
    {
        // Get the source string
        string data = (string) value;

        if (data.Length == 0)
            return new FilterSettings();

        // Split the string into parts
        string[] parts = data.Split(culture.TextInfo.ListSeparator[0]);
        if (parts.Length != NumOfMembers)
            throw new ArgumentException(
                    "Invalid FilterSettings object", "value");

        // Create a new FilterSettings object
        FilterSettings filter = new FilterSettings();

        // Part 0 is a string representing the FilterType property
        Type t = typeof(GaugeFilterType);
        filter.FilterType = (GaugeFilterType) Enum.Parse(t, parts[0]);

        // Part 1 represents the AlphaOpacity property (integer)
        TypeConverter cvInt;
        cvInt = TypeDescriptor.GetConverter(typeof(int));
        filter.AlphaOpacity = (int) cvInt.ConvertFrom(context, culture,
                    parts[1]);

        // Part 2 represents the GlowStrength property (integer)
        filter.GlowStrength = (int) cvInt.ConvertFrom(context, culture,
                    parts[2]);

        // Part 3 represents the GlowColor property (Color)
        TypeConverter cvColor;
        cvColor = TypeDescriptor.GetConverter(typeof(Color));
        filter.GlowColor = (Color) cvColor.ConvertFrom(context,
                    culture, parts[3]);

        return filter;
    }

    return base.ConvertFrom(context, culture, value);
}
```

The *GaugeFilterSettingsConverter* enables you to convert the *FilterSettings* object to and from strings, as you can infer from the implementation of the *CanConvertTo* and *CanConvertFrom* methods. A *FilterSettings* object is serialized to a string type by creating a string of separated tokens. The separator is defined in a culture-independent way—by using the comma, for most cultures.

You should note the use of ad hoc converters to obtain strings to represent of *Color* and *Integer* types.

```
TypeConverter cvInt = TypeDescriptor.GetConverter(typeof(int));
TypeConverter cvColor = TypeDescriptor.GetConverter(typeof(Color));
```

The use of these converters is not strictly necessary—you can use any algorithm to serialize members of the *FilterSettings* class to strings—but it helps to get a standard representation in the designer of commonly used types.

```
parts[2] = cvInt.ConvertTo(filter.GlowStrength, typeof(int));
parts[3] = cvColor.ConvertTo(filter.GlowColor, typeof(string));
```

Likewise, you convert from a comma-separated string to a new instance of the *FilterSettings* class by using type-specific converters for the various members, as shown here:

```
filter.GlowStrength = cvInt.ConvertFrom(context, culture, parts[2]);
filter.GlowColor = cvColor.ConvertFromString(context, culture, parts[3]);
```

The converter is not effective until you associate it with the *FilterSettings* class.

```
[TypeConverter(typeof(GaugeFilterSettingsConverter))]
public class FilterSettings
{
    ⋮
}
```

The Properties window now displays an entry for the *Filter* property, which now contains a comma-separated list of strings. The colors, in particular, are rendered with an integer that indicates the RGB representation of the color.

```
// 0=type, 25=opacity, 5=strength, -256=color
0,25,5,-256
```

To edit properties, you must type the new value directly in the text box. Admittedly, this is not practical; indeed, a more user-friendly solution exists.

Deriving from *ExpandableObjectConverter*

If you've worked with Visual Studio 2005, you know that to set font properties you select the *Font* property and expand it to see and edit the various subproperties, such as *Size* and *Name*.

The *Font* property is expandable and exposes all its subproperties as individual properties in the same window. How can we obtain the same behavior for a custom property?

The type converter for the property must inherit from a more specialized base class. The new base class is *ExpandableObjectConverter*.

The *ExpandableObjectConverter* class inherits from *TypeConverter* and provides a couple of additional overrides—*GetProperties* and *GetPropertiesSupported*. By simply replacing the base class, the type converter code shown previously provides a behavior identical to that of the *Font* property. This is demonstrated in Figure 15-6.

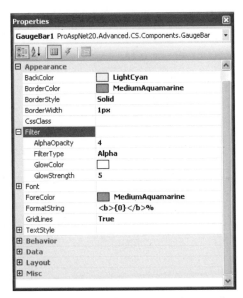

Figure 15-6 The *Filter* property just made expandable.

Each property in a class associated with a type converter should also be marked with the *NotifyParentProperty* attribute to notify the parent property (for example, *Filter*) of any changes. The following code snippet illustrates the metadata for the *Text* subproperty:

```
[Description("Gets and sets the type of filter to use")]
[NotifyParentProperty(true)]
public GaugeFilterType FilterType
{
    get { return _type; }
    set { _type = value; }
}
```

Figure 15-7 shows a sample page that uses the *GaugeBar* control with a glow filter applied.

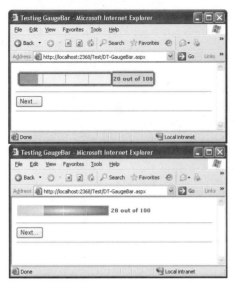

Figure 15-7   A *GaugeBar* control with glow and alpha filters applied in Internet Explorer.

Here is what the source code of the page that hosts the *GaugeBar* control looks like:

```
<expo:GaugeBar runat="server" ID="GaugeBar1"
      Width="200px"
      Height="20px"
      BackColor="LightCyan"
      Value="22"
      BorderStyle="Solid"
      BorderWidth="1px"
      BorderColor="MediumAquamarine"
      ForeColor="MediumAquamarine"
      GridLines="True"
      FormatString="<b>{0}</b>%"
      Filter-AlphaOpacity="4"
      Filter-FilterType="Glow"
      Filter-GlowColor="Blue"
      Filter-GlowStrength="5" >
</expo:GaugeBar>
```

As you can see, the subproperties of the *Filter* property are serialized in the standard format *Property-SubProperty*. To control the serialization of property values, you resort to serialization attributes such as the *DesignerSerializationVisibility* attribute that we first met in the declaration of the new *Filter* property.

Serialization Attributes

The attributes in Table 15-5 tell the designer how to serialize the control and its properties. The serialization process is important because it governs the creation of the HTML code for the control.

Table 15-5   Design-Time Serialization Attributes for Server Controls

Attribute	Description
DesignerSerializationVisibility	Specifies whether (and how) a property displayed in the Properties window should be persisted into code.
NotifyParentProperty	Specifies whether changes to subproperties should be bubbled up to the parent property. This attribute is used when the converted property is derived from *ExpandableObjectConverter*.
PersistChildrenAttribute	Indicates whether the nested contents of a control should be interpreted as properties (default) or child controls.
PersistenceMode	Specifies whether a property should be persisted as an attribute on the control's tag or as nested content.

The *DesignerSerializationVisibility* attribute can take any of the values listed in Table 15-6.

Table 15-6   Values for the *DesignerSerializationVisibility* Attribute

Value	Description
Content	This option causes the contents of the property (for example, *Filter*) to be serialized as a whole. All subproperties will be serialized using an ad hoc naming convention. The subproperties of a property are the child members of a complex type. For example, *FilterType* and *GlowColor* are subproperties of the property *Filter*. For the *FilterType* subproperty, an attribute named *Filter-FilterType* will be created.
Hidden	This option hides the property from serialization. The property will not be persisted in the markup code of the control.
Visible	Default value, causes the top-level property to be serialized. When this option is set, a property such as *Filter* is serialized as a comma-separated list of child values. All subproperties will not be saved individually but within a unique, all-encompassing attribute named *Filter*.

The *PersistChildren* attribute is set to *false* for a control derived from *WebControl*, and it's set to *true* if the control inherits from *Control*. When this attribute is set to *false*, the nested contents of a control are handled as properties. Each child tag is mapped to a property with the same name as the tag. For example, a child tag named *<ItemTemplate>* must have a corresponding *ItemTemplate* property. If this automatic mapping is disabled—that is, if *PersistChildren* is *true*—the child tag is considered an HTML element and a custom builder is required to properly handle its content; otherwise, a compile error is raised.

The *PersistenceMode* attribute indicates how to persist the content of a property. You can decide whether you want a given property to be serialized as a tag-level attribute or as a child tag. Acceptable values for the attribute are listed in Table 15-7.

Table 15-7   Values for the *PersistenceMode* Attribute

Value	Description
Attribute	The property is persisted as a tag's attribute. This is the default option.
EncodedInnerDefault-Property	The property is persisted as the only content of the tag. The content is HTML encoded.
InnerDefaultProperty	The property is persisted as the only content of the tag. The content is not encoded.
InnerProperty	The property is persisted as a child tag along with any other properties of the control.

If your control has template properties, you should change the default value of the *Persistence-Mode* attribute for each of them to prevent the designer from wiping out any nested contents whenever a property in the Properties window is saved. Here's the typical heading of a template property, as we saw in Chapter 14:

```
[TemplateContainer(typeof(TitleTemplateContainer))]
[PersistenceMode(PersistenceMode.InnerProperty)]
public ITemplate TitleTemplate
{
    get { return _titleTemplate; }
    set { _titleTemplate = value; }
}
```

The preceding code indicates that the *TitleTemplate* property must be saved as a nested tag with all the other properties of the control.

Creating a Type Editor

The Properties window doesn't provide much flexibility for editing values. Sure, the Properties window provides you with color palettes and drop-down lists for colors and enumerations; most other types, though, are editable only through text boxes.

If you're not satisfied with the default editing tools of the designer, you can create a made-to-measure editor and link it to the designer. The base class for type editors is *UITypeEditor*. You define a custom type editor class and use metadata attributes to inform the designer that a given property must be edited through the specified dialog box.

A type editor is a Windows Forms dialog box managed through a well-known interface. The dialog box supplies controls and facilities to make data editing as seamless as possible, and it fills a buffer with the string value for the Properties window.

Let's examine the case of the *Filter* property.

The *Filter* Property Editor

The following code shows how to replace the expandable converter with a user interface (UI) type editor for the *Filter* property.

```
[Editor(typeof(GaugeFilterSettingsEditor), typeof(UITypeEditor))]
public FilterSettings Filter
{
    ⋮
}
```

The *Editor* attribute indicates the dialog box to use to edit the value of the specified property. In this case, we'll use the *GaugeFilterSettingsEditor* custom class. The second argument to the attribute is the type of the base class for the editor. The .NET Framework defines several editor classes from which you can choose the predefined one that provides the features you want.

The *UITypeEditor* class is a base class that can be extended to provide custom editing capabilities for a particular property. Other built-in editors exist for collections, URLs, colors, and dates, just to name a few.

When a property is marked with the *Editor* attribute, the designer shows an ellipsis button close to the default text box (shown in Figure 15-8). By clicking that button, the user-defined dialog box shows up and the user can edit the value using a more comfortable user interface.

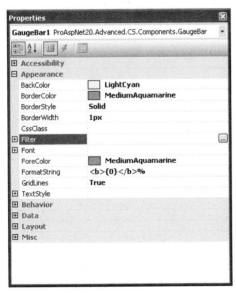

Figure 15-8   The *Filter* property and the ellipsis button that brings up the custom editor.

> **Note**   A UI type editor requires the *System.Windows.Forms* assembly. This assembly is a big one and significantly contributes to keeping the memory footprint of the control quite large. If you're going to define UI type editors, consider splitting run-time and design-time features into distinct assemblies.

Designing a Custom Type Editor

To create a custom type editor, you start by deriving a new class from *UITypeEditor* or from any other type editor. Next, you add a form class to the project and define the user interface of the dialog box. In doing so, you'll probably need to import one or more namespaces that relate to Windows Forms and designers. For example, you'll certainly reference the following namespaces:

```
using System.Drawing.Design;
using System.Windows.Forms;
```

Referencing Windows Forms classes, even from within an ASP.NET Web control project, is necessary to extend the user interface of the visual designer.

A type editor class will at least override the *GetEditStyle* and *EditValue* methods. The *GetEditStyle* method indicates the style of the editing required. Acceptable values are *DropDown* and *Modal*. The *EditValue* method takes care of displaying the dialog box and retrieves the value to pass on to the Properties window. The following listing details the code for the *GaugeFilterSettingsEditor* class.

```
public class GaugeFilterSettingsEditor : UITypeEditor
{
    public override UITypeEditorEditStyle GetEditStyle(
            ITypeDescriptorContext context)
    {
        return UITypeEditorEditStyle.Modal;
    }

    public override object EditValue(
            ITypeDescriptorContext context,
            IServiceProvider provider,
            object value)
    {
        // Create and display your Windows Forms dialog box here
        :

        // Use the return values of the dialog box to edit the value
        :

        return value;
    }
}
```

If the *GetEditStyle* method returns the *UITypeEditorEditStyle.DropDown* value, the designer prepares to display the specified control just below the property text box. If the modal style is set, the designer expects to have a modal dialog box to display.

The *EditValue* method is called to enable editing. In the preceding code, a new dialog window is created and displayed. When the window is dismissed, you can use global fields or properties on the dialog class to retrieve user information and store that to an internal variable. The value returned from the *EditValue* method is assigned to the property.

If you opt for a drop-down user interface, you must use the methods of the *IWindowsForms-EditorService* interface to display a custom control in the Properties window. In this case, you create a custom Windows Forms control instead of a form. The designer displays a down-arrow button instead of an ellipsis button (...).

```
public override object EditValue(
     ITypeDescriptorContext context,
     IServiceProvider provider,
     object value)
{
   object o = provider.GetService(typeof(IWindowsFormsEditorService));
   IWindowsFormsEditorService srv = (IWindowsFormsEditorService) o;
   if (srv != null)
   {
       // Display a custom control and retrieve the value
       MyControl myCtl = new MyControl(value);
       srv.DropDownControl(myCtl);
   }
}
```

You can also implement an owner-drawn mechanism by overriding the *GetPaintValue-Supported* and *PaintValue* methods. The *GetPaintValueSupported* method just returns a Boolean value; the *PaintValue* method is passed a rectangle that represents the area of the Properties window where a representation of the value is to be drawn. The *PaintValue* method also receives a *Graphics* object and can use all the power of GDI+ to create owner-drawn output.

Working with Custom Collections

Control properties implemented through collections enjoy a particular treatment from most designers. When you work with built-in controls, you might not be surprised to see that collection properties have a tailor-made UI editor. You click the ellipsis button and a dialog box appears that is similar to that shown in Figure 15-9.

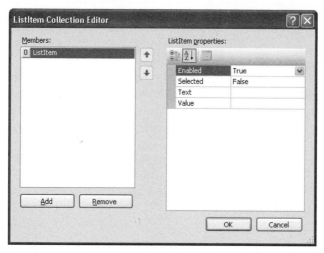

Figure 15-9 The standard collection editor used by most built-in controls.

The great news is that a similar dialog box can be inherited by custom collection properties without much effort.

Designing the Collection Class

The Visual Studio 2005 designer associates all classes that inherit from *ICollection* with the *CollectionEditor* class. This editor class is ultimately responsible for the user interface in Figure 15-9.

The collection must be formed by classes that expose properties and not by fields. In this case, the editor extracts members and fills the property grid on the right edge of Figure 15-9. You can use the controls in the dialog box to populate the collection. Added items appear in the list to the left with the description returned by the *ToString* method of the class that forms the collection.

Editing the *HyperLinkItemCollection* Collection

The *HyperLinkList* control that we created in Chapter 14 features a collection property named *Items* that contains a description of the links to display. Each link is represented with an object of type *HyperLinkItem*; the collection class is *HyperLinkItemCollection* and is defined as follows:

```
public class HyperLinkItemCollection : Collection<HyperLinkItem>
{
    ⋮
}
```

The *HyperLinkItem* class has three public properties—*Text*, *Url*, and *Tooltip*. By simply clicking on the *Items* ellipsis button in the Properties window, you get the dialog box shown in Figure 15-10 for any instance of the *HyperLinkList* control you have on a Web form.

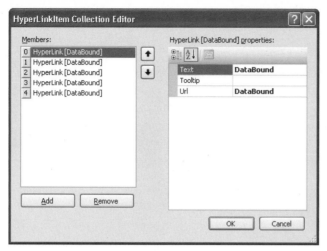

Figure 15-10   The standard collection editor working on *HyperLinkItemCollection* properties.

Custom Designers

Sometimes when you test a custom control, you mainly focus on its run-time behavior. You quickly arrange a test page and run it over and over again. When you're satisfied with the results, you turn your attention to the design-time behavior of the control and, more often than not, you get into trouble. The control might render well at run time, but it throws a rendering exception at design time.

In ASP.NET 2.0, the *Control* class features a new Boolean property named *DesignMode*. As the name suggests, the property returns *true* if the instance of the control is being hosted in a designer and *false* if it is being used at run time. In simple cases, an *if* statement in the *Render* method of the control solves most of the issues.

```
if (DesignMode)
{
    ⋮
}
else
{
    ⋮
}
```

In other cases, you must neatly separate the design-time rendering from the run-time rendering. The tool to leverage is a custom designer.

Built-in Designers

All ASP.NET controls are associated with a designer component that takes care of generating the markup to show in Visual Studio 2005. This base designer ensures that the control's markup is retrieved as a string and passed to the host environment.

Note that when hosted in Visual Studio 2005 (or in general in a host environment), a control doesn't go through the usual life cycle and doesn't receive events. The interaction between the host and the control is limited to the invocation of the *RenderControl* method.

There at least two reasons for needing a custom designer for a custom control. The first reason is that the control doesn't just render at design time as expected. This might be because of arguable choices you made while coding the rendering engine of the control. It might also be because the behavior of the control depends heavily on run-time data. How can you effectively simulate the run-time appearance of the control at design time? A custom designer can use fake data to give users a realistic preview of the control at run time.

The second reason is that you want to add messages or, especially in ASP.NET 2.0, give users a much richer experience and take advantage of the host capabilities—for example, adding AutoFormat lists, custom actions, and tasks.

Before we go any further with custom designers, let's briefly review a couple of built-in designers that are often used right before your eyes.

The *ControlDesigner* Class

The *ControlDesigner* class provides a base set of design-time capabilities that are inherited by all ASP.NET controls. *ControlDesigner* receives from the host designer the instance of the control to design and captures the control's markup to a memory stream. The following pseudo-code shows how it works internally:

```
// ctl is control instance hosted by the designer
StringWriter sw = new StringWriter();
HtmlTextWriter writer = new HtmlTextWriter(sw);
ctl.RenderControl(writer);
return sw.ToString();
```

The obtained string is then returned to Visual Studio 2005 and displayed in the Web form.

The heart of any control designer is the *GetDesignTimeHtml* method. The method takes no arguments and returns the HTML to use to represent the control at design time. The preceding code snippet comes from the *GetDesignTimeHtml* method as implemented in *ControlDesigner*. Quite often, custom designers are just classes that inherit from *ControlDesigner* and override *GetDesignTimeHtml*.

Designers for Data-Bound Controls

Built-in designers exist for all categories of data-bound controls. The primary goal of a data-bound designer is providing a realistic preview of the control's appearance when it gets bound to real data. The way designers accomplish this task is by loading fake data—mostly fixed strings such as "DataBound Item" or something like that. (We'll see an example soon.)

In ASP.NET 2.0, a control designer has additional goals, such as providing a rich design-time environment that sets up a kind of wizard to let users easily configure the control. Figure 15-11 shows the standard list of actions defined on data-bound controls.

Figure 15-11   The action list of a data-bound designer in ASP.NET 2.0.

When writing a designer for a data-bound control, the class to consider is *DataBoundControlDesigner*. Compared to *ControlDesigner*, this class has a more general architecture, but it's still centered on the *GetDesignTimeHtml* method.

The *DataBoundControlDesigner* class has a *DataBind* method that calls into a new method—*GetDesignTimeDataSource*. This method is responsible for providing the data to use at design time. If the control is bound to a fully configured data source control, the data is the real data set; otherwise, it is a fake data set much like in ASP.NET 1.x.

Writing Custom Designers

The base class for a Web control designer is *ControlDesigner*, and it's located in the *System.Web.UI.Design* namespace. The class defines a common behavior for designers and supplies methods that the design-time environment can call for a variety of purposes. *ControlDesigner* is the first concrete class in the hierarchy that you can use in your code. All designers for ASP.NET controls actually inherit from an abstract class named *HtmlControlDesigner*, which marks the difference between Web and Windows control designers.

HTML Control Designers

When hosted in a visual environment, a Web server control is not very interactive, does not fire postback events, and is limited to generating HTML output. If you want the control to provide a truly what-you-see-is-what-you-get (WYSIWYG) view, you should implement the rendering engine of the control directly in the *Render* method. Only this method, in fact, is called from within the visual designer to obtain the HTML of the control.

If you create a composite control and override the *CreateChildControls* method, the control will work great at run time but not at design time. In the designer, the sequence of calls is different and, in the end, a control structured in this way returns an empty HTML string to the designer. In ASP.NET 2.0, the base class *CompositeControl* has a fix for this situation; if you don't inherit from *CompositeControl* but still have a hierarchy of child controls, you should ensure that child controls are created in the *Render* method. Here's the pseudo-code for the *Render* method in the *CompositeControl* that you should replicate in your code for an effective design-time behavior:

```
protected internal override void Render(HtmlTextWriter writer)
{
    if (base.DesignMode)
        this.EnsureChildControls();
    base.Render(writer);
}
```

To control the appearance of the control in the visual designer, you can override a few methods, such as *GetDesignTimeHtml*. Writing a custom designer for a control is the most efficient way to provide special design-time features without affecting the run-time behavior.

Creating a Control Designer

A typical control designer derives from *ControlDesigner* and overrides a few methods (described in the following list) to control the HTML code displayed in the designer:

- **GetDesignTimeHtml**   This method returns the HTML markup code that is used to represent the control at design time. By default, the method returns the output generated by the *Render* method. By overriding this method, you can enhance that string or even provide a fixed representation for the control.

- **GetEmptyDesignTimeHtml**   This protected, overridable method gets the HTML markup code that is used to represent an empty control at design time. The base implementation of this method returns a string that contains the name of the control class and the ID.

- **GetErrorDesignTimeHtml**   This protected overridable method provides the HTML markup code that is displayed when a design-time error occurs in the control. The returned text typically provides information about the specific exception.

Other methods you can override or use in a custom control designer class are *AllowResize* and *CreatePlaceHolderDesignTimeHtml*. The *AllowResize* method returns a Boolean value that informs the designer about the availability of the control to be resized. Normally, there's no reason against making a control resizeable. However, in some situations you might opt for a fixed size—for example, when a templated control has an empty template.

The *CreatePlaceHolderDesignTimeHtml* method takes a message string and returns a block of HTML text with a look and feel consistent with that of standard ASP.NET controls. For example, you can use the method to provide an error message, as shown in the following code snippet (and in Figure 15-12):

```
protected override string GetErrorDesignTimeHtml(Exception e)
{
    return CreatePlaceHolderDesignTimeHtml("There was an error");
}
```

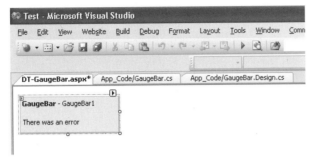

Figure 15-12 A design-time error message for a control.

If you don't like the standard user interface, or you just want to customize it further, you can simply return ad hoc HTML code, as discussed in the following example.

Generating Design-Time HTML

The following listing shows a sample implementation of a designer for the *GaugeBar* control. The class overrides three methods—*GetDesignTimeHtml*, *Initialize*, *OnClick*—and the *Auto-Formats* property. As a result, the control provides different views based on the settings made, detects user clicking, and supplies an AutoFormat menu. The *GetDesignTimeHtml* method takes the output of the control and inserts it in a table along with a short note.

```
public class GaugeBarDesigner : ControlDesigner
{
    private GaugeBar _controlInstance;
    private bool _addNote;
    private float _originalValue;

    public override void Initialize(IComponent component)
    {
        // Get a reference to the control to design
        _controlInstance = (GaugeBar) component;
        base.Initialize(component);
    }

    public override string GetDesignTimeHtml()
    {
        if (_controlInstance.Value < 0)
        {
            // Save the current (invalid) Value
            _originalValue = _controlInstance.Value;

            // Generate a random value. This assignment must
            // be undone on exit, otherwise it'll be saved to the ASPX
            _controlInstance.Value = GetRandomNumber();
            _addNote = true;
        }
        else
            _addNote = false;
```

```
            // If no valid Value is provided, add a note to the markup
            if (_addNote)
            {
                string template = "...";
                string message = "The <b>Value</b> property has no valid " +
                                 "value set. <br/>The displayed value has " +
                                 "been randomly generated to help " +
                                 "you form an idea about the control. <hr/>" +
                                 "<small>Courtesy of <b>Programming " +
                                 "Microsoft ASP.NET 2.0 Applications-" +
                                 "Advanced Topics</b></small>";
                string markup =  String.Format(template,
                    base.Component.GetType().Name,
                    base.Component.Site.Name,
                    base.GetDesignTimeHtml(),
                    message);

                // Restore the original value
                _controlInstance.Value = _originalValue;

                // Return
                return markup;
            }

            // Return the default markup
            return base.GetDesignTimeHtml();
        }

        protected override void OnClick(DesignerRegionMouseEventArgs e)
        {
            base.OnClick(e);

            // Re-render the control to a newly generated random number
            UpdateDesignTimeHtml();
        }

        public override DesignerAutoFormatCollection AutoFormats
        {
            get
            {
                DesignerAutoFormatCollection autoFormats;
                autoFormats = new DesignerAutoFormatCollection();
                autoFormats.Add(new SimpleAutoFormat());
                autoFormats.Add(new PercentageAutoFormat());
                return autoFormats;
            }
        }
        private  int GetRandomNumber()
        {
            Random rnd = new Random();
            return (int) rnd.Next(0, (int)_controlInstance.Maximum);
        }
    }
}
```

Figure 15-13 shows the *GaugeBar* control in the Visual Studio 2005 designer.

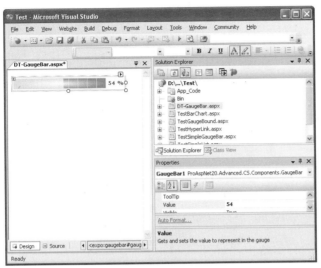

Figure 15-13   The *GaugeBar* control in action sited in the Visual Studio environment.

The designer adapts the returned markup based on the specified value of the *Value* property.

Adapting Markup to the *Value* Property

The output of the *GaugeBar* control depends for the most part on the *Value* property. If the *Value* property is set to a negative value at design-time (that is, the real value is known only at run time), users might not receive a realistic and useful preview. For this reason (and to demonstrate how custom logic can be embedded in a designer), let's force the *GaugeBar* to display a random value when the real *Value* property is negative. In addition, we'll add an explanatory note to inform the user about the choice we made.

As a result, the design-time HTML is composed of two parts—the effective output of the control, and a part with information and an extra copyright note. The information and copyright will not show up at run time.

You can give any form and appearance to this piece of HTML markup, and you can compose it using any technique you're familiar with, including *StringBuilder* and *String.Format*. To keep the final result as close as possible to standard messages you get from designers, I borrowed the HTML template string that is used by the *CreatePlaceHolderDesignTimeHtml* method and modified it slightly.

The HTML templates describe an HTML table with three rows that is populated with four parameters—the type of the control, the ID of the control, the default markup of the *GaugeBar* control, and a message for the user.

In the *Initialize* method, the *component* parameter represents a reference to the *GaugeBar* control created by Visual Studio 2005 for rendering purposes. You cache this reference and work with it to prepare the markup. You test the *Value* property; if it is negative, you change it to a random generated value. Note, though, that any settings on the control are persisted to the ASP.NET Web Form when the page is saved. So it is essential that you restore the original value of the *Value* property immediately after generating the markup. This technique is used by most data-bound control designers to provide a fake list of data for design-time rendering.

Figure 15-14 shows the design-time view of the *GaugeBar* when set to a negative value. Note that the real value of the *Value* property is that set in the Properties window, namely –1. This is the value that will be rendered at run time.

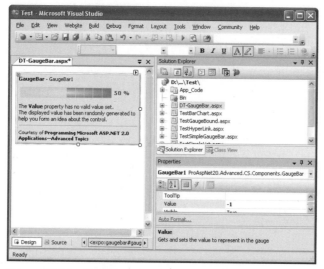

Figure 15-14   The *GaugeBar* control has the *Value* property set to an invalid value.

In ASP.NET 2.0, control developers can intercept and handle click events in the control's rectangle. The following code shows how to intercept clicks and generate another random number:

```
protected override void OnClick(DesignerRegionMouseEventArgs e)
{
    base.OnClick(e);
    UpdateDesignTimeHtml();
}
```

The *UpdateDesignTimeHtml* method refreshes the control's view to reflect any changes you might have made in the meantime. The *DesignerRegionMouseEventArgs* structure carries information about the location of the click that you can use to perform different actions.

Creating an AutoFormat List

Some built-in ASP.NET controls have an AutoFormat link just at the bottom of the Properties window. You can see it in Figure 15-14. The link appears automatically if the designer class returns a nonempty collection out of the *AutoFormats* property.

An auto-format collection is a list of classes that provide predefined design-time skins for the control. Each skin is a class that inherits from *DesignerAutoFormat*. The following code defines two formats:

```
DesignerAutoFormatCollection autoFormats;
autoFormats = new DesignerAutoFormatCollection();
autoFormats.Add(new SimpleAutoFormat());
autoFormats.Add(new PercentageAutoFormat());
```

Let's take a look at a sample auto-format class:

```
public class SimpleAutoFormat : DesignerAutoFormat
{
    public SimpleAutoFormat() : base("(Default formatting)")
    {
    }

    public override void Apply(System.Web.UI.Control control)
    {
        GaugeBar _gaugeBar = control as GaugeBar;
        if (_gaugeBar != null)
        {
            _gaugeBar.FormatString = "{0} out of {1}";
            _gaugeBar.Segments = 4;
            _gaugeBar.TextStyle.BackColor = Color.Transparent;
            _gaugeBar.TextStyle.Font.Name = "verdana";
            _gaugeBar.TextStyle.Font.Size = FontUnit.Point(8);
            _gaugeBar.TextStyle.DisplayTextAtBottom = true;
            _gaugeBar.TextStyle.RenderInsideTable = false;
        }
    }
}
```

The parameter passed to the base constructor is the description of the auto-format. The *Apply* method receives a reference to the control and simply sets some of its visual properties to predefined values.

The auto-format classes listed in the *AutoFormats* property are then used to set up the Visual Studio 2005 dialog box shown in Figure 15-15.

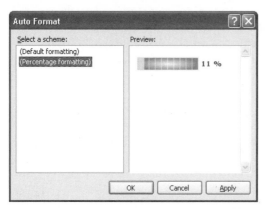

Figure 15-15 The AutoFormat window for the *GaugeBar* control.

Specifying the Designer for a Control Class

You associate a custom designer with a control using the *Designer* attribute, as shown in the following code snippet:

```
[Designer(typeof(GaugeBarDesigner))]
public class GaugeBar : DataBoundControl
{
    ⋮
}
```

The designer class will be loaded when the control is dropped onto a Web Form and its methods are called back by the visual designer.

In ASP.NET 1.x, you typically derive a designer from *ControlDesigner* and extend it by overriding a few methods. In ASP.NET 2.0, it is essential that you choose the base designer class that is closer to the characteristics of the control, such as *CompositeControlDesigner* or *DataBoundDesigner*. Note that the vast majority of ASP.NET 2.0 built-in controls have a tailor-made designer. When you plan a custom control, allow some extra time to plan its design-time support.

Conclusion

Applications written for the .NET Framework are for the most part component-based applications. ASP.NET applications are no exceptions, and several controls can be found working under the lid of Web pages. If you choose Visual Studio 2005 as your development environment, you end up assembling pages using a visual designer. Controls are picked from a palette and dropped onto a design surface. Once instantiated, controls can be configured declaratively through the Properties window. ASP.NET controls know how to integrate themselves into this environment, but their behavior can be further enhanced by resorting to a number of extensions.

In this chapter, we discussed three ways to improve the design-time capabilities of ASP.NET controls. You can assign a few metadata attributes to each property so that the property displays with an ad hoc description and in the most appropriate category. Setting attributes works great if the property value is of a simple type such as string, integer, or an enumeration type.

Properties with custom types need more work and possibly a type converter. A type converter is a sort of special serializer that renders the state of a class as a string. Normally, a type converter returns a comma-separated string in which each token is the value of a public property. A property associated with a converter can be rendered as an expandable object in the Properties window. To achieve that, you need to derive the custom type converter from a more specialized class, such as *ExpandableObjectConverter*.

In all these cases, though, the user interface employed for editing properties consists of a simple text-box control. If a plain text box is inadequate for your values, you can create a type or even a component editor. Editors are Windows Forms classes that are bound to the Properties window and shown when the user chooses to edit the value. A type editor class edits a particular property, whereas a component editor looks like a property page for the control and provides a single user interface to edit all properties in a more convenient way.

Finally, to control the aspect of the component in the designer you can create a made-to-measure designer class. A designer class consists of a few overrides aimed at controlling the HTML text being displayed in the environment for the control. By default, the design-time aspect of the control is nearly identical to its run-time look. However, there might be situations in which you want the control to provide a different output that is not a function of the current properties. In these cases, using a custom designer can do the trick.

Just the Facts

- A server control has two distinct sets of functionality—run-time and design-time capabilities.

- The design-time behavior of a control can be enhanced in three ways: setting predefined attributes, defining custom editors for properties, and adding a made-to-measure designer.

- Through attributes, you can decide how the control shows up in the Properties window.

- Attributes set through the Properties window are serialized to the ASP.NET page; the *PersistenceMode* attribute determines how and where they will be persisted.

- Type converters are classes derived from *TypeConverter* that are used to serialize the value of nonprimitive types to a string format that can be saved to an *.aspx* file.

- If you're not satisfied with the default editing tools of the designer, you can create a made-to-measure editor and link it to the designer. The base class for type editors is *UITypeEditor*.

- A control designer is a class that generates the markup that a control shows when hosted in Visual Studio 2005. All controls have a built-in control designer that you can change through an attribute.

- The *ControlDesigner* class defines a common behavior for controls designers. A custom designer derives from this class, either directly or indirectly.

Index

Symbols

<%#...%>. *See* data-binding
    expressions
* (asterisk), 107
: (colon), 228
#-expressions. *See* data-binding
    expressions
$-expressions. *See* dynamic
    expressions
? (question mark), 107
$ symbol, mobile applications and,
    351

A

AbortTransaction event, 472
abstract methods, 154
Access data stores, 32, 35
accounts. *See also* security
    ASPNET account, 5, 35
    NETWORK SERVICE account, 7
AcquireRequestState event, 82
Activator class, 401
Active Server Pages (ASP), 60
ActiveDirectoryMembershipProvide
    r provider, 156–157
ActiveX controls, 268
ActiveXControls property, 250
adapter pattern, provider, 150, 178
adaptive rendering, mobile
    application, 367–368
<add> element, 98, 184–185
Add Web Reference dialog box, 38
AddOnPrerenderCompleteAsync
    method
    asynchronous pages and,
      196–197
    multiple asynchronous tasks and,
      212–213
    Page_Load event and, 195, 196
    RegisterAsynTask method vs.,
      197, 222
administrative privileges,
    aspnet_compiler.exe utility
    and, 26
ADO.NET, 208
AdRotator mobile control, 341
Ajax.NET library, 279–286
    building sample page, 280–283
    callbacks and, 273
    implementation details, 283–284

overview, 279
remote procedure call vs.
    postback, 285–286
script callbacks vs., 284–286
setting up, 280
al.exe (Assembly Linker) utility, 36
<allow> section, 107
allowAnonymous attribute, 122, 185
AllowBaseType method, 236, 240
AllowClose property, 299
AllowCode property, 237
allowCollectionClass attribute, 44
AllowConnect property, 299
AllowControl method, 236,
    238–240
allowCustomSqlDatabase attribute,
    124
allowDefinition attribute, 98
AllowEdit property, 299
AllowHide property, 299
AllowLayoutChange property, 315
allowLocation attribute, 98, 102
AllowMinimize property, 299
allowOverride attribute, 99–100,
    101
allowPartialClass attribute, 44
AllowResize method, 622
AllowServerSideInclude method,
    236
AllowVirtualReference method, 236,
    240–241
AllowZoneChange property, 299
alpha filters, 604
AlternatingItemStyle property, 453
AlternatingItemTemplate property,
    453
ambiguous reference exceptions, 33
<anonymousIdentification> section,
    102, 104–105
apartmentThreading attribute, 114
App_Browsers folder, 32, 33
App_Code folder
    build providers and, 44
    <codeSubDirectories> section
      and, 30
    custom controls and, 534
    overview, 32, 34–35
    registering virtual path providers,
      54
App_Code_xxx.dll assembly, 34
App_Data folder, 32, 35

AppDomains (application domains)
    compilation and, 3
    HTTP pipeline and, 8, 9
    IIS 5.0 process model and, 5–6
    membership service providers
      and multiple, 157
    no-compile pages and, 32
    passing objects between, 401
    recompilation and, 15
    runtime information about, 15–16
    shadow copy feature, 113
    <trust> section and, 128
AppearanceEditorPart editor, 326
AppendDataBoundItems property,
    563
App_GlobalResources folder, 32,
    36–37, 230
AppInitialize method, 54
application domains. *See*
    AppDomains (application
    domains)
application precompilation, 24–29.
    See also compilation
    build providers and, 40
    deploy, 26–29
    dynamic page class creation
      first-hit delay and, 10
    in-place, 24–26
    in-place vs. deploy, 24
Application property, 471
ApplicationName property, 181, 187
applications. *See also* ASP.NET
    programming
    IIS 6.0 process model and
      application pool, 6
    mapped resource extensions, 4
    pools, 59
    precompilation. *See* application
      precompilation
    protection levels, 59
    recompilation and restarts, 15
    retrieving configuration settings,
      135
    runtime information about, 15–16
    scoping custom provider data to,
      187
    updating configuration settings,
      135–136
Application_Start event, 54
App_LocalResources folder, 32, 37

About the Author

Dino Esposito is the ASP.NET and ADO.NET expert at Solid Quality Learning, a premier training and consulting firm.

Dino writes the "Cutting Edge" column for *MSDN Magazine* and regularly contributes .NET Framework articles to the Microsoft ASP.NET and Visual Studio Developer Centers and other magazines, including *asp.netPRO Magazine*, *CoDe Magazine*, and *Dr. Dobb's ASP.NET-2-The-Max* newsletter. His books for Microsoft Press include *Programming Microsoft ASP.NET* (2003), *Building Web Solutions with ASP.NET and ADO.NET* (2002), *Applied XML Programming for Microsoft .NET* (2002), and *Programming Microsoft ASP.NET 2.0 Core Reference*. Up-to-date information about Dino's upcoming articles and books can be found in his blog at *http://weblogs.asp.net/despos*.

As a member of the International .NET Association (INETA) team of speakers, Dino is a frequent speaker at community events, particularly in Europe and the United States.

Before becoming a full-time author, consultant, and trainer, Dino worked for several top consulting companies. Based in Rome, Italy, he pioneered DNA systems in Europe and in 1994 designed one of the first serious Web applications—an image data bank. These days, you can find Dino at leading conferences such as DevConnections, DevWeek, WinDev, and Microsoft TechEd.

Additional Resources for Web Developers

Published and Forthcoming Titles from Microsoft Press

Microsoft® Visual Web Developer™ 2005 Express Edition: Build a Web Site Now!
Jim Buyens ● ISBN 0-7356-2212-4

With this lively, eye-opening, and hands-on book, all you need is a computer and the desire to learn how to create Web pages now using Visual Web Developer Express Edition! Featuring a full working edition of the software, this fun and highly visual guide walks you through a complete Web page project from set-up to launch. You'll get an introduction to the Microsoft Visual Studio® environment and learn how to put the light-weight, easy-to-use tools in Visual Web Developer Express to work right away—building your first, dynamic Web pages with Microsoft ASP.NET 2.0. You'll get expert tips, coaching, and visual examples at each step of the way, along with pointers to additional learning resources.

Microsoft ASP.NET 2.0 Programming
Step by Step
George Shepherd ● ISBN 0-7356-2201-9

With dramatic improvements in performance, productivity, and security features, Visual Studio 2005 and ASP.NET 2.0 deliver a simplified, high-performance, and powerful Web development experience. ASP.NET 2.0 features a new set of controls and infrastructure that simplify Web-based data access and include functionality that facilitates code reuse, visual consistency, and aesthetic appeal. Now you can teach yourself the essentials of working with ASP.NET 2.0 in the Visual Studio environment— one step at a time. With *Step by Step*, you work at your own pace through hands-on, learn-by-doing exercises. Whether you're a beginning programmer or new to this version of the technology, you'll understand the core capabilities and fundamental techniques for ASP.NET 2.0. Each chapter puts you to work, showing you how, when, and why to use specific features of the ASP.NET 2.0 rapid application development environment and guiding you as you create actual components and working applications for the Web, including advanced features such as personalization.

Programming Microsoft ASP.NET 2.0
Core Reference
Dino Esposito ● ISBN 0-7356-2176-4

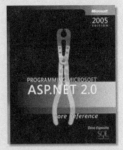

Delve into the core topics for ASP.NET 2.0 programming, mastering the essential skills and capabilities needed to build high-performance Web applications successfully. Well-known ASP.NET author Dino Esposito deftly builds your expertise with Web forms, Visual Studio, core controls, master pages, data access, data binding, state management, security services, and other must-know topics—combining definitive reference with practical, hands-on programming instruction. Packed with expert guidance and pragmatic examples, this *Core Reference* delivers the key resources that you need to develop professional-level Web programming skills.

Programming Microsoft ASP.NET 2.0
Applications: *Advanced Topics*
Dino Esposito ● ISBN 0-7356-2177-2

Master advanced topics in ASP.NET 2.0 programming—gaining the essential insights and in-depth understanding that you need to build sophisticated, highly func-tional Web applications success-fully. Topics include Web forms, Visual Studio 2005, core controls, master pages, data access, data binding, state management, and security considerations. Developers often discover that the more they use ASP.NET, the more they need to know. With expert guidance from ASP.NET authority Dino Esposito, you get the in-depth, comprehensive information that leads to full mastery of the technology.

Programming Microsoft Windows® Forms
Charles Petzold ● ISBN 0-7356-2153-5

Programming Microsoft Web Forms
Douglas J. Reilly ● ISBN 0-7356-2179-9

CLR via C++
Jeffrey Richter with Stanley B. Lippman
ISBN 0-7356-2248-5

Debugging, Tuning, and Testing Microsoft .NET 2.0 Applications
John Robbins ● ISBN 0-7356-2202-7

CLR via C#, Second Edition
Jeffrey Richter ● ISBN 0-7356-2163-2

For more information about Microsoft Press® books and other learning products, visit: **www.microsoft.com/books** *and* **www.microsoft.com/learning**

Additional Resources for C# Developers

Published and Forthcoming Titles from Microsoft Press

Microsoft® Visual C#® 2005 Express Edition: Build a Program Now!
Patrice Pelland • ISBN 0-7356-2229-9

In this lively, eye-opening, and hands-on book, all you need is a computer and the desire to learn how to program with Visual C# 2005 Express Edition. Featuring a full working edition of the software, this fun and highly visual guide walks you through a complete programming project—a desktop weather-reporting application—from start to finish. You'll get an unintimidating introduction to the Microsoft Visual Studio® development environment and learn how to put the lightweight, easy-to-use tools in Visual C# Express to work right away—creating, compiling, testing, and delivering your first, ready-to-use program. You'll get expert tips, coaching, and visual examples at each step of the way, along with pointers to additional learning resources.

Microsoft Visual C# 2005 *Step by Step*
John Sharp • ISBN 0-7356-2129-2

Visual C#, a feature of Visual Studio 2005, is a modern programming language designed to deliver a productive environment for creating business frameworks and reusable object-oriented components. Now you can teach yourself essential techniques with Visual C#—and start building components and Microsoft Windows®–based applications—one step at a time. With *Step by Step*, you work at your own pace through hands-on, learn-by-doing exercises. Whether you're a beginning programmer or new to this particular language, you'll learn how, when, and why to use specific features of Visual C# 2005. Each chapter puts you to work, building your knowledge of core capabilities and guiding you as you create your first C#-based applications for Windows, data management, and the Web.

Programming Microsoft Visual C# 2005 Framework Reference
Francesco Balena • ISBN 0-7356-2182-9

Complementing *Programming Microsoft Visual C# 2005 Core Reference*, this book covers a wide range of additional topics and information critical to Visual C# developers, including Windows Forms, working with Microsoft ADO.NET 2.0 and Microsoft ASP.NET 2.0, Web services, security, remoting, and much more. Packed with sample code and real-world examples, this book will help developers move from understanding to mastery.

Programming Microsoft Visual C# 2005 *Core Reference*
Donis Marshall • ISBN 0-7356-2181-0

Get the in-depth reference and pragmatic, real-world insights you need to exploit the enhanced language features and core capabilities in Visual C# 2005. Programming expert Donis Marshall deftly builds your proficiency with classes, structs, and other fundamentals, and advances your expertise with more advanced topics such as debugging, threading, and memory management. Combining incisive reference with hands-on coding examples and best practices, this *Core Reference* focuses on mastering the C# skills you need to build innovative solutions for smart clients and the Web.

CLR via C#, Second Edition
Jeffrey Richter • ISBN 0-7356-2163-2

In this new edition of Jeffrey Richter's popular book, you get focused, pragmatic guidance on how to exploit the common language runtime (CLR) functionality in Microsoft .NET Framework 2.0 for applications of all types—from Web Forms, Windows Forms, and Web services to solutions for Microsoft SQL Server™, Microsoft code names "Avalon" and "Indigo," consoles, Microsoft Windows NT® Service, and more. Targeted to advanced developers and software designers, this book takes you under the covers of .NET for an in-depth understanding of its structure, functions, and operational components, demonstrating the most practical ways to apply this knowledge to your own development efforts. You'll master fundamental design tenets for .NET and get hands-on insights for creating high-performance applications more easily and efficiently. The book features extensive code examples in Visual C# 2005.

Programming Microsoft Windows Forms
Charles Petzold • ISBN 0-7356-2153-5

CLR via C++
Jeffrey Richter with Stanley B. Lippman
ISBN 0-7356-2248-5

Programming Microsoft Web Forms
Douglas J. Reilly • ISBN 0-7356-2179-9

Debugging, Tuning, and Testing Microsoft .NET 2.0 Applications
John Robbins • ISBN 0-7356-2202-7

For more information about Microsoft Press® books and other learning products,
visit: **www.microsoft.com/books** *and* **www.microsoft.com/learning**

Additional Resources for Visual Basic Developers

Published and Forthcoming Titles from Microsoft Press

Microsoft® Visual Basic® 2005 Express Edition: Build a Program Now!
Patrice Pelland • ISBN 0-7356-2213-2

Featuring a full working edition of the software, this fun and highly visual guide walks you through a complete programming project—a desktop weather-reporting application—from start to finish. You'll get an introduction to the Microsoft Visual Studio® development environment and learn how to put the lightweight, easy-to-use tools in Visual Basic Express to work right away—creating, compiling, testing, and delivering your first ready-to-use program. You'll get expert tips, coaching, and visual examples each step of the way, along with pointers to additional learning resources.

Microsoft Visual Basic 2005 *Step by Step*
Michael Halvorson • ISBN 0-7356-2131-4

With enhancements across its visual designers, code editor, language, and debugger that help accelerate the development and deployment of robust, elegant applications across the Web, a business group, or an enterprise, Visual Basic 2005 focuses on enabling developers to rapidly build applications. Now you can teach yourself the essentials of working with Visual Studio 2005 and the new features of the Visual Basic language—one step at a time. Each chapter puts you to work, showing you how, when, and why to use specific features of Visual Basic and guiding as you create actual components and working applications for Microsoft Windows®. You'll also explore data management and Web-based development topics.

Programming Microsoft Visual Basic 2005 *Core Reference*
Francesco Balena • ISBN 0-7356-2183-7

Get the expert insights, indispensable reference, and practical instruction needed to exploit the core language features and capabilities in Visual Basic 2005. Well-known Visual Basic programming author Francesco Balena expertly guides you through the fundamentals, including modules, keywords, and inheritance, and builds your mastery of more advanced topics such as delegates, assemblies, and My Namespace. Combining in-depth reference with extensive, hands-on code examples and best-practices advice, this *Core Reference* delivers the key resources that you need to develop professional-level programming skills for smart clients and the Web.

Programming Microsoft Visual Basic 2005 Framework Reference
Francesco Balena • ISBN 0-7356-2175-6

Complementing *Programming Microsoft Visual Basic 2005 Core Reference*, this book covers a wide range of additional topics and information critical to Visual Basic developers, including Windows Forms, working with Microsoft ADO.NET 2.0 and ASP.NET 2.0, Web services, security, remoting, and much more. Packed with sample code and real-world examples, this book will help developers move from understanding to mastery.

Programming Microsoft Windows Forms
Charles Petzold • ISBN 0-7356-2153-5

Programming Microsoft Web Forms
Douglas J. Reilly • ISBN 0-7356-2179-9

Debugging, Tuning, and Testing Microsoft .NET 2.0 Applications
John Robbins • ISBN 0-7356-2202-7

Microsoft ASP.NET 2.0 *Step by Step*
George Shepherd • ISBN 0-7356-2201-9

Microsoft ADO.NET 2.0 *Step by Step*
Rebecca Riordan • ISBN 0-7356-2164-0

Programming Microsoft ASP.NET 2.0 *Core Reference*
Dino Esposito • ISBN 0-7356-2176-4

For more information about Microsoft Press® books and other learning products, visit: **www.microsoft.com/books** *and* **www.microsoft.com/learning**

What do you think of this book?
We want to hear from you!

Do you have a few minutes to participate in a brief online survey? Microsoft is interested in hearing your feedback about this publication so that we can continually improve our books and learning resources for you.

To participate in our survey, please visit:

www.microsoft.com/learning/booksurvey

And enter this book's ISBN, 0-7356-2177-2. As a thank-you to survey participants in the United States and Canada, each month we'll randomly select five respondents to win one of five $100 gift certificates from a leading online merchant.* At the conclusion of the survey, you can enter the drawing by providing your e-mail address, which will be used for prize notification *only*.

Thanks in advance for your input. Your opinion counts!

Sincerely,

Microsoft Learning

Learn More. Go Further.